Mind, Brain, and Language
Multidisciplinary Perspectives

Mind, Brain, and Language
Multidisciplinary Perspectives

Edited by

Marie T. Banich
University of Colorado at Boulder

Molly Mack
University of Illinois at Urbana–Champaign

LAWRENCE ERLBAUM ASSOCIATES, PUBLISHERS
2003 Mahwah, New Jersey London

Lawrence Erlbaum Associates, Inc., Publishers
10 Industrial Avenue
Mahwah, NJ 07430

Cover design by Kathryn Houghtaling Lacey

Library of Congress Cataloging-in-Publication Data

Mind, brain, and language : multidisciplinary perspectives / edited by Marie T. Banich, Molly Mack.
p. cm.
Includes bibliographical references and index.
ISBN 0-8058-3327-7 (cloth : alk. paper)
ISBN 0-8058-3328-5 (pbk. : alk. paper)
1. Biolinguistics. I. Banich, Marie T., 1957– II. Mack, Molly Ann.
P132 .M563 2002
401—dc21 2002069209
CIP

Books published by Lawrence Erlbaum Associates are printed on acid-free paper, and their bindings are chosen for strength and durability.

Printed in the United States of America
10 9 8 7 6 5 4 3 2

To my deceased dad, John Banich, the polyglot,
and to my brother John G. Banich, who by quietly always being there,
provides me freedom to pursue projects such as this book

~ and ~

To my father and mother, Robert and Gretchen Mack,
for their encouragement and support in so many ways large and small,
and to my aunts, Sisso and Jenny, whose enthusiasm for life
continues to inspire me.

In memory of Peter W. Jusczyk
1948–2001

Contents

Preface xi

Acknowledgments xiii

About the Contributors xv

I The Emergence, Influence, and Development of Language

1 Language Evolution and Innateness 3
Philip Lieberman

2 Language, Mind, and Culture: From Linguistic Relativity to Representational Modularity 23
Giovanni Bennardo

3 The Role of Speech Perception Capacities in Early Language Acquisition 61
Peter W. Jusczyk

II Models of Language and Language Processing

4 Dissociation and Modularity: Reflections on Language and Mind 87
Neil Smith

5 Linguistic Models 113
Geoffrey K. Pullum and Barbara C. Scholz

6 Connectionist Modeling of Language: Examples and Implications 143
David C. Plaut

III The Neurological Bases of Language

7 Language in Microvolts 171
Marta Kutas and Bernadette M. Schmitt

8 Functional and Structural Imaging in the Study of Auditory Language Processes 211
Robert J. Zatorre

9 Parallel Systems for Processing Language: Hemispheric Complementarity in the Normal Brain 229
Christine Chiarello

IV Language Disruption and Loss

10 Evidence From Language Breakdown: Implications for the Neural and Functional Organization of Language 251
Eleanor M. Saffran

11 The Neurocognitive Bases of Developmental Reading Disorders 283
Marie T. Banich and Paige E. Scalf

V Two Languages, One Brain

12 The Phonetic Systems of Bilinguals 309
Molly Mack

13 Differential Use of Cerebral Mechanisms in Bilinguals 351
Michel Paradis

Author Index 371

Subject Index 389

Preface

The major objective of this book is to provide, within one volume, an overview of how the structure of language influences the way we think and how the organization of the brain influences language. The contributors to this volume examine these issues from a variety of distinct disciplinary vantage points, ranging from linguistics and philosophy to psychology and neuroscience. The impetus for such an interdisciplinary volume comes from our belief that major insights in science result from interaction and cross–fertilization between the discrete conceptualizations and approaches that occur within individual disciplines. What can emerge from the convergence of different perspectives are central truths. Yet interdisciplinary studies are often difficult because they require a breadth of knowledge that is hard for any one individual to obtain. Gaining access to knowledge within a new discipline can be complicated not only because most scientific writings are geared to a reader trained within a specific domain but also because each traditional discipline has its own implicit assumptions and specialized vocabulary.

This volume is designed to address this problem by providing an entry point for individuals who are interested in an interdisciplinary approach to issues related to mind, brain, and language. To that end, each chapter is written not only to be comprehensible to a specialist within a particular field of inquiry, but to be accessible to a generally educated reader. Yet there was also the need to provide breadth and rigor. To meet that goal, each chapter has been written by a noted individual within a particular discipline, providing an expert perspective on what his or her field can teach us about the interrelationships between mind, brain, and language. These experts provide a glimpse, by discussing both their own work and that of others, into how relevant issues are conceptualized and into the methods employed to provide answers to questions within their fields.

Thus the chapters within this book address a broad range of the most fundamental questions dealing with the mind/brain/language relationship. These include, but are not limited to, the following: How did language evolve and how is it acquired by the child language learner? How does culture influence language? How does the brain process linguistic information and how is that information represented at the psycholinguistic and neurolinguistic levels? How do we obtain empirical evidence about how the brain produces and perceives language? How do computational models provide insights into mind and brain? What are some of the neurolinguistic and psycholinguistic consequences of brain injury? And what do we know about dual–language systems, such as language representation in the two cerebral hemispheres, and language representation in "the bilingual brain"? It is our intention that, after completing this book, the reader not only will have found some answers to these questions but also will have attained a greater appreciation of how important multidisciplinary interaction is in obtaining such answers.

Many years ago, Charles Evans Hughes, a Chief Justice of the Supreme Court, stated that "[i]n the highest ranges of thought, in theology, philosophy and science, we find differences of view on the part of the most distinguished experts.... The history of scholarship is a record of disagreements." It is our hope that amid the differences, the disparities, and the disagreements that are an inevitable consequence of communication across (and often within) disciplines, what will emerge will be a greater degree of understanding of three of the great mysteries of human existence–the workings of the human mind, the function of the mind's progenitor, the brain, and the mind's major achievement, language. We believe that the present volume represents a step toward achieving such an understanding.

Acknowledgments

This book came about because of support provided by the Center for Advanced Study at the University of Illinois at Urbana-Champaign. The center has as its core mission the goal of bringing together faculty to engage in a multidisciplinary dialogue. In the spring semester of 1998, the center sponsored a faculty–student seminar devoted to considering ways in which mind, brain, and language interact. This seminar brought together nearly 30 faculty members from a wide range of academic units at the University of Illinois. A conference on Mind, Brain, and Language, held at the University of Illinois on May 8–9, 1998, expanded the conversations started in this seminar to include notable researchers from other institutions. As a result of this conference, the current volume came into being.

We would like to thank a number of individuals who provided assistance in helping us bring what began as an idea from a valued colleague to fruition in the form of the present volume. We especially thank Braj B. Kachru, who, as then-director of the Center for Advanced Study at the University of Illinois, provided the impetus, strong support, and boundless enthusiasm for this project, and H. Jeanie Taylor, who, as Associate Director of the center, helped in many invaluable ways to make the vision of the seminar, the conference, and the book a reality. Without her guidance in planning these endeavors, they would not have been possible. Other individuals at the Center also provided much–welcomed assistance. Our ability to organize both the Mind, Brain, and Language seminar and conference was aided by funds from the Center for Advanced Study, which provided us with release time from teaching. The willingness of our home departments to release us from teaching responsibilities was also critical. Financial support for the conference was provided by funds from the Center for Advanced Study, the College of Liberal Arts and Sciences, and the Beckman Institute for Advanced Science and Technology. Wendy Baker, Donald Kilburg, Hyunjung Kim, Gabseon Lee, and Pavel Trofimovich also provided indispensable technical assistance in the preparation of this volume.

We also owe a debt to our faculty colleagues at the University of Illinois, who stimulated our thinking, expanded our knowledge, and helped make the seminar and conference that we co-chaired so rewarding. They include the following: Giovanni Bennardo, Janet Keller, Anthropology; Prahlad Gupta, Beckman Institute; Zong–qi Cai, Jerome Packard, East Asian Languages and Cultures; Gary Cziko, George W. McConkie, David Zola, Educational Psychology; Stephen Levinson, Electrical and Computer Engineering; J. Ronayne Cowan, English as an International Language; Jennifer Cole, Adele Goldberg, Georgia Green, Yamuna Kachru, Chin-Woo Kim, Jerry Morgan, Daniel D. Silverman, James Yoon, Linguistics; Paul Lauterbur, Medical Information Science; Robert Wilson, Philosophy; Ruthann Atchley, Kathryn Bock, Gary Dell, Cynthia Fisher, Susan Garnsey, William Greenough, Kevin Miller, Psychology; Bill VanPatten, Spanish, Italian and Portuguese; Charissa Lansing, Speech and Hearing Science.

Lastly, we would like to thank the contributors to this volume. To ensure that this volume would be accessible to the nonspecialist, we provided our contributors with many detailed comments on earlier versions of their chapters. The end result was, of course, more work for them. Yet our contributors complied with our suggestions willingly, without complaint, and with genuine good cheer. For that, and for their enthusiasm for this project, we are most appreciative.

—*Marie T. Banich*
—*Molly Mack*
March, 2002

About the Contributors

Marie Banich is Professor of Psychology at the University of Colorado at Boulder. She received her PhD in behavioral sciences from the University of Chicago in 1985. She then joined the Psychology Department at the University of Illinois at Urbana-Champaign, where she stayed until 2000. She has a large interest in interdisciplinary approaches to scientific questions. From 1994 to 2000, she was co-chair of the Biological Intelligence Major Research Theme of the Beckman Institute at the University of Illinois. The Beckman Institute is one of the largest multidisciplinary institutes in the world, designed to investigate intelligent behavior, whether manifested in systems composed of neurons or microchips. Her research interests lie in cognitive neuroscience and neuropsychology. She utilizes brain imaging techniques, such as functional magnetic resonance imaging (fMRI), to examine neural mechanisms of attentional control. She is author of a leading textbook in the area, *Cognitive Neuroscience and Neuropsychology, 2nd edition* (Houghton-Mifflin, 2003).

Giovanni Bennardo is Assistant Professor of Linguistic Anthropology and Cognitive Science at Northern Illinois University. He earned his PhD in anthropology (linguistic and cognitive) from the University of Illinois at Urbana-Champaign in 1996. His research and publications examine the relationship between language, culture, and the mind. Specifically, he is interested in cross-cultural semantics, spatial cognition, and cross-modular and cross-domain interactions. He has conducted research in the Kingdom of Tonga, Polynesia. He is currently investigating major features of the mental representations of space instantiated in various cultural realms such as exchange, navigation, kinship, land distribution, social networks, and politics.

Christine Chiarello received her PhD in linguistics from the University of California, Berkeley, in 1982. She then joined the Psychology Department at Syracuse University, where she pursued research in the areas of word recognition, lexical semantic processing, and cerebral hemispheric asymmetries. In 1996 she moved to the University of California, Riverside, where she is currently Professor of Psychology and a contributor to the neuroscience PhD program. Her current research addresses the role of the right hemisphere in language processing at the word and sentence level, and the means by which the stimulus environment can modulate the distribution of function between the left and right hemispheres. This work has been funded by the National Institutes of Mental Health, the National Science Foundation, and the US–Israel Binational Science Foundation. She has edited two volumes, *Right Hemisphere Contributions to Lexical Semantics* in 1988 and, with Mark Beeman, *Right Hemisphere Language Comprehension: Perspectives from Cognitive Neuroscience* in 1998.

Peter Jusczyk was Professor of Psychology and Cognitive Science at Johns Hopkins University. He received his BA from Brown University and his PhD in psychology from the University of Pennsylvania. He taught at Dalhousie University (1975–1980), the University of Oregon (1980–1990), and the State University of New York at Buffalo (1990–1996) prior to accepting a position at Johns Hopkins. He also worked at the Laboratory of Cognitive Science and Psycholinguistics at CNRS in Paris (1981–1982 and 1986–1988). He was a Fulbright Fellow at Catholic University in Lublin, Poland (1985), a Sloane Fellow at the University of Pennsylvania (1984), and a Visiting Scientist at the Max Planck Institute for Psycholinguistics in Nijmegen, the Netherlands (1989 and 1995). He held a Senior Scientist Award from the National Institute of Mental Health and served on a number of editorial boards (*Cognition, Child Development, Language and Speech, Syntax, Developmental Psychology, Infancy, Perception & Psychophysics*) and as Chairman of a National Institutes of Health Grant Panel (Sensory Disorders and Language). His research focused on infant speech perception capacities and their role in language acquisition. His book on this topic, *The Discovery of Spoken Language*, was published by the MIT Press. In addition, he co-edited two volumes, *The Nature of Thought* (with Raymond Klein) and *Developmental Neurocognition: The Development of Speech and Face Processing in the First Year of Life* (with Benedicte de Boysson-Bardies, Scania de Schonen, Peter MacNeilage, and John Morton).

Marta Kutas received her PhD in physiological psychology from the University of Illinois at Urbana-Champaign and has been at the University of California, San Diego, ever since, initially in the Department of Neurosciences and then in the newly founded Department of Cognitive Science. Her primary interest is how people make sense of their senses, with an emphasis on the interface between language and memory and the functional differences between the two cerebral hemispheres. Her laboratory uses a combination of behavioral and electrophysiological measurement techniques (electrical recordings from the human scalp) as a means of linking the mind, brain, and language. She is past President of the Society for Psychophysiological Research.

Philip Lieberman is Fred M. Seed Professor of Cognitive and Linguistic Sciences and Professor of Anthropology, Brown University. He received his BS and MS in electrical engineering at the Massachusetts Institute of Technology and his PhD in linguistics, also at MIT. His accomplishments include Fellow, American Association for the Advancement of Science, American Psychological Society, and American Anthropological Association, Guggenheim Fellow, Distinguished Lecturer of Academica Sinica, Taipei, NATO Visiting Professor, Lecturer of the Max Planck Institute for Psycholinguistics, Nijmegen, and Research Award recipient, the American Speech and Hearing Association. Two of his major written works are *Human Language and Our Reptilian Brain: The Subcortical Bases of Speech, Syntax, and Thought* (Harvard University Press) and *The Biology and Evolution of Language* (Harvard University Press).

Molly Mack received her PhD in Linguistics from Brown University where her doctoral work was supervised by Sheila Blumstein. She then held a position as a postdoctoral research associate working with Philip Lieberman in child-language acquisition at Brown University. Prior to taking her position at the University of Illinois at Urbana-Champaign, she conducted research on computer-generated speech and speech recognition with Ben Gold at the Massachusetts Institute of Technology Lincoln Laboratory. Her primary areas of interest are in the psycholinguistic and neurolinguistic aspects of bilingualism and second-language articulatory and acoustic phonetics. She has published in such journals as *The Acoustical Society of America*, *The Journal of Child Language*, *The Journal of Phonetics*, *Perception & Psychophysics*, and *World Englishes*. She has also contributed chapters in books on bilingualism and entries in *The Linguistics Encyclopedia* (Routledge). She is the recipient of a number of awards and grants, is listed in *Who's Who of American Women*, and has been both a Fellow and Associate in the University of Illinois Center for Advanced Study. At present, she is co-investigator in a large-scale, multi-site National Institutes of Health project designed to examine child–adult differences in the acquisition of second-language phonetic and morphosyntactic systems.

Michel Paradis, PhD (philosophy, McGill), PhD (neurolinguistics, Université de Montréal), is a Fellow of the Royal Society of Canada, Professor of Neurolinguistics, and is Professor Emeritus in the Department of Linguistics at McGill University. He is the author of 11 books and approximately 70 articles and chapters. Among these, *The Assessment of Bilingual Aphasia* and *The Bilingual Aphasia Test* are now available in over 65 languages and 170 specific language-pair combinations. He is also Chair of the Aphasia Committee of the International Association of Logopaedics and Phoniatrics and serves as editor of the *Journal of Neurolinguistics* and is on the editorial board of *Brain and Language, Folia Phoniatrica et Logopaedica, International Journal of Bilingualism,* and *Bilingualism: Language and Cognition.* He is currently investigating the cerebral mechanisms involved in simultaneous translation, the pragmatic deficits of right-hemisphere-damaged individuals, the cross-linguistic manifestations of genetic dysphasia, and the manifestations of aphasic symptoms as a function of the structure of different languages.

David Plaut is Associate Professor in the Departments of Psychology and Computer Science at Carnegie Mellon University, with a joint appointment in the Center for the Neural Basis of Cognition. He received his PhD in computer science at Carnegie Mellon in 1991. His research involves using computational modeling, complemented by empirical studies, to investigate the nature of normal and impaired cognitive processing in the domain of reading and language. He works within a connectionist or parallel distributed-processing framework, in which cognitive processes are implemented in terms of cooperative and competitive interactions among large numbers of simple, neuron-like processing units. Much of his work has been directed at understanding word reading, both in normal skilled readers and in brain-damaged patients with acquired reading disorders. His research interests also encompass normal and impaired semantic processing and phenomena related to phonological, morphological, and sentence-level processing.

Geoffrey K. Pullum did his undergraduate work in linguistics at the University of York, spent a year at Cambridge University as a research student, and then took up a job at the University of London, where he also earned his PhD in general linguistics. In 1981 he moved to the Department of Linguistics at the University of California, Santa Cruz, where he has worked ever since, serving as Dean of Graduate Studies and Research from 1987 to 1993. His research interests include English syntax and mathematical and computational aspects of linguistics and, more recently, the philosophy of linguistics. He is the author or coauthor of several books, including *Generalized Phrase Structure Grammar* (1985) and *The Cambridge Grammar of English*, in addition to many journal articles in a wide range of subfields of linguistics.

Eleanor M. Saffran received a PhD in psychology from the University of California, Berkeley, and then held a postdoctoral fellowship at the Institute for Neuroscience at the University of Pennsylvania. Her doctoral and postdoctoral work focused on electrophysiological studies of attention in rats, but she subsequently moved up the evolutionary scale to examine cognitive disorders resulting from brain lesions in humans, with a major focus on language. She worked at the Johns Hopkins Medical School for a number of years, then spent a sabbatical in London at the National Hospital for Nervous Diseases, and moved to Temple University in 1980. She is currently Professor of Communication Sciences, with adjunct professorships in the Departments of Neurology and Psychology. She is also director of Temple University's Center for Cognitive Neuroscience. Her current work focuses on disorders of semantic memory, word production, and syntax comprehension in aphasics.

Paige E. Scalf received undergraduate and graduate degrees in music at the University of Illinois at Urbana-Champaign before defecting to the field of biological psychology. She is currently working on her PhD at that institution. Her research focuses on visual and auditory attention, with an emphasis on linking cognitive theories of attention to the neural structures that support attentional function.

Bernadette M. Schmitt received her MA in cognitive psychology at the Carolo-Wilhelmina University of Braunschweig, Germany, in 1993. She carried out research on visual attention mechanisms. Her supervisors were Dirk Vorberg and Rainer Goebel. She then moved to the Netherlands, to the Max Planck Institute for Psycholinguistics, Nijmegen, where she received her Ph.D. in 1997 in the field of lexical access in the production of ellipsis and pronouns, supervised by Pim Levelt, Antje Meyer, and Rainer Goebel. In 1997 and 1998 she was a postdoctoral research fellow in the Department of Cognitive Science, University of California, San Diego. She did research in collaboration with Marta Kutas and Thomas Münte on the time course of lexical access in language production using event-related potentials (ERPs). The research—referred to in part in the present volume—was supported by the McDonnell–Pew Center of Cognitive Neuroscience and the German Academic Exchange Service (DAAD). Schmitt is currently Assistant Professor in the Department of Neurocognition, Faculty of Psychology, Maastricht University, the Netherlands.

Barbara C. Scholz teaches in the Department of Philosophy at San Jose State University in California. She has an MSc in cognitive science from the University of Edinburgh and earned her PhD in philosophy at the Ohio State University. Her doctoral research explored the implications of Kripke's Wittgensteinian rule-following paradox for contemporary linguistic theories. Since then she has done research on implicit functional definitions and holism as applied to several fields, including folk aesthetics, semantics, and structuralist linguistics. Her current work centers on the philosophy of the cognitive sciences, especially linguistics. She is the author of the article on the philosophy of linguistics in the *Encyclopedia of Cognitive Science* (Macmillan) and of several journal articles in various fields of philosophy and linguistics.

Neil Smith was educated at Trinity College Cambridge and University College London (UCL), where he received his PhD in linguistics. His research included a year of fieldwork among the Nupe in Nigeria. He did further research at MIT and UCLA while holding a Harkness Fellowship and, since 1972, has been at UCL where he is currently Professor of Linguistics. He was President of the Linguistics Association of Great Britain from 1980 to 1986, and of the Association of Heads and Professors of Linguistics from 1993 to 1994. His main books are *An Outline Grammar of Nupe* (1967), *The Acquisition of Phonology* (1973), *Modern Linguistics: The Results of Chomsky's Revolution* (with Deirdre Wilson, 1979), *The Twitter Machine: Reflections on Language* (1989), *The Mind of a Savant* (with Ianthi Tsimpli, 1995), and *Chomsky: Ideas and Ideals* (1999). He was elected Fellow of the British Academy in 1999 and Honorary Member of the Linguistic Society of America in 2000.

Robert Zatorre is a cognitive neuroscientist working at the Montreal Neurological Institute. His principal research interests relate to the neural substrate for perceptual and cognitive processes in the human brain. In particular, he has worked extensively on auditory processing, and is most interested in two complex and characteristically human abilities—speech and music. His training was obtained at Boston University, where he completed a degree in music and in psychology, and at Brown University where he earned his PhD under Peter Eimas. He then went on to do postdoctoral work at McGill University under Brenda Milner. He has worked for a number of years investigating the behavioral effects of focal brain lesions on cognitive and perceptual functions. Over the past decade, this work has been complemented by important developments in the field of brain imaging. He has been heavily involved in the development and implementation of functional imaging paradigms, including positron emission tomography (PET) and functional magnetic resonance imaging(fMRI), as a means of mapping cognitive function in the normal brain. These techniques have been successfully applied to study perceptual and cognitive functions, including auditory processes related to speech and music perception, as well as olfactory and gustatory perception. In addition, together with his colleagues, he has completed functional imaging studies on such diverse issues as auditory spatial attention, auditory imagery, absolute pitch, linguistic function in bilinguals, and brain organization for sign language in the deaf. Finally, he has also used structural brain imaging techniques to measure the morphology of the auditory cortex *in vivo* and to investigate hemispheric asymmetries.

I

The Emergence, Influence, and Development of Language

1

Language Evolution and Innateness

Philip Lieberman
Cognitive and Linguistic Sciences, Brown University

I propose a model for the evolution of human language that takes into account evidence derived by means of the comparative method introduced by Charles Darwin. We can only study the physical characteristics and behavior of living species. Stories based on conjecture, although entertaining, concerning the presumed life-styles of extinct hominids or our ancestors 150,000 years ago are no substitute. Therefore, studies of the physiology, brains, and behavior of chimpanzees, other animals, and human beings provide the only relevant database. We can conclude that human linguistic ability appears to involve quantitative increases in primitive capacities evident in living nonhuman primates and other species, plus "derived" features that must have evolved since the divergence of hominids from an ancestral species common to both apes and human beings. Evolutionary biologists use the term *primitive feature* to designate an attribute that can be traced back to the common ancestor of many related species. The five fingers of the human hand can be traced back in evolutionary time to the common ancestors of present day frogs and human beings. Derived features, such as a horse's hoof, are those that differentiate particular species.

Comparative studies of apes and human beings show that one of the primitive linguistic features shared by humans and apes is lexical ability; the ability to communicate by means of words using various nonvocal signals. The concept of a word entails an association between an arbitrary signal that have no inherent meaning with concepts rooted in life. Rudimentary syntactic ability has been demonstrated in the limited linguistic communications of both pygmy and common chimpanzees. The derived feature that differentiates human language from apes is vocal speech. Although the vocal signals of other species are "bound" to particular emotional states, humans are able to generate arbitrary speech sounds that signal words. The neural mechanisms regulating human speech allow us to generate arbitrary vocal signals that signal referential information. Moreover, recent neurobiological studies show that the neural mechanisms that regulate speech are also implicated in comprehending syntax and thinking. Comparative data and studies of both the fossil and archaeological record indicate that these derived attributes of human language developed gradually and may be linked. In other words, human speech, complex syntax, and abstract thought may have gradually evolved in concert. In this regard, the "proto-language" versus language distinction proposed by scholars positing an abrupt change in the course of hominid evolution deriving from an innate "universal grammar" does not appear to be a reasonable model for the evolution of human language. Moreover, neurobiological data rule out the claim that the details of grammar are innately specified.

EVOLUTIONARY BIOLOGY VERSUS EVOLUTIONARY PSYCHOLOGY

The methods of evolutionary biology introduced by Charles Darwin provide evidence that concerning the history of the neural bases of human language and thought. Studies of the brains and behavior of living humans show, beyond reasonable doubt, that primitive subcortical structures deep in the brain such as the basal ganglia, traditionally associated with motor control, support neuronal circuits regulating the comprehension of sentences and thinking (Lieberman, 2000). Functional basal ganglia occur in frogs where they generate appropriate motor responses to incoming sensory information. Comparative studies of other species provide insights on the operations that these subcortical structures perform and the probable evolution of unique, derived human behaviors. Comparative studies show a trend from the regulation of stereotyped innate to novel behavior as we proceed up the phylogenetic scale. Although basal ganglia regulate invariant, innate behavior in rodents, in primates they are implicated in the acquisition and regulation of learned activities that furnish rewards.

Current theories concerning the evolution of human language tend to mirror opposing views concerning the biological bases of human language. The linguistic theories developed by Noam Chomsky and advocated by those working in his tradition differ in detail but adhere to the claim that the human brain contains a "universal grammar," an innate store of knowledge that specifies the detailed syntax of all languages. Hypothetical language genes or a single gene specify the universal grammar. Although Chomsky for many years claimed that human language could not be the result of any Darwinian process, theories have been proposed by his followers that attempt to provide an evolutionary basis for this biological claim. Many of these theories ultimately reduce to unsupported scenarios describing the life-styles of extinct hominids and our immediate ancestors 50 thousand years to 2 million years ago. These scenarios for life in the past follow the methods of evolutionary psychology, which must be differentiated from the biological approach of this discussion.

I instead propose a Darwinian model for the evolution of human language. The evolutionary mechanisms that I believe yielded human language include first natural selection acting on the genetic variation that is present in any population. As Darwin noted,

> any variation, however slight and from whatever cause proceeding, if it be in any degree profitable to an individual of any species, in its infinitely complex relations to organic beings and to external nature, will tend to the preservation of that individual, and will generally be inherited by its offspring. The offspring, also, will thus have a better chance of surviving. I have called this principle, by which each small variation if useful is preserved by the term of Natural Selection. (1859-1964, p.61)

The second Darwinian mechanism that appears to have shaped the biological capacity for human language is as Darwin noted the process by which an

> organ might be modified for some other and quite distinct purpose. The illustration of the swimbladder in fishes is a good one, because it shows us clearly the highly important fact that an organ originally constructed for one purpose, namely flotation, may be converted into one for a wholly different purpose, namely respiration. (1859–1964, p. 190)

This process, which has been termed *predaptation* by Mayr (1982) can account for the sudden transitions that are apparent in both evolutionary record. As behavioral responses to the environment change, indeed in response to environmental changes, organs that have been adapted through natural selection to carry out one operation take on new roles. Natural selection for this new role then shapes the organ and behavior.

The evolutionary history of a species and its relationship to other species are often evident when we take stock of "primitive" properties that it shares with related species through its evolutionary history and the "derived" properties that differentiate it from related species. The model proposes that language involves different biological components, some of which are primitive in the evolutionary sense—in other words, components that have deep roots, that are evident when we study the brains and behavior of other related living species. Lexical ability and the ability to comprehend simple aspects of syntax can be seen in living apes, who, in all likelihood, retain some of the characteristics of the extinct 6-million-year-old common ancestor of humans and present-day apes. The distinction between the lexical ability of humans and that of apes, is more quantitative than qualitative. Apes can produce about 150 words using manual sign language or computer boards, roughly equivalent to the abilities of children between ages 2 and 21/2 years. Humans typically have vocabularies exceeding

10,000 words, sometimes exceeding 50,000. Chimpanzees can comprehend sentences in American Sign Language or spoken English that adhere to canonical forms, again roughly equivalent to the abilities of young children. However, other factors that mark human language appear to be the product of "derived" unique aspects of the human brain. Vocal language, the ability to produce novel sound sequences that signal words, is present today only in human beings. The human brain appears to have a species-specific system that regulates speech. Neurobiological studies of the human brain demonstrate that the brain bases that regulate speech are also implicated in the comprehension of distinctions of meaning conveyed by syntax and in other aspects of cognition.

However, we need not invoke unique mechanisms for the evolution of the neural substrate that regulate human speech. It again seems to derive from neural systems that were adapted for motor control. The human brain appears to have a "functional language system" (FLS) (Lieberman, 2000), a neural substrate that regulates human language. But components of the FLS also play a part in regulating motor control and emotion, reflecting its evolutionary history. I next discuss some of the studies that hint at the evolution of the brain mechanisms that allowed human beings to transcend the limits of nonhuman vocal communication, consisting of stereotyped calls bound to affect and emotion rather than words. Finally, I briefly review evidence that demonstrates, beyond reasonable doubt, that the human brain cannot contain a detailed, genetically determined universal grammar. We are not born "preloaded" with a "Chomsky operating system."

The nature of current proposals that attempt to account for the evolution of an innate Chomskian universal grammar is perhaps best exemplified by the current proposal of Derek Bickerton and William Calvin (2000). Their database exemplifies the principles of evolutionary psychology. The scenario they develop is deemed "evolutionary" because it involves *biological fitness*, the term used to designate the survival of one's progeny. The Bickerton-Calvin scenario first claims that our ancestors lived in groups 50 to 150,000 years ago (perhaps earlier, the exact time is not specified) in which all the females formed a harem for the exclusive sexual use of an "alpha male." The story claims that sexually deprived non-alpha males banded together, forming alliances in which some would distract the alpha male, while one lucky male quickly had sex with a compliant female or females. A hypothetical innate neural "cheater–detector" mechanism in the hominid brain allowed the males to keep score and take turns. These activities formed the basis of "reciprocal altruism," which, according to Bickerton, somehow was the basis for the basic noun-verb distinction of syntax, again somehow yielding an innate universal grammar. However, although Bickerton claims that chimpanzees and unspecified nonhuman primates mate in this manner, field studies refute this model. (The pattern of sexual behavior proposed by Bickerton and Calvin has been observed in dolphins. Therefore, we might expect dolphins to possess fully developed syntax according to this script.)

It is not surprising that the principles of evolutionary psychology have been endorsed by linguists following in Noam Chomsky's footsteps. Evolutionary psychologists posit genetic bases for virtually all aspects of human behavior, constructing scenarios for the life-styles of our ancestors. For example, Steven Pinker in a BBC interview (*The World* April, 1998) stated that human beings are genetically predisposed to prefer landscapes that portray open vistas filled with greenery. Pinker asserts that we prefer these landscapes to heavily forested regions, mountains, deserts, seascapes, and so on. We are informed that this preference is innate, deriving from genes shaped during the Pleistocene. According to Pinker, these vistas of open greenery portray the open savannas of southern Africa where hominids first evolved. The holdings of major museums of art refute the proposition that this is an innate, universal human preference. Consider the National Palace Art Museum in Taiwan, which contains the treasures of Chinese art, paintings of travelers in the mountains, or the Tate Gallery's London collection of Turner's seascapes, or Ansel Adam's mountain views, Edward Weston's desert scenes, and so on. Moreover, Pinker fails to take account of recent archaeological studies that show that early hominids did not all live in open grassy plains; 4-million-year-old hominid fossils lived in parts of Africa that were then heavily forested.

But Pinker's scenario and corresponding esthetic claims could readily be changed to account for these facts; Pinker could with equal certainty claim that we like to view seascapes and mountains because they portray the landscapes that our ancestors traversed as they migrated within and from Africa in past ages. In truth, the scenarios constructed by evolutionary psychologists are stories constructed, without supporting data, to justify a genetic basis for any aspect of human behavior. It is not surprising that linguists working in the Chomskian tradition accept the premises of evolutionary psychology, because it generalizes the nativist linguistic agenda introduced by Noam Chomsky—that the neural basis for the syntax of human language must be an innate, genetically transmitted property of the human brain.

BOUND BEHAVIOR VERSUS VOLUNTARY CONTROL AND "FREE WILL"

Apes can comprehend and produce a limited number of words using sign language or visual symbols. Recent studies of the communications of pygmy chimpanzees (Savage-Rumbaugh & Rumbaugh, 1993) and reanalyses of the manual sign language of common chimpanzees (Gardner & Gardner, 1994) show that they have limited syntactic ability. The data are discussed by Lieberman (1998, 2000). In contrast, human beings can comprehend and produce utterances that have complex syntax. Therefore, the task of those studying the evolution of human language must be to account for this derived property of human language. But there is another derived property of human language that qualitatively differentiates human beings from apes. Apes can't talk. Nor as I pointed out in 1994, can they even freely modulate their vocal signals to communicate novel events.

Acoustic analyses of chimpanzee calls show that they make use of phonetic "features" that play a linguistic role in human speech (Lieberman, 1968, 1975). For example, chimpanzees produce falling formant frequency transitions, by rounding their lips, that are similar to those that specify "labial" sounds like [b] and [w] in English. Chimpanzees also have functional larynges, and most of their calls are phonated. Therefore, chimpanzees could, in principle, produce the labial stop consonants [b] and [p], which are differentiated by means of the voice-onset-timing distinction discussed later. Moreover, chimpanzees have speech-producing anatomy that, in principle, could produce nasalized vowels similar to the human vowels [I], [U], [ae], and so on (Lieberman et al., 1972). Acoustic analyses confirm that some of their stereotyped vocal calls show the formant frequency patterns and transitions that specify different vowels and bilabial consonants of human speech (Lieberman, 1968). However, although many chimpanzees have been raised from infancy in proximity to humans speaking to them and to other humans and have been actively tutored (Gardner et. al., 1989), no chimpanzee has ever produced voluntary speech-like vocalizations to communicate even phonetically simple words such as *ma, no, bad, bat*, and so on; which the chimpanzee vocal apparatus could produce.

It is apparent that the acoustic features that constitute chimpanzee calls are bound together. Chimpanzees cannot voluntarily dissociate the bonds that link these elements together. Though their stereotyped vocalizations incorporate elements that could approximate many human words, chimpanzees are not able to "free" these elements from links to particular affective states or situations and produce voluntary speech. The most that nonhuman primates can do is to change the rate at which they produce some stereotyped utterance. In contrast, humans can say whatever they please, whether they're happy, hungry, feeding, frightened, and so on. In contrast, as many observers of chimpanzees and other nonhuman primates note, primate calls are part of a stereotyped response pattern that signals a particular effectual or emotional state (Goodall, 1986). Operant conditioning of nonhuman primates that changes their effectual state would also modify their calls. As the primates' affective state changes, so would their stereotyped calls, yet the calls would still be involuntary, stereotyped calls.

Likewise, the stereotyped vocal responses of infant and adult primates may differ as the result of either maturation or learning, but the end result is a stereotyped call that signals particular threats, rewards, and so on. The data presented by Cheney and Seyfarth (1990) and other studies of nonhuman primates do not demonstrate voluntary generation of vocalizations. As Goodall (1986) noted, chimpanzees can, at most, learn to suppress emotionally triggered vocalizations. If nonhuman primates had voluntary control of their vocalizations, we would expect to find them imitating human speech when they were raised in human environments. Yet as stated, they never produce any speech sounds despite the most intensive training. In contrast, any normal human child raised in any reasonably normal environment effortlessly acquires speech. We can conclude that chimpanzees and other nonhuman primates do not acquire any aspect of speech because they lack the appropriate neural substrate. A derived feature of the human brain clearly is the capacity to produce vocal signals that are "free" from particular emotional contexts or stereotyped situations. The neurobiological studies that I next briefly review suggest that this capacity may also be central to our ability to comprehend complex syntax and to think.

THE FUNCTIONAL LANGUAGE SYSTEM

The neurobiological research program that may yield some understanding of how our brains regulate language is far from complete. It ultimately derives from one of Karl Lashley's many prescient observations. Lashley, in 1951, proposed that the neural mechanisms that carry out the sequential operations necessary for controlled motor activity were the starting points for natural selection that ultimately yielded human language and cognition. In Lashley's words,

> temporal integration is not found exclusively in language; the coordination of leg movements in insects, the song of birds, the control of trotting and pacing in a gaited horse, the rat running the maze, the architect designing a house, and the carpenter sawing a board present a problem of sequences of action [each of which similarly requires syntactic organization] (Lashley, 1951, p. 113)

Lashley himself was following in the footsteps of Charles Darwin, who in 1859 pointed out that organs adapted for one function can take on new roles. The neurobiological research of the past two decades supports Darwin's general concept and Lashley's specific proposal.

Neural Circuits

It is evident that complex behaviors including language are regulated by neural circuits that integrate activity in many parts of the brain. Different parts of the brain perform particular operations. However, these operations are not in themselves coordinate with observed complex behaviors such as picking up a pencil, speaking a word, or recalling the meaning of a word. In other words, although we can differentiate and name various aspects of human behavior such as walking, eating, talking, and understanding a sentence, these names are not coordinate with activity restricted to one particular part of the human brain. There is no "center" of language.

Distributed circuits link the operations that occur in different parts of the brain to yield the neural basis for a complex behavior. Information is transferred in these neural circuits through populations of neurons in particular neural structures that project to neuronal populations in other parts of the brain (Mesulam, 1990). A particular structure, such as the putamen (part of the subcortical basal ganglia), can control similar sequencing operations in manual movements, speech production, the comprehension of syntax, and other aspects of cognition through segregated neuronal populations linked to different parts of the cortex (Alexander, Delong, & Strick; 1986; Cummings, 1993; Marsden & Obeso, 1994). I have proposed that the human brain has a specialized functional language system (FLS) adapted for the production and perception of spoken language (Lieberman, 2000), keeping in mind that the FLS can be redirected to regulate manual sign language.

The structure of the FLS can be understood by considering two aspects of the neurophysiological organization of the brain: (a) Particular neuroanatomical structures are implicated in different aspects of behavior through (b) circuits within and connecting these neuroanatomical structures that carry out particular activities that enhance biological fitness. Segregated neuronal populations in one neuroanatomical structure project (connect) to neuronal populations in different neuroanatomical structures that are globally involved in regulating different aspects of behavior. It is clear that the FLS involves subcortical structures as well as Broca's and Wernicke's areas, the areas of neocortex traditionally associated with human language. In fact, it can be safely said that the Broca's-Wernicke's area theory first proposed by Lichtheim in 1885 is wrong.

The primary evidence usually cited for Broca's and Wernicke's areas being the "seats" of human linguistic ability are the linguistic deficits, "aphasias," that occur after these cortical areas are damaged. Neuroanatomical studies clearly show that permanent aphasia does not occur absent subcortical damage; victims of strokes and other trauma that results in purely cortical damage recover, usually after a period of months (Elman et al., 1997). In contrast, subcortical brain damage can result in permanent linguistic deficits. This is not surprising because independent studies show that subcortical neural circuits involving basal ganglia support at least six different functional circuits in human beings (Alexander et al., 1986; Cummings, 1993). Neuronal basal ganglia populations project to prefrontal cortex to form part of the neural circuits implicated in cognition and the comprehension of syntax. Other segregated circuits regulate manual and speech motor control; still others affect and emotion. These different aspects of behavior appear to be regulated by neuronal basal ganglia circuits that project to different parts of the brain. Different circuits involving basal ganglia appear to regulate sequencing when people move their fingers (Cunnington, Iansek, Bradshaw, & Philips,), talk (Lieberman et al., 1992), attempt to comprehend distinctions in meaning conveyed by syntax (Lieberman, Friedman, & Feldman, 1990; Lieberman et al., 1992; Grossman et al., 1991, 1993; Natsopoulos et al., 1993), and solve cognitive puzzles (Morris et al., 1988). Because natural selection selects for timely responses to environmental challenges, functional neural systems channel sensory information to neuronal populations that mediate appropriate, rapid, motoric responses to stimuli. Therefore, the neuroanatomical structures implicated in comprehending syntax or accessing the meanings of words have direct access to useful sensory—that is auditory and visual information without intermediate levels of processing in "encapsulated" modules (Fodor, 1983).

It is appropriate to note, at this point, that the term *module* carries different weight among neurobiologists and most linguists and many behavioral scientists, including psycholinguists. Neurobiological studies generally use the term *module* to refer to a segregated neural circuit. In contrast, the hypothetical modules of most linguistic and psycholinguistic studies essentially reduce to "black boxes" that each carry out some domain-specific process (e.g., speech perception) or store a domain-specific knowledge base (e.g., the rules of syntax), independent of modules that perform other tasks. However, two of the properties of these hypothetical modules differ in a fundamental manner from the probable circuits of the FLS and the observed properties of neural circuits of other species. According to modular theory (Fodor, 1983), each module is "encapsulated." That is, it is impossible to influence the operations within a module with events outside the module. Modules, furthermore, have "shallow outputs": The input information available to a module is not preserved in the module's output. The processes carried out in these hypothetical modules are usually chained together to complete a functional operation, such as comprehending the meaning of a sentence. For example, according to some psycholinguistic modular theories, speech perception is carried out in a hypothetical module in which the incoming acoustic signal is transformed into a phonetic representation. The phonetic representation, in turn, is the input to a lexical module, which has no access to the primary acoustic information that was available to the phonetic module. Neither of these modular claims holds for human beings when they perceive speech (Lieberman, 2000).

BASAL GANGLIA FUNCTION AND FREE BEHAVIOR

The comparative method introduced by Charles Darwin provides the only reasonable source of data concerning the evolution of the human brain. The continuity of evolution is evident in the similar, primitive aspects of morphology and behavior that are evident when we compare living humans and other species. Likewise, differences between species hint at the evolution of the derived features that differentiate human beings from other animals. As shown next, studies of aphasia (the permanent impairment or loss of language in humans after brain damage), Parkinson's disease (PD), and other conditions show that subcortical basal ganglia are essential components of the human FLS. Studies of rodents and nonhuman primates suggest that subcortical basal ganglia are implicated in the release of speech motor activity from "bound behavior." The available studies are fragmentary, but they show a trend from the regulation of stereotyped innate to novel behavior as we proceed up the phylogenetic scale. Although the basal ganglia regulate invariant innate behavior in rodents, in primates they are implicated in the acquisition and regulation of learned activities that furnish rewards.

The Innate Syntax of Rat Grooming

The grooming movements of rats are innate, genetically transmitted, "syntactically" governed sequences. The "syntax" of the grooming sequence is regulated in the basal ganglia; damage to other parts of the rat brain does not affect the grooming sequence. In contrast, damage to parts of the basal ganglia disrupts the sequences that normally occur, but does not disrupt the individual gestures that make up a grooming sequence. Aldridge and his colleagues (Aldridge, Berridge, Herman, & Zimmer, 1993) confirmed the sequential role of the basal ganglia in rodent grooming patterns by monitoring the firing patterns of basal ganglia neurons in 11 rats using microelectrodes. The onset and offset times of more than 6,000 events were entered into a computer that correlated frame-by-frame analysis of the grooming sequences with the firing patterns. Aldridge et al. (1993) concluded that

> Hierarchal modulation of sequential elements by the neostratum may operate in essentially similar ways for grooming actions and thoughts, but upon very different classes of elements in the two cases. Our argument is that very different behavioral or mental operations might be sequenced by essentially similar neural processes. (p. 393)

In contrast to rodents, the basal ganglia in primates are implicated in acquiring and regulating sequential learned motor responses rather than innate ones. Comparative neurophysiological data on nonhuman primates confirm that the basal ganglia circuits that regulate learned behavior are shaped by associative learning. Kimura, Aosaki, and Graybiel (1993) studied the responses of basal ganglia interneurons as monkeys learned a conditioned motor task in which the monkeys had to associate an arbitrary sound with getting food. At the start of the conditioning process 10%-20% of the 201 neurons monitored showed small responses to the sound. After 3 weeks of conditioning, 60%-70% responded to the sound. Injection of a dopamine antagonist reduced response to 10% and the monkeys were unable to perform the task.

Graybiel and her colleagues (Graybiel, Aosaki, Flaherty, & Kimura, 1994) reviewed the data of a series of studies in which they mapped the circuitry between cortical areas and basal ganglia and studied the physiology of the response patterns of certain neurons. Their model of the functional organization of the striatum is a parallel processing system, adapted for supervised learning. The tracer studies of primate brains discussed in their review article show that inputs from cortical sites that represent a particular body part (e.g., a hand) in parts of the cortex project to "matrisomes" in the basal ganglia, populations of neurons in which "any given matrisome receives overlapping inputs from the same body-part representation in different subareas of the sensorimotor cortex, so that several sorts of information relevant to that body-part converge" (Graybiel et al., 1994, p. 1827). Their experiments show that injections of anterograde tracer in a site in the motor cortex that represents the foot project forward to multiple sites in the putamen. (Tracers are substances that reveal neural pathways; anterograde ones project forward from a population of neurons, and retrograde tracers project backward.) Injection of retrograde tracers in the globus pallidus (GP), the output stage of the basal ganglia, indicates that dispersed matrisomes in the putamen, in turn, converge to a small area of the GP. As Graybiel et al. (1994) pointed out,

> This divergence–reconvergence pattern suggests one way to have an overall parallel processing scheme for cortico-basal ganglia interactions and at the same time to maximize computational power within channels. (p. 1827)

The basal ganglia carry out similar functions in human beings. Cunnington et al. (1995) demonstrated the role of basal ganglia in human subjects executing sequential, self-paced, manual, motor-control tasks. Their experiment monitored the activity of the supplementary motor area of the cortex by means of movement-related potentials (MRPs) in both Parkinson's disease (PD) and normal subjects who executed both voluntary internally generated and voluntary externally cued manual sequential activity by pushing buttons with their index fingers. MRPs reflect the planning and execution of these movements. Cunnington et al. (1995) noted that

> The supplementary motor area receives its dominant input from the ventral lateral thalmus, which in turn receives projections almost exclusively from the globus pallidus—the major output unit of the basal ganglia. Consequently, basal ganglia function can be investigated by examining MRP's of supplementary motor area (p. 936).

The manual tasks executed by the normal control and PD subjects in this study included ones in which timing and/or spatial patterns were predictable. Increased pre-movement MRPs in normal subjects were present only when timing was predictable; premovement MRPs for PD subjects in these conditions were absent or greatly diminished. The detailed analysis of their data led Cunnington et al. (1995) to conclude that the basal ganglia

> provide an internal cue to terminate supplementary motor area activity following movement, and to activate the preparatory phase for the next submovement, thereby switching between components of a motor sequence. Since the basal ganglia and supplementary motor area are more involved in temporal rather than spatial aspects of serial movement, this internal cuing mechanism would coordinate the switch between

> motor components at the appropriate time, thus controlling the timing of submovement initiation. (p. 948)

Marsden and Obeso (1994), reviewing studies in which surgical lesions were made in human subjects to relieve some of the effects of Parkinson's disease also concluded the following:

> The role of the basal ganglia in controlling movement must give insight into their other functions, particularly if thought is mental movement without motion. Perhaps the basal ganglia are an elaborate machine, within the overall frontal lobe distributed system, that allow routine thought and action, but which responds to new circumstances to allows a change in direction of ideas and movement. Loss of basal ganglia contribution, such as in Parkinson's disease, thus would lead to inflexibility of mental and motor response. (p. 893)

EXPERIMENTS IN NATURE EXPLORING SPEECH AND SYNTAX

Because the intermediate stages of hominid evolution having brains that might have possessed partial human language are extinct, we must make inferences concerning the evolution of the human brain based on its present state. However, as many evolutionary biologists have noted, the historical "logic" of evolution is evident when we study living species (Mayr, 1982). The studies that I briefly review here (details are noted in Lieberman, 2000) show that subcortical basal ganglia structures that regulate the motor activity resulting in overt speech are also active when humans comprehend the meaning of a sentence or perform certain cognitive tasks.

The data of Lieberman et al. (1992) showed that the pattern of speech production deficits and syntax comprehension deficits in nondemented Parkinson's disease (PD) subjects was similar in nature to that noted for Broca's aphasia. Parkinson's disease affects the basal ganglia mostly sparing the cortex. Acoustic analysis of the speech of 40 PD subjects showed a breakdown in 9 subjects' ability to control the production of stop-consonant vowel sequences. The acoustic parameter that differentiates the syllable *ba* from *pa* is the time interval between the instant at which a person's lips open and the start of phonation generated by the larynx. Phonation results when the larynx produces periodic "puffs of air", the rate at which these occur is perceived as the "pitch" of a person's voice. Voice-onset time (VOT) differentiates these sounds as well as stop consonants in syllables such as ta, *da*, ga,and *ka*. The supralaryngeal airway is obstructed at the start of these syllables. The sequence in which it is opened relative to the start of phonation results in short VOTs for *ba*, *da*, and *ga* and long VOTs for *pa*, *ta*, and *ka*. Broca's aphasics lose the ability to control the sequence. The problem is not in timing alone because they can produce the distinctions in vowel length that signal the same consonants when the occur after a vowel

(Blumstein, Cooper, Goodglass, Statlender, & Gottlieb, 1980). The PD subjects, like Broca's aphasics, also had difficulty comprehending sentences that had relatively complex syntax or that were long. The number of VOT sequencing errors and number of syntax errors was highly correlated $r = .65, p < .01$) for these subjects.

A battery of cognitive tests was also administered as reported in Lieberman et al. (1992). The moderately impaired PD subjects made significantly more errors than mildly impaired PD subjects on the Odd-Man-Out test (Flowers & Robertson, 1985)—a sorting test that measures the ability to derive an abstract criterion necessary to solve a problem and then shift to a new criterion. The Odd-Man-Out test can be regarded as a probe of both visual and verbal working memory because it involves sorting both geometrical figures that differ in size and shape, and upper and lower case letters of the alphabet that appear to be represented and phonetically rehearsed in verbal working memory (Awh et al., 1996). The moderately impaired PD subjects also made significantly more errors than mildly impaired PD subjects on other tests involving working memory—that is, tests of short-term and long-term recall, delayed recognition and the Digit Span Backward test (a test in which a subject has to repeat a string of digits backward).

It would be reasonable to suppose that impaired laryngeal control rather than sequencing caused the VOT deficits noted for both PD and aphasia. Impaired laryngeal control, perceptually characterized as hoarse (termed *dysarthric*) speech, frequently occurs in Broca's aphasia and as extremely quiet speech, (termed*hypophonia*) in PD. These speech production problems may reflect disruption of the neural circuitry regulating laryngeal control, which in monkeys involves the dopamine-sensitive neural circuits. A study of Chinese-speaking PD subjects resolved the question of whether laryngeal function or sequencing underlies the VOT deficits noted in PD. Chinese and most other languages make use of "phonemic tones," controlled variations in F0, to differentiate words. The syllable [ma] produced with a level F0 contour in Mandarin Chinese, for example, signifies *mother*, whereas it signifies *hemp* when produced with a rising F0 contour. A study of Chinese-speaking PD subjects (Lieberman & Tseng, 1994) has replicated the VOT defits noted earlier. Although VOT sequencing was disrupted in these PD subjects when they had not received medication restoring the neurotransmitter deficits that occur in PD, the regulation of the phonemic "tones" that differentiate words in Chinese languages was not affected. The phonemic tones of Chinese involve the production of pitch contours, produced by laryngeal control. Because these pitch contours were preserved, we can conclude that laryngeal control was not impaired. The VOT performance of the Chinese speakers improved when they received their medication that restores the neurotransmitter depleted by PD.

The data of Lange et al. (1992) also demonstrate beyond reasonable doubt that basal ganglia dysfunction, in itself, produces cognitive deficits similar in nature to those associated with frontal-lobe dysfunction. The error rates and "thinking times" (the time necessary to plan the task's solution) of PD subjects were compared when they were unmedicated and medicated on the Tower of London test, which tests planning usually associated with frontal lobe function. Patients who suffer focal frontal-lobe damage have difficulty with this test. In this test the PD subjects saw a computer-generated "target" picture of three colored balls inside two hoops. The third hoop was empty. The subject's task was to move the balls in the two hoops of a second computer-generated image presented below the target image to match the target configuration. Error rates and thinking times were significantly higher and longer when the subjects were not medicated. Thinking times were calculated by subtracting the increases in the time required by PD subjects to move their fingers on the computer screen. A special procedure allowed the investigators to determine motor movement delays due to PD.

Focal Brain Damage

Further evidence for basal ganglia activity regulating sequencing in speech production, syntax, and cognition was noted by Pickett et al. (1998) in a subject who had suffered brain damage restricted to profound bilateral damage to the putamen and some damage to the anterior caudate nucleus (both structures are part of the basal ganglia). The subject showed impaired sequencing of the articulatory gestures that constitute the speech motor programs of English words. Acoustic analyses showed that the subject's speech was degraded due to inappropriate sequencing of anatomically independent articulatory structures, inappropriate nasalization, missynchronized consonantal bursts, and peculiar distributions of VOT sequencing. The subject was unable to properly sequence the intercostal muscles of the chest that regulate lung air pressure with upper airway articulation. Transient changes in amplitude occurred. However, intrinsic vowel and consonantal durations were maintained. The subject also had a 14% error rate when she was required to comprehend distinctions in meaning conveyed by syntax using a sensitive test instrument, the Test of Distinctions in Meaning Conveyed by Syntax (TMS). The subject's errors here also appeared to reflect an inability to shift conceptual sequences. High error rates occurred when she responded to probe questions concerning active sentences or questions in active voice concerning information presented in passive sentences. The subject also had problems terminating syntactic–semantic processing of embedded clauses, switching to the analysis of new material at clause boundaries. Cognitive deficits involving sequencing also occurred for this severely compromised subject; the subject had a 70% error rate on the Odd-Man-Out test (Flowers & Robertson, 1985; described earlier). Cognitive preservation occurred when the subject was asked to shift from sorting by shape to size or from size to shape. In contrast, performance was within normal ranges in tests of lexical access and memory. Damage to circuits supported in the putamen and anterior caudate nucleus clearly were the neurological bases for these behavioral deficits.

Verbal Working Memory, Speech, and Syntax

The apparent link between speech production and syntax that supports the probable existence of an FLS may derive from the role of verbal working memory in the comprehension of language. Baddeley (1986) proposed a model for the comprehension of language in which words of a sentence are maintained in a memory buffer while cognitive processing derives meaning taking into account syntax, context, and the meanings of the words. One of the mechanisms involved in maintaining the memory trace is "phonetic rehearsal"—a sort of silent speech in which the brain mechanisms involved in speech production are activated. Baddeley noted indirect evidence supporting this hypothesis, which has been confirmed by the data of subsequent brain imaging studies (Awh et al; 1996). Damage to the neural substrate that regulates speech production in PD and Broca's subjects having VOT sequencing deficits would necessarily disrupt the phonetic rehearsal mechanism of verbal working memory. Impaired phonetic rehearsal, in turn, could account for some of the sentence comprehension deficits noted for these subjects. Impaired phonetic rehearsal could also account for a portion of the deficits in cognitive tasks involving verbal working memory such as the Odd-Man-Out test and the Wisconsin Card Sorting Test, on which PD subjects perform poorly (Cummings, 1993).

Deficits in the comprehension of sentences by aged people are consistent with the claim that working memory capacity is limited by phonetic rehearsal. The phenomenon is not general; some people well into their eighties produce utterances and write books that have complex rich prose styles. A correlation between slow speech and the impaired comprehension of spoken sentences in aged people was found by Lieberman, Feldman, Aronson, and Engen (1989). The comprehension of distinctions in meaning conveyed by syntax was tested for people aged 71 to 93 years. Although older subjects as a group tended to have higher error rates, there was no consistent age-related increase in syntactic errors. Vowel duration was measured for 24 of the subjects. The procedure excluded tokens that had long durations due to emphatic stress or prepausal lengthening; the three shortest exemplars of the vowels [i] and [u] were measured. Older speakers tended to have longer vowel durations, but individual differences override this effect. For example, the longest (426 msec) and shortest (278 msec) average vowel durations were produced by 78-year-old subjects. The group of subjects who produced the longest average vowel durations (329 msec, *SD* 33) had the highest syntactic error rates (16% to 32% errors). The group of subjects who produced the shortest average vowel durations (277 msec, *SD* 48) made no errors on the sentence comprehension test. Slower speech production would inherently limit phonetic refreshment in working memory if the slow speech reflected neural processing rather than reduced muscle tone.

The phonetic rehearsal hypothesis receives some support from strong correlations between speech motor control deficits and the comprehension of distinctions of meaning conveyed by syntax in young, otherwise robust individuals who do not manifest deficits in nonlinguistic cognitive tests. Evidence for this was found in a study of mountain climbers ascending Mount Everest. The subjects showed co-occurring decrements in subjects' regulation of stop-consonant VOT, similar in nature but not as extreme as in PD, and in the time that it took to comprehend simple English sentences (Lieberman; Kanki, Protopapas, Reed, & Young, 1994; Lieberman, Kanki, & Protopapas, 1995). The ascent of Mount Everest by the "normal" South Col route involves a staying at a series of high camps over a 3-month period. A battery of speech, syntax and cognitive tests similar to those used to assess deficits in PD subjects (Lieberman et al., 1992) was administered to five climbers when they first reached each of these progressively higher camps. The mean VOT separation width that differentiates voiced stop consonants such as [b], [d], and [g] from "unvoiced" [p], [t], and [k] decreased from 26.0 to 6.4 msec. The time needed to comprehend spoken English sentences also increased. Response times were 54% longer at Camp Three for simple sentences that are readily comprehended by 6-year-old children. Sentence response time and VOT decrements were strongly correlated $r = -.774$, $p < .001$). In contrast, performance was not impaired on cognitive tests that involved the retrieval of words from memory, digit span forwards and backwards, and tests of reasoning.

The possible effects of extreme cold and fatigue were ruled out as causatives. Reduced activity in basal ganglia structures, which are sensitive to oxygen deprivation (Cummings, 1993), was the most likely cause of these speech and syntax deficits. The findings are significant because the subjects were in peak physical condition; the brain mechanisms implicated obviously were lightly stressed because the subjects were able to ascend to the summit of Mount Everest. Under these conditions a strong correlation between speech production and the comprehension of syntax was evident. Given the involvement of speech production in rehearsal (e.g., Baddeley, 1986; Awh et al., 1996), these highly correlated deficits in regulating speech motor timing and the comprehension of sentences is not surprising.

INNATENESS AND EVOLUTION

A complete specification of the brain mechanisms and neural circuitry of the functional language system is not possible, given our ignorance of how biological brains work. Although I have stressed the role of subcortical basal ganglia, it is apparent that these structures form part of a complex network involving the prefrontal cortex and areas of the primary visual and auditory cortex, as well as the traditional "language areas" of the brain and right- hemisphere homologues. How they evolved is not clear, but it is highly probable that the process was gradual. There appears to have been no "magic bullet" effect in the course of hominid evolution. For example, contrary to claims that human language derives from the disproportionate expansion of the prefrontal cortex (Deacon, 1988) or some other unspecified saltation that gave us better brains (Bickerton, 1990), quantitative studies show that the proportions of the human brain's frontal cortex are similar to those of apes, (Semendeferi et al., 1997). Since the relative proportions of the human frontal regions involved in motor control are not reduced compared to apes we can conclude that the human prefrontal cortex is not disproportionately large. Humans have bigger brains overall. The quantitative difference between the human and nonhuman primate brain may simply be the answer. For example, the quantitative difference between a supercomputer's logical components and the similar components of a hand-held calculator yields qualitative differences in the tasks that they can perform. Human manual dexterity, speech, language, and cognition all seem to be the result of the larger size and computing power of the human brain, and we can trace the gradual expansion of the hominid brain through the fossil record.

Other data argue for a long, gradual increment in linguistic ability. The enhancement of phonetic ability that follows from the restructuring of the human mouth, tongue, and throat yields more efficient speech. But as Edmund S. Crelin and I noted in 1971, the enhancement of human phonetic ability has a biological cost-less efficient swallowing. Humans can produce sounds that enhance the perception of speech, but the cost is increased susceptibility to choking to death while swallowing food. But natural selection enhancing speech communication could only occur if speech were already in place in the hominids who preceded anatomically modern *Homo sapiens*. Hence we can conclude that the hominid species ancestral to both anatomically modern human beings (us) and Neanderthals was already talking. *Homo erectus*, the ancestral species to both humans and Neanderthals also must have had limited syntactic ability because present-day apes have this ability. Because apes diverged from the common ancestor of all hominids and apes some 5 million years ago, some syntactic ability must have been present in all subsequent hominid species. Thus syntax, contrary to the claims of linguists like Derek Bickerton, was not the magic that changed "proto-language" to language. *Homo erectus* may have talked more slowly than we do and used simpler, shorter sentences, the evidence is not yet conclusive, but it is almost certain that the evolution of human language and thought was gradual. As for the selective pressures that shaped human language, paraphrasing Charles Darwin, it is clear that language enhances virtually all aspects of the infinitely complex ways in which we cope with external nature and other organisms. Thus it is futile, if not silly, to attempt to find "the" factor that provided the selective advantage for the evolution of human linguistic ability.

As for the issue of innateness, although the biological substrate of the functional language system clearly is genetically specified, it is clear that the details are not. The studies of Elizabeth Bates and her colleagues (1999) demonstrate, beyond reasonable doubt, that children acquire language after the destruction of virtually all of the cortical structures traditionally supposed to be the sites in which grammar is stored. Similar effects are now being observed in adults. There appears to be a preference for certain cortical regions to regulate language, but cortical plasticity allows other regions to assume these tasks (Elman et al., 1997). This explains the patterns of variation long evident in neurobiological studies of language, for example, in the cortical stimulation studies of George Ojemann and his colleagues (Ojemann, Ojemann, Letich, & Berger, 1989). Indeed, the constraints on the FLS seem to derive from relatively primitive subcortical structures that channel sensory information to neocortex. Thus the evolution of our human capacity for speech, language, and thinking is a demonstration of the continuity of evolution. Both primitive, phylogenetically ancient neural structures and derived structures that are largest in humans are involved. We are unique, but it is the uniqueness that defines any species.

REFERENCES

Aldridge, J. W., Berridge, K. C., Herman, M., & Zimmer, L. (1993). Neuronal coding of serial order: Syntax of grooming in the neostratum. *Psychological Science, 4,* 391–393.

Alexander, G. E., Delong, M. R., & Strick, P. L. (1986). Parallel organization of segregated circuits linking basal ganglia and cortex. *Annual Review of Neuroscience, 9,* 357–381.

Awh, E., Jonides, J., Smith, R. E., Schumacher, E. H., Koeppe, R. A., & Katz, S. (1996). Dissociation of storage and rehearsal in working memory: Evidence from positron emission tomography. *Psychological Science 17,* 25–31.

Baddeley, A. D. (1986). *Working memory.* Oxford: Clarendon Press.

Bates, E., Vicari, S., & Trauner, D. (1999). Neural mediation of language development: Perspectives from lesion studies of infants and children. In H. Tager-Flusberg (Ed.), *Neurodevelopmental disorders: Contributions to a new framework from the cognitive neurosciences.* Cambridge, MA: MIT Press.

Blumstein, S. E., Cooper, W., Goodglass, H., Statlender, H., & Gottleib, J. (1980). Production deficits in aphasia: A voice-onset time analysis. *Brain and Language, 9,* 153–170.

Bickerton, D. (1990). *Language and species.* Chicago: University of Chicago Press.

Bickerton, D. (1998). Paper presented at the 2nd International Conference on the Evolution of Language, London.

Cheney, D. L., & Seyfarth, R. M. (1990). *How monkeys see the world: Inside the mind of another species.* Chicago: University of Chicago Press.

Cummings, J. L. (1993). Frontal-subcortical circuts and human behavior. *Archives of Neurology, 50,* 873–880.

Cunnington, R., Iansek, R., Bradshaw, J. L., & Philips, J. G. (1995). Movement-related potentials in Parkinson's disease: Presence and predictability of temporal and spatial cues. *Brain, 118,* 935–950.

Darwin, C. (1964). *On the origin of species.* Cambridge: MA: Harvard University Press.(original work published 1964)

Deacon, T. W. (1988). Human brain evolution: Evolution of language circuits. In H. J. Jerison & I. Jerison (Eds.), *Intelligence and evolutionary biology* (pp. 363–382).Berlin: NATO ASI Series.

Elman J., Bates, E., Johnson, M., Karmiloff-Smith, A., Parisi, D., & Plunkett, K. (1997). *Rethinking innateness: A connectionist perspective on development.* Cambridge, MA: MIT Press/Bradford Books.

Flowers, K. A., & Robertson, C. (1985). The effects of Parkinson's disease on the ability to maintain a mental set. *Journal of Neurology, Neurosurgery, and Psychiatry, 48,* 517–529.

Fodor, J. (1983). *Modularity of mind.* Cambridge, MA: MIT Press.

Gardner, B. T., & Gardner, R. A. (in press). Development of phrases in the utterances of children and cross-fostered chimpanzees.*The ethological roots of culture.* In R. A. Gardner, B. T. Gardner, B. Chiarelli, & R. Plooj (Eds.), Boston: Kluwer.

Goodall, J. (1986). *The chimpanzees of Gombe: Patterns of behavior.* Cambridge, MA: Harvard University Press.

Graybiel, A. M., Aosaki, T., Flaherty, A. W., & Kimura, M. (1994). The basal ganglia and adaptive motor control. *Science, 265*, 1826–1831.

Grossman, M., Carvell, S., Gollomp S., Stern, M. B., Vernon, G., & Hurtig, H. I. (1991). Sentence comprehension and praxis deficits in Parkinson's disease, *Neurology, 41*, 160–1628.

Grossman, M., Carvell, S., Gollomp, S., Stern, M. B., Reivich, Morrison, D., Alavi, A., & Hurtig, H. L. (1993). Cognitive and physiological substrates of impaired sentence processing in Parkinson's disease. *Journal of Cognitive Neuroscience, 5*, 480–498.

Kimura, M., Aosaki, T., & Graybiel, A. (1993). Role of basal ganglia in the acquisition and initiation of learned movement. In N. Mano, I., Hamada, & M. R. DeLong (Eds.), *Role of the cerebellum and basal ganglia in voluntary movements* (pp. 83–87). Amsterdam: Elsevier.

Lashley, K. S. (1951). The problem of serial order in behavior. In L. A. Jefress (Ed.), *Cerebral mechanisms in behavior* (pp. 112–146). New York: Wiley.

Lichtheim, L. (1885). On aphasia. *Brain, 7*, 433–484.

Lieberman, P. (1968). Primate vocalizations and human linguistic ability. *Journal of the Acoustical Society of America, 44*, 1157–1164.

Lieberman, P. (1984). *The biology and evolution of language*. Cambridge, MA:Harvard University Press.

Lieberman, P. (1985). On the evolution of human syntactic ability: Its pre-adaptive bases—motor control and speech. *Journal of Human Evolution, 14*, 657–668.

Lieberman, P. (1991). *Uniquely human: The evolution of speech, thought, and selfless behavior.* Cambridge, MA: Harvard University Press.

Lieberman, P. (1994). Biologically bound behavior, free–will, and human evolution. In J. I. Casti (Ed.), *Conflict and cooperation in nature* (pp. 133–163). New York: John Wiley and Sons.

Lieberman, P., (2000). *Human languages and our ? Brain: The subcortual bases of speech, syntax and thought.* Cambridge, MA: Harvard University Press.

Lieberman, P., Feldman, L. S., Aronson, S., & Engen, B. (1989). Sentence comprehension, syntax and vowel duration in aged people. *Clinical Linguistics and Phonetics, 3*, 299–311.

Lieberman, P., Friedman, J., & Feldman, L. S. (1990). Syntactic deficits in Parkinson's disease. *Journal of Nervous and Mental Disease, 178*, 360–365.

Lieberman, P., Kako, E.T., Friedman, J., Tajchman, G., Feldman, L. S., & Jiminez, E. B. (1992). Speech production, syntax comprehension, and cognitive deficits in Parkinson's disease. *Brain and Language, 43*, 169–189.

Lieberman, P., & Tseng, C.-Y. (1994). Subcortical pathways essential for speech, language and cognition: Implications for hominid evolution. *American Journal of Physical Anthropology, 16*, 93–130.

Lieberman, P., Kanki, B. G., & Protopapas, A., Reed, E., & Youngs, J.W. (1994). Cognitive defects at altitude. *Nature, 372*, 325.

Lieberman, P., Kanki, B. G., Protopapas, A. (1995). Speech production and cognitive decrements on Mount Everest. *Aviation, Space and Environmental Medicine, 66*, 857–864.

Marsden, C. D., & Obeso, J. A. (1994). The functions of the basal ganglia and the paradox of sterotaxic surgery in Parkinson's disease. *Brain, 117*, 877–897.

Martin, A., Wiggs, C. L., Ungerleider, L. G., & Haxby, J. V. (1995). Neural correlates of category-specific knowledge. *Nature, 379*, 649–652.

Mesulam, M. M. (1990). Large–scale neurocognitive networks and distributed processing for attention, language, and memory. *Annals of Neurology, 28*, 597–613.

Mirenowicz, J., & Schultz, W. (1996). Preferential activation of midbrain dopamine neurons by appetitive rather than aversive stimuli. *Nature, 379*, 449–451.

Natsopoulos, D., Grouios, G., Bostantzopoulou, S., Mentenopoulos, G., Katsarou, Z., & Logothetis, J. (1993). Algorithmic and heuristic strategies in comprehension of complement clauses by patients with Parkinson's disease. *Neuropsychologia, 31*, 951–964.

Ojemann, G. A. Ojemann, F., Lettich, E., & Berger, M. (1989). Cortical language localization in left dominant hemisphere: An electrical stimulation mapping investigation in 117 patients. *Journal of Neurosurgery, 71*, 316–326.

Pinker, S. (1994). *The language instinct: How the mind creates language*. New York: William Morrow.

Savage-Rumbaugh, E. S., & Rumbaugh, D. (1993). The emergence of language. In K. R. Gibson & T. Ingold (Eds.), *Tools, language and cognition in human evolution* (pp. 86–100). Cambridge: Cambridge University Press.

Semendeferi, K., Damasio, H., Frank, R., & Van Hoesen, G. W. (1997). The evolution of the frontal lobes: A volumetric analysis based on three-dimensional reconstructions of magnetic resonance scans of human and ape brains. *Journal of Human Evolution, 32*, 375–378.

2

Language, Mind, and Culture: From Linguistic Relativity to Representational Modularity

Giovanni Bennardo
Department of Anthropology and Cognitive Studies Program
Northern Illinois University

Mayan speakers of Yucatec classify objects by paying more attention to substance (i.e., materials) than shape, contrary to what English speakers do (Lucy, 1992a). Yucatec is a classifier language,[1] and, according to Lucy, most Yucatec nouns are mass nouns (i.e., uncountable nouns). Because the meanings of mass nouns universally express substance, Lucy suggested that this linguistic feature determines the characteristics of the Yucatec object classification system. In other words, language affects thought.

Australian (North Queensland) Aboriginals speaking Guugu Yimithirr cannot describe the positions of objects in relation to themselves or the positions of two objects to each other without using the names of cardinal points (Levinson, 1997). That is, any object will be described as to the north, south, east, or west of the speaker or of another object. The language does not allow the speaker to use expressions such as "to the right of" or "in front of" simply because these expressions do not exist. Furthermore, Guugu Yimithirr speakers habitually organize the

[1]A classifier languages is a language in which morphemes called *classifiers* precede or follow lexical items to indicate that they belong to the same semantic class. Basis for classification can be number, shape, size, color, animacy, etc.

spatiality of their world in mental patterns similar to those expressed in their language (i.e., in absolute terms). Levinson (1997) posited a causal relationship between these linguistic and mental patterns; that is, language constrains thought.

Children speaking English, Spanish, German, or Hebrew as young as 3 years old, describe pictures illustrating a story by using rhetorical styles that are typical of the language they speak (Slobin, 1996). It seems that the language we acquire orients our apprehension of human—experiences, that is, **"affects the way we think while we are speaking"** (Slobin, 1996, p. 91 [bold in original]). Twenty-month-old Korean children correctly use different verbs for encoding spontaneous versus caused motion along a particular path, whereas English children correctly use the same prepositions (e.g., in, out, on, off) for both situations (Bowerman, 1996, p. 405). Explicit and complex characteristics of their languages (not just sound patterns) are learned and may shape children's apprehension of the world even before they can confidently walk.

These examples represent only some of the findings that have rekindled interest in linguistic relativity in the last decade. Traditionally, investigators working within the linguistic relativity paradigm, also referred to as the Sapir-Whorf hypothesis, claimed that the characteristics of the language spoken determine the way in which people think about the world. This claim has typically been referred to as the "strong" form of the linguistic relativity hypothesis. After being seriously challenged in the 1960s and 1970s, linguistic relativity has become again a significant part of the discourse in many disciplines about the relationship between language, mind, and culture. Because these new proposals do not claim "determinism" but only "constraining" phenomena, they are referred to as the "weak" form of linguistic relativity.

What is the paradigm that generates this (recent) revival of linguistic relativity (henceforth LR)? That is, are there common theoretical assumptions that unify the various types of research about LR? Is there a common methodological approach that would allow a cross-utilization of data and a cross-comparison of findings? And, most importantly, what is the broader significance of the various findings within the larger inquiry about the relationships between language, mind, and culture?

It may appear that the current research on LR is neither theoretically nor methodologically unified. The authors who make overt or implicit reference to the LR paradigm[2] are linguistic anthropologists (e.g., Lucy), psycholinguists (e.g., Slobin, Bowerman), and cognitive anthropologists (e.g., Levinson). They employ a variety of methods that either are specific to their disciplines or are cross-disciplinary hybrids. Is it possible to find shared assumptions behind these apparently diversified approaches?

The first goal of the present work is to clarify whether common assumptions underscore the various research projects within the LR paradigm. The second

---

[2]Typically LR has been called a *hypothesis*, or more precisely, the Sapir–*Whorf hypothesis*. I explain in the next section why I prefer to call it a *paradigm*.

goal is to introduce two alternative contemporary approaches to the relationship between language, mind, and culture. The third goal is to suggest and briefly delineate an approach to cognition with clear consequences for the description of mental, linguistic, and cultural phenomena.

This chapter begins with a very brief outline of the genesis of the LR paradigm. I continue by discussing three different areas of research that have challenged the paradigm—color, ethnobotany, and kinship. Then I discuss in detail some contemporary research within the LR paradigm. Most of these investigations give primacy to language over cognition and culture. Finally, I introduce two proposals about cognitive architecture, and I use them to offer my own suggestion regarding the relationship between language, mind, and culture.

In my proposal I argue for a perspective that considers language and culture as cognitive phenomena, that is, as essential organizing principles of mental representations of knowledge. These basic principles are relational and hence properly described as *structures*—that is relational properties are, in principle, descriptive algebras or theories (Bennardo, 1996; J. D. Keller & Lehman, 1991; Lehman, 1985). These principles (or theories) are computational because they have indefinite generative capacity (see Chomsky, 1995; Jackendoff, 1997). In other words, structure is not to be identified with a static grid matrix of fixed relations, but with a theory from which numbers of theorems can be produced.

THE LINGUISTIC RELATIVITY PARADIGM: BOAS, SAPIR, AND WHORF

In 1911, Boas, one of the generally recognized fathers of modern anthropology, wrote:

> Thus it appears that from practical, as well as from theoretical, points of view, the study of language must be considered as one of the most important branches of ethnological studies, because, on the one hand, a thorough insight into ethnology can not be gained without practical knowledge of language, and, on the other hand, the fundamental concepts illustrated by human languages are not distinct in kind from ethnological phenomena; and because, furthermore, the peculiar characteristics of languages are clearly reflected in the views and customs of the peoples of the world. (Boas, 1911, p. 69)

His call for closer attention to the languages of the peoples studied was motivated by an academic milieu in which ethnological research was mainly conducted by means of interpreters. One of his main theoretical contributions consists of the manifest statement that the similarity "in kind" of language and culture (both "mental" and "unconscious" in nature) ensures the possibility of describing characteristics of the latter by studying the former. However, he also stated:

> It does not seem likely ... that there is any direct relation between the culture of a tribe and the language they speak, except in so far as the form of the language will be molded by the state of culture, but not in so far as a certain state of culture is conditioned by morphological traits of the language. (Boas, 1911, p. 63)

Language is essential to ethnological studies because it is "molded" by the culture within which it is used. Language is simply "reflected" in culture. One of Boas's students, Edward Sapir, capitalized on these fundamental intuitions and started building what I have called the LR paradigm.

Sapir's main interest was language. He wrote extensively about it and his writings contributed substantively to the establishing of modern linguistics. Relevant are his discussion of the "phonemic" reality of language and his definition of grammar as a "formal procedure ... employed by the speakers of a language in order to build ... symbol sequences ... out of ... isolable units" (Sapir, 1949b, p. 9). Some of the core theoretical assumptions of linguistic structuralism are clearly summarized in this sentence (cf. de Saussure, 1959).

Sapir's deep knowledge of a variety of languages and his keen linguistic intuitions led him to suggest the isomorphism between the ontology expressed in language and a "possible" mental ontology. Thus, his often cited quote:

> [T]he "real world" is to a large extent unconsciously built up on the language habits of the group. No two languages are ever sufficiently similar to be considered as representing the same reality. The worlds in which different societies live are distinct worlds, not merely the same world with different labels attached. (Sapir, 1949a, p. 162)

Language carves "a" reality out of many possible ones. Linguistic practices affect thought and the construction of a worldview. This, however, does not entail that language affects culture; on the contrary, "there is no general correlation between cultural type and linguistic structure" (Sapir, 1949b, p. 26). Vocabulary is the only part of language that is "a very sensitive index of the culture of a people" (1949b, p. 27).

The writings of Benjamin Lee Whorf, a student of Sapir and a Boas admirer, brought to completion the edifice of the LR paradigm. Whorf defined what he called a "linguistic relativity principle" as follows:

> [U]sers of markedly different grammars are pointed by the grammars toward different types of observations and different evaluations of externally similar acts of observation, and hence are not equivalent as observers but must arrive at somewhat different views of the world. (Whorf, 1956, p. 221)

In line with Boas and Sapir, Whorf distinguished between "covert" and "overt" categories that characterize two different classificatory styles implicit in language.[3] The covert categories may interact with other mental activities and consequently contribute to the construction of "different views of the world." The great innovation that he introduced is the systematic and explicit attempt to consider discovered "covert" categories of English and Hopi languages as analogous to complex patterns of behavior in the two peoples speaking those languages. He defined his investigation in this way:

> This portion of the whole investigation here to be reported may be summed up in two questions: (1) Are our own concepts of "time," "space," and "matter" given in substantially the same form by experience to all men, or are they in part conditioned by the structure of particular languages? (2) Are there traceable affinities between (a) cultural and behavioral norms and (b) large-scale linguistic patterns? (Whorf, 1956, p. 138)

He answered the second question affirmatively, thus accepting that "cultural and behavioral norms" are partially conditioned by the way in which language structures the ontological categories of time and matter. Regarding "space" he said that "the apprehension of space is given in substantially the same form by experience irrespective of language" (Whorf, 1956, p. 158). It is very important to keep in mind not only the specific content of his proposal, but also the ontological categories to which he referred (time, matter, and space). We show later how they define the shape of much of the contemporary LR paradigm revival.

Finally, Whorf introduced the concept of "habitual thought," which he defined in this way:

> By "habitual thought" and "thought world" I mean more than simply language, i.e. than the linguistic patterns themselves. I include all the analogical and suggestive value of the patterns (e.g., our "imaginary space" and its distant implications), and all the give-and-take between language and the culture as a whole, wherein is a vast amount that is not linguistic but yet shows the shaping influence of language. In brief, this "thought world" is the microcosm that each man carries about within himself, by which he measures and understands what he can of the macrocosm. (Whorf, 1956, p. 147)

This "thought," in other words, is the one of everyday life, not the specialized one of experts or of specific restricted domains (see Lucy, 1992b, p. 7). It is proposed that it is within this type of mental activity that the influence of the language will be felt most strongly. This influence will affect people's behavior as well.

In summary, Boas opened the way to a treatment of language and culture as mental phenomena whose study could illuminate the contents and characteris-

---

[3]An "overt" category is always explicitly marked in the language. For example, number is always expressed in English, either by a plural marker or by the form of the verb, or by the use of articles. A "covert" category is not always expressed. For example, intransitivity of English verbs becomes transparent only when we realize that they cannot be used in certain specific forms—that is, they lack the passive participle (Whorf, 1956, pp. 88–90).

tics of both. Sapir suggested that the investigation of linguistic patterns would reveal a set of ontological choices. Thus, the construction of one's worldview would be affected by the choices inherent in one's language. Whorf set out to demonstrate empirically that these assumptions are conducive to valid explanations of both linguistic and behavioral patterns coexisting in two strikingly different cultures and languages—Hopi and English. It must be underlined that like Boas, both Sapir and Whorf assumed universal characteristics (either in the content or processes) of the human mind. This often-forgotten side of their suggestions anticipated and contributed to advance studies now under the rubric of cognitive science (see Furbee & Shaul, 1998, p. 52).

The proposals just outlined came to be erroneously labeled as the *Sapir-Whorf hypothesis* (Hoijer, 1954/1995; Lenneberg & Roberts, 1956). In reality, neither Sapir nor Whorf ever presented or discussed a distinct "hypothesis." Their ideas about the relationship between language, mind, and culture could be better characterized as a set of assumptions or axioms that may generate hypotheses (see Hill & Mannheim, 1992, p. 383). These could eventually be supported or not supported by a variety of investigations. It is for this reason that I have decided to call their proposals the LR *paradigm*.

Kuhn introduces and defines the concept of paradigm in this way:

> By choosing it [paradigm], I mean to suggest that some accepted examples of actual scientific practice ... provide models from which spring particular coherent traditions of scientific research. (1970, p. 10)

These "models" are accepted as the mold within which and by which research questions are generated. These questions may eventually be answered, but the paradigm will continue to be held as a viable construct. Only when "revolutions" occur is a new paradigm established.

Investigators in three research areas—color, ethnobotany, and kinship—have generated questions within the LR paradigm. Their findings have brought about significant changes in the study of the relationship between language, mind, and culture. These changes need to be interpreted within the revolutionary—in a Kuhnian sense—generative paradigm that characterizes many of the linguistic investigations since 1957, the date of the publication of Chomsky's *Syntactic Structures*.

In the generative paradigm, language as a mental phenomenon (i.e., competence) is chosen as the focus of the investigation. Structuralist discovery procedures applied to finite linguistic corpuses are abandoned as a consequence of the realization that data processing simply rearranges the data but does not explain them, and that any linguistic corpus is infinite. The goal is now to identify the finite set of rules used to govern the potentially infinite number of forms manifested in linguistic production (i.e., performance). Rule-governed behavior (linguistic in this case) is limited and constrained by well-formedness conditions, which can be empirically studied by looking at the behavioral regularities themselves. From a number of language-specific rules, some universal language rules and parameters can be evinced, and posited as features of a biological human endowment, including an innate language faculty or language acquisition device (LAD). The internal modularity of the language faculty (Chomsky, 1986, 1995) is considered a model on which is based the notion that the mind's architecture is modular (Fodor, 1983; Hirschfeld & Gelman, 1994; Jackendoff, 1997).

CHALLENGING THE PARADIGM: LEXICAL DOMAINS AND UNIVERSALS

The research on lexical domains is generated by one of the assumptions of the LR paradigm: At the lexical level, major cultural differences are represented (see Sapir, 1949b, p. 27). In this discussion I focus on work on the lexical domains of color, ethnobotany, and kinship. These domains are neither the investigators' arbitrary choices nor mine. Regarding the investigators' choices, these are some of the few domains whose borders are clearly delineated by a closed set of lexical items. Moreover, a number of members of these sets, even if minimal (two in the case of color), are universally found throughout the languages of the world. Regarding my choice, the findings about these particular domains are considered as the most challenging to the LR paradigm.

Color

It is well known that languages differ in the number of terms they have to cover the color spectrum. This difference has been used to argue in favor of LR (Lenneberg & Roberts, 1956). The difference in the number of linguistic terms in a particular language was interpreted as a different way of thinking about (i.e., conceptualizing) the domain of color by its speakers.

In 1969, Berlin and Kay published the results of an investigation of 98 languages (to which more were added later). They found that the possible number of "basic" color terms[4] present in any language ranged from 2 to 11. The second relevant finding was that languages increased their lexical terms to cover the color spectrum in seven (fixed) phases. This allowed investigators to predict which color term might be eventually added to the lexicon of a language found to be in any of the seven stages. Finally, the appearance of specific color terms at each phase was correlated with the physiology of color vision. Red, green, and blue (and then yellow) appear immediately after black and white (the only terms in the first phase) because they represent the wavelengths at which our

[4]A color term in order to be labeled *basic* must be monolexemic (its meaning cannot be predictable from the meaning of its part), its signification must not be included in other terms (*crimson* and *scarlet* are two types of *red*), it must not cover only a limited set of objects (*blonde* refers only to hair), and it must be psychologically salient (see Berlin and Kay, 1969, pp. 5–6).

cones in the retina are biologically wired to respond (Hubel, 1988; Kay & McDaniel, 1978). In other words, the acquisition of new linguistic terms covering the color spectrum is heavily constrained by universal characteristics of the physiology of vision. Thus, it is not language (color terms) that affects thought, but language that is constrained by mental processes directly linked to perception—visual perception in this case. The LR paradigm appears to be greatly undermined.

The research on color has been enriched by a variety of investigators who helped expand and refine Berlin and Kay's original hypothesis (see Hardin & Maffi, 1997, for a comprehensive treatment). Despite many criticisms (e.g., Lucy, 1997), the research on color contributed to a reevaluation of the assumptions of the LR paradigm. A strict relationship was established between universal characteristics of human vision and language. The psychological "space" between these two realms (physiology and language) is the area about which various theories are still proposed (see MacLaury, 1997).

Ethnobotany and Folk Biology

The findings of the research from two different lexical domains, ethnobotany and folk biology, are to be treated as an attempt to understand and describe the nature of that psychological "space." All languages have a set of terms used to categorize the botanical world. Despite differences in the number of terms and types of environments in which languages are spoken, Berlin (1972/1995) suggested that the taxonomic arrangement of these terms follows a universal pattern. Terms are arranged typically in a three-level taxonomy, sometimes expanded to five levels: unique beginner ("plant"), life form ("tree"), generic ("oak"), specific ("white oak"), and varietal ("California live oak"). In this domain too—in the same way as for color—the genesis of the ethnobotanical nomenclature is constrained to proceed or evolve along specific phases. Typically generic terms appear first, followed by the life-form and the specific terms, and then the varietal terms and the unique beginner term are added (these last two types of terms are not always present).

Dougherty (1978), adding to Berlin's proposal, demonstrated that the level of entry for the taxonomy varies as a function of the quality and extension of the interaction of members of different cultures with their environments. In other words, although for some cultures the generic terms are the most salient, as Berlin suggested, for others it is the life-form terms that are the most salient.

More recently, Atran (1990, p. 5) expanded the realm of the investigation started by Berlin to folkbiology. He looked at "some of the principal features of the common-sense background to natural history, focusing on how people the world over ordinarily classify locally perceived living kinds." One of Atran's major contributions is the suggestion that folk biology is based on the attribution of an "underlying hidden nature" to living things that separates them from technologically produced objects of any sort.

Investigators working on the lexical domains of ethnobotany and folk biology—domains that promised to be conducive to the discovery of relevant relativistic phenomena—have highlighted complex but universal mental organizations of knowledge. Taxonomic genesis and structuring of ethnobotanical nomenclature appear to be mentally organized in the same way in a variety of languages and cultures all over the world (Berlin, 1972/1995). Some basic core assumptions about folk biology are also universally shared (Atran, 1990). Cultural variation is possible, but in highly constrained ways (Dougherty, 1978). Again, the LR paradigm seems to need serious reexamination.

Kinship

Another traditional lexical domain that typically led to LR conclusions is that of kinship. A basic distinction is drawn between genealogical relationships (e.g., mother's brother, father's brother) that are commonly treated as universal, and linguistic terms that categorize the genealogical relationships (e.g., *uncle*). Because kinship terms are distributed differentially over the genealogical space (this is the space created by all the possible genealogical relationships), researchers within the LR paradigm argue that each individual would think (and act) about human relationships according to this specific linguistic categorization of the genealogical space.

However, starting in the 1960s (for earlier research see Goodenough, 1956, and Lounsbury, 1956), in opposition to the LR paradigm, investigators attempted to extract some of the underlying universal cognitive parameters that generate these kinship systems. They employed formal semantic analysis, that is, componential analysis, of the closed sets of terms constituting these kinship systems. Thus, universal units were proposed, that is, the relationship between mother and child (Goodenough, 1970), as were rewrite rules[5] acting on these units, such as Lounsbury's (1969, p. 221) Half-Sibling Rule: PCh → Sb, which reads as "parent's child equals sibling," in which a half-sibling is rewritten as a (full) sibling. It is apparent from these last two statements that the "new" generative paradigm in linguistics started having consequences outside the traditional linguistic realm. Specifically, in kinship studies, the new generative paradigm provides the theoretical focus—looking for universals—and the "language" or modality through which one can express the findings, such as rewrite rules.

[5]A rewrite rule is typical of generative grammar and takes the form X → Y. Both X and Y can be a unit or a string of units, and the arrow is an instruction to replace X with Y. These rules are usually read as "rewrite X as Y" (see Crystal, 1991, p. 301).

Some researchers pointed out the limitations of these componential analyses in representing psychological reality (Burling, 1969; Dougherty and C. M. Keller, 1985; Wallace, 1969). However, whatever validity these studies may still have, it cannot be denied that they had a profound impact in shifting the focus of the investigations about the relationship between language, mind, and culture to its cognitive aspect. Linguistic analyses are considered a privileged entry into the working of the mind, and because culture is also considered a mental phenomenon (or knowledge) by some (see Goodenough, 1957/1964; but also Boas, 1911), fruitful connections can be foreseen. Investigations of the kinship domain are now directed toward determining and understanding universal characteristics of the mind. The approach to kinship by Lehman and Witz (1974, 1979) is certainly to be seen within the new emerging paradigm (i.e., generative).

Although not denying the value of componential analysis of kinship terminologies, they attend to the formal characteristics of what they label *primary genealogical space* or PGS. They define this space as an axiomatized set of formal relationships (an algebra) that generates all possible (infinite) biological relations. PGS is mapped onto any system of kinship categories or terms, such that "the set of categories in question must simply be closed under that map" (Lehman, 1993, p. 97 [original in italics]). The proper formalism for such mapping is "a system of Category-Theoretic morphisms, where these only partially preserve dimensionality or order of relations." (1993, p. 96). In other words, not all the relations as well as the order of the relations possible in PGS are present in any kinship system. However, it is the content of PGS that generates any kinship system, as it becomes apparent when engaging any informant in describing those systems and/or solving genealogical problems.

It might seem that the new research questions now being generated and the new findings function as a death knell for the LR paradigm. This is not the case. After all, even if the research conducted within the LR paradigm never focused on universal aspects of language, mind, or culture, it always assumed language and culture to be phenomena identical "in kind" (Boas, 1911, p. 28), that is, mental. Neither Sapir not Whorf denied this assumption; they were only led by their assertions about language to overrate the value of their methodological approach in relating language to thought, and thought to culture. The so-called Chomskyan revolution and the birth of cognitive science revealed the limitations of the classical (Sapir-)Whorfian relativist line of investigation, and opened up a vista with a potential for richer (and more formal) descriptions of mental phenomena. Thus, although still considering language as one of the primary entry points into mental phenomena, the formal methods force our attention to empirical observations and levels of detail that old methods never made us notice, and it is these new facts that show the limitations of the relativist approach.

Compelling questions like: Are language and culture related and if so, how? Does language shape thought? Does language shape culture?—typical within the LR paradigm—have now shifted to ones of a different nature. Specifically, is the formal description of linguistic knowledge analogous to the formal description of cultural knowledge? Are the mental processes engaged in processing language compatible with those in other domains (e.g., vision, action, emotions)? What is the architecture of the mind that allows us as human beings to use language to speak about almost everything we experience?

Many investigations have tried to answer these questions. Some of their research has been cloaked in traditional LR paradigm terms (i.e., strong relativistic); some have come from new fields of linguistic investigation. And other research has been conducted along the lines of the interdisciplinary approach characterized by cognitive science. In the remaining sections of this chapter, I look at a representative sample of the research constituting a revival of the inquiry into the relationship between language, mind, and culture.

THE NEW INCARNATION OF THE LINGUISTIC RELATIVITY PARADIGM

The LR paradigm has reemerged in the last decade as a significant part of the study of the relationship between language, mind, and culture. A distinction is now made, though, between a "strong" relativism and a "weak" one. In other words, bold suggestions about language "straitjacketing" thought and world view are no longer made (i.e., "strong" relativism). However, carefully constructed studies are conducted in which forms of thought habituation are found to correlate with ontological choices expressed by linguistic systems (i.e., "weak" relativism).

Within the LR paradigm, ontological categories such as "time," "space," and "matter" are traditionally considered primary realms for investigation (see quotation from Whorf given earlier). The ways in which each language covertly (and overtly) organizes and expresses these categories are regarded as the building blocks for the construction of an individual"s world view. Typically, languages express these categories not only by means of a closed set of terms (as is the case for color or kinship), but also by means of various syntactic constructions.

The studies I discuss here claim to be generated within the LR paradigm, and boast to be explicitly unaffected by universalist claims (as in the generative paradigm) (see Levinson, 1996c, p. 134). I show that clear universalist concerns, both methodological and theoretical, are present in these studies. I also show that the studies inherit these universalist concerns from forgotten aspects of the LR paradigm.

A Canonical "New" Linguistic Relativity Research: Lucy and "Matter versus Form"

Lucy (1992a, 1992b) considered "Linguistic Relativity as an hypothesis to be tested" (Foley, 1997, p. 209). He regarded language and thought as two separate domains. Thus, in principle it is possible to test whether or not characteristics of one domain have any effect on the characteristics of the other domain.

Lucy paid great attention to the way in which salient differences in the two languages that he compares are determined. He said:

> [The] *languages* of the communities being studied must be contrasted as to how they differently construe a common reality. This will involve a formal analysis of the morphosyntactic categories of the language with special attention to their referential values, that is, their relationship to the contextual surround. (Lucy, 1992a, p. 2 [italics in original])

He compared English and Yucatec Maya and found a salient difference in the way "number" or "enumeration" is treated in the two languages. Yucatec is a classifier language and "all nouns are like our mass nouns in that they are neutral with respect to logical unit or shape" (Lucy, 1992a, p. 83). This makes it obligatory to express singularity and optional to express plurality. English, instead,

> divides its lexical nouns into two groups, those with presupposable unit as part of lexical structure and which may take Plurals and Singular marking with indefinite article [count nouns], and those lexical nouns which function like the Yucatec lexical nouns in requiring unitizers and lacking the plural [mass nouns]. (Lucy, 1992a, p. 83)

Lucy hypothesized that this linguistic difference affects the way in which speakers of the two languages attend to reality. To investigate this hypothesis; Lucy constructed two types of tasks. In the first type, subjects were asked to describe sets of pictures about familiar scenes containing repeated instances of objects, animals, and humans as well as a variety of materials and types of produce (e.g., wood, corn). In the second type, subjects were asked to make "similarity" choices among triads of objects carefully selected to contrast along the matter vs. shape dimension (e.g., a cardboard box, a plastic box, a piece of cardboard). The first type of task was intended to obtain information about the saliency of matter versus shape in linguistic production (guided by the scenes in the photos, but not constrained otherwise). The second type of task was intended to provide insights in the way in which differences between objects are psychologically/mentally constructed.

As expected, the difference in responses between the speakers of the two languages aligns with the linguistic differences. In other words, in the first task English speakers attend more often to countable objects in describing the scenes in the photos, whereas Yucatec speakers attend more to mass nouns. Further, in the second task, Yucatec speakers rely more on materials than shape in producing similarity judgments. For example, when asked whether a cardboard box was more like a plastic box of a similar shape or a piece of cardboard, English speakers generally opted for the plastic box, whereas Yucatec speakers opted for the piece of cardboard.

The detailed linguistic descriptions of the two languages compared were conducted independently of each other. The domains eventually chosen and compared were some of the salient ones within and across the two languages. Relevantly, however, "number" is one of the domains extensively investigated by Whorf (1956). The tasks could be made as ecologically valid as possible due to Lucy's deep familiarity with the cultural milieus of the two languages. It is clear that the nature of the two tasks employed for the collection of the empirical data was affected by the theoretical assumption of a possible separation between language and thought. In fact, the first type of task is intended to elicit linguistic descriptions of scenes, whereas the second one attempted to tap into a prelinguistic, cognitive activity preceding a similarity judgment.

Lucy was looking for "habitual thought" and it seems that he found it. Preferred linguistic encodings of ontological categories, such as "number," are conducive to habitual thinking patterns. There is a price to pay, though. How can we assume that language is separate from thought? Is the assumption here that language is not a mental activity? Only if we take a structuralist position about language can such an assumption be constructed. It is clear that this is Lucy's stand. However, language cannot be reified as an object that exists independent of a mind. Language production is mental before being realized (see Levelt, 1989). As such language and thought overlap (or better, are the same activity) before specific motor actions actually produce sounds with the characteristics of language. In other words, if language is a mental activity, and part of mental activity is language, then on what basis can we hypothesize the separation of language and thought? For now, I leave this question unanswered and I return to it later.

Linguistic Relativity and Empiricism: Levinson and "Space"

In 1996 Levinson advocated the following:

> The study of the language of space might play a fundamental role in the anthropology of space more generally.... The focus has been on collective representations, on cosmologies and the symbolic uses and associations of space, with little mention of the kind of notions in daily use to solve spatial problems. (Levinson, 1996a, p. 354)

This suggestion is perfectly in line with two fundamental points made by Whorf—one being the usefulness of the cross-cultural investigation of the ontological concept of space (Whorf, 1956, p. 138), and the other to be found in

Whorf's definition of and interest in habitual thought as part of everyday life, not a specialized type of thought (Whorf, 1956, p. 147). A third and most relevant Whorfian point is the conclusion Levinson eventually drew from his research with Australian (North Queensland) Aboriginals speaking Guugu Yimithirr.

> Not only Guugu Yimithirr speakers, at least of this older generation, speak a language that as a prerequisite requires storage and computation of orientation and absolute directions, but they can also be shown when engaged in speaking the language to think in a way that is concordant with it. (Levinson, 1997, p. 125)

How does he reach this conclusion? How are linguistic characteristics shown to be "concordant" with thinking? Why is this result considered a Whorfian effect? It is appropriate at this point to briefly discuss the methodology employed by Levinson in collecting his data, because it is revealing of some of his implicit theoretical assumptions.

Besides the acquisition of linguistic data from the available literature, his linguistic corpus was acquired mainly by means of carefully prepared tasks (Levinson, 1992; but also 1996b, 1997).[6] In these tasks linguistic production was elicited by engaging two participants in what can be defined as "games." The descriptions of carefully prepared photos or the production of instructions necessary for the manipulation of objects by another participant elicited language rich in spatial descriptions. These activities in small-scale space were accompanied by other ones in large-scale space, thus covering almost the full range of possible contexts in which spatial descriptions are produced.

When speaking about spatial relationships between objects and/or places, speakers of Guugu Yimithirr predominantly use expressions containing terms like north, south, east, and west that are associated with an absolute frame of reference.[7] They also have terms for left and right or front and back (commonly associated with the relative and the intrinsic frame of reference),[8] but they only use them for body parts and not for expressions referring to the relationships between objects and/or places. Do they also use only the absolute frame of reference when thinking about spatial relationships?

---

[6]He also conducted extensive fieldwork, thus securing an appropriate experience and knowledge of the linguistic and cultural milieu.

[7]A frame of reference is a set of coordinates (three intersecting axes: vertical, sagittal, and transversal) used to construct a space within which spatial relationships among objects are identified (Levinson, 1996b)

[8]A relative frame of reference is centered on a speaker and it remains centered on the speaker when the speaker moves. A linguistic encoding is: "The ball is in front of me." An intrinsic frame of reference is centered on an object and it remains centered on the object when the object moves. A linguistic encoding is: "The ball is in front of the car." See Levinson (1996b) for a typology of frame of reference, and Bennardo (1996, in preparation) for a revision of that typology.

In order to answer this question, Levinson used a set of other tasks in which no language production is required, but choices made by participants clearly show the use of a specific frame of reference, either absolute or relative. The results of these tasks demonstrate that Guugu Yimithirr speakers prefer the absolute frame of reference in solving the tasks. This finding clearly contrasts with the performance of Dutch speakers who were also tested (Levinson, 1997, p. 116) and who prefer the relative frame of reference. The concordance between the two types of findings—linguistic and cognitive—for Guugu Yimithirr speakers, and the contrast with the Dutch group,[9] are interpreted as support for a Whorfian effect. That is, the choices that speakers make because of the way in which their language expresses spatial relationships constrain their thinking processes so that they adopt the same mental organization for spatial relationships (Levinson, 1996b, p. 157).

Because the tasks used for collecting data about the conceptualization of space (i.e., thought) are distinct from the ones used for the collection of the linguistic data about space, it is obvious that, like Lucy, Levinson assumed a distinction between language and thought. It is also clear that a specific linguistic encoding of frames of reference was proposed as independent from either perceptual or cognitive encodings (Levinson, 1996b, pp. 133–134). In other words, he suggests that the choice of frame of reference at the linguistic level is made independently from the choices at the perceptual and conceptual levels (see also Levelt, 1989, 1996, and Carlson-Radvansky & Irwin, 1993).

Levinson later argued that "frames of reference are incommensurable" (1996b, p. 155)—that is, spatial information coded in one frame of reference cannot be converted into another. Thus, a language that expresses spatial relationships in only one frame of reference (e.g., speakers of Guugu Yimithirr only use the absolute frame of reference linguistically) can possibly cause a similar habitual representation (and choice) at the conceptual level (i.e., thought) (1996b, p. 157). The "Whorfian effect" chosen by Levinson to interpret his data seems to have found further support.

The cross-linguistic and cross-cultural investigations conducted by Levinson represent an extremely important step in the research about space. His methodology, data, and findings made the investigation of space one of the most innovative areas of research in cognitive anthropology and cognitive science in the 1990s.[10] His review of the literature about frames of reference and the proposed typology (1996b) are a constant point of reference for anyone interested in cross-cultural and monocultural research of space. Levinson's treat-

---

[9]Levinson (1996b, p.125) replicated these results with speakers of Tzeltal, a Mayan language spoken in Chiapas, Mexico.

[10]The Cognitive Anthropology Research Group at the Max Planck Institute for Psycholinguistics, Nijmegen, the Netherlands (now simply part of the institute), that he founded and directs has produced methodology, data, and findings involving several languages and cultures all over the world (see Baayen & Danziger, 1994; Brown, Senft, & Wheeldon, 1993; Pederson & Roelofs, 1995).

ment of the cognitive realm as compared to the linguistic realm and the perceptual realm, is more fully articulated than Lucy's and deserves close attention.

When talking about use of frames of reference across modalities, Levinson said:

> Put simply, we may ask whether the same frames of reference can in principle operate across all the modalities, and if not, whether at least they can be translated into one another. What we should mean by "modality" here is an important question. In what follows I shall assume that corresponding to (some of) the different senses, and more generally to input/output systems, there are specialized "central" representational systems, for example, an imagistic system related to vision, a propositional system related to language, a kinaesthetic system related to gesture, and so on (see, for example, Levelt 1989; Jackendoff 1991). (Levinson, 1996b, pp. 152–153)

These various "representational systems" are the cognitive realm driven by and at the same time driving either perception ("senses"), action, or language. We have already seen that each individual system can adopt a frame of reference independently of the other systems. Also, each system can adopt any of the three frames available: relative, intrinsic, and absolute (1996b, p. 152). The other important step in Levinson's reasoning is that once information has been coded in one of the three frames of reference, it is not possible to "translate" that same information in a format that uses another frame of reference (Levinson,1996b, p. 155). For example, if by using an intrinsic frame of reference we describe a dog as being "in front of" a car, we cannot translate that information into an expression that uses an absolute frame of reference (e.g., cardinal points) because we don't know if the dog is north, south, east, or west of the car.[11]

This problem of translatability or incommensurability between frames is definitely an interesting phenomenon. But is it possible to use it, as Levinson did, to argue for the possibility that a language that only expresses spatial relationships using one frame of reference (absolute in Guugu Yimithirr or Tzeltal) requires other representational systems to adopt the same frame? This is, in other words, the core of the Whorfian effect argument he suggested.

There are three major points that need attention at this juncture: When does the translatability problem emerge? What type of communication between representational systems is assumed by arguing that a choice of a frame of reference internal to a system will determine the adoption of a similar choice internally to another system? And what does it mean to assert that a language expresses "only" one type of spatial relationship, or better, "uses" only one frame of reference in linguistically referring to spatial relationships?

---

[11]The only time translation is possible is from either an absolute or a relative frame to an intrinsic frame (Levinson, 1996b, p.155).

First, when spatial information is perceptually acquired it is represented by one of the available frames of reference. Is the other information lost? Because we cannot recover spatial information across frames of reference, we must conclude that the other information is lost (for an opposite position see Kosslyn, 1996). Later, the linguistic representational system must use the same frame to encode the same information, because, again, the incommensurability problem prevents the system from encoding the "same" information in a different frame. Thus, it may follow that we speak about what we see only in the way dictated by our perceptual representational system. But how do we explain two persons speaking the same language, seeing the same scene, and describing it differently—using two different frames? Do they use two different perceptual representational systems? Clearly not.

Second, the process just described entails adopting an extreme encapsulated position regarding cognitive modularity (see Fodor, 1983). According to this position, the operations within a series of related cognitive subsystems—making up a system—are not influenced by the operations in another system—also made up of subsystems. According to Levinson, once language has represented some spatial information in a specific frame of reference, it will condition other representational systems to represent information in the same way. This could be true only under a particular condition: The two (or more) systems involved are to be considered subsystems and must be encapsulated. Is this what Levinson was advocating and/or assuming? This is not clear, but it certainly follows from some of his suggestions. Can speakers of a language that uses only an absolute frame of reference (e.g., Guugu Yimithirr) think about spatial relationships by using a relative frame of reference? From what Levinson was advocating, we must deduce that they cannot. Most of the literature about the developmental sequence (Clark, 1970; Cohen, 1985; Liben, Patterson and Newcombe, 1981; Moore, 1973; Pick, 1993; Stiles-Davis, Kritchevsky, & Bellugi, 1988;) points toward the primacy of a stage in infants—as early as 3-6 month of age—in which only the relative frame of reference is used. Do we have to conclude that the acquisition of a language eliminates this cognitive capacity? Clearly not.

Third, in discussing the way in which speakers of Tzeltal—a Mayan language spoken in Chiapas, Mexico—represent spatial relationships linguistically, Levinson said, "The intriguing fact here is that although notions like "front," "back," "left," "right" would seem to be inevitable concepts in human visual and bodily experience, they have been bypassed as the basis for systematic linguistic distinctions" (1996c, p. 138). Tzeltal speakers express linguistically spatial relationships only by using the absolute frame of reference. The Tzeltal phenomenon is very interesting and certainly rare among the world's languages. How is the lack of the use of those terms for "systematic linguistic distinctions" relevant to the relationship between language and thought? What is the meaning of this phenomenon for the cognition of space? What does it tell us about the relationship between spatial cognition and the language of space? Levinson's answer (that there is a Whorfian effect) assumed a simplified view of language that does not consider the full array of mental phenomena (i.e., mental representations, cognitive processes) that precede and underlie linguistic production.

An approach to cognition like Jackendoff's representational modularity (1997) (see next section) would compensate for some of Levinson's shortcomings. What is missing in Levinson's proposal about the architecture of cognition, in fact, is a central representational system or conceptual structures that mediate subsystems such as visual input, emotions, and language (among others) (Jackendoff, 1997, p. 44). It is at the level of conceptual structures that spatial knowledge and information are acquired and possibly encoded in any of the available frames of reference according to the specific need of the output systems, for example, language.[12]

The incommensurability problem, then, would only regard a terminal stage of a mental process in which a number of conceptual units of spatial information and knowledge (i.e., frames of reference) is encoded in linguistic forms. Where specific characteristics of the language spoken (i.e., use of only north, south, east, west in Guugu Yimithirr) demand a repeated use of one frame over the others, Levinson's proposal of a linguistic choice that "obliges" other modalities to adopt the same choice could be stated in a different way. Linguistic characteristics may "habituate" people to make specific choices at the conceptual structures level. This entails the repeated and *ad hoc* construction for linguistic purposes of specific frames of reference, leading to habituation.

Finally, a possibility that Levinson did not consider is that frames of reference may be conceptually "nested" into one another; thus an absolute one may have to rely on a relative one in order to be constructed and later expressed linguistically. An absolute frame of reference is based on fixed points of reference chosen in the environment of the speakers and socially and historically agreed on (e.g., the point where the sun rises, a mountain, the sea). Conceptually, before choosing a fixed point of reference, a field around the speaker must exist already. Such a field, or space, is constructed by what we call a relative frame of reference, that is, a set of coordinates centered on the speaker. Thus, conceptual "nesting" of the two frames is plausible. I discuss in the next section an approach to the na-

---

[12]In another work, Levinson considered a similar a solution and dismissed it:

> Why not, for example reverse the argument and claim that the cognitive system of absolute spatial conception drives the language? The answer is that there is no obvious way in which a community-wide cognitive practice of this sort could come to be shared except through its encoding in language and other communicative systems like gesture (see Haviland 1993). It is the need to conform to these communicative systems that requires convergence in cognitive systems, not the other way around. (1997, p. 125)

His desire to stay close to the empirical data seems to discourage him from attempting a more "abstract," but highly plausible, interpretation of the data (see also Levinson, 1996c, pp. 134–135).

ture of conceptual structures of space that allows for the possibility of spatial cognition and linguistic representations of spatial relationships to be related precisely in this way.

Language Acquisition and Relativity: Slobin and Bowerman

If language affects thought, then specific characteristics of one's language may influence one's world view very early in the language learning process. The psycholinguist Slobin focused his research on various stages of learning a mother tongue (and also a foreign language) in many languages including English, Spanish, German, and Hebrew. Slobin (1996, p. 76) believed that those aspects of reality that a language obliges a speaker to express become aspects of the part of thought that is activated when speech is produced. "Thinking for speaking" is the kind of LR that he proposed.

Slobin identified two domains in which the four languages differ substantially in the ontological distinctions obligatorily expressed. The two domains identified are aspect and motion. Aspect of a verb can be punctual if expressing a completed action like "sneeze," or durative if expressing an action extending over time like "sail" (or progressive forms of any verb). Regarding motion, English, for example, differs substantially from Spanish because in English, verbs of motion express only manner as in "running," and directionality is expressed by a prepositional phrase as in "to school." In Spanish, instead, verbs of motion express either manner as in *volar* "fly" or directionality as in *salir* "exit." Compounding manner and directionality of motion in a sentence takes place in different ways in English and Spanish. "English tends to assert trajectories, leaving resulting locative states to be inferred" (Slobin, 1996, p. 84), as in "The boy put the frog down into a jar." "Spanish tends to assert locations and directions, leaving trajectories to be inferred" (Slobin, 1996, p. 84), as in *El niño metió la rana en el frasco que habia abajo* "The boy inserted the frog *en* [=in/on] the jar that was below."[13]

Slobin asked groups of children of 3, 5, and 9 years of age to tell a story by using a set of pictures. The storytelling required the description and organization of events that could be attended to linguistically in a variety of ways. The interesting finding is that children of any age (including the 3-year-olds) preferred the rhetorical patterns typical of their native language. These results supported Slobin's hypothesis that thinking is concordant with specific linguistic characteristics when one is producing (or comprehending) language.

Another psycholinguist, Bowerman (1996), looked at how spatial concepts and relationships are realized cross-linguistically, specifically, in English, Korean, and Dutch. English, using Talmy's (1985, 1991) typology, is a "satellite-framed" language, that is, it expresses the notion of path by means of a constitu-

[13]Both sentences are from Slobin (1996, p. 84).

ent external to the main verb: that is, a prepositional phrase as in "to school." Different prepositions express different types of paths, such as "from," "through," "across." Korean instead is a "verb-framed" language, that is, the notion of path is expressed within the verb and different verbs are used to differentiate between different types of paths.

Both English and Korean children were observed. They had started using either verbs and prepositions (English) or only verbs (Korean) by the age of 14 months. By 20 months, the linguistic production of the two groups was closer to the characteristics of the input language than to each other. These and other findings did not lead Bowerman to question the role of prelinguistic development of spatial concepts. In fact, after a brief review of the literature (1996, pp. 387–391), she said,

> There can be little doubt, then, that non-linguistic spatial development plays an important role in children"s acquisition of spatial morphemes. But does the evidence establish that children map spatial words directly onto spatial concepts that are already in place? Here there is still room for doubt. (Bowerman, 1996, p. 391)

Because she argued for a clear separation of conceptualization (or cognition) and semantics (or language)—as did Lucy and Levinson—any early linguistic production that follows the semantics of space was eventually interpreted as a shaping effect of language over cognition (i.e., thought). Her findings about the early age at which children already express spatial concepts within the path laid out by their languages were then a powerful argument for speculations about a LR effect (i.e., a Whorfian effect).

Both Slobin's and Bowerman's studies provide extremely valuable cross-linguistic and cross-cultural data about spatial representations. Their data were obtained by means of sophisticated and standardized methods that are used for investigations in other linguistic and cultural environments. Again, however, a common unstated assumption is that of considering language (linguistic semantics for Bowerman) as a realm distinct from thought (conceptual semantics for Bowerman). It is not clarified, though, how this distinction obtains; neither is it made explicit how the two realms come to exchange information without substantial commonality of structure or organization. The results of these investigations, then, although important, do not point toward any specific direction for the relationship between language and thought, including the ones "thinking for speaking" and "the Whorfian effect" indicated by the two authors.

Linguistic Relativity Revival Revisited

What are then the common features of this LR revival? First and foremost, these studies share the empirical acquisition of cross-linguistic and cross-cultural data. They also consider essential to their investigations an appropriate knowledge and analysis of two or more languages. This knowledge determines the contrastive ontological domain (e.g., enumeration, space, time) within which the acquisition of the data to be compared is conducted. This procedure represents a clear debt to the positive examples provided by Boas, Sapir, and Whorf.

Second, the primacy and sophistication of the linguistic knowledge, depth of analyses, and theorizing are not balanced by similar sophistication and depth when speculating about mind, thought, or the architecture of cognition. Formal mental properties of language are not highlighted. No clear distinction or similarity is suggested and/or described between general conceptual structure and linguistic semantic structure. No linguistic or cognitive modularity is proposed (except by Levinson). Language seems to occupy nearly all areas of inquiry, thus obscuring the possible complexity of mind and thought. Actually, thought lives in the shadow of language and never becomes a coprimary object of investigation.

Third, common to all of these studies is the assumed separation between language and thought. This assumption is clearly part of the traditional LR paradigm (see discussion in second section). Because few details are assumed about the nature of thought, whenever data about thought are found to share properties with linguistic data, this is inevitably used to claim support for Whorfian effects. But we know that language is a mental activity; it must follow that some aspect of thought/cognition will be reflected in it. The point, then, is not to claim that aspects of language are present in thought processes. This is already part of generalized and obviously unstated premises about language. It may be more interesting to investigate those formal properties of language that can be hypothesized as universal and, as such, belong to human cognition/thought. In addition, detailed hypotheses about cognitive architecture may throw new light onto all the findings of the studies discussed.

BEYOND LINGUISTIC RELATIVITY

In this section I discuss and introduce two proposals about the nature of cognition and cognitive architecture. I use the framework that these proposals provide to arrive at a suggestion about the formal nature of the spatial representation module suggested by Jackendoff (1997, p. 44). The linguistic, cognitive, and ethnographic data presented were collected in a Polynesian culture, Tonga. Finally, I also attempt a possible reinterpretation of the data of the studies discussed above in light of these new perspectives on the relationship between language, mind, and culture.

Jackendoff and Representational Modularity

The first hypothesis about the architecture and nature of cognition I examine is Jackendoff's (1983, 1992, 1997) "Representational Modularity." In his own words:

> Representational Modularity is by no means a "virtual necessity." It is a hypothesis about the overall architecture of the mind, to be verified in terms of not only the language faculty but other faculties as well. I therefore do not wish to claim for it any degree of inevitability. Nonetheless, it appears to be a plausible way of looking at how the mind is put together, with preliminary support from many different quarters. (Jackendoff, 1997, p. 45)

In his attempt to widen the Chomskyan research project, Jackendoff devoted extensive attention to the investigation of the semantic component of language. He reached the conclusion that "*semantic structure* and *conceptual structure* denote the same level of representation" (Jackendoff, 1983, p. 95 [original italics]) that he called "conceptual structures." Furthermore, this single level of conceptual structures is the "level of mental representation onto which and from which all peripheral information is mapped" (Jackendoff, 1983, p. 19). In later works (1992, 1997) he refined his proposal and suggested the overall architecture presented in Fig. 2.1.

Conceptual structures remain central in this new architecture. They are propositional in nature and their modeling resembles linguistic/syntactic structures (see Jackendoff, 1983, 1990). However, three major innovations are introduced: correspondence rules (represented by bold double-headed arrows) or "interface modules" between modules, the "spatial representation" module,[14] and the "auditory information" module which also inputs conceptual structures. An interface module provides a link between major modules by being structurally compatible with the two modules it unites. This is accomplished by a structural core of the interface module made up of correspondence rules (not directly in contact with either modules to be linked), and two peripheral structures each compatible with the structures of one of the two modules linked (Jackendoff, 1997, pp. 21ff). The advantage of this proposal is that it allows for major modules to be substantially different in their structures, whereas information can still move between them.

The findings of the vast literature available on the visual system convinced Jackendoff to posit the module he called "spatial representation" as separate from the central module of conceptual structures (see also Jackendoff & Landau, 1992; Landau & Jackendoff, 1993). He said, "certain types of visual/spatial information (such as details of shape) cannot be represented propositionally/linguistically. Consequently visual/spatial representation must be encoded in one or more modules distinct from conceptual structures" (Jackendoff, 1997, p. 43). Furthermore, this module is also the center of reference for other modules connected exclusively and directly with conceptual structures in his previous proposals. These modules are "action," "haptic representation," and "proprioception." Finally, auditory information previously inputting only pho-

[14]Jackendoff had already introduced a module called "3D model structures" in 1992, (p. 14), but it was at that time only related to the "visual faculty" model.

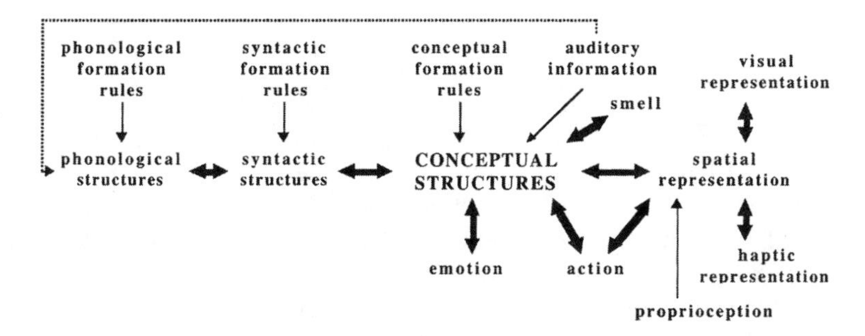

FIG. 2.1. Jackendoff's architecture of cognition.
(From Jackendoff 1977, pp. 39 and 44, adapted with permission)

nological structures is now also inputting conceptual structures. Thus, the architecture proposed has increased in complexity as a function of the increasing amount of new information about module interactions.

It is impossible in this work to summarize all the detailed linguistic analyses and literature Jackendoff brought forth in support of his proposal. One relevant feature of his architecture of the mind is that it is driven by the two largest bodies of knowledge recently accumulated about the functioning of the mind: linguistic knowledge and knowledge of the visual system. Jackendoff, however, made little use of another huge body of knowledge that accumulated over the last decades: cultural knowledge.

One problematic point in his proposal remains the collapsing of linguistic semantics with conceptual structures. Lehman and Bennardo (1992) clearly demonstrated why this is not appropriate. They argued for a conceptual content of English spatial prepositions that dictates the interpretation of their arguments as either Locus[15] or Place. An Object[16] is conceptually a Place when its geometrical characteristics count, and it is a Locus when it can be reduced to a Point because its geometric characteristics do not count. It is only when an Object (e.g., a noun like "building") is an argument of a spatial preposition (e.g., "to," "from," "between") that it will be considered either a Locus or a Place according to the specific preposition. The noun then acquires a specific linguistic meaning that is different from its dual potential conceptual meaning (either a Locus or a Place). Similarly, Broschart (1997) demonstrated that some Tongan lexical items are neither verbs nor nouns until they appear in a specific structural construction. That is, they acquire linguistic meaning in addition to their conceptual meaning. Thus, I will keep for now the distinction between linguistic meaning (i.e., semantics) and conceptual meaning (i.e., conceptual structures).[17]

---

[15]From here on, a capital letter indicates a concept.

[16]The concept Object is very abstract and can be a physical object, a place, or an abstract idea (Lehman & Bennardo, 1992).

[17]See also J. D. Keller and Lehman, 1991, p. 281, note 9 and 10) for a similar position.

Knowledge as Theory

The second hypothesis about the architecture and the nature of cognition I examine is the result of collaboration of Janet D. Dougherty (later J. D. Keller) with Charles M. Keller, and separately, with F. K. Lehman (Dougherty & C. M. Keller, 1985; J. D. Keller & C. M. Keller, 1993, 1996a, 1996b; J. D. Keller and Lehman, 1991, Lehman, 1985). Dougherty and C. M. Keller demonstrate that it is impossible to access cognition fully by using only linguistic data. Their focus on "conceptualization" led them to "characterize knowledge structures as constellations of conceptual units arising in response to a task at hand" (Dougherty & C. M. Keller, 1985, p. 165). These "constellations are ephemeral" (1985, p. 166); they are constructed only to tackle a "task" and do not bind the participating conceptual units beyond the duration of the task. When used repeatedly over a period of time they become "recipes," that is, habitual cognitive responses to tasks (J. D. Keller & C. M. Keller, 1996b, p. 91). The activated conceptual units include technical imagery, goals, and linguistic labels—that is, naming. None of these activated units, however, is independently sufficient to retrieve the conceptual constellation.

The two authors offer an anti-Whorfian argument by arguing that "the named class to which an object belongs for purposes of standard reference in general classification schemes has little influence over its occurrences in other constellations of applied knowledge" (Dougherty & C. M. Keller, 1985, p. 171). In other words, because cognition/thought works in task-oriented constellations that include a variety of conceptual units, it cannot be argued that language determines thought/cognition (although linguistic labels of objects are present).

This hypothesis about knowledge/cognition in action is very important, but leaves unaddressed the issue of the nature of knowledge, and unanswered the question of how it is possible for these "constellations" of units of knowledge to come together and constitute a well-connected unit eventually used in action. In other words, once it is demonstrated that knowledge is activated in bundles, the question arises of how this is possible. What is the nature of knowledge structures such that units of knowledge (i.e., concepts) can "bundle" together? Is there a common underlying structure/nature for knowledge from different sources (e.g., perceptual, visual, emotive, etc.)?

These questions are addressed in Lehman (1985) and J. D. Keller and Lehman (1991). They stated that their approach to cognition is "radically intensional" (J. D. Keller & Lehman, 1991, p. 272, note 1). In linguistic semantics, to adopt an "intensional" approach means to consider meaning as the defining properties of terms (intension) and not as the set of objects in the world to which terms are applied (extension; see Frege, 1975). Consequently, Keller and Lehman looked at cognition to discover its properties as mental/conceptual phenomena per se and not as defined by the external world phenomena to which they are related. They considered knowledge domains as theories, and concepts—units of knowledge—as generated within these theories (for similar positions see Murphy & Medin, 1985; Medin, 1989; Gelman, Coley, & Gottfried, 1994; but also Johnson-Laird, 1983; and Jackendoff, 1997).

They defined the internal computations of these theories not as a number "of binary features in a matrix whose dimensions are nothing but such features" (J. D. Keller & Lehman, 1991, p. 288), but as a number of relations—including cause-and-effect—that are possible given the axioms of the theory. In other words, theories are computational devices; that is, given a set of axioms, a number of theorems can be obtained (generated concepts can be considered theorems). Theories are also recursive computational devices. Once theorems have been obtained, they may function as axioms for other theories. Considering knowledge domains as theories and concepts as theorems (and due to recursiveness also mini-theories) explains how they can come together to become "constellations" of knowledge. This is possible only because they share this basic intra- and interstructure or nature.

Finally, J. D. Keller and Lehman provided an intentional analysis of two West Futuna Polynesian terms: *hkano* (Material Essence) and *ata* (Efficacious Image). In order to disambiguate these concepts they arrived at a "cosmological theory"—a theory about the existence of material and immaterial things, living or not living, and the relationships between them—for which seven axioms are hypothesized and within which concepts are generated (1991, pp. 279–280). The two concepts investigated were found to be generated by this theory. The construction of the "cosmological theory" required linguistic and cultural data that were patiently collected over a number of years by J. D. Keller during several field trips to West Futuna, Vanuatu, South Pacific, where a Polynesian language is spoken. These data were derived from long interviews with a great number of people. The theoretical position about cognition of the two authors, coupled with the painstaking methodology employed, allowed them to disambiguate the two concepts (*hkano* and *ata*) that are central to the understanding of Futunese thinking and provided supporting evidence for their approach to cognition.

Let me now make a proposal regarding the domain of space by integrating contributions from Jackendoff, Lehman, C. M. Keller, and J. D. Keller. I suggest a formal content for a subpart of Jackendoff"s spatial representation module. A relevant part of the data I discuss in making this proposal was collected in The Kingdom of Tonga, Polynesia.

Towards a Description of the Spatial Representation Module: Spatial Relationships in Tonga

Spatial relationships are realized linguistically in English mainly by means of spatial prepositions (between 80 and 100; see Jackendoff & Landau, 1992, p. 108). In contrast, Tongan (a Polynesian language) uses only three spatial prepositions. Intensional analyses of both English spatial prepositions and the three

Tongan spatial prepositions, five directionals (postverbal adverbs expressing direction of movement), and spatial nouns yielded a number of axioms for a partial theory of space, that is, for a substantial part of the content of Jackendoff's spatial representation module (see Bennardo, 1993, 1996, 2000).

The major axioms of this partial theory include concepts like Locus, Object, Vector, Path, Verticality, and Horizontality (for a full list and definitions see Bennardo, 2000). These axiomatic concepts of the partial theory of space are used to construct frames of reference (for a similar approach see Levinson, 1996b) that are part of the content of the spatial representation module. In other words, frames of reference are considered theorems derived from the major axiomatic content of the partial theory of space.

For example, given the following axioms: a Locus (the speaker), a Vector—a complex concept made up of a Locus (beginning point, in this case the speaker), a Body (repeated points), and Direction—the concept of Verticality, and the concept of Horizontality, a relative frame of reference can be generated by using also the Repeat Function—to repeat the construction of vectors and obtain axes.[18] I have described before (see note 7) a relative frame of reference as a set of coordinates—three axes: vertical, sagittal, and transversal—that create an oriented space centered on a speaker. Once generated as theorems of the partial axiomatic content of the spatial representation module, frames of reference can function as axioms of a partial theory of space that can be used to generate specific spatial descriptions as expressed in linguistic strings (see Miller & Johnson-Laird, 1976; Levelt, 1982, 1984; Levinson, 1996b) or other behavior (see Ellen & Thinus-Blanc, 1987; for animal behavior see Gallistel, 1993).

The conceptual/axiomatic content of the various frames of reference is given in Table 2.1. Notice that a concept/axiom like Orthogonality appears in the table, but was not present in the axioms mentioned above. This is possible because Orthogonality is derivable from some of the axioms listed and by using the concepts of Angle, Quantity, and Unit. Basically, Orthogonality represents a theorem (a compositional one) or, if you like, a short-cut label for a derivation from the axioms. Animacy, habitual Direction of Motion, and Habitual Use are also theorems derived partially from the introduced axioms and by the participation of other concepts/axioms from other domains/theories (e.g., a theory of living things).

Deducible from Table 2. 1 is that the conceptual content of the relative frame of reference is contained in the other two frames. As such, all the other frames represent further, more complex, conceptual constructions, all subsuming the basic relative frame.[19] For example, in order to construct conceptually the "cardinal points" subtype of the absolute frame of reference (we show later that two other subtypes exists: a "radial" one, and one based on a "single axis"), first the

[18]Please note that this process has been highly simplified for clarity of presentation.

[19]This differs from Levinson's (1996b) approach. For further discussion about this issue see Bennardo (1996, in press).

TABLE 2.1

Partial Conceptual /Axiomatic Content of the Three Frames of Refererence

Concept/Axiom	*Relative*[a]	*Intrinsic*	*Absolute*
Locus[b]	X (s/v/c)[d]	X (s/v/c)[d]	X (s/v/c)[d]
Object		1	4
Vector	6	10	6
Verticality	X	X	X
Horizontality	X	X	X
Orthgonality	X	X	X
Animacy[c]		X[a]	
Habitual use[c]		X[a]	
Habitual direction of motion[c]		X[a]	
Path			4
Choice function[e]	X	X	X
Repeat function[e]	X	X	X

Note. From Bennardo (in press-b), with permission.
[a]The other two subtypes of the relative frame of reference are not considered here.
[b]This concept, as well as others, may be used more than once.
[c]Only one of the three indicated is necessary.
[d]Speaker/viewer/cognizer.
[e]Cognitive process.

speaker's field must be constructed by means of a relative frame. Then four fixed points of reference need to be chosen by using the Choice and Repeat functions in the field of the speaker—or at least two initial ones like the rising and setting place of the sun, with an orthogonal axis defining two further points. In other words, in addition to the content of the relative frame of reference (a Locus/speaker; six Vectors: up, down, front, back, left, and right; etc.), four Objects/places are now needed. The concept of Path—by definition a Vector with an End (see Lehman & Bennardo, 1992)—is also part of the axioms used because conceptually the speaker is joined with the four places selected (i.e., east, west, north, south) by a Path for each Object chosen.

Although this whole conceptual computation may not be apparent, just think of the fact that once one identifies one of the cardinal points, it is always possible to derive the other points by thinking of going either left or right along the cardinal system. In other words, the basic relative frame is subsumed by the absolute frame (in this case, the "cardinal points" subtype).

The data I collected in Tonga led me to revise the content of Table 2. 1, specifically the part regarding the absolute frame of reference and its various subtypes. I used for part of the collection of the data the methodology produced by the Cognitive Anthropology Research Group at the Max-Planck Institute for Psycholinguistics, Njimegen, the Netherlands (CARG, 1992, but see also Levinson, 1992, and above discussion of Levinson in the prceding section). However, I was obliged by some challenging results—and by theoretical differences—to expand this methodology (see Bennardo, 1996, p. 129ff).

For linguistic production in which frames of reference are used, Tongans prefer the relative frame in small-scale space descriptions and move into a preference of the absolute frame in large-scale space descriptions. The results of the cognitive tasks, though, administered in small-scale space, point toward a clear preference for the absolute frame of reference. Thus, because the preference found in language production differs from the preference found by the cognitive tasks (in which no linguistic production is involved) in the same scale size (i.e., small-scale), I could not find support for any type of Whorfian effect as Levinson (1997) did.

In an attempt to disambiguate the cognitive results, which do not discriminate between subtypes of the absolute frame of reference, I administered other tasks, including memory tasks and the drawing of maps of one's village and island of residence. These activities yielded the use of a subtype of the absolute frame of reference that I labeled "radial" (see Bennardo, 1996, p. 276, and 2002). That is, only one fixed point of reference (i.e., the center) is chosen in the field of the speaker and then the figure/object[20] is described as toward the center (centripetally) or away from it (centrifugally). What renders this frame absolute is the fact that the center has a field of its own distinct from the field of the speaker.

This last point is demonstrated by the nondeictic use of one of Tongan directionals, *atu* "away from center"[21]

(1)*Hu atu.*

enter away-from-center

"Enter"

Both the speaker and the addressee were outside the place that would be entered (a Tongan house) when the sentence in (1) was produced. Moreover, the speaker was facing one of the addressee's sides (the left one) whereas the addressee was facing the entrance of the house. Thus, the center from which movement would eventually initiate could not possibly coincide with the speaker; it must have referred to the addressee.[22] Then, instead of glossing *atu* as

[20]The "figure" is the object whose spatial relationships are described, that is, the "ball" in "the ball is in front of the car." The "car" instead is the "ground." I am using the terms "figure" and "ground" according to Talmy (1983).

[21]The other four are *hake* "up," *hifo* "down," *mai* "towards center" and *ange* "away from center 2 (speaker and addressee)" (Bennardo, 1999).

[22]The case described here is just one of many examples that I witnessed and recorded during my fieldwork.

"to you" as typically done in the literature about Tongan (see Broschart, 1996; Churchward, 1953; Tchekhoff, 1990), I glossed *atu* as "away from center" (Bennardo, 1996, p. 182ff; see also Bennardo, 1999). This gloss includes the cases in which the center is the speaker and also the cases in which the center is other than the speaker. For the example presented in (1), I also hypothesized *atu* as expressing a "radial" absolute frame of reference, in which an independent field from the one centered on the speaker is used.

Another subtype of the absolute frame of reference used by Tongans is one in which only a single axis is addressed: the inland-sea axis.[23] This system is typical of many Oceanic languages (Florey, & Kelly, 2002; Hill, 1997; Hyslop, 2002; Ozanne-Rivierre, 1997;) and seems to be related to the relevance of the sea/land opposition in the island world of Oceania (see Palmer, 2002).

The proposed conceptual/axiomatic content for the three subtypes (radial, single axis, and cardinal points) of the absolute frame of reference are presented in Table 2. 2.

For all three subtypes there are two cases (Type 1 and Type 2 in Table 2. 2) to be considered. The first case is when the ground is the viewer, for example, "the mountain is north of me (the speaker)." The second case is when the ground is an object different from the speaker, for example, "the mountain is north of the highway." The two cases yield two different conceptual contents for each subtype. For example, the two cases of the Tongan directional *atu* "away from center" discussed earlier, are to be considered as realizing the conceptual content under Type 1 of the radial subtype when the center is the speaker. We only need a Locus for the speaker and a Vector for the direction of movement. When the center is other than speaker, Type 2, then we also need an Object that functions as the new center, and a Path. This Path is the conceptual joining of the speaker with this Object that takes place when the Object is chosen—by means of the Choice function.

The fundamental difference between a radial frame Type 1 and a radial frame Type 2 is that a new field is created around an Object that is chosen within the original field centered on the speaker. This difference is similar to the one between a relative frame and an intrinsic frame. For the intrinsic frame, an Object is chosen within the oriented field of the speaker (constructed with a relative frame), and the same characteristics (up, down, front, back, left, right) of the original oriented field are then constructed on this Object.

I used all the information so far only briefly introduced about the various frames of reference to organize them in a typology (Bennardo, in press-b). This typology is the content of Figure 2. 2.

The various frame of reference are organized in a top-down manner that signifies a simple-complex direction in terms of conceptual or axiomatic content.

---

[23]Other two single axis are also present: inland-town and inland-down (see Bennardo, 1996, pp. 246–251).

TABLE 2.2

Conceptual Content of Subtypes of the Absolute Frame of Reference

	Subtype of Absolute Frame of Reference					
Concept	*Radial*		*Single Axis*		*Cardinal Points*	
Axiom	*Type 1*	*Type 2*	*Type 1*	*Type 2*	*Type 1*	*Type 2*
Locus	X (s/v/c)[a]	X (s/v/c)[a]	X (s/v/c)[a]	X (s/v/c)[a]	X (s/v/c)[a]	X (s/v/c)[a]
Vector	1	1	6	6	6	6
Object		1	2	2 + 1	4	4 + 1
Path		1	2	3	4	5

Note. From Bennardo (in press–b), with permission.
[a]Speaker/viewer/cognizer.

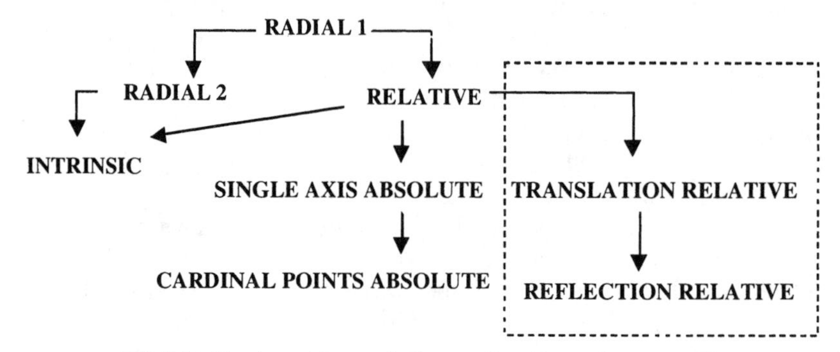

FIG. 2.2. Typology of frames of reference. From Bennardo (in press-b).

The arrows in Figure 2. 2 stand for a particular relationship between the two frames of reference they join. In fact, the frame of reference receiving the content of another frame of reference treats this latter as an axiom in its own conceptual content. This means that further conceptual material is specifically added at each stage. Thus, the necessity of a new label for that particular type of frame of reference arises. Each of these frames represents a theorem derivable from the axioms of the partial theory of space I suggested earlier. At the same time, each frame may become one of the axioms that generate a more complex frame. For example, the single-axis absolute frame of reference is generated from axioms like Locus, Object, Path, and necessarily a Relative Frame of Reference (capitalized to emphasize that it is now to be considered a single concept/axiom). In the same way, the relative frame subsumes a radial Type 1—that is, it uses this latter as one of its axioms (i.e., Radial 1, Repeat Function to obtain 6 Vectors, Verticality, Horizontality, and Orthogonality).

Two subtypes of the relative frame of reference are included in a dotted square. This indicates that I chose not to discuss these two subtypes in this work, nonetheless I acknowledge their existence (for a definition of these two subtypes see Levinson, 1996b). Notice also how the intrinsic frame utilizes as its axioms (conceptual content) both the radial frame 1 (for its two fields), and the relative frame (for its oriented field: up, down, front, back, left, right). Thus, I hypothesize nesting, penetrability, and complex interactions at the conceptual level between frames of reference. Finally, I propose the typology of frames of reference just outlined as a partial content of the spatial representation module suggested by Jackendoff (1997).

Language, Culture, and Mind

In light of the three proposals briefly presented in this section, I can now look back at the findings of the research I characterized as the "LR revival." Can we still assume that language is a phenomenon (or a system or module) separate from cognition (or thought), and thus search for the effect of language on thought, or even for the effect of language on culture? And how does culture relate to cognition and language? In order to answer these questions, we need to answer three more basic questions: What is language? What is culture? And what is cognition/thought?

Within the guidelines indicated by the authors discussed in this section, language is a module of the mind. It is propositional in nature and internally modular (see Chomsky, 1986, 1995). Internal modules are phonology, syntax, and semantics. The linguistic semantic submodule is suggested as different from the conceptual semantic (or conceptual structures) module. Language is connected to the conceptual structures module by means of an interface that shares only parts of its internal structure with both modules that it joins. The fundamental nature of the conceptual (or knowledge) structures module is not propositional—although it has propositional features—but is organized in a relational way that I have labeled "theory-like." This theory (or principles or structure) is computational because it has an indefinite generative capacity. I suggested the same structure or nature for the spatial representation module whose partial content was presented in Fig. 2. 2.

Culture is defined as a large subset of the content of the conceptual/knowledge structures module. As such, each culture shares basic organizational principles and partial content—including the content of the spatial representation module—with all other cultures. The distinct differences that characterize each individual culture (or language) are the result of the generative capacity of the internal structure of cognitive modules such as the conceptual structures module, the language module, and the spatial representation module.

Contrary to the authors in the LR revival discussed in the proceeding section, language and thought (or conceptual structures) are not assumed to be two separate systems eventually affecting each other. They are two modules in the general architecture of the mind. They exchange information, and consequently they must share some basic organizational principles (i.e., structures) for this to be possible at all. All meaning expressed linguistically must be present in conceptual structures, but not all conceptual meaning will be present in language. Linguistic meaning is the realization/instantiation of a meaning only potentially present in conceptual structures; that is, any meaning can only exist in language if it is in some or other form present in or potentially generated from conceptual structures. Recoverability can become easier and possibly faster—"recipe"-like (Keller & Keller, 1996b, p. 91)—when the process is repeated over and over in time.

If speakers of Guugu Yimithirr always use only an absolute frame of reference to linguistically express spatial relationships, it is to be expected that they will eventually develop a similar preference at the cognitive level. It would be more interesting, though, to ask what this phenomenon is telling us about the workings of the mind. How is it that a world perceived relatively is preferably represented absolutely and is linguistically expressed in the same way? What other knowledge is constraining the spatial information to follow this direction (from perceptual relative to conceptual and linguistic absolute)? Is it social, historical, or environmental—in other words, cultural—knowledge? Is cultural knowledge filtering the organization and content of the spatial information expressed linguistically?

This is the path I took in disambiguating contrasting results about linguistic use and cognitive organization of spatial relationships in Tongan (Bennardo, 1996, pp. 306ff). The ethnographic description of salient events—a variety of exchanges—in the Tongan cultural milieu allowed me to comprehend the cognitive preference for the "radial" subtype of the absolute frame of reference. These events provide the context for acquiring this preference, while at the same time revealing its existence. Obtaining these insights into another culture, that is, establishing relevant and meaningful relationships between linguistic and social behavior with thinking patterns and organization, is conceivable within the approach to language, mind, and culture I have just outlined: namely, considering the mind as modular with language as a mental module, the content of the various modules organized in theories, and culture existing as a large subset in the knowledge or conceptual structures module.

CONCLUSION

The LR paradigm has its roots in the works of Boas, Sapir, and Whorf. The linguistic knowledge about an enormous variety of languages (especially Native

American languages) acquired at the beginning of the century gave scholars access to different worldviews and thinking patterns. Both thought and culture were eventually regarded as being affected by the nature of linguistic form and content. Extremely relevant was the recognition of the similarity "in kind" of linguistic and cultural phenomena. Universal characteristics of the human mind were assumed, but the focus of the investigations was on establishing the existence of legitimate differences between languages, and on showing how these differences related to differences in thought and culture.

After decades of structuralism, the generative paradigm moved the focus of linguistic investigations—and of part of anthropological investigations as well—to the universal mental characteristics of language, seen again as a relevant part of the mind (or thought). The advances obtained in the study of other mental systems, such as the visual system and the auditory system, made possible proposals for a cognitive architecture that encompassed findings both about language—obtained by linguistic analyses—and about these other systems. Research within cognitive science now suggests intra and intermodular organization of these various systems (Hirschfeld & Gelman, 1994; Jackendoff, 1997; Pinker, 1997). This allows us to hypothesize, find substantial support for, and convincingly argue about new forms of relationships between language, conceptual (or knowledge) structures, spatial representation, and other modules—including action.

Why then do investigators still talk about linguistic relativity? It seems to me that there are three major reasons. First, the findings of linguistic analyses and knowledge about language still represent the greatest bulk of information that is available about the workings of the human mind. The second reason is the practice of thinking about the linguistic realm as being completely independent of the other cognitive realms. We have seen how assuming a clear separation between language and thought leads to the hypothesis that linguistic practices may affect thought processes. Third, the small amount of information exchanged across disciplines can lead to a limited point of view on the mind and its internal architecture.

In conclusion, a fully intensional (mentalistic) approach to language, culture, and mind dissipates the fog of linguistic relativity proposals. A modular architecture of the mind calls for a common internal structure of the various modules. At the same time, such a common structure has to be capable of generating and accounting for the vast array of linguistic and cultural realizations one encounters in this world. The proposal of regarding this common structure as a theory is coming from several corners of the cognitive science field and seems to be a productive one. Supporting evidence is starting to be provided—some was presented in this chapter—and will hopefully continue to be accumulated in the close future. I hope that this chapter, as well as this volume, helps to find not answers, but possibly better interdisciplinary questions to ask about the relationship between language, mind, and culture.

ACKNOWLEDGMENT

I thank Peter M. Gardner, Janet D. Keller, Kris K. Lehman, and the two editors of this book for reading and commenting on the first draft of this chapter. A warm thank you goes to Katharine L. Wiegele, who read, edited, and discussed the chapter with me before, during, and after its completion. Another thankful thought goes to my students in the "Language and Culture" class I taught at University of Missouri-Columbia in spring 1999, who suffered through many of the ideas contained in the chapter. All mistakes and omissions are my own.

REFERENCES

Atran, S. (1990). *Cognitive foundations of fatural history: Towards an anthropology of science*. Cambridge: Cambridge University Press.

Baayen, H., & Danziger, E. (Eds.). (1994). *Max Planck Institute for Psycholinguistics: Annual Report 14, 1993*. Nijmegen, the Netherlands: Max Planck Institute for Psycholinguistics.

Bennardo, G. (1993). *Towards a computational approach to spatial cognition: An investigation of relevant computations in the visual system and the linguistic system*. Cognitive Science Technical Report UIUC-BI-CS-93-05 (Language Series). Urbana: The Beckman Institute for Advanced Science and Technology, University of Illinois at Urbana-Champaign.

Bennardo, G. (1996). *A computational approach to spatial cognition: representing spatial relationships in Tongan language and culture*. Unpublished doctoral dissertation, University of Illinois at Urbana-Champaign, Urbana.

Bennardo, G. (1999). The conceptual content of Tongan directionals: Mental representations of space in Tongan. *Rongorongo Studies*, 9(2), 39–61. Published by the Institute of Polynesian Languages and Literatures, Auckland, New Zealand.

Bennardo, G. (2000). A conceptual analysis of Tongan spatial nouns: From grammar to mind. *Languages of the World, 12*., Munich: Lincom Europe.

Bennardo, G. (2002). Mental Images of the familiar: Cultural Strategies of Spatial Representations in Tonga. In G. Bennardo (Ed.), *Representing Space in Oceania: Culture in Language and Mind,* (pp. 159–177). Canberra, Australia: Pacific Linguistics, Research School of Pacific and Asian Studies, The Australian National University.

Bennardo, G. (in press). *A typology of frames of reference based on their axiomatic content*. Unpublished manuscript, Department of Anthropology, Northern Illinois University.

Berlin, B. (1995). Speculation on the growth of ethnobotanial nomenclature. In B. G. Blount (Ed.), *Language, culture, and society: A book of readings* (2nd ed., pp. 152–86). Prospect Heights, IL: Waveland Press. (Original work published 1972)

Berlin, B., & Kay, P. (1969). *Basic color terms: Their universality and evolution*. Los Angeles: University of California Press.

Boas, F. (1911). Introduction. *In Handbook of American Indian languages* (pp. 1–83). Bulletin 40, Part I, Bureau of American Ethnology. Washington, DC, Government Printing Office.

Bowerman, M. (1996). Learning how to structure space for language: A crosslinguistic perspective. In P. Bloom, M. A. Peterson, L. Nadel, & M. F. Garrett (Eds.), *Language and space* (pp. 385–436). Cambridge, MA: MIT Press.

Broschart, J. (1996). The social perception of space: Non-spatial determinants of the use of directionals in Tongan (Polynesia). In A. Frank & W. Kuhn (Eds.), *Spatial information theory* (pp. 443–462). Berlin: Springer.

Broschart, J. (1997). Why Tongan does it differently: Categorical distinctions in a language without nouns and verbs. *Linguistic Typology 1* (2).

Brown, P., Senft, G., & Wheeldon, L. (Eds.). (1993). *Max Planck Institute for Psycholinguistics: Annual Report 13, 1992*. Nijmegen, the Netherlands: Max-Planck Institute for Psycholinguistics.

Burling, R. (1969). Cognition and componential analysis: God's truth or hocus-pocus? In S. A. Tyler (Ed.), *Cognitive anthropology* (pp. 419–428). New York: Holt, Rinehart, and Winston.
CARG (Cognitive Anthropology Research Group). (1992). *Manual for the Space Stimuli Kit 1.1.* Nijmegen, the Netherlands: Max Planck Institute for Psycholinguistics.
Carlson-Radvansky, L. & Irwin, D. (1993). Frames of Reference in Vision and Language: Where is Above? *Cognition* 46: 223–244.
Chomsky, N. (1986). *Knowledge of language*. New York: Praeger.
Chomsky, N. (1995). *The minimalist program*. Cambridge, MA: MIT Press.
Churchward, C. M. (1953). *Tongan grammar.* Nuku'alofa, Tonga: Vava'u Press.
Clark, H. H. (1970). The primitive nature of children's relational concepts. In J. R. Hayes (Ed.), *Cognition and development of language*. New York: John Wiley & Sons.
Cohen, R. (Ed.). (1985). *The development of spatial cognition*. London: Lawrence Erlbaum Associates.
Crystal, D. (1991). *A dictionary of linguistics and phonetics*. Oxford: Blackwell.
de Saussure, F. (1959). *Course in general linguistics*. New York: McGraw-Hill.
Dougherty, J. D. (1978). Salience and relativity in classification. *American Ethnologist*, 5(1), 55–80.
Dougherty, J. D., & Keller, C. M. (1985). Taskonomy: A practical approach to knowledge structures. In J. D. Dougherty (Ed.), *Directions in cognitive anthropology* (pp. 161–174). Urbana: University of Illinois Press.
Ellen, P., & Thinus-Blanc, C. (Eds.). (1987) *Cognitive processes and spatial orientation in animal and man*. Boston: Martinus Nijhoff.
Florey, M. J. & Kelly, B. F. (2002). Spatial reference in Alune. In G. Bennardo (Ed.), *Representing Space in Oceania: Culture and Language and Mind* (pp. 11–46).
Fodor, J. (1983). *Modularity of mind*. Cambridge, MA: MIT Press.
Foley, A. W. (1997). *Anthropological linguistics: An introduction.* Oxford: Blackwell Publishers Ltd.
Frege, G. (1975). On Sense and Reference. In D. Davidson & G. Harman (Eds.), *The logic of grammar* (pp. 116–128). Encino, CA: Dickenson.
Furbee, L. N., & Shaul, D. L. (1998). *Language and culture*. Prospect Heights, IL: Waveland Press.
Gallistel, C. R. (1993). *The organization of learning*. Cambridge, MA: MIT Press.
Gelman, S. A., Coley, J. D., & Gottfried, G. M. (1994). Essentialist beliefs in children: The acquisition of concepts and theories. In L. A. Hirschfeld & S. A. Gelman (Eds.), *Mapping the mind: Domain specificity in cognition and culture* (pp. 341–366). Cambridge: Cambridge University Press.
Goodenough, W. (1956). Componential analysis and the study of meaning. *Language*, *32*, 195–216.
Goodenough, W. (1964). Cultural anthropology and linguistics. In Dell Hymes (Ed.), *Language in Culture and Society: A reader in linguistic anthropology* (pp. 36–39). New York: Harper & Row. (Original work published 1957)
Goodenough, W. (1970). *Description and comparison in cultural anthropology*. Chicago: Aldine.
Hardin, C. L., & Maffi, L. (Eds.). (1997). *Color categories in thought and language*. Cambridge: Cambridge University Press.
Hill, D. (1997). Finding your way in Longgu: Geographical reference in Solomon Islands' language. In G. Senft (Ed.), *Referring to Space: Studies in Austronesian and Papuan languages* (pp. 101–126). Oxford: Oxford University Press.
Hill, J. H., & Mannheim, B. (1992). Language and world view. *Annual Review of Anthropology*, *21*, 381–406.
Hirschfeld, L. A., & Gelman, S. A. (Eds.). (1994). *Mapping the mind: Domain specificity in cognition and culture*. Cambridge: Cambridge University Press.
Hoijer, H. (1995). The Sapir-Whorf Hypothesis. In B. G. Blount (Ed.), *Language, culture, and society: A book of readings* (2nd ed., pp. 113–215). Prospect Heights, IL: Waveland Press. (Original work published 1954)
Hubel, D. H. (1988). *Eye, brain, and vision*. New York: Scientific American Library.
Hyslop, C. (2002). Hiding behind trees on ambae: Spatial reference in an Oceanic language of Vanuatu. In G. Bennardo (Ed.), *Representing Space in Oceania: Culture and Language and Mind* (pp. 47–76). Canberra, Australia: Pacific Linguistics, Research School of Pacific and Asian Studies, Australian National University.
Jackendoff, R. (1983). *Semantics and cognition*. Cambridge, MA: MIT Press.
Jackendoff, R. (1990). *Semantic structures*. Cambridge, MA: MIT Press.
Jackendoff, R. (1991). Parts and boundaries. *Cognition*, *41*, 9–45.
Jackendoff, R. (1992). *Languages of the mind: Essays on mental representation*. Cambridge, MA: MIT Press.
Jackendoff, R. (1997). *The architecture of the language faculty*. Cambridge, MA: MIT Press.

Jackendoff, R., & Landau, B. (1992). Spatial language and spatial cognition. In R. Jackendoff (Ed.), *Languages of the mind: Essays on mental representation* (pp. 99–124). Cambridge, MA: MIT Press.
Johnson, M. (1987). *The body in the mind: The bodily basis of meaning, imagination, and reason*. Chicago: University of Chicago Press.
Johnson-Laird, P. N. (1983). *Mental models*. Cambridge, MA: Harvard University Press.
Kay, P., & McDaniel, C. (1978). The linguistic significance of the meanings of basic color terms. *Language, 54*, 610–646.
Keller, J. D., & Keller, C. M. (1993). Thinking and acting with Iron. In S. Chaiklin & J. Lave (Eds.), *Understanding practice: Perspectives on activity and context* (pp. 125–143). Cambridge: Cambridge University Press.
Keller, J. D., & Keller, C. M. (1996a). Imaging in Iron, or thought is not inner speech. In J. J. Gumperz & S. C. Levinson (Eds.), *Rethinking linguistic relativity* (pp. 115–129). Cambridge: Cambridge University Press.
Keller, J. D., & Keller, C. M. (1996b). *Cognition and tool use: The blacksmith at work*. Cambridge: Cambridge University Press.
Keller, J. D., & Lehman, F. K. (1991). Complex concepts. *Cognitive science, 15*(2), 271– 292.
Keller, J. D., & Lehman, F. K. (1993). Computational complexity in the cognitive modeling of cosmological ideas. In P. Boyer (Ed.), *Cognitive aspects of religious symbolism* (pp. 74–92). Cambridge: Cambridge University Press.
Kosslyn, S. M. (1996). *Image and brain: The resolution of the imagery debate*. Cambridge, MA: MIT Press.
Kuhn, T. S. (1970). *The structure of scientific revolutions* (2nd ed.). Chicago: University of Chicago Press.
Landau, B., & Jackendoff, R. (1993). "What" and "where" in spatial language and spatial cognition. *Behavioral and brain sciences. 16*(2), 17–38.
Lehman, F. K. (1985). Cognition and computation: On being sufficiently abstract. In J. W. D. Dougherty (Ed.), *Directions in cognitive anthropology* (pp. 19–48). Urbana: University of Illinois Press.
Lehman, F. K. (1993). The relationship between genealogical and terminological structure in kinship terminologies. *Journal of Quantitative Anthropology, 4*(1), 95–122.
Lehman, F. K., & Bennardo, G. (1992, November). A computational approach to the cognition of space and its linguistic expression. Prepared in advance for conference, The Relationship Between Linguistic and Conceptual Representation, Antwerp, Belgium.
Lehman, F. K., & Witz, K. (1974). Prolegomena to a formal theory of kinship. In P. Ballanoff (Ed.), *Genealogical mathematics* (pp. 111–134). The Hague: Mouton.
Lehman, F. K., & Witz, K. (1979). *A formal theory of kinship: The transformational component*. Report No. 11, Committee on Culture and Cognition. Urbana: University of Illinois at Urbana-Champaign.
Lenneberg, E., & Roberts, J. (1956). The language of experience, a study in methodology. Memoir 13. *International Journal of American Linguistics*. Indiana University Publications in Anthropology and Linguistics. Baltimore, MD: Waverly Press.
Levelt, W. J. M. (1982). Cognitive styles in the use of spatial direction terms. In R. J. Jarvella & W. Klein (Eds.), *Speech, place, and action: Studies in deixis and related topics* (pp. 251–270). New York: John Wiley & Sons.
Levelt, W. J. M. (1984). Some perceptual limitations on talking about space. In A. J. Van Doorn, W. A. Vander Grind, & J. Koenderink (Eds.), *Limits in perception* (pp. 323–358). Utrecht: VNU Press.
Levelt, W. J. M. (1989). *Speaking: From intention to articulation*. Cambridge, MA: MIT Press.
Levelt, W. J. M. (1996). Perspective taking and ellipsis in spatial descriptions. In P. Bloom, M. A. Peterson, L. Nadel, & M. F. Garrett (Eds.), *Language and space* (pp. 77–108). Cambridge, MA: MIT Press.
Levinson, S. C. (1992). Primer for the field investigation of spatial description and conception. *Pragmatics, 2*(1), 5–47.
Levinson, S. C. (1996a) Language and space. *Annual Review of Anthropology, 25*, 353– 382.
Levinson, S. C. (1996b). Frames of reference and Molyneaux's question: Cross-linguistic evidence. In P. Bloom, M. A. Peterson, L. Nadel, & M. F. Garrett (Eds.), *Language and space* (pp. 109–170). Cambridge, MA: MIT Press.
Levinson, S. C. (1996c). Introduction to Part II. In J. J. Gumperz & S. C. Levinson (Eds.), *Rethinking linguistic relativity* (pp. 133–144). Cambridge: Cambridge University Press.
Levinson, S. C. (1997). Language and Cognition: The cognitive consequences of spatial description in Guugu Yimithirr. *Journal of Linguistic Anthropology, 7*(1), 98–131

Liben, L. S., Patterson, A. H., & Newcombe, N. (Eds.). (1981). *Spatial representation and behavior across the life span*. New York: Academic Press.

Lounsbury, F. G. (1956). A semantic analysis of the Pawnee kinship Usage. *Language, 32*, 158–194.

Lounsbury, F. G. (1969). A formal account of the Omaha- and Crow-type kinship terminologies. In S. A. Tyler (Ed.), *Cognitive anthropology* (pp. 212–255). New York: Holt, Rinehart, and Winston.

Lucy, J. (1992a). *Grammatical Categories and Cognition : A Case Study of the Linguistic Relativity Hypothesis*. Cambridge: Cambridge University Press.

Lucy, J. (1992b). *Language diversity and thought: A reformulation of the linguistic relativity hypothesis*. Cambridge: Cambridge University Press.

Lucy, J. (1997). The linguistics of "color." In C. L. Hardin & L. Maffi. (Eds.), *Color categories in thought and language* (pp. 320–46). Cambridge: Cambridge University Press.

MacLaury, R. E. (1997). *Color and cognition in Mesoamerican languages: Constructing categories as vantage*. Austin: University of Texas Press.

Medin, D. L. (1989). Concepts and conceptual structure. *American Psychologist, 44*(12), 1469–1481.

Miller, G. A., & Johnson–Laird, P. N. (1976). *Language and perception*. Cambridge, MA: Harvard University Press.

Moore, T. E. (Ed.). (1973). *Cognitive development and the acquisition of language*. New York: Academic Press.

Murphy, G. L., & Medin, D. L. (1985). The role of theories in conceptual coherence. *Psychological Review, 92*(3), 289–316.

Ozanne-Rivierre, F. (1997). Spatial references in New Caledonian languages. In G. Senft (Ed.), *Referring to space: Studies in Austronesian and Papuan languages* (pp. 83–100). Oxford: Oxford University Press.

Palmer, S. (2002). Absolute spacial reference and the grammaticalisation of cognitively salient phenomena. In G. Bennardo (Ed.), *Representing Space in Oceania: Culture in Language and Mind* (pp. 107–157). Canberra, Australia: Pacific Linguistics, Research School of Pacific and Asian Studies, Australian National University.

Pederson, E., & Roelofs, A. (Eds.), (1995). *Max Planck Institute for Psycholinguistics: Annual Report 15, 1994*. Nijmegen, The Netherlands: Max Planck Institute for Psycholinguistics.

Pick, H. L. (1993). Organization of spatial knowledge in children. In N. Eilan, R. McCarthy, & B. Brewer (Eds.), *Spatial representation: Problems in philosophy and psychology* (pp. 31–42). Oxford: Basil Blackwell.

Pinker, S. (1997). *How the mind works*. New York: W. W. Norton.

Sapir, E. (1949a). The status of linguistics as a science. In D. G. Mandelbaum (Ed.), *The selected writings of Edward Sapir in language, culture, and personality* (pp. 160–166). Berkeley: University of California Press.(Original work published 1929)

Sapir, E. (1949b). Language. In D. G. Mandelbaum (Ed.), *The selected writings of Edward Sapir in language, culture, and personality* (pp. 7–32). Berkeley: University of California Press. (Original work published 1933).

Slobin, I. D. (1996). From "thought and language" to "thinking for speaking." In J. J. Guperz & S. C. Levinson (Eds.), *Rethinking linguistic relativity* (pp. 70–96). Cambridge: Cambridge University Press.

Stiles-Davis, J., Kritchevsky, M., & Bellugi, U. (Eds.). (1988). *Spatial cognition: Brain bases and development*. London: Lawrence Erlbaum Associates.

Talmy, L. (1983). How language structures space. In H. L. Pick & L. P. Acredolo (Eds.), *Spatial orientation: Theory, research, and application* (pp. 225–282). New York: Plenum Press.

Talmy, L. (1985). Lexicalization patterns: Semantics structure in lexical form. In T. Shopen (Ed.), *Language typology and syntactic description, Vol. 3, Grammatical categories and the lexicon* (pp. 57–149). Cambridge: Cambridge University Press.

Talmy, L. (1991). Path to realization: A typology of event conflation. *Proceedings of the Seventeenth Annual Meeting of the Berkeley Linguistic Society* (pp. 480–519). [Supplement in the *Buffalo Papers in Linguistics*, 91–101, 182–187.]

Tchekhoff, C. (1990). Discourse and Tongan *mai, atu, ange*: Scratching the surface. In J. H. C. S. Davidson (Ed.), *Pacific Island languages* (pp. 105–110). Honolulu: University of Hawai'i Press.

Wallace, A. F. C. (1969). The problem of the psychological validity of componential analyses. In S. A. Tyler (Ed.), *Cognitive anthropology* (pp. 396–418). New York: Holt, Rinehart, and Winston.

Whorf, B. L. (1956). *Language, thought, and reality: Selected writings of Benjamin Lee Whorf* (Ed. J. B. Carroll). Cambridge, MA: MIT Press. (Original works written 1927–1941)

3

The Role of Speech Perception Capacities in Early Language Acquisition

Peter W. Jusczyk
Departments of Psychology and Cognitive Science
Johns Hopkins University

Understanding how language acquisition occurs requires both a detailed description of the initial capacities of first language learners and an accurate characterization of the nature of the linguistic input they receive. Neither task is trivial. The researcher investigating the initial capacities faces many obstacles in determining the range of infants' cognitive and perceptual abilities. Devising appropriate methods to assess the perceptual capacities of infants has been difficult enough. How to delineate fully the nature of any abstract cognitive constraints that enter into language learning is far from clear. There are also serious difficulties to surmount in describing the nature of the effective linguistic input that learners receive. Not only are there practical problems in trying to record and transcribe the real input that learners receive, but there is the added difficulty in determining which aspects of the input are attended to and encoded by learners. Indeed, characterizing the latter requires some knowledge of learners' perceptual and cognitive capacities.

When language-acquisition research began in earnest in the early 1960s, little was known about the cognitive and perceptual capacities of young infants. Indeed, there were relatively few methods available for assessing these capacities in infants. Consequently, most language studies began at a point when language learners were producing their first words (10–12 months) or word combinations (around 18 months). As corpora of early productions from young language learners were collected, it appeared that even the earliest word combinations were not random, but structured in certain ways. By analogy to processes assumed to underlie adults' productions of sentences, language learners were thought to begin with a rudimentary grammar which then developed into the much more complex grammar of the target language they were acquiring (Braine, 1963; Brown, Cazden, & Bellugi, 1969; McNeill, 1966). Theorizing about an innate language acquisition device (LAD) typically focused more on elements of universal grammar than on the perceptual and cognitive capacities of language learners (Chomsky, 1965; Katz, 1966). As characterized by one influential proponent, "LAD must be equipped with knowledge of just those specific aspects of linguistic competence that cannot be extracted from overt speech, namely, appropriate generic grammatical classes and hierarchical structures" (McNeill, 1966, p. 50). Included in grammatical classes were notions such as basic categories, such as nouns, verbs, and adjectives. The hierarchical structure refers to the way such units can be combined into noun phrases and verb phrases, and ultimately into sentences. Because this knowledge was presumed to be part of one's innate endowment, and therefore a common starting point for all learners, it was referred to as universal grammar or UG (see also Pullum, chap. 5, this volume.) As syntactic theorizing changed over the years, so did assumptions about the nature of the information included in universal grammar (Chomsky, 1995; Roeper & Williams, 1987).

Present-day knowledge of the initial state of language learners is based on more than assumptions drawn from linguistic theorizing. Great strides have been made in understanding infants' perceptual and cognitive capacities and their development during the first few years of life. We have a much clearer picture of when infants become sensitive to various aspects of native language structure and organization. This new understanding of the range of infants' capacities has led to some re-thinking about how infants acquire language. In what follows, I review some of the key findings concerning infants' speech-processing abilities and the role that these may play in language acquisition.

BASIC SPEECH PERCEPTION CAPACITIES

A critical step in acquiring any language is being able to identify what its words are. Doing so requires some ability to discriminate utterances of one word from another, but it also demands some ability to ignore irrelevant differences in the acoustic characteristics of the word that might be introduced as a result of differences among talkers or speaking rates. The field of infant speech perception research began by focusing on the ability of young infants to discriminate differences in speech sounds. Eimas, Siqueland, Jusczyk, and Vigorito found that infants as young as 1 month could discriminate the voicing contrast that distinguishes [ba] from [pa] in English. In this case, voicing refers to whether the vocal chords are vibrating when the air is released from the lips (as in the case of [ba]) or whether they begin to vibrate about 50 msec later (as in the case of [pa]).

Subsequently, researchers began to explore the range of speech contrasts that young infants are able to discriminate. These studies demonstrated that infants' capacities for detecting speech contrasts were not limited to voicing contrasts, but extended to place of articulation—e.g., [b–d] and manner of articulation—e.g., [r–l] among consonants, and to various vowel distinctions—e.g., [i–I]. Moreover, evidence that young infants perceive phonetic contrasts not present in their native language indicated that a long period of prior experience was not necessary for discriminating such contrasts. Rather, infants' discriminative capacities appeared to be well-developed, right from birth.

The ability to discriminate one sound pattern from another is an important prerequisite for acquiring a vocabulary. However, it is also critical that a learner be able to recognize when different utterances are instances of the same word. Considerable acoustic variability is present in productions of the same words by different talkers, and even in the production of the same word by the same talker in different contexts. Thus, one critical task is to identify when some acoustic difference constitutes a meaningful distinction among words rather than variability in the production of the same word. Six-month olds display some ability to compensate for differences among talkers in their productions of the same vowel contrasts (Kuhl, 1979, 1983). Subsequent research extended this finding, demonstrating that 2-month-olds generalized across talker differences in the production of consonant-vowel-consonant (CVC) syllables, such as "bug" and "dug" (Jusczyk, Pisoni, & Mullennix, 1992). Similarly, infants at the same age also display some ability to compensate for acoustic variability caused by changes in speaking rates (Eimas & Miller, 1980a; Miller & Eimas, 1983). Hence, young infants appear to have, at least, a rudimentary ability to compensate for variability in the production of the same word across different talkers and speaking rates.

Taken together, young infants' discriminative capacities and their abilities to generalize across different sources of acoustic variability allow them to begin to categorize the input in ways that could potentially lead to the discovery of the structural organization of their native language. However, a number of other obstacles remain. Many infants grow up in environments in which more than one language is spoken. Without some way of separating utterances in one language from another, it would be impossible for infants to extract the right set of generalizations about the structural organization of their native language. Instead, generalizations about the nature of word and sentence forms would be based on disparate and unrelated utterances. However, evidence from several investigations suggests that even young infants have some ability to distinguish utterances in one language from another. Mehler et al., 1988) found that French newborns listening to an unfamiliar bilingual talker distinguished utterances in their mother's native language (French) from those of another language (Russian). Mehler et al. also demonstrated that American 2-month-olds discriminated English utterances from Italian. Similar results have also been reported for newborns and 5-month-olds listening to English and Spanish.

In their original investigation, Mehler et al. found that infants used prosodic information to distinguish utterances in the mother's native language from those in the foreign language. More recent investigations have supported and extended these observations. Nazzi, Bertoncini, and Mehler reported that French newborns were able to distinguish two foreign languages (English and Japanese). The rhythmic organization of these two languages differs: English is considered to be stress timed, whereas Japanese is mora timed. The mora is a rhythmic unit that can either be syllabic or subsyllabic. In English, a mora corresponds roughly to a CV syllable with a short vowel (e.g., "the" as opposed to "thee," which has a long vowel and thus two moras). Nazzi et al. found that French newborns tested on two foreign languages with a similar rhythmic organization (e.g., English and Dutch) did not discriminate utterances from the two languages. Nazzi et al. concluded that newborns initially distinguish utterances from different languages on the basis of their rhythmic organization. Thus, provided that learners receive input from languages with different rhythmic organization, they should be able to assign utterances to the appropriate linguistic category. However, what happens if the native language being learned has the same type of rhythmic organization as another language spoken in the same environment? Bosch and Sebastián-Gallés explored this issue by testing 4-month-olds exposed to Spanish and Catalan. The infants discriminated the utterances from these two languages. Bosch and Sebastián-Gallés suggested that information about the distribution of syllable types and their durational characteristics may have provided the basis for distinguishing utterances in Spanish and Catalan. More recent research indicates that discrimination of languages from within the same rhythmic class may require prior experience with at least one of the languages (Nazzi, Jusczyk, & Johnson, 2000). In particular, American 5-month-olds discriminate English from Dutch, but not Dutch from German, even though each of these languages is stress timed.

The critical finding from these studies is that, from birth, infants have some capacity to categorize utterances as belonging to different languages according to their rhythmic organization. By 4 months, they can go beyond gross rhythmic distinctions and use other kinds of information to distinguish utterances in their native language from those in another language with a similar rhythmic organization.

These early speech perception capacities are crucial for making sense of linguistic input. They provide a means of initially classifying utterances, which then may allow learners to pick up distributional patterns revealing the underlying structure and organization of the language. As powerful and important as these capacities are, they undergo considerable development before evolving to support the kinds of speech processing found in fluent users of a particular language. In particular, in the course of language acquisition, speech perception capacities are tailored to deal most optimally and efficiently with the typical structure of utterances in the native language (Cutler, Mehler, Norris, & Segui, 1986; Jusczyk, 1985, 1997; Mehler, Dupoux, & Segui, 1990).

NATIVE LANGUAGE INFLUENCES ON SPEECH PERCEPTION CAPACITIES

Cross-linguistic comparisons of infant speech perception capacities have noted few, if any, differences in infants before 6 months of age. However, there are indications that the nature of the linguistic input has a considerable impact on speech perception capacities during the second half of the first year. In their seminal study, Werker and Tees documented a decline in sensitivity to non-native speech contrasts between 6 and 12 months of age. English-learning infants were tested at three different ages (6–8 months, 8–10 months, and 10–12 months) on their ability to distinguish phonetic contrasts from the native language as well as two others: Nthlakapmx and Hindi. The youngest group easily discriminated all three types of contrasts. However, by 10–12 months of age, the foreign language contrasts were no longer reliably discriminated, even though discrimination performance remained high on the native-language contrast. The decline in sensitivity to the non-native contrasts appeared to stem from their absence in the linguistic input of the English learners, because Hindi and Nthlakapmx 12-month-olds continued to discriminate their native–language contrasts.

Although it appeared initially that lack of exposure to a particular contrast would ensure a decline in sensitivity to it, the picture has turned out to be considerably more complicated. For example, although, between 6 and 12 months, English learners, show a decline in sensitivity to a Zulu lateral fricative distinction, they do not show a similar decline to an Ethopian ejective distinction (Best, 1991), nor to a Zulu lateral vs. medial click distinction (Best, McRoberts, & Sithole, 1988). It is clear that other factors, such as the relation of the nonnative contrasts to native-language contrasts (Best, 1995), may affect whether perceptual sensitivity to the contrasts declines or not.

There have been suggestions that declines in sensitivity may occur sooner for some types of contrasts than for others. For instance, Polka and Werker found that English-learning 4- to 6-month-olds, but not 6- to 8-month-olds, discriminated the German vowel contrasts [U] versus [Y],(ü) and [u] versus [y]. Moreover, Werker and Polka also reported an asymmetry in their discrimination results. Specifically, infants only discriminated the contrasts when the vowel that was more distant from a native language vowel category served as the repeating background stimulus and the vowel nearer the native language category served as the target. This asymmetric discrimination pattern is similar to what Kuhl termed the "perceptual magnet effect" for native-language vowel perception.

Kuhl argued that native-language vowel categories are organized around prototypes, and that by 6 months, infants reflect this organization in their vowel categories. She hypothesized that the perceptual space around the prototype is distorted, shortening the perceptual distances between the center and the edges of the vowel category. New utterances of vowels close to the prototype of the category are drawn to the prototype (or perceptual magnet) and perceived as belonging to the category. Empirical support for the notion that perceptual magnet effects arise from infants' exposure to native-language input came from an investigation of American and Swedish 6-month-olds' perception of vowel contrasts. Both groups of infants were tested on English and Swedish vowel contrasts. The infants displayed a perceptual magnet effect only for their native language vowels.

Another recent investigation raises questions about both the extent and the sources of change in infants' vowel perception. Polka and Bohn explored the perception of an English [E]–[æ], and a German [u]–[y], vowel contrast by English and German-learning infants at two ages: 6–8 months and 10–12 months. No age differences were observed in the discrimination of either contrast, nor were differences found in the discrimination performance of English and German infants. English and German learners showed the same asymmetrical pattern of discrimination for each vowel contrast. Because the German contrast was one of the same ones used in the earlier study by Polka and Werker (1994), the findings raise doubts about the view that sensitivity to nonnative vowel contrasts declines earlier than for nonnative consonantal contrasts. Moreover, the findings also seem to undercut the view that asymmetries in the discrimination of vowel contrasts are the result of experience with input from a particular language. If language-specific experience is critical in producing such asymmetries, one would expect this pattern to occur only when infants are discriminating the vowel contrast from their own native language. Polka and Bohn suggest that the real source of such asymmetries may have to do with the fact that vowels that act as perceptual magnets (English [æ] and German [u] are located in more extreme positions along the front/back and high/low dimensions of the vowel space).

In conclusion, the full extent of declines in sensitivity for non-native contrasts is uncertain. However, there are some indications that, during the second half of the first year, infants' capacities for discriminating non-native contrasts are affected by the linguistic input that they receive.

INCREASED SENSITIVITY TO NATIVE LANGUAGE SOUND PROPERTIES

One potential explanation of any decline in perceptual sensitivity to non-native speech sound categories is that infants are beginning to focus their attention on prominent characteristics of their own linguistic input. Attention to dimensions of sound patterns that recur frequently in their own input may lead them to ignore other dimensions that do not figure as prominently, thus resulting in an apparent loss of sensitivity to these nonattended dimensions.

Even with the perceptual capacities that they possess, there are many facets of native-language sound organization that learners must discover. Not only must they apprehend what elementary sound categories (i.e., phonemes) are used to form words in the language, but they also need to learn about any constraints on the way that phonemes can be ordered in words (i.e., the phonotactic organization of the language). Learners must also master the prosodic organization of the language, such as the nature of any rhythmic patterns associated with words and phrases. In addition, because words in fluent speech are nearly always uttered without pauses in between them, infants have to learn how word boundaries are marked in utterances. There is evidence that learners make progress along all of these fronts during the second half of the first year.

Given infants' discriminative capacities, learning the phonemes of a language would be trivial if each phoneme had a single acoustic realization. However, phonemes typically are marked by different acoustic variants (i.e., allophones) in different contexts. For example, in English, the allophone of /t/ is not the same in "tap" as in "dot," nor are either of these the same as the one in "train," or the one in "writer." Moreover, which phones are treated as allophones of a particular phoneme vary from language to language. Thus, how phones are mapped to phonemes in their native language has to be learned. On the one hand, it is important that infants perceive differences among the allophones of a phoneme because knowing which contexts a particular allophone occurs in could provide information about word boundaries. On the other hand, learning the phonological organization of the language demands that learners come to treat these allophones as manifestations of the same phoneme.

Studies of young infants' discriminative capacities have sometimes tested infants on contrasts involving phones that are mapped to the same phoneme in the language being acquired. For example, Hohne and Jusczyk found that English-learning 2-month-olds could distinguish between two allophones of /t/ that could signal the presence or absence of a word boundary in fluent speech. Hence, young infants can discriminate allophonic differences. However, what had not been investigated until recently was when infants give evidence of treating two allophones as manifestations of the same phoneme. Pegg and Werker explored this issue with English-learning 6 to 8 and 10 to 12-month-olds. They presented the infants with a contrast between [da] and [$t^{=}$a]. The initial segment of the latter syllable is the allophone of /t/ that occurs as part of an initial cluster with [s], as in "sta" Adult listeners perceive [$t^{=}$a] as perceptually more similar to [da] than to [t^{h}a] (the initial sound in the word "top"), even though [$t^{=}$a] and [t^{h}a] are manifestations of /t/. Nevertheless, adults were able to discriminate [$t^{=}$a] from [da], as were the English-learning 6 to 8-month olds. By comparison, the 10 to 12-month olds did not discriminate this contrast. Pegg and Werker suggest that the failure of the older infants to discriminate the contrast is an indication that these infants are in the process of organizing phones into phoneme classes. Clearly, some sort of reorganization appears to be occurring at this time. However, the mapping that the 10-to-12 months are attempting (i.e., linking [t⁼a] with [da]) is not the correct one for English where [t⁼a] and [t^ha] are both mapped to /t/ and where /d/ is a separate phoneme. Therefore, although the beginnings of phoneme category formation may be occurring in the 10- to12-month olds, these infants still have not mastered the mappings that exist in the adult language.

There are stronger indications that infants at this age have begun to learn about the phonotactic organization of their native language. Jusczyk, Friederici, Wessels, Svenkerud, and Jusczyk explored this issue by testing infants on unfamiliar words from their native language and a foreign language. They chose two languages with similar prosodic structure but differing in phonetic and phonotactic properties—English and Dutch. With respect to their phonetic properties, each language contains elements that do not appear in the other language (e.g., the /r/ of English is not the same as /r/ in Dutch). Moreover, the languages differ in their phonotactic patterns. For instance, Dutch allows clusters, such as [vl], [kn], and [zw], at the beginnings of words; English does not (except in some proper nouns and lexical borrowings, such as "Vladimir"and "zwieback"). English allows words to end in the voiced stop consonants [b], [d], and [g]; Dutch does not. Jusczyk et al. created six lists for each language, consisting of unfamiliar, infrequently occurring words that violated the phonetic and phonotactic constraints of the other language. Each list was composed of different words. American 6-month-olds listened about equally long to each type of list (i.e., they showed no preference for the English over the Dutch lists). Thus, there was no indication that the 6-month-olds had yet discovered the phonetic and phonotactic properties of native language words. Several additional studies revealed that 9-month-olds behave differently. American 9-month-olds listened significantly longer to the English lists, whereas Dutch 9-month-olds listened significantly longer to the Dutch lists—even when the lists differed only in their phonotactic properties. As an additional check on whether the infants were relying on the phonotactic information, Jusczyk et al. tested 9-month-olds on lowpass filtered versions of their stimuli. Low-pass filtering blocks out the acoustic energy of frequencies above a certain threshold (in this case 400 Hz). Thus, lowpass filtering at 400 Hz eliminates most of the phonotactic and phonetic information from the stimuli. With the low–pass filtered stimuli, the infants showed no preference for either type of list. Hence, Jusczyk et al. concluded that sensitivity to the phonotactic properties of native language words develops between 6 and 9 months of age.

Infants' developing sensitivity to phonotactic properties goes well beyond what is necessary for discriminating native from foreign-language words. Friederici and Wessels found that Dutch 9-month-olds are sensitive to phonotactically legal onset and offset clusters in Dutch. Specifically, the infants listened significantly longer to lists with phonotactically legal sequences than they did to phonotactically illegal sequences. In another investigation, Jusczyk, Luce, and Charles-Luce (1994) reported that English-learning 9-month-olds, but not 6-month-olds, are sensitive to the frequency with which phonotactically legal sequences occur in native-language words. Specifically, when presented with lists of items containing either frequently occurring or infrequently occurring phonotactic sequences, 9-month-olds listened significantly longer to the former. These findings suggest that not only are infants between 6 and 9 months learning about native language phonotactic patterns, but they are also remarkably sensitive to the distributional frequencies of such patterns.

During this same period, infants also appear to be developing sensitivity to the prosodic characteristics of native-language words. Studies of the typical stress patterns of words used in English conversational speech indicate that a very high proportion of these words are either stressed monosyllables or ones that begin with a stressed (or strong) syllable followed by an unstressed (or weak) syllable. Hence, the predominant stress pattern of English words is said to be trochaic—that is, strong/weak. Jusczyk, Cutler, and Redanz explored when American infants might be sensitive to this property of English words. They created lists of bisyllabic low frequency English words that either observed the predominant strong/weak pattern (e.g., "falter") or observed the nondominant weak/strong stress pattern (e.g., "befall"). When presented with these different types of lists, American 6-month-olds showed no preference for either the strong/weak or weak/strong words. In contrast, American 9-month-olds had a clear preference for the lists of strong/weak words. Moreover, this preference for the strong/weak patterns was obtained even when the words were low-pass filtered to eliminate most of the phonetic and phonotactic information. Thus, between 6 and 9 months, English learners develop sensitivity to the predominant stress patterns of English words. As in the case of phonotactic patterns, this achievement may stem from their sensitivity to the distributional frequency of certain word-stress patterns in the input.

In summary, during the second half of the first year, infants become attuned to many features of the structure and organization of sound patterns in their native language. Sensitivity to these properties of the linguistic input may position learners to discover other aspects of the structure and organization of utterances in the language.

HOW KNOWLEDGE OF SOUND ORGANIZATION MAY ASSIST WORD SEGMENTATION

As noted in the previous section, one problem that language learners must solve is how their language marks word boundaries in fluent speech. Speakers rarely pause between words in utterances. Indeed, the problem of accurately determining word boundaries in fluent speech has been one of the biggest obstacles to the development of successful automatic speech recognition devices (Klatt, 1986, 1989). It has been suggested that human listeners may take advantage of certain regularities in native language sound patterns to predict the location of possible word boundaries in fluent speech. For example, information about the contexts in which certain allophones appear is a potential source of information about word boundary locations (Bolinger & Gerstman, 1957; Church, 1987; Lehiste, 1960; Brent & Cartwright, 1996; Cairns et al., 1997; Christiansen, Allen, & Seidenberg, 1997; Myers et al., 1996). Knowledge of phonotactic patterns has also been suggested as another possible cue to word boundary locations. Similarly, Cutler and her colleagues (Cutler, 1990, 1994; Cutler & Norris, 1988) have suggested that English-language listeners' knowledge of the predominant stress patterns of English words could serve as a basis for a metrical segmentation strategy (MSS) whereby strong syllables are identified as possible onsets for new words in fluent speech. Finally, others have suggested that a general sensitivity to the statistical probabilities with which certain sound patterns occur in the input could provide learners with potential cues to word boundaries. For example, the two-word string *hungrybaby,* consists of four syllables: *hun, gry, bay,* and *by*. The first two syllables (*hun* and *gry*) consistently appear together because they form a word, as do the latter two syllables (*bay* and *by*). However, the second and third syllables (*gry* and *bay*) occur together relatively rarely across a corpus of English. Thus, the syllable *gry* follows the syllable *hun* more frequently than the syllable *bay* follows the syllable *gry*, because many different words can follow the word *hungry*, but only a few syllables can follow *hun*. It is this greater predictability of word-internal syllables than syllables spanning word boundaries that may be helpful in discovering word boundaries.

The notion that English-language learners may use information about predominant stress patterns to segment words has received considerable support. Studies indicate that English-learning 6- to 9-month-olds benefit from rhythmic properties in grouping and segmenting syllables from longer strings (Morgan, 1994, 1996; Morgan & Saffran, 1995). For example, Morgan (1994) found that the presence of a trochaic pattern led infants to cluster sequences of syllables together from a three-syllable string. In a subsequent investigation using both trochaic and iambic (i.e., weak/strong) stress patterns, Morgan (1996) found that 9-month-olds perceived novel bisyllables as cohesive only when they constituted a trochaic pattern. In another study that used sequences of nonsense syllables, Echols, Crowhurst, and Childers (1997) also reported findings suggesting that English-learners appear to favor trochaic over iambic patterns when segmenting four-syllable sequences.

Another indication that English-language learners use stress cues in segmenting words from fluent speech comes from a series of studies using a longer and more complex set of stimulus materials (Jusczyk, Houston, & Newsome, 1999). Using a paradigm first developed by Jusczyk and Aslin (1995), Jusczyk et al. familiarized infants with pairs of English words and then tested their detection of these words in fluent speech passages. In one experiment, 7.5-month-olds were familiarized with a pair of words with strong/weak stress patterns (e.g., "doctor" and "candle" or "kingdom" and "hamlet"). Subsequently, the infants were tested on four different six sentence passages—two of which contained the familiarized words and two of which did not. The infants listened significantly longer to the passages with the familiarized target words, suggesting that they detected these words in the passages. An additional experiment was conducted to determine whether the infants were responding to the whole words or just to a portion of these words, such as their strong syllables (i.e., to "dock" and "can," rather than to "doctor" and "candle"). To test this possibility, infants were familiarized with only the strong syllables of the original bisyllabic words (i.g., "dock" and "can" or "king" and "ham") and then tested on the passages containing the whole bisyllabic words (i.e., "doctor," "candle," "kingdom," and "hamlet"). In contrast to the previous experiment, the infants did not listen significantly longer to the passages in which the strong syllables of the target words corresponded to familiarized items. Thus, when familiarized with strong/weak words, English-learning 7.5 month-olds match the whole words and not just the strong syllables.

These findings with strong/weak words are certainly consistent with the view that English-language learners are using something like a metrical segmentation strategy to locate words in fluent speech. However, a crucial test of this hypothesis is to determine how infants fare with weak/strong words. If infants follow some version of MSS, and posit a word boundary at the onsets of strong syllables, one would expect them to have difficulty in recovering weak/strong words from fluent speech. For instance, when learners hear a word in fluent speech such as "device," they may missegment it by inserting a word boundary before "vice." Jusczyk et al. investigated this possibility by familiarizing 7.5-month-olds with pairs of weak/strong words (e.g., "device" and "guitar"), then testing them on four passages, two of which included the targets and two of which did not. In contrast to the results for the strong/weak words, the infants did not listen any longer to the passages with the weak/strong target words. As a further check on whether the infants were missegmenting the weak/strong words, another group of infants was familiarized with just the strong syllables of these words (e.g., "vice" and "tar"). When tested on the passages with the corresponding weak/strong words, the infants did display a significant listening preference for the passages with weak/strong words whose strong syllables matched the familiarized targets. Thus, consistent with the predictions of MSS, English-learning 7.5-month-olds mis-segment weak/strong words at the onset of the strong syllable. Interestingly enough, English-language learners develop the ability to overcome these difficulties in relatively short order. When Jusczyk et al. tested English-learning 10.5-month-olds, they found that these infants correctly segmented weak/strong words from fluent speech.

Because of the high proportion of words in English conversational speech that begin with strong syllables, relying on some form of MSS will prove to be of some benefit to learners in identifying possible words in the speech stream. However, reliance on MSS will lead English-language learners to incorrect segmentations of the input every time words begin with weak syllables. What are the benefits of a word segmentation strategy that is bound to fail to identify a significant number of words in the input? How do English-lanuage learners manage to overcome their difficulties with weak/strong words so quickly? One possible answer to these questions is that breaking the input into smaller sized chunks at strong syllable onsets may facilitate the discovery of other elements in the sound stream that may serve as cues to word boundaries. Specifically, by attending to information at the edges of these chunks, learners are positioned to detect information about the distribution of allophones and phonotactic sequences that do and do not appear in these contexts (Jusczyk, 1999). As a number of recent computer simulation studies have shown, access to these additional sources of information greatly improves performance in correctly identifying word boundaries in fluent speech. Moreover, as noted earlier, infants' sensitivity to the phonotactic organization of their native language develops between 6 and 9 months.

There is evidence from two recent investigations that English-learning infants are beginning to put their knowledge of native language sound organization to use in segmenting words from fluent speech. Mattys, Jusczyk, Luce, and Morgan (1999) investigated English-learning 9-month-olds' sensitivity to the way that phonotactic sequences typically correspond to word boundaries in English utterances. They created lists of CVCCVC sequences in which the internal CC sequence was systematically manipulated. For half of the lists, the internal CC sequences occurred much more frequently within words than between successive words in a corpus of speech directed to children (e.g., [ft]). For the other half of the lists, the internal CC sequences were found much more frequently between successive words than within words (e.g., [vt]). All of the CVCCVC items were recorded with two different stress patterns: once as strong/weak items and once as weak/strong items.

In their first experiment, Mattys et al. used the strong/weak stress patterns. They assumed that infants would treat CVCCVC items with this stress pattern as single bisyllabic words. Consequently, they predicted that if infants have learned how phonotactic sequences are distributed within and at the edges of words, they would listen significantly longer to the lists with items in which the internal CC sequence occurred frequently within words. In fact, 9-month olds behaved in accord with this prediction. Next, Mattys et al. tested another group of 9-month-olds on the items with weak/strong stress. They assumed that infants might be inclined to impose a word boundary at the onset of the stressed second syllable, thus treating each CVCCVC sequence as two separate words, rather than as a single word. Hence, they predicted that for these weak/strong

CVCCVC sequences, the infants would actually show a preference for the items in which the internal CC occurred more frequently between words. Once again, the infants responded in accord with the prediction.

Further confirmation that English-learning 9-month-olds have discovered how phonotactic sequences typically line up with word boundaries came in a third experiment. Mattys et al. imposed a 500–ms silent pause between the internal CC sequence of the strong/weak items. They reasoned that this pause might lead the infants to treat each of these CVCCVC items as two separate words. Therefore, they predicted that the 9-month-olds would now display a preference for the items in which the internal CC sequence occurred more frequently between words. Again, the infants' listening behavior confirmed the prediction. Finally, in another experiment, Mattys et al. demonstrated that when stress and phonotactics provided conflicting information about word boundaries, 9-month-olds favor the stress-based cues, suggesting that, at this age, phonotactic cues may serve as a secondary source of information about word boundaries. Overall, the results of this investigation indicate that English-learning 9-month-olds are sensitive to the way that phonotactic sequences typically align with word boundaries.

Results of another investigation suggest that, between 9 and 10.5 months of age, English-language learners are also developing sensitivity to allophonic cues to word boundaries in fluent speech. Jusczyk, Hohne, and Bauman (1999) explored whether English-language learners could use allophonic cues to distinguish occurrences of "nitrates" and "night rates" in fluent speech. The first occurrence of "t" in "nitrates" is aspirated, released, and often retroflexed, and the following "r" is devoiced—suggesting that it is part of a cluster. In contrast, the first "t" in "night rates" is unaspirated, unreleased, not retroflexed, and sometimes glottalized, and the following "r" is voiced—suggesting that it is syllable-initial. Together the absence of aspiration for the first "t" in "night rates" and the voicing of the following "r" suggests that the phoneme /t/ is not syllable initial. Jusczyk et al. conducted an experiment in which they familiarized 9-month olds with pairs of items, such as "night rates" and "doctor" (or "hamlet" and "nitrates"), then tested their ability to detect these words in passages. With respect to familiarization with either "hamlet" or "doctor," the infants listened longer to the passage containing the familiarized word than they did to the passage with the other word. However, infants familiarized with "nitrates" listened as long to the "night rates" passage as they did to the "nitrates" passage, and similarly, for familiarization with "night rates." Consequently, 9-month-olds did not seem to use the allophonic differences between "night rates" and "nitrates" to recognize them in fluent speech contexts. However, older infants *can* use allophonic cues to detect these items in fluent speech. In particular, 10.5-month-olds tested on the same materials displayed significant listening preferences for the passages containing the member of the "night rates" "nitrates" pair that they had been familiarized with.

The picture emerging from these studies of early word segmentation by English-language learners is that these skills develop over the course of several months. The learner begins with some approximation of the word segmentation system that will ultimately be in place. The crude initial parsing strategy helps in discovering other potential word segmentation cues. As learners begin to use and integrate these different sources of information, they are better positioned to detect still other cues that help to refine their developing word segmentation skills. English-language learners may initially rely on stress-based cues as a first-pass strategy for word segmentation. The smaller sized units that infants derive serve to limit their search space and facilitate the detection of allophonic and phonotactic cues to word boundaries.

It is worth noting that during this developmental period, infants are often segmenting words prior to learning their meanings. However, a study by Jusczyk and Hohne (1997) revealed that infants do retain information about the sound patterns of words that they hear frequently for at least as long as 2 weeks. Thus, it appears that as infants begin to build up a lexicon for their native language, they sometimes store information about sound patterns of potential words, even before they learn their meanings. Of course, just how word recognition processes change as vocabulary growth takes off during the latter half of the second year is an interesting question. Studies in this area have only recently begun (e.g. Fernald, Pinto, Swingley, Weinberg, & McRoberts, 1998; Schafer & Plunkett, 1998). Some success has been attained in determining the timecourse of infants' processing of familiar lexical items (Swingley, Pinto, & Fernald, 1998). With respect to their speed and accuracy in responding to a spoken word, as measured by looking at a correct picture on a video screen, 24-month-olds perform at close to adult levels. Moreover, the reaction time data suggest that representations of known words include rather detailed phonetic information (Swingley, Pinto, & Fernald, 1999). In particular, 24-month-olds are more delayed in responding to the correct picture when a distracter picture's label overlaps phonetically with the target at onset (*dog* vs. *doll*) than when the distracter has no phonetic overlap (*dog* vs. *tree*). One goal for future research in this area is to explore just how the word segmentation skills of 7.5-month-olds evolve to support the kinds of processing abilities that are manifest in 24-month-olds.

USING THE SPEECH SIGNAL TO DISCOVER SYNTACTIC ORGANIZATION

The notion that learners may derive useful information about syntactic organization from information in the speech signal was first raised many years ago. McNeill considered and rejected the idea. Drawing on Lieberman's work, he noted that units derived from the speech signal do not always correspond to the critical units in the linguistic analysis of the utterances. However, some thoughtful reconsideration of how learners might benefit from information in the speech signal to learn about syntax rekindled interest in this possibility. A number of investigations revealed that were not only cues to the location of clause boundaries present in speech addressed to infants (Fisher & Tokura, 1996), but that infants are sensitive to the occurrence of such cues (Hirsh-Pasek er al., 1987; Kemler Nelson, Hirsh-Pasek, Jusczyk, & Wright-Cassidy, 1989). Moreover, sensitivity to clausal units affects how infants encode and remember speech information (Mandel, Jusczyk, & Kemler Nelson, 1994; Mandel, Kemler Nelson, & Jusczyk, 1996; Nazzi, Kemler Nelson, Jusczyk, & Jusczyk, 2000).

There is also some indication that English-learning infants are sensitive to the marking of subclausal units, such as phrases (Jusczyk, Hirsh-Pasek, Kemler Nelson, Kennedy, Woodward, & Piwoz, 1992). However, one problem noted about markers for phrases in the speech signal is that the units picked out are usually prosodic phrases, and these do not map perfectly onto syntactic phrases. For example, consider the following sentences:

(1) Mary / bought the cow.

(2) She bought / the cow.

In (1) the prosodic phrase boundary (indicated by "/") coincides with the syntactic boundary between the subject phrase and the predicate phrase. However, in (2), the prosodic phrase boundary occurs within the predicate phrase between the verb and its direct object. Given a conflict between prosodic phrase marking and syntactic phrase marking such as in (2), English-learning 9-month-olds display listening preferences that accord with the prosodic organization of utterances (Gerken, Jusczyk, & Mandel, 1994). Nevertheless, the prosodic boundary does coincide with a syntactic boundary in both cases, just not the same type of syntactic boundary.

Given such mismatches between prosodic and syntactic organization, one might be tempted to abandon the notion that the speech signal can help to bootstrap the acquisition of syntax. However, even with the imperfect correlation between prosodic and syntactic organization, attention to the speech signal may aid the discovery of syntactic organization. Recall that a similar situation holds with respect to the role that attention to prosodic features, such as word stress, plays in segmenting words. That is, the correlation between stressed syllables and word onsets is not perfect. However, as stated earlier, dividing the input into smaller chunks provides the learner with greater opportunities for learning about the distribution of other potential cues within these chunks. A similar case can be made with respect to grouping information in utterances into prosodic phrasal units. Access to smaller prosodic phrase packets may allow learners to pick up certain kinds of syntactic regularities within such units. For example, one possible source of information within prosodic phrases is the occurrence of grammatical morphemes. In English, certain function words are typically found only at certain locations inside phrasal units. Thus, "the" marks the beginning of a noun phrase, and would be extremely unlikely to occur as the last word of a phrasal unit. Hence, grouping the input into prosodic phrases and noting regularities in how certain morphemes are distributed within such phrases may help in delineating their syntactic roles.

Grammatical morphemes often mark relations among words that learners must track within phrasal units. Yet because such elements are unstressed and are often left out of early word combinations produced by children, it has been suggested that young learners may not attend to these elements in the input (Echols & Newport, 1992; Gleitman, Gleitman, Landau & Wanner, 1988). However, Gerken and her colleagues have shown that these kinds of omissions are attributable to constraints on production rather than on perception (Gerken, 1991, 1994; Gerken, Landau & Remez, 1990). Indeed, recent findings suggest that during their first year, infants are sensitive to the occurrence of typical function words in native language utterances. Using an electrophysiological measure, Shafer, Gerken, Shucard, and Shucard (1992) found that infants distinguished normal English passages from ones in which nonsense syllables (such as "gub") replaced function words (such as "was"). The task involved a tone probe technique, wherein evoked potentials to a series of tones were measured while infants listened to passages. Evoked potentials to the tone sequences were delayed when infants were listening to passages with the nonsense syllables as compared to when they were listening to the passages with the real function words.

Shady (1996) replicated and extended the findings of Shafer et al. First, Shady found that English-learning 10.5-month-olds listen significantly longer to passages with function words than to ones in which nonsense words were substituted for the function words. This result held even when the nonsense items were phonetically very similar to English function words. To check whether infants had simply responded to the presence of any nonsense words in the passages, Shady conducted another experiment. She substituted nonsense words adhering to English phonotactic constraints for the English content words of the same passages, but the function words were not altered. No significant listening preferences were observed for the passages with the content, as opposed to the nonsense words. This last result is not surprising since there are many real content words that infants do not already know.

It appears that by 10.5 months, English-language learners have developed some expectations about the kinds of function words likely to appear in utterances. However, do infants at this age have any expectations about where such function words are likely to appear within utterances? To investigate this issue, Shady created new pairs of passages that were identical except for the placement of certain function words. In the natural passages, each function word occurred in its proper sentential position. In the unnatural passages, the function words were misplaced by interchanging them with function words from another sentential position. In the following example of an unnatural passage, the interchanged function words are italicized.

> *Is* bike with three wheels *a* coming down the street. Johnny *that* seen *had* bike yesterday. *Was* lady with him *the* his aunt. *Was* red bike *this* missing for a day. *Had* cover *that* fallen on it. We *the* found *had* bike next to her garage.

The development of sensitivity to the typical location of function words in sentences occurs relatively late. In particular, only 16-month-olds, but not 10.5-, 12 nor 14-month-olds, showed a significant listening preference for the natural passages. Shady concluded that although 10.5-month-olds may have some idea of which function words belong in English utterances, it is not until between 14 and 16 months of age that they learn the typical locations of these function words in sentences.

The correct placement of function words within phrases is not the only type of regularity that learners may discover within prosodic groupings. For instance, parsing the input into prosodic groups may facilitate the discovery of other kinds of relations between elements within such groups. There are certain kinds of syntactic dependencies that occur among words in an utterance. In English, demonstratives such as "this" and "these" must agree in number with the nouns that they modify. Hence, we say "this cat" or "these cats," but not "this cats" or "these cat." Another kind of dependency occurs between certain auxiliaries and verb forms. We say "the boy is running" but not "the boy can running." For the learner, one of the interesting, and potentially problematic, properties of these dependencies is that the critical elements can occur at some remove from each other in an utterance. So, although we might say, "Everyone *is* bak*ing* bread," in which the critical elements occur almost adjacent to each other, we can also say, "Everyone *is* not very skillfully bak*ing* bread," in which the critical elements are separated by a five-syllable adverbial phrase. Given the amount of intervening material in the latter case, correctly relating the verb form back to the auxiliary is not trivial.

Santelmann and Jusczyk have been investigating the circumstances in which English-language learners begin to detect dependencies between auxiliaries and verbs. They first tested infants on passages in which the critical auxiliary element occurred adjacent to a monosyllabic verb stem with an "ing" ending. For the natural passages, the auxiliary "is" was used, whereas for the unnatural passages, the auxiliary "can" was substituted. For example, a natural passage included a sentence such as "Fred *is* eat*ing*," which became "John *can* eat*ing*"in the unnatural passage. Eighteen month-olds, but not 15-month-olds, listened significantly longer to the natural than to the unnatural passages. Thus, 18-month-olds have developed at least some sensitivity to this type of syntactic dependency. The next objective was to determine the conditions under which the infants respond to the dependency. In a series of follow-up experiments, Santelmann and Jusczyk systematically varied the distance between the auxil-

Bosch, L., & Sebastián-Gallés, N. (1997). Native-language recognition abilities in 4-month-old infants from monolingual and bilingual environments. *Cognition, 65,* 33–69.
Braine, M. D. S. (1963). The ontogeny of English phrase structure. *Language, 39,* 1–13.
Brent, M. R. (1999). Speech segmentation and word discovery: A computational perspective. *Trends in Cognitive Science, 3,* 294–300.
Brent, M. R., & Cartwright, T. A. (1996). Distributional regularity and phonotactic constraints are useful for segmentation. *Cognition, 61,* 93–125.
Brown, R., Cazden, C., & Bellugi, U. (1969). The child's grammar from I to III. In J. P. Hill (Ed.), *Minnesota Symposia on Child Psychology* (Vol. II, pp. 28–73). Minneapolis: University of Minnesota Press.
Brown, R., & Fraser, C. (1964). The acquisition of syntax. *Monographs of the Society for Research in Child Development, 29,* 9–34.
Cairns, P., Shillcock, R., Chater, N., & Levy, J. (1997). Bootstrapping word boundaries: A bottom-up corpus-based approach to speech segmentation. *Cognitive Psychology, 33,* 111–153.
Chomsky, N. (1965). *Aspects of the theory of syntax.* Cambridge, MA: MIT Press.
Chomsky, N. (1995). *The minimalist program.* Cambridge, MA: MIT Press.
Christiansen, M. H., Allen, J., & Seidenberg, M. S. (1998). Learning to segment speech using multiple cues: A connectionist model. *Language and Cognitive Processes, 13,* pp. 221–268.
Church, K. W. (1987). *Phonological parsing in speech recognition.* Dordrecht: Kluwer.
Cutler, A. (1990). Exploiting prosodic probabilities in speech segmentation. In G. T. M. Altman (Ed.), *Cognitive models of speech processing: Psycholinguistic and computational perspective* (pp. 105–121). Cambridge, MA: MIT Press.
Cutler, A. (1994). Segmentation problems, rhythmic solutions. *Lingua, 92,* 81–104.
Cutler, A., & Carter, D. M. (1987). The predominance of strong initial syllables in the English vocabulary. *Computer Speech and Language, 2,* 133–142.
Cutler, A., Mehler, J., Norris, D. G., & Segui, J. (1986). The syllable's differing role in the segmentation of French and English. *Journal of Memory and Language, 25,* 385–400.
Cutler, A., & Norris, D. G. (1988). The role of strong syllables in segmentation for lexical access. *Journal of Experimental Psychology: Human Perception and Performance, 14,* 113–121.
Echols, C. H., Crowhurst, M. J., & Childers, J. B. (1997). Perception of rhythmic units in speech by infants and adults. *Journal of Memory and Language, 36,* 202–225.
Echols, C. H., & Newport, E. L. (1992). The role of stress and position in determining first words. *Language Acquisition, 2,* 189–220.
Eimas, P. D. (1975). Auditory and phonetic coding of the cues for speech: Discrimination of the [r–l] distinction by infants. *Perception & Psychophysics, 18,* 341–347.
Eimas, P. D., & Miller, J. L. (1980a). Contextual effects in infant speech perception. *Science, 209* , 1140–1141.
Eimas, P. D., & Miller, J. L. (1980b). Discrimination of the information for manner of articulation. *Infant Behavior & Development, 3,* 367–375.
Eimas, P. D., Siqueland, E. R., Jusczyk, P. W., & Vigorito, J. (1971). Speech perception in infants. *Science, 171,* 303–306.
Ervin, S. (1964). Imitation and structural change in children's language. In E. Lenneberg (Ed.), *New directions in the study of language.* Cambridge, MA: MIT Press.
Fernald, A., Pinto, J. P., Swingley, D., Weinberg, A., & McRoberts, G. W. (1998). Rapid gains in the speed of verbal processing in the second year. *Psychological Science, 9,* 228–231.
Fisher, C. L., & Tokura, H. (1996). Acoustic cues to grammatical structure in infant–directed speech: Cross-linguistic evidence. *Child Development, 67,* 3192–3218.
Friederici, A. D., & Wessels, J. M. I. (1993). Phonotactic knowledge and its use in infant speech perception. *Perception & Psychophysics, 54,* 287–295.
Gerken, L. A. (1994). Young children's representation of prosodic phonology: Evidence from English–speakers' weak syllable omissions. *Journal of Memory and Language, 33,* 19–38.
Gerken, L. A., Jusczyk, P. W., & Mandel, D. R. (1994). When prosody fails to cue syntactic structure: Nine-month-olds' sensitivity to phonological versus syntactic phrases. *Cognition, 51,* 237–265.
Gerken, L. A., Landau, B., & Remez, R. E. (1990). Function morphemes in young children's speech perception and production. *Developmental Psychology, 25,* 204–216.
Gleitman, L., Gleitman, H., Landau, B., & Wanner, E. (1988). Where the learning begins: Initial representations for language learning. In F. Newmeyer (Ed.), *The Cambridge linguistic survey* (Vol. 3, pp. 150–193). Cambridge, MA: Harvard University Press.

Gleitman, L., & Wanner, E. (1982). The state of the state of the art. In E. Wanner & L. Gleitman (Ed.), *Language acquisition: The state of the art* (pp. 3–48). Cambridge: Cambridge University Press.
Grieser, D., & Kuhl, P. K. (1989). The categorization of speech by infants: Support for speech–sound prototypes. *Developmental Psychology, 25*, 577–588.
Hillenbrand, J. M., Minifie, F. D., & Edwards, T. J. (1979). Tempo of spectrum change as a cue in speech sound discrimination by infants. *Journal of Speech and Hearing Research, 22*, 147–165.
Hirsh–Pasek, K., Kemler Nelson, D. G., Jusczyk, P. W., Wright Cassidy, K., Druss, B., & Kennedy, L. (1987). Clauses are perceptual units for young infants. *Cognition, 26*, 269–286.
Hockett, C. F. (1958). *A course in modern linguistics.* New York: Macmillan.
Hohne, E. A., & Jusczyk, P. W. (1994). Two-month-old infants' sensitivity to allophonic differences. *Perception & Psychophysics, 56*, 613–623.
Jusczyk, P. W. (1977). Perception of syllable–final stops by two-month-old infants. *Perception and Psychophysics, 21*, 450–454.
Jusczyk, P. W. (1985). On characterizing the development of speech perception. In J. Mehler & R. Fox (Eds.), *Neonate cognition: Beyond the blooming, buzzing confusion* (pp. 199–229). Hillsdale, NJ: Lawrence Erlbaum Associates.
Juscyk, P. W. (1997). *The discovery of spoken language.* Cambridge, MA: MIT Press.
Juscyk, P. W. (1999). How infants begin to extract words from fluent speech. *Trends in Cognitive Science, 3*, 323–328.
Jusczyk, P. W., & Aslin, R. N. (1995). Infants' detection of sound patterns of words in fluent speech. *Cognitive Psychology, 29*, 1–23.
Jusczyk, P. W., Cutler, A., & Redanz, N. (1993). Perference for the predominant stress patterns of English words. *Child Psychology, 64*, 675–687.
Jusczyk, P. W., Friederici, A. D., Wessels, J., Svenkerud, V. Y., & Jusczyk, A. M. (1993). Infants' sensitivity to the sound patterns of native language words. *Journal of Memory and Language, 32*, 402–420.
Jusczyk, P. W., Hirsh-Pasek, K., Kemler Nelson, D. G., Kennedy, L., Woodward, A., & Piwoz, J. (1992). Perception of acoustic correlates of major phrasal units by young infants. *Cognitive Psychology, 24*, 252–293.
Jusczyk, P. W. & Hohne, E. A. (1997). Infants' memory for spoken words. *Science, 277*, 1984–1986.
Jusczyk, P. W., Hohne, E. A., & Bauman, A. (1999). Infants' sensitivity to allophonic cues for word segmentation. *Perception & Psychophysics, 61*, 1465–1476.
Jusczyk, P. W., Houston, D. M., & Newsome, M. (1999). The beginnings of word segmentation in English-learning infants. *Cognitive Psychology, 39*, 159–207.
Jusczyk, P. W., Luce, P. A., & Charles-Luce, J. (1994). Infants' sensitivity to phonotactic patterns in the native language. *Journal of Memory and Language, 33*, 630–645.
Jusczyk, P. W., Pisoni, D. B., & Mullennix, J. (1992). Some consequences of stimulus variability on speech processing by 2-month-old infants. *Cognition, 43*, 253–291.
Katz, J. J. (1966). *The philosophy of language.* New York: Harper.
Kemler Nelson, D. G., Hirsh-Pasek, K., Jusczyk, P. W., & Wright Cassidy, K. (1989). How prosodic cues in motherese might assist language learning. *Journal of Child Language, 16*, 55–68.
Klatt, D. H. (1979). Speech perception: A model of acoustic-phonetic analysis and lexical access. *Journal of Phoenetics, 7*, 279–312.
Klatt, D. H. (1986). The problem of variability in speech recognition an in models of speech perception. In J. S. Perkell & D. H. Klatt (Eds.), *Invariance and variability in speech processes,* (pp. 300–319). Hillsdale, NJ: Lawrence Erlbaum Associates.
Klatt, D. H. (1989). Review of selected models of speech perception. In W. Marslen-Wilson (Ed.), *Lexical Representation and Process* (pp. 169–226). Cambridge, MA: MIT Press.
Kuhl, P. K. (1979). Speech perception in early infancy: Perceptual constancy for spectrally dissimiliar vowel categories. *Journal of the Acoustical Society of America, 66*, 1668–1679.
Kuhl, P. K. (1983). Perception of auditory equivalence classes for speech in early infancy. *Infant Behavior and Development, 6*, 263–285.
Kuhl, P. K. (1991). Human adults and human infants show a "perceptual magnet effect" for the prototypes of speech categories, monkeys do not. *Perception & Psychophysics, 50*, 93107.
Kuhl, P. K., Williams, K. A., Lacerda, F., Stevens, K. N., & Lindblom, B. (1992). Linguistics experiences alter phonetic perception in infants by 6 months of age. *Science, 255*, 606–608.
Lasky, R. E., Syrdal-Lasky, A., & Klein, R. E. (1975). VOT discrimination by four to six and a half month old infants from Spanish environments. *Journal of Experimental Child Psychology, 20*, 215–225.

Lehiste, I. (1960). *An acoustic–phonetic study of internal open juncture.* New York: S. Karger.
Liberman, A. M., & Studdert-Kennedy, M. G. (1978). Phoenetic perception. In R. Held, H. Leibowitz, & H. L. Teuber (Eds.), *Handbook of sensory physiology: Perception* (Vol. 8, pp. 143–178). Berlin: Springer-Verlag.
Leiberman, P. (1963). Some effects of semantic and grammatical context on the production and perception of speech. *Language and Speech, 6*, 172–179.
Lieberman, P. (1965). On the acoustic basis of the perception of intonation by linguists. *Word, 21*, 40–54.
Mandel, D. R., Jusczyk, P. W., & Kemler Nelson, D. G. (1994). Does sentential prosody help infants to organize and remember speech information? *Cognition, 53*, 155–180.
Mandel, D. R., Kemler Nelson, D. G., & Jusczyk, P. W. (1996). Infants remember the order of words in a spoken sentence. *Cognitive Development, 11*, 181–196.
Mattys, S., Jusczyk, P. W., Luce, P. A., & Morgan, J. L. (1999). Word segmentation in infants: How phonotactics and prosody combine. *Cognitive Psychology, 38*, 464–465.
McNeill, D. (1966). Developmental psycholinguistics. In F. Smith & G. A. Miller (Eds.), *The genesis of language* (pp. 15–84). Cambridge, MA: MIT Press.
Mehler, J., Dupoux, E., & Segui, J. (1990). Constraining models of lexical access: The onset of word recognition. G. T. M. Altmann (Ed.), *Cognitive models of speech processing,* (pp. 236–262). Hillsdale, NJ: Lawrence Erlbaum Associates.
Mehler, J., Jusczyk, P. W., Lambertz, G., Halstead, N., Bertoncini, J., & Amiel-Tison, C. (1988). A precursor of language acquisition in young infants. *Cognition, 29*, 144–178.
Miller, J. L., & Eimas, P. D. (1983). Studies on the categorization of speech by infants. *Cognition, 13*, 135–165.
Moffitt, A. R. (1971). Consonant cue perception by twenty-to-twenty-four week old infants. *Child Development, 42*, 717–731.
Moon, C., Cooper, R. P., & Fifer, W. P. (1993). Two-day old infants prefer their native language. *Infant Behavior and Development, 16*, 495–500.
Morgan, J. L. (1986). *From simple input to complex grammar.* Cambridge, MA: MIT Press.
Morgan, J. L. (1994). Converging measures of speech segmentation in prelingual infants. *Infant Behavior & Development, 17*, 387–400.
Morgan, J. L. (1996). A rhythmic bias in preverbal speech segmentation. *Journal of Memory and Language, 35*, 666–688.
Morgan, J. L., Meier, R. P., & Newport, E. L. (1987). Structural packaging in the input to language learning: Contributions of prosodic and morphological marking of phrases to the acquisition of language? *Cognitive Psychology, 19*, 498–550.
Morgan, J. L., & Saffran, J. R. (1995). Emerging integration of sequential and suprasegmental information in preverbal speech segmentation. *Child Development, 66*, 911–936.
Morse, P. A. (1972). The discrimination of speech and nonspeech stimuli in early infancy. *Journal of Experimental Child Psychology, 13*, 477–492.
Myers, J., Jusczyk, P. W., Kemler Nelson, D. G., Charles-Luce, J., Woodward, A., & Hirsh-Pasek, K. (1996). Infants' sensitivity to word boundaries in fluent speech. *Journal of Child Language, 23*, 1–30.
Nazzi, T., Bertoncini, J., & Mehler, J. (1998). Language discrimination by newborns: Towards an understanding of the role of rhythm. *Journal of Experimental Psychology: Human Perception & Performance.*
Nazzi, T., Jusczyk, P. W., & Johnson, E. K. (2000). Language discrimination by English–learning 5-month-olds: Effects of rhythm and familiarity. *Journal of Memory and Language, 43*, 1–19.
Nazzi, T., Kemler Nelson, D. G., Jusczyk, P. W., & Jusczyk, A. M. (2000). Six-month-olds' detection of clauses embedded in continuous speech: Effects of prosodic well-formedness. *Infancy, 1*, 123–147.
Nespor, M., & Vogel, I. (1986). *Prosodic phonology.* Dordrecht: Foris.
Pegg, J. E., & Werker, J. F. (1997). Adult and infant perception of two English phones. *Journal of the Acoustical Society of America, 102*, 3742–3753.
Peters, A. (1983). *The units of language acquisition.* Cambridge: Cambridge University Press.
Polka, L., & Bohn, O. S. (1996). Cross-language comparison of vowel perception in English-learning and German-learning infants. *Journal of the Acoustic Society of America, 100*, 577–592.
Polka, L., & Werker, J. F. (1994). Developmental changes in perception of non-native vowel contrasts. *Journal of Experimental Psychology: Human Perception and Performance, 20*, 421–435.
Roeper, T., & Williams, E. (Eds.). (1987). *Parameter setting.* Dordrecht: D. Reidel.
Saffran, J. R., Aslin, R. N., & Newport, E. L. (1996). Statistical learning by 8-month-old infants. *Science, 274*, 1926–1928.

Saffran, J. R., Newport, E. L., & Aslin, R. N. (1996). Word segmentation: The role of distributional cues. *Journal of Memory and Language, 35*, 606–621.
Santelmann, L., & Jusczyk, P. W. (1998). Sensitivity to discontinuous dependencies in language learners: Evidence for limitations in processing space. *Cognition, 69*, 105–134.
Schafer, G., & Plunkett, K. (1998). Rapid word learning by 15-month-old infants under tightly controlled conditions. *Child Development, 69*, 309–320.
Selkirk, E. O. (1984). *Phonology and syntax: The relation between sound and structure.* Cambridge, MA: MIT Press.
Shady, M. E. (1996). *Infants-sensitivity to function morphemes.* Unpublished doctoral dissertation, State University of New York at Buffalo.
Shafer, V., Gerken, L. A., Shucard, J., & Shucard, D. (1992, November). *"The" and the brain: An electrophysiological study of infants sensitivity to English function morphemes.* Paper presented at the Boston University Conference on Language Development, Boston.
Streeter, L. A. (1976). Language perception of 2-month-old infants shows effects of both innate mechanisms and experience. *Nature, 259*, 39–41.
Suomi, K. (1993). An outline of a developmental model of adult phonological organization and behavior. *Journal of Phonetics, 21*, 29–60.
Singley, D., Pinto, J. P., & Fernald, A. (1998). Assessing the speed and accuracy of word recognition in infants. In C. Rovee-Collier, L. P. Lipsitt, & H. Hayne (Eds.), *Advances in infancy research* (Vol. 12, pp. 257–277). Stamford, CT: Ablex.
Swingley, D., Pinto, J. P., & Fernald, A. (1999). Continuous processing in word recognition at 24-months. *Cognition, 71*, 73–108.
Swoboda, P., Morse, P. A., & Leavitt, L. A. (1976). Continuous vowel discrimination in normal and at-risk infants. *Child Development, 47*, 459–465.
Tincoff, R., Santelmann, L., & Jusczyk, P. (2000). Auxiliary verb learning and 18-month-olds' acquisition of morphological relationships. In S. C. Howell, S. A. Fish, & T. Keith-Lucas (Eds.), *Proceedings of the 24th Annual Boston University Conference on Language Development* (pp. 726–737). Somerville, MA: Cascadilla Press.
Trehub, S. E. (1973). Infants' sensitivity to vowel and tonal contrasts. *Developmental Psychology, 9*, 91–96.
Trehub, S. E. (1976). The discrimination of foreign speech contrasts by infants and adults. *Child Development, 47*, 466–472.
Werker, J. F., & Tees, R. C. (1984). Cross-language speech perception: Evidence for perceptual reorganization during the first year of life. *Infant Behavior and Development, 7*, 49–63.

II

Models of Language and Language Processing

4

Dissociation and Modularity: Reflections on Language and Mind

Neil Smith
University College, London

It would be presumptuous to imagine that one could do more than scratch the surface of a subject as vast as that indicated by the subtitle of this chapter. Language, mind, and the relationship of one to the other have preoccupied many of the best thinkers for millennia, and I can hope neither to summarize nor to replace their conclusions in a few pages. There are, however, clear generalizations to be made, and I can at least gesture in what I think is the right direction. The essence is modularity; the evidence is dissociation.

MODULARITY

I adopt a view of cognitive architecture on which the mind is pervasively modular in the sense of Chomsky (1975, 1984) and Fodor (1983). There are significant differences between their positions, some of which I spell out here, but there is sufficient overlap to make a unified summary feasible. I begin with Fodor's now classical position, as put forward in *The Modularity of Mind.* Fodor differentiates the central system, which is responsible for higher cognitive activities, such as general problem solving and the fixation of belief, from the input systems, which provide grist for the central mill. He then argues that these input systems, which correspond in the first instance to the sensorium, but crucially also include the language faculty, share a number of further properties, and any component with these properties is then, by definition, a module. For instance, modules are *domain specific*, in that their operations are sensitive only to a subset of impinging stimuli—light waves for vision, sound waves for audition, and likewise for the other senses. They are relatively *fast*, in that it takes minimal time to see a person as a person, but much longer to decide what to buy one's mother as a birthday present. Modules operate *mandatorily*—you have no choice but to see a face as a face, or to understand a sentence of your native language; but you may choose to ignore what you have seen and heard. They are *ontogenetically deterministic*, in that their development typically unfolds in the same way across the species without the benefit of overt instruction. The visual systems of children from all over the world appear to grow in much the same way, irrespective of culture, and their linguistic systems characteristically go through comparable stages at comparable ages, irrespective of the language being acquired. Modules are subject to *idiosyncratic pathological breakdown*, in that brain damage can cause deafness or blindness or aphasia. This suggests further that modules are *subserved by specific neural architecture* which is probably genetically determined. Finally, the operations of modules seem to be largely impervious to the influence of the central system; they are "informationally encapsulated." The classic example is provided by the Müller-Lyer optical illusion, in which two lines, flanked by inward or outward pointing arrowheads are displayed as in Fig. 4.1. The visual system perceives the lower line as longer than the upper line. Even if you take a ruler and convince yourself that the two lines are indeed of identical length, your eyes still interpret them as being different. That is, the working of the visual system is impervious to the explicit knowledge provided by the central system.

All of these properties are, of course, the subject of debate and controversy, but it is generally agreed that the most important of them are domain specificity and informational encapsulation (Carston, 1996; Coltheart, 1999). As this is a position with which I disagree, it is also worth noting Fodor's claim that the central system is largely inaccessible to scientific investigation; hence he attributes to it virtually no internal structure. More recently, however (Fodor, 1992), he admitted some putative structure into the central system as well. A simplified schematic representation of Fodor's view is given in Fig. 4.2a. The transducers convert a physical stimulus, such as light waves, into a neural signal; the input systems then interpret transduced information for the central system to work on.

For Chomsky, the language faculty cannot be a Fodorian module for two reasons. First, we use language to speak as well as to understand, and if Fodor is correct in identifying modules with "input systems," then language, which is also an output system, cannot be a module. Second, and more importantly, the

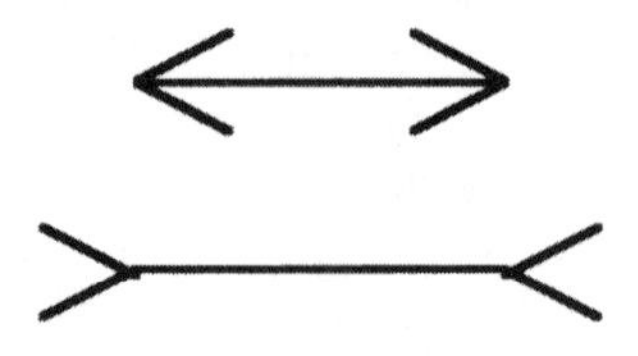

FIG. 4.1. The Müller–Lyer Illusion.

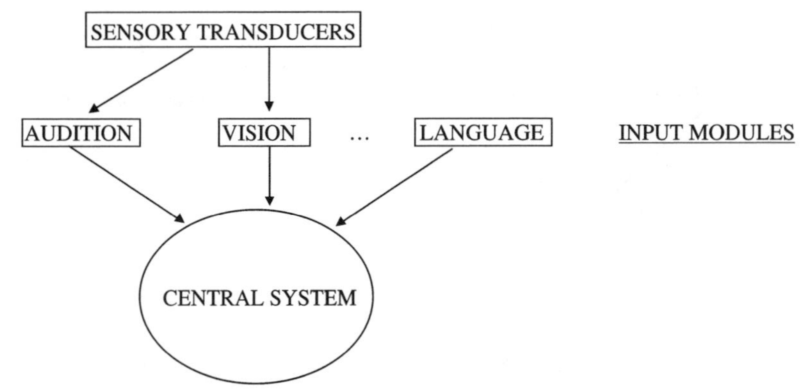

FIG. 4.2(a). Schematic representation of Fodor's Model.

language faculty must in some respects be "central" to accommodate the basic fact that it is a system of knowledge. Moreover, this knowledge constitutes a common store that is neutral as between speaker and hearer. That is, we draw on largely the same knowledge whether we are producing an utterance of our own or interpreting that of someone addressing us. If understanding (parsing) and production deployed different systems, we would expect it to be the case that someone could speak one language and understand only a different one. Moreover, Chomsky does not share Fodor's pessimism that the central system is essentially inscrutable, suggesting that a range of functions from moral judgment to face recognition falls within its purview, and language is just one such domain, albeit the one about which we know most. (For discussion, see Levy and Kavé, 1999, and Smith, 1999.) A simplified schematic representation of Chomsky's view is given in Fig. 4.2b. I return later to different kinds of modules.

Note that Chomsky has not committed himself to anything like this simplistic diagram, which is intended only to highlight some of the differences between him and Fodor. In Smith and Tsimpli (1995, p. 170) we propose and defend a more complex model of the mind in which the language faculty is partly inside and partly outside the central system. The "Central modules" here correspond to our "Quasi-modules."

DISSOCIATION

Although dissociation does not entail modularity, it is the case that modularity entails (possible) dissociation. Accordingly, a major kind of evidence for modularity is functional autonomy, as seen most obviously in dissociative pathology. If a system's operation is independent of other systems, that system is prima facie a candidate for having modular status. Such autonomy is characteristic of the senses: One can be deaf without being blind, blind without being deaf. Although there are conditions in which both afflictions occur simultaneously,

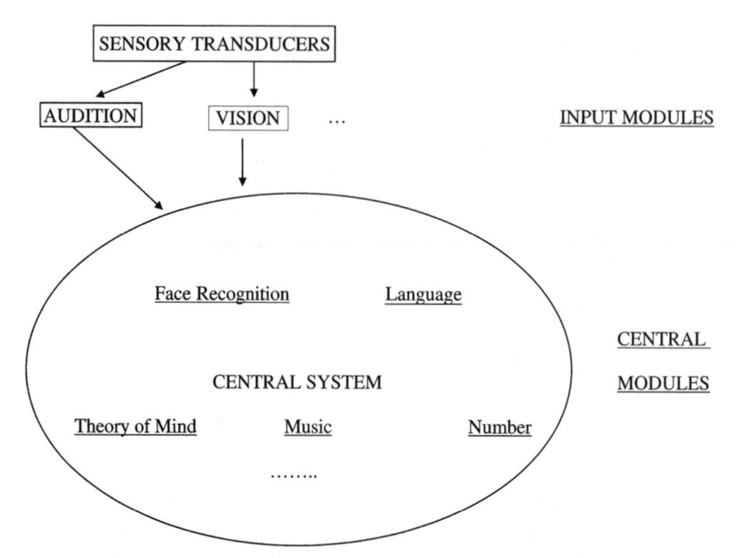

FIG. 4.2(b). Schematic representation of Chomsky's Model.

they can in principle dissociate, with the implication that the functions are independent of each other, subserved by different mechanisms, characterized by different generalizations, and liable to breakdown under different conditions. Not all dissociations are "double" or absolute in this way. Consider the incidence of hemophilia in the population. There are four logical possibilities—males with or without hemophilia, and females with or without hemophilia. In fact, the category of "females with hemophilia" is essentially nonexistent. Although females can carry the disease, they cannot suffer from it. Sex and hemophilia are only singly dissociable, not doubly dissociable, indicating that one property is dependent on the other.

This kind of dependency has been of central importance in discussions of the relation between language and other properties of mind, in particular of intelligence. It is (relatively) uncontroversial that three of the four logical possibilities are found: normal people exhibit the coexistence of language and intelligence; anencephalic subjects (those born with an absent or poorly developed cerebrum) develop neither language nor intelligence; and some aphasic conditions can result in the loss of language with intelligence unimpaired. An interesting example is given by Sloboda (1985, p. 260), who reported that after a stroke, the Russian composer Shebalin had severe difficulties with understanding and reproducing speech, but continued to compose and to teach his music students to the same high level as before. Such cases involving aphasia are hard to evaluate, as the inability to make manifest one's intelligence via one's linguistic ability may give a grossly misleading impression of one's competences. An extreme example is provided by "locked-in syndrome" of the kind poignantly described by

Bauby in his autobiography (1997). Bauby suffered a devastating stroke, resulting in mutism and quadriplegia, yet his book shows that his knowledge of French and his intelligence were obviously intact. Furthermore, the spontaneous intelligent behavior of the permanently language-less makes it plausible that the third category exists. Whether the fourth possibility occurs, where people manifest linguistic ability in the absence of (some specifiable level of) intelligence, has been less obvious.

If the category does not exist, and if there is therefore a crucial link between language and intelligence, we have two possibilities: Either the acquisition of language is dependent on the antecedent presence of particular conceptual abilities, or particular conceptual contrasts are available only in the presence of particular linguistic ability. The second of these views was put forward by Quine, who claimed that cognitive development is parasitic on language. His claim (1960, section 19) is that the syntax of quantification is prerequisite to understanding the difference between individuals and substances. For example, until children have mastered the syntactic differences between count and mass nouns, their grasp of the ontological distinction between substances like *water* and individuals such as *people* or *sticks* cannot be comparable with the adult's conception. Meticulous experimentation (Soja, Carey, & Spelke, 1991) has refuted this claim, demonstrating that from the very earliest stages of language acquisition, children exploit conceptual categories of substance and individual essentially equivalent to those that adults use. Because Quine's claim would seem to suggest that speakers of languages like Chinese, which make minimal or no use of the count/mass distinction, would be unable to conceptualize the contrast (which they can), this refutation came as no surprise to linguists and psychologists. More interestingly, such findings make the contrary claim, that intelligence is necessary for first language acquisition, even more plausible. This position has indeed been widely defended.

There is a long tradition, best exemplified by the work of the Genevan psychologist Piaget and his associates, that claims that the acquisition of language is dependent on the prior attainment of a particular level of cognitive ability; there are "cognitive prerequisites for the development of grammar," in Slobin's (1973) phrase. A typical observation from within this paradigm is that "Genevan psycholinguists tend to find the reason for [the late acquisition of the passive] in difficulties of a cognitive nature" (Inhelder, 1980, p. 135). To take a specific example, Piagetians hold that there is a correlation between the acquisition of comparatives and passives and the attainment of the "concrete operational" stage of cognitive development. This stage is marked by the achievement of the ability to pass "seriation" and "conservation" tasks. By seriation is meant the ability correctly to put in ascending or descending order the elements in an array of the kind seen in Fig. 4.3; by conservation is meant the ability to recognize the equivalence of two perceptually distinct stimuli—for instance, that a liquid poured from a tall thin glass into a short wide glass, as in

Fig. 4.4, retains a constant volume. It appears that the mastery of comparatives presupposes seriation, and the mastery of passives presupposes conservation.

If such Piagetian views were correct, they would constitute evidence against the autonomy, and hence the modularity, of the language faculty. In fact, there is evidence from children with Williams syndrome that such views are simply wrong. Williams syndrome, or infantile hypercalcemia, is a genetically determined condition that results in a variety of physical and psychological characteristics. Affected children suffer from hypertension and heart defects, and they have "an elfin-like face, with heavy orbital ridge, temporal dimples, full cheeks, retroussé nose, flat nasal bridge, flared nostrils, stellate iris pattern, wide mouth, and irregular dentition" (Karmiloff-Smith, Klima, Grant, & Baron-Cohen, 1995, p. 198). Psychologically, they are characterized by severe deficits in spatial cognition, number, and problem solving, but by proficiency in face recognition,

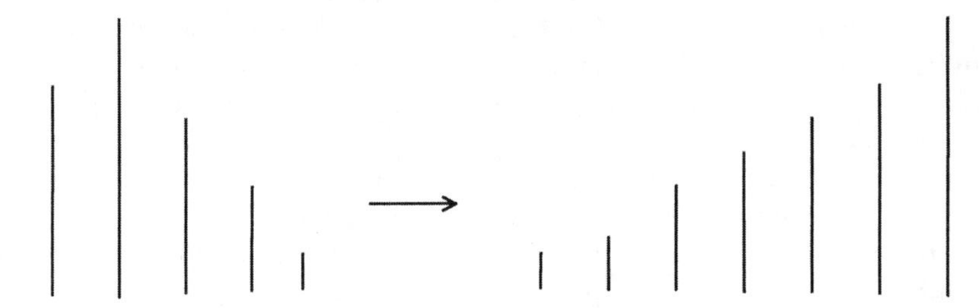

FIG. 4.3. Seriation.

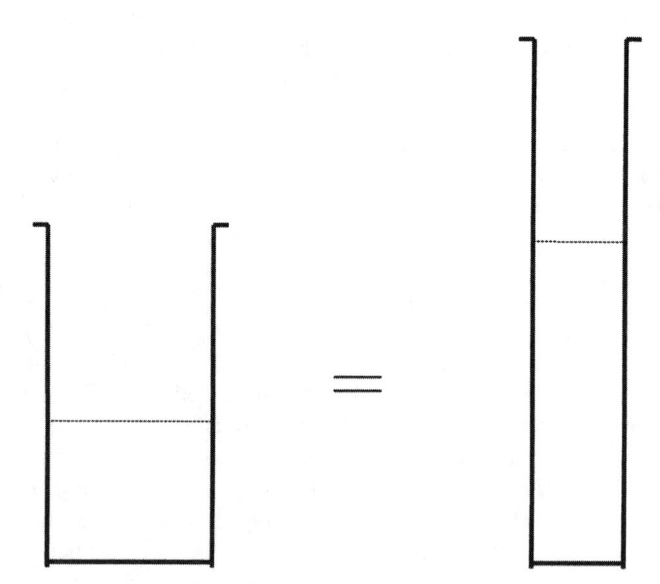

FIG. 4.4. Conservation of volume.

theory of mind, rote memory, and language. Of relevance here is that Bellugi and her colleagues (Bellugi, Marks, Bihrle, & Sabo, 1993) showed persuasively that Williams syndrome children have mastery of the syntactic constructions (passives and comparatives) whose acquisition is supposedly dependent on the achievement of the ability successfully to carry out seriation and conservation tasks, but that they consistently fail in these cognitive tasks. It is thus clear that in this population, language and intelligence dissociate.

Further evidence for such dissociation of language and intelligence, and for the putative modularity of the language faculty, comes from the "savant" syndrome, in particular from a man (Christopher) whom Ianthi Tsimpli and I have been studying for the past decade (Smith & Tsimpli, 1995, 1997; Tsimpli & Smith, 1991, 1998).

Christopher

Savants are people who have an island of talent in an ocean of disability. Typical examples are provided by calendrical calculators, who can tell you instantly the day of the week on which any named date falls; by athetoid musicians, who can play music while being unable to manipulate a spoon; and by retarded artists, who can draw magnificent animals or buildings while being unable to look after themselves. The traditional wisdom is that such people typically have minimal or no language ability (Treffert, 1989), so it was of great interest when we came across a savant whose talent is precisely in manipulating languages.

Born in January 1962, Christopher lives in sheltered accommodation because he is unable to look after himself. He is right-handed, but his hand–eye coordination is so impaired that everyday tasks like dressing or hanging a cup on a hook are serious chores for him; his psychological profile, outlined in Fig. 4.5,

Raven's Matrices:		75
WISC-R, UK:	Verbal:	89
	Performance:	42
Goodenough 'Draw a Man':		40

Peabody Picture Vocabulary Test
English - 121, German - 114, French - 110, Spanish - 89

Columbia Greystone Mental Maturity Scale: Score 68; Mental Age 9.2; IQ 56

Embedded Figures Test (Witkin): Responses random (perhaps 1/12 correct)

FIG. 4.5. Christopher's psychological background. Christopher's performance varied somewhat on different occasions of testing. For details, see Smith and Tsimpli (1995) and O'Connor and Hermelin (1991). In all cases except the last, the norm is 100.

shows a pattern of moderate to severe disability in performance tasks, but results close to normal in verbal tasks.

In addition, he is quite unable to master tick tack toe (noughts and crosses), and he fails Piagetian conservation-of-number tasks. For example, presented with two rows of beads, arranged either so that the beads on each string matched each other or so that those on one string were spread out to form a longer line as in Fig. 4.6, Christopher was consistent in claiming that whichever string the beads were spread out on contained more items than the other. Children usually conserve number correctly between the ages of 4 and 5 years.

Christopher also shows some, but not all of the signs of autism. On the "Sally-Anne" task, designed to test the subject's ability to impute false belief to others, Christopher usually fails, but on the superficially comparable Smarties test he is usually successful. In one version of the Sally-Anne test, the subject and another observer watch while the experimenter hides a toy. The observer is then sent out of the room and, in full view of the subject, the toy is moved from its first position and hidden in a new position. After ensuring that the subject was aware of where the toy was first hidden and of when the observer was last present, he or she is then asked where the observer will look for the toy on returning to the room. From about the age of 4, normal people indicate the first hiding place. Children under the age of 4, and autistic subjects, usually indicate the second hiding place, *where the toy actually is*. That is, they are unable to entertain the idea that someone else could have a representation of the world which deviates from reality; they cannot understand "false belief". In the Smarties test, subjects are shown a Smarties container (a well-known chocolate candy) and asked what they think is in it. When they reply "Smarties," they are shown that it really contains a pencil, and are then asked what their friends across the room will think is in it when they are asked. Again, autistic and very young children typically reply "a pencil"; older children, of course, reply correctly "Smarties." The standard explanation for this phenomenon is in terms of the absence or malfunctioning of a "theory-of-mind module" (more accurately a theory of other minds), a component of the mind that enables you to take someone else's point of view irrespective of whether that point of view conforms to reality. (For extensive discussion, including an explanation for Christopher's differential success, see Smith and Tsimpli, 1995, and especially Tsimpli and Smith, 1998.)

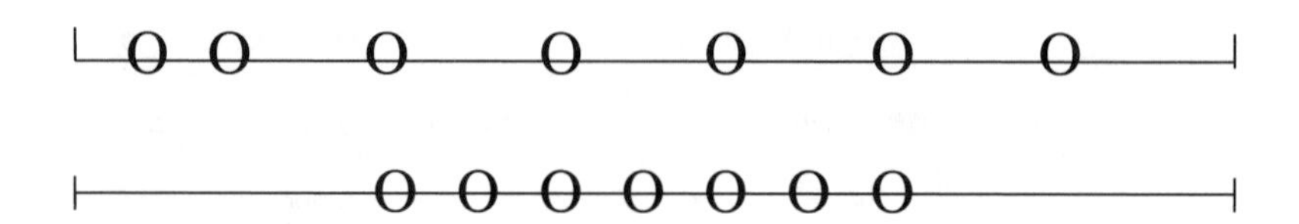

FIG. 4.6. Conservation of number.

Despite his poor or mixed performance on tests of this kind, Christopher has considerable encyclopedic and linguistic knowledge. He defined correctly such terms as *baht* (the unit of currency used in Thailand) and *han'gul* (the name of the Korean script); he identified the nationality and affiliation of various footballers (telling us, for instance, that Koeman used to play for Barcelona); and he recognizes public figures such as Margaret Thatcher, Saddam Hussein, and Melina Mercouri. On the linguistic side, he shows normal command of English syntax, as tested in production, comprehension, and wellformedness judgments of examples including relatives, clefts, questions, negatives, *that*-trace effects, control relations, and parasitic gaps. That is, he shows normal command of even the most complicated syntax, giving appropriate judgments on the acceptability of such examples as those in (1):

1a. Who do you think that arrived?

1b. Which book did you throw away without reading?

He correctly rejects as ungrammatical "*that*-trace effect" sentences like that in (1a), and he correctly accepts "parasitic gap" sentences like that in (1b). Moreover, despite the psychological profile given above, he can also integrate this linguistic knowledge into simple patterns of inferencing, correctly using both logical and contextual information in answering questions based on dialogues such as that in (2):

2. John said, "Would you like some coffee?"
Mary replied, "Coffee would keep me awake."
Do you think Mary accepted the coffee?
(Christopher's response: "No")

That this is not simply some kind of learned response is clear from his ability to vary his judgment for more complex examples, as illustrated in (3):

3. Mary said, "I have to work all night tonight."
John said, "Would you like some coffee?"
Mary replied, "Coffee would keep me awake."
Do you think Mary accepted the coffee?
(Christopher's response: "Yes")

What is most striking about Christopher is his considerable polyglot ability. He has some knowledge, ranging from a smattering to that of an average undergraduate, of Danish, Dutch, Finnish, French, German, Greek, Hindi, Italian, Norwegian, Polish, Portuguese, Russian, Spanish, Swedish, Turkish, and Welsh.

He may have some ability in several others on which we have not tested him. He has recently been exposed to speakers of Hungarian, Serbo-Croatian, and a variety of other languages, and is reportedly assimilating them rapidly, and we are currently giving him intensive instruction in British Sign Language. (Morgan et al., 2002) His knowledge of these various languages has been gleaned in a variety of ways. For some, such as the Scandinavian languages, it has been derived mainly from pedagogical grammar books; for others, such as Greek and Polish, it has arisen from reading and interacting with native speakers; for yet others, such as French and Spanish, it has come from all of these in combination with some formal school instruction. In every case we have consulted native speakers of the various languages to corroborate our judgment of his varying abilities. Detailed discussion and examples of his translational prowess in the languages listed above can be found in Smith & Tsimpli (1995:12–17).

It is worth noting that the languages he controls belong to groups that are unrelated historically or structurally, and that they are written in a variety of different scripts. It is also remarkable that Christopher is not a particularly good judge of his own abilities. After first asserting and then denying that he knew Russian, he was able to give a rough translation of the opening of a Russian short story written in Cyrillic script. It may be that his claims to "know X" are best interpreted as the ability—common to most linguists—to recognize that a passage comes from a particular language: He has correctly identified dozens of languages in this way, including, but not limited to, Arabic, Bengali, Chinese, Finnish, Georgian, Hungarian, Icelandic, Japanese, Korean, Letzeburgesch, and Mongolian.

His talent is impressive, but what is most remarkable about Christopher's second-language acquisition is the speed with which he masters the lexicon and the morphology. As part of our investigations we taught him two new languages under conditions of controlled input. That is, we controlled the nature and order of the input data, so that we had a complete record of every detail of the language to which he was exposed. One of these languages was Berber (Smith, Tsimpli, & Ouhalla, 1993), an Afro-Asiatic language of North Africa with a rich morphology, that is, with a wide variety of inflectional endings. On the basis of sets of sentences presented both orally (by a native speaker) and in written form, Christopher mastered the Berber system of subject agreement rapidly and with enthusiasm. It is noteworthy that both in Berber and in other languages, Christopher's mastery of morphology is characterized by the kind of overgeneralization that indicates that he is using inferred rules rather than just a prodigious memory. For instance, in Portuguese, abstract nouns typically end in *-ação*, where in English they end in *-ation*. Accordingly, in providing us with examples in Portuguese, he produced the "regular" but nonexistent form *examinação* ("examination") instead of the correct word *examen*. Similarly, he used the regularized sequence *Ime vlemmenos* ("I am seen") in Modern Greek, even though *vlemmenos* does not exist.

In contrast with his prodigious vocabulary and impressive morphological knowledge, and in contrast with his essentially flawless knowledge of the complexities of English syntax, Christopher's syntax in the various languages he has tackled seems soon to reach a plateau, beyond which he never proceeds. This suggests that the syntax of these languages is being somehow "filtered" through his native English. For instance, his Modern Greek is fluent, but after several years of exposure to a wide variety of data, and even to explicit teaching, he still makes systematic errors both in his performance and in his judgments of well-formedness on sentences involving the null subject parameter. That is, Greek—like Spanish and Italian, but unlike French and English—allows subject pronouns to be freely omitted if the referent is contextually recoverable. This phenomenon generally correlates with a wide variety of other syntactic characteristics, such as the *that*-trace effects mentioned earlier, and although Christopher can cope with the missing subject, he has persistent difficulty with the related constructions. Thus, although the Greek equivalent of (1a) is acceptable, Christopher judges it to be ungrammatical—as in English—despite his fluency in the language.

The mixture of talent and disability documented here is already evidence of the kind of dissociation of language and intelligence that was discussed earlier. Further evidence of a more striking kind is provided by two of the tests we carried out with him. The first of these is Christopher's reaction to a kind of fixed-ratio deletion cloze test; the second is his learning of an "impossible" invented language called Epun. Let us look at each in turn. For the first, we constructed anomalous prose passages by taking *n* consecutive words from a text, deleting the next *n* words, and so on repeatedly, producing second-order, fifth-order, seventh-order and 10-order approximations to English (Smith and Tsimpli, 1995, p. 73). We then presented these passages to Christopher to see what his reaction would be. Given the rather automaton-like manner in which he translates, we predicted that he would balk only at the most extreme divergences from coherent text. In fact, it was only with second-order approximations that he gave any indication that he found the examples anything but normal. Given the seventh-order sequence in (4), his reaction was immediately to try to translate it into French, as in (5), adding the comment in (6). A translation back into English of his translation is given in (5')—the item italicized was left in English.

4. The Pharaohs had enough stone to build enough papyrus, too, so there was nothing as large as floating islands. The papyrus a modest fifth of the Sphinx's length. Of the underworld of mummies and stood it made us realize what giant structures.

5. Les Pharaohs ont beaucoup de pierres pour, pour construire des papyrus, aussi, so il n'y était pas si grand comme le île flottante. Le papyrus, un modeste quinze—cinq de le longueur du Sphinx. Et je ne sais pas.

5'. The pharaohs have many stones to, to build some papyrus, also *so* it wasn't as big as the floating island. The papyrus, a modest fifteen—five of the length of the Sphinx. And I don't know.
[Note that "le île" should have been "l'île"; "cinq" should have been "cinquième"; "de le" should have been "du," as in the (correct) phrase "du Sphinx" immediately following.]

6. NVS What did you think of that passage?

C Très bon, très bon. ["Very good, very good"].

I take it that this reaction is abnormal and indicates at the very least an insensitivity to violations of coherence or rationality. His translation is not without mistakes (Smith & Tsimpli, 1995, p. 169), but it is clear from his linguistic profile, especially his expertise in providing grammaticality judgments, that his language faculty is operating more efficiently than his faculty of common sense, which here seems to be switched off.

Corroboration of the dissociation between his linguistic and general intellectual abilities came from the second area already mentioned-the acquisition of Epun. As well as teaching Berber to Christopher, we decided to teach him an invented language in which we could manipulate variables of interest. We were stimulated by Chomsky's (1991, p. 40) observation that "knowing something about UG [Universal Grammar—the innate endowment that the child brings to first language acquisition—NS], we can readily design "languages" that will be unattainable by the language faculty." Accordingly, after several months of teaching Christopher (and a group of controls) aspects of a perfectly possible if nonexistent language, we gradually introduced linguistically "impossible" but logically simple constructions. The hypothesis we wished to test was that although Christopher's remarkable language faculty should enable him to cope with anything natural languages could confront him with, his limited intelligence would prevent him coming up with the logically simple solutions to the problems we presented him. In contrast, normal undergraduate controls should be able to use their intelligence to learn what, by hypothesis, was beyond their language faculty. To investigate this possibility we used the pervasive and fundamental property of "structure dependence." Consider the example in (7):

7. The man who is tall is in the room

and the task of working out how to form questions from statements. Given a pair of sentences of the kind in (8):

8a. The man is tall.

B. Is the man tall?

a range of logically possible solutions is available. You could try moving the third word to the front; this works with (8a), but with "John is tall" it would give the impossible "tall John is?". You could try moving the first auxiliary verb to the front (auxiliaries are things like *is, can,* and *might*; in the present example *is* is the auxiliary), but with (7) this would give the ungrammatical result "Is the man who tall is in the room?" Mentioning the auxiliary is all right, but what is needed is a rule which refers not to mathematical notions like first and third, but exclusively to *structural* notions like "subject" and "auxiliary". To form a question in English you move the auxiliary immediately following the subject to the front of the sentence. The subject of (8a) is "*The man*"; the subject of (7) is "*The man who is tall*," not just "*The man.*" The example is trivial, but the moral is vital: All rules in all languages are "structure dependent" in this way.

We constructed a series of both structure-dependent and structure-independent examples and submitted them to Christopher and the controls (Smith et al., 1993; Smith & Tsimpli, 1995). A simple example of a structure-independent operation is given by the process of emphasis formation in (9), in which the element *-nog* is suffixed to the *third word* of the corresponding nonemphatic sentence: that is, the position of the suffix is arithmetically rather than structurally determined.

9a. Chi h-u-pat Lodo-p to miza kakol

Who Past-3MS-Pos Lodo-Obl and I see[1]

Who saw Lodo and me?

b. Chi h-u-pat Lodo-p-*nog* to miza kakol

Who Past-3MS-Pos Lodo-Obl-Emph and I see

Who did see Lodo and me?

Examples of structure-dependent, but nonetheless impossible, processes are provided by the syntax of tense and negation. Epun has the basic word order Subject Verb Object (SVO), but this changes depending first on whether the sentence is positive or negative, and second on the tense, so that we have the possibilities in (10):

10. SV(O)Positive (present and future)

VS(O)Negative (present and future)

(O)SVPositive (past)

(O)VSNegative (past)

The intuitive generalizations implicit here are that in negative sentences the verb moves to presubject position, and in transitive past-tense sentences the ob-

[1]The term "h-u-pat" is a positive auxiliary inflected for past and third person masculine singular; "-p" is the marker of oblique case. The word order is a function of tense and transitivity. Details can be found in the references cited.

ject is moved to initial position. The processes are "impossible" because in no language can negation be marked solely by a change in word order—it is always necessary that there be an overt negative morpheme such as "*not*" in English—and because there is no motivation for the movement of the object to initial position. In current linguistic theory (Chomsky, 1995), all movement has to be motivated by the presence of some morphological driving force, and we deliberately constructed the language so that this was absent. That is, the relations among the array of word orders in (10) are logically extremely simple, but they are nonetheless linguistically impossible. The idea was that controls would be able to induce these simple generalizations by a form of elementary problem solving, that is, by processes external to the language faculty, whereas Christopher would fail to induce them because his "central" problem-solving abilities were inadequate, and his linguistic abilities were (by hypothesis) irrelevant in a domain that lay outside the scope of linguistic theory.

The results provided partial confirmation of these predictions. Structure–independent operations of the kind shown in (9) proved impossible for Christopher, but they proved impossible for everyone else as well. Although the controls could solve such quasi-arithmetic problems in a nonlinguistic domain, in a linguistic context they appeared to be unable to suppress the architectural constraints of the language faculty and remained baffled by the process of emphasis formation. As we show in the discussion of connectionism that follows; this result has wider implications than might at first appear. Structure dependent, but linguistically impossible, operations were within the abilities of the control group but proved beyond Christopher in the initial stages, although he made some progress after prolonged exposure. Specifically, he showed partial mastery of the syntax of negation, but the peculiarities of the past tense proved totally insuperable, whereas the controls performed essentially flawlessly in both domains. I take it that these results support modularist claims about the dissociability of the cognitive and the linguistic systems.

MODIFIED MODULARITY

The language faculty is clearly domain specific and it is, at least in part, independent of other aspects of mind. But it is not just an input system in Fodor's sense, and it is furthermore necessary to attribute greater structure to the "central" system than Fodor allows for, so we need a more subtle ontology than one that just differentiates modules and the central system. Accordingly, Ianthi Tsimpli and I have suggested that it is desirable to draw a distinction between modules and what we call "quasi-modules" (Smith & Tsimpli, 1995; Tsimpli & Smith, 1998). Like Fodorian modules, quasi-modules are domain-specific, fast, and mandatory, but they are not informationally encapsulated and their vocabulary, which may differ from case to case, is conceptual not perceptual. We have argued extensively elsewhere (Tsimpli & Smith, 1998) for the claim that theory of mind is a quasi-module in this sense; other domains that partake of at least some of the same properties include face recognition, moral judgment, music, common sense, the number sense, the senses of social structure and of personality structure, and perhaps folk physics and folk biology. In addition, it is still necessary to maintain the notion of the "submodular" structure characteristic of the language faculty (and other domains) in which, for instance, we have Chomskyan modules[2] of Theta theory, Binding theory, Case theory, and so on. A full explanation of these theories is not essential to an understanding of the current discussion of modules and quasi-modules, but to give a flavor of the enterprise, consider Case theory. This module of the grammar accounts for the contrast between *he* and *him*, in "he saw him", and the dependence of such forms on differences of finiteness, as illustrated in (11):

11a. I believe him to be a werewolf.

b. I believe he is a werewolf.

In each of these examples *he/him* is the subject of the clause *be a werewolf*, but it has to appear in the oblique (accusative) form *him* when the verb (*be*) is nonfinite (that is, not marked for tense), and in the nominative form *he* when the verb (*is*) is finite.

In every case where a module or quasi-module is postulated, there arises the possibility of double dissociation. Concentrating on the case of Christopher, we can see a number of dissociations. Christopher illustrates the situation in which linguistic ability is generally spared and general intelligence is impaired, while aphasia provides evidence for the converse—impaired linguistic ability and spared general intelligence. A developmental parallel to such aphasia, where aspects of the language faculty are impaired but general intelligence is within the normal range, is provided by specific language impairment (SLI; for an overview, see Joanisse and Seidenberg, 1998). In this condition children fail to develop age-appropriate knowledge of language despite being cognitively normal in all or most other respects. In fact, this simple characterization is itself controversial: Many researchers have claimed that the deficit is not language specific but is rather a reflex of a general deficit in the processing of rapid sequential information (Tallal, 1990). Although some SLI subjects may show such deficits in addition to language problems, it is becoming clear that there is a population in whom the only difficulty is linguistic (Bishop, 1997; van der Lely, 1997; van der Lely & Stollwerck, 1997), where moreover the epidemiology shows that the deficit is genetically determined (Gopnik, 1997). Such cases provide an interesting contrast to that of Christopher, both in the double dissociation of the def-

[2]It is worth making explicit that Chomsky's use of the term *modular* varies according to context between an interpretation in which the language faculty is a module, and one in which, e.g., Case theory is a module.

icits involved, and also in the details of the putative linguistic problem. In addition to those like Joanisse and Seidenberg (1998), who argue that SLI is characterized by a general processing deficit rather than a purely linguistic one, there have been a number of attempts to pinpoint the precise nature of what the linguistic deficit in SLI is. The "Agreement Deficit of Clahsen, Bartke, and Gollner" (1997) predicts inter alia that there should be problems with person and number agreement on verbs, but not on nouns; Gopnik's (1994) "Implicit Rule Formation Deficit" claims that SLI children cannot construct grammatical rules; van der Lely's (1996) "Representational Deficit with Dependent Relationships" predicts specific problems with particular aspects of adjectival versus verbal passives—the difference between "*The girl was very frightened*" and "*The girl was cruelly frightened*" (for a comprehensive overview, see Levy & Kavé, 1999).

All of these suggestions have had difficulty in accounting for the fact that the production of SLI children is characteristically a mixture of the correct and the incorrect. That is, their utterances often give evidence that they have knowledge of the linguistic constructions on which they usually fail. In brief, they appear to obey linguistic constraints optionally. The most plausible explanation for this pattern seems currently to be that there is conflict between the principles of "Last Resort" and "Procrastinate" in the sense of Chomsky (1995). Last Resort stipulates that a grammatical operation of a particular kind, such as movement, can take place only if there is no alternative which will give rise to an acceptable output; Procrastinate stipulates that movement should be delayed as long as possible, with the result that it takes place preferentially at LF—the level of Logical Form—where its effects are largely invisible. The idea is that the incorporation of one but not the other of these principles in the pathologically developing grammar leads to the possibility of a range of optional choices that are normally excluded (Davies, 2002; van der Lely, 1998). What is of most current relevance is that the SLI population provides a double dissociation with regard to Christopher. SLI children may be of normal intelligence but have problems with that part of language—the inflectional morphology—at which Christopher, despite his intellectual impairment, is best.

Other dissociations abound. Just as intelligence and language are dissociable, so also is it possible to separate linguistic ability and "theory of mind" in the sense of Frith and her colleagues (Frith, 1989; Frith & Happé, 1994; Frith, Morton & Leslie, 1991; Leslie, 1987). Autistic subjects probably lack a theory of mind but—especially in the case of Asperger's syndrome (Frith, Smith, in press)—may control language within normal limits. Some Down syndrome children provide a contrary scenario, with their theory of mind being intact, so that they characteristically succeed on "false belief" tasks, but with their linguistic ability moderately to severely degraded.

That the language faculty and the number faculty dissociate can be seen from different kinds of savants. Uniquely, Christopher's ability is in language, and his numerical talent is minimal. By contrast, calendrical calculators and other mathematical prodigies are characteristically severely linguistically impoverished, often being unable to communicate more than basic needs (Hermelin & O'Connor, 1990; O'Connor & Hermelin, 2001). In the case of number, it appears that there is also evidence for submodular dissociation (Dehaene, 1997; Wynn, 1998), with addition and subtraction being both differentially affected in pathology and separately localized in imaging studies. Language and face recognition dissociate, with Williams syndrome children being remarkable at both (Karmiloff-Smith et al; 1995),[3] whereas Christopher's performance on face recognition tasks is (typically for someone who has autistic characteristics) extremely weak.

If we look at the linguistic domain, similar "submodular" dissociations within the language faculty are also manifest, providing corroborative support for any linguistic theory that postulates the kind of modules characteristic of most versions of a Principles and Parameters model. The most obvious of these dissociations is between the lexicon and the "computational system" (Chomsky, 1995; Clahsen, 1999), roughly, the contrast between vocabulary and grammar. As we saw earlier, Christopher's first language, English, is entirely normal, but it is striking that his talent in his numerous "second" languages is restricted largely to mastery of the morphology and the lexicon, while his syntactic ability rapidly peaks and then plateaus. This dissociation is significant in that it is precisely the syntax, the main domain of parametric variation, that is the subpart of the language faculty that is most likely to be genetically specified and develop or unfold during a particular "critical period" (Smith, 1998). If Christopher's "second" languages have all been learned after the end of this critical period, it suggests that his talent, however remarkable, is necessarily flawed. It also suggests that in interesting respects, Christopher's abilities are only partly "linguistic." Unlike first-language acquisition, second-language learning may crucially involve the deployment of general learning strategies that are ultimately correlated with attributes of the central system (Tsimpli & Smith, 1991). Christopher is then able to "relexify" the particular syntactic template of his first language, but he cannot modify that original template itself—a large proportion of his second–language activity consists in introducing items of vocabulary from a wide variety of languages into English syntactic structures. This makes Christopher strikingly different from talented second-language learners whose "ultimate attainment" is close to that of native speakers (Birdsong, 1992). Assuming nonetheless that there is an obvious linguistic component to Christopher's learning of "second" languages, the dissociation between morphology and syntax is reminiscent of the reverse dissociation found in the case of children with spinal muscular atrophy, who seem to develop a proficient syntactic rule system but have correspondingly greater difficulty with lexical development (Sieratzki & Woll, 1998).

---

[3]Williams syndrome children appear to achieve their remarkable feats of face recognition by processes distinct from those of normals, focussing on one trait rather than the whole facial gestalt.

ALTERNATIVES

Modularity is frequently adduced as support for the "innateness" of the language faculty, but, as has been frequently pointed out, modularity (as also sub-modularity and quasi-modularity) is compatible with a variety of noninnatist positions, and the boundaries of what constitutes a module (or submodule, quasi-module, etc.) are definable in a variety of ways. In this section I wish to look briefly at one or two alternatives to the position I have already outlined.

Karmiloff-Smith (1992) argued extensively for the view that modules are a function of constructivist, epigenetic development rather than of simple genetic determination. That is, "cognitive development is the outcome of a self-organizing system that is structured and shaped by its interaction with the environment" (Carston, 1996, p. 78), with the mind of the newborn being largely unstructured and knowledge free. She supports her position with a series of elegant explanations for developmental patterns in terms of the "Representational Redescription Hypothesis," where redescription involves the transfer from implicit, unconscious, representation to explicit—hence potentially conscious— representation. Her thesis is compatible with some patterns of meta-linguistic development in children, but it is inadequate for dealing with the regular emergence of the functional categories of syntax (at around the 2 years stage). Functional categories of the kind exemplified by determiners, such as "*the*," inflectional elements, such as the plural "*-s*," and complementizers, such as "*that*" and "*if*," seem to emerge at about the same age in all children learning all languages, largely independently of intelligence, context, and environment (Smith, 1994). Although it is obvious that triggering input is necessary, this uniform emergence points strongly to a genetic, rather than an epigenetic, etiology—a conclusion that is supported by two other considerations. First, many phonological parameters are set in the first year of life (Jusczyk, 1997,and chap. 3, this volume), and syntactic choices have been argued by Wexler (1998) to be available to the child from a stage before representational redescription can even get under way. Second, her account leaves mysterious why brain functions, in particular linguistic functions, should develop in such a way that they are localized similarly from person to person and from language to language. It is hard to see any appreciable role for the environment in such development.

A second alternative account of modularity is provided by Sperber (1994), who developed a position that also assigns considerable structure to the "central system" and that also makes a tripartite distinction among types of modules, but whose boundaries are somewhat different and which, I suspect, is flawed. His first division is into modules the size of concepts—the CAT module, the GOLDFISH module, and other "micro-modules" for every concept we have. Second, he postulates modules à la Fodor that are sensitive to particular kinds of percept: vision, audition, and so on. Third, he suggests that the central system is best characterized by a metarepresentational module (or modules), devoted to "representations of representations." There is no provision in this system for submodules of the kind found within the language faculty or within the number sense, but it is likely that Sperber would happily add such structure to his model. Where we differ is in the apparent equation of "concept" with "micromodule" and in the assumption that all of the central system is metarepresentational. There are two problems. The first is whether there are any identity criteria for "module" under his system, or whether it is simply an allusive "loose use" of terminology (Sperber & Wilson, 1986) with no definable content. The second is whether the central systems—"quasi-modules" in my terminology—all involve "metarepresentation"; that is, the second-order representation of another representation. If all quasi-modules were necessarily metarepresentational, Sperber could plausibly accommodate them within a suggested (1994, p. 64) extension of his system allowing his metarepresentational module to be fragmented into a number of sub-components. However, although moral judgment and a sense of social structure are plausibly metarepresentational in this way, it is not obvious that music, the number sense or face recognition are. For instance, face recognition is itself not unitary, as it involves at least two components—face recognition proper, and the emotional response to the retrieved percept. These components are independently subject to breakdown, as in prosopagnosia (the specific inability to recognize faces) and Capgras' Delusion (the failure to register an emotional response to the face recognized) respectively (Coltheart, Langdon, & Breen, 1997). Although the latter may be metarepresentational, it is not clear why one should consider the former to be so. If this interpretation is correct, then it removes one possible basis for the unification inherent in Sperber's model. (For further discussion, see Tsimpli and Smith, 1998.)

The most radical alternative to modularist theories is provided by Connectionism (Plaut, chap. 6, this volume). This approach denies the need for symbolic representations at all. All the complexities of human thought and language can emerge from interactions among a set of processing units which can take on different activation values. A connectionist network consists of a set of nodes that collect inputs from a variety of sources (both inside and outside the system), and transmit inputs to other nodes, thereby activating them in turn. The connections may be unidirectional or bidirectional, and are differently weighted so that the next node along may be either inhibited or excited. "Learning" results from training a network by repeatedly exposing it to vast numbers of examples of the pattern to be acquired. Importantly, there is no need to postulate any kind of initial domain-specific structure to the network, as the framework denies the need either for the innate schemata which are held to underlie modular accounts of linguistic ability, be these Fodorian or Chomskyan, or indeed for symbolic representation more generally. In this section I want to highlight what I perceive to be a serious problem for the spirit of connectionist accounts, and thereby lend indirect support to a modularist view (Bechtel & Abrahamson, 1991; Elman, 1993; Elman; 1996; for further discussion, see Clahsen, 1999 ; Marcus, 2001; Smith, 1997, 1999. Plaut, this volume, provides a radically different viewpoint on connectionist accounts of language).

It is not controversial that connectionist networks can serve as one possible form of implementation for symbolic theories, nor that the sophistication of current networks is sufficient to model almost anything one cares to throw at them, even though their achievements in rendering the complexities of syntax are so far minimal. Whether they have anything at all to offer in the way of a replacement for symbolic theories, however, is a matter of heated controversy. Whichever view one takes, there are several claimed advantages of connectionist systems that are worth listing: They are explicit, they have neural correlates, they are "interactive," statistically based, and self-organizing, they manifest graceful degradation, and they allow for plasticity. Some of these properties are clearly desirable, some are irrelevant, and others may be pernicious. Let us look at them in turn.

The first property, explicitness, is uncontroversially beneficial, but it does not provide a principled distinction between symbolic systems, such as formal grammars and connectionist systems. The second characteristic, the fact that neural networks are modeled on one aspect of the structure of the brain is of no greater relevance than it would be to model them on physicists' superstring models of the universe, on the grounds that they are ultimately realized in terms of quarks and the like. What is important is the nature of the generalizations that can be expressed in alternative systems, and there are few, if any, syntactic generalizations statable in terms of networks. Next, connectionist networks are interactive, in that their final properties emerge from interaction among component parts of the system. This may or may not be an advantage. There are interesting issues concerning the relations among input systems and what we have called quasi-modules (e.g., informational encapsulation), but what precisely these relations are is an open empirical issue, not one to be decided in advance by fiat. Similar remarks obtain with regard to the property of being self-organizing: If the organization that emerges is the same as that found in human beings, then it is an advantage, but to the extent that the organization has to be built in by ascribing initial weights to the various connections, it is an admission of the correctness of innatist assumptions. Likewise with plasticity: The fact that "region *x* can be co-opted to carry out the function usually effected by region *y*" is sometimes used as an argument against modular systems (e.g., by Elman et al., 1996). The idea is that the claimed innateness of modularity is undermined by the brain's ability to compensate for injury in one area by "redeploying" its forces. For example, if a child suffers damage to the language area (e.g., in the form of a left hemispherectomy), the language function may be taken over by the right hemisphere. It is supposed to follow that modularity cannot be (innately) prespecified but must emerge. But it is not clear why this is a problem for innateness hypotheses: invoking plasticity implicitly presupposes that regions *x* and *y* are, in the absence of pathological conditions, prespecified for the particular (modular) functions that connectionists are at pains to deny.

Although these critical observations should be taken into consideration in evaluating connectionist models, none of them provides particularly strong counterevidence to the theory. But there are two major objections to connectionism, relating to the other properties mentioned, which seem to me to be more problematic. The first is that connectionism is in principle inadequate for handling certain sorts of linguistic phenomena; the second is that it is in principle well designed to do things that it should not be able to do—that is, it is intrinsically too powerful. Networks typically use the method of gradient descent, but this militates against providing a sensible explanation for certain linguistic processes. Consider the phenomenon of "retreat," where a child who has internalized a grammar that overgenerates—as in Bowerman's (1987) example "don't giggle me"—retreats to a grammar in which this is, correctly, ungrammatical. That is, the child has to change its grammar from more general to less general. According to Elman, gradient descent "makes it difficult for a network to make dramatic changes in its hypotheses. Once a network is committed to an erroneous generalization it may be unable to escape" (Elman, 1993, p. 94). This unfortunately seems to make the problem of retreat insoluble.

It may be possible to alleviate this problem by modifying the learning rate or the momentum of the network, but the second kind of problem is more serious. It is of the essence of connectionist networks that they are sensitive to statistical data, and that structure emerges as a function of the frequency of elements of the input. I pointed out earlier that in the experiment in which Christopher and the controls had to learn Epun, none of them were able to infer the simple rule that emphatic sentences were produced by suffixing some element to the third word. This is something that connectionist networks are extremely good at doing, but which they ought not to be good at if they are accurately to replicate the normal abilities of human learners. Unlike networks, grammars can't count. That is, there is no phonological or syntactic rule in any of the world's languages, which requires reference to such notions as the third word, or the fourth segment. Rather, all rules of grammar refer either to structural configurations or to adjacency, and the course of linguistic development in the child seems to indicate that "structure dependence is the prerequisite to, not the outcome of, language acquisition" (Smith, 1997, p. 7). It is possible to impose additional constraints on a network so that it could not learn structure independent operations, correctly replicating the behaviour of human subjects. But such manipulation is contrary to the spirit of the enterprise and requires building in the "innate" structure that networks are supposed to be able to do without.

CONCLUSION

The mind is modular, but to put flesh on that skeletal statement it is necessary to distinguish different notions of "module." Input systems are modular in Fodor's sense, being sensitive to a subset of perceptually available stimuli; but *pace* Fodor, language is not just an input system, and it is also necessary to assign some structure to the "central" system, compartmentalizing it into a number of conceptual "quasi-modules" one of which is language. Both kinds of entities may be characterised by further "submodular," structure, corresponding to traditional notions such as morphology and syntax, and addition and multiplication, as well as some of the more recent constructs of linguistic theory, giving rise to the subtheories of a generative grammar, such as case and binding.

Modularity is in part genetically determined, but if language is modular, then the existence of different languages shows that it must also be in part the product of external input. The demarcations between what is learned and what is innate is contentious and the subject of ongoing research, but no one seriously doubts that both components are needed. There is ongoing healthy disagreement as to what the defining properties of modules are. I have suggested that some of the confusion and disagreement in the literature has arisen from a failure to make enough distinctions, and I have proposed a distinction between modules of the kind made famous by Fodor and quasi-modules, corresponding somewhat more closely to Chomsky's conception of the mind. I have defended these ideas on the basis of a wealth of dissociationist data, paying particular attention to the case of the polyglot savant, Christopher. Finally, I have argued that nonmodular (and nonsymbolic) rivals to modularity, specifically connectionist models, seem to have serious problems as replacements for theories of language and mind, even though they may remain viable as implementations for such theories. As of today, a modular conception of language, and of the structure of the mind more generally, is the most powerful and the most explanatory one available.

ACKNOWLEDGMENTS

I am grateful to the organizers of the conference "Mind, Brain, and Language," which was sponsored by the Center for Advanced Study at the University of Illinois at Urbana–Champaign. I am particularly indebted to both of the organizers and to the other participants in the conference for a variety of comments and questions. The work on Christopher has all been done in collaboration with Ianthi Tsimpli, and with the support of the Leverhulme Trust under grant number F.134.

REFERENCES

Bates, E., & Elman, J. 1996. Learning rediscovered. *Science, 274,* 1849–1850.
Bauby, J. D. (1997). *The diving-bell and the butterfly.* New York: Vintage Books.
Bechtel, W., & Abrahamson, A. (1991). *Connectionism and the mind: An introduction to parallel processing in networks.* Oxford: Blackwell.
Bellugi, U., Marks, S., Bihrle, A., & Sabo, H. (1993). Dissociation between language and cognitive functions in Williams syndrome. In D. Bishop & K. Mogford (Eds.), *Language development in exceptional circumstances* (pp. 177–189). Hillsdale, NJ: Lawrence Erlbaum Associates.
Birdsong, D. (1992). Ultimate attainment in second language learning. *Language, 68,* 706–755.
Bishop, D. V. M. (1997). *Uncommon understanding: Development and disorders of language comprehension in children.* London: Psychology Press.
Bowerman, M. (1987). The "no negative evidence" problem. How do children avoid constructing an overly general grammar? In J. Hawkins (Ed.), *Explaining language universals* (pp. 73–101). Oxford: Blackwell.
Carston, R. (1996). The architecture of the mind: Modularity and modularization. In D. Green and others (Eds.), *Cognitive Science: An Introduction* (pp. 53–83). Oxford, Blackwell.
Chomsky, N. (1975). *Reflections on language.* New York: Pantheon.
Chomsky, N. (1984). *Modular approaches to the study of mind.* San Diego: San Diego State University Press.
Chomsky, N. (1991). Linguistics and cognitive science: Problems and mysteries. In A. Kasher (Ed.), *The Chomskyan turn* (pp. 26–53). Oxford, Blackwell.
Chomsky, N. (1995). *The minimalist program.* Cambridge, MA: MIT Press.
Clahsen, H. (1999). Lexical entries and rules of language: A multidisciplinary study of German inflection. *Behavioral and Brain Sciences, 22,* 991–1060.
Clahsen, H., Bartke, S., & Gollner, S. (1997). Formal features in impaired grammars: A comparison of English and German SLI children. *Essex Research Reports in Linguistics, 14,* 42–75.
Coltheart, M. (1999). Modularity and cognition. *Trends in Cognitive Sciences, 3,* 115–120.
Coltheart, M., Langdon, R., & Breen, N. (1997). Misidentification syndromes and cognitive neuropsychiatry. *Trends in Cognitive Sciences, 1,* 157–158.
Davies, L. (2002). Specific language impairment as principle conflict: Evidence from negation. *Lingua, 112,* 281–300.
Dehaene, S. (1997). *The number sense.* London: Allen Lane.
Elman, J. (1993). Learning and development in neural networks: The importance of starting small. *Cognition, 48,* 71–99.
Elman, J., Bates, E., Johnson, M., Karmiloff-Smith, A., Parisi, D., & Plunkett, K. (1996). *Rethinking innateness: A connectionist perspective on development.* Cambridge, MA: MIT Press.
Fodor, J. (1983). *The modularity of mind.* Cambridge, MA: MIT Press.
Fodor, J. (1992). A theory of the child's theory of mind. *Cognition, 44,* 283–296.
Frith, U. (1989). *Autism: Explaining the enigma.* Oxford: Blackwell.
Frith, U. (1991). Asperger and his syndrome. In U. Frith (Ed.), *Autism and Asperger syndrome* (pp. 1–36). Cambridge: Cambridge University Press.
Frith, U.,& Happé, F. (1994). Language and communication in autistic disorders. *Philosophical Transactions of the Royal Society of London B, 346,* 97–104.
Frith, U., Morton, J., & Leslie, A. (1991). The cognitive basis of a biological disorder. *Trends in Neuroscience, 14,* 433–438.
Gopnik, M. (1997). Language deficits and genetic factors. *Trends in Cognitive Sciences, 1,* 5–9.
Hermelin, B. (2001). *Bright splinters of the mind.* London: Jessica Kinglsey Publishers.
Hermelin, B., & O'Connor, N. (1990). Factors and primes: A specific numerical ability. *Psychological Medicine, 20,* 163–169.
Inhelder, B. (1980). Language and knowledge in a constructivist framework. In M. Piattelli-Palmarini (Ed.), *Language and learning: The debate between Jean Piaget and Noam Chomsky* (pp. 132–141). Cambridge MA: Harvard University Press.
Joanisse, M., & Seidenberg, M. (1998). Specific language impairment: A deficit in grammar or processing? *Trends in Cognitive Sciences, 2,* 240–247.
Jusczyk, P. (1997). *The discovery of spoken language.* Cambridge, MA: MIT Press.

Karmiloff-Smith, A. (1992). *Beyond modularity*. Cambridge, MA: MIT Press.
Karmiloff-Smith, A., Klima, E., Grant, J., & Baron–Cohen, S. (1995). Is there a social module? Language, face processing, and theory of mind in individuals with Williams syndrome. *Journal of Cognitive Neuroscience, 7*, 196–208.
Leslie, A. (1987). Pretense and representation: The origins of "Theory of Mind." *Psychological Review, 94*, 412–426.
Levy, Y., &. Kavé, G. (1999). Language breakdown and linguistic theory: A tutorial overview. *Lingua, 107*, 95–143.
Marcus, G. (2001). *The algebraic mind: Reflections on connectionism and cognitive science*. Cambridge, MA: MIT Press.
Morgan, G., Smith, N. V., Tsimpli, I. M., & Woll, B. (2002). Language against the odds: The learning of British Sign Language by a polyglot savant. *Journal of Linguistics, 38*, 1–41.
O'Connor, N., & Hermelin, B. (1984). Idiot savant calendrical calculators: Maths or memory? *Psychological Medicine, 14*, 801–806.
O'Connor, N., & Hermelin, B. (1991). A specific linguistic ability. American Journal of Mental Retardation, 95, 673–680.
Piaget, J., & Inhelder, B. (1968). *The psychology of the child.* London: Routledge.
Quine, W. V. O. (1960). *Word and object*. Cambridge, MA: MIT Press.
Sieratzki, J. S., & Woll, B. (1998). *Toddling into language: Precocious language development in motor–impaired children with spinal muscular atrophy*. In A. Greenhill, M. Hughes, H. Littlefield, & H. Walsh (Eds.), Proceedings of the 22nd annual Boston University Conference on Language Development, (Vol. 2, pp. 684–694). Somerville, MA: Cascadilla Press.
Slobin, D. (1973). Cognitive prerequisites for the development of grammar. In C. Ferguson & D. Slobin (Eds.), *Studies of child language development* (pp. 175–208). New York: Holt Rinehart & Winston.
Sloboda, J. (1985). *The musical mind: The cognitive psychology of music*. Oxford: Clarendon Press.
Smith, N. V. (1994). Review article on A. Karmiloff–Smith (1992). *European Journal of Disorders of Communication, 29*, 95–105.
Smith, N. V. (1997). Structural eccentricities. *Glot International, 2*, 8. Reprinted in Smith, 2002, pp. 110–115.
Smith, N. V. (1998). Jackdaws, sex and language acquisition. *Glot International, 3*, 7. Reprinted in Smith, 2002, pp. 95–99.
Smith, N. V. (1999). Chomsky: Ideas and ideals. Cambridge: Cambridge University Press.
Smith, N. V. (2002). *Language, bananas and bonobos*. Oxford: Blackwell.
Smith, N. V. (in press). Wonder. *Glot International*, 6.
Smith, N. V., & Tsimpli, I.-M. (1995). The mind of a savant: Language-learning and Modularity. Oxford: Blackwell.
Smith, N. V., & Tsimpli, I.-M. (1997). Reply to Bates: Review of Smith & Tsimpli, 1995. *The International Journal of Bilingualism, 2*, 180–186.
Smith, N. V., Tsimpli, I.-M., & Ouhalla, J. (1993). Learning the impossible: The acquisition of possible and impossible languages by a polyglot *savant*. *Lingua, 91*, 279–347.
Soja, N., Carey, S., & Spelke, E. (1991). Ontological categories guide young children's inductions of word meaning: Object terms and substance terms. *Cognition, 38*, 179–211.
Sperber, D. (1994). The modularity of thought and the epidemiology of representations. In L. Hirschfeld & S. Gelman (Eds.), *Mapping the mind: Domain specificity in cognition and culture* (pp. 39–67). Cambridge: Cambridge University Press.
Sperber, D., & Wilson, D. (1986). Loose talk. *Proceedings of the Aristotelian Society, NS LXXXVI*, 153–171.
Tallal, P. (1990). Fine-grained discrimination deficits in language learning impaired children are specific neither to the auditory modality nor to speech perception. *Journal of Speech and Hearing Research, 33*, 616–617.
Treffert, D. A. (1989). *Extraordinary people*. London: Black Swan.
Tsimpli, I.-M., &Smith, N.V. (1991). Second language learning: Evidence from a polyglot savant. *University College London Working Papers in Linguistics, 3*, 171–183.
Tsimpli, I.-M., & Smith, N.V. (1998). Modules and quasi-modules: language and theory of mind in a polyglot savant. *Learning and individual differences, 10*, 193–215.
van der Lely, H. K. J. (1996). Specifically language impaired and normally developing children: Verbal passive *vs.* adjectival passive sentence interpretation. *Lingua*, 98, 243–272.

van der Lely, H. K. J. (1997). Language and cognitive development in a grammatical SLI boy: Modularity and innateness. *Journal of Neurolinguistics*, *10*, 75–107.

van der Lely, H. K. J. (1998). SLI in children: Movement, economy and deficits in the computational syntactic system. *Language Acquisition*, *72*, 161–192.

van der Lely, H. K. J., & Stollwerck, L. (1997). Binding theory and grammatical specific language impairment in children. *Cognition*, *62*, 245–290.

Wexler, K. (1998). The unique checking constraint and the extended projection principle as the explanation for the optional infinitive stage: very early parameter–setting, maturational mechanisms and variation in grammatical development. *Lingua*, *106*, 23–79.

Wynn, K. (1998). Psychological foundations of number: Numerical competence in human infants. *Trends in Cognitive Sciences*, *2*, 296–303.

5

Linguistic Models

Geoffrey K. Pullum
Barbara C. Scholz

This chapter is about natural languages, their structure, and their grammars. The concentration is entirely on syntax (the structure of sentences, clauses, and phrases), setting aside phonology (sound structure) and morphology (word structure), as well as issues of semantics and pragmatics. We consider a class of grammars that encompasses almost all current research in syntax, point out two rather deep conceptual problems for grammars of that sort, and sketch the outlines of some recent work that promises a resolution of these problems.

We begin with an is a no-prerequisites introduction to one simple kind of grammar. This section may be skimmed by linguists familiar with phrase structure grammars, although there are references in the rest of the chapter to the grammars and languages cited as examples there.

We then survey several types of grammar that have played a significant role in recent linguistics. A plethora of different kinds of grammar has emerged in the literature, driven by different attempts to optimize over many conflicting desiderata: clarity, generality, economy, descriptive adequacy, explanatory power, and the need to interface successfully with semantics. Our survey is designed for readers unfamiliar with the last four decades of research on syntax (particularly what is known as generative grammar). For those linguists who are acquainted with this literature it will be merely a review. However, we draw from the survey a key point that is important to the subsequent sections. We show that the various grammar types we sketch all have one thing in common, namely, that they generate sets. We call them *generative–enumerative grammars*.

Next, we raise a general problem for generate–enumerative grammars: They do not adequately describe the gradience of syntactic deviance. It is well known to syntacticians that English, for example, is not appropriately described by categorically distinguishing between the perfectly grammatical and the utterly ungrammatical. Many expressions are partially grammatical and partially not.

They are largely structured in accord with grammatical principles, yet not completely. Such partial deviance is recognized by ordinary speakers as well as by grammarians. But the grammars surveyed in the third section do not assign grammatical structure to any expression that they do not generate. Hence they do not describe this well-known phenomenon adequately. We show how a modification (already quite widely adopted by many linguists for a variety of descriptive purposes other than this one) partially solves the problem.

We then turn to a more intractable problem, emanating from mathematical learning theory, that is extremely problematic for contemporary linguistics. An elementary proof, dependent only on basic recursive function theory, appears to show that language learning as we know it is outright impossible. This presents a paradox, because of course languages are readily learned by all neurophysiologically normal human beings at the toddler stage. We argue that the problem posed by these results is far more serious than many linguists seem to think. But again we point to a possible solution. It involves the introduction of an alternative kind of grammar—and it is based on the solution offered for the problem in the previous section.

After that, we introduce this alternative kind of grammar. The goal is not to provide a thorough introduction to the relatively new area of linguistics involved, but simply to show two things. First, the new kind of grammar fully supports the solution to the problem of gradient deviance. Second, it promises to dissolve the unlearnability paradox as well. The grammars in question, which we call *model-theoretic grammars*, are not generative–enumerative. Their most significant property—oddly unnoticed by their advocates—is that they do not entail that natural languages are sets at all. They describe and represent the properties of expressions, not of sets. This is the key to dissolving the unlearnability paradox of the previous section.

SIMPLE PHRASE STRUCTURE GRAMMARS

We begin by briefly describing a particularly simple and familiar kind of grammar, which we refer to as a *simple phrase structure grammar.* (For a somewhat fuller elementary introduction to the issues we cover in this section, see Lasnik, 2000, chap. 1.) A grammar of this kind, referred to in the technical literature as a context-free phrase structure grammar in Chomsky normal form, represents the syntactic structure of a language by means of rules defined over the *words* that occur in expressions together with symbols that name certain categories of expression. We distinguish *lexical categories*, to which words belong (just as in a traditional grammar each word is assigned by the dictionary to a "part of speech"), and *phrasal categories*, to which different types of phrase belong (noun phrases, preposition phrases, clauses, and so on). Grammatical rules represent for each phrasal category what components a phrase of that sort has, and for each lexical category, which words belong to it.

The rules of a phrase structure grammar have two different interpretations (which are provably equivalent if certain conditions are met). On the first, the rules function like rules of inference in logic. Each rule licenses an inference step in a proof that a certain word sequence is grammatical. Such a proof is called a *derivation*. A derivation implicitly represents a grammatical structure for the derived word sequence. On the second interpretation, rules are templates for directly checking that certain linguistic structures are grammatical.

The simplest way to see how such grammars describe syntactic structure is to examine a grammar for a simple invented language. In (2) we give a complete grammar for the syntax of an invented language called *Little-English*. Little-English expressions are like certain English expressions, but Little-English has only six words (*boy*, *girl*, *met*, *that*, *thinks*, and *this*). The categories of Little-English are represented by the labels listed in (1).

(1) Lexical categories

N	noun
Det	determinative
V_c	clausally complemented verb (that is, a verb such as **think** which may be accompanied by a tensed subordinate clause)
V_t	transitive verb (that is, a verb such as **met** which may be accompanied by a direct object NP)

Phrasal categories

NP	noun phrase
VP	verb phrase
S	sentence or clause (a sentence is basically a clause standing alone)

The rules are stated in the form "$\alpha \rightarrow \beta$", where α is the name of some syntactic category (lexical or phrasal) from the list in (1) and β is either a word or a sequence of exactly two category symbols. The entire syntax for Little-English is stated in (2).

(2) A grammar for Little-English

a. S → NP VP	f. Det → that
b. NP → Det N	g. N → boy
c. VP → V_t NP	h. N → girl
d. VP → V_c S	i. V_t → met
e. Det → this	j. V_c → thinks

Each formula in (2) is a grammatical rule. Rule (2a), for example, says that a clause consists of a noun phrase followed by a verb phrase (these are the traditional "subject" and "predicate"of the clause). Rule (2c) says that a verb phrase of Little-English may consist of a transitive verb followed by a noun phrase. Rule (2h) says that "*girl*" is a member of the lexical category of nouns in Little-English.

To see how such rules function to license inferences in proofs of grammaticality, consider the sample derivation in (3). It begins with line (3a), consisting of the name of the category of the expression that is to be proved grammatical, and ends with the sequence of words (3p). Each line is derived from its predecessor by the application of some rule. For example, rule (2a) says that in a derivation of a Little-English expression a line "... NP VP ..." can be inferred from a line "... S ..." (i.e., the only difference is that "S" is replaced by "NP VP"). This means that, for example, step (3h) can legitimately follow (3g).

(3)	a.	S	(assumption)
	b.	NP VP	(NP VP inferred from S, by rule (2a))
	c.	Det N VP	(Det N inferred from NP, by rule (2b))
	d.	this N VP	(this inferred from Det, by rule (2e))
	e.	this girl VP	(girl inferred from N, by rule (2h))
	f.	this girl V_c S	(V_c S inferred from VP, by rule (2d))
	g.	this girl thinks S	(thinks inferred from V_c, by rule (2j))
	h.	this girl thinks NP VP	(NP VP inferred from S, by rule (2a))
	i.	this girl thinks Det N VP	(Det N inferred from NP, by rule (2b))
	j.	this girl thinks that N VP	(that inferred from Det, by rule (2f))
	k.	this girl thinks that boy VP	(boy inferred from N, by rule (2g))
	l.	this girl thinks that boy V_t NP	(V_t NP inferred from VP, by rule (2c))
	m.	this girl thinks that boy met NP	(met inferred from V_t, by rule (2i))
	n.	this girl thinks that boy met Det N	(Det N inferred from NP, by rule (2b))
	o.	this girl thinks that boy met that N	(that inferred from Det, by rule (2f))
	p.	this girl thinks that boy met that girl	(girl inferred from N, by rule (2h))

By virtue of (3a–p), the word sequence (3p) is demonstrated to be a representation of a grammatical Little-English expression of the category S. (It is helpful in the next section to keep in mind that in a sentence like this, *that boy met that girl* is referred to as a *subordinate* clause.)

The derivation in (3), like any phrase structure grammar derivation, also implicitly defines the syntactic structure of the word sequence derived. This structure may be graphically represented in the form of a *tree*. A tree is a kind of graph, that is, a set of points called *nodes*, some connected to others by lines called *branches*. Each node has a category symbol as its *label*. If "Q" is a category symbol, a node having "Q" as its label is called a *Q node*. A tree represents two syntactically relevant structural relations between parts of expressions. First, one part of an expression can *precede* another, as "*this*" precedes "*girl*" in (3p). This relation is represented by left-to-right order across the page. Second, one part of an expression can be a *subpart* of another, as "*girl*" is a subpart of "*this girl*" in (3p). This is shown by branches between the labels of the parts and the labels of the wholes. The structure of (3p) as described by the rules in (2) can be represented by (4).

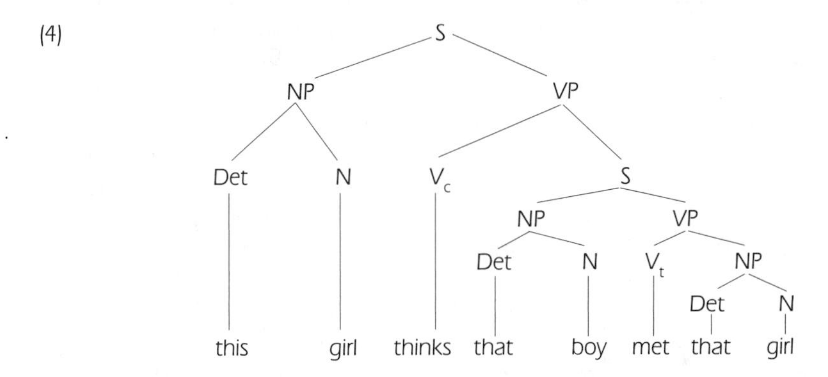

All the structural information in (4) is implicit in the derivation in (3), although we will not show this in detail here (see Lasnik, 2000, chap. 1, for an accessible account). The S node at the top is known as the *root* node, and represents the whole expression (which is not a subpart of anything). Where a Det node and an N node (in that order) are shown both connected to an NP node above them, that part of the tree represents a noun phrase composed of a determinative preceding a noun. The word sequence across the bottom of the tree represents the sequence of words in the expression as it would be uttered in spoken or written form. (Note also that it will be useful at a couple of points later on to refer to the sequence of lexical category labels immediately above the words, in this case "Det N V_c Det N V_t Det N", as the *lexical category sequence* for this expression.)

We mentioned earlier that there is a second interpretation of phrase structure rules. Suppose expressions of a language are taken to have structure representable in tree form. The rules of a grammar such as (2) can be interpreted to represent Little-English structure directly, no derivation being involved. Under this interpretation, rule (2b), for example, says that a minimal piece of tree structure (a piece consisting of one node and the nodes connected immediately below it by branches) represents a well-formed part of a Little-English expression if it is labeled thus:

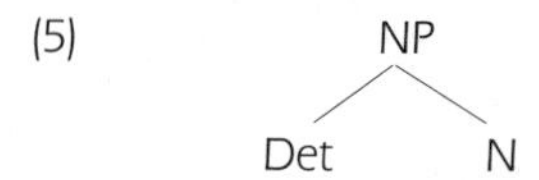

A whole tree represents a well-formed expression if and only if all of its subtrees represent well-formed parts. For example, the tree in (4) has exactly 15 minimal pieces. For each of them some rule in (2) states that it represents a well-formed expression part. Therefore the whole tree represents a well-formed expression. Under this interpretation of the grammar in (2), all those word sequences that occur at the bottom line of some tree represent well-formed expressions.

Although Little-English is a language with only six words in its vocabulary, and its syntax is described by the grammar in (2) using only 10 rules, nonetheless infinitely many word sequences (hence infinitely many trees) are defined as grammatical by (2). The reason is that the rules place no upper bound on the length of word sequences (or the size of trees). In terms of derivations, rule (2d) justifies deriving a line containing "S" from a line containing "VP", as in line (3f). That "S" can then give rise to another occurrence of "VP", and so on without limit. Every derivation is finite, because any proof that a sequence of words is a grammatical expression of a language must, by definition, end with the derived sequence of words. However, because there is no bound on either the length of derivations (number of steps) or their width (number of symbols in the longest line), infinitely many expressions are represented as grammatical. And putting it in terms of trees, rule (2d) allows a tree with an S node as its root to contain a subtree with an S node as its root, and this may again contain an S node, and so on.

A SURVEY OF GENERATIVE–ENUMERATIVE GRAMMARS

All explicit grammars describe the syntactic structure of expressions, but simple phrase structure grammars do it in a particular way. They are an example of a much wider range of grammar types, all having one thing in common: they describe syntactic structure by defining the membership of a certain set of expressions. Various terms are used in logic and formal language theory for the way grammars of this sort define sets: stating the characteristic function of a set, giving a recursive definition or recursive enumeration of it, or generating it. We will say that a grammar is *generative–enumerative* if and only if the grammar is interpreted as defining or generating a *set* of representations of the syntactic structure of a language, and that set is claimed to be the model or reconstruction of the language being described.

Some work in linguistics does not lay out its assumptions with sufficient explicitness for it to be determined whether it counts as generative–enumerative, but it has been consistently clear in the work of Chomsky that this is the view he takes: "the syntactic component of the grammar generates an infinite set of abstract structures" each of which is assigned a representation at three different levels (roughly phonological, syntactic, and semantic) and "Each expression of the language determined by the grammar is assigned representations at these three levels" (Chomsky, 1981, p. 4), so there are infinitely many expressions of the language. See also the similar remarks (differing mainly in terminology) in Chomsky (1995, pp. 14–15).

Generative–enumerative grammars were first used to describe natural languages in Chomsky (1957). They were first developed by mathematical logicians such as Axel Thue and Emil Post to define artificial languages. In the case of artificial languages, the distinction between the way they are and the way they are defined to be is arguably a distinction without a difference. Such languages (sets of logical or mathematical expressions) are identified solely by the grammars that define them. As a later section makes clear, we believe this to be the Achilles heel of generative–enumerative grammars. Chomsky's early work imported the assumptions of mathematical logic and formal language theory wholesale into the study of natural languages, despite the clear difference between invented languages (which have exactly the properties ascribed to them by the inventor) and natural languages (which are already in use before the linguist commences description of them).

Many varieties of generative–enumerative grammars for natural languages have been developed and defended over the last half century. Here we discuss just a few important ones. (The reader who wishes to learn more may find it helpful to study Sag and Wasow [1999] especially chapter 2, "Some Simple Theories of Grammar", and Appendix B, "Generative Grammar: An Historical Overview." A substantially deeper historical perspective on theories of syntax may be found in Seuren [1998].

Expressions as Trees

The simple phrase structure grammars sketched earlier describe expressions as complex entities whose syntactic structure is represented by trees. The language is the set of all those trees that the grammar defines. Gazdar, Klein, Pullum, and Sag (1985) presented a more elaborate kind of grammar that has the same property of defining a set of trees. The grammars they advocated are in a precise sense exactly equivalent to simple phrase structure grammars.

An alternative way to represent the expressions of a language in idealized form as a set of trees, one that is not necessarily equivalent to any simple phrase structure grammar, was developed by Aravind Joshi and his colleagues under the name *tree adjoining grammar* (TAG). A TAG defines a set of trees by listing a finite set of "initial trees", which directly represent certain structurally simple expressions, together with a finite set of templates called "auxiliary trees" that may be adjoined to certain nodes in initial trees to derive more complex trees (see Joshi [1987] for a survey). The language described is the set of all trees that may be built from initial trees by adjoining auxiliary trees at appropriate nodes, so this too is a generative–enumerative type of grammar.

Expressions as Trees with Complex Node Labels

So far, we have considered only grammars that use atomic labels for nodes in trees to represent syntactic structure. The labels are atomic in the sense of being unanalyzable. Although the label "NP" might look composite (N for noun and P for phrase), it is not. The grammar in (2) does ensure that every noun is contained within a noun phrase, but not because the labels "NP" and "N" represent complex structure. The presence of the letter "N" in the two-letter label "NP" is merely a mnemonic convenience. "NP" and "N" could be replaced throughout by "X" and "Y", and the grammar would define the same trees and word sequences (with a merely typographical difference in node labels). However, there are other kinds of grammar that describe expression structure with more elaborate node labels. These labels represent relations between syntactic categories, in that some syntactic categories are represented as intersections of other more general categories.

As a simple example, consider the label of the topmost VP node in (4), which is the label of the expression "*thinks that boy met that girl*". A more detailed and revealing label for this sort of phrase would convey considerably more information than just "VP", namely, the additional information that the phrase contains a verb in the present tense that displays agreement with a noun phrase of singular number and third person. This information could be represented concisely as follows (for a detailed account of such complex symbols, and their role as category labels in different syntactic theories, see Gazdar et al., 1988).

(6)

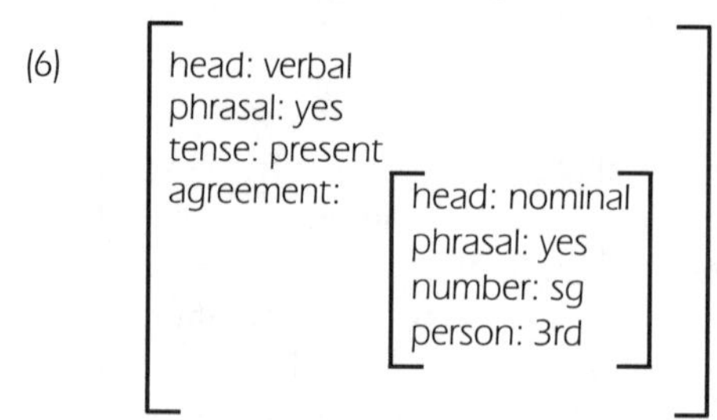

The items before the colon are names of dimensions along which syntactic categories can differ, and are usually called *features*. The items after the colon are called *values*, and represent distinct points on these dimensions. A feature paired with a value (as when we write head: verbal) is called a *feature specification*. Thus in (6) the feature tense takes the value present. What this means is that tense is one of the ways in which verb phrases can differ from each other, and this one is in the present tense. The combination tense: present represents the category of all present tense expressions. Similarly, phrasal: yes represents all expressions that are phrases (rather than single words).

Notice that the feature agreement in (6) has a complex value. The feature specification containing agreement and its value describes the expression with this label as agreeing with a third person singular noun phrase.

A full grammar of English would exploit such notations to represent verbal agreement in number and person with the subject of that clause (*I am*, *you are*, *she is*, and so on). In English it is an oversimplification to say that a clause consists of a noun phrase and a verb phrase, as rule (2a) says (for Little-English). A well-formed clause contains a noun phrase together with the *right kind* of verb phrase. If the noun phrase were third person singular, the right kind of verb phrase would be one with the label shown in (6).

Generalized phrase structure grammar (GPSG), first developed around 1978–1980, and its successor *head-driven phrase structure grammar* (HPSG) both make extensive use of complex category labels of the sort seen in (6) to represent syntactic information (see Gazdar et al. [1985] for a detailed presentation of GPSG, and Sag & Wasow [1999] for an introduction to syntax based mainly on HPSG). There are many differences between them, but they both define an infinite set of trees. The language described is reconstructed as the set of all the trees defined by the grammar as well-formed.

Categorial grammar (see Adjukiewicz [1935], Montague [1974], Steedman [1999]) also employs complex node labels. A categorial grammar defines a set of derivations of word sequences in much the same way as phrase structure grammars do, and is also interpreted as defining a set of trees. Some types of categorial grammar are equivalent to simple phrase structure grammars and others are not; one variety is proved by Vijay-Shanker and Weir (1994) to be equivalent to TAGs.

There is an intuitive sense in which a categorial grammar turns phrase structure grammar on its head. A phrase structure grammar is stated as a set of principles answering for each category the question "In what way is this composed of less inclusive subparts?" whereas categorial grammar answers the question, "In what way do words combine to make more inclusive wholes?" Consider the simple phrase structure grammar in (2), for instance. Transitive verbs, like *met*, belong to a category V_t. It is the function of rules (2a) and (2c) to show how the more inclusive unit corresponding to "VP" is composed of less inclusive units like V_t and NP, and thus show where a V_t can occur in a clause. A typical categorial grammar, on the other hand, represents *met* as a member of a category that if combined with an NP on its right forms a phrase of a type that can combine with an NP on its left to make an S. The notation for the lexical category label of *met* would be "(S\NP)/NP". The idea is that "S" and "NP" are basic-level categories, and whenever α and β are categories, α/β and $\alpha\backslash\beta$ are categories too. Moreover, their syntactic roles are fully determined. Anything of the category $\alpha\backslash\beta$ combines with a β to its right, and anything of the category α/β combines with a β on its left, the result in each case being an expression of the category α.

Thus no phrase structure rules are needed to describe how words can combine in a categorial grammar. Rather, there is just one entirely tacit rule saying that words and phrases are combined as determined by their categories. In the case of the present example, an item categorized as (S\NP)/NP combines with a following phrase of the category NP to make a phrase of the category S\NP, and an S\NP phrase combines with a preceding NP to make an S.

The set of strings or trees defined by a categorial grammar contains all and only those that are composed from categorized lexical items in a way that respects this principle. The single combination rule suffices to define the entire set of trees, and thus categorial grammars are generative–enumerative. Other kinds of grammar have been based on categorical grammars; see e.g. Chomsky (1995) and Keenan and Stabler (1996).

Expressions as Tree Sequences

Transformational-generative (TG) grammar was introduced by Chomsky (1957) to remedy some of what he took to be the shortcomings of phrase structure grammar descriptions of natural languages. A TG grammar includes as a subcomponent a simple phrase structure grammar (or its equivalent), which defines a set of trees. But there are also rules called *transformations*, which map trees to other trees (see Lasnik, 2000, chap. 2, for a simple exposition that is particularly faithful to Chomsky's early ideas). The full structural representation of an expression is a sequence of trees. Transformational rules play a role in the description by specifying the ways in which pairs of trees adjacent in a sequence may differ.

In the version of TG grammar introduced in Chomsky (1965), sometimes referred to as the standard theory, the first tree in the sequence is called the *deep structure* of the expression and the last is called its *surface structure*. Various other versions were subsequently developed, but in all of them a language is a set. If an expression is taken to be a word sequence, then the language defined by a TG grammar is the set of all word sequences that are the bottom line of some surface structure tree. If an expression is taken to be represented by a surface structure tree, then the language defined is the set of all surface structures that the transformations derive from deep structures. And if an expression is taken to be represented by a tree sequence, the language defined is the set of all tree sequences permitted by the transformations.

What is important here is that in each case the grammar generates a set of expression representations, and that set is claimed to be the language described, and thus all TG grammars are generative–enumerative grammars.

Generative–enumerative grammars with constraints

Generative–enumerative grammars have been modified by some syntacticians to describe languages in two stages. Under this modification, a generative–enumerative grammar defines a set of candidate expressions or trees that have to meet certain further requirements to represent only the well-formed expressions of the language. These additional necessary conditions on expression structure will be called *constraints* (following Perlmutter [1971] they are called *filters* in Postal, [1972] and Chomsky & Lasnik [1977].

To see that constraints could be a useful descriptive device, consider a completely artificial example. Suppose that (implausibly) we wanted a description of the syntactic structure of all and only the expressions of Little-English except for those that are eight words long. Revising the phrase structure rules in (2) to describe exactly those expressions is not impossible, but it requires changing the set of phrasal categories and adding several new rules. And the gerrymandered rule set, once achieved (we leave it as an exercise for the reader to do this), does not preserve the tree structure found in Little-English: The modified grammar will represent all expressions containing more than eight words as differing structurally from the word-for-word identical expressions of Little-English. (The reason is that we have to introduce a new category for verb phrases that contain just one V_c, and make sure that the S in those verb phrases contain at least one additional V_c. This new category will appear in all but the five-word expressions.)

There is an alternative way to describe the same set of expressions. We can use the rules in (2) to represent the structure of a set of *candidates* for expressionhood, and then rule out all the eight-word candidates with the following constraint:

(7) If a V_c occurs in a clause then an adjacent clause also contains a V_c.

The resultant two-stage grammar perspicuously describes the intended set—and it gives every expression in the set the same tree structure that it has in Little-English. (The reason the constraint works is that expressions satisfying it either have *met* as the only verb, and thus contain just five words, or contain *thinks* at least twice, and thus contain 11 words or more.)

This is a highly artificial example. But generative–enumerative grammars with constraints have been used to describe ordinary and familiar features of natural language expressions, such as pronoun-antecedent relationships in English. An intrasententially anaphoric pronoun is one that has the same referent as some other noun phrase, known as its antecedent, in the same sentence. For example, in the English expression *This girl thinks she met that boy*, the pronoun *she* may have the same referent as *this girl*, and if it does, it is intrasententially anaphoric. It was noted by Langacker (1969) that an intrasententially anaphoric pronoun must either follow its antecedent or be in a clause that is subordinate to the antecedent. For various reasons, TG grammarians found that it was not easy to use phrase structure rules and transformations to describe this restriction perspicuously. But the generative–enumerative part of the grammar can be used to generate candidate tree sequences in which the surface structure tree represents pronouns as occurring anywhere a noun phrase can occur. A constraint can then be imposed on surface structures to the effect that a candidate surface structure must satisfy the following condition in order for it to be in English:

(8) An intrasententially anaphoric pronoun precedes its antecedent only if the pronoun is contained in more clauses than the antecedent.

The expression *This girl thinks she met that boy* satisfies (8) with the pronoun *she* having *this girl* as its antecedent. The condition is also satisfied by *After she left the school, this girl met that boy* if *this girl* is the antecedent of *she* (the pronoun precedes the antecedent but is contained within an additional clause, the subordinate clause with the VP *left the school*, to which the antecedent does not belong). But *She thinks this girl met that boy* does not satisfy (8) if *she* has *this girl* as its antecedent (in other words, *she* must refer to someone other than the person *this girl* refers to).

Recent varieties of TG syntax have exploited constraints quite heavily. For example, Chomsky (1981) employed a set of statements (referred to as "the binding theory") paraphrasable as follows:

(9)a. Reflexive pronouns must have antecedents within their most immediately containing constituents (so **This girl hurt herself** is grammatical but *__This girl thinks [that boy hurt herself]__ is not, the problem being that the bracketed part is required to contain an antecedent for **herself** but it does not).

b. Anaphoric pronouns must not have antecedents within their most immediately containing constituents (so **This girl hurt her** is only interpretable as being about two different girls, while **This girl thinks that boy hurt her** may describe a situation in which there is only one girl).

c. NPs that are not pronouns cannot have antecedents at all (so **This girl saw this girl** cannot be understood as meaning that this girl saw herself).

Another set of constraints assumed in Chomsky (1981) requires every NP to have (in the terminology employed earlier in this section) a specification for the feature "case", the specification being case:nominative on an NP that occurs with a VP that has a "tense" specification, and "case:accusative" on an NP that occurs with a V_t.

Still other constraints have been posited to describe the fact that in English *What did you open the door with?* is grammatical but **What did you open the door and?* is not. (This is not just a semantic problem, as can be seen by comparing these paraphrases: *You opened the door with some tool and I want to know what tool*; *You opened the door and something else and I want to know what else*.)

It will be important below to keep in mind that generative–enumerative grammars with constraints still generate sets. The only function of the constraints is to exclude certain elements from the generated set. But a unique set is still exactly defined, and is taken to be the entire language.

Representing gradient ungrammaticality

Generative–enumerative grammars without constraints (henceforth, *pure* generative–enumerative grammars) represent all the grammatical expressions of a language and none of the ungrammatical ones. In this section we argue that generative–enumerative grammars with constraints, in addition to having descriptive advantages we have already noted, have another virtue. They can also describe the syntactic structure of natural-language expressions that are less than fully grammatical. This is something any descriptively adequate grammar for a natural language must do, yet no pure generative–enumerative grammar (without constraints) can do it.

An expression is represented as grammatical given a generative–enumerative grammar if and only if, starting with the root node label ["S" in the case of (2)] that expression can be derived using the rules of the grammar. If a word sequence is fully grammatical, the grammar defines at least one derivation for it (or defines at least one tree for it as well-formed), but otherwise it does not. Consequently, the structure of an expression exhibiting a single intuitively minor syntactic solecism is not distinguished from complete gibberish. No pure generative–enumerative grammar can represent any structure for a word sequence that has no derivation.

The point is not about whether ordinary speakers apply the concepts of grammaticality and ungrammaticality rather vaguely, or about whether they mistakenly say things that they do not themselves regard as grammatical. The issue is what syntactic structure different types of grammars can and cannot describe. Intuitively, the point is that (at least some) ungrammatical expressions have a certain amount of grammatical structure, and an adequate grammar should be able to describe it. For example, **I am wanting to use please your telephone* is not fully grammatical in English, but it surely should be described by a grammar for English as being a close approximation: It has *I* as the subject of the main clause, *am* correctly agreeing with the subject, *want* in the progressive form, the adverb *please* between the verb *use* and its object noun phrase, and so on. A pure generative–enumerative grammar of English would not describe these facts, because it would not say anything about the word sequence **I am wanting to use please your telephone* at all.

It is not controversial that ungrammaticality is gradient rather than absolute. Syntacticians frequently cite facts about degrees of ungrammaticality, and use them as evidence for or against certain grammars (see Schütze, 1996, pp. 41–48 for discussion). On the uncontroversial assumption that an adequate grammar must at least be able to represent the evidence that supports it, no pure generative–enumerative grammar is adequate. This has been recognized before. Chomsky (1961) directly responds to the point, proposing a solution that depends on a classification of all the word sequences *not* generated by a pure generative–enumerative grammar, corresponding to three degrees of ungrammaticality. The idea is that the ungrammaticality of a word sequence not in the set defined by the grammar is proportional to its degree of similarity to expressions in the set created by the grammar. We can illustrate with three simple examples:

(10) a. ?Chess plays Sandy.
b. *Sandy elapses chess.
c. **Elapses chess amuses.

Example (10a) is only slightly odd; some linguists would say it is strange merely because of its obvious falsity. It consists of an inanimate noun, a transitive verb requiring an animate subject and an inanimate object, and an animate noun. We can match this in a fully acceptable sentence like *Sandy plays chess* if we ignore just the mentions of animacy, which are only semantically relevant in English. The ungrammaticality of (10b) is more salient. It consists of an animate noun, an intransitive verb requiring an inanimate subject, and an inanimate noun. We can find a match for this sequence in expressions like *Sandy dislikes chess*, but only if we overlook both animacy and the significant syntactic property of transitivity (*elapse* is strictly intransitive, and should not be followed by an object). And finally (10c) is more ungrammatical still: It consists of an intransitive verb requiring an inanimate subject, an inanimate noun, and a transitive verb. This does not match even the gross lexical category sequence of any grammatical English expression at all. It is these three situations that Chomsky uses to define his three degrees of grammatical deviance.

Far from remedying the failure of pure generative–enumerative grammars to describe the structure of less-than-fully-grammatical expressions, this proposal only emphasizes that failure. First, partially grammatical expressions are not described by the grammar of the language; they are word sequences that do not belong to the language (but have certain defined degrees of similarity to sequences that do.) Second, the grammar plays no role at all in describing the degree of ungrammaticality of the three classes of ungrammatical word sequences. The definitions of the three degrees of ungrammaticality are given quite independently of any grammar, by means of quantification over the entire set of lexical category sequences that occur in derivations of expressions defined by the grammar, and comparison of them with lexical category sequences that correspond to ungrammatical word sequences. It is not even formally decidable, given an arbitrary TG grammar, whether a lexical category sequence of the relevant form occurs in some derivation in the language. Third, nothing in the proposal describes a word sequence as having a higher degree of ungrammaticality if it contains more than one configuration that violates the principles of grammar for the language: **The quick brown fox jumped over the lazy went* intuitively has just one problem (*went* is not a noun), while **Went lazy the over jumped fox brown quick the* is complete gibberish, yet Chomsky's proposal would evaluate them as having the same degree of ungrammaticality (all that can be said is that neither matches the lexical category sequence of any grammatical sentence).

The latter point is a special case of a more general problem. Chomsky's proposal entails that there are only three degrees of ungrammaticality. This is not true. To see this, consider the examples in (11).

(11)
a. Why am I charged a higher rate when my car is similar to yours?
b. *Why am I charged a higher rate when my car is similar from yours?
c. *Why is I charged a higher rate when my car is similar from yours?
d. *Why is I charged a higher rate when my car am similar from yours?
e. *Why is me charged a higher rate when my car am similar from yours?
f. *Why is me charged a higher rate when car my am similar from yours?
g. *Why is me charged a higher rate when car my am similar yours from?
.
.
.
z. *Me is why rate car a is charged similar higher yours when my am?

Example (11a) is a fully grammatical expression of English. In (11b) there is just one small departure from full grammaticality: The adjective *similar* in English takes a preposition phrase complement with *to*, not with *from*. Example (11c) shares this property, but in addition the first verb does not agree with its subject (**is I* instead of *am I*), and (11d) has not just one but two verbs not agreeing (**my car am* instead of *my car is*). All of the foregoing also holds in (11e), but in addition it has the accusative pronoun *me* where the nominative *I* is required. In (11f) we find all the previously mentioned properties but in addition *my* follows *car* instead of preceding it. And (11g) additionally has the preposition *from* following its complement noun phrase *yours* (English requires that prepositions precede their complements).

Notice that although each example departs just a bit further from full grammaticality than the previous one, (11g) is drastically worse than (11a).

And of course this series could be extended: among the more than 87 billion orders in which these 14 words can be arranged there are many that are utterly incomprehensible arbitrary words sequences like (11z).

These facts cannot be described under Chomsky's (1961) proposal. Much the same can be said of the other proposals that were advanced around the same time (there is a substantial literature in linguistics and psychology; see in particular chaps. 13–14 of Fodor & Katz, 1964; Chomsky, 1965, p. 148ff; Fillmore, 1972, p. 7ff; Schütze, 1996, chap. 3). We want to point out that a partial solution is available in virtue of a hitherto unrecognized property of grammars with constraints.

To see how generative–enumerative grammars with constraints can represent degrees of ungrammaticality in a way that pure generative–enumerative grammars cannot, consider a grammar with a set generating component and also a number of independent constraints, each stating a condition that expressions are required to satisfy in order to be fully grammatical. An arbitrary word sequence (or tree, or tree sequence) might satisfy all of the constraints, or it might violate one of them, or violate two of them, or violate any larger number up to the point of violating all of them. Degree of ungrammaticality can be correlated with number of constraints violated.

Suppose, to make this specific, that all of the following elements of English grammar were described using constraints: (a) grammatical determination of preposition choices, (b) verb agreement, (c) case of pronouns, and (d) order of phrases within a containing phrase. Then (11b) could be represented by a tree just like the one for (11a) except that it violates one constraint at one point (the one requiring *to* with *similar*); (11c), with a similar tree, would violate two constraints (there is also a verb that does not agree with its subject); (11d) would have three violations (one preposition choice and two failures of subject-verb agreement); (11e) would have four (it also violates the requirement for nominative case on subject pronouns); (11f) would have five (there is in addition a word order violation, a genitive pronoun after the head noun instead of before it); and (11g) would have six (all the foregoing plus a violation of the constraint placing prepositions first in the preposition phrase).

In other words, if key syntactic structures of the language are described by means of constraints, rather than by means of the generative–enumerative apparatus (phrase structure rules, transformations, and the like), we immediately obtain a description of gradient ungrammatically. We get this simply by adopting an over-generating grammar plus a sufficiently rich set of constraints. The description of the structure of the language relies on the idea that the more constraints an expression violates, the less grammatical it is.

Of course, the description of ungrammaticality could be modified and refined in many ways. For instance, some constraints could be assigned a higher weighting so that violating them counted for more than violating others. There might in principle be an elaborate or even total ranking defined on grammatical statements (see Keller [1998] for an interesting study based on this idea). But the point is that although a pure generative–enumerative grammar offers no promising approach at all to the description of degrees of ungrammaticality, a generative–enumerative grammar with constraints offers a very promising basis for research.

Notice that, importantly, the degree of gradience describable by generative–enumerative grammars with constraints is directly proportional to the amount of structure described by the constraints. As the constraints describe more and more of the structure of the language, finer degrees of ungrammaticality are described. The role of the set–generating part of the grammar is concomitantly attenuated. In this kind of grammar the constraints are applied to candidates, and if the structure of an ungrammatical expression is to be represented, the relevant candidate must be generated. The limiting case is a grammar with a set generating part that generates every possible candidate—for example, the set of all finite word sequences (or trees, or tree sequences) over a certain vocabulary. The function of the set generating part of the grammar then would be simply to ensure that there was a well-defined set of candidates from which the constraints would select a well-defined set of expression representations to constitute the language defined.

Generative–enumerative grammars with constraints therefore have a distinct descriptive advantage over pure generative–enumerative grammars, but they still create and exactly delimit the membership of sets of expression representations. In the next section we argue that this is a key failing.

LOGICAL PROBLEMS OF LANGUAGE ACQUISITION

Natural languages are learned, and grammars that represent their structure must be in principle compatible with their being learned. This is not to say that a grammar of a natural language is supposed to carry with it a precise psychological theory of *how* a speaker learns a language. A minimal criterion of adequacy for any description of the structure of a natural language would be that the grammar representing that structure should be learnable. Certainly, grammars must not be incompatible with language learning. That is, linguists should not be describing languages with a type of grammar for which there is a proof that no method exists for grammar learning under plausible conditions.

Gold (1967) presented a mathematical investigation of the conditions under which set generating grammars may be learned. Of Gold's two main sets of results, the result that is usually thought most relevant to the learning of natural languages pertains to *learning from text* (Gold's term was "language identification in the limit from text"). The learner's experience is idealized as a *text* that is, a never-ending succession of expressions (in arbitrary order, perhaps with repetitions) that ultimately exhausts the target language. Notice that this idealization strongly favors success: No specific time limit is assumed, and any expression that is in the language will eventually be presented, with no speech errors or mishearings. The real world does not offer such favorable conditions, of course. Actual learning is temporally limited, perhaps to just a few years, and there is no guarantee that any particular expression of the language will ever be heard. So Gold's idealizations are biased in favor of learning, not against it.

The procedure the learner is assumed to use, as idealized, is tantamount to iterated conjectures and refutations. With each new expression encountered, the learner "hypothesizes" a generative–enumerative grammar (consciously or unconsciously; mathematically it does not matter which). A new and previously unconsidered grammar is hypothesized if the most recently presented expression is not in the set created by the currently considered grammar. Otherwise the current hypothesis is retained.

Success is defined as eventually hypothesizing a grammar that exactly describes the target language, and retaining it permanently thereafter. A language is learned from text by a learning procedure if the procedure always succeeds in some finite amount of time, when presented with any text for the language. And a class of languages is *learnable from text* if there is a single, general learning procedure by which any language in the class can be learned from any text for that language.

The theorem of Gold's that is most often cited concerns learning classes of languages that have the property of being *superfinite*, which means classes containing all the finite languages, and at least one infinite language, over some fixed finite vocabulary. The theorem is stated in (12).

(12) If a class of languages is superfinite, it is not learnable from text.

We omit the proof, but the intuition behind it can be straightforwardly sketched. Consider two imaginary learners, Cautious Connie and Bold Bonnie, each trying to learn from text some language belonging to a superfinite class. Cautious Connie is highly conservative. She always succumbs to the temptation of continuing to hypothesize grammars for larger and larger finite languages, just to be safe. If the target language is actually infinite, she will never succeed. Bold Bonnie, on the other hand, is a risk-taker. She will sometimes hypothesize an infinite language—an infinite proper superset of the set of all expressions observed so far. If the target language is actually finite, no examples can reveal her error, so she will never succeed. Neither boldness nor caution, nor any combination thereof, leads invariably to success on any superfinite class of languages.

Unfortunately, every generative–enumerative type of grammar allows for the possibility of the natural languages being a superfinite class. Consider again the grammar we presented in (2). If rule (2d) were removed or altered to prevent S from being reintroduced arbitrarily many times in a derivation that starts from S, the grammar in (2) would generate a finite language. Any finite language could be generated by a simple phrase structure grammar. Yet if we have a rule like (2d), the language defined is an infinite set. So even very simple types of grammar define superfinite classes of languages. And adding devices like transformations to create more complex and expressive grammars does not change this.

It therefore follows, given the Gold theorems, that the class of languages defined by a class of generative–enumerative grammars will not be learnable from text, which amounts to saying that the languages generated by such grammars simply cannot be learned from experience. This has been taken to a powerful a priori version of what has been called the *argument from poverty of the stimulus* (Pullum & Scholz, [2002], Scholz & Pullum, [2002]). If the conditions of the Gold theorems are satisfied, then learners cannot learn a language from experience alone. Yet infants do learn. Some linguists therefore conclude that human infants must rely on some additional assistance, such as innate information concerning the character of the languages to be learned or the grammars to be hypothesized (see Neil Smith, chap. 4, in this volume).

The Gold theorems are so general that they can be applied to learning in nonlinguistic domains. The results can be applied not only to language learners inducing grammars from utterance sequences, but also to (for instance) scientists inducing theories from experimental result sequences. Indeed, learners are called "scientists" throughout the presentation of Gold-style learning theory in Jain, Osherson, Royer, and Sharma (1999). Gold is widely understood to have formalized "empiricist" learning, because learning is represented as being from experience only, and the learning procedures considered utilize innate language-specialized information that is the hallmark of linguistic nativist theories.

But many linguists, psychologists, and philosophers have failed to understand the scope and robustness of the results. For example, Demopoulos (1989, p. 81) commented that "for all the theorem on unlearnability from text data shows, it would suffice if the learning function considered only infinite cardinality languages as candidate natural languages." But this is true only if narrowly applied to the theorem we stated as (12). It does not actually point to a way out, because there are classes of infinite languages that are unlearnable from text; theorem (12) is only an expositorily useful special case. (For an exact characterization of the classes of languages that are learnable from text, see Angluin, [1988]).

A slightly different misunderstanding was implied when Fiona Cowie wrote, in similar terms: "for all Gold has shown, general-purpose constraints such as 'Prefer more general hypotheses,' or 'Make a tentative universal generalization that all Fs are Gs if you've encountered *n* instances of Fs that are Gs' would do the trick to ensure the learnability of natural languages" (Cowie, 1999, p. 195). This too is false. Gold actually established that no general hypothesis selection strategy can reliably facilitate learning. Every strategy turns out in some situations to prevent learning rather than assist it.

To see this, compare the task of learning Little-English, as defined in the second section, with the task of learning the language consisting of just those Little-English sentences that have a prime number of words. There is no question that the latter language is vastly more difficult. (It is provably impossible to describe with a simple phrase structure grammar, although other classes of grammar can describe it.) Given a class of grammars that includes a grammar for each of these two languages, a preference for generality will *preclude* success, because when the prime-length subset of Little-English is the target language a grammar for little English will be incorrectly hypothesized instead (because it will be simpler, and compatible with the same data). No data from the prime-length subset language can ever refute that hypothesis. A preference for simplicity and generality will cause a learner to fall prey to Bold Bonnie's problem.

Most of the discussion of whether the Gold theorems are relevant to natural language learning have centered on whether actual language learners really learn a grammar purely from text—from nothing more than hearing expressions that belong to the target language. Gold studied a condition for language learning that differs from learning from text in that the learner is systematically supplied with information about what is *not* in the language as well as what is (or more technically, the learner is supplied with a text for the complement of the language as well as a text for the language). This is called *learning from an informant*. A vast range of interesting classes of languages that are not learnable from a text are learnable from an informant. So language acquisition researchers have been very interested in the question of whether or not human infants take in and utilize information about ungrammatical expressions, which is generally called *negative evidence*. The large literature on negative evidence (usefully surveyed by Cowie, 1999, §9.5, pp. 222–237) does not offer a conclusive result. At the very least, we certainly cannot assume that every child who learns a language receives systematic and comprehensive information about the expressions the target does not contain.

An idea that has occurred to a number of people is that the force of theorem (12) might be evaded, without rejecting the assumption of text learning, if learners actually *inferred* negative evidence from their experience, using information about what structures they have not encountered so far. For example, suppose a learner noted (perhaps subliminally) that although expressions like those in (13) were encountered with comparable frequencies, those in (14) were not; expressions like (14a) were heard but expressions like (14b) never were.

(13) a. After dinner I'll read a story to you.
b. After dinner I'll read you a story.

(14) a. After dinner I'll explain a puzzle to you.
b. *After dinner I'll explain you a puzzle.

Expressions like (13a) and (13b) exemplify the use of *read*, and expressions like (14a) exemplify the use of *explain*. The problem is that no examples of what is grammatical can directly provide the learner with the crucial information that (14b) is not in the set of English expressions—or more generally, that *explain* never takes two object noun phrases in any English expression. To say that this negative evidence might be inferred is to suggest that, putting it intuitively, a learner might (subconsciously) notice that expressions like (14b) are not encountered, and draw inferences from that. The gap in the pattern of experience could serve as circumstantial evidence for the ungrammaticality of the type of expression that would fill it. Systematic use of such inferences could yield a goldmine of information about what is not grammatical in the language.

At this point we have to carefully separate the real learning situations from the idealized learning situations that Gold explored. It would be possible to use the statistical properties of children's actual linguistic experiences as the basis for statistical inference procedures, exploiting the vast database of probabilities of occurrence for expression types in the kind of discourse that children hear. The research program of statistical learning theory that follows this line is not discussed here (see Charniak, 1993, for an elementary introduction to some of the statistical language learning literature, and Haussler, 1996, for a much more technical survey of the field). Suffice it to say that statistical approaches to learning are achieving major successes under the assumption that children learn entirely from experience. But there are no frequencies of occurrence in Gold's paradigm. His resolutely nonstatistical formulation poses greater difficulties for the idea that children learn solely from experience. Under the conditions Gold defines, procedures that rely on inferring negative evidence from positive data simply fail.

The reason they fail is that negative evidence is vastly too abundant. Consider a learner who has never heard the words *pterodactyl* and *teaspoon* in the same clause, and concludes from this absence that these words cannot occur together in English clauses. In any text there will be indefinitely many such accidental absences of evidence. A learner using this procedure will be seduced into pursuing infinite sequences of incorrect hypotheses, and this will preclude success.

Given some kinds of possible linguistic experience, a learner who forms hypotheses about what is not in the language from gaps in her experience will be led into an endless sequence of wrong guesses. For example, if she has heard examples like (13a) but, purely by accident, has not heard any like (13b), this strategy will lead her to conclude (incorrectly) that expressions like (13b) are not in the target language. When she subsequently hears something like (13b), this hypothesis will have to be abandoned. But some other accidental absence may suggest a new incorrect negative inference. And so on and so on, through a potentially never-ending sequence of wrong guesses, which is incompatible with success under to Gold's definitions.

Far from facilitating learning, then, inference from absence of evidence to evidence of absence can actually *prevent* language learning. The learner who draws inferences from telltale gaps in her experience will be prey to Cautious Connie's problem.

Cowie (1999, p. 224) mentioned "a second, more interesting, way in which nonoccurrence can serve as negative evidence." There is good reason, she observed, for adopting a procedure that disregards the nonoccurrence of (15a) as negative evidence, but treating the nonoccurrence of (15b) as evidence of absence from the language.

(15) a. Steve enjoyed the curry
b. *Enjoyed curry Steve the.

What is different about (15a) is that "strings of that kind" occur in English: (15a) has the same structure as a large class of expressions like *Mom fixed the bike*, *Bob cooked the burgers*, *Pete took my pencil*, *You deserve a break*, etc., which as a very rough approximation is a token of the lexical category sequence in (16a). The same is not true of (15b); it is a token of the lexical category sequence (16b), which is not the lexical category sequence of any English sentence at all.

(16) a. N V_t Det N
b. V_t N N Det

Thus the failure to experience (15b) is evidence of the absence of expressions with that lexical category sequence in English, whereas the failure to experience (16a) is not evidence that English has no expressions with that lexical category sequence.

But this suggestion fails too, because Gold's theorems also hold for the language of expressions using the lexical category vocabulary (N, V_t, Det,...). Gold proved that *no* superfinite class of languages is learnable from text. It makes no difference whether the vocabulary is the one in (17a) or the one in (17b).

(17) a. {a, bike, Bob, break, burgers, cooked, curry, deserve, enjoyed, fixed, mom, my, pencil, Pete, pterodactyl, Steve, the, teaspoon, took, you,...}
b. {Det, N, V_c, V_t,...}

In order for Cowie's procedure to succeed, the learner must infer that (15b) does not occur in English on the basis of the absence of expressions with the lexical category sequence (16b). Thus the learner must already know the syntax of English over the vocabulary of (17b). But this assumes what was to be accounted for.

Hopes of assistance from negative evidence extracted from positive data are misplaced. Gold's result is too robust for this enticing defense of learning from experience to succeed. We are left with a mathematical demonstration that learning a generative–enumerative grammar purely from experience is literally impossible. Given that children do learn languages, it is perhaps not surprising that some (see Matthews, 1984) have taken the Gold theorems as the basis of an a priori argument for linguistic nativism—the view that language learning requires both innate linguistic information and specialized cognitive structures specific to linguistic information processing. This is a view that some linguists have enthusiastically endorsed (see Neil Smith's contribution to this volume, chap. 4, for one example). But expecting it to offer an escape from the consequences of Gold's work represents just one more misunderstanding.

Gold was talking about whether certain classes of *languages* are learnable—his term is "identifiable"—in the limit. Languages are represented as sets of expressions. The question is whether access to an unending and ultimately exhaustive sequence of presentations of expressions suffices to permit some algorithmic procedure to guess which language from a given class is the source of the expressions. Now, the notion of an algorithm is a very broad one. An algorithm is a finitely statable exact instruction (or sequences of instructions) for performing some computation. The usual theoretical model for algorithms is the Turing machine, and any Turing machine can incorporate a finite database of arbitrary complexity as part of the basis for its computations. Specifically, any body of universal truths about grammar could be stored in the program of a Turing machine to guide its operations. So imagine we have a full, true, and complete description of universal grammar, embodying what all grammars for natural languages share, and it is built into a Turing machine that aims to identify languages in the limit from text. Learning under Gold's idealizations is still impossible if the class of languages has a structure that makes it unlearnable. Any superfinite class of languages, for example, remains unlearnable whether a database of universal grammatical truths is appealed to or not. A result about algorithms for text-based identification of grammars from some class cannot be vitiated by describing what those grammars have in common.

In the final section of this chapter we point out that there remains another possibility: abandoning the assumption that success in learning a language consists in identifying a generative–enumerative grammar that exactly generates it.

MODEL-THEORETIC GRAMMARS AND THEIR IMPLICATIONS

Natural languages are not necessarily sets. They are represented as such by generative–enumerative grammars, but explicit descriptions of the syntactic structure of natural language expressions need not define a set of expressions. Instead of *generating* a set of syntactic structures, a grammar can describe the syntactic structure shared by expressions. The structure can be represented in idealized form by trees, tree sequences, or other appropriate sorts of structural representation, but the grammar does not have to generate them: the trees are representations of structure that expressions actually have. The grammar describes what is true of trees (or other representations) with that structure.

In model theory, which is the branch of logic that is concerned with relating invented logical languages to their interpretations, a structure of which some statement is true is said to be a *model* of it. The grammars we are considering in this section, which we will call *model-theoretic grammars*, consist of sets of statements (referred to as *constraints*) for which individual expressions are the models. Perhaps the easiest way to understand what model-theoretic grammars are like is simply to recall the generative–enumerative grammars with constraints that we discussed earlier, and consider the effect of simply eliminating the *set–generating part altogether.*

This is not a novel idea, but it is decidedly under-explored. An early precursor can be found in Lakoff (1971), which proposed what is in effect a constraint grammar that reformulates of some of the content of TG descriptions using tree sequences as models. It was much more fully developed in Johnson and Postal (1980), where the models for the constraints were not trees or tree sequences but "pair networks", which are rather complex configurations representing grammatical relations. The explicitly model-theoretic stance of Johnson and Postal inspired some recent work reviving this approach to use the term "model-theoretic syntax" (Blackburn & Meyer-Viol, 1997; Rogers, 1997, p. 722n). Rogers (1997) restated many of the key points of GPSG in constraint-grammar terms, and Rogers (1998) did the same for much of the content of TG grammars in the style of Chomsky (1981). And recent expositions of HPSG are framed as constraint grammars (see Sag & Wasow, 1999, chap. 16, for a clear and useful introduction).

There are probably other examples of recent syntax that should be included under the heading of constraint grammars. The "construction grammar" of Charles J. Fillmore and Paul Kay is one example. The informal exposition in Kay and Fillmore (1999) nowhere suggests that grammars are devices generating a set of expressions. All descriptive devices are couched as statements. The "subset principle", for instance, says: "Set values of a head daughter are subsets of corresponding values of its mother." The models for this statements and the other constraints they give are objects called "attribute-value matrices" or AVMs (equivalent to trees with complex node labels as described in the third section). The subset principle states a condition that an AVM may either satisfy or not satisfy, but it is not part of a system for generating a specific infinite set of AVMs.

However, in none of the literature just cited is it noted that constraint grammars remove the role of set generation from descriptions of the syntactic structure of natural languages altogether. A constraint grammar does not, in and of itself, generate a unique set containing all and only the expressions that conform to the constraints. In fact, there is a sense in which, given an appropriate language for the statement of constraints, a constraint grammar *cannot* address language size issues. Suppose, for concreteness, we take expression structures to be represented as trees, and we describe expression structure with a constraint grammar that states certain necessary conditions on trees—properties that a tree must have if it is to represent a well-formed expression according to the grammar. This kind of grammar needs to be framed in terms that refer to nodes, their properties, and the relations that hold between them. For example, the constraints for English would have to include (or entail) statements like those informally paraphrased as follows. (N.B.: A *daughter* of a node is another node further from the root and connected to it by a single branch.)

(18)
a. The root node is labeled "S"
b. Every S-node has exactly one VP-node daughter.
c. A lexical category node precedes a phrasal category node if they are both daughters of the same node.

But it is not possible to use statements about nodes and their relations to state that there are at most 37 trees, or that for any natural number n there are more than n trees. Statements about language size are not about nodes and their properties and relations at all, but about trees as wholes. If constraints are stated in a language that has trees as models, the constraints do not, in and of themselves, define a set having all and only the expressions in the natural language as members. Their statements are about nodes and their properties and relations, and statements about relations between nodes in a tree do not imply anything about how many trees there are.

The idea that natural languages are sets is very deeply entrenched, because linguists have thought of natural languages as sets of expressions for half a century, ever since Chomsky began using Post's production systems to describe natural languages. But model-theoretic grammars do not entail any such identification. They state *necessary* conditions on the structure of expressions, but not *sufficient* conditions for set membership. In contrast, generative–enumerative grammars like the one we exhibited in (2) state both necessary and sufficient conditions for set membership. All the strings or trees generated as the result of some derivation are in the language, and nothing else is.

Adopting model-theoretic grammars does not mean denying the mathematical existence of any set, of course. Arbitrary sets of trees (or other models) can be defined as necessary. Given a set of constraints for English, one could use the resources of logic and set theory to define the set of all constraint-satisfying finite trees over a certain vocabulary, or the set of all constraint-satisfying tree-like objects whether finite or not, or the set of all constraint-satisfying trees that belong to some very large finite set (like the set of all trees with less than a million nodes, or the set of all trees representing expressions that have been printed in the *New York Times*). The point is not that such sets do not exist, but rather that the structure of English expressions can be described without taking any specific set to *be* English.

What *are* natural languages, then, if they are not sets of expressions? They are ways or styles of structuring expressions. English is a style of structuring expressions. The English way of structuring expressions, to a large extent shared by all English speakers, should not be equated with the unique set containing all the expressions that are structured that way. Making such an equation would be like confusing a humorous style of writing with the set of all (possible or actual) amusing literary works, or confusing cubism with a certain set of (possible or actual) paintings.

This means that pure generative–enumerative grammars are inherently unsuited to capturing the ordinary notion of what natural languages are. They are not well suited to the scientific study of natural language either. One reason was noted earlier: Pure generative–enumerative grammars offer no account of expressions with partially well-formed syntactic structure. We also pointed out there that the addition of constraints to generative–enumerative grammars suggests a remedy—though in a way that vitiates the point of the set-generating mechanisms. Greater or lesser degrees of ungrammaticality can be correlated with violations of larger or smaller numbers of constraints. The range of degrees of ungrammaticality that can be described is in inverse proportion to the descriptive work done by the set–generating component of the grammar.

Maximal flexibility for describing gradient ungrammaticality is attained with model-theoretic grammars. Model-theoretic grammars make no distinction between candidate structures, which are generated by the set-generating component and potentially grammatical, and structures that are entirely undescribed (not generated, hence not even candidates). Instead, every structure either satisfies or fails to satisfy a larger or smaller number of the constraints. The notion "in the English manner" that is reconstructed by a model–theoretic grammar of English is a fully gradient concept, just as data like (11) suggest it should be. There are indefinitely many degrees of variation between utter gibberish and perfect Englishness, and constraint grammars automatically describe that variation.

But the most dramatic consequence of this shift of view about what grammars are (or rather what they are not) is that it dissolves the puzzle of the Gold theorems for linguistics. The proofs of the Gold theorems depend entirely on languages being sets with definite cardinalities. If languages are not sets, then neither sets nor the grammars that generate them have to be identified by the learner. Learning will instead be a matter of learning what syntactic properties expressions have, based on the structure of individual expressions actually encountered, thus rendering as-yet unencountered expressions syntactically analyzable just in case they are models of at least some of the constraints developed so far. But there is no reason to envisage the learner having to decide on which unique *set* of expressions is the language as a whole. This is tantamount to requiring the learner to make tacit decisions about the correct answers to questions like "From which set are all the expressions so far presented being drawn?" or "How many expressions are there in the unique set from which these examples are all taken?" But there is no reason to think that the ability to answer questions like this has anything to do with knowledge of the structure of the expressions of a language.

Chomsky (1959) remarked over four decades ago in his review of B. F. Skinner's *Verbal Behavior* that "there is little point in speculating about the process of acquisition without much better understanding of what is acquired," and he was surely right. The plausibility of claims about what is learnable or unlearnable will change as linguists and psychologists discover more about what the learner must ultimately acquire. The Gold theorems are irrelevant to language learning under the claim that what has to be acquired by the learner is not a generative–enumerative grammar but a collection of constraints.

A new research program is now being developed, one that takes learning to be an incremental process of incrementally acquiring a set of constraints on expression structure from evidence provided by exposure to expressions in context. The viability of this program will be determined by future research. Whether it will vindicate nativism or reconfirm empiricism is an entirely open question. But there is a difference between this new program and the old one (the one that assumes the learner identifies a set of expressions by discovering a grammar that exactly generates it): The new program does not start out burdened by a mathematical demonstration of its impossibility.

CONCLUSION

The negative point made in this chapter is that linguists have been modeling natural languages wrongly. The grammars they have devised describe sets of expressions rather than expressions, and in consequence have two very serious but unacknowledged problems: They do not describe gradient ungrammaticality, and they engender (under one set of assumptions) a paradox about learnability.

The positive point we have more briefly made is that there is a different type of grammar available, model-theoretic grammar, which offers solutions to both of these problems. Moreover, there is an intermediate step that eases the transition, because model-theoretic grammars can be understood, to a first approximation, by taking generative–enumerative grammars with constraints and jettisoning the set-generating component. We believe that greater insight into the character of natural languages results from adopting model–theoretic grammars, with their emphasis on modeling not entire sets of expressions but the structure of individual expressions. The enhanced understanding extends not only to the areas we have specifically mentioned here—gradient ungrammaticality and learnability from text—but to other areas, such as the correspondence between what scientific linguistics studies and the commonsense idea of a language, two things that have hitherto been very much at odds.

REFERENCES

Adjukiewicz, K. (1935). Die syntaktische Konnexität. *Studia Philosophica, 1,* 1–27. [Reprinted in translation in S. McCall (Ed.). (1967). *Polish logic 1920–1939.* Oxford: Oxford University Press.]

Angluin, D. (1988). Inductive inference of formal languages from positive data. *Information & Control, 45,* 117–135.

Blackburn, P., & Meyer-Viol, W. (1997). Modal logic and model-theoretic syntax. In M. de Rijke (Ed.), *Advances in intensional logic*. Dordrecht: Kluwer Academic.

Charniak, E. (1993). *Statistical language learning*. Cambridge, MA: MIT Press.

Chomsky, N. (1957). *Syntactic Structures.* The Hague: Mouton.

Chomsky, N. (1959). Review of B. F. Skinner, *Verbal behavior. Language, 35,* 26–58.

Chomsky, N. (1961). Some methodological remarks on generative grammar. *Word, 17,* 219–239. [Section 5 reprinted as "Degrees of grammaticalness" in Fodor & Katz, 1964, pp. 384–389.]

Chomsky, N. (1965). *Aspects of the theory of syntax*. Cambridge, MA: MIT Press.

Chomsky, N. (1981). *Lectures on Government and Binding.* Dordrecht: Foris.

Chomsky, N. (1995). *The minimalist program.* Cambridge, MA: MIT Press.

Chomsky, N., & Lasnik, H. (1977). Filters and control. *Linguistic Inquiry, 8,* 425–504.

Cowie, F. (1999). *What's within? Nativism reconsidered.* New York: Oxford University Press.

Demopoulos, W. (1989). On applying learnability theory to the rationalism-empiricism controversy. In R. J. Matthews & W. Demopoulos (Eds.), *Learnability and linguistic theory.* (pp. 77–88). Dordrecht, The Netherlands: Kluwer.

Fillmore, C. W. (1972). On generativity. In P. S. Peters (Ed.), *Goals of linguistic theory* (pp. 1–19). Englewood Cliffs, NJ: Prentice Hall.

Fodor, J. A., & Katz J. J. (Eds.). (1964). *The structure of language: Readings in the philosophy of language.* Englewood Cliffs, NJ: Prentice Hall.

Gazdar, G., Klein, E., Pullum, G. K., & Sag, I. A. (1985). *Generalized phrase structure grammar.* Cambridge, MA: Harvard University Press.

Gazdar, G., Pullum, G., Carpenter, R., Klein, E., Hukari, T. E., & Levine, R. D. (1988). Category structures. *Computational Linguistics, 14,* 1–19.

Gold, E. M. (1967). Language identification in the limit. *Information and Control, 10,* 447–474.

Haussler, D. (1996). Probably approximately correct learning and decision-theoretic generalizations. In P. Smolensky, M. C. Mozer, & D. E. Rumelhart (Eds.), *Mathematical perspectives on neural networks* (pp. 651–718). Mahwah, NJ: Lawrence Erlbaum Associates.

Jain, S., Osherson, D., Royer, J. S., & Sharma, A. (1999). *Systems that learn: An introduction to learning theory* (2nd ed.). Cambridge, MA: MIT Press.

Johnson, D. E., & Postal, P. M. (1980). *Arc pair grammar.* Princeton, NJ: Princeton University Press.

Joshi, A. (1987). An introduction to tree adjoining grammars. In A. Manaster-Ramer (Ed.), *Mathematics of language.* (pp. 87–114). Amsterdam: John Benjamins.

Kay, P., & Fillmore, C. W. (1999). Grammatical constructions and linguistic generalizations: The *What's X doing Y?* construction. *Language, 75,* 1–33.

Keenan, E. L., & Stabler, E. (1996). Abstract syntax. In A.-M. DiSciullo (Ed.), *Configurations: Essays on structure and interpretation* (pp. 329–344). Somerville, MA: Cascadilla Press.

Keller, F. (1998). Gradient grammaticality as an effect of selective constraint re-ranking. In M. C. Gruber, D. Higgins, K. S. Olson, & T. Wysocki (Eds.), *Papers from the 34th meeting of the Chicago Linguistic Society, Vol. 2: The panels* (pp. 95–109). Chicago: Chicago Linguistic Society.

Lakoff, G. (1971). On generative semantics. In D. Steinberg & L. Jakobovits (Eds.), *Semantics: An interdisciplinary reader in philosophy, linguistics and psychology* (pp. 232–296). Cambridge: Cambridge University Press.

Langacker, R. W. (1969). On pronominalization and the chain of command. In D. A. Reibel & S. A. Schane (Eds.), *Modern Studies in English,* 160–186. Englewood Cliffs, NJ: Prentice Hall.

Lasnik H. (2000). Syntactic Structures *revisited.* Cambridge, MA: MIT Press.

Matthews, R. J. (1984). The plausibility of rationalism. *Journal of Philosophy, 81,* 492–515.

Montague, R. (1974). *Formal philosophy.* Ed. R. Thomason. New Haven, CT: Yale University Press.

Perlmutter, D. M. (1971). *Deep and surface structure constraints in syntax.* New York: Holt Rinehart & Winston.

Peters, P. S. (Ed.). (1972). *Goals of linguistic theory.* Englewood Cliffs, NJ: Prentice Hall.

Postal, P. M. (1972). The best theory. In P. S. Peters (Ed.), *Goals of linguistic theory* (pp. 131–70). Englewood Cliffs, NJ: Prentice Hall.

Pullum, Geoffrey K., & Scholz, B. C. (2002). Empirical assessment of stimulus poverty arguments. *The Linguistic Review, 19*, 9–50.

Rogers, J. (1997). "Grammarless" phrase structure grammar. *Linguistics and Philosophy, 20*, 721–746.

Rogers, J. (1998). *A descriptive approach to language-theoretic complexity.* Stanford, CA: CSLI.

Scholz, B. C., & Pullum, G. K. (2002). Searching for arguments to support linguistic nativism. *The Linguistic Review, 19*, 185–223.

Schütze, C. (1996). *The empirical base of linguistics.* Chicago: University of Chicago Press.

Seuren, Pieter A. M. (1998). *Western linguistics: An historical introduction.* Oxford: Basil Blackwell.

Steedman, M. (1999). Categorial grammar. In R. A. Wilson & F. C. Keil (Eds.), *The MIT encyclopedia of the cognitive sciences.* (pp. 101–104). Cambridge, MA: MIT Press.

Valiant, L. (1984). A theory of the learnable. *Communications of the* ACM *27*, 1134–1142.

Vijay-Shanker, K. & Weir, D. J. (1994). The equivalence of four extensions of context-free grammars. *Mathematical Systems Theory, 27*, 511–546.

6

Connectionist Modeling of Language: Examples and Implications

David C. Plaut
Departments of Psychology and Computer Science
Carnegie Mellon University

Researchers interested in human cognitive processes have long used computer simulations to try to identify the principles of cognition. The strategy has been to build computational models that embody putative principles and then to examine how well such models capture human performance in cognitive tasks. Until the 1980s, this effort was undertaken within the context of the "computer metaphor" of mind. Researchers built computational models based on the conceptualization that the human mind operated as though it were a conventional digital computer. However, with the advent of so-called connectionist, neural network, or parallel distributed processing models (Anderson, Silverstein, Ritz, & Jones, 1977; Hinton & Anderson, 1981; McClelland & Rumelhart, 1981; McClelland, Rumelhart, & the PDP Research Group, 1986; Rumelhart, McClelland, & the PDP Research Group, 1986), researchers began exploring the implications of principles that are more broadly consistent with the style of computation employed by the brain.

In connectionist models, cognitive processes take the form of cooperative and competitive interactions among large numbers of simple, neuronlike processing units. Unit interactions are governed by weighted connections that encode the long-term knowledge of the system and are learned gradually through experience. The activity of some of the units encodes the input to the system; the resulting activity of other units encodes the system's response to that input. The patterns of activity of the remaining, so-called *hidden* units constitute learned, internal representations that mediate between inputs and outputs. Although each unit exhibits nonlinear spatial and temporal summation, units and connections are not generally considered to be in one-to-one correspondence with actual neurons and synapses. Rather, connectionist systems attempt to capture the essential computational properties of the vast ensembles of real neuronal elements found in the brain, through simulations of smaller networks of units. In this way, the approach is distinct from computational neuroscience (Sejnowski, Koch, & Churchland, 1989), which aims to model the detailed neurophysiology of relatively small groups of neurons. Although the connectionist approach uses physiological data to guide the search for underlying principles, it tends to focus more on overall system function or behavior, attempting to determine what principles of brain-style computation give rise to the cognitive phenomena observed in human behavior. The approach enables developmental, cognitive, and neurobiological issues to be addressed within a single, integrated formalism, providing new ways of thinking about how cognitive processes are implemented in the brain and how disorders of brain function lead to disorders of cognition.

The simplest structure for a connectionist network is a *feedforward* architecture, in which information flows unidirectionally from input units to output units, typically via one or more layers of hidden units. Although such networks can provide important insights into many cognitive domains, they are severely limited in their ability to learn and process information over time, and thus are relatively ill-suited for domains, such as language, that involve complex temporal structure (Elman, 1990). A more appropriate type of network for such domains is a *recurrent* architecture, with no a priori constraints on interactions among units. In one type of recurrent network, termed an *attractor* network, units interact in such a way that, in response to a fixed input, the network as a whole gradually settles to a stable pattern of activity representing the network's interpretation of the input (including any associated response). Recurrent networks can also learn to process sequences of inputs and/or to produce sequences of outputs. For example, in a *simple recurrent* network (Cleeremans, Servan-Schreiber, & McClelland, 1989; Elman, 1990, 1991), the internal representation generated by a given element of a sequence is made available as input to provide context for processing subsequent elements. Critically, the internal representations themselves adapt so as to provide and make effective use of this context information, enabling the system to learn to represent and retain relevant information across multiple time scales.

In fact, an issue of central relevance in the study of cognition in general, and language in particular, is the nature of the underlying representation of information. Some connectionist models use *localist* representations, in which individual units stand for familiar entities such as letters, words, concepts, and propositions (e.g., Dell, 1986; McClelland & Rumelhart, 1981). Others use *distributed* representations in which such entities are represented by alternative patterns of activity over large numbers of units rather than by the activity of a single unit (e.g., Hinton & Shallice, 1991; Seidenberg & McClelland, 1989). Although distributed representations are more difficult to think about, they offer a rich and powerful basis for understanding learning, generalization, and the flexibility and productivity of cognition (van Gelder, 1990).

The key to the effectiveness of distributed representations is the use of patterns whose similarity relations correspond to the similarities in the roles the patterns play in cognition, given that similar patterns tend to have similar consequences in connectionist models (see Hinton, McClelland, & Rumelhart, 1986, for discussion).[1] In very simple tasks, the similarities among the representations provided by the environment may be sufficient to guide behavior. However, in most cognitive domains, such as language, the functional relationships that must govern effective performance are often quite different from the similarities among surface forms. For example, the words CAT and CAP look and sound very similar but have entirely unrelated meanings. Consequently, the inputs to the system must be re-represented, perhaps via successive transformations across multiple intermediate layers of units, as new patterns of activity whose relative similarities abstract away from misleading surface similarity and, instead, capture the underlying structure of the domain. Traditional approaches to understanding cognition make very strong and specific assumptions about the structure of these internal representations and the processes that manipulate them. For example, it is often assumed that underlying linguistic knowledge takes the form of explicit rules that operate over discrete, symbolic representations (Chomsky, 1957; Chomsky & Halle, 1968; Fodor & Pylyshyn, 1988; Pinker, 1991) and, moreover, that this knowledge is, in large part, innately specified (Chomsky, 1965; Crain, 1991; Pinker, 1994).

In contrast, the connectionist approach places much greater emphasis on the ability of a system to *learn* effective internal representations. Learning in a connectionist network takes the form of modifying the values of weights on connections between units in response to feedback on the behavior of the network. Various specific learning procedures are employed in connectionist research; most that have been applied to cognitive domains, such as back-propagation (Rumelhart, Hinton, & Williams, 1986), take the form of error correction: Change each weight in a way that reduces the discrepancy between the correct response for a given input and the one actually generated by the system. In this process, internal representations over hidden units are learned by calculating how to change each unit's activation to reduce error and then modifying its incoming weights accordingly. Although it is unlikely that

[1]This property arises because the input to each unit is typically a weighted sum of the activations of units from which it receives connections. A similar pattern of activity over the sending units, summed across the same weights, will generally produce a similar input to the receiving unit and, hence, a similar activation. This bias toward giving similar responses to similar inputs can be overcome by having large weights on particular connections, but this takes time to develop and will happen only if it is required to perform the task.

the brain implements back-propagation in any direct sense (Crick, 1989), there are more biologically plausible procedures that are computationally equivalent (see, e.g., O'Reilly, 1996).

The emphasis on learning within the connectionist approach has fundamental implications for the nature of the explanations offered for cognitive behavior. Instead of attempting to stipulate the specific form and content of the knowledge required for performance in a domain, the approach instead stipulates the *tasks* the system must perform, including the nature of the relevant information in the environment, but then leaves it up to learning to develop the necessary internal representations and processes (McClelland, St. John, & Taraban, 1989). In some contexts, the resulting solution may bear a close relationship to more traditional mechanisms, but it is more often the case that learning develops representations and processes that are radically different from those proposed by traditional theories, and that generate novel hypotheses and testable predictions concerning human cognitive behavior.

Connectionist models have been applied to the full range of perceptual, cognitive, and motor domains (see McClelland et al., 1986; McLeod, Plunkett, & Rolls, 1998; Quinlan, 1991). It is, however, in their application to language that they have evoked the most interest and controversy (see, e.g., Pinker & Mehler, 1988). This is perhaps not surprising in light of the special role that language plays in human cognition and culture. It also stems in part from the considerable divergence of goals and methods between linguistic versus psychological approaches to the study of language. This rift goes deeper than a simple dichotomy of emphasizing competence versus performance (Chomsky, 1957); it cuts to the heart of the question of what it means to know and use a language (Seidenberg, 1997). From a connectionist perspective, performance is not an imperfect reflection of some abstract competence, but rather the behavioral manifestation of the internal representations and processes of actual language users: Language is as language does. The goal is not to abstract away from performance but to articulate computational principles that account for it.

A major attraction of the connectionist approach to language, apart from its natural relation to neural computation, is that the very same processing mechanisms apply across the full range of linguistic structure, including phonology, morphology, and syntax. The remainder of this chapter discusses three specific connectionist models, each applied to one of these levels. The first model (Plaut & Kello, 1999) is directed at central issues in phonological development, the second (Joanisse & Seidenberg, 1999) accounts for neuropsychological data in inflectional morphology, and the third (St. John & McClelland, 1990) addresses the integration of syntax and semantics in sentence comprehension. Beyond the use of common computational machinery, these models are all similar in that they learn internal representations that mediate between input and output surface forms and their underlying meanings. None of them provides a fully adequate account of the relevant phenomena in its domain. Nonetheless, they collectively illustrate both the breadth and depth of the approach. The concluding section highlights some of the limitations of current models and identifies important directions for future research.

PHONOLOGICAL DEVELOPMENT: PLAUT AND KELLO (1999)

Phonology is concerned with the sound structure of a language, and with how contrasts in meaning are conveyed by contrasts in the surface forms of words. The development of phonological representations plays a key role in the acquisition of both speech comprehension and production. In comprehension, time-varying acoustic input must be mapped onto a stable representation of the meaning of the utterance. This process poses a considerable challenge to the infant due to the considerable variability in the speech signal across talkers and contexts, and because, at the morphemic level, the relationship of spoken words to their meanings is largely arbitrary. In production, a meaning representation must generate appropriate time-varying articulatory output. Here, the infant must learn to produce comprehensible speech without any direct feedback or instruction from caretakers as to what articulatory movements are required to produce particular sound patterns. Moreover, although abilities in comprehension tend to precede those in production (for reviews see Jusczyk, 1997 and Vihman, 1996) these two processes must nonetheless converge on a mutually consistent solution to ensure that the infant comes to speak the same language(s) that he/she hears.

Plaut and Kello (1999) proposed a connectionist framework for phonological development in which phonology is a learned, internal representation that mediates among acoustic, articulatory, and semantic representations in the service of both comprehension and production. In support of the framework, Plaut and Kello developed an implementation in the form of a simple recurrent network, depicted in Fig. 6.1, that learned to understand and produce isolated spoken words in the absence of explicit articulatory feedback.

The framework instantiates two key assumptions. The first is that both comprehension and production are subserved by the same underlying phonological representations. These representations develop initially under the pressure of mapping acoustics to semantics in the course of learning to understand adult speech, but become increasingly refined by articulatory factors as skill in production develops. By sharing common underlying phonological representations, structure learned in the service of comprehension is available to guide production (see Vihman, 1996), and refinements driven by the demands of articulation automatically apply within comprehension (see Liberman, 1996).

The second key assumption is that feedback needed to guide the development of speech production is derived from the comprehension system—that is, from the acoustic, phonological, and semantic consequences of the system's

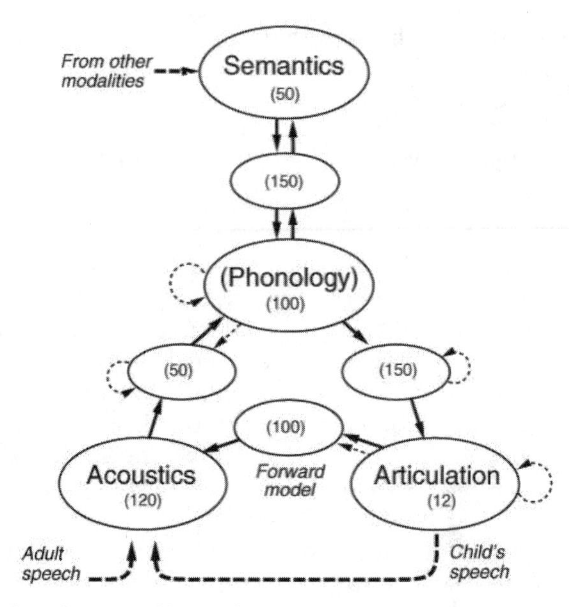

FIG. 6.1. The architecture of the simple recurrent network used by Plaut and Kello (1999). Solid arrows indicate standard projections of full connectivity between groups; dashed arrows indicate projections from "context" units whose states are copied from the previous time step. For the sake of clarity, context projections are depicted as coming from the source of the copied states rather than from separate context units. The number of units in each group is given in parentheses. Adapted from Plaut and Kello (1999), with permission.

own articulations (Locke, 1983; Menn & Stoel-Gammon, 1995; Studdert-Kennedy, 1993). This can be accomplished by first learning an internal *forward* model of the physical processes relating specific articulations to the acoustics they produce (Jordan & Rumelhart, 1992; Perkell et al., 1995). Such a model can be learned by executing a variety of articulations, predicting how they will sound, and then adapting the model based on the discrepancy or error between this prediction and the actual resulting acoustics. In the infant, the forward model is assumed to develop primarily as a result of canonical and variegated babbling in the second half of the first year (see Vihman, 1996, for review, and Houde & Jordan, 1998, for empirical support for the existence of such a forward model).

The importance of learning an articulatory-acoustic forward model is that it can be used to convert acoustic and phonological feedback (i.e., whether an utterance sounded right) into articulatory feedback that can improve speech production. The approach assumes that learning to produce speech takes place largely in the context of attempts to imitate adult speech. In imitation, the system first derives acoustic and phonological representations for an adult utterance during comprehension. It then uses the resulting phonological representation as input to generate a sequence of articulatory gestures. These gestures, when executed, result in acoustics that are then mapped back onto phonology via the comprehension system. The discrepancies between the resulting representations and the original acoustic and phonological representations generated by the adult constitute the error signals that ultimately drive articulatory learning. In order for this to work, however, these "distal" errors in acoustics and phonology must be converted to "proximal" errors in articulation. This is done by propagating phonological and acoustic error across the forward model to derive error signals over articulatory states. These error signals are then used to adapt the production system (i.e., the mapping from stable phonological representations onto articulatory sequences) to better approximate the acoustics and phonology generated by the adult.

The implementation developed by Plaut and Kello necessarily incorporated a number of simplifications to keep computational demands within reasonable limits. Two of these are most critical. First, the implementation used discrete rather than continuous time. The time-varying acoustic input and articulatory output were described in terms of sequences of events marking points of significant change. There were approximately as many events in an utterance as phonemes (plosives, affricates and diphthongs corresponded to two events) although, due to coarticulatory influences, information about a given segment was spread out over a number of adjacent events.

Second, the implementation used artificial rather than real speech. Acoustic events were encoded in terms of 10 variables: the first three formants (1–3) and their rates of change (4–6), amount of frication (7) and bursting (8), loudness (9), and degree of jaw openness (10). The last variable is, strictly speaking, visual/proprioceptive rather than acoustic but has been shown to be a important source of information in infant speech acquisition (Locke, 1995; Meltzoff & Moore, 1977). Articulatory events were similarly encoded in terms of six variables: degree of oral (1) and nasal constriction (2), place of oral constriction (3), tongue height (4) and backness (5), and amount of voicing (6). Finally, the physical processes relating articulation to acoustics were approximated by a set of complex, coupled equations that map any combination of values for the articulatory variables onto the corresponding values for the acoustic variables. Considerable effort was spent to make these representations and equations as realistic as possible while staying within the constraints of computational efficiency.

In the simulation, the value of each articulatory variable was represented by the difference in activity between contrasting units (corresponding to the ends of the continuum). Each acoustic value was represented by the mean of a Gaussian pattern of activity over a bank of 12 units; the total activity of the Gaussian encoded the strength of the information. For illustration purposes, Fig. 6.2 shows the articulatory and acoustic representations for the closure and release of the /p/ in the word SPIN.

The training vocabulary for the network was the 400 highest frequency monosyllabic nouns and verbs in the Brown corpus (Kucera & Francis, 1967)

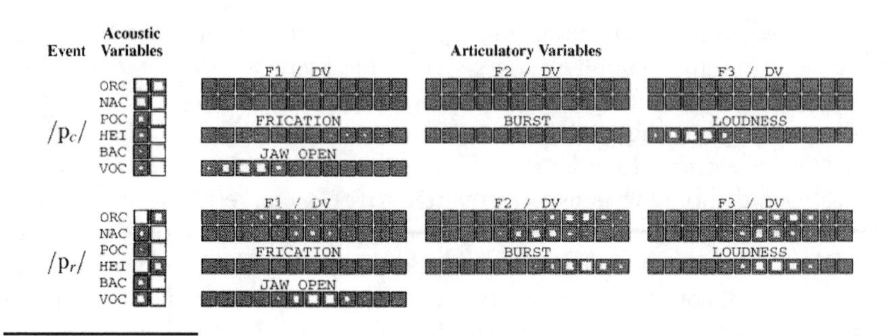

FIG. 6.2. The articulatory (left) and acoustic (right) events corresponding to the closure and release of /p/ in an utterance of the word SPIN. Adapted from Plaut and Kello (1999), with permission.

with at most four phonemes (mean = 3.42). Words were selected for presentation during training in proportion to a logarithmic function of their frequency of occurrence.

The network underwent three kinds of training episodes: babbling, comprehension, and imitation. Intentional naming is also mentioned because the network was tested on this task even though it was not trained on it explicitly.

Babbling. Babbling served to train the articulatory-acoustic forward model (see Fig. 6.1). Pseudo-random articulatory sequences, designed to mimic a bias toward mandibular (jaw) oscillation in infants (MacNeilage & Davis, 1990), were generated and passed through the articulation-to-acoustics equations to produce a sequence of acoustic patterns. The articulations also served as input to the forward model, which generated a sequence of predicted acoustic patterns. The discrepancy or error between the actual and predicted acoustics at each step was then back-propagated through the forward model and used to adjust its connection weights to improve its ability to predict the acoustic outcomes of the given articulations. In this way, the forward model gradually learned to mimic the physical mapping from articulatory sequences to acoustic sequences (as instantiated by the articulation-to-acoustics equations).

Comprehension. Comprehension involved deriving the semantic representation of a word from the acoustic sequence produced by an adult utterance of the word. Adult utterances were generated by applying the articulation-to-acoustics equations to the sequences of canonical articulatory events for words, subject to intrinsic variability and coarticulation. Each resulting sequence was then mapped from acoustics via phonology to semantics, and the error between the generated semantics at each step and the correct semantics for the word was back-propagated to change the weights between acoustics and semantics.[2] Gradually, the network learned to activate the correct semantic pattern for the acoustic sequences corresponding to each word; in doing so, the final pattern of activity over phonology constituted the network's internal phonological representation of the word.

Imitation. Imitation involved using a phonological representation derived from an adult utterance as input to drive articulation, and comparing the resulting acoustic and phonological representations with those of the adult utterance. Specifically, after hearing an adult utterance, the network used its derived phonological representation as input to generate a sequence of articulatory representations. This sequence was then mapped both by the forward model to generate predicted acoustics, and by the articulation-to-acoustics equations to generate actual acoustics. The latter were in turn mapped via the comprehension system to phonology (and semantics). The error between the acoustic and phonological representations generated by the network and those generated by the adult was then back-propagated from phonology to acoustics and then back across the forward model to derive error feedback for articulation. (Note that the forward model plays the critical role here of converting acoustic error into articulatory error.) This feedback was then back-propagated to phonology and used to modify the weights in the production system to improve its ability to reproduce the acoustics and phonology of the adult utterance.

Note that, in learning to imitate, the network is provided only with the acoustics of adult utterances. It must learn to adapt its own articulations based solely on how similar to the adult utterances they *sound*.

Intentional Naming. Intentional naming involved generating an articulatory sequence given the semantic representation of a word as input. Although the network was not trained specifically to perform this task, it can be tested on it in a way that is similar to imitation. The only difference is that the initial phonological representation is generated from semantics top-down rather than from an adult utterance bottom-up.

The network was tested for its ability to comprehend, imitate, and intentionally name words after every 500,000 word presentations, up to a total of 3.5M (million) presentations.[3] Figure 6.3 shows the levels of correct performance on these tasks over the course of training. Performance was measured in terms of whether the semantics generated by the network was more similar to the correct semantics of the word than to those of any other word. Comprehension per-

---

[2]The semantic representations were generated artificially to cluster into categories and assigned to words randomly (see Plaut & Kello, 1999, for details). Although the relationship between the surface forms of words and their meanings was arbitrary, no attempt was made to approximate the actual meanings of the words themselves.

[3]Although this may seem like an excessive amount of training, children speak up to 14,000 words per day (Wagner, 1985), or over 5 million words per year.

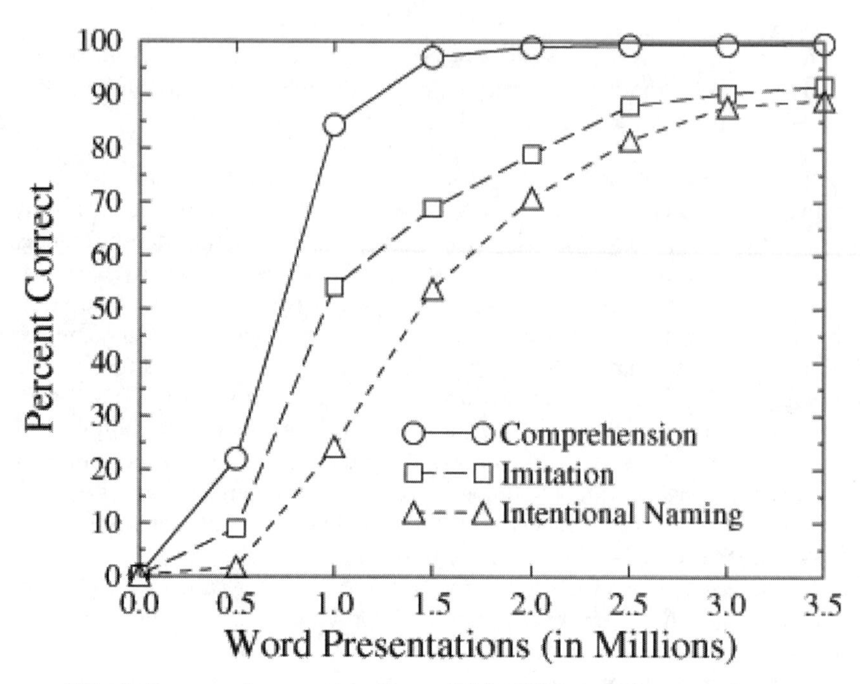

FIG. 6.3. Correct performance of the Plaut and Kello (1999) network on comprehension, imitation, and intentional naming, over the course of training. Adapted from Plaut and Kello (1999), with permission.

formance improved relatively rapidly, reaching 84.3% correct by 1M word presentations and 99.6% by 3.5M presentations. This level of performance is impressive given the lack of systematicity in the mapping between acoustics and semantics and the considerable intrinsic variability of adult utterances. Relative to comprehension, production developed more slowly: the network was only 54.2% correct at imitation by 1M presentations, although it did achieve 91.7% correct by 3.5M presentations. Intentional naming was slightly poorer than imitation throughout training, eventually reaching 89.0% correct. This is not surprising as the task involves mapping through the entire network and was not trained explicitly.

Thus, the network achieved quite good performance at both comprehension and production. The fact that comprehension precedes production in the model stems directly from the fact that learning within the production system is driven by comparisons over representations within the comprehension system. The excellent performance on imitation demonstrates that feedback from the comprehension system via a learned forward model can provide effective guidance for articulatory development.

Plaut and Kello also carried out an analysis of the errors produced by the network. In general, the network showed a strong bias toward phonological similarity in its errors compared with the chance rate, for both comprehension and imitation. At the phoneme level, there were far more errors on consonants than on vowels and, among consonants, a relatively higher error rate on fricatives, affricates (e.g., /tS/), and /N/ (as in RING). These errors involved both additions and deletions; when they were deleted, they were often replaced by a plosive. In fact, plosives accounted for over half of the total number of insertions. By contrast, the liquids /r/ and /l/ were deleted occasionally, but never inserted. These characteristics are in broad agreement with the properties of early child speech errors (e.g., Ingram, 1976).

In summary, Plaut and Kello (1999) developed a connectionist framework in which phonology is a learned internal representation mediating both comprehension and production, and in which comprehension provides production with error feedback via a learned articulatory-acoustic forward model. An implementation of the framework, in the form of a simple recurrent network, learned to comprehend, imitate, and intentionally name a corpus of 400 monosyllabic words. Moreover, the speech errors produced by the network showed tendencies similar to those of young children. Although only a first step, the results suggest that the approach may ultimately form the basis for a comprehensive account of phonological development.

INFLECTIONAL MORPHOLOGY: JOANISSE AND SEIDENBERG (1999)

The second example of a connectionist model of language processing is from recent work by Joanisse and Seidenberg (1999) in the domain of English inflectional morphology. The past-tense system of English verbs is a classic example of a *quasi-regular* domain, in which the relationship between inputs and outputs is systematic but admits many exceptions. Thus, there is a single regular "rule" (add –ed; e.g., WALK => "walked") and only about 150 exceptions, grouped into several clusters of similar items that undergo a similar change (e.g., SING => "sang", DRINK => "drank") along with a very small number of very high–frequency, arbitrary forms (e.g., GO => " went" ; Bybee & Slobin, 1982).

The traditional view of the language system (e.g., Pinker, 1984, 1991) is that the systematic aspects of language are represented and processed in the form of an explicit set of rules. Given that most domains are only partially systematic, however, a separate mechanism (e.g., an associative network; Pinker, 1991) is required to handle the exceptions. The distinction between a rule-based mechanism and an exception mechanism, each operating according to different computational principles, forms the central tenet of so-called " dual-route" theories of language.

Rumelhart and McClelland (1986) argued for an alternative view of language in which all items coexist within a single system whose representations and processing reflect the relative degree of *consistency* in the mappings for different items (Plaut, McClelland, Seidenberg, & Patterson, 1996; also see Seidenberg & McClelland, 1989). They developed a connectionist model that learned a direct association between the phonology of all types of verb stems and the phonology of their past-tense forms. Pinker and Prince (1988) and Lachter and Bever (1988), however, pointed out numerous deficiencies in the model's performance and in some of its specific assumptions, and argued more generally that the applicability of connectionist mechanisms in language is fundamentally limited (also see Fodor & Pylyshyn, 1988). Subsequent simulation work has addressed many of the specific limitations of the Rumelhart and McClelland model (Cottrell & Plunkett, 1991, 1995; Daugherty & Seidenberg, 1992; Hoeffner, 1992; MacWhinney & Leinbach, 1991; Plunkett & Marchman, 1991, 1993, 1996) and has extended the approach to address language disorders (Hoeffner & McClelland, 1993; Marchman, 1993) and language change (Hare & Elman, 1995).

More recently, proponents of dual-route theories have identified neuropsychological dissociations in processing regular versus irregular inflectional morphology, both in the performance of brain-damaged patients (Marslen-Wilson & Tyler, 1997; Ullman et al., 1997) and in the regional cerebral blood flow of normal subjects (Jaeger et al., 1996, although see Seidenberg & Hoeffner, 1998, for criticism). These dissociations have been interpreted by these authors as supporting the existence of separate mechanisms for rule–governed versus exceptional items. For example, Ullman et al. (1997) found that patients with Alzheimer's disease were relatively impaired in generating the past tense of irregular verbs (60% correct) compared with regular verbs (89% correct) and novel verbs (e.g., CUG; 84% correct). In contrast, patients with Parkinson's disease were relatively impaired on the novel verbs (65% correct) compared with both the regular and irregular verbs (80 and 88% correct, respectively). A similar contrast in performance on novel versus irregular verbs held among aphasic patients with either posterior lesions (novel 85%; irregular 71%) or anterior lesions (novel 5%; irregular 69%). Ullman and colleagues interpreted these findings as implicating two separate mechanisms: a posterior "mental dictionary" needed to retrieve irregular inflections, and a frontal/basal–ganglia grammatical rule system needed to inflect novel verbs.

An alternative account is that the double dissociation of novel versus irregular inflectional morphology is due to damage to different types of information within a single mechanism that processes all types of items (also see Plaut, 1995). In particular, irregular morphology may be particularly sensitive to semantic damage whereas novel inflections may be particularly sensitive to phonological damage. In fact, the same proposal has been made in the domain of word reading (Patterson & Hodges, 1992; Patterson & Marcel, 1992; Plaut et al., 1996) where analogous dissociations occur: Surface dyslexic patients (see Patterson, Coltheart, & Marshall, 1985) are impaired in pronouncing exception words (e.g., PINT) but not pseudowords (e.g., RINT), whereas phonological dyslexic patients (see Coltheart, 1996) are impaired in pronouncing pseudowords relative to both regular and exception words. In fact, there is independent evidence for semantic impairments with posterior (temporal) involvement in Alzheimer's disease (Schwartz, 1990) and in surface dyslexic patients (Graham, Hodges, & Patterson, 1994), and for phonological impairments with frontal involvement in Parkinson's patients (e.g., Grossman, Carvell, Stern, Gollump, & Hurtig, 1992) and in phonological dyslexic patients (Patterson & Marcel, 1992).

Joanisse and Seidenberg (1999) developed a connectionist simulation of inflectional morphology in support of this account. The architecture of their network is shown in Fig 6.4. Note that it is broadly similar to the framework proposed by Plaut and Kello (1999): Spoken input interacts via a common internal representation both with semantics and with spoken output. Here, though, the surface forms of words are represented in more abstract form. Input and output phonology are represented in terms of sequences of phonemes of the form CCCVVCCVC (where some slots may be empty). Thus, the past tense of STOP is -sta-pt—and the past tense of WANT is—wa-nt-Id. Within each of the nine slots, a phoneme is coded in terms of 18 phonetic features, yielding a total of 162 units.

Verb meanings were not encoded explicitly; rather, each verb was assigned a localist representation of a single unit. An additional "past-tense" unit in se-

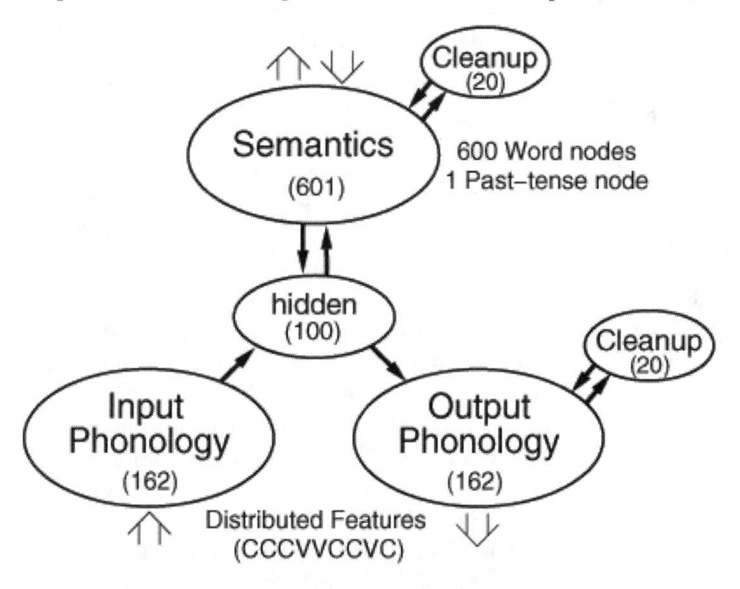

FIG. 6.4. The architecture of the network used by Joanisse and Seidenberg (1999) to model inflectional morphology. The large arrows identify input and output layers. The number of units in each layer is indicated in parentheses.
Adapted from Joanisse & Seidenberg with permission (1999).

mantics indicated that the phonological output of the verb should be the past (as opposed to present) tense. The network was trained on 600 randomly selected verbs (weighted by their frequency), including 64 irregular verbs; it thus contained 601 semantic units. In addition, the network contained two groups of 20 "cleanup" units, one interacting with semantics and one with output phonology. These groups are additional hidden units that learn to help semantics and output phonology settle into correct, stable (attractor) states.

The network was trained with back-propagation through time (Rumelhart, Hinton, & Williams, 1986) to perform four tasks (on the indicated proportion of trials):

Hearing (40%). Given the input phonology of a verb (present or past), activate the corresponding semantic unit (and the past-tense unit if it was in the past tense).

Repeating (30%). Given the input phonology of a verb, reproduce it over output phonology. To facilitate learning English phonology, in addition to the 600 verbs in semantics, the network was trained to repeat an additional 596 verbs in both present and past tense.

Speaking (20%). Given the semantics of a verb (possibly including the past-tense unit), generate the correct output phonology.

Transforming (10%). Given the input phonology of a verb in present tense and activation of the past-tense unit in semantics, generate the past-tense output phonology of the verb.

After 2.7 million training trials, the network was 99.5% correct on hearing, 98.2% correct on repetition, 99.8% correct on speaking, and 99.3% correct on transforming present to past. In addition, the network was 85% correct when tested for its ability to transform the phonology of the novel verbs from the Ullman et al. (1997) study. Thus, although the network did not contain separate mechanisms for regular versus irregular morphology, it nonetheless was capable of highly accurate processing of both types of verbs, as well as reasonably accurate generalization in transforming novel verbs.

Joanisse and Seidenberg then tested their network's performance after either semantic or phonological lesions. Semantic lesions involved adding Gaussian noise with $SD = 0.22$ to the activations of the semantic units and randomly eliminating 22% of their connections from cleanup units. Phonological lesions involved adding Gaussian noise with $SD = 0.30$ to the activation of the output phonology units and randomly eliminating 15% of their connections from cleanup units. Fig 6.5 shows the performance of the model, averaged over 10 instances of each such lesion, in transforming the present to past tense of regular, irregular, and novel verbs. Also included are the Ullman et al. (1997) data for the corresponding patient groups. As with Alzheimer's patients, semantic lesions in the model have a much more detrimental effect on irregular verbs than on regular or novel verbs. In contrast, in Parkinson's patients and for the model after phonological lesions, novel verbs are the most impaired (although the dissociation is not as strong as for semantic lesions).

In the model, semantic damage impairs irregulars the most because interactions with semantics are required to override the strong consistency in the regular inflection for these items. In contrast, phonological damage impairs novel verbs the most because, unlike both regular and irregular verbs, such verbs receive no support from interactions with semantics. Thus, due to these learned specializations, lesions to semantics versus phonology in the model replicate the empirical double dissociation of performance in inflecting irregular versus novel verbs that Ullman and colleagues observed among the patients. Consequently,

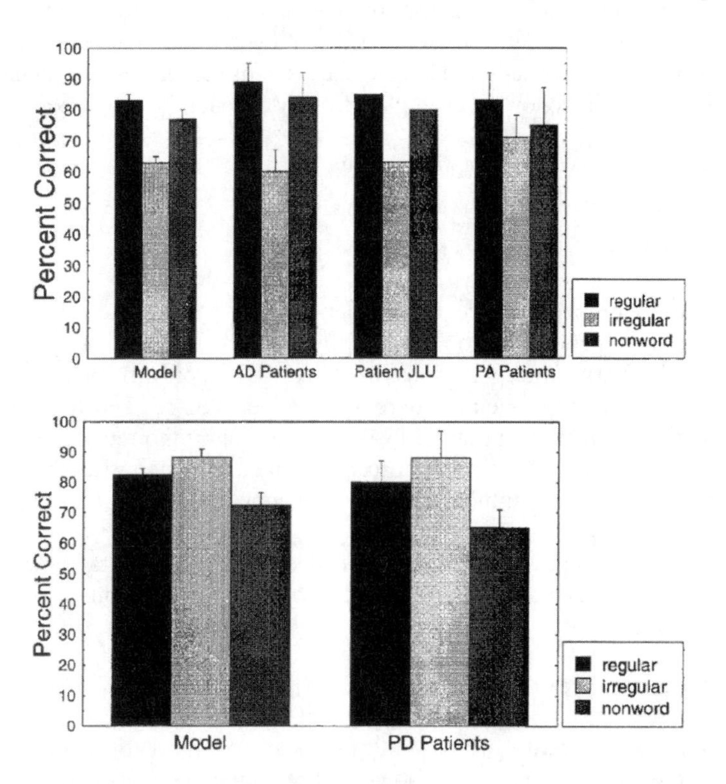

FIG. 6.5. The effects of lesions to semantics (top) or to phonology (bottom) on the performance of the Joanisse and Seidenberg (1999) network in transforming regular, irregular, and novel verbs, and the corresponding data for patients with Alzheimer's disease (AD) or Parkinson's disease (PD) from Ullman et al. (1997).
Adapted from Joanisse & Seidenberg with permission (1999).

the dissociations do not provide support for dual-route theories of language processing, and can be accounted for naturally by a distributed connectionist system in which multiple sources of information interact in processing all types of items.

SENTENCE COMPREHENSION: ST. JOHN AND MCCLELLAND (1990)

Having discussed connectionist models that have been applied to issues in phonology and morphology, we now consider how the approach can provide important insights at the level of the syntax and semantics of sentences. Traditional linguistic theory has focused on grammar as the essential element of linguistic knowledge, abstracting away from semantic and pragmatic influences on performance (Chomsky, 1957, 1965, 1985, 1995). This view has spawned psychological models (e.g., Ferreira & Clifton, 1986; Frazier, 1986; Marcus, 1980) that include an initial syntactic parse that is insensitive to lexical/semantic constraints (apart from word class information). And yet, from a computational point of view, a parser divorced from real-world knowledge runs into a number of difficult problems. Consider the following examples (from McClelland et al., 1989):

1. The spy saw the policeman with a revolver
2. The spy saw the policeman with binoculars
3. The bird saw the birdwatcher with binoculars

As these sentences are structurally identical, the attachment of the prepositional phrase depends solely on the meanings of the words and the relative adequacy of alternative interpretations. In (1) versus (2), only the binoculars are a plausible instrument of seeing, whereas a revolver is more likely to belong to a policeman. In (3), the fact that birdwatchers but not birds often possess and use binoculars reverses the attachment in (2). Indeed, every constituent in a sentence can potentially influence the role assigned to a prepositional phrase (Oden, 1978).

Conversely, just as word meaning is needed to influence syntactic processes, so sentence-level syntax and semantics must be used to determine word meanings. This can be seen clearly in considering ambiguous words, as in

4. The pitcher threw the ball

in which every content word has multiple meanings in isolation but an unambiguous meaning in context. It also applies to vague or generic words, such as "container," which can refer to very different types of objects in different contexts (Anderson & Ortony, 1975), as in

5. The container held the apples
6. The container held the cola

Finally, at the extreme end of context dependence are implied constituents which are not even mentioned in the sentence but nonetheless are an important aspect of its meaning. For example, from

7. The boy spread the jelly on the bread

most people infer a knife as instrument (McKoon & Ratcliff, 1981).

These and other considerations have lead a number of researchers to question claims for the autonomy of syntax. Instead, sentence comprehension is envisioned as a constraint satisfaction process in which multiple sources of information from both syntax and semantics are simultaneously brought to bear in constructing the most plausible interpretation of a given utterance (see, e.g., MacDonald, Pearlmutter, & Seidenberg, 1994; McClelland & Kawamoto, 1986; Seidenberg, 1997; Tanenhaus & Trueswell, 1995).

St. John and McClelland (1990; McClelland et al., 1989) developed a connectionist model of sentence comprehension that instantiates this key idea and that, at least in limited form, addresses the challenges just raised. The architecture of the model, in the form of a simple recurrent network, is shown in Fig. 6.6. The task of the network was to take as input a single-clause sentence as a sequence of surface constituents, and to derive an internal representation of the event described by the sentence, termed the *sentence gestalt*. Critically, this representation was not predefined but was learned from feedback on its ability to

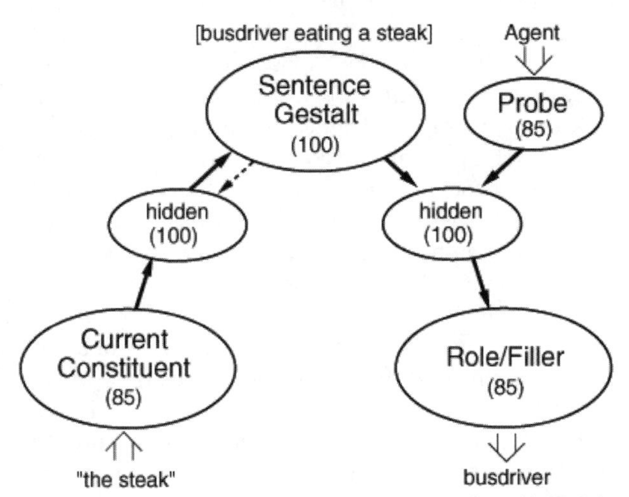

FIG. 6.6. The architecture of the simple recurrent network used by St. John and McClelland (1990) to model sentence comprehension. The number of units in each layer is shown in parentheses. The large arrows identify input and output layers. The dashed arrow indicates a projection from "context" units (omitted for clarity) whose states are copied from the Sentence Gestalt layer for the previous time step. Adapted from St. John & McClelland, (1990), with permission.

generate appropriate thematic role assignments for the event (given either roles or fillers as "probes").

Events were organized around actions and had a probabilistic structure. Specifically, each of 14 actions had a specified set of thematic roles, each of which was filled probabilistically by one of the possible constituents. In this process, the selection of fillers for certain roles biased the selection for other roles. For example, for eating events, the bus driver most often ate steak whereas the teacher most often ate soup, although occasionally the reverse occurred. The choice of words in the construction of a sentence describing the event was also probabilistic. The event of a bus driver eating a steak with a knife might be rendered as THE-ADULT ATE THE-FOOD WITH-A-UTENSIL, THE-STEAK WAS-CONSUMED-BY THE-PERSON, SOMEONE ATE SOMETHING, and so on (where the hyphenated phrases are constituents). Overall, given the probabilistic event structures and the lexical and syntactic options for describing events as sentences, there were a total of 120 different events (of which some are much more likely than others) and 22,645 different sentence–event pairs.

During training, sentence–event pairs were generated successively and the constituents of each sentence were presented one at a time over the Current Constituent units (see Fig 6.6). For each constituent, the network updated its Sentence Gestalt representation and then attempted to use this representation as input to generate the full set of role/filler pairs for the event. Specifically, with the Sentence Gestalt fixed and given either a role or a filler over the "Probe" units, the network had to generate the other element of the pair over the "Role/Filler" units. For example, after the presentation of THE-STEAK in the sentence THE-STEAK WAS-EATEN-BY THE-BUSDRIVER, the network was trained to output, among other things, the agent (bus driver), the patient (steak), the action (eating), and the instrument (fork). It was, of course, impossible for the network to do this with complete accuracy, as these role assignments depend on constituents that have yet to occur or are only implied. Even so, the network could do better than chance. It could attempt to predict missing information based on its experience with the probabilistic dependencies in the event structures. More specifically, it could (and, in fact, did) generate distributions of activity over roles and fillers that approximated their frequency of occurrence over all possible events described by sentences that start with THE-STEAK. Note that these distributions could, in many cases, be strongly biases towards the correct responses. For example, steaks typically fill the patient role in eating events and (in the environment of the network) are most commonly eaten by bus drivers using a fork. In this way, the training procedure encouraged the network to extract as much information as possible as early as possible, in keeping with the principle of *immediate update* (Eberhard, Spivey-Knowlton, & Tanenhaus, 1995; Marslen-Wilson & Tyler, 1980; van Dijk & Kintsch, 1983). Of course, the network also had to learn to revise the Sentence Gestalt appropriately in cases where its predictions were violated, as in THE-STEAK WAS-EATEN-BY THE-TEACHER.

The network was trained on a total of 630,000 sentence–event pairs, in which some pairs occurred frequently and others, particularly those with atypical role assignments, were very rare. Figure 6.7 shows the performance of the model on sentences of various types as a function of training experience. In general, active voice was learned before passive voice, and syntactic constraints (implied by word order) were learned before semantic constraints (implied by event statistics). By the end of training, when tested on 55 randomly generated sentence–event pairs with unambiguous interpretations, the network was correct in 1,699 of 1,710 role/filler assignments (99.4% correct).

St. John and McClelland also carried out a number of more specific analyses intended to establish that the network could handle more subtle aspects of sentence comprehension. In general, the network succeeded at using both semantic and syntactic context a) to disambiguate word meanings (e.g., for THE PITCHER HIT THE BAT WITH THE BAT, assigning flying bat as patient and baseball bat as instrument); b) to instantiate vague words (e.g., for the teacher kissed someone, activating a male of unknown age as patient); and c) to elaborate implied roles (e.g., for THE TEACHER ATE THE SOUP, activating spoon as the instrument; for THE SCHOOLGIRL ATE), activating a range of foods as possible patients). The network also demonstrated the ability to recover from semantic "garden paths," in which early predictions had to be revised in light of later evidence (see Fig 6.8).

In summary, St. John and McClelland (1990) present a connectionist model in which semantic and syntactic constraints are integrated to support online sentence comprehension. Although there are significant limitations in the complex-

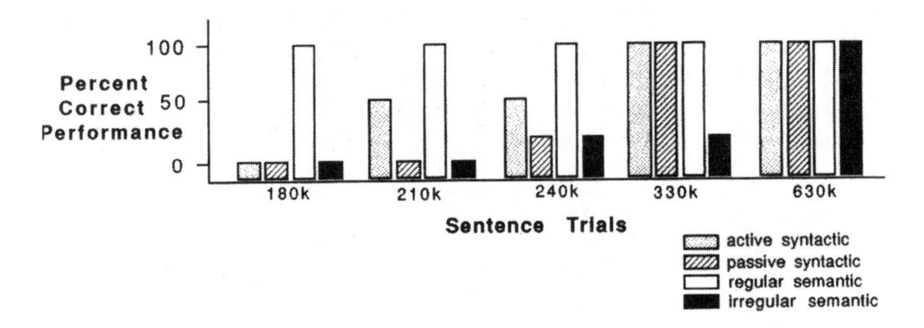

FIG. 6.7. Performance of the St. John and McClelland (1990) network in thematic role assignment for four classes of sentences: *active syntactic* (e.g., the busdriver kissed the teacher), *passive syntactic* (e.g., the teacher was kissed by the busdriver), *regular semantic* (e.g., the busdriver ate the steak), and *irregular semantic* (e.g., the busdriver ate the soup). (From St. John and McClelland (1990), with permission.

ity of the language on which the model was trained, it nonetheless instantiates and provides support for a theory of sentence comprehension as probabilistic constraint satisfaction (MacDonald et al., 1994; Seidenberg, 1997). This perspective stands in sharp contrast to traditional linguistic (Chomsky, 1965) and psycholinguistic theories (Ferreira & Clifton, 1986; Frazier, 1986) that espouse a clear separation of grammar from the rest of cognition.

SUMMARY AND CONCLUSIONS

Connectionist modeling is attractive as a framework for understanding cognition in general, and language in particular, because it provides an account of the flexi-

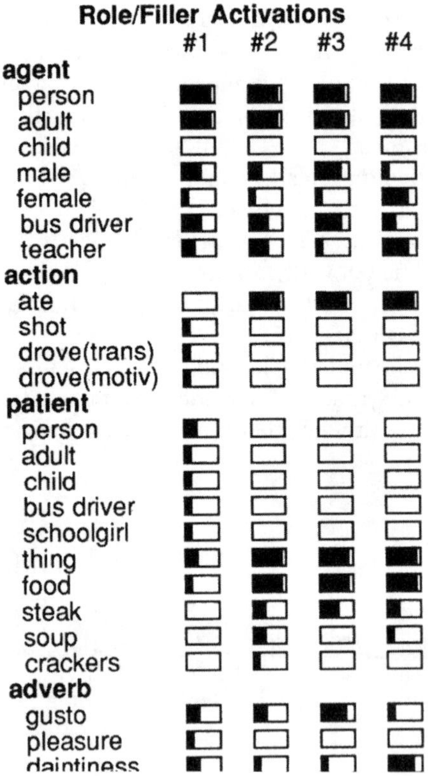

FIG. 6.8. The activations (as black bars) of possible fillers for selected roles generated by the St. John and McClelland (1990) network after processing each of the four constituents in the sentence the–adult #1) ate #2) the–steak #3) with–daintiness #4). After processing the–steak, the network instantiates the–adult as the bus driver, but when with–daintiness is encountered, the network must reinterpret the–adult to mean the teacher (given the statistics for eating events). From St. John and McClelland (1990), with permission.

bility and productivity of human performance through the development of internal representations that capture the underlying structure in a domain, and because it suggests how such representations and processes might actually be learned and carried out by the brain. This chapter discussed three examples of connectionist models, each applied to a different level of language structure. At the phonological level, the Plaut and Kello (1999) model provides an account of how comprehension and production are coordinated in phonological development, and how production can be trained by feedback from the comprehension system via a learned articulatory-acoustic forward model. At the morphological level, the Joanisse and Seidenberg (1999) model demonstrates that neuropsychological dissociations in inflecting regular (and novel) versus irregular English verbs do not implicate separate rule-based and associative mechanisms, but arise naturally from damage to semantic versus phonological processes within a single, distributed system that processes all types of items. At the sentence level, the St. John and McClelland (1990) model illustrates how a system can learn both semantic and syntactic knowledge from its experience with sentences and the events they describe, and bring this knowledge to bear in an online, integrated fashion to construct the most plausible interpretation of a given sentence.

Each of these models has important limitations in its theoretical scope and empirical adequacy. The Plaut and Kello model was applied only to isolated monosyllables, which were assigned very abstract distributed semantic representations. Moreover, the articulatory and acoustic representations, and the equations that relate them, provide only a coarse approximation to the richness of the information and constraints in these domains. The Joanisse and Seidenberg model, similarly, employed a limited vocabulary of isolated verbs, highly restrictive phonological representations, and made no attempt to capture similarities among verb meanings. The St. John and McClelland model was trained on sentences restricted to single clauses without embeddings and preparsed into syntactic constituents. The use of event structures composed of probabilistic assignment to fixed thematic roles was also highly simplified.

A more general limitation that spans all three models is the approximation of temporal processing in terms of discrete sequences of events. Although networks with continuous-time processing have been applied in language-related domains (e.g., Harm & Seidenberg, 1999; Plaut et al., 1996), typically these networks have been trained only to settle to stable attractor states given fixed inputs. An important goal for future work is to establish that such networks can learn to carry out more sophisticated temporal processing, such as interpreting continuously varying acoustic input in speech comprehension, and producing continuous articulatory trajectories in speech production.

Another important goal for future work is to develop models that span linguistic levels. Currently, the most connectionist models of language are restricted to processing single (often monosyllabic) words, whereas models that processes sentences adopt highly simplified (often localist) surface representations for words (also see Elman, 1993; Rohde & Plaut, 1999). In principle, the phonological model of Plaut and Kello could be extended to processes multiword utterances, and the sentence-level model of St. John and McClelland could be elaborated with more phonologically structured inputs.

It should be clear that none of the three models described in this chapter, nor any other existing connectionist model, accounts for all of the relevant empirical findings in its domain. In considering this, it is important to think of a model as a demonstration of key theoretical principles in the service of supporting an underlying theory, rather than as a proposal for exactly how the human cognitive system operates in every detail. In this respect, the three models are quite successful, although much work remains in refining the principles and in applying them to increasingly realistic tasks.

Connectionist models provide the means of exploring the implications of a set of computational principles that are closely tied to neurophysiology and yet have important implications for cognition. In this way, the approach offers a computational bridge between mind and brain.

ACKNOWLEDGMENTS

This research was supported by the National Institute of Mental Health (grant MH47566) and the National Science Foundation (Grant 9720348). I thank Marlene Behrmann and Marc Joanisse for helpful comments.

REFERENCES

Anderson, J. A., Silverstein, J. W., Ritz, S. A., & Jones, R. S. (1977). Distinctive features, categorical perception, and probability learning: Some applications of a neural model. *Psychological Review, 84*, 413–451.

Anderson, R. C., & Ortony, A. (1975). On putting apples into bottles: A problem of polysemy. *Cognitive Psychology, 7*, 167–180.

Bybee, J. L., & Slobin, D. L. (1982). Rules and schemas in the development and use of the English past tense. *Language, 58*, 265–289.

Chomsky, N. (1957). *Syntactic structures*. The Hague: Mouton.

Chomsky, N. (1965). *Aspects of the theory of syntax*. Cambridge, MA: MIT Press.

Chomsky, N. (1985). *Knowledge of language: Its nature, origin, and use*. New York: Praeger.

Chomsky, N. (1995). *The minimalist program*. Cambridge, MA: MIT Press.

Chomsky, N., & Halle, M. (1968). *The sound pattern of English*. New York: Harper & Row.

Cleeremans, A., Servan-Schreiber, D., & McClelland, J. L. (1989). Finite state automata and simple recurrent networks. *Neural Computation, 1*, 372–381.

Coltheart, M. (Ed.). (1996). Special issue on phonological dyslexia. *Cognitive Neuropsychology, 13*, 749–934.

Cottrell, G. W., & Plunkett, K. (1991). Learning the past tense in a recurrent network: Acquiring the mapping from meaning to sounds. In *Proceedings of the 13th Annual Conference of the Cognitive Science Society* (pp. 328–333). Hillsdale, NJ: Lawrence Erlbaum Associates.

Cottrell, G. W., & Plunkett, K. (1995). Acquiring the mapping from meanings to sounds. *Connection Science, 6*, 379–412.

Crain, S. (1991). Language acquisition in the absence of experience. *Behavioral and Brain Sciences, 14,* 597–650.

Crick, F. H. C. (1989). The recent excitement about neural networks. *Nature, 337,* 129–132.

Daugherty, K., & Seidenberg, M. S. (1992). Rules or connections? The past tense revisited. In *Proceedings of the 14th annual conference of the Cognitive Science Society* (pp. 259–264). Hillsdale, NJ: Lawrence Erlbaum Associates.

Dell, G. S. (1986). A spreading–activation theory of retrieval in sentence production. *Psychological Review, 93,* 283–321.

Eberhard, K. M., Spivey-Knowlton, M. J., & Tanenhaus, M. K. (1995). Eye movements as a window into real–time spoken language comprehension in natural contexts. *Journal of Psycholinguistic Research, 24,* 409.

Elman, J. L. (1990). Finding structure in time. *Cognitive Science, 14,* 179–211.

Elman, J. L. (1991). Distributed representations, simple recurrent networks, and grammatical structure. *Machine Learning, 7,* 195–225.

Elman, J. L. (1993). Learning and development in neural networks: The importance of starting small. *Cognition, 48,* 71–99.

Ferreira, F., & Clifton, C. (1986). The independence of syntactic processing. *Journal of Memory and Language, 25,* 348–368.

Fodor, J. A., & Pylyshyn, Z. W. (1988). Connectionism and cognitive architecture: A critical analysis. *Cognition, 28,* 3–71.

Frazier, L. (1986). Theories of sentence processing. In J. Garfield (Ed.), *Modularity in knowledge representation and natural language processing* (pp. 291–307). Cambridge, MA: MIT Press.

Graham, K. S., Hodges, J. R., & Patterson, K. (1994). The relationship between comprehension and oral reading in progressive fluent aphasia. *Neuropsychologia, 32,* 299–316.

Grossman, M., Carvell, S., Stern, M., Gollump, S., & Hurtig, H. (1992). Sentence comprehension in Parkinson's disease: The role of attention and memory. *Brain and Language, 42,* 347–384.

Hare, M., & Elman, J. L. (1995). Learning and morphological change. *Cognition, 56,* 61–98.

Harm, M., & Seidenberg, M. S. (1999). Phonological representations, reading, and dyslexia: Insights from a connectionist model. *Psychological Review, 106,* 491–528.

Hinton, G. E., & Anderson, J. A. (Eds.). (1981). *Parallel models of associative memory.* Hillsdale, NJ: Lawrence Erlbaum Associates.

Hinton, G. E., McClelland, J. L., & Rumelhart, D. E. (1986). Distributed representations. In D. E. Rumelhart, J. L. McClelland, & the PDP Research Group (Eds.), *Parallel distributed processing: Explorations in the microstructure of cognition. Volume 1: Foundations* (pp. 77–109). Cambridge, MA: MIT Press.

Hinton, G. E., & Shallice, T. (1991). Lesioning an attractor network: Investigations of acquired dyslexia. *Psychological Review, 98,* 74–95.

Hoeffner, J. (1992). Are rules a thing of the past? The acquisition of verbal morphology by an attractor network. In *Proceedings of the 14th annual conference of the Cognitive Science Society* (pp. 861–866). Hillsdale, NJ: Lawrence Erlbaum Associates.

Hoeffner, J. H., & McClelland, J. L. (1993). Can a perceptual processing deficit explain the impairment of inflectional morphology in developmental dysphasia? A computational investigation. In E. V. Clark (Ed.), *Proceedings of the 25th annual Child Language Research Forum* (pp. 38–49). Stanford, CA: Center for the Study of Language and Information.

Houde, J. F., & Jordan, M. I. (1998). Sensorimotor adaption in speech production. *Science, 279,* 1213–1215.

Ingram, D. (1976). *Phonological disability in children.* London: Edward Arnold.

Jaeger, J. J., Lockwood, A. H., Kemmerer, D. L., Van Valin, Jr., R. D., Murphy, B. W., & Khalak, H. G. (1996). A positron emission tomographic study of regular and irregular verb morphology in English. *Language, 72,* 451–497.

Joanisse, M. & Seidenberg, M. S. (1999). Impairments in verb morphology after brain injury: A connectionist model. *Proceedings of the National Academy of Science, 96,* 7592–7592.

Jordan, M. I., & Rumelhart, D. E. (1992). Forward models: Supervised learning with a distal teacher. *Cognitive Science, 16,* 307–354.

Jusczyk, P. W. (1997). *The discovery of spoken language.* Cambridge, MA: MIT Press.

Kucera, H., & Francis, W. N. (1967). *Computational analysis of present–day American English.* Providence, RI: Brown University Press.

Lachter, J., & Bever, T. G. (1988). The relation between linguistic structure and theories of language learning: A constructive critique of some connectionist learning models. *Cognition, 28,* 195–247.
Liberman, A. M. (1996). *Speech: A special code.* Cambridge, MA: MIT Press.
Locke, J. L. (1983). *Phonological acquisition and change.* New York: Academic Press.
Locke, J. L. (1995). Development of the capacity for spoken language. In P. Fletcher & B. MacWhinney (Eds.), *The handbook of child language* (pp. 278–302). Oxford: Blackwell.
MacDonald, M. C., Pearlmutter, N. J., & Seidenberg, M. S. (1994). The lexical nature of syntactic ambiguity resolution. *Psychological Review, 101,* 676–703.
MacNeilage, P. F., & Davis, B. L. (1990). Acquisition of speech production: The achievement of segmental independence. In W. J. Hardcastle & A. Marchal (Eds.), *Speech production and speech modelling* (pp. 453–476). Dordrecht: Kluwer Academic.
MacWhinney, B., & Leinbach, J. (1991). Implementations are not conceptualizations: Revising the verb learning model. *Cognition, 40,* 121–153.
Marchman, V. A. (1993). Constraints on plasticity in a connectionist model of the English past tense. *Journal of Cognitive Neuroscience, 5,* 215–234.
Marcus, M. P. (1980). *A theory of syntactic recognition for natural language.* Cambridge, MA: MIT Press.
Marslen-Wilson, W., & Tyler, L. K. (1980). The temporal structure of spoken language understanding. *Cognition, 8,* 1–71.
Marslen-Wilson, W. D., & Tyler, L. K. (1997). Dissociating types of mental computation. *Nature, 387,* 592–594.
McClelland, J. L., & Kawamoto, A. H. (1986). Mechanisms of sentence processing: Assigning roles to constituents of sentences. In J. L. McClelland, D. E. Rumelhart, & the PDP Research Group (Eds.), *Parallel distributed processing: Explorations in the microstructure of cognition. Volume 2: Psychological and biological models* (pp. 272–325). Cambridge, MA: MIT Press.
McClelland, J. L., & Rumelhart, D. E. (1981). An interactive activation model of context effects in letter perception: Part 1. An account of basic findings. *Psychological Review, 88,* 375–407.
McClelland, J. L., Rumelhart, D. E., & the PDP Research Group. (Eds.). (1986). *Parallel distributed processing: Explorations in the microstructure of cognition. Volume 2: Psychological and biological models.* Cambridge, MA: MIT Press.
McClelland, J. L., St. John, M., & Taraban, R. (1989). Sentence comprehension: A parallel distributed processing approach. *Language and Cognitive Processes, 4,* 287–335.
McKoon, G., & Ratcliff, R. (1981). The comprehension processes and memory structures involved in instrumental inference. *Journal of Verbal Learning and Verbal Behaviour, 20,* 671–682.
McLeod, P., Plunkett, K., & Rolls, E. T. (1998). *Introduction to connectionist modelling of cognitive processes.* Oxford: Oxford University Press.
Meltzoff, A. N., & Moore, M. K. (1977). Imitation of facial and manual gestures by human neonates. *Science, 198,* 75–78.
Menn, L., & Stoel-Gammon, C. (1995). Phonological development. In P. Fletcher & B. MacWhinney (Eds.), *The handbook of child language* (pp. 335–359). Oxford: Blackwell.
Oden, G. (1978). Semantic constraints and judged preference for interpretations of ambiguous sentences. *Memory and Cognition, 6,* 26–37.
O' Reilly, R. C. (1996). Biologically plausible error–driven learning using local activation differences: The generalized recirculation algorithm. *Neural Computation, 8,* 895–938.
Patterson, K., Coltheart, M., & Marshall, J. C. (Eds.). (1985). *Surface dyslexia.* Hillsdale, NJ: Lawrence Erlbaum Associates.
Patterson, K., & Hodges, J. R. (1992). Deterioration of word meaning: Implications for reading. *Neuropsychologia, 30,* 1025–1040.
Patterson, K., & Marcel, A. J. (1992). Phonological ALEXIA or PHONOLOGICAL alexia? In J. Alegria, D. Holender, J. Junca de Morais, & M. Radeau (Eds.), *Analytic approaches to human cognition* (pp. 259–274). New York: Elsevier.
Perkell, J. S., Matthies, M. L., Svirsky, M. A., & Jordan, M. I. (1995). Goal–based speech motor control: A theoretical framework and some preliminary data. *Journal of Phonetics, 23,* 23–35.
Pinker, S. (1984). *Language learnability and language development.* Cambridge, MA: Harvard University Press.
Pinker, S. (1991). *Rules of language.* Science, 253, 530–535.
Pinker, S. (1994). *The language instinct.* New York: Morrow.
Pinker, S., & Mehler, J. (Eds.). (1988). *Connections and symbols.* Cambridge, MA: MIT Press.

Pinker, S., & Prince, A. (1988). On language and connectionism: Analysis of a parallel distributed processing model of language acquisition. *Cognition, 28,* 73–193.

Plaut, D. C. (1995). Double dissociation without modularity: Evidence from connectionist neuropsychology. *Journal of Clinical and Experimental Neuropsychology, 17,* 291–321.

Plaut, D. C., & Kello, C. T. (1999). The interplay of speech comprehension and production in phonological development: A forward modeling approach. In B. MacWhinney (Ed.), *The emergence of language* (pp. 381–415). Mahwah, NJ: Lawrence Erlbaum Associates.

Plaut, D. C., McClelland, J. L., Seidenberg, M. S., & Patterson, K. (1996). Understanding normal and impaired word reading: Computational principles in quasi–regular domains. *Psychological Review, 103,* 56–115.

Plunkett, K., & Marchman, V. A. (1991). U–shaped learning and frequency effects in a multi-layered perception: Implications for child language acquisition. *Cognition, 38,* 43–102.

Plunkett, K., & Marchman, V. A. (1993). From rote learning to system building: Acquiring verb morphology in children and connectionist nets. *Cognition, 48,* 21–69.

Plunkett, K., & Marchman, V. A. (1996). Learning from a connectionist model of the acquisition of the English past tense. *Cognition, 61,* 299–308.

Quinlan, P. (1991). *Connectionism and psychology: A psychological perspective on new connectionist research.* Chicago: University of Chicago Press.

Rohde, D. L. T., & Plaut, D. C. (1999). Language acquisition in the absence of explicit negative evidence: How important is starting small? *Cognition, 72,* 67–109.

Rumelhart, D. E., Hinton, G. E., & Williams, R. J. (1986). Learning representations by back–propagating errors. *Nature, 323,* 533–536.

Rumelhart, D. E., & McClelland, J. L. (1986). On learning the past tenses of English verbs. In J. L. McClelland, D. E. Rumelhart, & the PDP Research Group (Eds.), *Parallel distributed processing: Explorations in the microstructure of cognition. Volume 2: Psychological and biological models* (pp. 216–271). Cambridge, MA: MIT Press.

Rumelhart, D. E., McClelland, J. L., & the PDP Research Group. (Eds.). (1986). *Parallel distributed processing: Explorations in the microstructure of cognition. Volume 1: Foundations.* Cambridge, MA: MIT Press.

Schwartz, M. F. (Ed.). (1990). *Modular deficits in Alzheimer–type dementia.* Cambridge, MA: MIT Press.

Seidenberg, M. S. (1997). Language acquisition and use: Learning and applying probabilistic constraints. *Science, 275,* 1599–1603.

Seidenberg, M. S., & Hoeffner, J. H. (1998). Evaluating behavioral and neuroimaging data on past tense processing. *Language, 74,* 104–122.

Seidenberg, M. S., & McClelland, J. L. (1989). A distributed, developmental model of word recognition and naming. *Psychological Review, 96,* 523–568.

Sejnowski, T. J., Koch, C., & Churchland, P. S. (1989). Computational neuroscience. *Science, 241,* 1299–1306.

St. John, M. F., & McClelland, J. L. (1990). Learning and applying contextual constraints in sentence comprehension. *Artificial Intelligence, 46,* 217–257.

Studdert-Kennedy, M. (1993). Discovering phonetic function. *Journal of Phonetics, 21,* 147–155.

Tanenhaus, M. K., & Trueswell, J. (1995). Sentence processing. In P. Eimas, & J. L. Miller (Eds.), *Handbook of perception and cognition: Language* (pp. 217–262) New York: Academic Press.

Ullman, M. T., Corkin, S., Coppola, M., Hicock, G., Growdon, J. H., Koroshetz, W. J., & Pinker, S. (1997). A neural dissociation within language: Evidence that the mental dictionary is part of declarative memory and that grammatical rules are processed by the procedural system. *Journal of Cognitive Neuroscience, 9,* 266–276.

van Dijk, T. A., & Kintsch, W. (1983). *Strategies of discourse comprehension.* New York: Academic Press.

van Gelder, T. (1990). Compositionality: A connectionist variation on a classical theme. *Cognitive Science, 14,* 355–384.

Vihman, M. M. (1996). *Phonological development: The origins of language in the child.* Oxford: Blackwell.

Wagner, K. R. (1985). How much do children say in a day? *Journal of Child Language, 12,* 475–487.

III

The Neurological Bases of Language

7

Language in Microvolts

Marta Kutas
University of California, San Diego

Bernadette M. Schmitt
Maastricht University

Language mediates between thoughts and motor commands in a speaker, and between acoustic or visuospatial signals and thoughts in a listener. This mediation takes place in the brain. The brain is the machine that takes sounds, letter strings, or hand shapes as input and somehow yields the phenomenological sense of understanding. The brain is also the machine that controls the mouth or the hand in sign language so as to generate a linguistic utterance. Understanding language is one of the major integrative acts at which the human brain excels. The brain must integrate different kinds of language representations, such as semantic, syntactic, phonological knowledge of words, and discourse information, in real time during the process of understanding and speaking. It is thus to the brain in action that electrophysiologists turn for answers to fundamental questions about the nature of language representations and operations on them, and about the relationships among language and other cognitive processes.

There are more than 4,000 languages in the world. However, it is believed that their comprehension and production can be analyzed similarly in terms of a number of different kinds of representations (such as semantic, syntactic, and phonological knowledge) and a set of seemingly rule-based operations on these representations (such as accessing phonological, syntactic, and semantic information about words and sentences). The questions addressed by psycholinguistics examine what operations are performed on which representations at what point(s) in time. Psycholinguists argue about whether certain language abilities result from dedicated insular brain areas each specialized for specific kinds of linguistic representations and processes (modular approach), or whether these abilities are more accurately described in terms of interactions among different linguistic levels distributed across multiple brain regions (interactive or parallel distributed processing approach). They also argue about when in the processing stream the various representations make contact with each other, if ever. More recently, in addition to linguistic and psycholinguistic methods, various neuroimaging techniques have been used to investigate where, how, and when language processing takes place.

Functional brain imaging techniques differ widely in their ability to delineate separate physiological processing events, and to map these events onto both their spatially defined neuroanatomical substrates and their temporally defined place in the causal chain that guides thought and behavior. Those that depend on physiological changes related to energy metabolism in the brain (such as positron emission tomography [PET] and functional magnetic resonance imaging [fMRI] have illuminated important anatomical substrates of language processing. However, these metabolically based functional imaging techniques have not been as successful in elucidating the orchestration of these areas because they occur on the order of at least 2 seconds—much too slow to reflect changes crucial to the language processes that occur on the order of tens to a few hundreds of milliseconds. Because they depend on blood flow, PET and fMRI measures do not have the temporal resolution to index neural changes occurring for less than a second. The scalp-recorded electrical or magnetic fields produced by the brain, on the other hand, have had fewer applications in terms of anatomical mapping but enjoy a much higher temporal resolution (in milliseconds instead of seconds). Techniques with millisecond resolution, such as event related-brain potentials (ERPs) and their magnetic counterpart, the magnetoencephalogram (MEG), can be used to track the availability of different sorts of linguistic information and the temporal course of their interactions, and, thereby help to reveal how language processing unfolds over time.

AN INTRODUCTION TO ERPs

The general approach of electrophysiological studies assumes that (a) language processes take place in different anatomical and physiological substrates, (b) engagement of these substrates generates distinct patterns of biological activity (in this case, ion flow across neural membranes), and (c) these patterns (in this case, of electromagnetic activity) can be recorded inside and outside the head. The remainder of this chapter provides illustrations of how this type of research is carried out. We begin with an introduction to the ERP technique. We then review some ERP data concerning what goes on in the brain/mind of the language comprehender and the language producer (see also Brown & Hagoort, 2000; Brown, Hagoort, & Kutas, 2000; Kutas & Van Petten, 1994; Osterhout & Holcomb, 1995).

The Talking Cell

Comprehending and producing language are brain functions that require the coordinated activity of large groups of neurons. Neurons (nerve cells) have a sophisticated electrochemical system for communicating with each other. At rest, each neuron has a difference in its electrical charge due to an uneven distribution of positive and negative ions inside and outside of it. This is known as the resting potential. This potential can be disturbed by a change in the permeability of the membrane to certain ions, such as occurs when a cell is stimulated. The consequence of stimulation is an all-or-none action potential or spike that travels down an axon (a neuron's output). This spike signal is passed onto the next neuron via the release of neurotransmitter, which is a chemical substance that affects the next neuron by diffusing across a space between neurons, known as the synapse. Some neurotransmitters alter the permeability of the receiving cell's membrane to certain ions (i.e., altering the shape of proteins in the cell's membrane so as to allow some ions to get in and to keep others out), thereby increasing the likelihood that it will fire, whereas others have the opposite effect. These voltage-changes are reflected in the receiving cell in excitatory postsynaptic potentials (EPSPs), which increase the likelihood that the cell will fire, and inhibitory postsynaptic potentials (IPSPs), which decrease the likelihood that the cell will fire. Any given cortical cell receives hundreds of synaptic inputs, mostly on its dendritic arbor, a branch-link structure that receives information from other neurons, or on its soma (body). The postsynaptic potential generated at each of these synapses is not large enough to cause the cell to fire; however, these postsynaptic potentials sum in space and time. When the sum surpasses a neuron's threshold it will fire, thereby sending the signal via its axon to the next neuron, and so on.

The neural communication that underlies human communication thus involves the flow of charged particles across the neural membrane, which generates an electric potential in the conductive media both inside and outside the cell. These current flows across neuronal membranes are the basis for the electrophysiological recordings at the scalp. The electric potential at any given moment depends on the membrane currents only at that moment. What this means is that it is possible to monitor the neurons talking to each other, as it were, on a moment-by-moment basis.

It is possible to measure this activity by placing at least two electrodes somewhere on the head and recording the voltage difference between them. These measurements are much more sensitive to the currents at this receiving end (the EPSPs and IPSPs in the dendritic arbor of a cell) than to the spike generated down the axon that is used to communicate with the next cell. What we see at the scalp is the sum of these EPSPs and IPSPs for many neurons acting in concert in like manner. In fact, much of the activity seen at the scalp is probably that of the pyramidal cells of the neocortex because their dendritic arbors, when activated synchronously, tend to align in the same orientation thereby allowing the summation of their activity to be observed as a signal at the scalp (Kutas & Dale, 1997; Martin, 1991; Nunez, 1981).

Many Cells Telling Each Other What They Saw, Heard, Thought, or Felt

The brain is particularly sensitive to transient changes. Thus, if a picture, for example, of an aardvark were suddenly to appear in front of your eyes, your brain would process this patterned visual input, as it would a word, and so on. Cells in the parts of the brain that process visual information (i.e., primary & secondary visual cortices) and are involved in object recognition (i.e., inferotemporal cortex) would fire and within a few hundred milliseconds you would "know" that you had seen an animal, whether or not you knew exactly which one it was. At the same time, cells in other areas of the brain also would fire (see Mason & Kandel, 1991). Perhaps a little later you might come to realize that you once knew the name of this type of animal and would actively search your mind for it. You might fail, even if you knew that its name has two syllables and rhymes with "ark". On another occasion you might simply have uttered "aardvark" almost immediately. Whatever the case, there would be a flow of neural activity that could be traced from the retina through the visual pathways and into the higher areas of the brain and back and forth, (see e.g. McCarthy, Nobre, Bentin, & Spencer, 1995; Tanaka, 1996).

If one of these scenarios had taken place in an experimental laboratory setting, it would be considered an event or trial, and the electrical activity synchronized in time to the picture's appearance would be the evoked response (EP) to that event. The brain's response to such an event is what an electrophysiologist wants to measure so as to track what the brain does with the event. In so doing we can find out to which stimulus, cognitive, and response parameters the brain is sensitive. In addition, we can look at *when* in the temporal course of the event under investigation the brain reacts. However, the response to a single event is quite small relative to all the other ongoing electrical activity in the brain as well as in the eyes, muscles, and heart. We can, however, take advantage of the fact that the specific activity we want to measure is locked in time to the event we are interested in. Accordingly, we can record the evoked response to many such events (either physically or conceptually similar) and average them. At any given moment the electrical activity that is not time-locked to the event of interest is just as likely to be positive as negative, so with enough events, this "noise" from the various trials cancels out. What remains is the average EP or event-related brain potential—the ERP, as shown in Fig. 7.1 (for a detailed introduction on ERP see Coles & Rugg, 1995; Kutas & Federmeier, 1998; Kutas & King, 1996; Kutas & Van Petten, 1994).

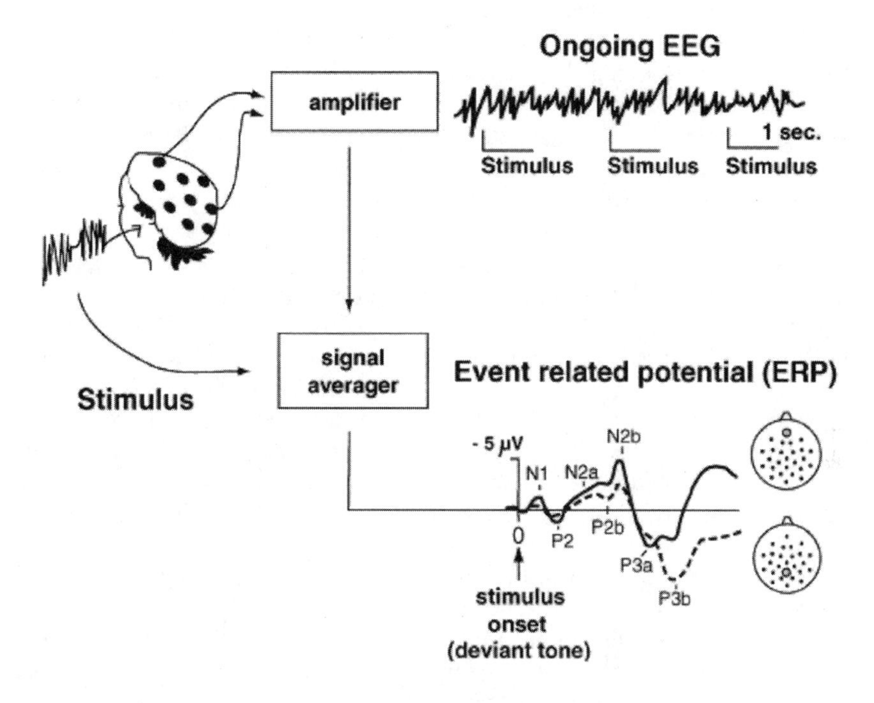

FIG. 7.1. Derivation and component structure of the event-related potential (ERP) to a deviant stimulus. The analog-recorded electric potentials at the scalp are shown as the ongoing electroencephalogram or EEG (top) is amplified and digitized. The ERP is generally too small (amplitudes of about 5–20µV, where 1V is 1 millionth of a volt; by comparison consider that an average flashlight battery is 1.5µV) to be detected in the EEG (amplitudes of about 100µV), and thus requires computer averaging over many stimulus presentations to achieve adequate signal-to-noise ratios. After averaging, time-locked to the onset of the stimulus, the ERP emerges as a waveform with a variety of positive and negative peaks (components). The solid line represents recordings from a midline frontal site and the dashed line the recording from a midline parietal site. Circles on the head icon represent electrode locations. Larger gray circles represent the electrode sites for which the average waveform is displayed; Negative is plotted upwards in this and all subsequent figures; potentials above the baseline are negative-going relative to activity prior to the stimulus whereas those below the baseline are positive going. Whether components are negative or positive at the scalp is a function of the location of the electrodes used for the recording and thus does not have any significance per se (after Näätänen, 1982, and Hillyard & Kutas, 1983). Note that a stimulus could also be a picture that has to be named, or a specific word in a sentence that has to be read or heard. Linguistic stimuli usually elicit specific ERP components that occur later in time than those shown here. Language related components (such as N280, N400, P600/SPS, LRP, N200) are described in more detail later in this chapter.

The Cells' Gossip Creates Waves

We record the electroencephalograph (EEG) at multiple sites on the scalp, each marked by a circle on the head icon in Fig. 7. 1. The EEG activity at each of these locations is averaged to yield an average ERP for that recording site. The average ERP is typically looked at as a waveform—a plot of the variations in voltage over time relative to the stimulus onset. There is one ERP waveform for each recording site. Such a waveform consists of a series of positive and negative-going waves (relative to baseline activity prior to event onset).

These waveforms can be analyzed in terms of their morphology (shape), the latency in time of their peaks, or the onsets of positive or negative-going waves, amplitude (size) of their peaks, distribution across the scalp, and duration of salient waveform pattern. The tradition is to measure the peaks, although there is nothing special about peaks; in principle, every moment of the waveform could be equally informative as it merely reflects neural activity at that instant.

Until quite recently, electrophysiological investigations of language have focused on relatively fast (high frequency), transient responses elicited by some "linguistic" event (e.g., picture or written or spoken word in a list or within a sentence); more recently, much slower potentials that develop across sentences and clauses have also been monitored.

Written words, spoken words, visuo-gestural words as in American Sign Language, and pictures each elicit a characteristic pattern of waves also known as components. The components are labeled in terms of their polarity as either negative (N) or positive (P) and in terms of their order of appearance (e.g., N1 first negative peak, N2 second negative peak, etc.) or in terms of their typical or actual latency (N100 at 100 msec, or N120), relative to stimulus onset. The initial components (e.g., P1, N1) are very sensitive to stimulus parameters (intensity, duration, spatial frequency, location in visual field) and attentional manipulations and are often seen as obligatory responses to stimuli. The later components are more task dependent as they show less sensitivity to physical stimulus parameters and greater sensitivity to variables that are neither strictly sensory nor strictly motor; they are optional depending on how the stimulus or event is processed.

When visually presented words are the events of interest, a typical average ERP may include P1, N1, P2, and other components, that are occasionally labeled by their proposed functional significance or scalp location; thus, FSN is frequency sensitive negativity, LRP is lateralized readiness potential, SPS is syntactic positive shift, CEN is clause ending negativity, and LAN is left anterior negativity.

Specifically, the FSN (referred to as LPN within the context of words) is a negativity over the left side of the front of the head occurring between 250 and 400 msec after a word's onset with a latency depending on the eliciting word's frequency of usage. The P2 component between 150 and 220 msec (sometimes together with a P3) occurs a little later and varies with the amount of attention directed at the features of the eliciting event. Note that these early components are elicited by nonlinguistic visual and auditory stimuli as well. However, especially the FSN can vary with the frequency of daily usage of words, and because it does so, it seems to be informative for linguistic processing (see the later section Representation and Processing Speed: The LPN for more details). The N400 (250–450 msec) is sensitive to a word's (or picture's) analysis at a semantic level. The SPS (or P600) varies with aspects of syntactic processing. The N400–700 is a later, slow potential seen prominently over the front of the head, that has been linked to anticipation of upcoming syntactic constructions (such as anticipation of a prepositional phrase following a preposition) in sentences (for review, see Hillyard & Picton, 1987; Kutas, Federmeier, Coulson, King, & Münte, 2000; Kutas & King, 1996; Osterhout & Holcomb, 1995). We discuss some of these in greater detail later.

Is Component X = Component X?

Before reviewing some specific examples of how ERP measurements are used to make inferences about various psycholinguistic issues, we wish to bring up one of the more difficult aspects of this type of research, namely, that of component identification. Is the negativity observed in one experimental condition the same as that observed in another condition? The answer, of course, depends on what one means by "the same" (reflection of same neural generator, same functional process). To begin, it is next to impossible, even for an experienced ERP researcher, to be shown a plot of an ERP waveform and asked to interpret it without more information. It is not even clear that one could say with certainty that the response was from a human. Given a plot of waveforms across the scalp surface of a human, the best one can do is to guess the modality (visual, auditory) of the eliciting stimulus. But beyond this, deciphering the waveform is difficult because for isolated events, the typical ERP consists of activity in a time window of a second or two, wherein there are a number of positive- and negative-going waves. The presence of large late potentials (300 msec plus) is often a sign of some "cognitive" processing, but it could also be a sign of drowsiness or that the person was asleep. A 30-year history of ERP research shows that ERPs are best interpreted in the context of the experimental conditions in which they were collected. ERP research has enumerated the types of ERP effects that are routinely seen in response to certain types of manipulations of attention, decision making, matches, mismatches, improbable events of various types, semantic variables, syntactic variables, how words look, how words sound, pseudowords, items in and out of context, encoding, and so on (e.g., Rugg & Coles, 1995).

Within each experiment or task, the safest reading of the ERPs comes out of contrasts between two or more waveforms, i.e., the effect as a difference of two experimental conditions. For example, although one might know that an unexpected word in a sentence context will elicit a negativity peaking at around 400 msec, one feels safer labeling it an N400 if the ERP it is a part of can be compared to that of a control word. The control word usually should be of the same part of speech (e.g., noun or verb) and it should have approximately the same within modality frequency of daily usage as the target word. Furthermore, both the control word and the target word should occur in the same position in the sentence. The two words should differ only in one experimental dimension, such as whether or not the word makes sense in the sentence (i.e., semantic expectancy). Moreover, one could feel on safer ground if the waveform has certain characteristics that one typically observes for an N400: a negativity that starts around 200 msec, lasts for a few hundred milliseconds, is larger posteriorly than anteriorly, and is larger over the right than the left hemisphere. However some N400s peak at 500 ms (as in elderly individuals or sentences presented at fast rates; see King & Kutas, 1995c) and some N400s are not as posterior or as lateralized as the one initially described for semantic violations. Yet they are considered N400s nonetheless. Moreover, not all negativities peaking at 400 msec are N400s. Would that it were that simple!

Part of the problem in identifying components stems from the inability to locate the neurons that are responsible for an ERP pattern. It is impossible to determine what subset of neurons generated some particular pattern of potentials at the scalp if the only information available is the pattern itself. In principle, the same pattern at the scalp could be created by various combinations of different neural generators, because the potential fields of active neuronal generators sum linearly. Thus, in the same way that one cannot tell from the number 7 how the total came about (e.g., 6 + 1, 5 + 2, 4 + 1 + 1+ 1, 8–1, etc.), the brain sources for the scalp potentials remain a mystery during the interpretation of a component at the scalp. We would be safe if we knew that only one generator were active at a time, because this generator would have a spatial signature at the scalp each time it was engaged. However, from what we know of how the brain works, this is highly unlikely. Usually, more than one generator is involved in complex cognitive tasks. Intracranial recordings from electrodes in the brains of epileptic patients (McCarthy et al., 1995), and on the scalp of individuals with various kinds of brain damage can help to localize a component's generators as can magnetic recordings combined with various modeling techniques (Dale & Sereno, 1993; Dale et al., 2000).

Although intracranial recordings are usually made prior to neurosurgery in individuals with seizure activity (and may thus be abnormal), in many cases, the implanted electrodes may be closer to the neural generators of the component in question. Various aspects of the recorded potentials such as its polarity and its polarity relative to those of potentials at nearby electrodes (same or opposite) as well as the relative amplitudes of potentials at electrodes nearby versus farther away all can be used to infer the likelihood that the generator of the recorded potential is close by. Likewise, although a compromised brain may yield uninterpretable brain activity because it is damaged, whether or not, and if so how, damage to a particular brain region influences the potentials at the scalp can be used to infer whether that area is essential for, or at least involved in, some aspect of the generation of modulation of the component of interest.

In summary, the ERP is a biological tool that can be used to measure a variety of cognitive processes. It is essential to interpret the ERP component in the context of the experiment and its specific manipulations. The experimental comparison does not reveal the anatomical locus of a component but does constrain the likelihood that it is the same as another component with the same functional characteristics. In addition, because of the ERP's high temporal resolution it is especially well suited to address issues concerning timing and interaction in high-speed processes, such as language. Next we discuss how ERPs are used to investigate language comprehension.

FROM THE EARDRUMS TO THE MEANING: ERPS IN COMPREHENSION

The recognition of spoken language begins with the extraction of acoustic and phonetic information from the speech signal. This is a nontrivial problem, given that the acoustic signal includes no obvious cue as to where a word begins or ends (for a review see Lively, Pisoni, & Goldinger, 1994). What information then does the listener use to extract meaning from an essentially continuous acoustic stream? Are there units of perception, and if so, are they acoustic-phonetic features (such as the length of vowels), phonemes, syllables, and/or prosodic patterns? Reaction time studies show shorter recognition latencies for "well-" as opposed to "ill-formed" patterns based on each of these units of analysis, thereby giving them some psychological reality (for a review see Altmann & Shillcock, 1993; Caplan, 1992; McQueen & Cutler, 1997). But there is still no consensus on whether the brain actually categorizes acoustic input in these ways nor about how these units might feed into or interact with higher order cognitive processes such as meaning integration.

One assumed source of meaning is the mental "lexicon"—an abstract store of knowledge about words. Psycholinguists commonly use the term *lexical access* as a metaphor for the process of looking up or activating language-related information in this lexicon. The fastest way of looking up the German word "Erdferkel" in a German-English dictionary is to use the alphabetic coding system. So doing reveals that "Erdferkel" is the German equivalent of an "earthpig" or 'aardvark'. Besides phonological information, syntactic information becomes available, such as that the word is a noun. Furthermore, for a native English speaker, the translation would automatically provide access to the word's denotative meaning. Thus, you may find that an aardvark is a large burrowing nocturnal mammal—an animal that has an extensile tongue, powerful claws, large ears, a heavy tail, and an appetite for termites. If you are a student in the cognitive science department at the University of California at San Diego you may also be reminded of the fact that it is the name of the department's sports teams.

Although there is consensus that word knowledge is stored, there is less agreement on exactly what information about words is stored in the mental lexicon, the internal structure of the store, how it is used during comprehension or production, or how it is implemented in neural tissue. It has been suggested that, like a real dictionary, the mental lexicon holds different types of information about words, such as phonological information (maybe in term of cohorts; see Colombo, 1986), semantic information (in terms of networks or category relations; see Collins & Loftus, 1975; Miller & Fellbaum, 1991; Saffran & Sholl, 1999), and syntactic information, although none necessarily in a single location. In fact, the same "word" may be represented multiply along different dimensions, which normally come together when that "word" is accessed. Presumably each of these dimensions is structured because this aids error-free access. A fast, error-free access is needed, because in a typical conversation a normal speaker produces about five to six syllables per second (Deese, 1984), and up to150 words per minute (Maclay & Osgood, 1959), and a listener has to segregate the incoming speech stream very quickly in order to keep up with the speaker.

Reaction-time studies indicate that before a speech sound is recognized as a particular word, several lexical candidates consistent with the available input become activated (accessed); this cohort is progressively winnowed until only one candidate that is consistent with the acoustic input is selected as the word heard (Marslen-Wilson, 1987, 1990; Marslen-Wilson & Welsh, 1978; Zwitserlood, 1989). At issue is whether or not phonological, syntactic, or semantic information is involved in reducing the initial cohort. Interactive models (such as TRACE; see McClelland & Elman, 1986) say semantic and phonological information influences speech perception whereas autonomous models (such as SHORTLIST; see Norris, 1994) say semantic information does not influence speech perception. As currently implemented, both types of models can account for lexical effects in a variety of experimental tasks, thereby leaving the question of autonomous versus interactive processing still open (see McQueen & Cutler, 1997). The need for convergent data from other methods, such as from ERP investigations of speech processing, is obvious (see Van Petten, Coulson, Rubin, Plante, & Parks, 1999).

Because of its exquisite temporal resolution, the ERP can be used to track the time course of the brain's sensitivity to various information types—phonological, semantic, syntactic—in the acoustic stream. By the time an effect of a variable is evident in the ERP, it must have been registered—hence, the onset latency of the ERP effect provides information about when specific cognitive processes are performed. At times the pattern of ERPs recorded also can be revealing about the extent to which various information types are or are not integrated. An added benefit of the ERP technique is that no extra task (such as categorization or lexical decision in reaction time experiments) above and beyond listening, reading, or comprehending needs to be imposed to garner a dependent variable. On the pathway from the eardrums to the mind, we address ERPs in phonological processing first and than delve more deeply into the mind by addressing semantic, syntactic, and discourse processes.

Is the ERP Sensitive to the Time Course of Phonological Access?

If ERPs are to be useful in studies of the sound patterns of human language, we first need to know whether or not they are sensitive to phonological information. There are several reasons why the ERP at the scalp may not show sensitivity to any particular variable, in this case, phonological information. For instance, it may be that phonology is processed in a brain area whose activity is not readily seen at the scalp. This could be because the active regions of the neurons involved in the ERP's generation are aligned so that the potentials cancel each other (as in a closed field). This could also be because the phonological processing does not occur in the same temporal synchrony with the eliciting stimulus across trials. However, if we find that some parameter of the scalp-recorded ERP does vary with phonological information, then we can use the timing of the effect as an estimate of the upper limit on when the brain must have registered the information. Thus, we can use the ERP to ask when phonological information becomes available during natural speech processing. We may also use the ERP's sensitivity to phonological information to examine a controversial aspect of theories of lexical access—namely, whether phonological processing occurs prior to and independent of semantic processing, as suggested by an autonomous approach, or whether semantic information can influence phonological encoding, as suggested by an interactive approach.

Rhyme Time: When in Comprehension Does Phonological Information Become Available?

The words "cat" and "cab" share the same initial phonemes. "Cat" and "hat," on the other hand, share word-medial and word-final phonemes; that is, they rhyme. When does a listener notice these relationships, and is the ERP sensitive to the perception of these phonological relations? And is the onset relation noticed earlier than the rhyme relation, as might be expected given the serial nature of acoustic input? Praamstra, Meyer, and Levelt (1994) used ERPs to examine this question by presenting participants with pairs of spoken words that had either an onset relation, rhyme relation or no phonological relation (e.g., "cat"–"sun"). After a slight delay subjects indicated whether the stimulus was a real word or not. The ERP of interest was time-locked to the beginning of the second stimulus.

As can be seen in Fig. 7.2, all acoustic words elicited a similar waveform with an early negativity at around 100 msec (N1) followed by a large negativity peaking at around 400 ms. The late negativity was largest in amplitude for unrelated words; it was reduced in amplitude for both types of phonologically related second words. The reduction was evident early, between 250 and 450 msec relative to word onset for the onset relation, and, later, between 450 and 700 msec for the rhyming relation (for similar ERP rhyming data, see Barrett & Rugg, 1990; Rugg, 1984a, 1984b; Rugg & Barrett, 1987).

Because the rhyme and the onset versions were carried out in separate experiments using different materials, the timing differences must be interpreted with caution. In any case, however, the results show that the ERP is sensitive to phonological processing. Moreover, if we assume (as the authors did) that the same ERP component is varying in both conditions, then the results indicate that its latency is sensitive to the time course of phonological encoding (showing an early effect for word onset, and a late effect for rhyme relations). The data show that phonological encoding takes places serially.

Furthermore, the observed phonological effect is similar in timing (between 200 and 600 msec) and scalp distribution to the N400 component, usually ob-

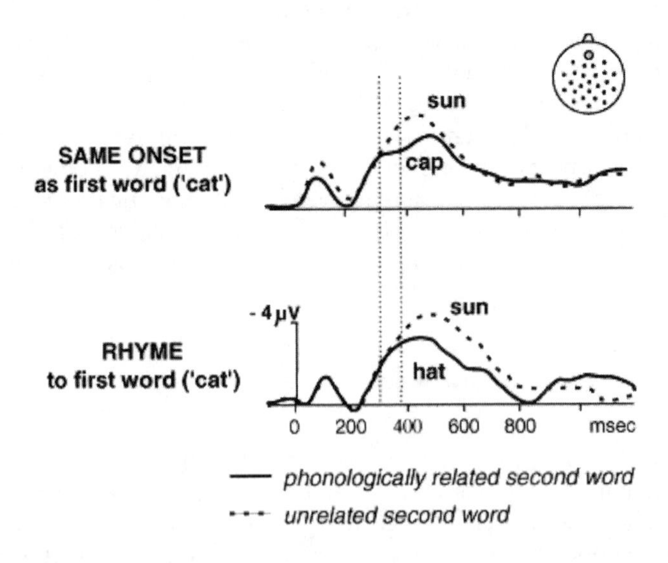

FIG. 7.2. Comparison of the grand average ERPs elicited by a second word of a phonologically related and unrelated spoken word-pair (the same 24 participants in all conditions; 40 trials per condition). The top panel shows an early phonological effect when the second word shares the same onset phonemes with the first word. The bottom panel shows a later phonological effect when the second word rhymed with the first, that is, shared final phonemes. (Adapted from Praamstra et al., 1994, with permission).

served in semantic tasks (Pritchard, Shappell, & Brandt, 1991). What might this similarity mean? If the phonological N400 is the same as the semantic N400, one could argue that phonological and semantic processes are not independent. However, even if this negativity is not an N400, the data indicate a temporal overlap in the processing of phonological and semantic information. Whatever the case turns out to be, the described experiment illustrates how the fine-grained temporal aspects of the ERP make it an excellent tool for investigating the time course of phonological processing, which is closely aligned in time and perhaps interactive with semantic processing.

From other experiments like this we know that the ERP is also sensitive to (a) identity relations, so that processing "cat" after "cat" is different from "cat" after "sun" (Doyle, Rugg, & Wells, 1996; Rugg, 1985; Van Petten, Kutas, Kluender, Mitchiner, & McIsaac, 1991); (b) morphological relations, so that "jump" after "jumped" is different than "jump" after "look" (Münte, Say, Clahsen, Schiltz, & Kutas, 1999); and (c) semantic relations, so that "cat" after "dog" is different from "cat" after "ink" (Holcomb, 1988; Kutas & Hillyard, 1989). The phonological, morphological, and semantic effects all occur by about 200 msec. So although it is not a direct empirical test of the question we raised about the role of meaning in phonological processing, these data are more in line with parallel then serial processing models of phonological, morphological, and semantic information during comprehension.

The Brain's Response to Meaning: The N400

The mind's extraction of meaning has been examined not only within word–pair tasks but also using "violation" paradigms. Our brains are very sensitive to violations of meaning. Specifically, a written, a spoken, or a signed word that does not make sense relative to its context elicits a large negativity between 200 and 500 msec that peaks around 400 msec (Kutas & Hillyard, 1980a, 1980b, 1980c). Even a semantically anomalous picture seems to elicit an N400–like response. In such studies, sentences are presented visually to volunteers one word at a time for comprehension. The sentences might vary, depending on the degree of expectancy of the final word, as in the following example:

He was stung by a bee.	(expected ending)
He was stung by a hive.	(unexpected, but semantically related)
He was stung by a mile.	(unexpected and semantically unrelated)

The ERPs to these final words (for an average of 25 words per condition), are depicted in Fig. 7. 3. The expected word elicits a positivity between 200 and 500 msec, the semantically anomalous word elicits a large N400, and the anomalous but semantically or associatively related word elicits an N400 of intermediate amplitude (Kutas & Hillyard, 1980a, 1980b, 1980c, 1982; Kutas, Van Petten &

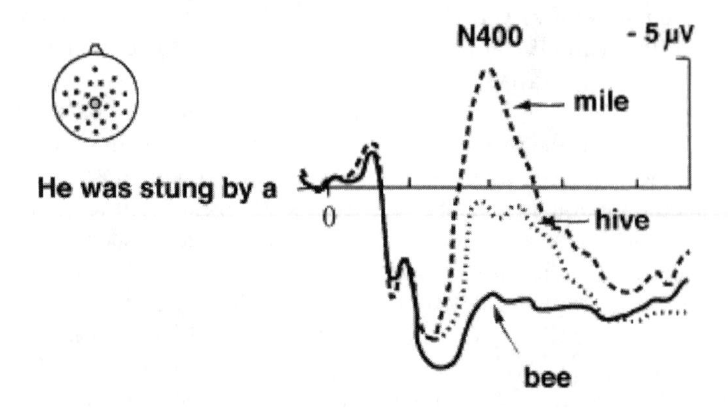

FIG. 7.3. Grand average ERPs elicited by visually presented sentence–final words, showing a positivity between 250 and 500 msec (solid line) for a predictable word, and an N400 between 200 and 500 msec for a semantically anomalous word (thick dashed line). When the final word is semantically incongruent but semantically related to the expected final word (dotted line), it elicits an N400 of intermediate amplitude (After Kutas and Hillyard 1984), with permission.

Besson, 1988; for a review see Kutas & King, 1996 and Kutas & van Petten, 1994). Fortunately for its utility as a tool for investigating semantic processing, N400 elicitation is not driven solely by semantic anomalies. In fact, in a sentence context all words seem to elicit some N400 activity, with the amplitude determined by how expected a word is and thus how readily it can be integrated with the current context at a semantic level. In the absence of context, N400 amplitude is determined by word frequency (larger for low-frequency words according to Francis & Kucera, 1982, among others), concreteness (larger for concrete than abstract words), and other properties of the words. With minimal context such as in a word pair, the N400 to the second word is reduced by repeating the same word exactly or by a word that is semantically related. Within a sentence, with all else held constant, the amplitude of the N400 to any content (meaning–bearing) word such as an adjective, adverb, noun, or verb becomes smaller and smaller the further into the sentence it occurs. Studies using words in semantically anomalous sentences (meaningless, but syntactically correct sentences, such as "Colorless green ideas sleep furiously") show no such reduction in N400, regardless of the word's intrasentential position. This suggests that it is the semantic rather than syntactic constraints that conspire to reduce the N400 in normal prose.

The N400 occurs within 200 msec after presentation of the critical word, thereby supporting theoretical models of sentence processing that assume relatively immediate online integration of a word's meaning into sentence context (Gernsbacher & Hargreaves, 1988; Just & Carpenter, 1980). The N400's timing does not support models which propose that word meanings are buffered for use at phrase boundaries, clause boundaries, or the ends of sentences rather than analyzed on a word-by-word basis with respect to the immediate context (see Fodor & Bever, 1965; Garrett, Bever & Foder, 1966; Just & Carpenter, 1980; for a review, Kutas & Van Petten, 1994).

Data from several studies show that the important context for modulating N400 amplitude is not just a related word earlier in the sentence, or the many words of a sentence, but also that of the larger context of the discourse of which a sentence may be but a part. As single sentences, both "The aardvark went quickly into its burrow," and "The aardvark went slowly into its burrow" are equally plausible and the words within them should elicit about the same level of N400 activity. However, put into a larger discourse context, such as, "It was a quiet summer day. The aardvark was surprised by the sudden appearance of the tiger and went ... " the two adverbs (quickly, slowly) are no longer equally expected. If discourse information comes into play relatively early during sentence processing, then one might expect a larger N400 to the word "slowly," because it is less expected in the context; this is what Van Berkum, Hagoort, and Brown (1999) found for similar materials in Dutch (see Fig. 7. 4).

Whatever else this might mean, such results show that discourse-level information can influence how words in a sentence are processed. Moreover, discourse-level effects appear to come into play about the same time that a single

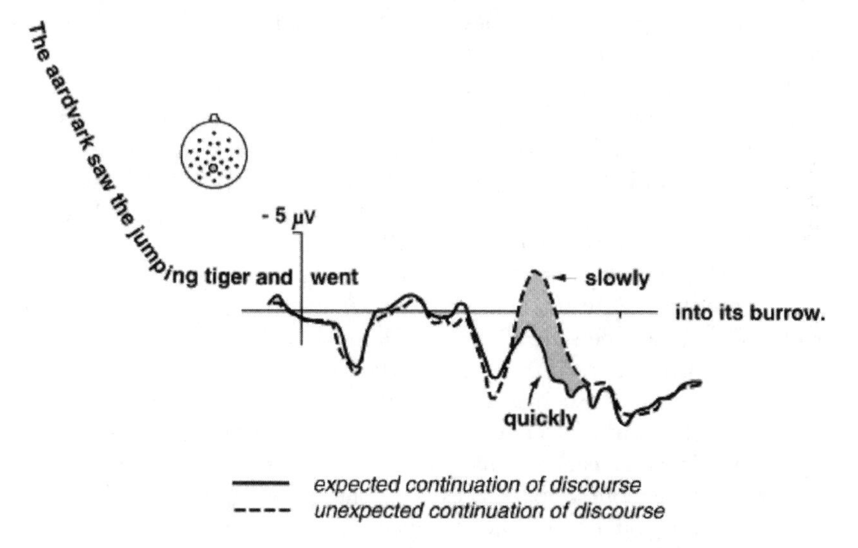

FIG. 7.4. Grand average ERPs (24 participants, 40 trials per participant) elicited by three words in a sentence; the second word is either an expected or an unexpected adverb, where the expectancy is based on discourse level information. The solid line shows the ERP to an expected continuation of a sentence in the discourse. The dashed line represents an unexpected continuation. The shaded area depicts the discourse level effect on N400 elicited by the unexpected adverb. After Van Berkum, Brown, and Hagoort, (1999), with permission.

related word would have its effect or that prior words in a sentence would have their effects. These results are clearly at odds with a serial view of processing that makes a clean separation between a word's processing and the larger sentential or discourse context with which it has to be reconciled. In summary, the N400 is a very robust index of semantic processing at the lexical, sentential, and discourse levels.

Representation and Processing Speed: The LPN

Although we do not yet know exactly how words are extracted from the speech signal, we can nonetheless ask whether words, once detected as such, differ from each other, in either their representation or their processing. Are nouns, because they refer to objects, and verbs, because they refer to actions, differentially represented in the brain (e.g., Pulvermüller, 1996)? Is the brain's response to nouns and other meaningful, content-bearing words different from its response to function words, such as articles, conjunctions, prepositions, auxiliaries, which tend to have less meaning and to serve the function of relating the content words to each other? From a linguistic point of view, different parts of speech clearly do play different functional roles, and thus some have argued that indeed they are stored in different brain regions and, at least for content versus function words, are accessed from the mental lexicon in qualitatively different ways (as proposed by Swinney, Zurif, & Cutler, 1980; see also Patterson & Shewell, 1987; Shillcock & Bard, 1993).

On the face of it, ERPs to different word classes do differ. The responses to function and content words differ from one another, as do the responses to nouns versus verbs and pronouns versus articles, among others. For example, open class words, which are content words, have larger P200s and N400s than function words when both types are embedded in a sentence (King & Kutas, 1995a; Kluender & Kutas, 1993; Neville, Mills, & Lawson, 1992; Van Petten & Kutas, 1991). In fact, no one denies that different lexical classes are associated with different ERP patterns. They do, however, disagree over what this means about how their members are represented in the brain and/or how they are accessed. It is difficult to answer this question because content and function words vary in important ways, such as word length and word frequency, which are in and of themselves known to have big effects on a word's processing.

For example, both reaction time and eye movement testify to the fact that longer words take more time to access than shorter words and that frequently used words are understood and produced more quickly than rare words (Jescheniak & Levelt, 1994; Just & Carpenter, 1980). These differences alone could account for the observed differences between the ERPs to content and function words, as function words are typically much shorter and of much higher frequency than content words (Gordon & Caramazza, 1985; Thibadeau, Just, & Carpenter, 1983). In fact, we have found that frequency does account for one of the proposed ERP differences between the two word classes (King & Kutas, 1995a, 1998). Contrary to the suggestion that there is a negative potential around 280 msec (N280) that is a marker for closed class words, we find that taking into account the frequency of a word reveals that the ERPs to all words include a negativity at left frontal recording sites. Thus, regardless of lexical class, the ERPs to all words contain a negativity somewhere between 250 and 400 msec, whose latency varies with a word's frequency of usage (See Fig. 7.5.)

On average, closed class words show this negativity (called the lexical processing negativity or LPN, or frequency sensitive negativity or FSN, indicating the possibility that the negativity may not be specific to words) at 280 msec and open class words, which are longer and lower frequency, show it about 50 msec later at 330 msec. This index of a word's frequency of usage is present to all words as they are read naturally for comprehension; no other overt response is needed. Even if the LPN/FSN does not reflect lexical access from the mental lexicon (because it might reflect other processes involved, such as working memory), it is strongly correlated with the process of lexical access. Thus, the LPN/FSN can be used as a dependent variable in investigations of how quickly or easily words are retrieved.

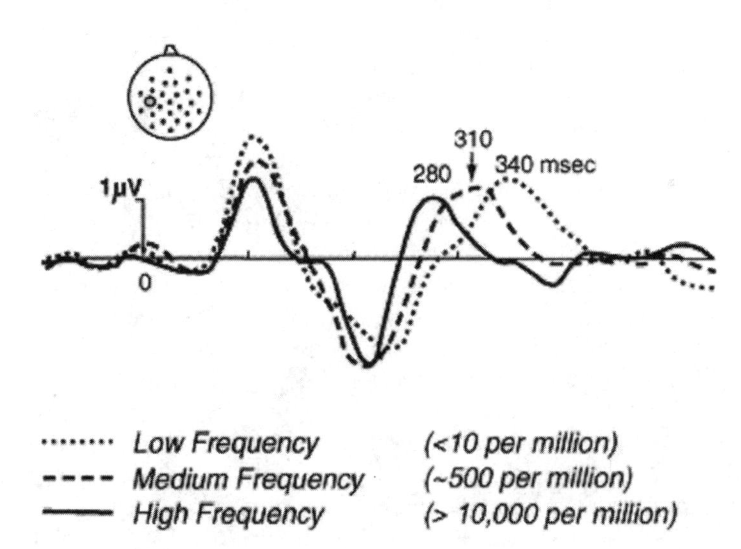

FIG. 7.5. Grand average ERPs elicited by words of different frequency of usage (bandpass–filtered, 4–20 Hz). High frequency words (solid line) elicit a negativity peaking at about 280 ms after word onset. This peak latency is earlier than for medium frequency words (dashed line, 310 msec) and low frequency words (dotted line, 340 msec). The negativity is called the lexical processing negativity or LPN, or even more generally the frequency sensitive negativity or FSN. (After King and Kutas, 1998), with permission.

WHEN SYNTACTIC VIOLATIONS DIFFER WHAT DOES IT MEAN?: THE SPS/P600

Until recently, most of the neuroimaging work on language processing has focused on the processing of single words, usually as part of word pairs or a longer list. But language is much more than a string of isolated words. Most of our communicative acts occur in sentences or beyond, as in discourse. Linguists tell us about the hierarchical structure of utterances—that is, what orders of words in a sentence are acceptable and which are not, as well as the grammatical roles that these words play. Psycholinguists propose various strategies that describe how a comprehender determines the proper structural analysis of a sentence—that is, how he or she parses the sentence. Many of the more recent ERP studies of language have been designed to test among alternative theories of parsing (see Pullum & Scholz, this volume; also chap. 5, Fodor, 1989, 1995; Garnsey, 1993; Garnsey, Tanenhaus, & Chapman, 1989; Garrett, 1995). These investigations capitalize on the observation that ERPs are sensitive to manipulations of at the level of syntax (relations between words in a sentence) and the nature of the effect differs qualitatively from that observed to more lexico–semantic manipulations.

In search of the functional significance of the N400 component, Kutas and Hillyard (1983) found that a syntactically or grammatically incorrect word such as a singular verb following a plural noun (e.g., "turtles eats") did not elicit a large N400, like a semantic anomaly, but rather small fronto–central negativity together with a small late positivity. Ten years later two laboratories independently identified a late positivity that is reliably elicited by a variety of syntactic violations. This positivity, variously called the syntactic positive shift (Hagoort, Brown, & Groothusen, 1993) or P600 component (Osterhout & Holcomb, 1992), can occur anywhere between 300 to 800 msec postword onset and is widely distributed across the scalp. Figure 7.6 shows the contrast between syntactically correct and incorrect sentences, wherein the violation is the grammatical number marking on the verb ("My pet aardvark prefer/prefers to eat potatoes").

As can be seen in the figure, this morphosyntactic violation elicits a positivity, large over posterior sites, that starts at around 500 msec after the violating word was presented and lasts for 300 msec or so. Similar effects have been noted for other violations including reflexive–antecedent gender agreement (e.g., "The momma aardvark sees himself as a potato lover"), reflexive-antecedent case agreement, phrase-structure violations (e.g., "The aardvark was fascinated by the emotional rather response of its mother"), constraints on the movement of sentence constituents ("What was a proof of criticized by the scientist?"), and verb subcategorization. Similar effects have been observed for violations occurring in written and spoken sentences in English, Dutch, German, and Finnish (e.g., Friederici, Pfeifer, & Hahne, 1993; Hagoort & Brown, 2000; Osterhout & Holcomb, 1993). Importantly, the P600 is seen whether the subject's task is to make an acceptability or grammaticality

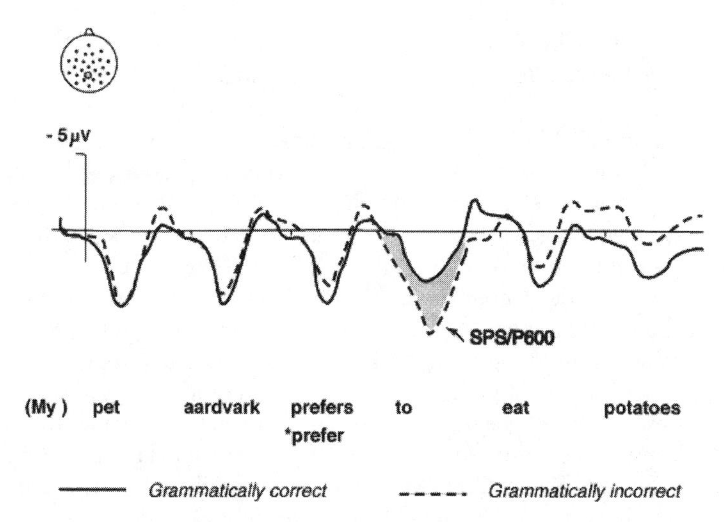

FIG. 7.6. Grand average ERPs elicited by a syntactic violation of subject–verb–number agreement. The solid line shows the ERP to syntactically correct sentences, the dashed line to syntactically incorrect sentences. The shaded area indicates the effect of this violation, known as the syntactic positive shift (SPS), or P600. After Hagoort, Brown, and Groothusen (1993), with permission.

judgment or merely to read or listen to the sentence (for review see Osterhout, McLaughlin, & Bersick, 1997).

The presence of P600 across a wide variety of grammatical violations has been used to argue for its syntactic sensitivity, although it also makes it difficult to pin down exactly what aspect of processing the component reflects. Among the proposed functional interpretations of the P600 are:

1. It is a general-purpose (non-linguistic) process such as the P3 elicited whenever enough information, of any type, has accumulated so as to require an updating of working memory (e.g. Coulson, King, & Kutas, 1998; Gunter, Stowe, & Mulder, 1997);
2. It is a reflection of specifically grammatical processing, related to (re)analysis whenever the parser fails to find a meaningful parse (Friederici & Mecklinger, 1996; Hagoort et al., 1993; Osterhout, 1994).
3. It is a re-analysis involving semantic processes (Münte, Matzke, & Johannes, 1997).

In some sense, it does not matter because in most of the linguistic settings, the response is clearly driven, in large part, by grammatical processing. As long as conditions (attention, meaning) are held constant and only syntactic processing is manipulated, a syntactic violation can be counted on to elicit some P600 activity, whose presence and timing can therefore be used to investigate various theories of parsing.

Most importantly, the P600 is not just a syntactic violation detector; it appears to be elicited at points of syntactic ambiguity (Brown, Hagoort, & Kutas, 2000; Hagoort & Brown, 1994). These are points in which the sentence can be interpreted in different ways, as at the word "coyote" in "The aardvark saw the ant and the coyote spotted the snake behind the rock"; here "coyote" could be what the aardvark saw or "coyote" could be who was doing the spotting of the snake. The fact that there are these two possible readings of the same set of words suggests different ways of structuring the words into sentence constituents. One interprets "the coyote" as a conjoint noun phrase, and the other interprets it as the beginning of a new sentence. The resolution of ambiguity in the example is at the verb "spotted", and is reflected in P600 activity. As can be seen in Figure 7.7 (data from Brown, Hagoort, & Kutas, (2000), an ambiguous reading (without a comma) reveals a P600, in contrast to an unambiguous reading (with comma).

For the moment we do not know exactly what processes are reflected in the P600 at the point of disambiguation. One idea, proposed by Brown, Hagoort, &

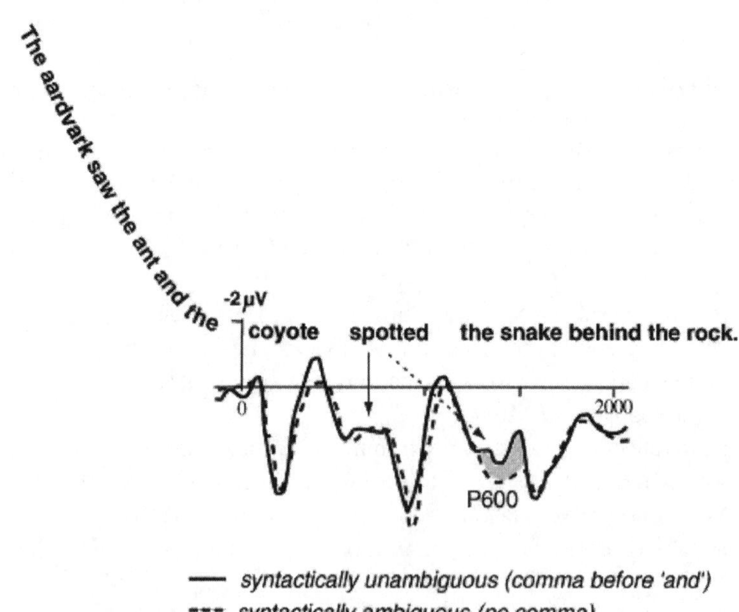

FIG. 7.7. Grand average ERPs to three words within syntactically ambiguous (dashed line) versus syntactically unambiguous (solid line) sentences: the syntactically ambiguous word, the disambiguating word, and the word following. Note the greater P600 or SPS to the disambiguating word ("spotted") relative to the same word, when a comma before "and" prevented an ambiguity. After Brown, Hagoort, and Kutas, (2000), with permission.

Kutas, (2000), is that the parser uses one reading as default and has to change the interpretation at the moment the critical verb signals that only the second reading is possible. In the parsing literature it has been suggested that the conjoined noun phrase reading is a default (preferred) reading, for two reasons: (a) the syntactic structure is assumed to be less complex than for sentence conjunctions, and (b) the parser prefers less complex readings. Thus, the P600 effect might reflect the process of shifting from the default to an alternative reading, among other possibilities.

One of the stronger arguments in favor of the hypothesis that the P600 reflects some aspect of syntactic processing is the finding that it is elicited by violations of number agreement even in syntactic prose (i.e., semantically anomalous sentences) presented visually, one word at a time with punctuation as needed. As can be seen in Figure 7. 8 (top), a P600 is elicited by the verb in "Two mellow graves freely sinks by the litany" when it is marked singular with an "s" relative to when it is without the "s." Clearly, a sentence need not make sense to elicit some P600 activity. Thus, it would seem there is a purely syntactic representation of a sentence that can be violated. However, some data by Münte, Matzke, and Johannes (1997) suggest that a crucial element in the picture may be the possibility that a sentence might make sense (even if it does not). Take, for example, syntactic prose wherein real words are replaced by pseudowords (e.g., "Twe mullow grives freoly senks by the litune."). For these types of sentences, the ERP to the verb number violation does not elicit a P600 (see Fig. 7.8, bottom).

The lack of the P600 effect, however, was not because the brain is unaware that something is potentially amiss, because the violation is associated with a frontal negativity (not shown in the figure). The presence of the P600 in strings of words and its absence in strings of pseudowords suggest that the P600 may not be wholly independent of semantic processing.

But in the context of a meaningful sentence presented one word at a time visually or as natural speech, a syntactic violation or ambiguity resolution will elicit a P600. Thus, its presence or absence, amplitude, and/or latency can be used to test alternative accounts of how a sentence is parsed, what the preferred parse is, and the type of information that can override the preferred parse. Evidence, not detailed here, indicates that, at least sometimes, semantic and discourse information can influence the initial syntactic ambiguity of a sentence. For example, there would be no P600 to "spotted" in "The radio played the music and the coyote spotted the snake behind the rock," even though it includes a syntactic ambiguity, because radios do not "play coyote." So at times, semantic information can override the syntactic parse (see, e.g., Brown, Van Berkum, & Hagoort, 2000).

Sentence Processing and Working Memory: The Ultraslow Potentials

The temporal resolution of the ERP is such that it can be used to look at not only the very fast stop-consonant transitions such as those that differentiate a "g"

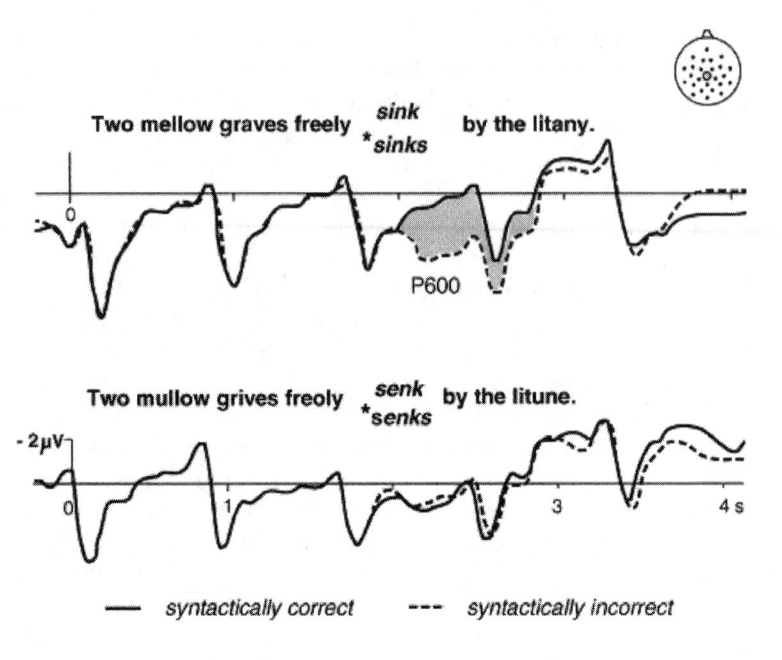

FIG. 7.8. Grand average ERPs elicited by morphosyntactic (subject–verb–number agreement) violations in meaningless sentences (prose). The solid lines show ERPs to syntactically correct sentences, and the dashed lines to incorrect sentences, wherein the verbs do not agree in number with their subject. At the top panel, the sentences are so-called syntactic prose. A syntactic violation in this case elicits a P600 effect (shaded area). In contrast, in the bottom panel, syntactic prose made of pseudowords is shown. Syntactic violations in pseudoword prose do *not* elicit a P600 effect. After Münte, Matzke, and Johannes (1997), with permission.

from a "d" but also the relatively slower processes that are needed to determine who did what to whom within a sentence or even discourse. By recording over an entire clause, we find a variety of very slow potentials (low frequency) on which the specific, transient evoked responses to the individual words are superimposed. The nature of the slow potential and the factors that seem to affect its behavior vary across the head (King & Kutas, 1995b). For visual stimuli there is a long-standing negativity over the visual areas at the back of the head. For auditory materials there is a long-standing negativity over the auditory areas located more centrally. For both written and spoken sentences, there is an ultraslow positivity over the frontal regions of the head (Müller, King, & Kutas, 1997). This ultraslow positivity has been hypothesized to reflect the linking of linguistic information and world knowledge in working memory during discourse processing (for reviews of discourse processing see Clark, 1994; Ericsson & Kintsch, 1995; Kintsch, 1994).

The interaction of linguistic processes and working memory can be seen in the comparison of simple and complex sentences. Sentences within sentences, that is, sentences with relative clauses, are typically more difficult to comprehend than those without embeddings because they are assumed to be more demanding on working memory. And even for relative clauses a distinction can be made in terms of complexity. In object-relative clauses as "The aardvark that the cop really scared ran into the bushes," several words pass before the reader/listener knows what grammatical or thematic role "aardvark" plays in the sentence. That is, several words must be read/heard before one can know what, if anything, the "aardvark" did or what, if anything, was done to the "aardvark" and if so by whom. This means the word "aardvark" has to stay in working memory for quite some time. This is not the case in subject-relative clauses, such as "The aardvark that really scared the cop ran into the bushes." Here, the same word "aardvark" is the subject of the main clause as well as of the relative clause.

As depicted in Figure 7.9, the ERP waveforms spanning entire clauses in these two sentence types show a divergence as soon as there is a difference in working memory load, with greater negativity observed for the more demanding sentence type. This difference is most pronounced over frontal sites of the left hemisphere. This general pattern holds whether the sentences are read one word at a time or naturally spoken (King & Kutas, 1995b; Müller et al., 1997).

At the level of the ERP to individual words, greater working memory load seems to be associated with negativity over the frontal regions of the left side of the head. In the example just given, the ERP to the main clause verb ("ran") would show relatively greater negativity between 200 and 800 msec after onset of the individual words when the "aardvark" did the running and the "cop" did the scaring than when the "aardvark" did both; this is the so-called left anterior negativity or LAN.

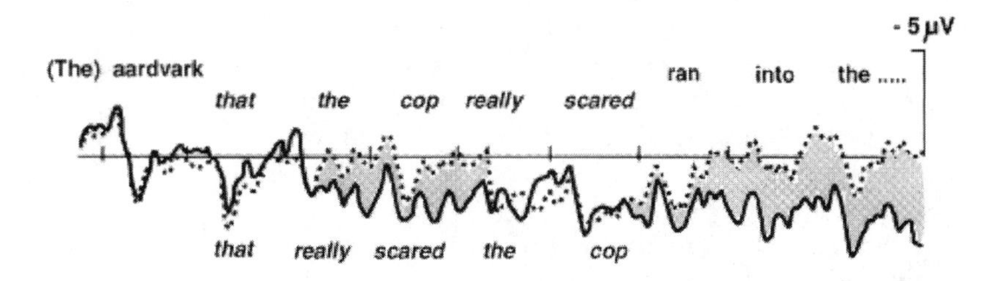

FIG. 7.9. Comparison of the grand-average cross-sentence ERPs elicited by subject relative (solid line) and object relative (dotted line) sentences recorded over a left frontal location. Words were visually presented one at a time every 500 ms for 200 ms each. The shading represents areas of where object relative sentences are reliably more negative than subject relative sentences (after King & Kutas, 1995b).

We observed a similar pattern of ERP effects to sentences designed to investigate how real-world knowledge and linguistic knowledge interact during sentence processing (Münte, Schiltz, & Kutas, 1998). Specifically, we examined how people's conceptions of time as flowing linearly influences their processing such that they might find it easier to understand (read) sentences that describe events in their natural order than sentences that describe events counter to their actual order of occurrence (i.e., a later event before an earlier event). We pursued this simply by changing the first words of sentences, all of which had two clauses. The sentences began either with the word "Before" or the word "After" as in "Before/After the scientist finished her lecture, the aardvark chewed the pointer." Linguistic and experience-based knowledge tells us how temporal conjunctions like "before" and "after" are normally used. Both of these temporal terms signal that part of the process of forming a discourse representation of this sentence will involve determining the temporal order of events in a discourse. "After" nearly always signals that events will be expressed in their natural order (consistent with real-world knowledge). "Before" nearly always signals that events will be expressed counter to their natural order. If real-world knowledge had no effect on sentence processing, then the brain's processing of the two sentence types should not differ. However, if world knowledge does affect language processing, then the two sentence types are likely to make different demands on working memory, with "before" sentences being more demanding.

As we show in Figure 7.10, world knowledge and sentence processing interact, at least in those individuals with high verbal working memory spans. (See top panel of the figure.) Within 300 msec of the onset of the first word of the sentence, the ERPs diverge and the difference only gets larger as the sentence proceeds. The nature of the difference is similar to that seen for sentences with embeddings. For individuals with low verbal working memory span, the effect is not present (as the bottom panel in Fig. 7.10 reveals). Their ERPs suggest that they find both sentence types quite demanding. Thus, we think the observed negativity reflects the added load on working memory processes, in this case for the building of a message or discourse representation, affected by both world knowledge and linguistic information (Goldman-Rakic, 1996; Just, Carpenter, Keller, Eddy, & Thulborn, 1996; Owen, 1997; Petrides, 1996; Stromswold, Caplan, Alpert, & Rauch, 1996).

In summary, ERPs provide insights into how world knowledge and linguistic knowledge meet in working memory. But most importantly, these data reveal when the different information sources meet, namely, quite early. A relatively high-level process at the discourse level influences how a word and then a sentence is processed by the brain, almost from the outset. These data effectively rule out any strictly serial model of language comprehension wherein the influence of a discourse-level representation would hardly be

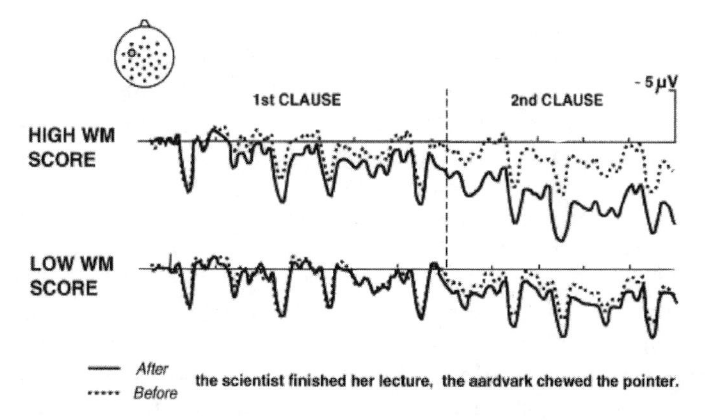

FIG. 7.10. Over-sentence ERPs from the left frontal recording site elicited by visually presented sentences that are equivalent in all respects except their initial word, either 'after' (solid lines) or 'before' (dotted lines). The top trace represents the responses of individuals with high working memory score (based on Daneman & Carpenter, 1980); while the bottom trace comes from individuals with low working memory scores. Individuals with higher working memory span show a more pronounced difference between 'before' and 'after' sentences than those with lower working memory span. These differences are seen within 300 ms of the response to the initial word (after Münte, Schiltz, & Kutas, 1998). Verbal working memory span is an estimate of an individual's temporary buffer for holding and processing of verbal information, presumably used during sentence processing. Loosely, it can be considered the number of language-like items that an individual can maintain for a few seconds without rehearsal.

expected to manifest itself at the first word, whether written or spoken, much less only 300 msec after its appearance.

Next stop on this journey through the brain/mind: the language production system.

FROM MIND TO MOUTH: LANGUAGE PRODUCTION

In our daily lives; we continually express thoughts and ideas in words. We talk about the present, the past, the future. We talk about what if, and about things that do not exist or never happened or never will. However, unless we encounter someone who stutters, has an accent, is too young to talk, is too demented to talk clearly, talks with difficulty due to a stroke, or does not want to talk, we take the ability to talk for granted. We do not think about how some abstract idea in the mind becomes a linguistic utterance that someone else must decipher.

Some psycholinguists, however, are very much concerned with how a concept in the mind comes to be a meaningful utterance. Broadly speaking, theories of language production agree that going from an idea to an utterance involves knowledge (at the least) at the level of (a) meaning, (b) syntax, and (c) phonological form (Bock, 1982, 1995; Dell, 1986, 1988; Garrett, 1975, 1988; Kempen & Huijbers, 1983; Levelt, 1989; Levelt, Roelofs, & Meyer, 1999). Research on patients with brain damage supports the assertion that there is a distinction between the semantic and syntactic levels (Rapp & Caramazza, 1995). Speech-errors (Dell, 1986, 1990, Dell & Reich, 1981;) and reaction-time data (Levelt, et al.,1991a, 1991b; Schriefers, Meyer, & Levelt, 1990) both support a distinction between semantic and phonological knowledge, as do findings on the tip-of-the-tongue phenomenon (Brown, 1991).

There is little agreement, however, on the time course or independence of the different processes that operate on these information types during natural speech production (e.g., Levelt et al., 1991a, 1991b, 1999; O'Seaghdha & Marin, 1997, for reviews). Some theories favor a serial view wherein conceptual/semantic information first activates syntactic information that in turn activates phonological encoding (Levelt et al., 1991a, 1991 Roelofs, 1992b; Schriefers et al., 1990). Others espouse a more interactive model of speech production with both top-down processing and bottom-up information flow (Dell & O'Seaghdha, 1991, 1992). Both positions are supported by empirical data. For instance, picture-word interference data show early semantic and late phonological activation of a picture's name during naming (Schriefers et al., 1990). However, the very existence of some types of errors (e.g., mixed errors—saying "rat" instead of the intended "cat" when viewing a picture of a cat) has been taken to suggest that semantic (animals) and phonological (rhyming) activation not only take place in parallel but can influence each other during speech production (Dell, 1990; but see also Levelt et al., 1999, for a different view).

This serial versus interactive activation debate hinges on issues of relative timing and thus would seem quite amenable to ERP research. But the act of speaking generates many electrical artifacts (muscle activity, tongue potentials) that can swamp the recorded brain activity (Brooker & Donald, 1980; Wohlert, 1993). Recently, however, Van Turennout, Hagoort, and Brown (1997, 1998, 1999) developed a method for examining preparation for speech production using the lateralized readiness potential (LRP). The LRP circumvents this problem of speech-related artifacts by focusing on preparation to speak rather than the speaking per se.

The LRP is derived from and related to the well-understood readiness potential (RP). The RP develops about a second or so before a voluntary hand movement as a negative-going potential, and is most prominent over central sites (Kornhuber & Deecke, 1965). Approximately half a second before the actual movement, the RP becomes lateralized, with larger amplitudes over the hemisphere contralateral to the moving hand (e.g., Kutas & Donchin, 1974). The LRP is derived from the RP, but is time-locked to the stimulus to which a response is given. By averaging the activity for responses made with the left and right hand (given contralateral vs. ipsilateral recordings), lateralized activity that is not related to response preparation cancels out. What remains is the lateralized part of the readiness potential; this LRP reflects the average amount of lateralization specifically related to the motor preparation of the responding hands. The LRP allows researchers to see motor-related brain activity prior to an overt response, even when the response is never realized (Miller, Riehle, & Requin 1992; Mulder, Wijers, Brookhuis, Smid, & Mulder, 1994; Osman, Bashore, Coles, Donchin, & Meyer, 1992). In essence, scientists can peer into the mind/brain and determine when it begins to prepare to respond and which type of response is going to be carried out (e.g., pressing a response button with the left or the right index finger [go response], or not responding at all [nogo response]). These features make the LRP an especially apt brain measure with which to study the time course of the encoding of various levels of information during speech production.

Sometimes Meaning Beats Phonology by a 120 msec: The LRP

Using the LRP, Van Turennout et al. (1997) showed that semantic encoding precedes phonological encoding during picture naming. In one experiment, Dutch participants were asked to name pictures of animals and objects. On half of the trials, 150 msec after the appearance of the picture a frame appeared around it, cuing the participants to postpone their naming response and to perform a binary decision, known as a go/nogo task. The instruction was, for example, to press the left button if the picture was of an animal and the right button if it was of an inanimate object. However, the button response was to be executed only if the name of the pictured item ended with an "r," and was to be withheld if the picture name ended with an "s." (For an illustration of the design in English, see Fig. 7.11.)

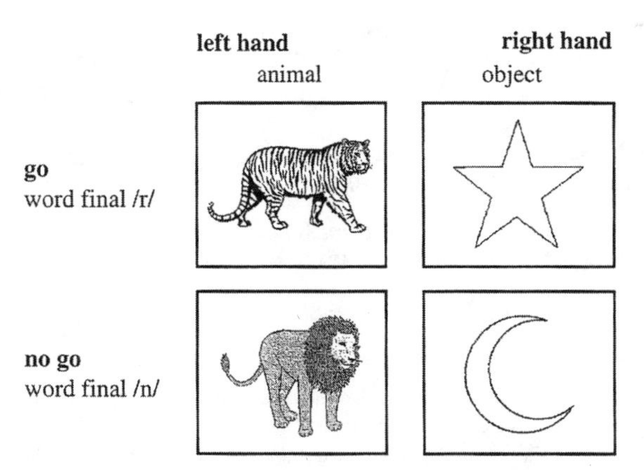

FIG. 7.11. An illustration of the design used in the first experiment of Van Turennout et al. (1997). The response hand was contingent on semantic information. The go–nogo response was contingent on phonological information. In the second experiment, the pictures were the same but the response contingencies were reversed: The response hand was contingent on phonological information. The go–nogo response was contingent on semantic information (after Van Turennout, Hagoort, & Brown, 1997).

The logic of the paradigm is as follows: It is assumed that people prepare to respond as soon as they have some information about what hand they are going to use. If semantic encoding precedes phonological encoding (as is assumed in serial models of speech production), and the responding hand is contingent on semantic information, then an LRP indicating preparation should develop for both go and nogo trials alike. Then, as soon as the phonological information is encoded indicating that no response is to be made, the LRP for go and nogo trials should diverge from each other, and the LRP for nogo trials should drop back to baseline. This was exactly the pattern of data Van Turennout et al. observed, as shown in the top panel of Figure 7.12.

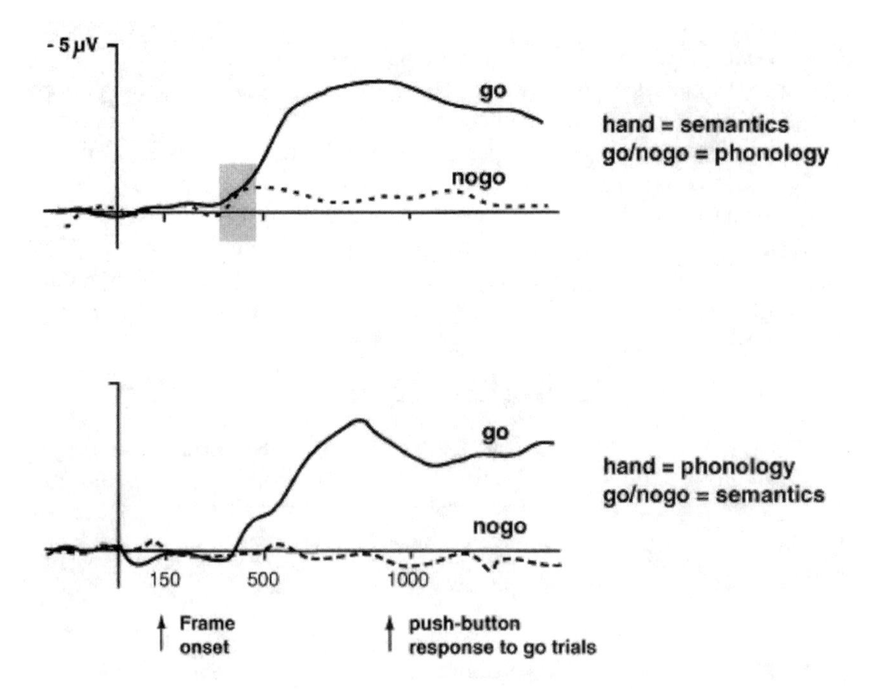

FIG. 7.12. Grand average lateralized readiness potential (LRP) on go (solid lines) and nogo trials (dashed lines) in a dual task that involves semantic and phonological decisions on picture names. The LRP is time-locked to picture onset. The top panel shows LRPs that were recorded when the outcome of the semantic decision determined the response hand, and the outcome of the phonological decision determined whether a response was required (go) or not (nogo). The shaded area indicates the interval during which the nogo LRP is reliably different from the baseline, and equivalent in amplitude to the go LRP. In the bottom panel are shown LRPs that were recorded when the response contingencies were reversed (phonological information determined the responding hand, and semantic decision whether or not a response was required). No reliable nogo LRP developed in this task (after Van Turennout, Hagoort, & Brown, 1997).

Van Turennout et al. also carried out a second experiment wherein the task instructions were reversed: The responding hand was contingent on the outcome of the phonological decision, and the decision about whether or not to respond was based on the semantic information. According to a serial model, no LRP should develop on nogo trials in this control experiment. This would be expected because the semantic information, which indicates that no response is to be given, would be available earlier than the phonological information, which would determine which response is to be given, thereby forestalling any preparation. As depicted in the bottom panel of Fig. 7. 12, Van Turennout et al. found no LRP on nogo trials. The authors thus concluded that semantic encoding precedes phonological encoding, in support of more serial-like models of speech production (e.g., Levelt et al., 1991a, 1991b, 1999; see also Van Turennout et al., 1998, 1999; Schmitt, Münte, & Kutas, 2000). These results demonstrate the sensitivity of the LRP as a tool for tapping into the time course of information access during (tacit) picture naming.

A Neural Stop: The N200

The ERPs associated with a go–nogo paradigm also offer another means of monitoring the time course of semantic, syntactic, and phonological processes during speech production. When an individual is asked to respond to one class of stimuli (go trials) and not to respond to another class (nogo trials), the ERPs to nogo (relative to go) trials are characterized by a large negativity (N200), especially over frontal sites (Gemba & Sasaki, 1989; Pfefferbaum, Ford, Weller, & Kopell, 1985; Sasaki, Gemba, Nambu, & Matsuzaki, 1993; Simson, Vaughan, & Ritter, 1977). While the functional significance of N200 is not yet clear (Eimer, 1993; Näätänen, 1982, 1992; Pfefferbaum et al., 1985), there is a consensus that it is elicited when a potential response is withheld. The N200 amplitude, therefore, is seen as a function of neuronal activity required for "response inhibition" (Jodo & Kayama, 1992; Sasaki & Gemba, 1993). This assumption is supported by studies that examined surface and depth (2–3 mm) recordings from the prefrontal cortex of monkeys (Sasaki, Gemba, & Tsujimoto, 1989), as they performed a go–nogo task on color discrimination. (That is, they pushed a button if a red light went on, and did not respond if a green light went on.) Nogo responses were associated with a cortical N200. Moreover, when this cortical area was stimulated electrically during a go trial at the time when the N200 would have been elicited, the go response was suppressed (see also Sasaki & Gemba, 1993, for a comparison of human and monkey data).

By defining the information on which the go–nogo decision is based, the peak latency of the N200 effect can be used to determine *when* the specific information is encoded, as shown by Thorpe, Fize, and Marlot (1996) for picture processing. Furthermore, by varying the information on which the go–nogo decision is based, this characteristic of the N200 can be used to delineate the temporal course of the availability of different information types during speech production. An early N200 means that the information that blocked the response on nogo trials was available early and vice versa.

Under Some Conditions Semantics Outperforms Syntax by 93 msec

Recently, we used the N200 to a nogo paradigm to investigate the availability of semantic and syntactic information during speech production (Schmitt, Schiltz, Zaake, Kutas, & Münte 2001). German-speaking participants were initially trained in the naming of simple line drawings of animals and objects. The training guaranteed that the participants actually knew and therefore would use the intended name of the pictures later in the main experiment. Afterwards, they saw the pictures again, and they either made a semantic decision (e.g., animal vs. object) or a syntactic judgment (e.g., whether the item's name has masculine or feminine gender).On different trials, the responding hand was contingent on semantic information and the go–nogo judgment was contingent on the syntactic information or vice versa. For example, volunteers might be given the following instructions: "Press left if the drawing is of an animal and press right if it is an object, but in both cases press only if the name has masculine gender" in one condition or "Press left if the name has masculine gender and press right if it has feminine gender, but in both cases press only if it is the name of an animal" in another condition. If semantic encoding takes precedence over syntactic encoding, then the information to stop should be available earlier when it is linked to semantic than to syntactic decisions. The ERPs of interest time-locked to the onset of the picture are shown in Fig. 7.13.

At the top left column are shown the ERPs elicited by the go–nogo trials when the responding hand (left versus right) was contingent on syntax and the semantics determined whether or not any response was executed. At the top of the right column are shown the ERPs when the response contingencies were reversed: The responding hand was contingent on semantics, the go–nogo response was based on syntax. In both cases, nogo trials elicited a large N200, albeit at different latencies. At the bottom panel, the N200 effect (the difference derived by subtracting go from nogo ERPs) in these two cases is compared directly. This comparison reveals that the N200 occurs much earlier (~90 msec) when the decision not to respond is governed by semantic rather than by syntactic information. This pattern of data supports serial models of speech production that assume initial semantic encoding followed by syntactic encoding (Bock & Levelt, 1994; Levelt et al., 1999).

However, it is also possible that, in this case, the semantic decision was simply easier and therefore occurred faster than the syntactic one, and it was this differential in decision difficulty that was reflected in the timing of the N200 effects. Naturally, we need to rule out this possibility in order to make sure that

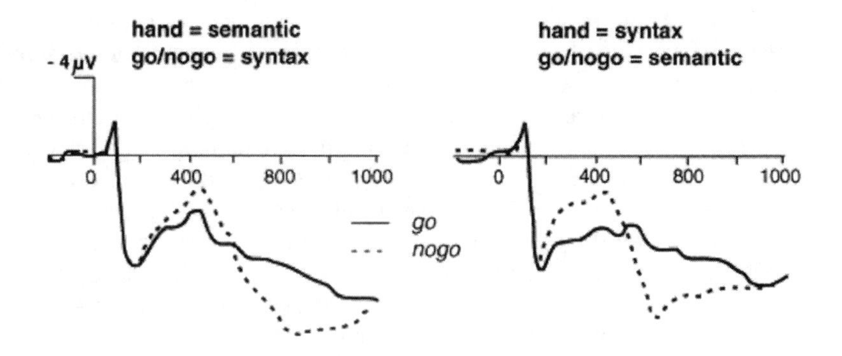

Response inhibition (difference nogo - go)

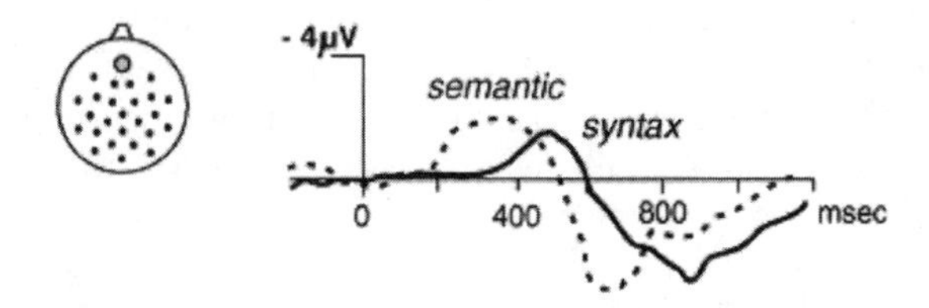

FIG. 7.13. Grand average ERPs on go and nogo trials in a dual task that involves semantic (animateness) and syntactic (syntactic gender in German) decisions on picture names. The ERPs are time locked to picture onset. At the top left figure are ERPs elicited in a condition, where the response hand was contingent on semantic information and the go–nogo decision was contingent on syntactic information. At the top right are ERPs where the response contingencies were reversed. Both conditions were associated with a frontal negativity (N200) that was more negative for nogo than for go trials. At the bottom, the difference waveforms (nogo minus go, interpreted as response inhibition) for the two conditions are shown superimposed. The solid line represents response inhibition when syntactic information determines the withholding of a response. The dashed line shows response inhibition when the semantic information determines the withholding of the response. The peak latencies for semantic response inhibition (i.e., N200 effect) are about 90 msec earlier than for syntactic response inhibition (Schmitt, Schiltz, Zaake, Münte, & Kutas, 2001).

the observed difference in the latencies of the N200 effects indeed tells us something about the timing of information access during speech processing and not just something about general decision making. Schmitt, Schiltz, Zaake, Kutas, and Münte (2001) ruled out this possibility in a follow-up study by showing that the N200 occurs much earlier (~80 msec) when the decision not to respond is governed by semantic rather than syntactic information, even when these two decisions were equated in difficulty when performed in isolation.

The N200 paradigm also has been successfully applied to a within-subject comparison of tacit picture naming and spoken word comprehension (Rodriguez-Fornells, Schmitt, Münte, & Kutas, 2000). Participants either saw pictures or heard the names of the pictured items. In both conditions on each trial they performed a dual choice go/nogo task that was based on semantic information (animal versus object) and on phonological information (picture's name begins with a vowel or a consonant sound). For tacit picture naming, the results replicated the study described earlier showing that the N200 effect based on semantics preceded that based on phonological information (in this case by ~190 msec); however, for spoken word comprehension the latencies of the N200 effects showed a reversed pattern. The N200 effect based on phonology preceded that based on semantic information (by ~100 msec), indicating that during comprehension phonological encoding comes first, as would be expected by speech comprehension models. Thus although comprehension and production both seem to access phonological and semantic information in a serial manner, the seriality appears to be more salient during production than comprehension.

In any case, the N200 component of the ERP is a very powerful tool for investigating temporal processes. The N200 reveals response-planning processes before response preparation (LRP), again even if no response is executed. Unlike the relatively small LRP elicited by nogo events, the N200 is quite robust. It may serve psycholinguists well as a tool for discerning fine–grained differences in rapidly occurring and closely related processes, such as those that characterize much of language production.

WHAT THE SYNCHRONOUS CACOPHONY OF NEOCORTICAL CELLS HAS TOLD US SO FAR

This overview of ERP findings of language processing shows that the method is an especially powerful tool for tapping the time course of language comprehension and production, including lexical/semantic, syntactic, and discourse-level processes.

The data obtained thus far suggest that there is a significant amount of temporal overlap and interaction not only among various linguistic representations but also between these and nonlinguistic knowledge representations during language comprehension. On the other hand, the data suggest that there is relatively more seriality, or at least a cascade of processes, during language production. By looking at various ERPs, (a) we can begin to catalog which sentence types are likely to be easier to comprehend, (b) we can point to the locations where the problems in comprehension might arise, and (c) we can establish what types of information might help reduce ambiguities or points of difficulty.

ERPs, such as the LRP or the N200, allow a view of the mind/brain as it plans to speak which is more direct than any other existing methodology. In fact, ERPs are more informative than simply asking a person what is going on in his or her head during language! Electrophysiological studies such as these thus afford researchers a means of combining information about the mind, the brain, and language in a natural way, thereby revealing the nature of the links between language and other cognitive domains, and between language and other cognitive functions.

We may need to leave it to future researchers to make sense of what various converging measures say about how human language works, but thank nature for the fact that it does so relatively effortlessly and that we can talk about "aardvarks" whenever the fancy to do so strikes us.

ACKNOWLEDGMENTS

Some of the research cited herein was supported by grants HD22614, AG08313, and MH52893 to M. Kutas. B. Schmitt was supported by a postdoctoral fellowship from the San Diego McDonnell-Pew Cognitive Neuroscience Institute. We thank K. Federmeier and A. Senkfor for their comments on a previous version of this chapter, and M. Lauer and editors of this book for their editorial assistance.

REFERENCES

Altmann, G., & Shillcock, R. (Eds.). (1993). *Cognitive models of speech processing: The second Sperlonga Meeting.* Hove, UK: Lawrence Erlbaum Associates.

Barrett, S. E., & Rugg, M. D. (1990). Event–related potentials and the phonological matching of picture names. *Brain and Language, 38,* 424–437.

Bock, J. K. (1982). Toward a cognitive psychology of syntax: Information processing contributions to sentence formulation. *Psychological Review, 89,* 1–47.

Bock, J. K. (1995). Sentence production: From mind to mouth. In J. L. Miller & P. D. Eimas (Eds.), *Handbook of perception and cognition: Vol. 11. Speech, language, and communication* (pp. 181–216). San Diego, CA: Academic Press.

Bock, K., & Levelt, W. (1994). Language production: Grammatical encoding. In M. A. Gernsbacher (Ed.), *Handbook of psycholinguistics* (pp. 945–984). San Diego: Academic Press.

Brooker, B. H., & Donald, M. W. (1980). Contribution of the speech musculature to apparent human EEG asymmetries prior to vocalization. *Brain and Language, 9,* 226–245.

Brown, A. S. (1991). A review of the tip–of–the–tongue experience. *Psychological Bulletin, 109,* 204–223.

Brown, C. M., & Hagoort, P. (2000). On the electrophysiology of language comprehension: Implications for the human language system. In M. Crocker, M. Pickering, & C. Clifton (Eds.), *Architectures and mechanisms for language processing* (pp. 213–237). Cambridge: Cambridge University Press.

Brown, C. M., Hagoort, P., & Kutas, M. (2000). Postlexical integration processes in language comprehension: Evidence from brain–imaging research. In M. S. Gazzaniga (Ed.), *The new cognitive neurosciences* (2nd ed., pp. 881–895). Cambridge, MA: MIT Press.

Brown, C. M., Van Berkum, J. J. A., & Hagoort, P. (2000). Discourse before gender: An event–related brain potential study on the interplay of semantic and syntactic information during spoken language understanding. *Journal of Psycholinguistic Research, 29,* 53–68.

Caplan, D. (1992). *Language: Structure, processing, and disorders.* Cambridge: MIT Press.

Clark, H. H. (1994). Discourse in production. In M. A. Gernsbacher (Ed.), *Handbook of psycholinguistics* (pp. 985–1021). San Diego, CA: Academic Press.

Coles, M. G. H., & Rugg, M. D. (1995). Event–related brain potentials: An introduction. In M. D. Rugg & M. G. H. Coles (Eds.), *Electrophysiology of mind: Event–related brain potentials and cognition* (pp. 1–26). New York: Oxford University Press.

Collins, A. M., & Loftus, E. F. (1975). A spreading–activation theory of semantic processing. *Psychological Review, 82,* 407–428.

Colombo, L. (1986). Activation and inhibition with orthographically similar words. *Journal of Experimental Psychology: Human Perception and Performance, 12,* 226–234.
Coulson, S., King, J. W., & Kutas, M. (1998). Expect the unexpected: Event–related brain response to morphosyntactic violations. *Language and Cognitive Processes, 13*(1), 21–58.
Dale, A. M., & Sereno, M. I. (1993). Improved localization of cortical activity by combining EEG and MEG with MRI cortical surface reconstruction: A linear approach. *Journal of Cognitive Neuroscience, 5,* 162–176.
Dale, A. M., Liu, A. K., Fischl, B. R., Buckner, R. L., Belliveau, J. W., Lewine, J. D., & Halgren, E. (2000). Dynamic statistical parametric mapping: Combining fMRI and MEG for high–resolution imaging of cortical activity. *Neuron, 26,* 55–67.
Daneman, M., & Carpenter, P. A. (1980). Individual differences in working memory and reading. *Journal of Verbal Learning and Verbal Behavior, 19,* 450–466.
Deese, J. (1984). *Thought into speech: The psychology of a language.* Englewood Cliffs, NJ: Prentice Hall.
Dell, G. S. (1986). A spreading–activation theory of retrieval in sentence production. *Psychological Review, 93,* 283–321.
Dell, G. S. (1988). The retrieval of phonological forms in production: Tests of predictions from a connectionist model. *Journal of Memory and Language, 27,* 124–142.
Dell, G. S. (1990). Effects of frequency and vocabulary type on phonological speech errors. *Language and Cognitive Processes, 5,* 313–349.
Dell, G. S., & O'Seaghdha, P. G. (1991). Mediated and convergent lexical priming in language production: A comment on Levelt et al. (1991). *Psychological Review, 98,* 604–614.
Dell, G. S., & O'Seaghdha, P. G. (1992). Stages of lexical access in language production. *Cognition, 42,* 287–314.
Dell, G. S., & Reich, P. A. (1981). Stages in sentence production: An analysis of speech error data. *Journal of Verbal Learning and Verbal Behavior, 20,* 611–629.
Doyle, M. C., Rugg, M. D., & Wells, T. (1996). A comparison of the electrophysiological effects of formal and repetition priming. *Psychophysiology, 33,* 132–147.
Eimer, M. (1993). Effects of attention and stimulus probability on ERPs in a go/nogo task. *Biological Psychology, 35,* 123–138.
Ericsson, K. A., & Kintsch, W. (1995). Long–term working memory. *Psychological Review, 102,* 211–245.
Fodor, J. D. (1989). Empty categories in sentence processing. *Language and Cognitive Processes, 4,* 155–209.
Fodor, J. D. (1995). Comprehending sentence structure. In L. R. Gleitmann & M. Libermann (Eds.), *Language: An invitation to cognitive science* (2nd ed., Vol. 1, pp. 209–246). Cambridge: MIT press.
Fodor, J. A., & Bever, T. G. (1965). The psychological reality of linguistic segments. *Journal of Learning and Verbal Behavior, 4,* 414–420.
Francis, W. N. & Kucera, H. (1982). *Frequency analysis of English usage: Lexicon and grammar.* Boston: Houghton Mifflin.
Friederici, A. D., & Mecklinger, A. (1996). Syntactic parsing as revealed by brain responses: First–pass and second–pass parsing processes. *Journal of Psycholinguistic Research, 25,* 157–176.
Friederici, A. D., Pfeifer, E., & Hahne, A. (1993). Event–related brain potentials during natural speech processing: Effects of semantic, morphological and syntactic violations. *Cognitive Brain Research, 1,* 183–192.
Garnsey, S. M. (1993). Event–related brain potentials in the study of language: An introduction. Special issue: Event–related brain potentials in the study of language. *Language and Cognitive Processes,* 8, 337–356.
Garnsey, S. M., Tanenhaus, M. K., & Chapman, R. M. (1989). Evoked potentials and the study of sentence comprehension. Special issue: Sentence Processing. *Journal of Psycholinguistic Research, 18,* 51–60.
Garrett, M. F. (1975). The analysis of sentence production. In G. H. Bower (Ed.), *The Psychology of Learning and Motivation: Advances in Research and Theory* (Vol. 9, pp. 133–177). New York: Academic Press.
Garrett, M. F. (1988). Processes in language production. In F. J. Newmeyer (Ed.), *Linguistics: The Cambridge survey: Vol. 3. Language: Biological and psychological aspects* (pp. 69–96). Cambridge: Cambridge University Press.
Garrett, M. F. (1995). The structure of language processing: Neuropsychological evidence. In M. S. Gazzaniga (Ed.), *The cognitive neurosciences* (pp. 881–899). Cambridge, MA: MIT Press.

Garrett, M. F., Bever, T. G., & Foder, J. A. (1966). The active use of grammar in speech perception. *Perception & Psychophysics, 1,* 30–32.
Gemba, H., & Sasaki, K. (1989). Potential related to no–go reaction of go/no–go hand movement task with color discrimination in human. *Neuroscience Letters, 101,* 263–268.
Gernsbacher, M. A., & Hargreaves, D. J. (1988). Accessing sentence participants: The advantage of first mention. *Journal of Memory and Language, 27,* 699–711.
Goldman-Rakic, P. S. (1996). The prefrontal landscape: implications of functional architecture for understanding human mentation and the central executive. *Philosophical Transactions of the Royal Society of London. Series B: Biological Sciences, 351,* 1445–1453.
Gordon, B., & Caramazza, A. (1985). Lexical access and frequency sensitivity: Frequency saturation and open/closed class equivalence. *Cognition, 21,* 95–115.
Gunter, T. C., Stowe, L. A., & Mulder, G. M. (1997). When syntax meets semantics. *Psychophysiology, 34,* 660–676.
Hagoort, P., & Brown, C. M. (1994). Brain responses to lexical ambiguity resolution and parsing. In C. Clifton, L. Frazier, & K. Rayner (Eds.), *Perspectives on sentence processing* (pp. 45–80). Hillsdale, NJ: Lawrence Erlbaum Associates.
Hagoort, P., & Brown, C. M. (2000). Semantic and syntactic ERP effects of listening to speech compared to reading. *Neuropsychologia, 38,* 1531–1549.
Hagoort, P., Brown, C. M., & Groothusen, J. (1993). The syntactic positive shift as an ERP–measure of syntactic processing. *Language and Cognitive Processes, 8,* 439–483.
Hillyard, S. A., & Kutas, M. (1983). Electrophysiology of cognitive processing. *Annual Review of Psychology, 34,* 33–61.
Hillyard, S. A., & Picton, T. W. (1987). Electrophysiology of cognition. In F. Plum (Ed.), *Handbook of physiology: The nervous system* (Vol. 5, pp. 519–584). Bethesda, MD: American Physiological Society.
Holcomb, P. J. (1988). Automatic and attentional processing: An event–related brain potential analysis of semantic priming. *Brain & Language, 35,* 66–85.
Jescheniak, J. D., & Levelt, W. J. M. (1994). Word frequency effects in speech production: Retrieval of syntactic information and of phonological form. *Journal of Experimental Psychology: Learning, Memory, and Cognition, 20,* 824–843.
Jodo, E., & Kayama, Y. (1992). Relation of a negative ERP component to response inhibition in a go/no–go task. *Electroencephalography and Clinical Neurophysiology, 82,* 477–482.
Just, M. A., & Carpenter, P. A. (1980). A theory of reading: From eye fixations to comprehension. *Psychological Review, 87,* 329–354.
Just, M. A., Carpenter, P. A., Keller, T. A., Eddy, W. F., & Thulborn, K. R. (1996). Brain activation modulated by sentence comprehension. *Science, 274,* 114–116.
Kempen, G., & Huijbers, P. (1983). The lexicalization process in sentence production and naming: Indirect election of words. *Cognition, 14,* 185–209.
King, J. W., & Kutas, M. (1995a, November). A brain potential whose latency indexes the length and frequency of words. *Newsletter of the Center for Research in Language, 10*(2), 3–9.
King, J. W., & Kutas, M. (1995b). Who did what and when? Using word– and clause–related ERPs to monitor working memory usage in reading. *Journal of Cognitive Neuroscience, 7,* 378–397.
King, J. W., & Kutas, M. (1995c). Do the waves begin to waver? ERP studies of language processing in the elderly. In P. Allen & T. R. Bashore (Eds.), *Age differences in word and language processing* (pp. 314–344). Amsterdam: Elsevier.
King, J. W., & Kutas, M. (1998). Neural plasticity in the dynamics of human visual word recognition. *Neuroscience Letters, 244,* 61–64.
Kintsch, W. (1994). The psychology of discourse processing. In M. A. Gernsbacher (Ed.), *Handbook of psycholinguistics* (pp. 721–739). San Diego, CA: Academic Press.
Kluender, R., & Kutas, M. (1993). Subjacency as a processing phenomenon. Special Issue: Event–related brain potentials in the study of language. *Language & Cognitive Processes, 8,* 573–633.
Kornhuber, H. H., & Deecke, L. (1965). Hirnpotentialänderungen bei Willkürbewegungen und passiven Bewegungen des Menschen: Bereitschafts–Potential und reafferente Potentiale [Brain potential changes associated with voluntary and passive movements in humans: Readiness potential and reafferent potentials]. *Pflügers Archive, 284,* 1–17.
Kutas, M., & Dale, A. (1997). Electrical and magnetic readings of mental functions. In M. D. Rugg (Ed.), *Cognitive neuroscience* (pp. 197–242). Hove, UK: Psychology Press.

Kutas, M., & Donchin, E. (1974). Studies of squeezing: Handedness, responding hand, response force, and asymmetry of readiness potential. *Science, 186*, 545–548.
Kutas, M., & Federmeier, K. D. (1998). Minding the body. *Psychophysiology, 35*, 135–150.
Kutas, M., Federmeier, K. D., Coulson, S., King, J., & Münte, T. F. (2000). Language. In John T. Cacioppo, L. G. Tassinary, & G. Bernston (Eds.), *Handbook of psychophysiology* (pp. 576–602). New York: Cambridge University Press.
Kutas, M., & Hillyard, S. A. (1980a). Event–related brain potentials to semantically inappropriate and surprisingly large words. *Biological Psychology, 11*, 99–116.
Kutas, M., & Hillyard, S. A. (1980b). Reading between the lines: Event–related brain potentials during natural sentence processing. *Brain and Language, 11*, 354–373.
Kutas, M., & Hillyard, S. A. (1980c). Reading senseless sentences: Brain potentials reflect semantic incongruity. *Science, 207*, 203–205.
Kutas, M., & Hillyard, S. A. (1982). The lateral distribution of event–related potentials during sentence processing. *Neuropsychologia, 20*, 579–590.
Kutas, M., & Hillyard, S. A. (1983). Event–related brain potentials to grammatical errors and semantic anomalies. *Memory & Cognition, 11*, 539–550.
Kutas, M., & Hillyard, S. A. (1984). Brain potentials during reading reflect word expectancy and semantic association. *Nature, 307*, 161–163.
Kutas, M., & Hillyard, S. A. (1989). An electrophysiological probe of incidental semantic association. *Journal of Cognitive Neuroscience, 1*, 38–49.
Kutas, M., & King, J. W. (1996). The potentials for basic sentence processing: differentiating integrative processes. In T. Inui & J. L. McClelland (Eds.), *Attention and performance XVI* (pp. 501–546). Cambridge, MA: MIT Press.
Kutas, M., & Van Petten, C. K. (1994). Psycholinguistics electrified: Event–related brain potential investigations. In M. A. Gernsbacher (Ed.), *Handbook of psycholinguistics* (pp. 83–143). San Diego, CA: Academic Press.
Kutas, M., Van Petten, C., & Besson, M. (1988). Event–related potential asymmetries during the reading of sentences. *Electroencephalography and Clinical Neurophysiology, 69*, 218–233.
Levelt, W. J. M. (1989). *Speaking: From intention to articulation*. Cambridge, MA: MIT Press.
Levelt, W. J. M., Roelofs, A., & Meyer, A. S. (1999). A theory of lexical access in speech production. *Behavioral and Brain Sciences, 22*, 1–75.
Levelt, W. J. M., Schriefers, H., Vorberg, D., Meyer, A. S., Pechmann, T., & Havinga, J. (1991a). The time course of lexical access in speech production: A study of picture naming. *Psychological Review, 98*, 122–142.
Levelt, W. J. M., Schriefers, H., Vorberg, D., Meyer, A. S., Pechmann, T., & Havinga, J. (1991b). Normal and deviant lexical processing: Reply to Dell & O'Seaghdha (1991). *Psychological Review, 98*, 615–618.
Lively, S. E., Pisoni, D. B., & Goldinger, S. D. (1994). Spoken word recognition: Research and theory. In M. A. Gernsbacher (Ed.), *Handbook of psycholinguistics* (pp. 265–301). San Diego, CA: Academic Press.
Maclay, H., & Osgood, C. E. (1959). Hesitation phenomena in spontaneous English speech. *Word, 15*, 19–44.
Marslen-Wilson, W. (1987). Functional parallelism in spoken word–recognition. *Cognition, 25*, 71–102.
Marslen-Wilson, W. (1990). Activation, competition, and frequency in lexical access. In G. T. M. Altmann (Ed.), *Cognitive models of speech processing* (pp. 148–172). Cambridge, MA: MIT Press.
Marslen-Wilson, W., & Welsh, A. (1978). Processing interactions and lexical access during word recognition in continuous speech. *Cognitive Psychology, 10*, 29–63.
Martin, J. H. (1991). The collective electrical behavior of cortical neurons: The electroencephalogram and the mechanisms of epilepsy. In E. R. Kandel, J. H. Schwartz, & T. M. Jessell (Eds.), *Principles of neural science* (3rd ed., pp. 777–791). New York: Elsevier.
Mason, C., & Kandel, E. R. (1991). Central visual pathways. In E. R. Kandel, J. H. Schwartz, & T. M. Jessell (Eds.), *Principles of neural science* (3rd ed., pp. 420–439). New York: Elsevier.
McCarthy, G., Nobre, A. C., Bentin, S., & Spencer, D. D. (1995). Language–related field potentials in the anterior–medial temporal lobe: I. Intracranial distribution and neural generators. *Journal of Neuroscience, 15*, 1080–1089.

McClelland, J. L., & Elman, J. L. (1986). Interactive processes in speech perception: The TRACE model. In J. L. McClelland & D. E. Rumelhart (Eds.), *Parallel distributed processing: Explorations in the microstructure of cognition.* (Vol. 2, pp. 58–121). Cambridge, MA: MIT Press/Bradford Books.

McQueen, J. M., & Cutler, A. (1997). Cognitive processes in speech perception. In W. J. Hardcastle & J. Lawer (Eds.), *The handbook of phonetic sciences* (pp. 566–585). Oxford: Blackwell.

Miller, J., Riehle, A., & Requin, J. (1992). Effects of preliminary perceptual output on neuronal activity of the primary motor cortex. *Journal of Experimental Psychology: Human Perception and Performance, 18,* 1121–1138.

Miller, G. A., & Fellbaum, C. (1991). Semantic networks of English. *Cognition, 41,* 197–229.

Mulder, G., Wijers, A. A., Brookhuis, K. A., Smid, H. G. O. M., & Mulder, L. J. M. (1994). Selective visual attention: Selective cuing, selective cognitive processing, and selective response processing. In: H.-J. Heinze, T. F. Münte, & G. R. Mangun (Eds.), *Cognitive electrophysiology* (pp. 26–80). Boston: Birkhäuser.

Müller, H. M., King, J. W., & Kutas, M. (1997). Event–related potentials to relative clause processing in spoken sentences. *Cognitive Brain Research, 5,* 193–203.

Münte, T. F., Matzke, M., & Johannes, S. (1997). Brain activity associated with syntactic incongruities in words and pseudo-words. *Journal of Cognitive Neuroscience, 9,* 300–311.

Münte, T. F., Say, T., Clahsen, H., Schiltz, K., & Kutas, M. (1999). Decomposition of morphologically complex words in English: Evidence from event–related brain potentials. *Cognitive Brain Research, 7,* 241–253.

Münte, T. F., Schiltz, K., & Kutas, M. (1998). When temporal terms belie conceptual order. *Nature, 395,* 71–73.

Näätänen, R. (1992). *Attention and brain function.* Hillsdale, NJ: Lawrence Erlbaum Associates.

Näätänen, R. (1982). Processing negativity: An evoked–potential reflection of selective attention. *Psychological Bulletin, 92,* 605–640.

Neville, H. J., Mills, D. L., & Lawson, D. S. (1992). Fractionating language: Different neural subsystems with different sensitive periods. *Cerebral Cortex, 2,* 244–258.

Norris, D. (1994). Shortlist: A connectionist model of continuous speech recognition. *Cognition, 52,* 189–234.

Nunez, P. L. (1981). *Electric fields of the brain.* New York: Oxford University Press.

O'Seaghdha, P. G., & Marin, J. W. (1997). Mediated semantic–phonological priming: Calling distant relatives. *Journal of Memory and Language, 36,* 226–252.

Osman, A., Bashore, T. R., Coles, M. G. H., Donchin, E., Meyer, D. E. (1992). On the transmission of partial information: Inferences from movement–related brain potentials. *Journal of Experimental Psychology: Human Perception and Performance, 18,* 217–232.

Osterhout, L. (1994). Event–related brain potentials as tools for comprehending sentence comprehension. In C. Clifton, L. Frazier, & K. Rayner (Eds.), *Perspectives on sentence processing* (pp. 15–44). Hillsdale, NJ: Lawrence Erlbaum Associates.

Osterhout, L., & Holcomb, P. J. (1992). Event–related brain potentials elicited by syntactic anomaly. *Journal of Memory and Language, 3,* 785–806.

Osterhout, L., & Holcomb, P. J. (1993). Event–related potentials and syntactic anomaly: Evidence of anomaly detection during the perception of continuous speech. *Language and Cognitive Processes, 8,* 413–437.

Osterhout, L., & Holcomb, P. J. (1995). Event–related potentials and language comprehension. In M. D. Rugg & M. G. H. Coles (Eds.), *Electrophysiology of mind: Event–related brain potentials and cognition* (pp. 171–215). New York: Oxford University Press.

Osterhout, L., McLaughlin, J., & Bersick, M. (1997). Event–related brain potentials and human language. *Trends in Cognitive Sciences, 1,* 203–209.

Owen, A. M. (1997). The functional organization of working memory processes within human lateral frontal cortex: The contribution of functional neuroimaging. *European Journal of Neuroscience, 9,* 1329–1339.

Patterson, K., & Shewell, C. (1987). Speak and spell: Dissociations and word–class effects. In M. Coltheart, G. Sartori, & R. Job (Eds.), *The cognitive neuropsychology of language* (pp. 273–295). London: Lawrence Erlbaum Associates.

Petrides, M. (1996). Specialized systems for the processing of mnemonic information within the primate frontal cortex. *Philosophical Transactions of the Royal Society of London. Series B: Biological Sciences, 351,* 1455–1461.

Pfefferbaum, A., Ford, J. M., Weller, B. J., & Kopell, B. S. (1985). ERPs to response production and inhibition. *Electroencephalography and Clinical Neurophysiology, 60*, 423–434.

Praamstra, P., Meyer, A. S., & Levelt, W. J. M. (1994). Neurophysiological manifestations of phonological processing: Latency variation of a negative ERP component time–locked to phonological mismatch. *Journal of Cognitive Neuroscience, 6*, 204–219.

Pritchard, W. S., Shappell, S. A., & Brandt, M. E. (1991). Psychophysiology of N200/N400: A review and classification scheme. In J. R. Jennings, P. K. Ackles, & M. G. H. Coles (Eds.), *Advances in psychophysiology* (Vol. 4, pp. 43–106). London: Jessica Kingsley.

Pulvermüller, F. (1996). Hebb's concept of cell assemblies and the psychophysiology of word processing. *Psychophysiology, 33*, 317–333.

Rapp, B. C., & Caramazza, A. (1995). Disorders of lexical processing and the lexicon. In M. S. Gazzaniga (Ed.), *The Cognitive Neurosciences* (pp. 901–913). Cambridge, MA: MIT Press.

Rodriguez-Fornells, A., Schmitt, B. M., Münte, T. F., & Kutas, M. (2000, April). *Electrophysiological estimates of the time course of semantic and phonological encoding during listening and naming.* Poster presented at the seventh annual meeting of the Cognitive Neuroscience Society (CNS), San Francisco.

Roelofs, A. (1992). A spreading–activation theory of lemma retrieval in speaking. *Cognition, 42*, 107–142.

Rugg, M. D. (1984a). Event–related potentials in phonological matching tasks. *Brain and Language, 23*, 225–240.

Rugg, M. D. (1984b). Event–related potentials and the phonological processing of words and non–words. *Neuropsychologia, 22*, 435–443.

Rugg, M. D. (1985). The effects of semantic priming and word repetition on event–related potentials. *Psychophysiology, 22*, 642–647.

Rugg, M. D., & Barrett, S. E. (1987). Event–related potentials and the interaction between orthographic and phonological information in a rhyme–judgment task. *Brain and Language, 32*, 336–361.

Rugg, M. D., & Coles, M. G. H. (Eds.). (1995). *Electrophysiology of mind: Event–related brain potentials and cognition*. New York: Oxford University Press.

Saffran, E. M., & Sholl, A. (1999). Clues to the functional and neural architecture of word meaning. In C. Brown & P. Hagoort (Eds.), *The Neurocognition of Language* (pp. 241–272). Oxford: Oxford University Press.

Sasaki, K., & Gemba, H. (1993). Prefrontal cortex in the organization and control of voluntary movement. In T. Ono, L. R. Squire, M. E. Raichle, D. I. Perrett, & M. Fukuda (Eds.), *Brain mechanisms of perception and memory: From neuron to behavior* (pp. 473–496). New York: Oxford University Press.

Sasaki, K., Gemba, H., & Tsujimoto, T. (1989). Suppression of visually initiated hand movement by stimulation of the prefrontal cortex in the monkey. *Brain Research, 495*, 100–107.

Sasaki, K., Gemba, H., Nambu, A., & Matsuzaki, R. (1993). No–go activity in the frontal association cortex of human subjects. *Neuroscience Research, 18*, 249–252.

Schmitt, B. M., Münte, T. F., & Kutas, M. (2000). Electrophysiological estimates of the time course of semantic and phonological encoding during implicit picture naming. *Psychophysiology, 37*(4), 473–484.

Schmitt, B. M., Schiltz, K., Zaake, W., Kutas, M., & Münte, T. F. (2001). An electrophysiological analysis of the time course of conceptual and syntactic encoding during tacit picture naming. *Journal of Cognitive Neuroscience, 13*(4), 510–522.

Schriefers, H., Meyer, A. S., & Levelt, W. J. M. (1990). Exploring the time course of lexical access in language production: Picture–word interference studies. *Journal of Memory and Language, 29*, 86–102.

Shillcock, R. C., & Bard, E. G. (1993). Modularity and the processing of closed–class words. In G. Altmann & R. C. Shillcock (Eds.), *Cognitive models of speech processing: The second Sperlonga Meeting* (pp. 163–185). Hove, UK: Lawrence Erlbaum Associates.

Simson, R., Vaughan, H. G., & Ritter, W. (1977). The scalp topography of potentials in auditory and visual go/nogo tasks. *Electroencephalography and Clinical Neurophysiology, 43*, 864–875.

Stromswold, K., Caplan, D., Alpert, N., & Rauch, S. (1996). Localization of syntactic comprehension by positron emission tomography. *Brain and Language, 53*, 452–473.

Swinney, D. A., Zurif, E. B., & Cutler, A. (1980). Effects of sentential stress and word class upon comprehension in Broca's aphasics. *Brain and Language, 10*, 132–144.

Tanaka, K. (1996). Representation of visual features of objects in the inferotemporal cortex. *Neural Networks, 9*, 1459–1475.

Thibadeau, R., Just, M. A., & Carpenter, P. A. (1983). A model of the time course and content of reading. *Cognitive Science, 6*, 157–203.

Thorpe, S., Fize, D., & Marlot, C. (1996). Speed of processing in the human visual system. *Nature, 381,* 520–522.
Van Berkum, J. J. A., Hagoort, P., & Brown, C. M. (1999). Semantic integration in sentences and discourse: Evidence from the N400. *Journal of Cognitive Neuroscience, 11,* 657–671.
Van Petten, C., & Kutas, M. (1991). Influences of semantic and syntactic context on open and closed class words. *Memory and Cognition, 19,* 95–112.
Van Petten, C., Kutas, M., Kluender, R., Mitchiner, M., & McIsaac, H. (1991). Fractionating the word repetition effect with event–related potentials. *Journal of Cognitive Neuroscience, 3(2),* 131–150.
Van Petten, C., Coulson, S., Rubin, S., Plante, E., & Parks, M. (1999). Time course of word identification and semantic integration in spoken language. *Journal of Experimental Psychology: Learning, Memory, and Cognition, 25,* 394–417.
Van Turennout, M., Hagoort, P., & Brown, C. M. (1997). Electrophysiological evidence on the time course of semantic and phonological processes in speech production. *Journal of Experimental Psychology: Learning, Memory, and Cognition, 23,* 787–806.
Van Turennout, M., Hagoort, P., & Brown, C. M. (1998). Brain activity during speaking: From syntax to phonology in 40 Milliseconds. *Science, 280,* 572–574.
Van Turennout, M., Hagoort, P., & Brown, C. (1999). The time course of grammatical and phonological processing during speaking: Evidence from event–related brain potentials. *Journal of Psycholinguistic Research, 28,* 649–676.
Wohlert, A. B. (1993). Event–related brain potentials preceding speech and nonspeech oral movements of varying complexity. *Journal of Speech and Hearing Research, 36,* 897–905.
Zwitserlood, P. (1989). The locus of the effects of sentential–semantic context in spoken–word processing. *Cognition, 32,* 25–64.

8

Functional and Structural Imaging in the Study of Auditory Language Processes

Robert J. Zatorre, PhD
Montreal Neurological Institute
McGill University

The relative ease with which most human beings comprehend and produce speech belies the complexity of the psychological and neuronal systems that underlie its processing. The past few years have seen notable advances in our understanding of the neural substrate for speech and language processing, particularly thanks to the development of functional brain imaging techniques. In this chapter I will review some work relevant to these questions from our laboratory and provide a sketch of some of the major theoretical conclusions that can be drawn from this work to date.

Functional imaging research into speech perception takes place, of course, in the context of many years of study of speech disturbances following brain damage, and of work in experimental psychology devoted to this topic. A review of this vast literature is beyond the scope of this chapter, but certain salient points that are relevant to the studies to be discussed should be mentioned. Among the most obvious findings from over a century of aphasia and related research is the identification of anterior and posterior speech areas in the left cerebral hemisphere of most right-handed individuals. The most common functional attribution of these regions is that there is a specialization involving the left posterior temporal area, often referred to as Wernicke's area, for speech perception, and the left frontal area, often referred to as Broca's area, in speech production (see Fig. 8.1). Yet despite the solidity of this textbook-standard statement, there

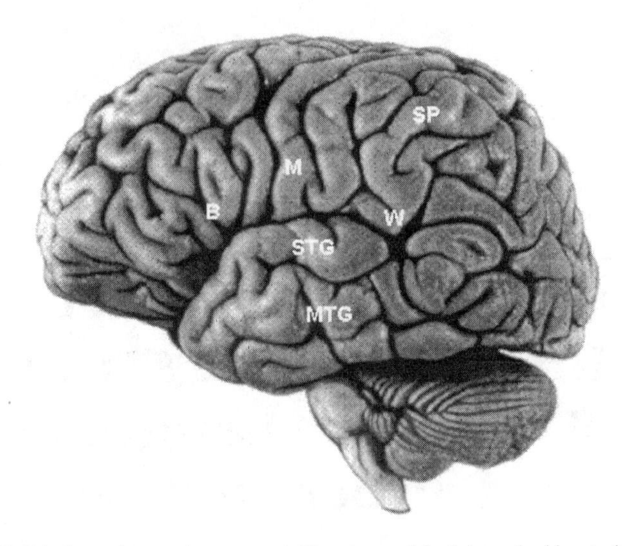

FIG. 8.1. Lateral view of an anatomical specimen of the left cerebral hemisphere. Letters indicate approximate location of structures referred to in the text. B, Broca's area; M, primary motor cortex; SP, superior parietal area; STG, superior temporal gyrus; MTG, middle temporal gyrus; W, Wernicke's area.

is remarkably little agreement on precisely what the nature of the underlying computations might be within these regions. Even the conventional description of comprehension deficits specifically following damage to the posterior speech area does not necessarily find consistent support in the aphasia literature (see, e.g., Blumstein, 1994, for evidence that anterior lesions cause disturbances in speech perception), nor is it corroborated by cortical stimulation studies, (Ojemann, 1991; Penfield & Roberts, 1959), which also report comprehension difficulties from stimulation of anterior as well as posterior speech zones.

In addition, there continues to be debate about the anatomical boundaries of the posterior temporal speech area, with much evidence indicating that it may extend beyond the classical Wernicke area of the posterior superior temporal gyrus (STG), to include tissue more inferiorly, in the middle temporal gyrus (e.g., Binder, Frost, Hammeke, Rao, & Cox, 1996; see Fig. 8.1). Much of the uncertainty stems from the necessarily uncontrolled nature of the lesions that produce aphasic disturbance which may vary considerably from individual to individual, and the difficulties in establishing anatomofunctional correlations prior to the development of in vivo structural brain imaging techniques. Other problems stem from the complexity of speech perception itself, and of the many component processes that may be involved even by seemingly simple tasks such as comprehending a basic command. These issues have led at least some authors to a genuine questioning of the standard neuronatomical model, and there is some consensus that it is in need of profound revision.

Functional imaging refers to techniques that allow one to visualize the physiological or hemodynamic activity pattern in the brain as a person performs some cognitive or behavioral task. These methods (positron emission tomography [PET] and functional magnetic resonance imaging [fMRI] have now emerged as essential tools to study the functional anatomy of many cognitive processes, and especially language. Although imaging techniques are limited in numerous ways, and cannot by themselves provide solutions to all the questions that may be raised, there is a general consensus in the scientific community that our understanding of the neuronal bases of uniquely human processes such as language has been improved considerably by the advent of imaging techniques. As these tools continue to develop and improve, it is worth reiterating that a complete understanding of such complex systems as language evidently will require the integration of knowledge from many domains of scientific inquiry, including traditional methods of lesion analysis and psycholinguistics.

Our laboratory began studying speech perception using PET in the early 1990s. This imaging technique measures cerebral blood flow (CBF), an indirect but nonetheless valid index of neuronal activity. These PET studies were particularly informative at the time because it was the first methodology to allow full-brain three-dimensional imaging of the pattern of regional changes of CBF associated with performing a cognitive task in normal volunteers. Our initial studies were motivated by several independent concerns. The first question that we wished to address related to the functional dissociation of primary from secondary auditory cortex in the processing of speech. These cortical areas are distinguishable based on their pattern of connectivity and cytoarchitecture, but we wished to see if they could be distinguished based on their functional properties. Several brain imaging studies (Binder et al., 1996; Peterson et al., 1991; Wisc et al., 1991) had demonstrated CBF increases in the STG bilaterally during the presentation of speech materials as compared to a baseline with no auditory stimulation, with some indication of a left-sided bias. These data indicate that the acoustic cues present in speech sounds engage neural systems within both left and right STG, but do not directly clarify to what extent these areas may be specialized for speech processing per se, as opposed to more general classes of stimuli.

A second question concerned the identification of cerebral regions specifically involved in phonetic processing. Some models from the psychological literature on speech perception have maintained that such a process would require a specialized speech module, distinct from perceptual mechanisms involved in processing other types of sounds. One specific model of speech processing further emphasizes the possible role of motor-articulatory codes in the perception of speech; according to this model, phonetic units are processed according to their underlying articulatory representations, so that the /d/ in "dog" and that in "dip" are perceived as similar not because of their acoustic properties, which differ as a function of the vowel, but because they are both articulated in the same way. Until recently, it has proven difficult to obtain direct evidence bearing on this question, particularly in terms of specifying the neural bases of these mechanisms. Thus, an additional aim of these initial studies was to clarify possible motor contributions to phonetic perceptual processes.

Finally, we attempted to dissociate linguistic from nonlinguistic processing by requiring judgments of pitch changes in the speech syllable. We hypothesized that pitch processing would involve right-hemisphere mechanisms, based on other data from our laboratory , in which we had consistently found that right temporal-lobe and frontal-lobe lesions caused disturbances in making judgments of pitch.

In our first PET study (Zatorre, Evans, Meyer, & Gjedde, 1992), we tested 10 normal right-handed volunteers using two types of stimuli: pairs of noise bursts, which had been matched acoustically (in terms of duration, intensity, and temporal envelope) to the syllables to be used subsequently, and pairs of consonant–vowel–consonant real speech syllables (e.g.: "fat–dig"). The vowels in any given syllable pair were always different, but the final consonant differed in half of the pairs. The difference in vowel is important, because the acoustic realization of the consonant is different when the vowel is different; we predicted that a specialized mechanism would therefore be necessary to accomplish the discrimination task in this condition. In addition to the difference in phonetic structure, the second syllable of each pair always had either a higher pitch (fundamental frequency) in half the pairs, or a lower pitch in the other half. The study included five conditions arranged in a subtractive hierarchy. According to this approach, first developed by Petersen et al. (1988), each condition is designed to add a small number of discrete processing components to the previous condition. Subtraction of successive conditions should thus isolate patterns of activity associated with specific task components. Such a hierarchical approach implies a number of assumptions that are often not entirely met; however, as a first approximation it serves a useful heuristic purpose.

The silent condition, at the bottom of the hierarchy, was a baseline condition in which no auditory input was presented and no response was elicited; in the second condition subjects listened to pairs of noise bursts and pressed a key (as a control for the motor aspect of the subsequent tasks). In the passive speech condition subjects listened to the syllables without making an explicit judgment, and pressed a key to alternate stimulus pairs. Two active conditions were also run in which subjects were asked to make explicit judgments. In the phonetic condition subjects listened to the same speech stimuli as before but responded only when the stimuli ended with the same consonant sound (e.g., a positive response would be given to the syllables "bag" and "pig"). In the pitch condition subjects once again listened to the same syllables, but responded only when the second item had a higher pitch than the first.

When the results from the silent baseline condition were subtracted from the noise condition, activation was observed bilaterally approximately within the transverse gyri of Heschl, corresponding to primary auditory cortex (Penhune,

Zatorre, MacDonald, & Evans, 1996; see Fig. 8.2), as predicted. Because the primary cortex is thought to subserve basic auditory processes, presentation of noise should activate it, and indeed it does. Subtraction of the noise condition from the passive speech activation pattern yielded several foci along the STG bilaterally. This region contains several distinct cortical fields that are known to be responsive to auditory stimulation. They also receive auditory input from other auditory cortical processing regions, as well as from the auditory portion of the thalamus, the relay point for incoming acoustic information from the periphery . These areas are therefore likely to be involved in higher–order auditory processing of complex signals that contain amplitude and frequency modulations, such as speech. One left-lateralized focus in the posterior STG, within the planum temporale, was also identified in this comparison. This finding is important in that it implicates this portion of the left temporal lobe, roughly falling within the classical posterior speech region, as being automatically engaged in the processing of speech signals.

Perhaps the most surprising results were obtained in the two active conditions, in which subjects were asked to make specific judgments of either pho-

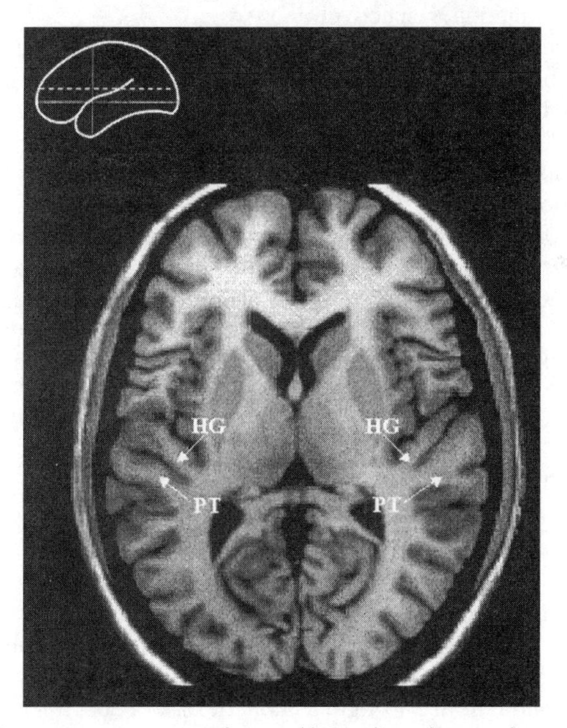

FIG. 8.2. Magnetic resonance image of a normal human brain showing a horizontal section (position of section indicated by dotted line on lateral view shown in insert) through the region of Heschl's gyrus, marked HG, and the planum temporale, marked PT. Note the thicker configuration of the left HG compared to the right HG.

netic identity or pitch. In the phonetic condition minus passive speech subtraction, activity was largely confined to the left hemisphere: The largest increase was observed in part of Broca's area near the junction with the premotor cortex, and additionally in a superior parietal area. This was surprising in terms of the conventional view of Broca's area as a speech output area (cf. Saffran, chap. 10, this volume), because no speech output occurred. However, it supported the interpretation that articulatory codes might be used in determining that the /g/ in "bag" and "pig" are the same phonetic unit.

The prediction that pitch processing would involve right-hemispheric mechanisms was confirmed in the pitch condition minus passive speech subtraction, with two foci observed in the right prefrontal cortex. This latter finding fits with earlier lesion studies in which we observed that damage to the right frontal cortex caused pitch processing deficits (Zatorre & Samson, 1991). In these latter two subtractions, both stimuli and responses were identical; only the nature of the required cognitive processing changed as a function of the instructions. The dissociable patterns of activity observed must therefore reflect the fundamentally different nature of the neural mechanisms involved in analysis of phonetic and pitch information, respectively.

These results were subjected to further scrutiny in a second study aimed at replicating and extending the first set of findings. In particular, the finding of increased CBF in a frontal region close to the conventionally defined Broca's area was of special significance, because its involvement in a purely perceptual task has implications for models of speech processing. However, data from any single PET activation comparison must be viewed cautiously, as many different, and perhaps uncontrolled, task dimensions may be responsible for the observed effect. For example, comparing an active discrimination to a passive listening condition entails many differences in cognitive demands. Because two items must be compared in the active discrimination task but not in the passive task, there is an additional working memory component that allows one item to be held online until the next is presented for comparison. Such a task also requires the subject to pay more attention to the stimuli than merely passively listening. Also; the motor demands of deciding which of two keys to press are different in the active task as compared to the passive one. All of these issues could have influenced the initial set of results—hence the importance of replicating results under different conditions.

In order to assess these issues, we carried out a new study with a separate set of subjects using both the original task and a different task that required monitoring of a given target phoneme within a stream of speech syllables (e.g., pressing a key whenever a [b] was perceived). This task is slightly different in its cognitive demands from the original phonetic task (it does not require comparison of pairs of stimuli, for example) but should engage the same phonetic processing system as was recruited by the first task. We reasoned that the Broca/premotor area would be engaged whenever a phonetic unit had to be isolated from the syllable, because this segmentation is accomplished by accessing an articulatory code, and therefore predicted that the monitoring task would result in activation of the area in question. A comparison of this monitoring task to passive listening of syllables did indeed yield very similar activation within the region close to Broca's area previously observed. The replication using the original phonetic task also gave similar results. Furthermore, we carried out a reanalysis of the previous study to compare the phonetic task to the pitch task. Our reasoning was that both tasks require active comparison and decision processes, but differ in terms of the crucial phonetic processing component which we wished to isolate. Once again, this comparison yielded a similar left frontal cortex response.

A spatial comparison of the various foci from our two studies, together with data from two similar experiments conducted by Démonet et al. (1992; Démonet, Price, Wise, & Frackowiack, 1994), reveals that the foci all cluster fairly closely together, despite coming from different studies with different subjects in different laboratories (Fig. 8.3). It is interesting that all of these foci con-

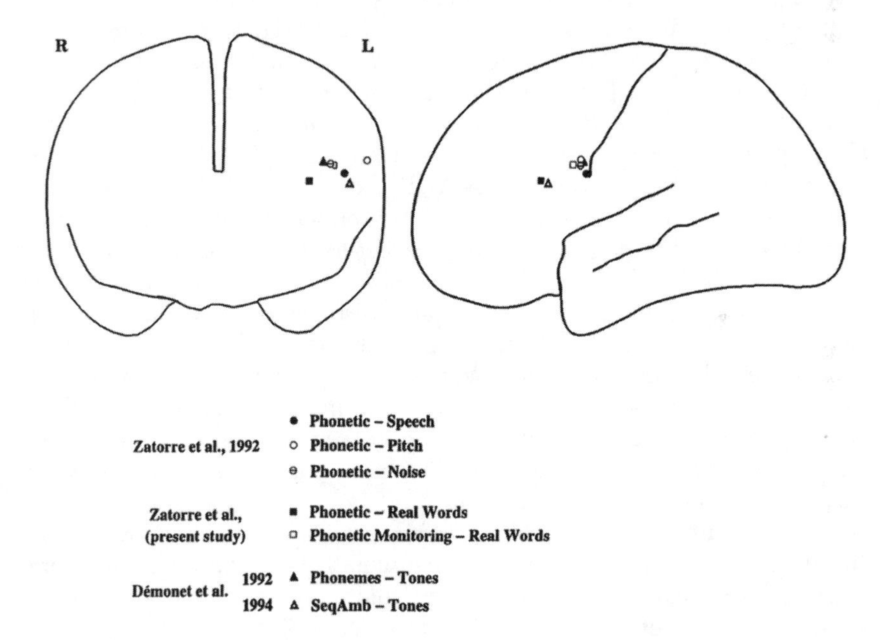

FIG. 8.3. Summary diagram demonstrating the location of foci near Broca's area identified in PET activation studies by Zatorre et al. (Zatorre, Evans, Meyer, & Gjedde, 1992; Zatorre, Meyer, Gjedde, & Evans, 1996) placed on coronal (front view) and saggital (lateral view) projections of a left hemisphere. For comparison purposes, the location of foci described by Démonet et al. (1992; Démonet, Price, Wise, & Frackowiack, 1994) in phonetic discrimination tasks is also shown. The symbols represent the center (most significant voxel) of extended regions of CBF increase identified in each comparison. The brain outlines and major sulci were generated from an average MRI data set, transformed into stereotaxic space (Talairach & Tournoux, 1988). From Zatorre et al. (1996, with permission).

sistently cluster in the most superior and posterior aspect of cytoarchitectonic area 44, near the border with the premotor cortex, rather than to the inferior aspect of the third frontal convolution more traditionally associated with Broca's area. The highly consistent anatomical placement of the region shown in Fig. 8.3 may possibly indicate the existence of a functional subregion within Broca's area related to phonetic operations.

More recently, two new studies have provided remarkable converging evidence and have extended our understanding of the role of left anterior regions in speech perception. Gandour, Wong, & Hutchins (1998) used a pitch–judgment task among speakers of Thai, for whom pitch changes are phonemically relevant. When discriminating pitch patterns in Thai words, native speakers of that language (but not English speakers) show significant activity in a left Broca/premotor area, within a few millimeters of the region identified in the previous studies from Démonet's and our own laboratories. Moreover, Gandour et al. showed that pitch judgments of low-pass filtered syllables, which are not perceived as speech but which contain the same pitch information as speech syllables, do not produce activity within this region. Thus, this left frontal region participates in processing pitch, but only when pitch is used as part of the phonetic inventory of a language. An even more recent study (Burton, Small, & Blumstein, 2000) replicated the earlier results and showed that the Broca/premotor region is specifically recruited when phonetic units must be segmented from the syllable, as predicted by Zatorre et al. (1996). That is, Burton et al. found that no Broca activation was present when subjects discriminated two syllables that were identical except for the initial consonant (e.g., "dip–tip"), but that the Broca/premotor area was recruited when subjects were asked to make the same initial-consonant discrimination in syllables that differed from one another in all segments (e.g.., "dip–tad"). Thus, the latter condition requires that the individual phonetic units be segmented from one another, which apparently is accomplished by accessing an articulatory representation. Conversely, the first condition does not require segmentation, since the vowel is the same, and hence the phonetic discrimination can be carried out without a need for any articulatory code.

The conclusion that part of Broca's area participates in phonetic processing does not imply that other regions, particularly the left posterior temporal region, do not play a role in the phonetic analysis of speech sounds. As mentioned earlier, experimental conditions in which subjects listen to speech syllables have often yielded asymmetric left posterior temporal CBF increases, as well as bilateral activation in the anterior portion of both left and right STG (Petersen et al., 1988; Price et al., 1992; Wise et al., 1991; 1992; Zatorre et al., 1992). Functional magnetic resonance imaging (MRI) data have also corroborated this finding (Binder et al., 1994). Thus, when passive listening is used as the baseline state, any neural activation in these regions would be subtracted out. It seems clear that "passive" listening would include an important phonetic processing component that would be engaged automatically, but that is not observable in subtractions using passive listening as a baseline.

How, then, are we to understand the difference in the roles that anterior and posterior speech regions play in phonetic processing? One possibility is that posterior regions are involved in the analysis of speech sounds, perhaps at the syllable level, whereas anterior regions are involved in analysis of individual phonemes when these must be segmented from the speech stream. It is reasonable to assume that neural processes in the STG are initially responsible for perceptual analysis of the incoming speech stream, because neurophysiological studies of auditory cortices reveal the presence of neuronal populations sensitive to acoustic features that are present in speech sounds, such as frequency modulation and bandwidth (e. g. Rauschecker et al., 1997; Whitfield & Evans, 1965), or onset times (e. g. Steinschneider, Schroeder, Arezzo, & Vaughan, 1995). It is therefore likely that the CBF activation in the left and right anterior superior temporal area observed during "passive" speech reflects the operation of such neural systems. The posterior region of the left STG likely plays a some role in speech processing, because this region is not activated by tone patterns or noise bursts (Zatorre, Evans, & Meyer, 1994; Zatorre et al., 1992), or by auditory tonal discrimination tasks (Démonet et al., 1992, 1994; Zatorre et al., 1994) but is consistently activated by speech stimuli. The processing carried out within this left posterior temporal area is not fully understood, but probably involves the analysis of speech sounds leading to comprehension, and may be specifically sensitive to rapidly changing acoustic information (Belin et al., 1998; Tallal, Miller & Fitch, 1993; see further discussion).

This aspect of speech processing appears to be distinct, however, from processes that engage the network that includes the portion of Broca's area identified earlier. In the phonetic tasks in question, a relatively abstract pattern–extraction process must take place, because individual phonetic units belonging to the same category may have very different acoustic manifestations (e. g. the /d/ in "dig" versus the /d/ in "dog"). It is therefore apparently insufficient to rely on a syllable-level representation to perform this type of task; rather, recourse must be made to a specialized mechanism that is able to compute the similarity between phonetic segments that are differently encoded acoustically by virtue of being embedded in syllables with different vowels (Liberman & Mattingly, 1985). We would argue that this type of judgment calls into play the specialized articulatory recoding system whose neural manifestation is activity in a portion of Broca's area, an argument that finds strong empirical support in the recent data of Burton et al. (2000).

A quite different approach to understanding the possible role of anterior and posterior cortical areas in speech processing was taken by Paus, Perry, Zatorre, Worsley, and Evans (1996), who examined how feedback mechanisms might be linked to the role of the left temporal cortex in speech. The premise in this case was somewhat different from previous studies, as the aim was to maintain a neutral, constant auditory input throughout all conditions, while varying the rate of speech output. The authors reasoned that if speech output and input mechanisms were functionally linked, then varying the rate of production should have similar effects on CBF in anterior and posterior speech areas (i.e., the CBF values should covary with one another). In order to test this hypothesis they devised a paradigm in which subjects were asked to articulate two meaningless speech syllables ([ba] and [lu]) repeatedly at each of seven different rates. Auditory input was held physically constant in all conditions by presenting continuous white noise that masked any speech perception. The PET data were analyzed by searching the image volume for significant sites of covariation as a function of output rate.

The most relevant finding was that an area of left posterior STG, just posterior to Heschl's gyrus, and within the planum temporale, showed a significant positive covariation with articulation rate, indicating that this region is involved in speech processing independently of any actual physical speech input (because auditory input was masked by white noise). The left precentral gyrus, a motor area directly related to speech production, also covaried with rate.

To complement the covariation analysis, a subtraction analysis was also performed comparing all the speech production conditions to a baseline containing white noise input but no speech output. This analysis was expected to reveal the network of brain areas involved in motor production of speech. As expected, several brain areas that are part of a complex motor network were strongly active in the subtraction, including not only a region in the left precentral gyrus, but also the primary motor cortex bilaterally, the supplementary motor area, the putamen, and the cerebellum. In contrast, this subtraction analysis did not reveal a significant CBF increase in the left temporal cortex, indicating that the net CBF change in this area is either very small or absent, and confirming that auditory input was not driving the response. Thus, the covariation analysis reveals a subtle effect of modulation in this region, an effect not reflected in any overall increase or decrease in CBF.

Finally, a further analysis of interregional covariation was performed. This type of analysis searches for loci in the scanned brain volume that covary with a preselected anatomical location; it is therefore useful in helping to identify regions whose CBF changes in concert with one another, and that are therefore presumably functionally related. This analysis was conducted by selecting a region of interest in the left STG, because that was the region whose CBF changed as a function of speech rate; the authors predicted that if this region is functionally interconnected with anterior regions, there should be significant covariation between these areas. As expected, the interregional analysis revealed that CBF in the STG covaried significantly with CBF in the motor areas, notably the left precentral gyrus, putamen, and cerebellum. Therefore, the authors concluded that the left STG area is specifically involved in a feedback loop, related perhaps to corollary discharge originating in the left premotor region. Although the precise functional role of this area remains an open question, the findings implicate this region of sensory cortex in perceptuo–motor integration.

At the functional level, the interaction between output and sensory processing systems may serve various purposes. A feedback mechanism could provide information about the precise timing and pattern of motor activity, for example, thus serving to modulate and correct speech output based on the match between expected and produced sound pattern. One may speculate that such a mechanism might also be important in inner speech, or imagery: motor-to-sensory discharges might activate phonological representations and thus underlie some aspects of speech imagery in the absence of actual sound input.

Taken together with the findings discussed earlier that implicate the left premotor area in phonetic perceptual processing, the findings of Paus et al. (1996) may be seen as providing complementary evidence. It is striking that these data illustrate precisely reverse roles for anterior and posterior speech areas than might have been predicted on the basis of classical functional models: The anterior region appears to be consistently active in certain purely perceptual tasks, whereas the posterior region is demonstrated to be involved in a production task in which auditory input was masked. Thus, although the premotor and temporal areas of the left hemisphere may continue to be considered as primarily motor and sensory cortices, respectively, the data would seem to argue that their functional roles are not so distinct: Motor areas play a role in perception, and sensory areas play a role in production, hence forming an integrated functional network. This conclusion is mirrored by the views of some investigators in the field of aphasia, who have recently challenged the classical view in which speech production is subserved by anterior brain structures and speech perception is subserved by posterior regions, but who instead insist on the distributed and interactive nature of the left-hemisphere cortical language system (Blumstein, 1994). Clearly, there remains a great deal of work to do before a more complete understanding of these complex systems emerges, but it would appear that we are at a better point than at any time in the recent past to make significant progress toward this goal.

We conclude the survey of our research into the correlates of human auditory processing by presenting some recent data pertaining to structural measures of auditory cortex (Penjune et al., 1996). The anatomical measures of auditory cortex present a complementary approach to the functional methods discussed earlier, and shed light on the functional characteristics of this region. The specific aim of this research was to characterize the shape, volume, and position of the human primary auditory cortical region in vivo, rather than relying on postmortem analysis. The findings were somewhat surprising, and have possibly important implications for a better understanding of functional differences.

The approach taken was to use anatomical MRI scans from groups of normal right-handed volunteer subjects, and to label the region of Heschl's gyrus using interactive software that permits three-dimensional viewing, which greatly facilitates accurate anatomical delineation. It has been established with postmortem methods (Rademacher, Caviness, Steinmetz, & Galaburda, 1993) that the primary auditory cortex is generally confined to the medial two–thirds of the most anterior Heschl's gyrus. These data thus indicate that visible landmarks may serve as consistent boundaries to define the region of interest. The results from our MRI-based morphometric measures therefore represent an estimate of the position and extent of primary auditory cortex in the human brain, but it is important to note that they also necessarily include non-primary cortical fields (particularly near the lateral edge of the gyrus), because there are no gross morphological features that would permit an exclusion of such areas.

Two sets of data were obtained, each on a different sample of 20 volunteer subjects; the first set underwent MR scanning using a 2-mm slice thickness, and the second underwent a higher resolution scanning protocol in which 1-mm thick slices were obtained. Images were acquired and then transformed to the standardized stereotaxic space of Talairach and Tournoux using an automatic algorithm (Collins, Meelin, Peters, & Evans, 1994); this transformation involves scaling (expanding or contracting) each individual MRI in each of the three spatial dimensions so that it fits within a standard template. Heschl's gyrus was then identified and labeled according to anatomical features visible in the three-dimensional dataset. This procedure yielded a set of points within the same standardized stereotaxic space for each subject, which may be superimposed to create a probabilistic map of the structure in question, in this case Heschl's gyrus (see Penhune et al., 1996, for further details). In addition, the second, higher resolution sample of MRI scans also allowed for automatic segmentation of the labeled volumes into the two tissue types of the brain: gray matter (containing cell bodies) and white matter (containing axonal fibers). The gray/white boundary was calculated from the histogram of intensity values for each point by taking the midpoint between peak values corresponding to gray and white matter.

The result of greatest relevance to the present review is that there were differences in the volume of Heschl's gyrus between the two hemispheres. These differences cannot be accounted for by any overall differences in brain size or shape because of the stereotaxic normalization procedure. In the first sample of 20, the volume of the left Heschl's gyrus was significantly greater than that of the right (Fig. 8.4. left), with 17 of the 20 subjects demonstrating a difference of 10% or more favoring the left side. This finding was replicated in the second sample of subjects, in which the asymmetry was slightly less marked but still highly significant (Fig. 8.4, right). Most interesting of all was the outcome of the gray/white segmentation analysis: the differences in volume were found to be confined to the white matter underlying Heschl's gyrus, and not to the volume of cortical tissue within the structure (Fig. 8.5).

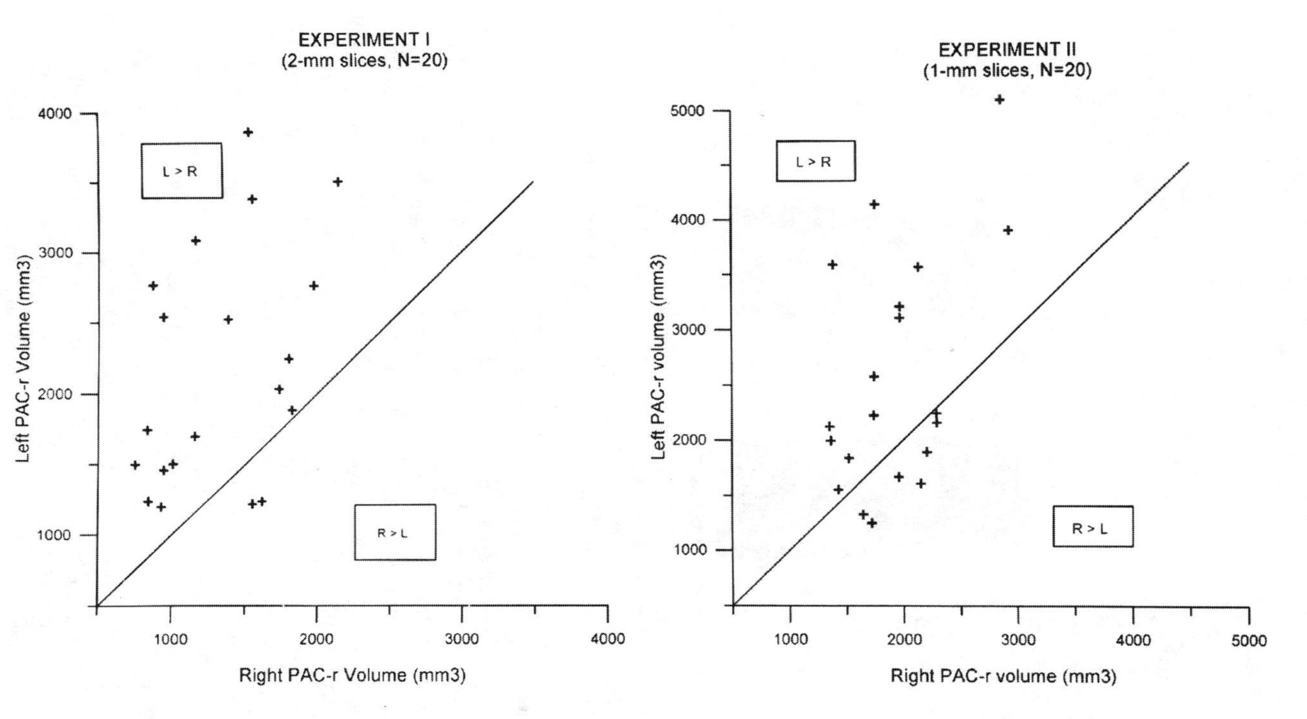

FIG. 8.4. Scatterplots for volume of Heschl's gyrus, or primary auditory cortex region in left and right hemispheres for two samples of subjects. The solid line represents values of equal left and right volume; each point represent measures from a single individual. Points that fall above the line represent subjects whose left volume was greater than right, and vice versa. PAC–r, primary auditory cortex region. From Penhune, Zatorre, MacDonald, and Evans (1996), with permission.

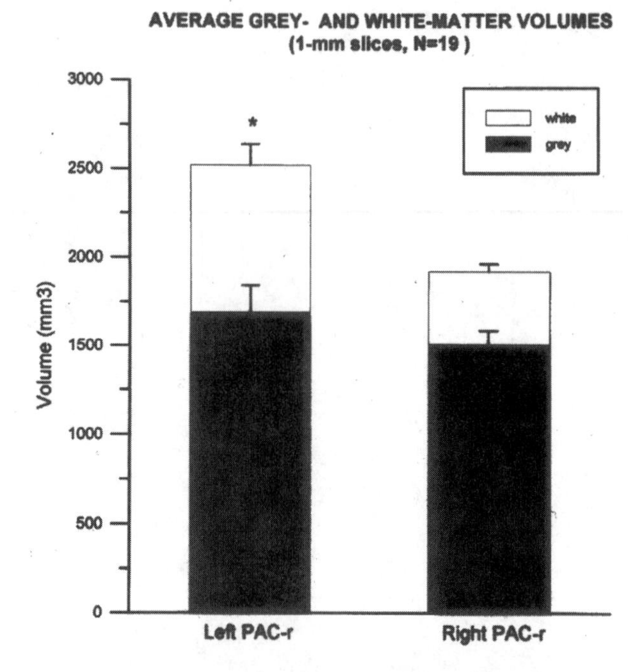

FIG. 8.5. Average volumes of gray and white matter for left and right Heschl's gyrus in second sample of 20 subjects scanned with high-resolution MRI protocol; standard errors displayed as vertical bars. From Penhune et al. (1996), with permission.

Because the differences between the hemispheres were confined to white matter, this indicates that the anatomical asymmetry arises not from the number of neurons in the area, but from a difference in the volume of fibers that carry information to and from the primary auditory cortex, and surrounding regions. However, the asymmetry in white matter may reflect any of a number of underlying neuronal structural differences. With in vivo MRI we cannot ascertain, for example, whether the asymmetry reflects connections going to and coming from other cortical areas, or whether they relate to inputs and outputs from subcortical regions such as the thalamus. We also cannot determine if the increased white-matter volume is a consequence of a greater number of fibers entering and exiting the primary cortical region, or if it may indicate a higher degree of myelination of these fibers. Research so far suggests that both possibilities are viable. Seldon (1981, 1982), for example, found that cell columns in the left primary auditory cortex are both wider and more widely spaced than those on the right. Also; Hutsler and Gazzaniga (1996) recently showed that the left primary auditory region has larger cells in certain cortical layers, which would be likely to form larger columns and to send out thicker or more heavily branched axons to other regions of auditory cortex, hence resulting in more white matter.

The functional significance of such structural asymmetries is not yet clearly established, but it is interesting to speculate that they may be directly related to some of the functional asymmetries observed in many of the studies described in the preceding sections of this chapter. In particular, several investigators (e.g., Tallal et al., 1993) have noted that the acoustic parameters necessary to process speech sounds entail rapid changes, particularly when tracking formant transitions (which correspond to spectral resonances of the vocal cavity associated with different speech sounds). Conversely, musical stimuli typically involve much slower rates of frequency change. Data from the MRI study (Penhune et al., 1996) would be consistent with this general explanation if the white-matter volume measures are related to degree of myelination. That is, a greater degree of left-sided myelination could lead to faster transmission of acoustically relevant information, thereby permitting a specialization of left auditory cortices in the fine-grained analysis of temporal aspects of the signal, which would be highly relevant for decoding of speech sounds. Confirmation of greater myelination of left auditory cortical regions comes from a recent postmortem electron microscopy study showing that the myelin sheath is significantly thicker in the left than in the right posterior temporal cortex (Anderson, Southern, & Powers, 1999).

This hypothesis has also received support from a PET study by Belin, et al. (1998), in which the rate of formant transitions in a pseudospeech sound—not perceived as speech—was either 40 or 200 msec. CBF changes in the left auditory region were found for both types of stimuli, indicating a capacity for processing spectral change over a wide range of durations; in contrast, regions in the right auditory cortex responded only to the slower rates, and not to the faster rate. Thus, the right auditory cortex seems unable to respond to fast formant transitions, whereas the homologous area on the left is better able to track rapidly changing acoustic information, which would be relevant for speech processing. The fact that the stimuli used were not perceived as speech and yet engaged the left auditory areas is also important, in that it points to a low-level perceptual mechanism that is independent of more cognitive linguistic systems that would be engaged by speech stimuli.

A complementary hypothesis to that just proposed may also be offered: We may speculate that there is a tradeoff between speed of response and spectral selectivity, and that different neural systems are best able to respond to these features. Neural systems in the left hemisphere would have a fast rate of response, but their spectral tuning function would therefore necessarily be fairly wide-band, as would be appropriate to speech sounds. The right-hemisphere system would have narrower tuning functions, and thus be well suited to the processing of stimuli containing small frequency differences, but would have a slower rate of integration in the temporal domain. This reciprocal relationship between bandwidth and speed reflects a fundamental physical limitation, because precision in the spectral domain requires greater temporal sampling, hence reducing time resolution, and vice versa (Joos, 1948). This model could explain why many aspects of pitch processing relevant to music might be predominantly processed by right auditory cortical mechanisms (Zatorre, 1988; Zatorre et al., 1994; Zatorre & Samson, 1991), because musical stimuli generally contain relatively slower changes, but small frequency differences are important. Recent PET data from our laboratory tend to confirm the idea that relative difference exists between the temporal and spectral resolution of auditory cortical areas in the two hemisphere (Zatorre & Belin, 2001; see Zatorre, Belin & Penhune, 2002, for additional discussion of this idea).

This account of the possible relation between structural and functional asymmetries in the human auditory cortex is at this stage very preliminary and necessarily highly speculative. It is important to put forth such ideas, however, in that they should be testable and verifiable. Perhaps more important, they point to the type of integration of evidence from multiple types of studies (behavioral, functional, structural) that will become more feasible in the near future, thanks to advances in functional imaging, the development of new in vivo imaging technologies, and more traditional physiological and anatomical knowledge.

ACKNOWLEDGMENT

Support for the research described in this chapter comes from grants awarded to the author from the Canadian Institute for Health Research, and the McDonnell-Pew Cognitive Neuroscience Program.

REFERENCES

Anderson, B., Southern, B. D., & Powers, R. E. (1999). Anatomic asymmetries of the posterior superior temporal lobes: A postmortem study. *Neuropsychiatry, Neuropsychology, & Behavioral Neurology, 12*, 247–254.

Belin, P., Zilbovicius, M., Crozier, S., Thivard, L., Fontaine, A., Masure, M. C., & Samson, Y. (1998). Lateralization of speech and auditory temporal processing. *Journal of Cognitive Neuroscience, 10*, 536–540.

Binder, J., Frost, J., Hammeke, T., Rao, S., & Cox, R. (1996). Function of the left planum temporale in auditory and linguistic processing. *Brain, 119*, 1239–1247.

Binder, J. R., Rao, S. M., Hammeke, T. A., Yetkin, F. Z., Jesmanowicz, A., Bandettini, P. A., Wong, E. C., Estkowski, L. D., Goldstein, M. D., Haughton, V. M., & Hyde, J. S. (1994). Functional magnetic resonance imaging of human auditory cortex. *Annals of Neurology, 35*, 662–672.

Blumstein, S. E. (1994). The neurobiology of the sound structure of language. In *The Cognitive Neurosciences*, M. S. Gazzaniga, (Ed.), pp. 915–929. Cambridge, MA: MIT Press.

Burton, M. W., Small, S. L., & Blumstein, S. E. (2000) The role of segmentation in phonological processing: An fMRI investigation. *Journal of Cognitive Neuroscience, 12*, 679–690.

Collins, D., Neelin, P., Peters, T., & Evans, A. (1994). Automatic 3D intersubject registration of MR volumetric data in standardized Talairach space. *Journal of Computer Assisted Tomography, 18*, 192–205.

Démonet, J. F., Chollet, F., Ramsay, S., Cardebat, D., Nespoulous, J. L., Wise, R., Rascol, A., & Frackowiak, R. (1992). The anatomy of phonological and semantic processing in normal subjects. *Brain, 115*, 1753–1768.

Démonet, J. F., Price, C., Wise, R., & Frackowiack, R. S. J. (1994). A PET study of cognitive strategies in normal subjects during language tasks. *Brain, 117*, 671–682.

Gandour, J., Wong, D., & Hutchins, G. (1998). Pitch processing in the human brain is influenced by language experience. *NeuroReport, 9*, 2115–2119.
Hutsler, J., & Gazzaniga, M. (1996). Acetylcholinesterase staining in human auditory and language cortices—regional variation of structural features. *Cerebral Cortex, 6*, 260–270.
Joos, M. (1948) Acoustic phonetics. *Language, 24*, (suppl. 2).
Liberman, A. M., & Mattingly, I.G. (1985). The motor theory of speech perception revised. *Cognition, 21*, 1–36.
Ojemann, G. A. (1991). Cortical organization of language. *Journal of Neuroscience, 11*, 2281–2287.
Paus, T., Perry, D., Zatorre, R., Worsley, K., & Evans, A. (1996). Modulation of cerebral blood–flow in the human auditory cortex during speech: Role of motor–to–sensory discharges. *European Journal of Neuroscience, 8*(11), 2236–2246.
Penfield, W., & Roberts, L. (1959). *Speech and brain mechanisms.* Princeton, NJ: Princeton University Press.
Penhune, V. B., Zatorre, R. J., MacDonald, J. D., & Evans, A. C. (1996). Interhemispheric anatomical differences in human primary auditory cortex: Probabilistic mapping and volume measurement from magnetic resonance scans. *Cerebral Cortex, 6*, 661–672.
Petersen, S., Fox, P., Posner, M., Mintun, M., & Raichle, M. (1988). Positron emission tomographic studies of the cortical anatomy of single-word processing. *Nature, 331*, 585–589.
Price, C., Wise, R., Ramsay, S., Friston, K., Howard, D., Patterson, K., & Frackowiak, R. S. J. (1992). Regional response differences within the human auditory cortex when listening to words. *Neuroscience Letters, 146*, 179–182.
Rademacher, J., Caviness, V. S., Steinmetz, H., & Galaburda, A. M. (1993). Topographical variation of the human primary cortices: Implications for neuroimaging, brain mapping and neurobiology. *Cerebral Cortex, 3*, 313–329.
Rauschecker, J. P., Tian, B., Pons, T., & Mishkin, M. (1997). Serial and parallel processing in rhesus monkey auditory cortex. *Journal of Comparative Neurology, 382*, 89–103.
Seldon, H. (1981). Structure of human auditory cortex II: Axon distributions and morphological correlates of speech perception. *Brain Research, 229*, 295–310.
Seldon, H. (1982). Structure of human auditory cortex III: Statistical analysis of dendritic trees. *Brain Research, 249*, 211–221.
Steinschneider, M., Schroeder, C., Arezzo, J., & Vaughan, H. (1995). Physiologic correlates of the voice onset time boundary in primary auditory cortex of the awake monkey: Temporal response patterns. *Brain and Language, 48*, 326–340.
Talairach, J., & Tournoux, P. (1988). *Co-planar stereotaxic atlas of the human brain*. New York: Thieme.
Tallal, P., Miller, S., & Fitch, R. (1993). Neurobiological basis of speech: A case for the preeminence of temporal processing. *Annals of the New York Academy of Sciences, 682*, 27–47.
Whitfield, I. C., & Evans, E. F. (1965). Responses of auditory cortical neurones to stimuli of changing frequency. *Journal of Neurophysiology, 28*, 655–672.
Wise, R. J., Chollet, F., Hadar, U., Friston, K., Hoffner, E., & Frackowiak, R. (1991). Distribution of cortical neural networks involved in word comprehension and word retrieval. *Brain, 114*, 1803–1817.
Zatorre, R. J. (1988). Pitch perception of complex tones and human temporal–lobe function. *Journal of the Acoustical Society of America, 84*(2), 566–572.
Zatorre, R. J., Evans, A. C., & Meyer, E. (1994). Neural mechanisms underlying melodic perception and memory for pitch. *Journal of Neuroscience, 14*(4), 1908–1919.
Zatorre, R. J., Evans, A. C., Meyer, E., & Gjedde, A. (1992). Lateralization of phonetic and pitch processing in speech perception. *Science, 256*, 846–849.
Zatorre, R. J., Meyer, E., Gjedde, A., & Evans, A. C. (1996). PET studies of phonetic processing of speech: Review, replication, and re–analysis. *Cerebral Cortex, 6*, 21–30.
Zatorre, R. J., & Samson, S. (1991). Role of the right temporal neocortex in retention of pitch in auditory short–term memory. *Brain, 114*, 2403–2417.
Zatorre, R. J., Belin, P., (2001). Spectral and temporal processing in human auditory cortex. *Cerebral Cortex 11*, 946–953.
Zatorre, R. J., Belin, P., & Penhune, V. B. (2002) Structure and function of auditory cortex: Music and speech. *Trends in Cognitive Science* 6, 37–46.

9

Parallel Systems for Processing Language: Hemispheric Complementarity in the Normal Brain

Christine Chiarello
University of California, Riverside

Human language is a multi-faceted entity. From single-word utterances to intricately structured discourse and from political slogans to poetry, language provides the primary medium through which we communicate, cogitate, and connect ourselves to past, present, and future individuals. Understanding how such a complex function is organized in the human brain will require a variety of theoretical perspectives, as well as converging evidence from diverse populations and experimental techniques. To approach this question, it is useful to consider the multiple levels of organization that comprise the nervous system.

Fig. 9.1, adapted from Churchland and Sejnowski (1992), makes it clear that the nervous system is organized and can be understood at multiple scales, ranging from the behavior of individual molecules, single neurons, and small networks of interacting neurons, on through rather distributed neural systems that coalesce to mediate significant behavioral functions such as vision. No single level can provide a complete picture of brain function, and selecting a level of analysis highlights some brain properties while blurring over (i.e., temporarily ignoring) others. Of course, this hierarchical scheme is not intended to be strictly reductionist—that is, it is not assumed that all properties of a given level can be reduced to those of units at the next lowest level. For example, although local neural networks consist of individual neurons, the behavior of the net-

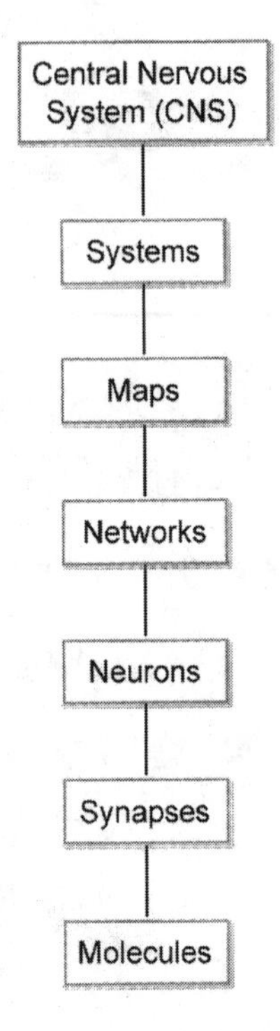

FIG. 9.1. Levels of organization of the nervous system, adapted from Churchland and Sejnowski (1992). Properties at lower levels of analysis constrain those of the next level up, but new properties emerge at each level. For example, neural activity can be analyzed in terms of the behavior of individual molecules (bottom of figure). Molecular function constrains the behavior of synapses (sites of communication between neurons), but not all aspects of synaptic function can be reduced to the activity of individual molecules. Thus each successive level (from bottom to top) represents a unique level of brain function, amenable to analysis using techniques that target activity at that level. In this chapter, it is argued that the left and right hemispheres represent parallel *systems* for processing language.

work is not completely predictable from the behavior of single cells. In other words, each level of analysis is distinguished by some emergent properties that result from complex *interactions* among units at the next lowest level.

This chapter focuses on a systems-level approach to understanding language, premised on the ideas that the left and right cerebral cortices represent parallel and distinct information processing systems and that each of these systems contributes in some way to nearly all linguistic behavior. Hence, normal language will require hemispheric collaboration. Making this claim in no way argues against the view that there are important levels of organization within each hemisphere: Functional neuroimaging research provides particularly striking evidence for distinct functional regions within each hemisphere (see Zatorre, chap. 8, this volume). However, the hemispheric-systems view postulates that some equally important aspects of brain organization will emerge only when we focus on system-level properties of the left and right hemispheres.

The most compelling evidence supporting the hemispheric-systems view comes from the study of commissurotomized or "split-brain"patients. In these patients the cortical connections between each hemisphere are surgically severed (i.e., the interhemispheric fiber tracts—corpus callosum, anterior commissure—that normally transmit information between the left and right cortices are cut), and we can examine the performance of each hemisphere in isolation (Sperry, Gazzaniga, & Bogen, 1969). Due to the anatomy of the visual system, presenting stimuli to one visual half-field (the area of visual space to the left or right of where an individual is fixating) directly stimulates the opposite hemisphere (see Fig. 9.2). So items presented to the left visual field (LVF) will be directed to the right hemisphere (RH), and vice versa. Because each hemisphere also controls the actions of the opposite hand, we have the opportunity to examine the capabilities and limits of cognitive processing carried out by each hemisphere in isolation.

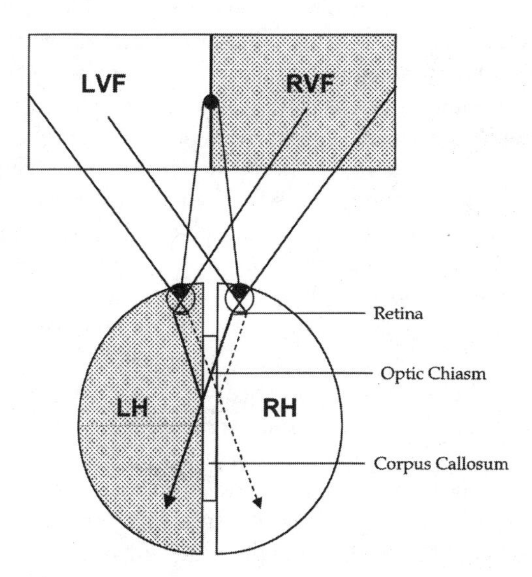

FIG. 9.2. Projection of visual information to the human cerebral cortex. The left visual half-field (LVF) consists of all information to the left of a person's point of fixation (fixation point indicated by the black dot). Any visual stimulus presented to the LVF will be directly transmitted to the visual cortex in the right hemisphere (RH); likewise stimuli in the right visual half-field (RVF) will be transmitted to the left hemisphere (LH). The corpus callosum allows information lateralized to a single hemisphere to be shared with the opposite hemisphere. When the corpus callosum and other cerebral commissures are cut as in split–brain surgery, the isolated processing of a single hemisphere can be studied.

As is well known, data obtained from testing split-brain patients reinforced views of hemispheric specialization obtained from the neurology clinic: The isolated left hemisphere (LH) is far superior for language processing and is critical for speech production, whereas the isolated right hemisphere is frequently superior when high-level perceptual and spatial functions are examined (Bradshaw & Nettleton, 1983; Gazzaniga & Sperry, 1967; Sperry, 1974). However, the real breakthrough represented by such studies was not to further document hemisphere asymmetries, but rather to conclusively demonstrate that each hemisphere represents a complete information-processing system. That is, each isolated hemisphere was shown to have its own perceptual experiences, memories both personal and semantic, problem-solving skills, and the ability to select and emit appropriate behavioral responses (Sperry et al., 1969; Sperry, Zaidel, & Zaidel, 1979). This fact, coupled with the evidence for functional asymmetries, strongly suggests that human cognition is dependent on these parallel, but differently organized, processing systems.

I next focus on how this hemispheric-systems approach can inform our view of language and mind by highlighting what has been learned to date from studying the normal brain. Here we can assume that both the left and right hemisphere systems are operating with maximal capacity, but in a highly interactive fashion. Yet when processing is initiated in either the left or right hemisphere, we frequently observe qualitative differences in processing, even though the two sides are not isolated from each other (Hellige, 1993). Close examination of such asymmetries can allow us to infer how processing proceeds within each hemisphere. Identifying the unique processing mechanisms that are recruited by the left hemisphere for language use can help us understand why language is critically dependent on an intact left hemisphere, and what auxiliary support the right hemisphere can provide.

The split–brain studies first provided hints that the right hemisphere might have greater than expected language potential (Nebes, 1974; Zaidel, 1990), and we now know that injury to the right hemisphere can disrupt a variety of linguistic and metalinguistic functions (Beeman & Chiarello, 1998; Joanette, Goulet, & Hannequin, 1990). For example, prosody (variations in the melody or pitch of speech that convey grammatical differences [question vs. statement] or the speaker's mood), discourse comprehension (understanding a group of sentences that describes a sequence of events, as in a story or conversation), figurative language (nonliteral words and phrases such as metaphors and idioms), and some word meaning judgments can be impaired after right hemisphere injury. However, examining the normal brain provides a unique contrast of left- and right-hemisphere processing within an intact individual and enables us to focus on and identify the differing computations that produce the distinct system-level behavior exhibited by each hemisphere.

Using methods from split–brain studies to present verbal information to the LH or RH in the normal brain first of all demonstrates a strong advantage for words directed to the LH via the RVF (see Chiarello, 1988, for review)[1]—that is, words are responded to more quickly and accurately when shown in the RVF than when shown in the LVF. This RVF/LH advantage in the processing of words is extremely robust and almost impossible to eliminate, remaining virtually unchanged over a range of different viewing conditions (Chiarello, Senehi, & Soulier, 1986), and it occurs to a similar extent for languages such as English or Hebrew which employ very different scripts and reading directions (Chiarello, Nuding, & Pollock, 1988; Faust, Kravetz, & Babkoff, 1993). However, the hemispheric systems approach is not oriented toward demonstrating which hemisphere may be superior overall in a given situation, but rather to discovering the differing ways in which each hemisphere accomplishes a given computational task such as word recognition. For this reason, the studies described herein all employ more indirect measures where we can examine qualitative differences in how a given task is performed when processing is initiated by one hemisphere as compared to another. Thus this approach is oriented toward demonstrating the differing *manners* in which information is processed within each hemisphere (qualitative effects), rather than simply asking whether processes or tasks are performed better by one hemisphere than another (quantitative differences).

VISUAL AND AUDITORY PROCESSES IN WORD RECOGNITION

It is typically assumed that once sensory information reaches the brain, it is transformed into different codes or types of information. For example, the visual features that specify a word will be encoded into orthographic (letter identities), phonological (linguistic sound patterns), grammatical (part of speech), and semantic (meaning) codes. By convention, codes that retain information from the sensory pattern are referred to as "early," and those that are based on meaning are said to reflect "deeper" or "later" processes. One of the goals of cognitive neuroscience is to specify the brain mechanisms that are used for each type of information transformation.

There are hemisphere asymmetries in the relatively early processes that occur after a spoken or written word reaches those areas of the brain that analyze auditory and visual patterns, respectively. Marsolek and colleagues (Marsolek, Kosslyn, & Squire, 1992; Marsolek, Schacter, & Nicholas, 1996) showed that the

---

[1]Unless indicated otherwise, the participants in the experiments descibed herein were neurologically normal right-handed individuals (in most studies 20-30 individuals are tested per condition). Although sex differences in cerebral lateralization are sometimes reported (Springer & Deutsch, 1998), we have not found evidence for this in our studies on language processing, nor have sex differences been reported in the other studies described in this chapter.

LH and RH rely on distinctly different representations of visual words. In their studies, subjects read a series of words that are printed in upper or lower case (e.g., triangle, combat, deliver ...) and are later shown word stems such as "com" in the RVF or LVF. The task is to complete the stem with "the first word that comes to mind". For words presented to either hemisphere, a priming effect is found: Given a word stem such as "com," participants are more likely to complete it with a word previously seen, such as "combat," rather than another possible completion such as "comfort." However, in the LVF/RH much greater priming is found when the original words and word stems are presented in the same case than when the cases differ, whereas in the RVF/LH equivalent priming is obtained regardless of whether or not the cases match (Marsolek et al., 1992).

Marsolek argued that the right hemisphere relies on representations of the word that preserve the specific details of its visual appearance, whereas the left hemisphere relies on a more abstract representation based on letter identity independent of its specific visual form. A slightly different interpretation of this finding is that words received by the left hemisphere very rapidly achieve deeper or more abstract encodings, without the maintenance of lower level representations, whereas words received by the right hemisphere maintain and perhaps even amplify early encodings even when deeper level codes become available. In any case, the issue here is not whether one hemisphere is superior to the other in visual form priming, but rather that the differential biases of each hemispheric system result in complementary encodings of the printed word, with the right hemisphere preserving information about visual details and the left hemisphere generalizing over the specific visual form in which a word is presented.

In the auditory domain, it was once believed that the right hemisphere had little or no ability to phonetically decode speech sounds or to discriminate between syllables differing in initial consonants. The only documented RH role in speech perception involved the processing of suprasegmental information such as intonation (e.g., Blumstein & Cooper, 1974; Ley & Bryden, 1982). However, recent studies by Ivry (Ivry & Lebby, 1998; Ivry & Robertson, 1998) hint that processing within the LH and RH may differentially amplify high versus low speech frequencies, respectively. This implies that the RH may be particularly involved when discriminating sounds based on low-frequency information.

The experimental technique involves presenting consonant-vowel syllables (such as /da/) to the left or right ear. When different sounds are simultaneously presented to the each ear, it appears that left ear information is preferentially processed by the right hemisphere and vice versa (for further discussion of the methodological issues surrounding this dichotic listening technique, see Springer & Deutsch, 1998). Ivry and Lebby (1998) synthesized syllable pairs such as /ba/ and /da/ that differed based on higher frequency components, and pairs such as /ba/ and /pa/ that differed based on lower frequency components[2] (in these studies, on each trial, one ear received the syllable pair while the other received noise). Subjects had to discriminate between different tokens of each contrast. Performance was better for the /ba–da/ contrast (distinguished by high-frequency information) when the syllables were presented to the right ear/LH, but for the /ba–pa/ discriminations (dependent upon low-frequency information) performance was enhanced when the syllables were directed to the left ear/RH.

These very recent findings are intriguing but will require replication. However, it's interesting that Molfese has repeatedly shown electrophysiological evidence for greater RH sensitivity to distinctions such as /pa/ versus /ba/, but not for distinctions such as /pa/ versus /da/ (Molfese, Molfese, & Parsons, 1983; Simos, Molfese, & Brenden, 1997), complementing the behavioral research. Ivry's idea that the RH amplifies low frequency components of speech (Ivry & Robertson, 1998) can also encompass the greater right hemisphere role in processing prosody because such information is also carried by modulation of the lower speech frequencies.

The important point to glean from the data described thus far is that the hemispheric systems appear to complement each other in some of the early perceptual processes involved in language comprehension. To take things a step further, it is necessary to examine word-level processes.

When people are asked to recognize a letter such as D, their performance is enhanced when the letter occurs within a word (CIDER) than when it occurs within a nonsense syllable (ERDIC). This phenomenon, known as the word superiority effect, indicates that word-level information is being used to assist letter identification (McClelland & Rumelhart, 1981). Word context reduces errors when the word strings are presented to the RVF/LH, but not when presented to the LVF/RH (Krueger, 1975). This indicates that letter strings directed to the LH very rapidly contact lexical or word-level codes and that this information influences the identification of component letters, whereas lexical information may not become available within the RH until after letter identification is complete. This interpretation is consistent with other data showing that identification of words presented to the LVF/RH is always limited by word length; that is, performance drops off as number of letters in the word increases. In contrast, RVF/LH word recognition speed is much less influenced by the length of the word (Eviatar & Zaidel, 1991; Iacaboni & Zaidel, 1996; Young & Ellis, 1985). These data may be another indication that the left hemisphere rapidly achieves the deepest level encodings of words in situations in which the right hemisphere is maintaining information based on lower level analyses.

---

[2]These contrasts can also be described based on the way in which the sounds are articulated. Distinctions such as /ba/–/da/ result from differences in the place within the vocal tract where the airflow is briefly occluded (at the lips for /ba/, behind the teeth for /da/). Distinctions such as /ba/–/pa/ result from differences in the timing of vocal cord vibration relative to the release of air (e.g., voice–onset time).

UNDERSTANDING WORD MEANINGS

Although the right hemisphere seems to retain information about the perceptual characteristics of words, we do know that words presented to either hemisphere are comprehended (although not necessarily in the same way). Hence word meaning access is bilateral. Not only do the split-brain data indicate this (Nebes, 1974; Zaidel, 1990), but numerous studies with normal subjects using the semantic-priming technique demonstrate that word meanings are accessed within each hemisphere, but in differing ways (reviewed by Chiarello, 1991; 1998). In such studies a target word such as CAT, to which a subject must respond, is preceded by a prime word, which may be related (DOG) or unrelated (JAR) to it in meaning. Semantic priming is indicated by faster responding following a related, than following an unrelated, prime word, and this indicates that the meaning of the prime word has been accessed (Neely, 1991). When the prime and target words have similar meanings, recognition of the prime word will activate semantic features shared with the target (e.g., four-legged, furry, domesticated), thereby facilitating the subsequent comprehension of related words (Masson, 1995; McRae, deSa, & Seidenberg, 1997). We and others have repeatedly shown semantic priming for words directed to either the RH or LH (via presentation to the LVF or RVF, respectively; Chiarello, 1991, 1998; Walker & Ceci, 1985).[3]

For example, in one study equal priming was obtained in each VF/hemisphere regardless of whether the prime words were abstract or concrete (Chiarello, Senehi, & Nuding, 1987, Exp. 3), and many other studies have shown similar bilateral priming (e.g., Eglin, 1987; Walker & Ceci, 1985). However, although word meanings appear to be bilaterally activated, meaning access proceeds rather differently within each hemisphere. At least two factors underlie these differences—the scope of word meanings activated within each hemisphere, and how the availability of word meanings changes over time. The following examples illustrate these principles.

Several studies indicate that a wider set of word meanings is activated within the RH than within the LH. For example, my colleagues and I have compared priming for strongly related words such as ARM–LEG, words that are members of the same category and strongly associated, to priming for words such as ARM–NOSE, which, although still members of the same category, are not associated and share fewer semantic features (Chiarello, Burgess, Richards, & Pollock, 1990). Equivalent priming was obtained across VFs/hemispheres for the strongly related category associates, but the more distantly related category pairs were primed only within the LVF/RH (see also Chiarello & Richards,

[3]In these studies the stimuli are usually presented on a computer screen for a brief period (100–200 msec), and the participant is asked to pronounce or make a word–nonword decision (via a key press) to the target stimulus. Both the speed and accuracy of the response are recorded.

1992). We interpreted this to indicate that when a word is recognized by the LH, only the most strongly related words are activated, whereas within the RH a much broader set of meanings becomes available. This could point to a special role for the right hemisphere in capturing word meaning relationships that are more distant. Some interesting work done by Beeman supports this idea.

In his study each target word was preceded by three prime words, each of which was chosen to be only very weakly related to a given target word (Beeman, Friedman, Grafman, Perez, Diamond, & Lindsay, 1994). So, for example, the words "foot–cry–glass" might precede a target word such as "cut." Beeman referred to this as summation priming because the target is primed by activation summing across several weak lexical semantic relations. If the RH is much more sensitive than the LH to such weak or distant relations, then we would expect greater summation priming within the LVF/RH, and this is what was found (see Beeman et al., 1994, for additional details and discussion).

Beeman (1998) proposed that words activate broader semantic fields within the RH than within the LH, and hence the actual interpretation of a word could be somewhat different within each hemisphere. In addition, broader semantic fields might be better able to capture certain types of semantic relations, those that depend on the overlap of rather distantly related meanings. This conceptualization fits with data from RH-injured patients who frequently show alterations in their ability to appreciate figurative meanings (reviewed by Burgess & Chiarello, 1996). Further, it has been demonstrated, using electrophysiological methods, that priming for distantly related word pairs is disrupted in RH-injured patients (Hagoort, Brown, & Swaab, 1996; Swaab, Baynes, & Knight, 1998).

The idea that LH processing might extract narrower but more precise word meanings, whereas RH processing derives broader and less distinct word meanings, has to be understood within the context of processing systems in which the availability of different kinds of information changes over time. Thus, we need to ask whether these hemisphere differences in the availability of word meanings remain constant during different moments of language processing. In priming studies this can be addressed by varying the interval between the presentation of the prime and target word (stimulus onset asynchrony, SOA). By varying the interval before the target appears, one can determine the earliest onset of word meaning activation and also for how long meanings activated by the prime are maintained. Several studies indicate that the unique RH priming of more distant relations is found at later in processing (i.e., at prime-target intervals of ½ sec or more).

Recall that our research shows priming for the more distantly related category pairs (ARM–NOSE) in the RH only (Chiarello et al., 1990; Chiarello & Richards, 1992). Because these experiments all employed prime–target intervals of approximately 600 msec, it is unclear what might have occurred at an earlier period. Koivisto (1997) recently followed up on these results in Finnish, by varying the SOA from 165 msec, to 750 ms, using the more distantly related category pairs (e.g., ARM–NOSE). At the briefest SOA (165 msec), priming for the distantly related pairs was found only in the RVF/LH (see also Abernethy & Coney, 1996). However, at much longer SOAs (500 and 750 msec), Koivisto replicated our result of exclusive LVF/RH priming. These data suggest that the left hemisphere may initially activate distant word meanings, but that these meanings are rather rapidly discarded and not maintained for later processes. In contrast, the right hemisphere may take longer to activate these same meanings, but appears to maintain these remote meanings during periods when they are no longer available within the LH. A similar time course pattern has been reported for other types of distant semantic relations (see Table 9.1).

Another way to examine the time course of semantic processing is to investigate priming for ambiguous words such as BANK. Burgess and Simpson (1988) took this approach by examining priming for both the dominant (e.g., financial institution) and subordinate (e.g., river side) meanings of such words. At a brief 35-msec SOA, the less common subordinate meanings (BANK–RIVER) were primed only within the RVF/LH, whereas at a 750 msec interval they remained accessible only within the LVF/RH. Here "distant" semantic relationship refers to the least frequent meaning of an ambiguous word, yet the temporal pattern was quite similar to that observed when semantic "distance" may reflect the extent of semantic feature overlap (Koivisto, 1997).

TABLE 9.1

Semantic Priming of Distantly Related Word Pairs in Experiments Contrasting Two or More Stimulus Onset Asynchronies (SOAs) for Words Presented to the Left (LH) or Right (RH) Hemisphere

	Short SOA	*Long SOA*
"Distant" category pairs (Koivisto, 1997) ARM–NOSE	LH only	RH only
Subordinate meaning of ambiguous word (Burgess & Simpson, 1988) BANK–RIVER	LH only	RH only
Metaphorical pairs (Anaki et al., 1998) STINGING–INSULT	LH + RH	RH Only

Anaki, Faust, and Kravetz (1998) examined priming for words related in a more figurative or metaphorical way, such as "stinging insult," and compared these to priming for literally related pairs such as "stinging mosquito." Bilateral priming of the metaphorical pairs was obtained at a brief (200 msec) SOA, but at a longer interval (800 msec) the metaphorical meaning was only available within the LVF/RH, again implying that the LH rather rapidly suspends processing of distantly related word meanings.

It is worth considering what may be occurring at the longer intervals where this characteristic RH priming pattern is observed. Many theories of comprehension claim that a wide set of word meanings may be activated early in processing, followed by a selection process in which the most contextually appropriate meaning is selectively maintained while other contextually irrelevant meanings are discarded (Gernsbacher, 1990; Kintsch, 1988). A variety of evidence suggests that this selection process occurs primarily within the LH (reviewed by Richards & Chiarello, 1997). Thus, the eventual loss within the LH of subordinate or metaphorical word meaning activation is accompanied by selective LH maintenance of the dominant or literal meaning of the word (Anaki et al., 1998; Burgess & Simpson, 1988). Meanwhile the RH continues to maintain more distant meanings, which may be only peripherally related to the ongoing topic, but which could be essential in cases where recovery of alternate meanings is necessary. The continued activation of such information by the RH may also serve some discourse functions, by providing the information needed to draw inferences and maintain coherence (Beeman, 1998).

There are two interesting theoretical accounts for the slower RH onset of "distant" meanings. On the one hand, the RH lag might simply reflect the internal dynamics of semantic activation within this hemisphere. Perhaps meaning activation is "noisier" within the RH, requiring greater time to "settle" into a stable pattern of activation when there is weaker meaning overlap between words. On the other hand, it may be that more distant meanings are activated within the RH only after they have been discarded by the LH. This would imply that some aspects of RH semantic processing may depend on the outcome of LH semantic analyses. Although the current data cannot conclusively discriminate between these possibilities, the latter interpretation receives some support from the finding that RH maintenance of subordinate ambiguous word meanings is not observed when the LH has failed to select the dominant meaning (Hasbrooke & Chiarello, 1998).

UNDERSTANDING SENTENCES

Thus far we have considered evidence for differential hemispheric processing of language for perceptual, lexical, and semantic processing of individual words. What happens at the sentence level, where word meanings are syntactically combined and modified to yield a higher level meaning representation? Faust reported a programmatic series of studies looking at the differential effects of sentence primes on Hebrew target words presented to the LVF or RVF (reviewed in Faust, 1998). In all cases, both hemispheres benefit from related sentence primes; however, right-hemisphere priming seems to be based only on word-level relations, whereas left-hemisphere priming additionally makes use of syntactic and semantic integration at the sentence level (see Table 9. 2).

In one study (Faust, Babkoff, & Kravetz, 1995, Exp. 2) the primes were either well-structured sentences or the same words presented in a scrambled order ("The rider saddled the horse" vs. "The saddled the rider horse"). Words presented to the RVF/LH obtained much greater priming (i.e., facilitation of response speed) from normal than from scrambled sentences, indicating a benefit from syntactic organization. However, words presented to the LVF/RH obtained equal priming across these conditions, suggesting that this hemisphere only benefited from the semantic relations between words, and not the sentence structure itself.

Two subsequent studies contrasted the effects of sentence and word–level relatedness, by including incongruous sentences that nevertheless contained related words. For example, in the sentence "The patient swallowed the medicine" the final target word "medicine" is related to a prior word in the sentence ("patient") and is also congruent with the meaning of the entire sentence. However, the sentence "The patient parked the medicine" still contains a related word, but now the sentence meaning is incongruent. For RVF/LH target words, much greater priming was obtained in the congruent sentence condition. However, for LVF/RH target words, priming was equivalent in congruent and incongruent sentences (Faust et al., 1995, Exp. 3). This suggests that al-

TABLE 9.2

Representative Sentence Priming Results for Words Presented to the Left (LH) or Right (RH) Hemisphere.

	LH	*RH*
Sentence structure		
Normal vs. "scrambled" sentences	Normal > scrambled	Normal = scrambled
(Faust et al., 1995)		
Sentence Congruity		
"The patient swallowed/parked the medicine"	Congruent only	Congruent + incongruent
(Faust et al.,1995)		
Ambiguous word meaning		
(Faust & Chiarello, 1998)	Congruent only	Congruent + incongruent

though word meanings are accessed within the right hemisphere, this does not result in an integrated meaning representation for the sentence as a whole. In contrast, LH processes do benefit from meaning relations that emerge at the sentence level. This conclusion does not conflict with the notion that the RH plays an important role in discourse comprehension. Discourse processes subserved by the RH (such as drawing predictive inferences while reading texts) do not depend on the achievement of integrated sentence meanings, but rather on the less constrained activation of word meanings within and across the sentences comprising the discourse (see Beeman, 1998; Beeman, Bowden, & Gernsbacher, 2000).

Finally, consider hemisphere differences in the processing of sentences that contain ambiguous words. The word-priming study of Burgess and Simpson (1988) suggested that without any other context, the LH would eventually select the dominant meaning of a word like BANK, and discard the subordinate meaning, while the RH continued to maintain both meanings. However, in many sentences the subordinate or less frequent meaning is the appropriate one. To investigate the role of sentence context in the maintenance of ambiguous word meanings, we presented sentences such as "She stood in line and was second." In isolation the final word is ambiguous, and but here the sentence primed the subordinate meaning (Faust & Chiarello, 1998). The priming sentence was followed by a congruent related target such as NUMBER or an incongruent related target such as TIME. Sentences that primed the dominant meaning of the final word were also included. In all cases, priming in the RVF/LH was based on sentence congruity; priming was only seen for the contextually appropriate meaning of the ambiguous word regardless of whether it was dominant or subordinate. However, all meanings of the ambiguous word were primed in the RH, regardless of whether or not they were congruent with the sentence (see also Faust & Gernsbacher, 1996).

The sentence priming data indicate that LH processing of word meanings is conditioned by their sentence context. Word meanings that are consistent with the sentence context are maintained and become part of an integrated meaning representation for the entire sentence; those that do not cohere with this context are not maintained in an accessible state. However, there is thus far little evidence that sentence-level processes alter the availability of word meanings in the right hemisphere (Faust, 1998). This suggests that RH processing derives a rather different kind of meaning from sentences. Instead of a single meaning for the sentence as a whole, a set of possibilities suggested by the multiple meanings of the words comprising the sentence may be maintained. Although this clearly cannot produce a single coherent sentence interpretation, it may be critical for situations in which multiple interpretations must be evaluated. In addition, it appears that the ability to draw inferences during discourse comprehension may depend on the activation of broader word meanings within the right hemisphere (Beeman, 1998).

CONCLUSIONS

To summarize, I highlight some generalizations about salient differences in how language is processed by these two rather different hemispheric systems. First, across many different language domains there is evidence that LH processing rapidly contacts the deepest level encodings of language that are relevant in a given task situation. So LH processing appears to rapidly abstract away from superficial differences among letter appearances to contact more abstract letter identity codes. In addition, when words are presented, lexical knowledge is rapidly recruited to assist in letter identification, and word meanings are exhaustively accessed but quickly narrowed down to those most likely to be relevant in the current context. When the input is a sentence, syntactic and semantic integration processes are efficiently utilized to extract a single unified meaning. This language-processing system is best characterized as rapid, deep, and narrow.

In contrast, RH language processing is slow, somewhat superficial, and broad. Thus RH processing often appears to maintain more superficial or shallow encodings of information, such as details of the visual forms of letters, even when the task does not require reliance on such information. Furthermore, deeper level encodings don' t seem to affect how lower level information is maintained. For example, word context does not affect letter recognition, and sentence context does not affect the availability of word meanings in the RH. However, this very lack of constraint results in broader interpretations of word and sentence meaning than those produced by LH processes, and this may prove useful in some discourse situations where extracting the "gist" of a conversation or text is more important than the precise details being expressed.

Second, these two systems also seem to operate differently in time. In many respects processing by the RH seems to lag behind that of the LH, almost as if the RH provides an echo of the prior processing done by the LH. This seems to be the case both in terms of some perceptual analyses, as well as in the activation of distantly related word meanings[4]. Although some types of information are available to both hemispheres simultaneously, in other cases we see that asymmetries in how processing unfolds over time yield qualitative differences in the kinds of information available to each hemisphere at any given moment.

Third, there are clear hemisphere differences when we consider the continuum between selectivity and maintaining a range of alternatives. LH language processing places a premium on rapid selection and elimination of other potentially viable alternate representations. In contrast, RH language processing takes a different tack, and seems designed to maintain a range of alternate representations without selection. Because there's always some type of risk in-

[4]However, examination of the time course of activation for *strongly* related word meanings argues against a *generalized* RH lag (Chiarello, Liu, Shears, Quan, & Kacinik, in press).

volved in selection, since the discarded information might later prove relevant, RH maintenance of alternatives may provide a safety net allowing the rapid recovery of alternate interpretations in such cases.

It would be unwise, however, to attempt to reduce these three themes (hemisphere differences in depth of encoding, time course, and selectivity) to a single dichotomy. If we take seriously the claim that each hemisphere represents a rather complete information-processing system, then there is no reason to assume that all the outputs of a given system can be reduced to a single factor. Complex systems by definition can produce a variety of behaviors—and the claim here is that each hemisphere is a complex system unto itself.

In closing, it is important to consider how this line of research can inform more global views of mind, brain, and language. First, the hemispheric systems view strongly implies that language, and other complex cognitive functions, utilize parallel but differently organized processing systems. The fact that the left hemisphere is critical for normal language use does not mean that the right hemisphere is uninvolved in the processing of language. In the normal brain both hemispheres are processing all kinds of information all of the time. What differs is just how this processing is done, and how useful the outcome of each hemisphere's processing may be for various tasks. This view is not compatible with strictly modular views of language processing in the brain. Rather, language appears to recruit a wide variety of processing mechanisms distributed across both the left and right cortex.

It is also important to note that these two systems are continually interacting in the normal brain. Although the emphasis here was on the parallel but distinct processing done by each hemisphere, this does not imply hemispheric isolation. Indeed the seamless language behavior we all exhibit has to imply a great deal of interhemispheric coordination if we accept the premise that parallel systems are recruited for nearly all types of language behavior.

Finally, the view that language is "special", that it requires the use of dedicated and perhaps even innately dedicated neural machinery, has always been intertwined with the notion of LH specialization for language. Closely examining the contrast between LH and RH processing of language can illuminate this issue. On the one hand, one could argue that the left hemisphere is a much more efficient and effective processor of language because it relies on some mechanisms specific to language that the right hemisphere cannot employ. According to this view, the right hemisphere is a less efficient language processor because it must rely on more general purpose mechanisms that are never quite good enough to efficiently subserve linguistic functions. There's a lot to be said for this view, and it's one that I have articulated in the past (see Chiarello, 1998). But, on the other hand, claiming that the left hemisphere is specialized for language requires one to articulate just what these specialized mechanisms are, and here is where this approach runs into some difficulty.

If we think back to the generalizations about LH and RH language processing offered earlier, none of them refers to domain–specific processes. For example, consider the contrast between LH selectivity and RH maintenance of alternatives. The propensity to select one from among a set of competing alternatives is hardly a process restricted to language, and it's likely to be important for other types of cognitive functions as well. In fact, some of the hemisphere differences described herein have analogs in nonlinguistic domains (see Ivry & Robertson, 1998; Burgund & Marsolek, 1998). Further if one examines the entire field of hemisphere asymmetries, it's the case that none of the computational mechanisms that have been identified to underlie these asymmetries appears to be domain specific (Hellige, 1993; Ivry & Roberston, 1998). However, we really need many more studies that attempt to contrast the use of similar processing mechanisms in linguistic and nonlinguistic domains in order to settle this debate.

Continued exploration of the contrast between right and left hemisphere processing systems can help us discover just what it is that makes the left hemisphere pre-eminent for language, and also how this system is supported by the very different kind of processes subserved by the right hemisphere. The benefits of both systems are available to the normal brain, enabling a wide variety of linguistic functions to be exploited as needed. The simplest as well as the most complex achievements of the human mind may depend on the distinct duality of the supporting brain systems.

ACKNOWLEDGEMENTS

The preparation of this chapter was supported by National Science Foundation grant SBR-9729009. I thank Natalie Kacinik for assistance in preparation of the figures.

REFERENCES

Abernethy, M., & Coney, J. (1996). Semantic category priming in the left cerebral hemisphere. *Neuropsychologia, 34*, 339–350.

Anaki, D., Faust, M., & Kravetz, S. (1998). Cerebral hemispheric asymmetries in processing lexical metaphors. *Neuropsychologia, 36*, 353–362.

Beeman, M. (1998). Coarse semantic coding and discourse comprehension. In M. Beeman & C. Chiarello (Eds.), *Right hemisphere language comprehension: Perspectives from cognitive neuroscience* (pp. 255–284). Mahwah, NJ: Lawrence Erlbaum Associates.

Beeman & Chiarello, C. (Eds.). (1998). *Right hemisphere language comprehension: Perspectives from cognitive neuroscience*. Mahwah, NJ: Lawrence Erlbaum Associates.

Beeman, M. J., Bowden, E., & Gernsbacher, M. (2000). Right and left hemisphere cooperation for drawing predictive and coherence inferences during normal story comprehension. *Brain and Language, 71*, 310–336.

Beeman, M., Friedman, R. B., Grafman, J., Perez, E., Diamond, S., & Lindsay, M. B. (1994). Summation priming and coarse coding in the right hemisphere. *Journal of Cognitive Neuroscience, 6*, 26–45.

Blumstein, S. E., & Cooper, W. E. (1974). Hemispheric processing of intonation contours. *Cortex, 10*, 146–158.
Bradshaw, J. L., & Nettleton, N. C. (1983). *Human cerebral asymmetry*. Englewood Cliffs, NJ: Prentice Hall.
Burgess, C., & Chiarello, C. (1996). Neurocognitive mechanisms underlying metaphor comprehension and other figurative language. *Metaphor & Symbolic Activity, 11*, 67–84.
Burgess, C., & Simpson, G. B. (1988). Cerebral hemispheric mechanisms in the retrieval of ambiguous word meanings. *Brain and Language, 33*, 86–103.
Burgund, E. D., & Marsolek, C. J. (1998, April). *Viewpoint–dependent priming for familiar objects in the right cerebral hemisphere*. Poster session presented at the annual meeting of the Cognitive Neuroscience Society, San Francisco, CA.
Chiarello, C. (1988). Lateralization of lexical processes in the normal brain: A review of visual half-field research. In H. Whitaker (Ed.), *Contemporary reviews in neuropsychology* (pp. 59–69). New York: Springer–Verlag.
Chiarello, C. (1991). Lateralization of lexical processes in the normal brain: A review of visual half-field research. In H. H. Whitaker (Ed.), *Contemporary reviews in neuropsychology* (pp. 59–69). New York: Springer–Verlag.
Chiarello, C. (1998). On codes of meaning and the meaning of codes: Semantic access and retrieval within and between hemispheres. In M. Beeman & C. Chiarello (Eds.), *Right hemisphere language comprehension: Perspectives from cognitive neuroscience* (pp. 141–160). Mahwah, NJ: Lawrence Erlbaum Associates.
Chiarello, C., Burgess, C., Richards, L., & Pollock, A. (1990). Semantic and associative priming in the cerebral hemispheres: Some words do, some words don't ... sometimes, some places. *Brain and Language, 34*, 302–314.
Chiarello, C., & Richards, L. (1992). Another look at categorical priming in the cerebral hemispheres. *Neuropsychologia, 30*, 381–392.
Chiarello, C., Liu, S., Shears, C., Quan, N., & Kacinik, N. (in press). Priming of strong semantic relations in the left and right visual fields: A time course investigation. *Neuropsychologia.*
Chiarello, C., Nuding, S., & Pollock, A. (1988). Lexical decision and naming asymmetries: Influence of response selection and response bias. *Brain and Language, 34*, 302–314.
Chiarello, C., Senehi, J., & Nuding, S. (1987). Semantic priming with abstract and concrete words: Differential asymmetry may be post-lexical. *Brain and Language, 31*, 43–60.
Chiarello, C., Senehi, J., & Soulier, M. (1986). Viewing conditions and hemisphere asymmetry for the lexical decision. *Neuropsychologia, 24*, 521–529.
Churchland, P. S., & Sejnowski, T. J. (1992). *The computational brain*. Cambridge, MA: MIT Press.
Eglin, M. (1987). Interference and priming within and across visual fields in a lexical decision task. *Neuropsychologia, 25*, 613–625.
Eviatar, Z., & Zaidel, E. (1991). The effects of word length and emotionality on hemispheric contribution to lexical decision. *Neuropsychologia, 29*, 415–428.
Faust, M. (1998). Obtaining evidence of language comprehension from sentence priming. In M. Beeman & C. Chiarello (Eds.), *Right hemisphere language comprehension: Perspectives from cognitive neuroscience* (pp. 161–186). Mahwah, NJ: Lawrence Erlbaum Associates.
Faust, M., & Chiarello, C. (1998). Sentence context and lexical ambiguity resolution by the two hemispheres. *Neuropsychologia, 36*, 827–836.
Faust, M., Babkoff, H., & Kravetz, S. (1995). Linguistic processes in the two cerebral hemispheres: Implications for modularity versus interactionism. *Journal of Clinical and Experimental Neuropsychology, 17*, 171–192.
Faust, M., Kravetz, S., & Babkoff, H. (1993). Hemispheric specialization or reading habits: Evidence from lexical decision research with Hebrew words and sentences. *Brain and Language, 44*, 254–263.
Faust, M. E., & Gernsbacher, M. A. (1996). Cerebral mechanisms for suppression of inappropriate information during sentence comprehension. *Brain and Language, 53*, 234–259.
Gazzaniga, M. S., & Sperry, R. W. (1967). Language after section of the cerebral commissures. *Brain, 90*, 131–148.
Gernsbacher, M. A. (1990). *Language comprehension as structure building*. Hillsdale, NJ: Lawrence Erlbaum Associates.

Hagoort, P., Brown, C. M., & Swaab, T. (1996). Lexical-semantic event-related potential effects in patients with left hemisphere lesions and aphasia, and patients with right hemisphere lesions without aphasia. *Brain, 119,* 627–649.

Hassbrooke, R., and Chiarello, C. (1998). Bihemispheric processing of redundant bilateral lexical information. *Neuropsychology, 12,* 78–94.

Hellige, J. B. (1993). *Hemispheric asymmetry: What's right and what's left.* Cambridge, MA: Harvard University Press.

Iacaboni, M., & Zaidel, E. (1996). Hemispheric independence in word recognition: Evidence from unilateral and bilateral presentations. *Brain and Language, 53,* 121–140.

Ivry, R., & Lebby, P. C. (1998). The neurology of consonant perception: Specialized module or distributed processors. In M. Beeman & C. Chiarello (Eds.), *Right hemisphere language comprehension: Perspectives from cognitive neuroscience* (pp. 13–26). Mahwah, NJ: Lawrence Erlbaum Associates.

Ivry, R. B., & Robertson, L. C. (1998). *The two sides of perception.* Cambridge: MIT Press.

Joanette, Y., Goulet, P., & Hannequin, D. (1990). *Right hemisphere and verbal communication.* New York: Springer-Verlag.

Kintsch, W. (1988). The role of knowledge in discourse comprehension: A construction-integration model. *Psychological Review,* 95, 163–182.

Koivisto, M. (1997). Time course of semantic activation in the cerebral hemispheres. *Neuropsychologia, 35,* 497–504.

Krueger, L. E. (1975). The word-superiority effect: Is its locus visual-spatial or verbal. *Bulletin of the Psychonomic Society,* 6, 465–468.

Ley, R. G., & Bryden, M. P. (1982). A dissociation of right and left hemisphere effects for recognizing emotional tone and verbal content. *Brain and Cognition, 1,* 3–9.

Marsolek, C. J., Kosslyn, S. M., & Squire, L. R. (1992). Form-specific visual priming in the right cerebral hemisphere. *Journal of Experimental Psychology: Learning, Memory, & Cognition, 18,* 492–508.

Marsolek, C. J., Schacter, D. L., & Nicholas, C. D. (1996). Form-specific visual priming for new associations in the right cerebral hemisphere. *Memory and Cognition, 24,* 539–556.

Masson, M. E. J. (1995). A distributed memory model of semantic priming. *Journal of Experimental Psychology: Learning, Memory, & Cognition, 21,* 3–23.

McClelland, J. L., & Rumelhart, D. E. (1981). An interactive activation model of context effects in letter perception: Part 1. An account of basic findings. *Psychological Review,* 88, 375–407.

McRae, K., deSa, V. R., & Seidenberg, M. S. (1997). On the nature and scope of featural representations of word meanings. *Journal of Experimental Psychology: General, 126,* 99–130.

Molfese, V. J., Molfese, D. L., & Parsons, C. (1983). Hemispheric processing of phonological information. In S. J. Segalowitz (Ed.), *Language functions and brain organization,* (pp. 29–50). New York: Academic Press.

Nebes, R. D. (1974). Hemispheric specialization in commissurotomized man. *Psychological Bulletin, 81,* 1–14.

Neely, J. H. (1991). Semantic priming effects in visual word recognition: A selective review of current findings and theories. In D. Besner & J. W. Humphreys (Eds.), *Basic processes in reading: Visual word recognition* (pp. 264–336). Hillsdale, NJ: Lawrence Erlbaum Associates.

Richards, L., & Chiarello, C. (1997). Activation without selection: Parallel right hemisphere roles in language and intentional movement? *Brain and Language, 57,* 151–178.

Simos, P. G., Molfese, D. L., & Brenden, R. A. (1997). Behavioral and electrophysiological indices of voicing–cue distinctions. *Brain and Language, 57,* 122–150.

Sperry, R.W. (1974). Lateral specialization in the surgically separated hemispheres. In F. O. Schmidt & F. G. Worden (Eds.), *The neurosciences: Third study program* (pp. 5–19). Cambridge, MA: MIT Press.

Sperry, R.W., Gazzaniga, M. S., & Bogen, J. E. (1969). Interhemispheric relationships: The neocortical commissures: Syndromes of hemispheric disconnection. In P. J. Vinken & G. W. Bruyn (Eds.), *Handbook of clinical neurology* (pp. 273–290). New York: Wiley–Interscience.

Sperry, R.W., Zaidel, E., & Zaidel, D. (1979). Self–recognition and social awareness in the deconnected minor hemisphere. *Neuropsychologia, 17,* 153–166.

Springer, S. P., & Deutsch, G. (1998). *Left brain, right brain: Perspectives from Cognitive Neuroscience.* New York: W. H. Freeman.

Swaab, T., Baynes, K., & Knight, R. T. (1998, April). *Coarse semantic coding in the right hemisphere: An ERP study.* Poster session presented at the annual meeting of the Cognitive Neuroscience Society, San Francisco, CA.

Walker, E., & Ceci, S. J. (1985). Semantic priming effects for stimuli presented to the right and left visual fields. *Brain and Language, 25*, 144–159.

Young, A.W., & Ellis, A.W. (1985). Different methods of lexical access for words presented in the left and right visual fields. *Brain and Language, 24*, 326–358.

Zaidel, E. (1990). Language functions in the two hemispheres following complete cerebral commissurotomy and hemispherectomy. In F. Boller & J. Grafman (Eds.), *Handbook of Neuropsychology*, (Vol. 4, pp. 115–150). Amsterdam: Elsevier.

IV

Language Disruption and Loss

10

Evidence From Language Breakdown: Implications for the Neural and Functional Organization of Language

Eleanor M. Saffran
Temple University

Although studies of bird song and primate communication have contributed to knowledge of the biological bases for communication, human language represents so significant an advance beyond these systems that animal models have thus far provided little understanding of its functional or anatomical organization. Until the recent development of methods for imaging ongoing brain activity, the study of language-brain relationships drew primarily on associations between lesion sites and language deficits in brain damaged individuals.[1] These are, of course, accidents of nature, not subject to the controls that can be exercised over experimental materials. In particular, the lesions of patients who manifest roughly similar deficits are subject to a good deal of variability (for examples, see Kertesz, 1979). Nevertheless, the functional perturbations can often be quite specific, and studies of individuals with acquired language impairments have contributed much of what we know about the organization of

[1]Although not exclusively: Some information with respect to localization came from studies in which electrical stimulation was applied to the cortex during surgical procedures (e.g., Penfield & Roberts, 1959); other data with respect to hemispheric responsibility for language came from the selective anesthesia of one hemisphere or the other, a technique that involves injecting sodium amytal into the artery (internal carotid) that supplies the lateral cortical circulation in that hemisphere

language in the brain. Although less widely recognized, these breakdown patterns also have implications for theories of language function.

THE STUDY OF BRAIN-LANGUAGE RELATIONSHIPS: A BRIEF HISTORY

People must have sustained injuries to one side of the head or the other since the inception of human language, but it took a very long time before anyone thought to link sites of injury to their consequences for behavior. In classical Greece and Rome, for example, the human capacity for language was ascribed to the tongue—a necessary organ, to be sure, but hardly a sufficient one. Systematic observations of the effects of brain damage had to await the emergence of an empirical mind set in the 18th and 19th centuries. Curiously, the attempt to localize human brain functions originated with a pseudo-science, phrenology, that emerged in the early 1800s. Bumps on the skull were taken to reflect areas of enlargement in the brain below, with the size of a particular protuberance serving as the measure of the designated capacity. Although most of the functions that phrenologists attempted to localize—generosity and secretiveness, for example—appear fanciful to us today, language was among the more sensible inclusions. The phrenological map associated language with the bony protrusion just below the eye, and hence with brain tissue at the tip of both frontal lobes. This attribution rested on scant data: The founder of phrenology, Franz Gall, recalled a verbally gifted schoolmate who happened to have bulging eyes!

The validity of this linkage of brain to language was one of the questions that a young French physician, Paul Broca, sought to address in the early 1860s. Broca was skeptical about the significance of bumps on the skull, believing that clues to the localization of function were more likely to be found in the convolutions of the cerebral cortex. He had observed a patient, M. Leborgne, who could utter only a single monosyllable due to a stroke suffered some years earlier. When Broca examined Leborgne's brain at autopsy, he observed an old area of damage in the left frontal lobe that was located rather more posteriorly than the site assigned to language on the phrenologists' map, specifically, at the foot of the third frontal convolution—the region now known as Broca's area (see Fig. 10.1). He identified additional cases of brain-damaged individuals over the next several years, all with limited expressive abilities and seemingly preserved comprehension. On the basis of these observations, he hypothesized that an area in the inferior frontal lobe of the left hemisphere (Fig. 10.1) was the substrate for "articulate language" (Broca, 1865). This region lies anterior to the area of motor cortex that transmits commands to the muscles of the face, tongue, and larynx; the syndrome associated with damage to this region of the brain is designated Broca's aphasia. Broca further concluded that the lateralization of language function was related to the left hemisphere's control of the dominant right hand.

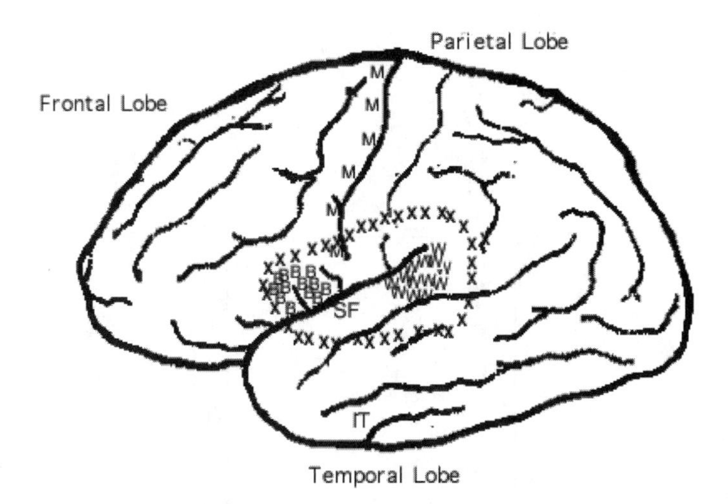

FIG. 10.1. Diagram of the left cerebral hemisphere of the brain. B, Broca's area; W, Wernicke's area; M, motor cortex; area enclosed by Xs indicates perisylvian area; SF, sylvian fissure; IT, anterior inferotemporal area.

A few years later, a German physician, Carl Wernicke, observed a relationship between the loss of language comprehension and damage to an area of the left superior temporal lobe, extending to its border with the parietal lobe (Wernicke, 1874, see Fig. 10.1). The brain area that Wernicke identified (part of the auditory association cortex of the left hemisphere, where meaningful signals are extracted from auditory input) adjoins the primary auditory cortex, the area that receives auditory input from lower brain centers. Although the syndrome of what came to be known as Wernicke's aphasia is often described as a receptive language deficit, there are significant expressive features as well. Wernicke's aphasics speak fluently at normal or even rapid rates, but their speech is often hard to understand. They have difficulty retrieving words, often substituting other words, and may produce combinations of sounds that are neologisms—not words at all. There are also pragmatic and discourse-level problems that further complicate interpretation of the speech of these patients. An example of this pattern can be found in Appendix 1.

Wernicke concluded that the superior temporal area affected in his patients was the site at which auditory word images are stored. Recognizing that people have to learn the sounds of words in order to produce them, he proposed that auditory word images are involved in word production, most likely by transmitting instructions to the motor speech area identified by Broca. Wernicke stressed the importance of connections between these two centers, an idea that was elaborated several years later by Ludwig Lichtheim. Lichtheim proposed a model of language (Fig. 10.2) in which the areas identified by Broca and Wernicke were connected to one another, as well as to a concept center—a re-

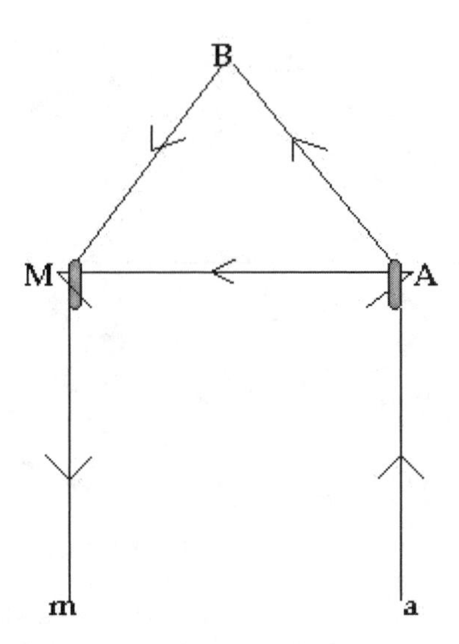

FIG. 10.2. Lichtheim's model: a, source of auditory input; A, Wernicke's area; B, concept center; M, Broca's area; m, speech motor output. Arrows indicate direction of information flow.

pository of information that gives meaning to words—which he regarded as diffusely represented in the brain (Lichtheim, 1885). This was a critical addition, as the concept center served not only as the endpoint of the comprehension process, translating sounds into thought, but also as the source of the messages ultimately produced by the speaker. On the basis of the postulated connections among the three centers and the input and output pathways that conduct information to Wernicke's area and from Broca's area, Lichtheim predicted a number of aphasic syndromes that had not yet been described—predictions that were subsequently borne out. One of the hypothesized disorders was transcortical sensory aphasia, a condition in which the language area is isolated from the concept center. This disconnection interferes with the capacity to generate meaningful speech and to comprehend it, but the preservation of Broca's and Wernicke's areas along with the connections between them allows the patient to repeat the speech of others. Although repetition has a limited role in adult language, the ability to repeat is an important distinguishing feature among several aphasic syndromes and remains a critical part of the aphasia examination to this day. Thus, for example, preserved repetition distinguishes transcortical sensory from Wernicke's aphasia, where repetition is impaired. This approach to brain-cognition relationships, which accounts for symptoms in terms of associations between centers committed to specific functions, came to be known as connectionism, and was subsequently extended to disorders such as the loss of reading ability (Dejerine, 1892). (It should be noted that in contemporary use, "connectionism" refers to computational [computer–implemented] models of cognitive function, where connections between different stages of processing also figure importantly.) Although the connectionist approach appeared to be productive, it was not long before it gave way to holistic views of language organization (see Caplan, 1987, for a historical review).

One of the early critics of connectionist theories was Sigmund Freud, who saw Lichtheim's model as too simple to account for a capacity as complex as human language (Freud, 1891/1953; for other critiques, see Marie, 1906, and Head, 1926). Those who are familiar with contemporary linguistic and psycholinguistic views of language function would surely agree with Freud. The model's most glaring limitation is its focus on single words; the production and comprehension of sentences, which involves knowledge of grammatical structure (syntax), is completely neglected. From the perspective of current psycholinguistic models (e. g., Levelt, 1992), the connectionists' treatment of single word processing as simply a matter of transforming a concept into sound would also be viewed as simplistic, as these models conceptualize word production as a multiple-stage process.

Still, the core findings embodied in the Wernicke-Lichtheim model have stood the test of time. The accumulation of data from brain-damaged individuals affirms the role of the left frontal area identified by Broca in speech production, as well as the role of Wernicke's area in the perception and the generation of speech (Goodglass, 1993; Kertesz, 1979). These findings have been confirmed by other methods, such as functional brain imaging (see Habib & Demonet, 1996, for a review) and electro-cortical stimulation of the brain prior to surgery (Boatman, Lesser, & Gordon, 1995). As Lichtheim's model predicted, lesions that deprive Wernicke's area of input result in a disorder (pure word deafness) in which speech cannot be understood or repeated, although language production remains intact or nearly so (e.g., Saffran, Marin, & Yeni-Komshian, 1976). The deficits of Wernicke's aphasics also provide support for the involvement of the left superior temporal area in comprehension and production. Patients who have incurred damage to this brain region are impaired in understanding single words as assessed, for example, by word-picture matching tests, particularly when the choices are semantically related to the target (e.g., for strawberry, other kinds of fruit). Concomitantly, there is difficulty in word production, manifested in errors (see Appendix 1) such as the substitution of semantically related words (e.g., "Polish" for *Russian*), phonological errors that may resemble the target in varying degrees (e.g., "thay" for *say*), so–called abstruse neologisms that cannot be traced to a target (e.g., "ryediss"), and the overuse of nonspecific terms, such as "place" or "thing." These patients are deficient in sentence-level comprehension and production as well.

More recent evidence indicates, however, that the brain regions involved in language function are more extensive than the connectionists had supposed (e.g., Goodglass & Wingfield, 1997). Data from pathological cases implicate what has been termed the perisylvian cortex of the left hemisphere in the processing of language, that is, the cortex that abuts both sides of the Sylvian fissure that separates the temporal lobe from the frontal and parietal lobes (Fig. 10. 1). The perisylvian area includes cortical tissue that lies between Broca's and Wernicke's areas, and extends posteriorly and inferiorly into the parietal and temporal lobes. It should also be noted that the lesions that impede particular language functions are often larger than the early investigators had assumed. For example, the full–blown syndrome of Broca's aphasia, in which speech is sparse, effortful, poorly articulated, and stripped of much of its grammatical structure, requires a lesion that extends well beyond the foot of the third frontal convolution—the area identified by Broca (although it should be noted that the lesion in his patient extended beyond this area as well). Damage restricted to Broca's area gives rise to an articulatory impairment that is generally transient (Mohr et al., Duncan & Davis, 1978). It is also recognized that damage to Wernicke's or Broca's areas is not the only source of difficulty in word production. Lesions in the left parietal area (supramarginal gyrus) result in frequent phonological errors, involving the misselection and sometimes the misordering of phonemes in a word (e.g., for *pretzel*, "trep ... tretzle ... trethle, tredfle"; from Goodglass, 1993, p. 142); these symptoms are associated with the syndrome of conduction aphasia, where repetition and oral reading are similarly affected (e.g., Caplan, Vanier, & Baker, 1986). The errors suggest that the parietal area is involved in maintaining and/or assembling the sequence of phonemes—individual sounds like /k/or /o/—that guides assembly of the motor programs for speech. Patients with damage to this area are also impaired on verbal short-term memory tasks; for example, their ability to reproduce lists of digits is reduced by four or more from the normal complement of about seven (e.g., Shallice & Vallar, 1990). As we show later, other areas involved in the representation of word meaning, postulated but not identified in Lichtheim's model, are also critical for word production and comprehension.

THE DISRUPTION OF SYNTACTIC PROCESSING

As noted, syntactic aspects of language were largely ignored by the 19th century aphasiologists, despite their familiarity with Broca's aphasia, the syndrome most striking for what appear to be syntactic limitations in production ("agrammatism"). An example of the agrammatic production pattern is provided in Appendix 2. In severe cases, output is essentially holophrastic; that is, the speaker produces one word at a time. Verb retrieval appears difficult, and output is biased toward nouns (e.g., Miceli, Silveri, Villa, & Caramazza, 1984). In less impaired patients, sentences are simple and often lack critical grammatical morphemes—bound morphemes such as inflections (such as the past tense markered on verbs) and free morphemes such as auxiliary verbs (*are*, *have*), determiners (*a*, *the*), and prepositions (*to*, *in*, *with*). In other languages, like Hebrew, where morphemes such as verb inflections are obligatory—they constitute the vowels in Hebrew verbs, and are therefore essential for pronunciation—the pattern involves substitutions of incorrect elements rather than omissions (Grodzinsky, 1984).

In psycholinguistic models of sentence production, syntactic structure is implemented in the form of a frame that specifies the sequence of the types of words in the sentence (e.g., Garrett, 1980). For example, the frame for the sentence "The dog chases the cat" is as follows (where spaces indicate slots for word insertion)[2]:

the ——*Noun*——*Verb (present, singular)* the ——*Noun*

The frame comes into play at the point where the sounds of words are retrieved and inserted into the appropriate locations in the utterance. As the frontal lobe is involved in sequencing other types of motor functions (and speech, involving the articulatory musculature, is a motor function), it would not be surprising to find that it is also involved in the sequencing of speech sounds. The evidence from aphasia is consistent with this view. Patients with anterior (frontal) left hemisphere lesions speak less fluently and often with some articulatory impairment, and produce shorter utterances and utilize simpler syntactic structures than those with posterior (temporal and parietal) lesions (e.g., Bird & Franklin, 1996). This is not to say that the utterances of patients with temporal or parietal lesions are always grammatically well formed; these patients do make errors, characterized as "paragrammatic," which generally involve the substitution of other grammatical elements. (For examples, see Appendix 1.) Their utterances may also show less structural elaboration than those of normal speakers (Bird & Franklin, 1996), although they tend to be more complex than those of agrammatic aphasics.

What about the grammatical morphemes that are also affected in agrammatism? It appears that some of these elements must be specified at a fairly late stage of the production process, as the forms they take depend on the contexts in which they appear. In English, for example, the indefinite determiner takes the form "a" if it precedes a consonant, and "an" if it precedes a vowel. Studies of normal speech errors have shown that the form selected is appropriate to the error, not the word that was intended (e.g., "an errant curgument," for *a current argument*; from Fromkin, 1973). One current theory of speech production asserts that stress patterns—the prosodic aspects of speech—are not implemented until grammatical morphemes are inserted, as these elements are uttered together with (that is, without pausing) the substantive words (nouns, verbs, adjectives) of the utterance (e.g., theboy isgoing ...)

---

[2]Whether the grammatical morphemes are completely specified within the frame, as suggested here, or retrieved in a separate operation is a question that remains open (e.g., Bock & Levelt, 1994).

(Levelt, Roelofs & Meyer, 1999). As left anterior cortex is involved in later stages of speech production, the late specification of the phonological form of grammatical morphemes, together with the deficient retrieval of these elements in Broca's aphasia, suggests the involvement of the frontal language area in the retrieval of grammatical elements. But it is unlikely that frontal cortex bears full responsibility for syntactic morphology, as damage to the posterior language area gives rise to paragrammatic errors, which generally involve the substitution of one grammatical morpheme for another.

The source of the agrammatic manifestations of Broca's aphasia also remains controversial. One early interpretation was that these patients adopt a simplified speech pattern as a means of reducing the struggle and effort associated with their articulatory impairment. This view has been revived in recent times, although from a somewhat different perspective. Kolk and his colleagues have proposed that there are difficulties in coordinating structural information with lexical retrieval, which give rise to a compensatory strategy that involves utterance simplification; thus, for example, the verb must be available for insertion at the point when the verb slot has to be filled (Kolk, 1995). An alternative view was that Broca's area served as the repository of syntactic knowledge (e.g., Berndt & Caramazza, 1980). This account, the "central syntactic deficit hypothesis," was based on the finding that agrammatic Broca's aphasics,[3] whose comprehension is reasonably good at the single word level, are impaired in understanding certain types of sentences. Postulating a central syntactic deficit hypothesis implies that syntactic aspects of comprehension as well as production depend on information stored in frontal language cortex. In many contexts, these patients appear to comprehend well. Thus, they have little or no difficulty when the interpretation of the sentence is constrained by its lexical content, but their performance often breaks down when it is not — that is, when the sentence is "semantically reversible" (e.g., Caramazza & Zurif, 1976). Compare "John loves books" with "John loves Mary" and with "Mary loves John." The meaning of the first sentence is constrained by the fact that John, but not books, is capable of loving. The other two sentences are not subject to this constraint; either person could conceivably love the other. And critically, despite their identical lexical content, these sentences do not have the same meaning. The interpretation of the John/Mary sentences depends on the sequence of the nouns around the verb (or other morphosyntactic elements in some types of sentences, such as the passive voice sentence "Mary is loved by John")—in other words, on syntactic structure. Some agrammatic patients have difficulty understanding simple reversible active voice sentences, like "John loves Mary" (Berndt, Mitchum & Haendiges, 1996). Others do well on

[3]Not all patients diagnosed as Broca's aphasics demonstrate the agrammatic speech pattern. Some Broca's patients exhibit articulatory impairments and slow, nonfluent speech, but speak in full sentences (albeit simply structured ones; see Saffran, Berndt & Schwartz, 1989, for evidence on this point).

these sentences, which conform to the subject-verb-object order that is dominant in English, but have problems when this pattern is violated, as in the case of passives and object relatives ("Mary is loved by John"; "The girl that John loves is tall"). Evidence that syntactic comprehension was impaired along with sentence production in agrammatic Broca's aphasics suggested that both processes depend on a syntactic knowledge base located in the left frontal language area.[4] Other evidence that implicates this brain region in syntactic processing comes from patients with progressive, degenerative diseases that attack frontal cortex. These patients demonstrate impairments in sentence comprehension, along with syntactic deficits in production (Hodges & Patterson, 1996). Functional imaging studies also demonstrate that anterior language areas are activated in sentence comprehension tasks administered to normal subjects (Just, Carpenter, Keller, Eddy, & Thulborn, 1996; Stromswold, Caplan, Alpert, & Rauch, 1996).

The central syntactic deficit hypothesis elicited much interest, but it was soon challenged by other findings. First, there were reports of dissociations between production and comprehension: some patients with agrammatic production patterns did not demonstrate impairment in sentence comprehension tasks (e.g., Miceli, Mazzucchi, Menn, & Goodglass, 1983). Second, it was found that agrammatics who had difficulty comprehending reversible sentences remained sensitive to many grammatical violations (Linebarger, Schwartz, & Saffran, 1983; see examples in Table 10. 1). These errors could not be detected without knowledge of English syntax, and implementation of this knowledge in processing sentences. Other evidence comes from on-line tasks, in which subjects respond as soon as they detect the target, in many cases by pressing a button when a previously specified word occurs in a sentence (e.g., Tyler, 1992). This task, termed *word monitoring,* has the virtue of simplicity: the aphasic does not need to ponder whether the sentence is grammatical or meaningful. Nevertheless, it is a useful and sensitive measure, in that response time decreases in the presence of syntactic constraints and semantic coherence, and increases following a syntactic error. The rapidity of word detection therefore reflects the patient's ability to process the sentence in which the word is embedded.

If patients are indeed capable of recovering syntactic information from the sentences they hear, what accounts for their comprehension problem? One view is that the difficulty does not lie in computing syntactic structures, as was

---

[4]It should be noted that the sentence comprehension pattern is not restricted to agrammatic Broca's aphasics. Aphasics in general are affected by semantic reversibility, as well as complexity of syntactic structure (e.g., Caplan & Hildebrandt, 1988). It is not clear, however, whether the underlying causes of these deficits are the same across all aphasic patients. Although some have contended that they are (e. g., Miyake, Carpenter & Just, 1994, attribute all such aphasic limitations to a decrease in working memory capacity), there are reasons to think otherwise. The difficulties of patients who are impaired in comprehending single words are likely to differ from those whose have no difficulty at the single word level. Evidence from a study by Schwartz et al. (1987) indicated, for example, that length had a greater impact on the sentence comprehension performance of posterior patients compared to agrammatic aphasics.

TABLE 10.1

Examples of Violations that Agrammatic patients Were Able to Detect

1. Left branch condition. * How many did you see birds in the park?
2. Empty elements. * The workmen were expected would finish by noon.
3. Gapless relative clauses. * Mary ate the bread that I baked a cake.
4. Phrase structure rules. * The paper was full mistakes.
5. Subject-aux inversion. * Did the old man enjoying the view?

Note. From Linebarger et al. (1983).

originally thought, but in utilizing syntactic information to recover the meaning of the sentence. In many sentences, this entails determining who is doing what to whom. To extract this information, it is necessary to link the nouns in the sentence to functions specified by the verb. These functions are termed thematic roles, such as the doer ("agent") or recipient ("patient") of the action. Syntactic information is critical here, as can readily be appreciated from the distinction between " John loves Mary" and "John is loved by Mary." In other words, nouns are assigned to thematic roles on the basis of their syntactic roles in the sentence, together with information retrieved from the lexicon regarding the verb—the thematic roles it sanctions, and the relationships between those roles and syntactic functions. (Often, in English, the first noun, or subject, is the doer or agent, as in the case of "John gives ...," but there are exceptions, as in the case of receive, where John in "John receives ... " is the recipient rather than the agent.) The "mapping deficit hypothesis" locates the comprehension impairment in the processes that utilize syntactic structure along with information specified by the verb to assign thematic roles (Linebarger, 1995; Schwartz, Linebarger, Saffran, & Pate, 1987). However, the factors underlying the putative mapping deficit are not yet clear. One possibility is that damage to frontal language cortex places limits on the capacity to integrate these various forms of information. But other accounts have been proposed, including the loss of specific components of the syntax (Grodzinsky, 1990; Hickok, Zurif, & Conseco–Gonzalez, 1993; Mauner, Fromkin, & Cornell, 1993), limitations on the ability to keep information in working memory (Haarmann, Just, & Carpenter, 1997; Miyake, Carpenter, & Just, 1994), and slowing of processing operations (Haarmann & Kolk, 1991). The latter two accounts assume that some critical information is lost before sentence interpretation can be completed.

One consequence of the failure to fully implement syntactic structure is that agrammatics place undue emphasis on factors other than syntax in interpreting sentences. Interpretation of the preverbal noun as the subject of the verb is one strategy that might account for the success that many patients have with active-voice sentences (e.g., Caplan & Futter, 1986). The fact that the patients do well with nonreversible sentences indicates that semantic constraints are also influential. The power of these constraints is particularly evident in tasks where patients are asked to judge the plausibility of sentences. Agrammatics were only 44 % correct in detecting anomalies like "The movie was frightened by the children," and succeeded in detecting only 57% of the anomalies in simple active voice sentences such as "The children frightened the movie" (Saffran, Schwartz, & Linebarger, 1998). In these sentences, the semantic bias against assigning emotion to an inanimate object competes with the structurally mandated thematic assignment; in many cases, it appears that the semantic constraint wins out over syntactic structure. In contrast, the agrammatics were highly successful (96 percent correct) in rejecting statements like "The water folded the sheet", where there are no thematic assignments that yield a plausible solution (Saffran et al., 1998). The mapping deficit account receives additional support from the finding that these patients have difficulty detecting violations that depend on links between semantic information and particular positions in a sentence. For example, they demonstrate insensitivity to gender violations that involve the noun and pronoun in reflexive constructions (e.g., "While opening the can, the woman hurt himself") (Linebarger, 1995; Linebarger et al., 1983). It appears that the patients are able to recover information about the structural elements in a sentence (in purely structural terms, the reflexive sentence passes muster, as it contains the necessary elements in the correct sequence) but do not necessarily implement this knowledge for the purpose of semantic interpretation.

Although there is evidence that posterior (temporoparietal) and anterior (frontal) speech areas are both involved in sentence-level comprehension and production, the data do not resolve the localization of particular language processes—with exceptions such as the involvement of the frontal lobe in articulation and speech fluency, and that of posterior language cortex in the receptive processing of words and the retrieval of substantive words (particularly nouns) for production.[5] It is clear that sentence production is compromised by damage to both regions, but at this point it is only possible to speculate about the specific contributions of these areas to syntactic functions.

Although the utterances of both Broca's and Wernicke's aphasics are reduced in syntactic complexity, relative to normal speech, the Broca patients are generally more impaired in this respect (Bird & Franklin, 1996). However, the factors responsible for these deficits have yet to be elucidated. Given the programming functions of the frontal cortex in relation to motor activity, it seems reasonable to assume that this brain region has special responsibility for assem-

[5]There is some evidence that implicates subcortical structures—the basal ganglia, in particular—in syntactic processing (see Lieberman, chap. 1, in this volume). As the basal ganglia have important projections to areas of the frontal lobe, it is not clear whether the deficits specifically reflect basal ganglia dysfunction, as opposed to disruption of frontal lobe processes due to inadequate input from these structures.

bling words into sentence form. But it is not clear that the sentence production deficit in agrammatism is fundamentally syntactic. There is evidence, for example, that agrammatics have the capacity to produce more complex structures than is apparent, although they seldom do so spontaneously. Given experience in repeating sentences such as passives—the experiment involves alternating sentence repetition and the description of unrelated pictures (after Bock, 1990)—agrammatic patients show increased production of these forms, although their attempts are often morphologically deviant (e.g., a typical utterance might be "The girl is stinging to the bee" instead of "The girl is stung by the bee"; Saffran & Martin, 1997). In view of the damage to frontal language cortex in these patients, this finding suggests that posterior areas are involved in the storage and retrieval of sentence frames, which are the same for the correct and deviant versions of this sentence, and that anterior areas may have at least partial responsibility for retrieving grammatical morphology. Another complicating factor is the difficulty that many agrammatics have in retrieving verbs (see Appendix 2); sentences cannot be formulated without verbs. There is evidence that some patients improve when the verb is provided, whereas others do not (see Berndt, 1998, for discussion of this point). There may also be restrictions on the number of lexical items that can be activated for the purpose of assembling an utterance. This finding is consistent with the approach taken by Kolk (1995), which postulates difficulty in coordinating lexical retrieval with sentence frame information. It appears, then, that there are a number of factors that contribute to the agrammatic deficit in production.

With respect to comprehension, there is evidence that a good deal of syntactic information is retrieved in the course of processing individual lexical items in the sentence. It appears, for example, that the lexical entry for the verb contains information about the frequency of the syntactic contexts in which the verb appears, and that the sentence processor utilizes this knowledge by initially constructing the structure that occurs most frequently (e.g., MacDonald, Pearlmutter, & Seidenberg, 1994). These findings point to the lexical functions of posterior language cortex in the recovery of syntactic information. But lexically stored specifications are clearly not sufficient. Most aspects of syntactic structure entail the compilation of information across a series of words. (Consider, for example, the distinction between cleft subject and object constructions, as in "It is the dog that is chasing the cat "vs." It is the dog that the cat is chasing.") There is little evidence that bears on the localization of such operations, although the sensitivity of agrammatic patients to violations of syntactic constraints suggests that these operations are more likely to depend on posterior than frontal language cortex. Nevertheless, damage to the frontal language area does have an impact on sentence interpretation. It is possible that frontal cortex plays an important role in maintaining the linkages among the various types of information that are critical for sentence comprehension (e.g., binding lexical items and their semantic specifications to syntactic components), as well as integrating these elements. Evidence from functional imaging studies suggests that areas of the frontal lobe are involved in maintaining information that is represented posteriorly in parietal cortex. For example, frontal areas are activated in tasks that require information with respect to spatial location, which is represented in areas of the parietal lobe (e.g., Smith et al.,1995). It is conceivable that frontal language cortex plays a similar role in receptive language function by contributing to the activation of posterior language areas (temporal and possibly parietal), thereby facilitating the integration of the several types of information that enter into sentence comprehension. Functional imaging studies of normal subjects undergoing sentence comprehension tests indicate, for example, that the frontal language area becomes increasingly activated as sentence structure grows more complex (Just et al., 1996; Stromswold et al., 1996). An activating role, which might promote integration, is one possible instantiation of the mapping deficit hypothesis outlined above. It is also conceivable that a decrease in the activation of posterior language cortex contributes to the lexical as well as morphosyntactic retrieval deficits in agrammatic production.

To conclude this section, current evidence suggests that many aspects of syntactic processing are more likely to be subserved by posterior than frontal language cortex. However, damage to frontal areas clearly limits both the ability to produce and comprehend sentences, although the nature of this limitation—whether it is truly syntactic—remains an open question. Clarification of the relationship between the anterior and posterior language cortices, as well as further delineation of their specific functions, are important directions for future research.

IMPLICATIONS OF RECENT DATA FOR FUNCTIONAL AND NEURAL ARCHITECTURE: CONCEPTUAL INFORMATION

Recall that Lichtheim envisioned a concept center,[6] diffusely represented in the brain, that would serve as the endpoint for language comprehension as well as the generative source for language production. Due in large part to data from brain-damaged patients, we are now in a position to evaluate this proposal.

In 1975, Warrington published a ground-breaking study that showed that semantic (or conceptual) knowledge could be selectively impaired while other cognitive functions remained relatively intact. She reported data from three patients who suffered from a progressive loss of conceptual information. This dis-

[6]The term *conceptual knowledge* is sometimes used to refer to information that is not stored linguistically, whereas *semantics* is sometimes reserved for linguistic knowledge. In this section I use these terms interchangeably, following on psychologists' use of the term *semantic memory* to refer to a general knowledge base that is not differentiated along these lines.

order, now termed *semantic dementia* (Hodges, Patterson, Oxbury, & Funnell, 1992; Snowden, Goulding, & Neary, 1989), is the product of a progressive, degenerative brain disease that targets the inferior and middle portions of the temporal lobes, for some time sparing the superior temporal area that Wernicke identified as critical for language. Although semantic dementia patients have no difficulty repeating what is said to them, they are seriously limited in retrieving words (e.g., in picture naming tasks) and in comprehending them. They are also deficient on measures of conceptual knowledge that employ pictorial materials (for example, determining that a pyramid goes with a palm and not a pine tree). In Lichtheim's terms, these individuals suffer from a disorder of the "concept center," although core receptive and expressive language capacities remain intact. Thus, phonology is spared, at least for a long period of time; words that the patient is able to retrieve are produced correctly, and the ability to repeat is maintained. Syntactic abilities are also preserved, as assessed by grammaticality judgment, sentence comprehension, and online tasks such as word monitoring (e.g., Breedin & Saffran, 1999; Hodges & Patterson, 1996; Schwartz, Marin & Saffran, 1979). In the early stages of the disease, semantic errors are common; for example, a patient might identify a horse as a cow in a picture naming task, and make similar errors in comprehension. As the disorder progresses, the errors bear a more distant relationship to the target; the horse might be termed an animal or a vehicle. In comprehension tasks, such as word-picture matching, the patient also begins to make choices that are completely unrelated to the target (Hodges, Graham, & Patterson, 1995; Schwartz et al., 1979).

Pathological changes in anterior, inferior regions of the temporal lobes (particularly the left) are associated with two more specific forms of semantic loss. Damage to this region occasionally gives rise to a disturbance in which abstract words are better preserved than concrete words (Breedin, Saffran & Coslett, 1994; Saffran & Sholl, 1999). This pattern is contrary to the normal advantage for concrete words that is demonstrated in learning and memory tasks (Paivio, 1991). It is also exceptional in that the concreteness advantage is frequently magnified as a result of left hemisphere damage. Aphasics in general (Goodglass, Hyde, & Blumstein, 1969), as well as patients with certain acquired reading (e.g., Coltheart, 1980) and word repetition disorders (e.g., Katz & Goodglass, 1990), demonstrate marked discrepancies that favor concrete words. To this point, seven cases of abstract word superiority have been reported. Patients who had undergone imaging studies showed bilateral temporal lobe involvement; in the best documented cases, the areas most affected were the anterior, inferior temporal lobes (inferotemporal cortex; see Fig. 10. 1), more so on the left than on the right (Saffran & Sholl, 1999). Superior performance with respect to abstract words has been demonstrated in tasks such as providing definitions for words, judgments of similarity of word meaning, and word-to-picture matching. The abstract word advantage in word-to-picture matching is particularly impressive in that the matches to abstract words entail inferential processing (e.g., the target for the word *disparity* was a pair of mittens of two different sizes), whereas the targets for concrete words (e.g., *donkey*) simply depict the named items (Breedin et al., 1994).

How do we account for the abstract word advantage? Abstract and concrete concepts can be distinguished, in large part, by the importance of perceptual properties in the case of the latter: Names for concepts characterized by semantic concreteness are associated with objects that have shape and color, tactile properties, and sometimes characteristic sounds as well. To investigate the role of perceptual information in the advantage for abstract words, patients' knowledge of perceptual properties (how things look, feel, and sound) has been contrasted with their knowledge of other characteristic features (associative/ encyclopedic properties, such as the location in which the object is found, whether it is dangerous, etc.). The patients who were tested in this manner were disproportionately impaired on perceptual features, suggesting that it is the loss of perceptual characteristics that accounts for the disproportionate impairment on concrete words (Breedin et al., 1994; Marshall, Pring, Chiat, & Robson, 1996). The inferotemporal area implicated in these cases lies just anterior to brain regions that support visual object recognition; in addition, inputs from many association areas of the brain converge in the inferior temporal lobe, en route to structures such as the hippocampus. It has been speculated that anterior inferotemporal cortex serves as a convergence point for the various forms of information that specify the perceptual properties of concrete objects (Breedin et al., 1994; Gainotti, Silveri, Daniele, & Giustolisi, 1995; Srinivas, Breedin, Coslett, & Saffran, 1997).

There is a second pattern of impairment that reflects a distinction within the domain of concrete objects, specifically, a dissociation between living and man-made things. Some patients (including five of the seven who demonstrated an abstract superiority effect; Saffran & Sholl, 1999) show greater loss of knowledge of living (animals, fruits and vegetables) as compared with nonliving things (tools and artifacts). Other patients show the opposite pattern, performing better on living than on nonliving things. The patients impaired on living things also tend to be deficient on foods, even if man-made, while those impaired on artifacts demonstrate impairment on body parts, which belong to living things. The tasks that provide evidence of these impairments include object naming, defining words, providing words for definition, and word-to-picture matching. It is important to note that the lesion sites in these two disorders differ: In almost all cases, those impaired on living things have had anterior, inferior temporal lesions (most of them due to herpes simplex encephalitis, which often affects this area of the brain), whereas those impaired on artifacts and body parts have had left frontoparietal damage (and are consequently aphasic) (e.g., Gainotti et al., 1995; Saffran & Schwartz, 1994). Examples of these patterns may be found in Table 10.2.

TABLE 10.2
Examples of Impairments on Living and Nonliving Things

Patient	*Task*	*Data (% correct)*	*Lesion Site*
Patient impaired on living things			
JBR	Definitions	Living: 8	Bilateral temporal
(Warrington & Sallice, 1984)		Nonliving: 79	
SBY (Warrington & Shallace, 1984)	Nonliving: 52		
LA	Picture	Living: 20	Bilateral frontotemporal
(Silveri & Gainotti, 1988)	Naming	Nonliving: 79	
Felicia	Pictures	Animals: 33	Bilateral frontal inferotemporal
(DeRenzi & Lucchelli, 1994)	Naming	Objects: 90	
Patients imparied on nonliving things			
VER	Word-Object	Animals: 86	Left frontoparietal
(Warrington & McCarthy, 1983)	Matching	Objects: 63	
YOT	Word–Pix	Living: 87	Left frontoparietal
(Warrington & McCarthy, 1987)	Matching	Manipulable	
CW	Picture	Living: 95	Left frontoparietal
(Sacchett & Humphreys, 1992)	Naming	Nonnliving +	Body Parts: 35
JJ	Picture	Living: 92	
(Hillis & Caramazza, 1991)	Naming	Nonliving+ Body parts: 45	Left temporal, basal ganglia

What is the significance of these breakdown patterns? First of all, the fact that different lesion sites give rise to different disorders suggests that conceptual information is distributed in the brain, in keeping with Lichtheim's early notion. Although it is possible that these patterns reflect categorical principles for the organization of knowledge, the categories implicated in these patterns are rather broad and in some respects counterintuitive. For example, why should living things pattern with manufactured food, and artifacts with body parts? An alternative possibility is that these patterns do not reflect categorical organization per se, but differences across categories in the kinds of information that distinguish category members from one another. Warrington and her colleagues proposed that perceptual information is strongly weighted in the representations of living things and foods, whereas functional information is particularly significant for artifacts and body parts (Warrington & Shallice, 1984; Warrington & McCarthy, 1987). For example, unless you were a gamekeeper, it would be difficult to differentiate lions from leopards and tigers on the basis of their behavior patterns; for most of us, the distinction rests on differences in appearance that remain stable in nature. Foods also share a common function, and are distinguished largely by their perceptual characteristics. In contrast, consider the variegated forms that radios take today; although vastly different in form (e.g., a table radio vs. a car radio vs. a headset), we classify them on the basis of their common function. In fact, evidence in support of the "differential weighting assumption" comes from a study in which participants listed object properties that were cited in dictionary definitions; for living things, the ratio of perceptual to other characteristics was considerably higher than it was for artifacts (Farah & McClelland, 1991).

Neuropsychologists have used a range of tasks to test the hypothesis that patients impaired on living things show disproportionate loss of, or access to, the perceptual properties of objects (the "perceptual deficit hypothesis"). Among them are tasks in which patients are asked to color or draw named objects, and verbal tasks in which they are queried about specific characteristics of things (e.g., Does a whale have legs? Does a whale live in the water?). On the coloring tasks, patients have consistently demonstrated loss of color information. On the drawing tasks, the product is much the same—the drawing of a generic, mammalian four-legged creature—whether the patient is asked to draw a cow or a parrot (e.g., Sartori, Job, & Coltheart, 1993). On the verbal questions, some of the patients impaired on living things have performed worse on perceptual properties, although others have done equally poorly on associative/encyclopedic characteristics (see Saffran & Sholl, 1999). The finding that patients impaired on living things do not always perform worse on perceptual than other properties has led some investigators to dismiss the "perceptual deficit hypothesis." Caramazza and Shelton (1998) suggested an alternative—that the living things deficit reflects damage to a cortical area (which they do not specify) that is innately committed to the representation of plants and animals. They argue that recognition of these entities is essential to life, and point out that infants learn quickly how to discriminate between animate and inanimate objects. Caramazza and Shelton proposed that the deficit for artifacts arises by default, as man-made objects are excluded from the area committed to plants and animals, and not because any area of cortex is dedicated to representing these entities or their properties.

Abandoning the perceptual deficit hypothesis on the basis of the finding that some patients do not perform worse on perceptual than other features may be premature. It is possible to account for these results on the following type of model: Assume that the properties of an object are represented across subsystems specialized for particular types of features, that these properties are linked by connections across these subsystems, and that these linkages allow representations in one subsystem to activate those in another (as in Fig. 10.3, from Allport, 1985). One consequence of this arrangement is that damage to a subsystem that carries a great deal of information about the object will decrease the activation levels of features represented in other subsystems, rendering these properties less accessible. Farah and McClelland (1991) produced just such a result by selectively removing perceptual information in a computational model that assumed greater weighting of perceptual properties in the representations of living things.

The account put forth by Warrington and her colleagues attributes the impairment on nonliving things to a loss of functional information about objects. The co-occurring deficit on body parts could be given a similar explanation: As with tools and utensils, body parts serve unique functions. Because the patients who demonstrate this deficit are aphasics who tend to be more impaired on abstract than concrete concepts (e.g., Goodglass et al., 1969), it is conceivable that the deficit reflects the greater abstractness of functional compared with perceptual information (Keil, 1989). There is, however, an alternative possibility: That is, the problem with artifacts may reflect loss of knowledge of the ways in which objects are manipulated. Buxbaum and Saffran (1998) have been investigating this hypothesis through the use of similarity judgments. Aphasic patients are given sets of three words (or pictures), and are instructed to choose the item that is least similar in terms of manner of manipulation (e.g.,

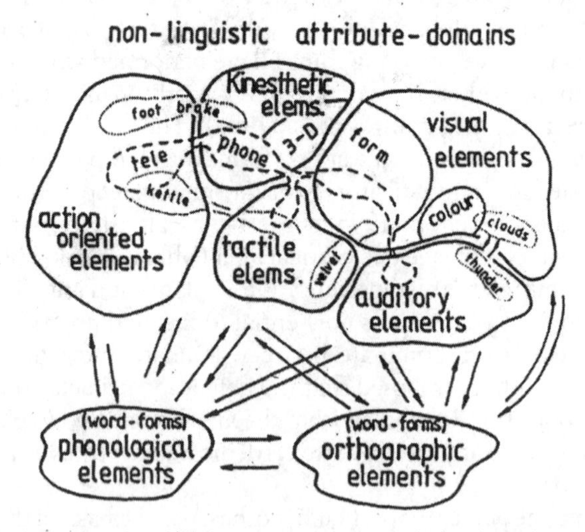

FIG. 10.3. A distributed model of semantic memory, in which only nonlinguistic areas of knowledge representation are marked. Note that information about an object, such as a telephone, is represented across several subsystems. (From Allport (1985), with permission.

lawnmower, baby carriage, wagon) on some trials, or function (e.g., *mop, shovel, plow*) on others. The subjects are aphasics who have also been assessed on tests of praxis (the ability to demonstrate how an object is used). Patients impaired on the praxis tests had significantly more difficulty with the manner of manipulation trials, and tended to be more impaired on tool similarity judgments than on animals. In contrast, patients who did well on the praxis measures performed equivalently on manner of manipulation and function trials; they also performed worse on animals than tools. These data suggest that the impairment of artifacts reflects loss of information about the manner in which objects are handled. The results are also consistent with the involvement of left fronto-parietal cortex in the artifacts deficit, as this area supports sensorimotor functions that are critical for object use. Other evidence that supports the dissociation of function and manipulational information in brain-damaged subjects comes from semantic dementia patients with inferotemporal damage, who cannot name objects or indicate their properties; nevertheless, these patients perform well on tests of object use (e.g., Buxbaum, Schwartz & Carew, 1997). And a patient with anterior temporal damage, in this case resulting from herpes simplex encephalitis, was able to demonstrate how to manipulate a pictured object, although he had lost knowledge of its function; for example, he indicated the correct motion for manipulating an iron, although he said it was used to glue objects together (Sirigu, Duhamel, & Poncet, 1991).

The patterns of semantic impairment just described provide support for a distributed model of the conceptual system, in which the various components of the network represent different types of information (e.g., Allport, 1985; Shallice, 1988). Data from recent functional imaging studies are in accord with this view, demonstrating left frontal activation in response to tools and greater inferotemporal activation in response to living things (Grafton, Fadiga, Arbib, & Rizzolatti, 1997; Martin, Wiggs, Ungerleider, & Haxby, 1996; Perani et al., 1995). The distributed model suggests that the manner in which information is stored reflects the modality in which it was acquired (e.g., visual input is stored in a visual format, kinesthetic input in sensorimotor form, etc.). This view is appealing in that it implies continuity with nonverbal creatures whose knowledge of the world is completely dependent on nonverbal input. For example, monkeys with ablations of inferotemporal cortex show visual recognition deficits despite the fact that they can see ("psychic blindness," one manifestation of the Kluver-Bucy syndrome), manifested by the tendency to put objects in their mouths in order to identify them (Kluver & Bucy, 1939). Evolution of the capacity for language created the necessity for associations between these non-verbal properties and the language system, and hence the possibility of disorders that reflect the disruption of these linking pathways. For example, McCarthy and Warrington (1988) described a patient who was able to provide information about objects presented visually (e.g., a picture of a dolphin), although he was unable to respond when given the names of the same objects.

The data that are emerging from the study of semantically impaired patients provide general support for Lichtheim's view that the "concept center" is diffusely represented in the brain, and, more specifically, that it comprises a number of subsystems dedicated to information deriving from different modalities of input. As noted, however, the factors that underlie a distributed knowledge system remain controversial (Caramazza & Shelton, 1998; Coltheart et al., 1998; Saffran & Sholl, 1999).

EVIDENCE FOR THE ORGANIZATION OF THE LEXICON

The organization of the mental lexicon—the internal dictionary—has been an active area of investigation in recent years. It is generally agreed that the lexicon serves as the interface between word sound and word meaning, and carries syntactic information as well—including specifications as to the syntactic category of the word (noun, verb, adjective, etc.), grammatical gender (in some languages), and the syntactic contexts that it requires (e.g., transitive and intransitive verbs mandate different structures, some verbs take complements whereas others do not, etc.). Word retrieval, for the purpose of language production, is currently conceptualized as a multistage process: A concept activates a lemma—an abstract representation of the word, essentially a node that connects it to other properties—which, in turn, activates its syntactic features as well as its phonology. Evidence from language breakdown bears on at least one controversial matter concerning the architecture of lexical organization.

One much-debated issue concerns the factors that affect selection of the correct lemma: specifically, whether or not this process is influenced by the sound of a word. If phonological information enters into the process, activation must feed back from the phonemes activated by lemmas to the lemma level. One phenomenon that is readily accommodated by a model that allows feedback is the frequency of "mixed" errors, that is, errors that reflect both a semantic and phonological relationship to the target word (e.g., *skeleton*→"skull"). People have collected large numbers of errors that arise in normal speech, either by writing down errors as they hear them (Dell & Reich, 1981; Garrett, 1980), or in the context of laboratory experiments designed to elicit errors (e.g., Martin, Weisberg & Saffran, 1989). In both sets of data, the rate of production of mixed errors is higher than would be expected if semantic and phonological influences were independent of one another. The mechanism for generating mixed errors is built into the architecture of models that allow feedback from the phoneme level, which afford the opportunity for semantic and phonological influences to summate at the lemma level (e.g., Dell, 1986). Summation, plus the addition of random activation from noise in the lexical network, sometimes allows an error (like "skull") to be more strongly activated than the target lemma ("skeleton"). However, arguing on the grounds of simplicity, some psycholinguists favor "independent stage" models in which lemmas are immune from phonological influences (e.g., Levelt, 1992). Indeed, in tasks that examine the time course of word production, early stages show semantic influences exclusively, whereas later stages show only phonological influences (e.g., Schriefers, Meyer & Levelt, 1990), although a model that allows semantic and phonological summation can also accommodate these findings (Dell & O'Seaghda, 1991). Advocates of "independent stage" models invoke internal monitoring of planned output to account for the prevalence of mixed errors. They claim that mixed errors are less likely to be detected than other error types because of their dual—semantic as well as phonological—similarity to the target word (e.g., Levelt, 1992).

The methods used to collect speech error data have drawn criticism, on the grounds that some types of errors are more likely to be noticed when they arise in casual conversation, and that the pools of items used in experimental studies contain relationships, such as semantic and/or phonological similarity across words, that might promote confusion among the items, resulting in the production of mixed errors (Levelt, 1992). Language-impaired individuals generate errors at much higher rates than normal speakers, easing the task of collecting an error corpus. In a recent study, Martin, Gagnon, Schwartz, Dell, and Saffran (1997) analyzed the errors produced by aphasics (as well as normal subjects) in a picture-naming task. The subjects' responses were taped and transcribed, eliminating the possible problems that may arise in casual data collection, when errors must be noticed by listeners and written down. This study also lacked the groupings of similar words that may have generated mixed errors in other experiments. The actual rates of mixed semantic and phonological errors were compared with chance rates calculated by randomly pairing targets and responses. Both aphasic and normal subjects demonstrated mixed errors at rates that significantly exceeded chance levels, supporting the reality of this phenomenon, as well as the natural account of mixed errors provided by the interactive model.

Of course, adherents of independent stage models could appeal to the alleged insensitivity of the error monitor to account for these data. Another set of findings that may be more difficult to accommodate on an independent stage model comes from computer simulations of the picture naming error patterns of individual aphasic patients, implementing a model that allows feedback from phonemes to the lemma level. Dell, Schwartz, Martin, Saffran, and Gagnon (1997) examined the rates at which patients generated particular kinds of errors in a picture naming task. The error types included words semantically related to the target (e.g., *king* → "queen"), words related to the target in their phonological properties (formal paraphasias, such as *basket* → "banquet"), words both phonologically and semantically related to the target (mixed errors, such as *train* → "truck"), unrelated words, and nonwords. The first step was to simulate naming data for normal subjects, obtained on the same task; this enabled the selection of parameters that would reproduce the normal error pattern in computer simulations. Dell et al. were able to show that altering one or two parameters from their normal settings—either decreasing the strength of the connections that determine the flow of activation from level to level, or increasing the rate of decay of activation in the lexical network—accurately simulated the error distributions of 21 aphasic patients. Although the model was developed to simulate normal naming performance, demonstrating that it can accommodate the deviant performance of aphasic individuals provides support for the assumption of phonological feedback to the lemma level. Comparable tests of an independent stage model have yet to be conducted.

OPPOSING VIEWS OF LANGUAGE ORGANIZATION

As noted, the attempts to uncover the relationships between language and brain structure began with the identification of brain areas that appeared to support different aspects of language function. This perspective was displaced, early in the 20th century, by more global views of the representation of language in the brain (Caplan, 1987). A similar polarization of views on language representation continues to the present. In 1965, the neurologist Norman Geschwind revived the approach of the 19th-century connectionists, accounting for a range of language and other cognitive deficits in terms of disconnections between brain regions specialized for particular functions (Geschwind, 1965a). At around the same time, some aphasia researchers argued against specialization within the language system, basing this conclusion on factor analyses conducted on data from successive patients who were tested on an aphasia battery (Schuell, Jenkins & Carroll, 1962). These analyses utilize mathematical methods to extract sets of behaviors that correlate with one another, thereby identifying a "factor" held in common across them. Although distinctions are routinely observed in clinical settings, the Schuell et al. analyses yielded only a single factor and hence no evidence for subtypes of aphasia. The reasons for these negative results are unclear; perhaps the tests were not sufficiently sensitive, or the sample may have included many patients with large lesions. If the latter, the damage would involve a number of brain regions, precluding specific impairments.

The controversy persists, fueled on the one hand by the strongly modular views of language organization held by many linguists and cognitive scientists (e.g., Fodor, 1983; Frazier, 1990), and by the powerful tools of computational modeling on the other. The modular viewpoint assumes that distinct brain regions subserve specific language functions. In contrast, connectionist models (see Plaut, chap. 6, this volume) assume that language information can be distributed throughout a system whose parts do not have specialized functions. For example, some researchers have developed computational models in which a single network acquires syntactic as well as semantic information (McClelland, St. John, & Taraban, 1989). Such models erase any distinction between the units that learn to distinguish between syntactic forms such as active and passive voice and those that acquire semantic information, such as the food preferences of bus drivers; the two types of information are "inextricably interwoven in the connections" (McClelland et al., 1989, p. 313). Others have proposed that the retrieval of lexical items and the retrieval of syntactic structure are similar processes that draw on "different kinds of linguistic information (phonological, lexical morphological, syntactic) ... represented together in a common format" (Devescovi et al., 1997, p. 546).

The evidence suggests, to the contrary, that the selective impairments of brain-damaged patients are more consistent with models in which components are specialized for particular tasks. The assumption that there are regions of specialization within the language system does not entail the assumption that these subcomponents must operate independently of one another, as some theorists have claimed (for example, Fodor, 1983). Evidence for the interaction of various forms of linguistic information (e.g., Dell et al., 1997; MacDonald et al., 1994) indicates that at least some components must be highly interconnected. Allowing interaction among components is not equivalent to collapsing various types of information into a single undifferentiated system. In the case of an undifferentiated model, the only way to generate selective impairments is to vary the amount of information represented in the system, and/or the extent of damage to the system: If the system represents more information of type X than type Y, X is less susceptible to disruption. In contrast, a model with specialized components assumes qualitative distinctions: Information type X is represented differently from information type Y. This distinction implies that information is represented across different sets of neurons, allowing the possibility of disrupting one function independently of the other. (See Shallice, 1988, for further discussion of this point.)

Evidence from other cognitive systems is relevant to this discussion. With respect to brain organization, the best studied system is that of vision, where the task of analyzing the visual world is divided among many specialized components: Color, form, movement, object identity, and location are computed by distinct subsystems, subserved by different brain regions (e.g., Maunsell & Newsome, 1987). Under normal circumstances, the perceiver is completely unaware of these parallel computations; experientially, the separate analyses are bound into a seamless whole. Although different brain regions are specialized for different aspects of visual processing, phenomenologically the visual system seems to function in an undifferentiated manner, and it is this aspect of the language system that is perhaps being captured in connectionist models. However, these systems can be selectively affected by brain lesions, leaving an individual unable to perceive color or movement, or in some cases unable to identify objects or to locate them in space.

Are there essential differences between the mechanisms that underlie visual as opposed to language function? The systems differ in important respects; some forms of visual information remain distinct from one another as they are transmitted through the nervous system, whereas there appears to be a single input pathway for spoken language. Nevertheless, the language system does respect the fundamental distinction between sensory and motor functions, assigning certain purely receptive and purely motor aspects of language processing to different brain regions. Are there other differences among the various forms of linguistic information that would be difficult to accommodate within a homogeneous representational system? Consider, for example, what a word entails: A word is a link between an arbitrary set of sounds and meaning that also takes on syntactic properties (e.g., part of speech, the syntactic contexts in which the word can occur, and so on). For concrete words, the association between meaning and sound is directly given by experience: Someone points to an object you have never seen before and utters its name, and the brain registers this co-occurrence. Syntactic properties are different, in that they are not given directly by sensory input but must be inferred, either from the linguistic context or from similarities between this particular word and others. This mediational requirement suggests that syntactic properties are acquired differently than the links between sounds and meanings, and implies that they are likely to be represented differently as well.

Evidence from aphasics, as well as from normal subjects in tip-of-the-tongue states where the meaning of a word is known but its sound remains elusive, indicates that these various aspects of word knowledge can dissociate. Often, aphasics seem to have adequate knowledge of the meaning of a word (as indicated by their ability to provide an adequate definition or description of an object), despite their inability to access its phonological form (e.g., Goodglass, 1993). It has recently been demonstrated that patients (and normals in tip-of-the-tongue states) can provide syntactic information about a word (such as its gender, in languages such as French and Italian) or the particular auxiliary that goes with a verb, although they are unable to retrieve the sounds that comprise it (e.g., Henaff Gonon, Bruckert, & Michel, 1989; Miozzo & Caramazza, 1997). Moreover, the ability to retrieve gender information appears to be unrelated to the ability to provide some phonological information about the word (Caramazza & Miozzo, 1997). The dissociability of these forms of lexical information indicates that components of the lexical entry are not tightly linked; the fact that they can be retrieved independently argues against a common form and locus of storage. The distribution of these specifications across different subsystems is consistent with the finding that word retrieval deficits are ubiquitous in aphasics, irrespective of lesion site or type of aphasia (e.g., Goodglass & Wingfield, 1997). Although one could argue that this reflects the distribution of a single network over an extensive area of the brain, the differences in error patterns across patients suggest otherwise. Some are prone to semantic error, others to phonological error, and so on. There are also dissociations involving parts of speech, nouns and verbs in particular; agrammatics (and some other patients) tend to be more impaired on verbs, whereas nouns may be more affected in other (anomic) aphasics (e.g., Berndt, Mitchum, Haendiges, & Sandson, 1997). Although the basis for these deficits remains controversial (e.g., Breedin, Saffran, & Schwartz, 1998; Hillis & Caramazza, 1995), the selective nature of these impairments further supports the argument for distinctions in manner of representation and retrieval.

In contrast, Bates and her colleagues have provided some data that point to a single system underlying the retrieval of lexical and syntactic information in sentence production (Bates, Harris, Marchman, Wulfeck, & Kritchevsky, 1995). These investigators demonstrated that structural simplification and word retrieval deficits co-occur in patients with Alzheimer's disease; specifically, impairments in picture naming were accompanied by decreased use of structures such as the passive. On the basis of these findings, they argued that both functions are supported by the same system. In support of a common mechanism, Bates et al. point out that the retrieval of lexical items and syntactic frames are both sensitive to frequency of use. Frequency of use facilitates retrieval, and offers some protection against brain damage; because syntactic structures (relatively few in number) have higher frequencies of occurrence than most individual lexical items, they may be more resistant to loss. But frequency dependence is a general characteristic of processes that reflect learning (that is, use strengthens representations and facilitates access to them) and does not, in itself, constitute an argument for commonality in representational format and mode of retrieval.

Evidence that is interpreted differently comes from a longitudinal study of Wernicke's aphasics, whose utterances increased in complexity and well-formedness as their ability to retrieve words increased (Bird & Franklin, 1996). The authors of this study attribute their findings to a causal relationship between the availability of lexical items and the ability to construct complex utterances. This seems a reasonable supposition, in that the ready availability of lexical items would seem to be essential for the construction of complex sentences.

There are additional factors that differentiate syntactic and lexical operations. Although syntactic specifications for words are accessed via the lexicon, we have already seen from consideration of the tip-of-the-tongue phenomenon that retrieval of this information is not tightly linked to the retrieval of phonological form. Most crucially, the factors that influence word retrieval are not equivalent to those that affect syntactic complexity. The production system selects words on the basis of the concepts to be expressed in the utterance. The selection of a syntactic frame, although subject to conceptual influences, is also governed by other factors, which include discourse considerations (such as which entity should receive emphasis) as well as the words that will appear in the sentence (e.g., Bock, 1990). Although the lemma, the intermediate stage between conceptual and phonological encoding in word retrieval, must be connected to phonological representations, the syntactic frame is not; the slots in the frame are specified for words of a particular syntactic category, but not for specific lexical items. These distinctions suggest that the various types of information required for sentence production are represented differently and retrieved differently.

Finally, consider the attempt to collapse semantic and syntactic information into a common network in which both types of representations are inextricably intertwined (McClelland et al., 1989). The dissociation of syntactic and semantic abilities in semantic dementia patients, whose loss of conceptual knowledge is severe, presents a challenge for this proposal. There is no indication that syntactic deficiency accompanies the disintegration of semantic knowledge in these patients. There is evidence that such patients continue to perform well (even at normal levels) on sentence comprehension tasks, as long as the participants are sufficiently differentiated (as in the case of sentences like "The boy is followed by the dog"); there is also evidence that they retain their sensitivity to grammatical violations (Breedin & Saffran, 1999). Data from online studies, in which processing is tracked by probing for word recognition within sentences, indicates that these patients compute syntactic information with normal efficiency (Breedin & Saffran, in press). Note in addition that the brain area implicated in semantic dementia—the inferior and middle regions of the temporal lobes (Hodges et al., 1992)—is distinct from the classical language areas (Wernicke's, Broca's) implicated in the disorders that compromise syntactic functions.

In conclusion, it is difficult to see how the selective deficit patterns that emerge in brain damaged patients could arise in a language system that was completely undifferentiated. To take one example, how could such a system be damaged to create verb impairments in some cases and noun impairments in others? The evidence from brain-damage appears more consistent with an architecture in which sub-regions are specialized for representing particular information types and/or carrying out specific functions. Those inclined against this approach are challenged to take up the task of accommodating these breakdown patterns within the framework of a unitary computational model—one that allows particular breakdown patterns to be simulated on the computer.

CONCLUDING COMMENTS

In sum, then, I have tried to show how these uncontrolled accidents of nature can provide information relevant to the anatomical and functional organization of the language system. The evidence from language breakdown patterns points to a differentiated system, in which particular areas are committed to particular functions, although these subcomponents may in some cases interact with one another as opposed to operating independently. Nevertheless, there are a number of issues that remain controversial. Along with the study of normal individuals, the study of language-impaired individuals should contribute to the resolution of these matters.

ACKNOWLEDGMENT

Preparation of this chapter was supported by grant DC00191 from the National Institutes of Health.

APPENDIX 1

Patient FL responds to a question about what he liked to cook (see Schwartz, Saffran, Bloch, & Dell, 1994, for a complete transcript). Words and nonwords in italics represent errors; represents word that was omitted.

I I don't know how there is any single way, there's so many thing, you know, that I like. I like meats, I have liked beef, the Germans, you know, and what, well the French you *koot* the whole, I can't recall the word that I can't *thay*. It was the where you make all the food, you make it all up today and keep it till the next day. With the French, you know, uh, what is the name of the word, God, public *serpinz* they talk about, uh but I have had that, it was *ryediss*, just before the *storage* you know, seven weeks, I had personal friends that, that, I would cook an' *food* the food and serve *fer* four or six *mean* for an evening.

APPENDIX 2

An agrammatic patient tells story of Cinderella.

Long ago Cinderella. One time many years ago two sisters and one stepmother. Cinderella is washing clothes and mop floor. One day big party in the castle. Two girls dresses is beautiful. Cinderella is poor. Two sisters left. In the castle Cinderella is ... Godmother. Oh, what's wrong? No money. A little mouse. Cinderella hurry. Queen. Magic wand. Mouses. Oh big men now. Magic wand pumpkin then chariot. Cinderella dresses no good. Cinderella. Oh my god beautiful now. Next time, twelve o'clock, hex. Then Cinderella party. Many women at the party. Prince is ... no good. Oh, prince is ... Cinderella. Dance dance. Two hours. Dance dance dance. Twelve o'clock, oh my god. Cinderella. What's wrong? I leave, I leave, I leave. One shoe slip. Cinderella is twelve o'clock. Poor again. Tomorrow, prince slipper. Village many houses. One house, knock, knock. What's wrong. Prince is ... One, two kids, OK, OK. First one too small. Second was too big. Hey wait a minute, wait a minute. Prince. You. What's wrong. Hey, slip it on. Oh. Does fit. Godmother. Magic wand. New gown again. Then magic prince and godmother went in the castle.

REFERENCES

Allport, D. A. (1985). Distributed memory, modular subsystems and dysphasia. In S. K. Newman & R. Epstein (Eds.), *Current perspectives in dysphasia* (pp. 32–60). Edinburgh: Churchill Livingstone.

Bates, E., Harris, C., Marchman, V., Wulfeck, B., & Kritchevsky, M. (1995). Production of complex syntax in normal aging and Alzheimer's disease. *Language and Cognitive Processes, 10*, 487–544.

Berndt, R. S. (1998). Sentence processing in aphasia. In M. Sarno (Ed.), *Acquired aphasia* (3rd ed., pp. 229–267). New York: Academic Press.

Berndt, R. S., & Caramazza, A. (1980). A redefinition of the syndrome of Broca's aphasia: Implications for a neuropsychological model of language. *Applied Linguistics, 1*, 225–278.
Berndt, R. S., Mitchum, C., & Haendiges, A. (1996). Comprehension of reversible sentences in "agrammatism"; a meta-analysis. *Cognition, 58*, 289–308.
Berndt, R. S., Mitchum, C., Haendiges, A., & Sandson, J. (1997). Verb retrieval in aphasia: 1. Characterizing single word impairments. *Brain and Language, 56*, 68–106.
Bird, H., & Franklin, S. (1996). Cinderella revisited: A comparison of fluent and non–fluent aphasic speech. *Journal of Neurolinguistics, 9*, 187–206.
Boatman, D. F., Lesser, R. P., & Gordon, B. (1995). Auditory speech processing in the left temporal lobe: An electrical interference study. *Brain and Language, 51*, 269–290.
Bock, K. (1990). Structure in language: Creating form in talk. *American Psychologist, 45*, 1221–1236.
Bock, K., & Levelt, W. (1994). Language production: Grammatical encoding. In M. A. Gernsbacher (Ed.), *Handbook of psycholinguistics*. San Diego: Academic Press.
Breedin, S. D., & Saffran, E. M. (1999). Sentence processing in the face of semantic loss: A case study. *Journal of Experimental Psychology: General, 128*, 1–16.
Breedin, S. D., Saffran, E. M., & Coslett, H. B. (1994). Reversal of the concreteness effect in a patient with semantic dementia. *Cognitive Neuropsychology. 11*, 617–660.
Breedin, S. D., Saffran, E. M., & Schwartz, M. F. (1998). Semantic factors in verb retrieval: An effect of complexity. *Brain and Language, 63*, 1–35.
Broca, P. (1865). Sur le siege de la faculte de langage articule. *Bulletin d'Anthropologie, 5*, 377–393.
Buxbaum, L., & Saffran, E. M. (1998). Knowing "how" vs. "what for": A new dissociation. *Brain and Language, 65*, 73–76.
Buxbaum, L., Schwartz, M. F., & Carew, T. G. (1997). The role of semantic memory in object use. *Cognitive Neuropsychology, 14*, 219–254.
Caplan, D. (1987). *Neurolinguistics and linguistic aphasiology*. Cambridge, MA: Cambridge University Press.
Caplan, D., & Futter, C. (1986). Assignment of thematic roles to nouns in sentence comprehension by an agrammatic patient. *Brain and Language, 27*, 117–134.
Caplan, D., & Hildebrandt, N. (1988). *Disorders of syntactic comprehension*. Cambridge, MA: MIT Press.
Caplan, D., Vanier, M., & Baker, C. (1986). A case study of reproduction conduction aphasia: 1. Word production. *Cognitive Neuropsychology, 3*, 99–128.
Caramazza, A., & Miozzo, M. (1997). The relation between syntactic and phonological knowledge in lexical access: Evidence from the "tip-of-the-tongue" phenomenon. *Cognition, 84*, 309–343.
Caramazza, A., & Shelton, J. R. (1998). Domain-specific knowledge systems in the brain: The animate-inanimate distinction. *Journal of Cognitive Neuroscience, 10*, 1–34.
Caramazza, A., & Zurif, E. B. (1976). Dissociation of algorithmic and heuristic processes in language comprehension: Evidence from aphasia. *Brain and Language, 3*, 572–582.
Coltheart, M. (1980). Deep dyslexia: A review of the syndrome. In M. Coltheart, K. E. Patterson, & J. C. Marshall (Eds.), *Deep dyslexia* (pp. 22–48). London: Routledge and Kegan Paul.
Dejerine, J. J. (1892). Contribution a l'etude anatomo–pathologique et clinique des differentes varietes de cecute verbale, *Memoires societe biologique, 4*, 61–90.
Dell, G. S. (1986). A spreading activation theory of retrieval in sentence production. *Psychological Review, 93*, 283–321.
Dell, G. S., & O'Seaghda, P. G. (1991). Mediated and convergent lexical priming in language production: A comment on Levelt et al. *Psychological Review, 98*, 604–614.
Dell, G. S., & Reich, P. A. (1981). Stages in sentence production: An analysis of speech error data. *Journal of Verbal Learning and Verbal Behavior, 20*, 611–629.
Dell, G. S., Schwartz, M. F., Martin, N., Saffran, E. M., & Gagnon, D.A. (1997). Lexical access aphasic and non-aphasic speakers. *Psychological Review, 104*, 811–838.
DeRenzi, E., & Lucchelli, F. (1994). Are semantic systems separately represented in the brain? The case of living category impairment. *Cortex, 30*, 3–25.
Devescovi, A., Bates, E., D'Amico, S., Hernandez, A., Marangolo, P., Pizzamiglio, L., & Razzano, C. (1997). An on-line study of grammaticality judgements in normal and aphasic speakers of Italian. *Aphasiology, 11*, 543–579.
Farah, M. J., & McClelland, J. (1991). A computational model of semantic memory impairment: Modality specificity and emergent category specificity. *Journal of Experimental Psychology: General, 120*, 339–357.
Fodor, J. A. (1983). *The modularity of mind*. Cambridge, MA: MIT Press.

Frazier, L. (1990). Exploring the architecture of the language processing system. In G. T. M. Altmann (Ed.), *Cognitive models of speech processing* (pp. 409–433). Cambridge, MA: MIT Press.
Freud, S. (1953). *On aphasia*. New York: International Universities Press. (Original work published 1891)
Fromkin, V. A. (1973). *Speech errors as linguistic evidence*. The Hague: Mouton.
Gainotti, G., Silveri, M. C., Daniele, A., & Giustolisi, L. (1995). Neuroanatomical correlates of category–specific semantic disorders: A critical survey. *Memory, 3*, 247–264.
Garrett, M. (1980). Levels of processing in sentence production, In B. Butterworth (Ed.), *Language production: Vol. 1, Speech and talk* (pp. 177–220). London: Academic Press.
Geschwind, N. (1965a). Disconnection syndromes in animals and man. Part I. *Brain, 88*, 237–294.
Geschwind, N. (1965b). Disconnection syndromes in animals and man. Part II. *Brain, 88*, 585–644.
Goodglass, H. (1993) *Understanding aphasia*. San Diego: Academic Press.
Goodglass, H., Hyde, M. R., & Blumstein, S. E. (1969). Frequency, picturability and availability of nouns in aphasia. *Cortex, 5*, 104–119.
Goodglass, H., & Wingfield, A. (1997). Word–finding deficits in aphasia: Brain–behavior relations and clinical symptomatology. In H. Goodglass & A. Wingfield (Eds.), *Anomia: Neuroanatomical and clinical correlates*, San Diego: Academic Press.
Grafton, S. T., Fatigue, L., Arbib, M. A., & Rizzolatti, G. (1997). Premotor cortex activation during observation and naming of familiar tools. *Neuroimage, 6*, 231–236.
Grodzinsky, Y. (1984). The syntactic characterization of agrammatism. *Cognition, 16*, 99–120.
Grodzinsky, Y. (1990). *Theoretical perspectives on language deficits*. Cambridge, MA: MIT Press.
Haarmaan, H. J., Just, M. A., & Carpenter, P. A. (1997). Aphasic sentence comprehension as a resource deficit: A computational approach. *Brain and Language, 59*, 76–120.
Haarmann, H. J., & Kolk, H. H. J. (1991). A computer model of the temporal course of agrammatic sentence understanding: The effects of variation in severity and sentence complexity. *Cognitive Science, 15*, 49–87.
Habib, M., & Demonet, J.-F. (1996). Cognitive neuroanatomy of language: the contribution of functional neuroimaging. *Aphasiology, 10*, 217–234.
Head, H. (1926). *Aphasia and kindred disorders of speech*. Cambridge: Cambridge University Press.
Henaff Gonon, M., Bruckert, R., & Michel, F. (1989). Lexicalization in an anomic patient. *Neuropsychologia, 27*, 391–407.
Hickock, G., Zurif, E., & Conseco-Gonzales, E. (1993). Structural description of agrammatic comprehension. *Brain and Language, 45*, 371–395.
Hillis, A. E., & Caramazza, A. (1991). Category-specific naming and comprehension impairment: A double dissociation. *Brain, 114*, 2081–2094.
Hillis, A. E., & Caramazza, A. (1995). Representation of grammatical categories of words in the brain. *Journal of Cognitive Neuroscience, 7*, 396–407.
Hodges, J. R., Graham, N., & Patterson, K. 1995. Charting the progression of semantic dementia: Implications for the organisation of semantic memory. *Memory, 3*, 463–495.
Hodges, J. R., & Patterson, K. (1996). Nonfluent progressive aphasia and semantic dementia: A comparative neuropsychological study. *Journal of the International Neuropsychological Society, 2*, 511–524.
Hodges, J. R., Patterson, K., Oxbury, S., & Funnell, E. (1992). Semantic dementia: Progressive fluent aphasia with temporal lobe atrophy. *Brain, 115*, 1783–1806.
Just, M. A., Carpenter, P. A., Keller, T. A., Eddy, W. F., & Thulborn, K. R. (1996). Brain activation modulated by sentence comprehension. *Science, 274*, 114–116.
Katz, R., & Goodglass, H. (1990). Deep dysphasia: An analysis of a rare form of repetition disorder. *Brain and Language, 39*, 153–185.
Keil, F. C. (1989). *Concepts, kinds and cognitive development*. Cambridge, MA: MIT Press.
Kertesz, A. (1979). *Aphasia and associated disorders*. New York: Grune and Stratton.
Kluver, H., & Bucy, P. C. (1939). Preliminary analysis of the functions of the temporal lobes in monkeys. *Archives of Neurology and Psychiatry, 42*, 979–1000.
Kolk, H. (1995). A time-based approach to agrammatic production. *Brain and Language, 50*, 282–303.
Levelt, W. J. M. (1992). Accessing word in speech production.: Stages, processes and representations. *Cognition, 42*, 1–22.
Levelt, W. J. M., Roelofs, A., & Meyer, A.S. (in press). A theory of lexical access in speech production. *Behavioral and Brain Science*.
Lichtheim, L. (1885). On aphasia. *Brain, 7*, 433–484.
Linebarger, M. (1995). Agrammatism as evidence about grammar. *Brain and Language, 50*, 52–91.

Linebarger, M., Schwartz, M. F., & Saffran, E. M. (1983). Sensitivity to grammatical structure in so–called agrammatic aphasics. *Cognition, 13*, 641–662.

MacDonald, M. C., Pearlmutter, N. J., & Seidenberg, M. S. (1994). The lexical nature of syntactic ambiguity resolution. *Psychological Review, 101*, 676–703.

Marie, P. (1906). Revision de la question de l'aphasie: La troisieme convolution frontale gauche ne joue aucun role speciale dans la fonction du langage. *Semaine Medicale (Paris), 21*, 241–247.

Marshall, J., Pring, T., Chiat, S., & Robson, J. (1996). Calling a salad a federation: An investigation of semantic jargon. Part I—Nouns. *Journal of Neurolinguistics*, 9, 237–250.

Martin, A., Wiggs, C. L., Ungerleider, L. G., & Haxby, J. V. (1996). Neural correlates of category-specific knowledge. *Nature, 379*, 649–652.

Martin, N., Gagnon, D. A., Schwartz, M. F. , Dell, G. S., & Saffran, E. M. (1997). Phonological facilitation of semantic errors in normal and aphasic speakers. *Language and Cognitive Processes, 11*, 257–282.

Martin, N., Weisberg, R., & Saffran, E. M. (1989). Variables influencing the occurrence of naming errors: Implications for models of lexical retrieval. *Journal of Memory and Language, 28*, 462–485.

Mauner, G., Fromkin, V. A., & Cornell, T. L. (1993). Comprehension and acceptability judgments in agrammatism: Disruptions in the syntax of referential dependency. *Brain and Language, 45*, 340–370.

Maunsell, J. H. B., & Newsome, W. T. (1987). Visual processing in monkey extrastriate cortex. *Annual Review of Neuroscience, 10*, 363–401.

McCarthy, R., & Warrington, E. K. (1988). Evidence for modality-specific meaning systems in the brain. *Nature, 334*, 428–430.

McClelland, J., St. John, M., & Taraban, R. (1989). Sentence comprehension: A parallel districuted processing approach. *Language and Cognitive Processes, 4*, 287–336.

Miceli, G., Mazzucchi, A., Menn, L., & Goodglass, H. (1983). Contrasting cases of Italian agrammatic aphasics without comprehension disorder. *Brain and Language, 19*, 56–97.

Miceli, G., Silveri, M. C., Nocentini, U., & Caramazza, A. (1988). Patterns of dissociation in comprehension and production of nouns and verbs. *Aphasiology, 2*, 351–358.

Miozzo, M., & Caramazza, A. (1997). On knowing the auxiliary of a verb that cannot be named: Evidence for the independence of grammatical and phonological aspects of lexical knowledge. *Journal of Cognitive Neuroscience,* 9, 160–166.

Miyake, A., Carpenter, P. A., & Just, M. A. (1994). A capacity approach to syntactic comprehension disorders: Making normal adults perform like aphasic patients. *Cognitive Neuropsychology, 11*, 671–717.

Mohr, J. P., Pessin, M. S., Finkelstein, S., Funkenstein, H. H., Duncan, G.W., & Davis, K. R. (1978). Broca's aphasia: Pathological and clinical. *Neurology, 28*, 311–324.

Paivio, A. (1991). Dual coding theory: Retrospect and current status. *Canadian Journal of Psychology, 45*, 255–287.

Penfield, W., & Roberts, L. (1959). *Speech and brain mechanisms*. Princeton, NJ: Princeton University Press.

Perani, D., Cappa, S. F., Bettinardi, V., Bressi, S., Gorno-Tempini, M., Matarrese, M., & Fazio, F. (1995). Different neural systems for the recognition of animals and man–made tools. *NeuroReport,* 6, 1637–1641.

Sacchett, C., & Humphreys, G. W. (1992). Calling a squirrel a squirrel but a canoe a wigwam: A category-specific deficit for artifactual objects and body parts. *Cognitive Neuropsychology,* 9, 73–86.

Saffran, E. M., Berndt, R. S., & Schwartz, M. F. (1989). A scheme for the quantitative analysis of agrammatic production. *Brain and Language, 37*, 440–479.

Saffran, E. M., Marin, O. S. M., & Yeni–Komshian, G. (1976). An analysis of speech perception in word deafness. *Brain & Language*, 3, 209–228.

Saffran, E. M., & Martin, N. (1997). Effects of structural priming on sentence production in aphasics. *Language and Cognitive Processes, 12*, 877–882.

Saffran, E. M., & Schwartz, M. F. (1994). Of cabbages and things: Semantic memory from a neuropsychological perspective: A tutorial review. In C. Umilta & M. Moscovitch (Eds.), *Attention and performance XV: Conscious and nonconscious information processing* (pp, 507–536). Cambridge, MA: MIT Press.

Saffran, E. M., Schwartz, M. F., & Linebarger, M. (1998). Semantic influences on thematic role assignment: Evidence from normals and aphasics. *Brain and Language, 62*, 255–297.

Saffran, E. M., & Sholl, A. (1999). Clues to the functional and neural architecture of word meaning. In C. M. Brown & P. Hagoort (Eds.), *The neurocognition of language* (pp. 241–272). Oxford: Oxford University Press.

Sartori, G., Job, R., & Coltheart, M. (1993). The organization of object knowledge: Evidence from neuropsychology. In D. E. Meyer & S. Kornblum (Eds.), *Attention and performance XIV* (pp. 451–466). Cambridge, MA: MIT Press.
Schriefers, H., Meyer, A. S., & Levelt, W. J. M. (1990). Exploring the time–course of lexical access in production: Picture-word interference studies. *Journal of Memory and Language, 29,* 86–102.
Schuell, H., Jenkins, J. J., & Carroll, J. M. (1962). Factor analysis of the Minnesota Test for differential diagnosis of aphasia. *Journal of Speech and Hearing Research, 5,* 439–369.
Schwartz, M. F., Linebarger, M., Saffran, E. M., & Pate, D. S. (1987). Syntactic transparency and sentence interpretation in aphasia. *Language and Cognitive Processes, 2,* 85–113.
Schwartz, M. F., Marin, O. S. M., & Saffran, E. M. (1979). Dissociation of language function in dementia: A case study. *Brain and Language, 7,* 277–306.
Schwartz, M. F., Saffran, E. M., Bloch, D. E., & Dell, G. S. (1994). Disordered speech production in aphasic and normal speakers. *Brain and Language, 47,* 52–88.
Shallice, T. (1988). *From neuropsychology to mental structure.* Cambridge: Cambridge University Press.
Shallice, T., & Vallar, G. (1990). The impairment of auditory-verbal short-term storage. In G. Vallar & T. Shallice (Eds.), *Neuropsychological impairments of short–term memory* (pp. 11–53). Cambridge, MA: Cambridge University Press.
Silveri, M. C., & Gainotti, G. (1988). Interaction between vision and language in category-specific semantic impairment. *Cognitive Neuropsychology, 5,* 677–709.
Sirigu, A., Duhamel, & Poncet, M. (1991). The role os sensorimotor experience in object recognition: A case of multimodal agnosia. *Brain, 114,* (pp. 2555–2573).
Smith, E. E., Jonides, J., Koeppe, R. A., Awh, E., Schumache, E. H., & Minoshima, S. (1995). Spatial vs. object working memory: PET investigations. *Journal of Cognitive Neuroscience, 7,* 337–356.
Snowden, J. S., Goulding, P. J., & Neary, D. (1989). Semantic dementia: A form of circumscribed cerebral atrophy. *Behavioural Neurology, 2,* 167–182.
Srinivas, K., Breedin, S. D., Coslett, H. B., & Saffran, E. M. (1997). Intact perceptual priming in a patient with damage to the anterior inferior temporal lobes. *Journal of Cognitive Neuroscience, 9,* 490–511.
Stromswold, K., Caplan, D., Alpert, N., & Rauch, S. (1996). Localization of syntactic comprehension by positron emission tomography. *Brain and Language, 52,* 452–473.
Tyler, L. K. (1992). *Spoken language comprehension: An experimental approach to disordered and normal processing.* Cambridge, MA: MIT Press.
Wada, J. (1949). A new method of identifying the dominant hemisphere for language: Intra-carotid sodium amytal injection in man. *Medical Biology, 14,* 221–222.
Warrington, E. K. (1975). The selective impairment of semantic memory. *Quarterly Journal of Experimental Psychology,* 27, 635–657.
Warrington, E. K., & McCarthy, R. A. (1983). Category-specific access dysphasia. *Brain, 106,* 859–878.
Warrington, E. K., & McCarthy, R. A. (1987). Categories of knowledge: Further fractionation and an attempted integration. *Brain, 100,* 1273–1296.
Warrington, E. K., & Shallice, T. (1984). Category-specific semantic impairments. *Brain, 107,* 829–853.
Wernicke, C. (1974). The aphasic symptom complex: A psychological study on a neurological basis. In R. S. Cohen & M. W. Wartofsky (Eds.), *Boston studies in the philosophy of science, Vol. 4.* Boston: Reidel. (Original work published 1974)

11

The Neurocognitive Bases of Developmental Reading Disorders

Marie T. Banich
Department of Psychology, University of Colorado at Boulder

Paige E. Scalf
Department of Psychology, University of Illinois at Urbana-Champaign

The goal of this chapter is to provide an overview of the neurocognitive bases of *developmental dyslexia*, a developmental reading disorder. The traditional definition of developmental dyslexia assumed that such individuals had reading skills at a level substantially below age level (e.g., 2 years below) in the face of otherwise normal intelligence, sensory, and language functioning, an environment adequate to support the acquisition of reading skills, and sufficient motivation to acquire reading skills (e.g., Rutter & Yule, 1975). More recently, a number of the assumptions underlying this view have been challenged. For example, it has been suggested that specific problems in reading occur even in the absence of a significant discrepancy between reading skills and overall IQ (e.g., Siegel, 1989, 1998). Furthermore, as discussed later in this chapter, certain aspects of language functioning, such as the ability to identify the individual sounds in words, are seriously compromised in children with specific reading disabilities. At present, the definition of developmental dyslexia is in a state of flux. What appears to be the cardinal symptom however, is an inability to acquire the skills involved in reading.

In an effort to understand developmental dyslexia, it is useful to consider knowledge about the neurocognitive bases of language processing garnered over the past 150 years. Much of this knowledge has been derived from examinations of the pattern of language deficits shown by individuals who have suffered brain damage (see Saffran, chap. 10, this volume). More recently, this knowledge has been augmented by brain imaging techniques that allow us to observe either the electrophysiological (e.g., Kutas & Schmitt, chap. 7, this volume) or metabolic activity (e.g., Zatorre, chap. 8, this volume) of brain regions in neurologically intact individuals during the performance of specific language tasks. Results from such studies indicate that specific aspects of language processing are each supported by distinct brain regions. For example, anterior brain regions have been suggested to play a role in syntactic processing and speech production, whereas posterior regions are implicated in the acoustic analysis of phonological information and interpreting a word's meaning. Reading is no exception to this pattern of regional specificity, as a well-defined region of the left hemisphere, known as the angular gyrus, has been implicated as playing a critical role in the reading process (see Fig. 11.1). Damage to this region produces a specific inability to read despite intact auditory language processing (e.g., Henderson, 1986), whereas engaging in the process of reading leads to increased activation of this region (Bavelier et al., 1997; Horwitz, Rumsey, & Donohue, 1998).

In this chapter, we review three major theoretical viewpoints regarding the neurocognitive bases of developmental reading disorders. One viewpoint suggests that developmental reading disabilities can be considered relatively analogous to reading disorders acquired in adulthood—the brain regions that are dysfunctional in individuals with developmental dyslexia are the same regions that, when damaged in adults, result in an inability to read. This viewpoint posits that developmental dyslexia occurs because the basic neural machinery required to read is defective.

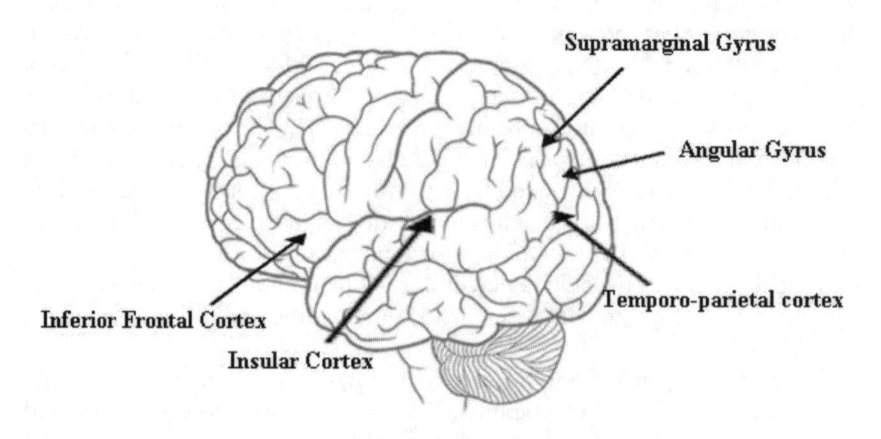

FIG. 11.1. Brain regions involved in reading and language.

Other researchers, however, have argued that models of reading derived from the results of injury to the adult brain cannot be simply imported, unmodified, to explain developmental disorders. They argue that models of adult disorders are inappropriate because adult disorders result from insult to a particular component of an intact language system whereas developmental reading disorders occur within a language system that has never been intact. Rather, these researchers focus on what type of neural disorganization would prevent the acquisition of reading, a skill that is learned readily by most children or adults when some basic instruction is provided.

Many accounts of developmental dyslexia posit that the difficulty in acquiring reading is caused by a deficit in *phonological awareness*—the ability to identify, think about, and manipulate the individual sounds in words. This ability requires the capacity to break a word down into phonemes, the smallest units of language that influence meaning (e.g., /b/ that distinguishes between the word "bat" and "cat," each of which has a different meaning). Because reading relies on linking graphemes (i.e., the smallest units of writing that carry phonemic information, such as "b") to their corresponding phonemes, phonological awareness is critical to reading acquisition.

Although many agree that phonological awareness is lacking in dyslexics, there is disagreement as to exactly why such awareness is lacking. Some researchers claim that phonological awareness relies on language-specific processors, and it is dysfunction of these specific processors themselves that causes difficulty in reading acquisition. However, learning to associate graphemes with phonemes and then interpreting a series of phonemes as a word relies on a variety of perceptual and linguistic functions. Hence, others suggest that disruption of these supporting processes, such as deficits in auditory-temporal or visual processing, causes difficulty in learning phonological awareness (or grapheme-to-phoneme correspondence), which in turn hinders reading acquisition. Still another perspective is provided by those who argue that because reading requires sequential processing, deficits in attentional control, rather than a modality-specific sensory deficit, contribute to dyslexia. Does developmental dyslexia occur because brain systems that provide input critical to reading acquisition are defective, or because the brain systems that specifically support reading are dysfunctional? This is an issue hotly debated in current research on dyslexia.

The final conceptual viewpoint posits that all the component brain regions required for reading are intact, but that there is a "disconnection syndrome" between these regions. From this perspective, even though the component neural machinery for reading is intact, the interconnections between the components are disrupted or defective, leading to reading disability.

In this chapter we explore the evidence for all of these viewpoints in turn. First we examine the degree to which developmental reading disorders are similar to reading disorders acquired in adulthood. Then we examine the degree to which developmental dyslexia results from poor phonological awareness, which could be caused either by (a) disrupted linguistic processing of phonological information, (b) poor perceptual/temporal processing that is a prerequisite for phonological awareness, or (c) disrupted attentional function. Finally, we examine whether dyslexia results from faulty or defective communication between intact brain regions.

A CONTINUITY BETWEEN READING DIFFICULTIES IN CHILDHOOD AND THOSE ACQUIRED IN ADULTHOOD

There is a variety of evidence suggesting that the same brain region that is affected in dyslexia is associated with *alexia,* the specific loss of reading ability (but not spoken language) as a result of brain injury in adulthood. In fact, as far back as 100 years ago, some individuals suggested that developmental dyslexia is caused by a congenital lesion in the angular gyrus (e.g., Hinshelwood, 1896), the same region that, when damaged in adults, leads to an inability to read. Studies of the neuroanatomical structure of the brains of dyslexic individuals indicate there are anatomical anomalies not only in the angular gyrus but in other regions throughout the left hemisphere of the brain in both dyslexic men (Galaburda & Kemper, 1978; Galaburda, Sherman, Rosen, Aboitiz, & Geschwind, 1985) and women (Humphreys, Kaufmann, & Galaburda, 1990). In particular, postmortem studies find that these regions are replete with *ectopias*, which are nests of misplaced neurons that interrupt the laminar organization of neurons in the cortex. Also observed are cortical scars indicative of damage to the brain. The source of such damage is generally unknown. However, in animals such anomalies can be induced if there is insult to the brain specifically during the time period when neurons are migrating from their site of origin to the particular layer of cortex in which they should eventually reside (e.g., Rosen et al., 1992).

Other evidence also suggests a commonality between developmental and acquired reading disorders. The same regions of the brain that are activated during reading in neurologically intact individuals are either not engaged in dyslexics or only engaged ineffectively (e.g., Rumsey et al., 1992, 1997; Shaywitz et al., 1998). Even more importantly, the more the left angular gyrus is activated in normal readers, the better are their reading scores on a variety of single-word reading tests. In contrast, the more this area is activated in dyslexics, the poorer are their reading scores (Rumsey et al., 1999). The positive correlation observed for normal readers suggests that activation of this region aids (or is critical for) good reading performance. The negative correlation in dyslexics suggests that the neural machinery in this region is defective, and the more it is invoked, the less likely it is that reading will be successfully accomplished. Interestingly, in dyslexics, better reading scores were associated with a specific region of the *right* hemisphere. This finding raises the possibility that whatever reading skills are acquired by dyslexic individuals rely on an alternate neural mechanism than that utilized by normal readers.

DYSLEXIA IS CAUSED BY AN INABILITY TO PERFORM PHONOLOGICAL ANALYSIS

The Role of Phonological Analysis in Reading

Reading requires that visual stimuli be analyzed and interpreted; in order for this to occur, however, the individual learning to read must have the ability to break spoken language into its constituent sounds. As mentioned earlier, a critical component of reading acquisition is phonological awareness, which is the ability to break a word down into phonemes, the smallest units of language that influence meaning. This ability involves the capacity to segment, insert, or delete information at the phonemic level. The ability to decode information phonologically in reading can be assessed in various ways. One method is to determine an individual's ability to restructure words based on a rule-governed manipulation of phonemes. One task of this type is the children's game of Pig Latin, in which the initial consonant or consonant cluster is moved to the end of the word and the "ay" sound is appended to that (e.g., "pig" becomes "igpay"). Another way to examine phonological awareness is to assess the ability to rhyme or to read pronounceable nonwords. To understand that a non-word such as "blean" rhymes with "frean", requires the ability to break words into parts. One must realize that /bl/ and /fr/ sound different but that the /ean/ portions of the words are identical.

Gaining access to the meaning of words by "sounding out" the word and then linking that to knowledge about what the sound means (e.g., /c/ /a/ /t/ = "cat" = the family pet that likes to chase mice) is referred to as the *phonological route* to meaning. Such a route must be used for words that are new and unknown in print, or for pseudowords (also called nonwords), such as "glome" that could be words in a given language because they follow the rules of orthography and phonology, but are not. Learning to read is critically dependent on the phonological route to reading, at least for languages that are alphabetic, such as English, because it allows new words encountered in print to be linked via sound to words already known orally.

A Disruption of Phonological Awareness in Dyslexia

Numerous studies across many different languages indicate that phonological awareness is an important predictor of success in reading and spelling (e.g., Cossu, Shankweiler, Liberman, Katz, & Tola, 1988; Lundberg, Wall, & Olofsson, 1980; Wagner, Torgensen, & Rashotte, 1994) and may be a prerequisite for learning to read (e.g., Liberman, Shankweiler, Fisher, & Carter, 1974). The inability to adequately process phonemes appears to be a core deficit in dyslexia (Pennington, Lefly, Van Orden, Bookman, & Smith, 1987). Adult dyslexics retain such a deficit (Pennington, Van Orden, Smith, Green, & Haith, 1990) and remain deficient in this skill relative to younger normal readers at a similar reading ability (Bruck, 1992).

However, the phonological route is not the only means via which access to word meaning can be gained from the written word. An alternative is the *direct route*, so-called because access to meaning is derived directly from the printed word. Such a route must be used for *irregular words* (sometimes referred to as *exception words*), which are those that cannot be understood by "sounding out" because they do not follow the regular phoneme-to-grapheme conversion rules. English is one language in which a sizable proportion of words must rely on this route. For example, one can only learn that "colonel" refers to a high-ranking military officer by using the direct route. If one were to rely on using grapheme-to-phoneme conversion rules in sounding out the word "colonel," it would be pronounced "cullonell," which would not provide access to the meaning of the word.

The brain regions activated during reading vary depending on whether a reading task stresses segmenting words into their constituent sounds (i.e., a task that would emphasize the phonological route) or deriving meaning from them (i.e., a task that would emphasize the direct route). In particular, regions near the angular gyrus are activated for reading tasks that are likely to rely on the direct route, whereas other regions such as temporo-parietal cortex, are more activated when phonology is emphasized (Price, Moore, Humphreys, & Wise, 1997). Those regions that are important for phonological processing are the ones that appear to show atypical activation in dyslexics (e.g., Georgiewa et al., 1999).

Some scientists have argued that the dichotomy between the phonological and direct routes may be a false one. For example, there is a high correlation (between .66 and .90) between the ability to read nonwords and irregular words both in normal (Gough & Walsh, 1991) and dyslexic readers (Rack, Snowling, & Olson, 1992). Such findings suggest a common unitary mechanism underlying access to meaning for both these types of words (see Plaut, chap. 6, this volume, for a connectionist model that suggests such a unitary mechanism).

Information regarding the genetic bases of dyslexia can be informative when trying to determine whether a dual-route or unitary model of reading is more plausible. It has been known for quite some time that dyslexic individuals often have similarly affected family members (e.g., Hallgren, 1950). To examine the genetic contribution to reading disability, the degree of concordance for dyslexia between monozygotic twins, who share the same genes, is compared to that of dizygotic twins, who share only half their genes. A significantly higher concordance rate for monozygotic than dizygotic twins suggests a significant genetic contribution. Such twin studies suggest a strong genetic component to deficits in phonological awareness (Olson, Wise, Conners, Rack, & Fulker, 1989), consistent with the idea that phonological processing deficits make a significant contribution to dyslexia. However, they also suggest that the ability to decode the orthography (i.e., visual form) of language (Olson, Forsberg, & Wise, 1994) has a strong genetic component, which suggests that the direct route to reading may also be affected in dyslexia. Further study indicated that although both of these genetic factors contribute separately to reading disability, there is also a common shared component (Olson, Datta, Gayan, & DeFries, 1999). Overall, genetic studies suggest that there may be a common mechanism for reading both regular and exception words, as posited by the single-route model, but also, at the same time, that there may be distinct mechanisms, as suggested by proponents of the dual-route model (e.g., Gayan & Olson, 2001).

It should also be noted that these genetic models suggest some commonality between regular reading and the disrupted reading of dyslexia. Evidence from studies examining the genetic bases of dyslexia suggests that the degree of genetic contribution to reading skills and the genetic mechanisms by which these are conveyed are similar in normal and abnormal readers. Given that writing systems are a relatively new invention in human history, having first appeared during the past 5000 years, it is highly unlikely that enough time has passed in human history to allow for a high degree of selection for individuals with regard to reading skills, especially considering that even today a large portion of the world's population is illiterate. Rather, there appear to be a number of sites on different genes that contribute to the variation across humans in the skills that are important for reading, and these genes are similar for normal and dyslexic readers. Hence dyslexics inherit genetic material that is unfavorable to the acquisition of reading and/or are in an environment unfavorable to acquiring reading, leading them to have much poorer than average acquisition of language (see Pennington, 1999, for an excellent discussion of these points).

Although there is large agreement that phonological processing is disrupted in dyslexia, there is much less agreement about the underlying cause of such impairment. Evidence that the difficulties are indeed language-specific impairment would be provided if it could be demonstrated that processing deficits do not extend to nonlinguistic information (see e.g., Bishop, Carlyon, Deeks, & Bishop, 1999). Because the disruption of language abilities in adults can be separate from other cognitive abilities (see Saffran, chap. 10, this volume), it is often assumed that such modularity occurs in the developing brain as well. However, others have questioned whether the phonological processing deficits are indeed language specific and suggested alternatively that they might reflect underlying problems in perceptual processing critical for phonological processing. It is to these issues that we now turn our attention.

Perceptual/Temporal Processing Deficits Preclude the Acquisition of Phonological Awareness

Rather than deficits in phonological awareness resulting from a specific difficulty within the domain of language processing, an alternate possibility is that phonological awareness cannot develop because the requisite perceptual mechanisms for acquiring such a skill are disrupted. The two types of perceptual processing most often cited as being potential problems in dyslexia are disruptions in the auditory-temporal processing, and disruptions in visual processing. Interest in exploring how these two domains of perceptual skill might contribute to dyslexia has been motivated, in part, by the heterogeneity of expression of dyslexia. For example, one classification system distinguishes between dyslexics who are dysphonetic, or impaired at phonological processing, those who are dyseidetic, or show visual impairments, and those who are dysphonoeidetic, or impaired both at phonological processing and visual processing (Boder, 1973).

Difficulties in Auditory/Temporal Processing. One group of dyslexics show a major deficit in identifying the phonemes of words, whether spoken or written. These children routinely mispronounce common words, such as pronouncing the word "elbow" as "oboe" and shoulder as "soldier." They also frequently confuse closely related semantic terms, despite their very different phonemic contents (Fawcett, 1994). One possible cause of their difficulty with phoneme identification could be impairments in temporal processing, especially for auditory information (see Farmer & Klein, 1995, and Studdert-Kennedy & Mody, 1995, for differing viewpoints on this issue). It has been suggested that the left hemisphere is specialized for language, not because it is specialized for language per se, but because language requires the fine temporal analysis of auditory information (e.g., Schwartz & Tallal, 1980). For example, the difference in the timing of the critical acoustic parameter that differentiates between a /ba/ and a /pa/ is a mere 40 msec. The ability to parse language into the constituent sounds appears to be a prerequisite for reading in that reading requires one to learn to associate a particular graphic form (e.g., "b") with a particular sound (e.g., /ba/). If one cannot perceptually discriminate between the acoustic parameters of different linguistic sounds, the acquisition of language will be adversely affected (e.g., Tallal et al., 1996). Of all language processing tasks, reading would be especially vulnerable because the segmentation process is critical to making a connection between a grapheme and a phoneme. Furthermore, because other aspects of auditory perception do not rely on such fine temporal discrimination, deficits in those other tasks will be relatively minor or nonexistent. For example, many nonverbal auditory stimuli, such as a train whistle, have steady-state components, meaning that the information critical for discriminating between distinct sounds stays fairly constant and does not rely on rapid acoustic transitions.

As discussed by Wright, Bowen, and Zecker (2000), a variety of evidence suggests that individuals with reading impairment have difficulty with a variety of aspects of auditory processing. For example, dyslexics have trouble determining the timing of pairs of tones when embedded in other tones (e.g., Kujala et al., 2000) and in processing the order of sequential sounds (e.g., Helenius, Uutela, & Hari, 1999). They exhibit difficulty in being able to perceive fluctuation in the frequency (pitch) of sounds (e.g., Witton et al., 1998) and cannot detect tones embedded within noise (McAnally & Stein, 1996).

Some interesting recent evidence suggests that some of these problems may exist at birth, implying that being born with less than optimal neural machinery for distinguishing between similar sounds may later influence the ability to acquire reading. Electrophysiological responses of newborn infants to simple speech sounds such as /gi/ and /bi/ can predict their reading ability 8 years later (Molfese, 2000). For example, the latency of the N1 ERP component recorded over frontal regions of the left hemisphere in infancy occurs earlier in those infants who subsequently became normal readers than for those who became poor or dyslexic readers. Furthermore, the amplitude of the N1 in these latter two groups was reduced relative to children who went on to become normal readers. As discussed by Kutas and Schmitt (chap. 7, this volume), the N1 is associated with sensory characteristics of a stimulus, such as its intensity, duration, and spectral characteristics. Such findings suggest that both the degree to which and the speed with which certain brain regions respond to speech signals in dyslexic children are differentially affected by the time of birth. These findings are consistent with the reports, discussed earlier, of neuroanatomical abnormalities in the brains of dyslexics that occur prenatally. Hence much evidence points to the fact that the neural substrate required for reading is never fully functional in the dyslexic brain. Problems, however, do not become obvious until later, at the age at which reading would be expected to be acquired.

Another way in which temporal processing deficits might be linked to dyslexia is through motor production. At least some dyslexics have difficulty with fine motor sequencing of the fingers or mouth (e.g., Wolff, Michel, Ovrut, & Drake, 1990). It has been proposed that speech sounds are linked to the articulatory motor commands for producing such sounds, and that this linkage is critical to speech perception (see Liberman & Whalen, 2000). To the degree that dyslexic individuals have a poor ability to produce a target speech sound, they cannot easily integrate what they do with the auditory feedback they receive. The ability to have good, stable phonological representations is thereby compromised (Heilman, Voeller, & Alexander, 1996). This viewpoint, like the others discussed just before it, suggests that phonological representations are disrupted in dyslexia because of damage to a neural system that is peripheral to language but nonetheless influences it.

Difficulties in Visual Processing. Another body of research suggests that developmental dyslexia results from a different perceptual deficit, one that is visual in nature rather than acoustic and temporal. To understand the nature of these visual processing problems, it is helpful to know a little about how the brain segregates different types of visual information. In the mammalian brain, processing of visual information is divided into two main processing streams: the parvocellular system and the magnocellular system. A detailed description of these systems is beyond the scope of the present chapter (see Livingstone & Hubel, 1988, for a brief overview). Broadly speaking, the parvocellular system, which originates mainly from the cones in the retina of the eye, is a system that is important for form discrimination, relatively sensitive to color and relatively insensitive to quick changes in the level of light that is critical for detecting visual motion. The parvocellular system excels at resolving fine visual details. In contrast, the magnocellular system, which processes information collected primarily by the rods in the retina, is insensitive to color and can resolve only gross visual detail. It is, however, extremely sensitive to rapid changes in brightness and contrast. The magnocellular system is therefore also responsible for tracking the temporal order of visual stimuli. During fluent reading, the eyes move in a series of fixations across the text. Reading therefore requires processing from both of these systems; the parvocellular system resolves the fine visual detail of the text, whereas the magnocellular system is necessary to integrate and sequence the visual detail acquired across fixations.

Currently, there is much debate over the suggestion that dyslexic individuals have a specific disruption of processing in the magnocullear system (e.g., Stein, Talcott, & Walsh, 2000; Stein & Walsh, 1997), whereas functioning of the parvocellular system performance, as measured by color and fine-form discrimination tasks, is relatively intact (e.g., Chase & Jenner, 1993; Lovegrove, 1994). An extensive overview of the evidence on this issue derived from psychophysical, neuropsychological, and functional imaging studies is beyond the scope of this chapter, so only some illustrative examples are provided.

Although certain sources of data support the existence of magnocellular processing impairments in dyslexic individuals, the scope of the deficits, the degree to which these impairments can explain reading problems in dyslexia, and the proportion of dyslexics who exhibit such impairments are still a matter of debate. Despite a body of research that finds evidence for dysfunction of the magnocellular system in dyslexics, there is also a large body of work that fails to demonstrate such dysfunction (for a review, see Skottun, 2000). Discrepancies may arise across studies because the magnocellular system is often discussed throughout this literature as a homogeneous neural pathway, although it too is comprised of multiple subsystems. Therefore, the absence of evidence of a deficit in any one given task does not indicate an intact magnocellular system, as a limited dysfunction in the magnocellular system will not necessarily affect every task that requires magnocellular processing. Many results cited as inconsistent with a magnocellular deficit (e.g., Skottun, 2000) might be construed as consistent with a hypothesis that posits a limited deficit in the magnocellular system that would only become apparent when the demands placed on the magnocellular system are very high (e.g., Stein, Talcott, & Walsh, 2000). We suggest that as the magnocellular subsystems and their functions become better understood, investigations examining possible deficits in dyslexic individuals will become more focused, and subsequently the conclusions drawn from these investigations will then become more consistent.

Deficits in magnocellular processing have been proposed to influence reading in three major ways. First, it has been suggested that poor transmission of information about the timing of visual events or the inability to integrate visual events that occur within a given time frame as a result of a defective magnocellular system could cause impairments in the ability to determine the order in which visual stimuli are perceived. Second, it has been suggested that in normal reading, activation of the magnocellular system inhibits processing of the parvocellular system at critical time points to reduce visual confusion, but that this mechanism fails in dyslexic readers (Lovegrove, 1994). Although this hypothesis has been largely abandoned (Stein & Walsh, 1997; Richardson, Fowler, & Stein, 2000), new research (Castet & Masson, 2000) suggests that it should be revisited. Third, a compromised magnocellular system could cause failures in eye movement control itself, confusing the process of visual perception. We discuss each of these possibilities in detail and explain more specifically how these deficits might impair reading.

The first proposal is that dysfunction of the magnocellular system in dyslexics leads to difficulty with the temporal integration of visual events. Evidence of such dysfunction comes from a variety of arenas. Dyslexic individuals have different sensitivity to visual contrast as a function of flicker rate than do normal controls (Martin & Lovegrove, 1987, 1988). The pattern of performance exhibited by dyslexics is indicative of high visual persistence within the magnocellular system. Neurons within that system continue responding to a visual stimulus for an unusually long time. Because neurons continue responding to an initial stimulus after it is no longer physically present, they are unable to respond to the onset of a second stimulus, leaving the viewer unaware that anything in the visual environment has changed. Dyslexics also exhibit disrupted perception of motion (Slaghuis & Ryan, 1999). Because the perception of motion relies critically on perceiving changes in location with time, this impairment also suggests difficulty in the temporal integration of visual information.

The neuroanatomical loci of these effects are not yet clear. Some evidence suggests that the problem arises relatively early on in the magnoceullar system, in particular in the lateral geniculate nucleus (LGN) of the thalamus, a subcortical structure that is a relay point for neural information between the retina and the cortex. One of the primary responsibilities of the LGN is to perform an initial "sorting" of raw visual information as it travels from the retina to the brain. The LGN has multiple cell layers, and postmortem examination of the brains of dyslexic individuals indicates that those layers of the LGN responsible for organizing information from cells of the magnocellular system are thinner, have fewer cell bodies, and are less organized than those of normal controls (Galaburda et al., 1985; Livingstone, Rosen, Drislane, & Galaburda, 1991). Another portion of the magnocellular system that appears to be dysfunctional in dyslexics is area V5/MT (located in the posterior parietal cortex), which is responsible for processing the movement of visual objects. When making judgments about group motion or relative stimulus velocity, dyslexic individuals show poorer performance and reduced activation in area V5/MT relative to that shown by neurologically-intact individuals (Demb, Boynton, Best, & Heeger, 1998; Eden, 1996).

Although much of the foregoing evidence suggests that visual information cannot be temporally integrated in a rapid manner, there is also evidence that the magnocellular system can become overwhelmed by too much visual information at one time. Motion detection is especially impaired in dyslexics when there were a large number of changes that needed to be integrated in order to perceive that motion (Raymond & Sorenson, 1998). The speed with which stimuli are presented, however, does not affect dyslexics' perception of motion. This evidence suggests that although the magnocellular system of dyslexics can temporally integrate information at the proper speed, it cannot properly integrate multiple visual events.

Regardless of whether the magnocellular system is unable to correctly represent the timing of changes in information contained across different fixations, or simply cannot integrate a number of fixations into a coherent series of events, deficits in reading could result. In both cases, reading would be adversely affected by causing an incorrect coding of the order in which visual information is acquired. Such insufficiencies in the magnocellular system would both confuse the order in which stimuli were viewed (making grapheme-to-phoneme correspondences difficult to resolve) and cause general visual confusion (Slaghuis & Ryan, 1999).

The second way in which a disrupted magnocellular system has been proposed to influence reading is by interfering with the processing of the parvocellular system. Masking paradigms (in which the presentation of one stimulus makes the perception of another more difficult) have been utilized to examine whether the magnocellular system inhibits parvocellular processing. These studies have suggested that the magnocellular system is less able to inhibit processing in the parvocellular system in dyslexics than in normal readers (Breitmeyer & Ganz, 1976; Williams, Molinet, & LeCluyse, 1989). One hypothesis suggests that the activity within the magnocellular system inhibits the processing of information gathered by the parvocellular system during saccades—the eye movements that occur during normal reading. This hypothesis proposes that dyslexics have slow rates of information transmission within the magnocellular system, and hence fail to suppress parvocellular information at critical times during saccades (Lovegrove, 1994). Such a problem would in turn create persistence of visual information in the parvocellular system that would almost certainly create visual confusion, making reading difficult. This hypothesis has been discarded, however, due to the conclusion that the magnocellular system itself is suppressed during saccades (Stein & Walsh, 1997; Stein et al., 2000). Very recent evidence, however, indicates that the magnocellular system is in fact active during eye movements (Castet & Masson, 2000), making this issue one that deserves reinvestigation.

A third way in which magnocellular dysfunction could hinder reading acquisition is by impairing the coordination and control of eye movements (Stein, 1994). Although many studies have indicated that dyslexics show abnormal eye movements during reading, most of these measurements are considered reflective of the difficulty dyslexics have in reading rather than a cause of the difficulty (for a review, see Rayner, 1999). There are aspects of eye movement control, however, that could result from compromised processing of magnocellular information. One of these is binocular vergence control, which is the ability of the two eyes to remain fixated at a single location in space and bind the information collected in that instant as a single object. When the visual items being focused are in close range, as they are in reading, information about the same aspect of a visual stimulus can appear at widely different points on the two retinas, which means that very different information is gathered by the two eyes (Stein, 1994). There is disagreement as to whether dyslexic children do indeed exhibit unstable binocular fixation compared to age-matched and reading-matched controls (Fowler & Stein, 1980; Stein, Riddel, & Fowler, 1986, 1987, 1988) or not (e.g., Ygge, Lennerstrand, Rydberg, Wijecoon, & Pettersson, 1993). Reading problems caused by binocular instability should theoretically be alleviated when a dyslexic child reads monocularly, because gathering information from a single eye should eliminate competition between the visual information received from the different eyes. In fact, there are reports that nonword reading errors by dyslexic children are reduced when they read with one eye occluded (Cornelissen, Bradley, Fowler, & Stein, 1992).

Difficulties in Attentional Functioning. Dysfunction in attentional regulation is another possible contribution to reading problems in dyslexic children. Letter and word identification require not only that an individual correctly receive sensory information about the visual stimulus, but also that the individual be able to reconstruct this information into a meaningful percept. Colors, line orientation, and the spatial position of visual objects all get processed in distinct portions of the visual system. Thus, when the image of a red chair falls on the retina, one channel codes that the color red is located somewhere in the visual field, another channel codes the orientation of the lines that make up the chair, and yet another channel codes the spatial position of the chair's parts. Directing visual attention to the chair allows those distinct visual elements to be bound together and reconstructed into a single percept of a red chair (Triesman & Gelade, 1980). Some theories (e.g., Vidyasagar, 1999; Vidyasagar & Pammer, 1999) suggest that dyslexics have an attentional deficit that prevents them from correctly linking together the distinct aspects of visual stimuli.

Such deficits in dyslexic children in binding together the component parts of visual information can be directly demonstrated by asking them to locate a visual target of a specific shape and color amongst a number of similar items. Searching for such targets (e.g., a blue circle), given that other items either share the target's shape or its color (e.g., amongst blue triangles and red circles), requires visual features to be conjoined into a single percept. Dyslexic children require more search time to locate the target than do normal readers (Vidyasagar & Pammer, 1999). Such an attentional deficit could affect reading because the perception of letters requires the conjoining of simple visual attributes, such as horizontal, diagonal, and curved lines. Moreover, such a deficit might manifest itself most obviously in reading, because reading requires the rapid conjunction of much visual information.

Attentional deficits in dyslexics might also influence reading because the conjoining of visual features by attention is not instantaneous. In order for features to be combined into a coherent percept, the spotlight of attention must remain on these features until the conjunction is complete. A key feature of the concept of attention as a spotlight is that the spotlight can be independent of where the eyes are fixated (e.g., Hoffman & Subramaniam, 1995). Dyslexic children appear to be slow at making covert shifts of attention, or shifts of attention without corresponding eye movement (Facoetti, Paganoni, Turatto, Marzola, & Mascetti, 2000). These difficulties may be due, in part, to decreased sensitivity to events that should be detected by the magnocellular system. They are also less able to sustain the focus of attention at a given location than are their age-matched counterparts. Such deficits could impair reading in two ways. First, slow shifting of attention could impair the coordination and control of eye movements because the eyes tend to follow the attentional spotlight. Alternatively, the attentional spotlight of a dyslexic child may not remain on a group of letters long enough for them to be identified. Measurements of eye movements in dyslexic college students indicate that dyslexics show more variability in the time required to generate an eye movement toward a target, and show less control over whether or not an eye movement is initiated (Biscaldi, Gezeck, & Stuhr, 1998). Both of these anomalies would be expected if attentional shifting processes were disturbed in dyslexic individuals.

There are also some hints that dyslexic children may exhibit deficits in visuospatial attention. Some reports suggest that dyslexic children manifest signs of "left-sided" neglect in that they tend to ignore information on the left side of space on a variety of tests designed to measure visual attention (Stein, 1994) and are less likely to attend to objects on the left side of space than are normal readers (Eden, Stein, & Wood, 1993). Typically, this phenomenon is observed in adults who have sustained damage to the right posterior parietal cortex. Although none of these neglect symptoms point directly to a specific reading disorder, they do support the idea that dyslexic individuals may have a compromised attentional system.

All the attentional deficits in dyslexics discussed so far are those related to difficulties specifically in the control of visual attention. Yet there is other evidence that attentional deficits in dyslexia may be more extensive. It has been found that dyslexia and attentional deficit disorder have a significant rate of comorbidity, meaning that they co-occur quite frequently (Willcutt, Pennington, & DeFries, 2000). It is useful to consider whether some of these attentional problems might account for the deficits observed on tests of psychophysical function. If there are short lapses of attention, this might be more likely to affect visual systems that require faster integration of information over time, as is the case for the magnocellular system, than those that require less precise temporal integration, as is the case for the parvocellular system. At present, more research is needed to more clearly delineate the degree and type of attentional problems that might compromise the ability to acquire the skill of reading.

DYSLEXIA IS CAUSED BY A DISCONNECTION SYNDROME

The last theory regarding the cause of dyslexia that we consider in this chapter is the one suggesting that dyslexia results from a disconnection between areas that are critical to the reading process, even though the regions themselves are intact. One variant of this type of theory suggests that dyslexia results from an inability to adequately transfer information between the cerebral hemispheres. The idea that dyslexia is caused by a disruption in processing between the hemsipheres is not new. Back in the 1930s, Orton suggested that dyslexia resulted because the left hemisphere did not adequately dominate the right (Orton, 1937). A more recent variant proposed that dyslexia resulted from a lack of integration between processing of graphical information in the right hemisphere and phonological information in the left hemisphere (e.g., Bakker, 1973). It was suggested that when learning to read, children must rely on the right hemisphere to do the type of visual analysis that would enable differentiation between similar-looking letters (e.g., b and d). Such an idea is consistent with reports that the right hemisphere is generally superior at tasks that require visuospatial processing (e.g., Banich & Heller, 1998) and is important for the initial stages of letter processing (e.g., Hellige & Webster, 1979; Petersen, Fox, Synder, & Raichle, 1990). The role of the left hemisphere in phonological processing is a well-established fact; one of the most striking asymmetries of the brain is that the left hemisphere can process phonological information whereas the right hemisphere cannot (e.g., Raymond & Zaidel, 1991; Zaidel, 1978).

Dyslexia would occur if the outputs of processing of graphical information performed by the right hemisphere could not be transferred to or integrated with phonological processing performed by the left hemisphere.

Given this hypothesis, numerous researchers have examined whether the corpus callosum, the main nerve fiber tract that allows information between the cerebral hemispheres to be integrated, exhibits either atypical structure or atypical function in dyslexics. Those examining morphology have obtained quite divergent results. Some studies have found that portions of the corpus callosum in dyslexics are smaller than in normal individuals (Duara et al., 1991), whereas different studies have found that other portions are relatively larger (Rumsey et al., 1996). Still other studies have found no differences between the corpus callosa of neurologically intact and dyslexic individuals (Larsen, Hoeien, & Oedegaard, 1992).

There may be a variety of reasons for this discrepancy across studies. First, as reviewed by Beaton (1997), there is evidence that gender and handedness are related to the morphology of the corpus callosum. Hence, unless normal readers and dyslexics are closely matched on these variables, spurious differences between the groups may be observed. Second, there are various methods for measuring the size of the corpus callosum, and in particular for parceling it into different regions. Variability in methods across studies may also account for some of the discrepancies.

Because there are discrepancies across studies with regard to the typicality or atypicality of callosal morphology in dyslexics, more convincing evidence that the corpus callosum is related to dyslexia would be provided by data indicating that the morphology of the corpus callosum has a significant relationship to reading ability. In fact, a number of authors have reported such a relationship. Hynd et al. (1995) observed a moderate correlation between reading achievement with the size of the very anterior portion of the callosum, the genu, and with the very posterior portion, the splenium. Robichon and Habib (1998) found that the overall size of the midsection of the corpus callosum (in particular the isthmus) was larger in dyslexics than normal readers. More importantly, however, the size of the anterior and posterior regions of the isthmus correlated with the phonological processing abilities of dyslexics. As discussed earlier in this chapter, phonological processing is the linguistic process conceived as critically disrupted in dyslexia.

Because it is difficult to make inferences about neural function based solely on neuroanatomy, it is important to have complimentary data that directly examine the degree to which the corpus callosum is capable of transferring information between the hemispheres. Data from such behavioral paradigms are consistent with the results of neuroanatomical investigations in pointing to disrupted interaction between the hemispheres in dyslexic individuals. For example, there are numerous reports that compared to normal readers, dyslexics have poorer bimanual coordination (e.g., Gladstone, Best, & Davidson, 1989;

Wolff, Cohen, & Drake, 1984). This finding is of import because research with split-brain patients has shown that an intact corpus callosum is critical for bimanual coordination, especially when hand movements are asynchronous (e.g., Prielowski, 1972). Dyslexics have also been shown to be impaired relative to normal readers when performing a finger localization task that requires interhemispheric cooperation for tactile–motor integration (Moore, Brown, Markee, Theberge, & Zvi, 1996).

One might question whether deficits in motor integration between the hemispheres would directly impact reading. However, other researchers have demonstrated a more specific relationship between interhemispheric functioning and reading ability. Poor rhyming ability in both dyslexics and nondyslexics has been associated with poorer performance on trials that require callosal transfer of information about the spatial localization of information (Moore et al., 1996). Interestingly, the two studies that explicitly examined the transfer between the hemispheres of visual information related to letters have not found any specific problem in dyslexics compared to normal readers (Giraud & Habib, 1999; Markee, Brown, Moore, & Theberge, 1996). Although it may seem unusual that integration between the hemispheres of motor but not letter-related information is compromised in dyslexia, it must be remembered that different types of information are transferred across different sections of the corpus callosum. Recent evidence suggests that transfer of word information occurs via a very specific portion of the callosum, the ventroposterior end of the splenium (Funnell, Corballis, & Gazzaniga, 2000; Suzuki et al., 1998). Hence, dyslexia may only affect certain portions of the callosum and not others, accounting for the seemingly disparate results.

Although the foregoing studies mainly examined how *well* information can be transferred between the hemispheres, the integrity of the corpus callosum can also be measured by determining how *quickly* information can be transferred between the hemispheres. Using electrophysiological measures, Davidson and Saron (1992) estimated the time to transfer simple visual information (i.e., light flashes) between the hemispheres. Compared to normal readers, dyslexic individuals showed faster transfer of information from the right hemisphere to the left than did nonimpaired readers. When information transfer was measured from left to right, however, normal readers showed faster transfer rates than did dyslexic individuals. These measures were moderately correlated with reading skill, such that faster right-to-left hemisphere transfer was associated with poorer performance on a variety of reading measures, whereas left-to-right hemisphere transfer was associated with better performance. In contrast, when similar methods were used to examine the speed of transfer in a letter-matching task, it was found that dyslexics had slower transfer time between the hemispheres than did normal readers (Markee et al., 1996). These seemingly contradictory results may be reconciled by the fact, as discussed earlier, that different types of information are likely to be transferred by distinct sections of the callosum. Hence, the relationship between reading ability and callosal function in dyslexic and normal readers may vary depending on what section of the callosal is required for the reading-related function under investigation.

On the whole, the evidence is suggestive of a disruption of interaction between the hemispheres of dyslexic individuals. Whether these findings indicate that the transfer of graphical information from the right hemisphere to the left is disrupted or that some other aspect of interhemispheric interaction is disturbed remains an open question. There is also another possible reason for the relationship between dyslexia and callosal structure and function. Interaction between the hemispheres plays a role in attentional functioning, especially when tasks are demanding (see Banich, 1998, for a review). Hence, it is also possible that atypical morphology and function of the corpus callosum in dyslexic individuals is indicative of attentional disregulation that interferes with the reading process.

More recently, researchers have been examining whether disconnection between regions within the left hemisphere itself (rather than disconnection between the hemispheres) might account for reading disorders. For example, Paulesu et al., (1996) found that dyslexics exhibited activation in temporo-parietal and inferior frontal areas during language tasks, just as did normal readers. However, during a phonological short-term memory task, dyslexics mainly exhibited temporo-parietal activation, whereas during a rhyming task they primarily exhibited frontal activation. In contrast, normal controls showed activation in both regions during both tasks. Although normal controls activated the entire language network during these phonologically related tasks, dyslexics activated only a subset of those regions. Of most importance, regions of insular cortex (refer back to Fig. 11.1), which connect these two brain areas, were active in normal controls but not dyslexics. These results suggest that there is a lack of functional connectivity in dyslexic adults between brain regions in the left hemisphere that are important for phonological processing.

More recent investigations have provided a possible neuroanatomical basis for the disconnection between these regions of the left hemisphere in dyslexics. This research has relied on a new method, diffusion tensor magnetic resonance imaging, to provide information about the thickness of white-matter tracts. White-matter tracts are essentially bundles of neurons that have a fatty sheath, called *myelin* (which is white in appearance). Myelin allows for fast communication between brain regions that are distant from one another. Although basic brain anatomy is similar in dyslexics and normal readers, a higher degree of myelination in left temporo-parietal regions of the brain is correlated with higher reading scores in both normal and dyslexic readers (Klingberg et al., 2000). Because this correlation exists both for normal and for dyslexic readers, it raises the question of whether such white-matter tracts are a prerequisite for good reading skill, or whether myelination of these regions increases as reading skills increase. Recent evidence has suggested that learning to read may indeed influence myelination of the corpus callosum. Regions of the callosum that connect parietal regions of the two hemispheres are thinner in illiterate than in literate adults (Castro-Caldas et al., 1999).

CONCLUSION

As should be clear from the brief review provided by this chapter, the potential neurocognitive causes of specific reading disability are many. It is quite possible that none of the proposed causes will turn out to be the "definitive" mechanism that explains developmental reading disorders. Rather, as has been discussed for quite some time, dyslexia may turn out to be a constellation of syndromes, as the specific patterns of performance across reading tasks may vary among individuals (e.g., some individuals have more trouble reading nonwords, whereas others have more difficulty reading irregular words). In fact, recent work suggests that the genetic contribution to dyslexia may vary across subtypes of dyslexic individuals (e.g., Castles, Datta, Gayan, & Olson, 1999). Hence, some of the putative neurocognitive causes of dyslexia discussed in this chapter are likely to be more prominent for certain subgroups of dyslexics as compared to others. Because a variety of different genes have been associated with reading disability, there could be a diversity of mechanisms that lead to the same end—reading disability. Each genetic mechanism may have associated with it a unique neural manifestation. Furthermore, although causes of reading disability may be genetic, others may be the result of environmental influences, such as insult during critical stages of brain development. Hence, although much progress has been made, there remain many threads to untangle before we will obtain a clear understanding of how brain anatomy and function are related to dyslexia.

ACKNOWLEDGMENTS

We thank Richard Olson for helpful comments on a prior version of the chapter and helpful discussions on some issues discussed in this chapter.

REFERENCES

Bakker, D. J. (1973). Hemispheric specialization and stages in the learning-to-read process. *Bulletin of the Orton Society, 23,* 15–27.

Banich, M. T. (1998). The missing link: The role of interhemispheric interaction in attentional processing. *Brain & Cognition, 36,* 128–157.

Banich, M. T., & Heller, W. (1998). Evolving perspectives on lateralization of function. *Current Directions in Psychological Science, 7,* 1–2.

Bavelier, D., Corina, D., Jezzard, P., Padmanabhan, S., Clark, V. P., Karni, A., Prinster, A., Braun, A., Lalwani, A., Rauschecker, J. P., Turner, R., & Neville, H. (1997). Sentence reading: A functional MRI study at 4 tesla. *Journal of Cognitive Neuroscience* 9, 664–686.

Beaton, A. A. (1997). The relation of planum temporale asymmetry and morphology of the corpus callosum to handedness, gender, and dyslexia: A review of the evidence. *Brain & Language, 60,* 255–322.

Biscaldi, M., Gezeck, S., & Stuhr, V. (1998). Poor saccadic control correlates with dyslexia. *Neuropsychologia, 3,* 1189–1202.
Bishop, D., Carlyon, R., Deeks, J., & Bishop, S. (1999). Auditory temporal processing impairment: Neither necessary nor sufficient for causing language impairment in children. *Journal of Speech, Language, and Hearing Research, 42,* 1295–1310.
Boder, E. (1973). Developmental dyslexia: A diagnostic approach based on three reading–spelling patterns. *Developmental Medicine and Child Neurology, 15,* 663–687.
Breitmeyer, B. G., & Ganz, L. (1976). Implications of sustained and transient channels for theories of visual pattern making, saccadic suppression and information processing. *Psychological Review, 83,* 1–36.
Bruck, M. (1992). Persistence of dyslexics phonological awareness deficits. *Developmental Psychology, 28,* 874–886.
Castet, E., & Masson, G. S. (2000). Motion perception during saccadic eye movements. *Nature Neuroscience, 3*(2), 177–183.
Castles, A., Datto, H., Gayan, J., & Olson, R. K. (1999). Varieties of developmental reading disorder: Genetic and environmental influences. *Journal of Experimental Child Psychology, 72,* 73–94.
Castro-Caldas, A., Miranda, P. C., Carmo, I., Reis, A., Leote, F., Ribeiro, C., & Dicla-Soares, E. (1999). Influence of learning to read and write on the morphology of the corpus callosum. *European Journal of Neurology, 6,* 23–28.
Chase, C., & Jenner, A. R. (1993). Magnocellular deficits affect temporal processing of dyslexics. *Annals of the New York Academy of Sciences, 682,* 326–329.
Cornelissen, P., Bradley, L., Fowler, M. S., & Stein, J. F. (1992). Covering one eye affects how some children read. *Developmental Medicine and Child Neurology, 34,* 296–304.
Cossu, G., Shankweiler, D., Liberman, I. Y., Katz, L., & Tola, G. (1988). Awareness of phonological segments and reading ability in Italian children. *Applied Psycholinguistics, 9,* 1–16.
Davidson, R. J., & Saron, C. D. (1992). Evoked potential measures of interhemispheric transfer time in reading disabled and normal boys. *Developmental Neuropsychology, 8,* 261–277.
Demb, J. B., Boyton, G., Best, M., & Heeger, D. J. (1998). Psychophysical evidence for a magnocellular pathway deficit in dyslexia. *Vision Research, 38,* 1555–1559.
Duara, R., Kushch, A., Gross-Glenn, K., Barker, W. W., Jallad, B., Pascal, S., Loewenstein, D. A., Sheldon, J., Rabin, M., Levin, B., et al. (1991). Neuroanatomic differences between dyslexic and normal readers on magnetic resonance imaging scans. *Archives of Neurology, 48,* 410–416.
Eden, G. F., & Zeffiro, T. A. (1996). Looking beyond the reading difficulties in dyslexia, a vision deficit. *Journal of NIH Research, 8,* 31–35.
Eden, G. F., Stein, J. F., & Wood, F. B. (1993). Visuospatial abiltiy and language processing in reading disabled and normal children. In S. E. Wright (Ed.), *Studies in Visual Information Processing* (pp. 321–335). Amsterdam: North Holland.
Eden, G. F., VanMeter, J. W., Rumsey, J. M., Maisog, J. M., Woods, R. P., & Zeffiro, T. A. (1996). Abnormal processing of visual motion in dyslexia revealed by functional brain imaging. *Nature, 382,* 66–69.
Facoetti, A., Paganoni, P., Turatto, M., Marzola, V., & Mascetti, G. (2000). Visual-spatial attention in developmental dyslexia. *Cortex, 36,* 109–123.
Farmer, M. E., & Klein, R. M. (1995). The evidence for a temporal processing deficit linked to dyslexia: A review. *Psychonomic Bulletin & Review, 2,* 460–493.
Fawcett, A. (1994). Dyslexia: A personal view. In A. Fawcett & R. Nicolson (Eds.), *Dyslexia in children: Multidisciplinary perspectives* (pp. vii–xi). Hemel Hempstead, Hertfordshire: Harvester Wheatsheaf.
Fowler, S., & Stein, J. (1980). Visual Dyslexia. *British Orthoptic Journal, 37,* 11.
Funnell, M. G., Corballis, P. M., & Gazzaniga, M. S. (2000). Insights into the functional specificity of the human corpus callosum. *Brain, 123,* 920–926.
Galaburda, A. M., & Kemper, T. L. (1978). Cytoarchitectonic abnormalities in developmental dyslexia: A case study. *Annals of Neurology, 6,* 94–100.
Galaburda, A. M., Sherman, G., Rosen, G. D., Aboitiz, F., & Geschwind, N. (1985). Developmental dyslexia: Four consecutive cases with cortical anomalies. *Annals of Neurology, 18,* 222–233.
Gayan, J., & Olson, R. K. (2001). Genetic and environmental influences on orthographic and phonological skills in children with reading disabilities. *Developmental Neuropsychology, 20,* 483–507.
Georgiewa, P., Rzanny, R., Hopf, J.-M., Knab, R., Glauche, W., Kaiser, W.-A., & Blanz, B. (1999). fMRI during word processing in dyslexic and normal reading children. *Neuroreport: For Rapid Communication of Neuroscience, 10,* 3459–3465.

Giraud, K., & Habib, M. (1999). Callosal function in developmental dyslexia: Evidence of interhemispheric sharing. *Brain & Cognition, 40,* 129–132.

Gladstone, M., Best, C. T., & Davidson, R. J. (1989). Anomalous bimanual coordination among dyslexic boys. *Developmental Psychology, 25,* 236–246.

Gough, P. B., & Walsh, M. A. (1991). Chinese, Phoenicians, and the orthographic cipher of English. In S. A. Brady & D. P. Shankweiler (Eds.), *Phonological processes in literacy* (pp. 199–209). Hillsdale, NJ: Lawrence Erlbaum Associates.

Hallgren, B. (1950). Specific dyslexia (congenital word-blindness): A clinical and genetic study. *Acta Psychiatrica et Neurologica Supplement, 65,* 1–287.

Hellige, J. B., & Webster, R. (1979). Right hemisphere superiority for initial stages of letter processing. *Neuropsychologia, 17*(6), 653–660.

Heilman, K. M., Voeller, K., & Alexander, A. W. (1996). Developmental dyslexia: A motor-artciulatory feedback hypothesis. *Annals of Neurology, 39,* 407–412.

Helenius, P., Uutela, K., & Hari, R. (1999). Auditory stream segregation in dyslexic adults. *Brain, 122,* 907–913.

Henderson, V. W. (1986). Anatomy of posterior pathways involved in reading: A reassessment. *Brain and Language, 29,* 119–133.

Hinshelwood, J. (1896). A case of dyslexia: A peculiar form of word-blindness. *Lancet, 2,* 1451–1454.

Hoffman, J. E., & Subramaniam, B. (1995). The role of visual attention in saccadic eye movements. *Perception and Psychophysics, 57,* 787–795.

Horwitz, B., Rumsey, J. M., & Donohue, B. C. (1998). Functional connectivity of the angular gyrus in normal reading and dyslexia. *Proceedings of the National Academy of Sciences, USA, 95,* 8939–8944.

Humphreys, P., Kaufmann, W., & Galaburda, A. (1990). Developmental dyslexia in women: Neuropathological findings in three patients. *Annals of Neurology, 28,* 727–738.

Hynd, G. W., Hall, J., Novey, E. S., Eliopulos, D., et al. (1995). Dyslexia and corpus callosum morphology. *Archives of Neurology, 52,* 32–38.

Klingberg, T., Hedehus, M., Emple, E., Satz, T., Gabrieli, J. D. E., Moseley, M. E., & Poldrack, R. A. (2000). Microstructure of temporo-parietal white matter as a basis for reading ability: Evidence from diffusion tensor magnetic resonance imaging. *Neuron, 25,* 493–500.

Kujala, T., Myllyviita, K., Tervaniemi, M., Alho, K., Kallio, J., & Naatanen, R. (2000). Basic auditory dysfunction in dyslexia as demonstrated by brain activity measurements. *Psychophysiology, 37,* 262–266.

Larsen, J. P., Hoeien, T., & Oedegaard, H. (1992). Magnetic resonance imaging of the corpus callosum in develomental dyslexia. *Cognitive Neuropsychology, 9,* 123–134.

Liberman, A. M., & Whalen, D. H. (2000). On the relation of speech to language. *Trends in Cognitive Sciences, 4,* 187–196.

Liberman, I. Y., Shankweiler, D., Fisher, F. W., & Carter, B. (1974). Explicit syllable and phoneme segmentation in the young child. *Journal of Experimental Child Psychology, 18,* 201–212.

Livingstone, M., & Hubel, D. (1988). Segregation of form, colour, movement and depth: Anatomy, physiology, and perception. *Science, 240,* 740–749.

Livingstone, M., Rosen, G., Drislane, F., & Galaburda, A. (1991). Physiological and anatomical evidence for a magnocellular deficit in developmental dyslexia. *Proceedings of the National Academy of Sciences, USA, 80,* 7943–7947.

Lovegrove, B. (1994). Visual deficits in dyslexia. In A. Fawcett & R. Nicolson (Eds.), *Dyslexia in children: Multidisciplinary perspectives* (pp. 113–135) Hemel Hempstead, Hertfordshire: Harvester Wheatsheaf.

Lundberg, I., Wall, S., & Olofsson, A. (1980). Reading and spelling skills in the first school years predicted from phonemic awareness skills in kindergarten. *Scandinavian Journal of Psychology, 21,* 159–173.

Markee, T., Brown, W. S., Moore, L. H., & Theberge, D. C. (1996). Callosal function in dyslexia: Evoked potential interhemispheric transfer time and bilateral field advantage. *Developmental Neuropsychology, 12,* 409–428.

Martin, F., & Lovegrove, W. (1987). Flicker contrast sensitivity in normal and specifically disabled readers. *Perception, 16,* 215–221.

Martin, F., & Lovegrove, W. (1988). Uniform and field flicker in control and specifically disabled readers. *Perception, 17,* 203–214.

McAnally, K., & Stein, J. (1996). Auditory temporal coding in dyslexia. *Proceedings of the Royal Society of London, B: Biological Sciences, 263,* 961–965.

Molfese, D. L. (2000). Predicting dyslexia at 8 years of age using neonatal brain responses. *Brain & Language, 72,* 238–245.

Moore, L. H., Brown, W. S., Markee, T. E., Theberge, D. C., & Zvi, J. C. (1996). Callosal transfer of finger localization information in phonologically dyslexic adults. *Cortex, 32,* 311–322.

Olson, R. K., Datta, H., Gayan, J., & DeFries, J. C. (1999). A behavioral-genetic analysis of reading disabilities and component processes. In R. M. Klein & P. A. McMullen (Eds.), *Convering methods of understanding reading and dyslexia* (pp. 133–153). Cambridge, MA: MIT Press.

Olson, R. K., Forsberg, H., & Wise, B. (1994). Genes, environment, and the development of orthographic skills. In V. W. Berninger (Ed.), *The varieties of orthographic knowledge I: Theoretical and developmental issues* (pp. 27–71). Dordrecht, the Netherlands: Kluwer.

Olson, R. K., Wise, B., Conners, F., Rack, J., & Fulker, D. (1989). Specific deficits in component reading and language skills: Genetic and environmental influences. *Journal of Learning Disabilities, 22,* 339–348.

Orton, S. T. (1937). *Reading, writing, and speech problems in children.* New York: Norton.

Paulesu, E., Frith, U., Snowling, M., Gallagher, A., Morton, J., Frackowiak, R. S. J., & Frith, C. D. (1996). Is developmental dyslexia a disconnection syndrome? Evidence from PET scanning. *Brain, 119,* 143–157.

Pennington, B. F. (1999). Towards an integrated understanding of dyslexia: Genetic, neurological, and cognitive mechanisms. *Development and Psychopathology, 11,* 629–654.

Pennington, B. F., Lefly, D. L., Van Orden, G. C., Bookman, M. O., & Smith, S. D. (1987). Is phonology bypassed in normal or dyslexic development? *Annals of Dyslexia, 37,* 62–89.

Pennington, B. F., Van Orden, G. C., Smith, S. D., Green, P. A., Haith, M. M. (1990). Phonological processing skills and deficits in adult dyslexics. *Child Development, 61,* 1753–1778.

Petersen, S. E., Fox, P. T., Snyder, A. Z., & Raichle, M. E. (1990). Activation of extrastriate and frontal cortical areas by visual words and word-like stimuli. *Science, 249,* 1041–1044.

Preilowski, B. (1972). Possible contribution of the anterior forebrain commissures to bilateral coordination. *Neuropsychologia, 10,* 267–277.

Price, C. J., Moore, C. J., Humphreys, G. W., & Wise, R. J. S. (1997). Segregating semantic from phonological processes during reading. *Journal of Cognitive Neuroscience, 9,* 727–733.

Rack, J., Snowling, M., & Olson, R. (1992). The non-word reading deficit in developmental dyslexia: A review. *Reading Research Quarterly, 27,* 28–53.

Rayman, J., & Zaidel, E. (1991). Rhyming and the right hemisphere. *Brain & Language, 40,* 89–105.

Raymond, J. E., & Sorensen, R. E. (1998). Visual motion perception in children with dyslexia: Normal detection but abnormal integration. *Visual Cognition, 5,* 389–404.

Rayner, K. (1999). What have we leaned about eye movements during reading? In R. Klein & P. McMullen (Eds.), *Converging methods for understanding reading and dyslexia* (pp. 23–56). Cambridge, MA: MIT Press.

Robichon, F., & Habib, M. (1998). Abnormal callosal morphology in male adult dyslexics: Relationships to handedness and phonological ability. *Brain & Language, 62,* 127–146.

Rosen, G. D., Sherman, G. F., Richman, J. M., Stone, L. V., & Galaburda, A. M. (1992). Induction of molecular layer ectopias by puncture wounds in newborn rats and mice. *Developmental Brain Research, 67,* 285–291.

Rumsey, J. M., Casanova, M., Mannheim, G. B., Paronas, N., DeVaughn, N., Hamburger, S. D., & Aquino, T. (1996). Corpus callosum morphology, as measured with MRI, in dyslexic men. *Biological Psychiatry, 39,* 769–775.

Rumsey, J. M., Andreason, P., Zametkin, A. J., Aquino, T., King, A. C., Hamburger, S. D., Pikus, A., Rapoport, J. L., & Cohen, R. M. (1992). Failure to activate the left temporo-parietal cortex in dyslexia: An oxygen 15 positron emission tomographic study. *Archives of Neurology, 54,* 1481–1489.

Rumsey, J. M., Horwitz, B., Donnohue, B. C., Nace, K. L., Maisog, J. M., & Andreason, P. (1999). A functional lesion in developmental dyslexia: Left angular gyral blood flow predicts severity. *Brain and Language, 70,* 187–204.

Rumsey, J. M., Nace, K., Donohue, B. C., Wise, D., Maisog, J. M., & Andreason, P. (1997). A positron emission tomographic study of impaired word recognition and phonological processing in dyslexic men. *Archives of Neurology, 54,* 562–573.

Rutter, M., & Yule, W. (1975). The concept of specific reading retardation. *Journal of Child Psychology and Psychiatry, 16,* 181–197.

Schwartz, J., & Tallal, P. (1980). Rate of acoustic change may underlie hemispheric specialization for speech perception. *Science, 207,* 1380–1381.

Shaywitz, S. E., Shaywitz, B. A., Pugh, K. R., Fulbright, R. K., Constable, R. T., Mencl, W. E., Shankweiler, D. P., Liberman, A. M., Skudlarsi, P., Fletcher, J. M., Katz, L., Marchione, K. E., Lacadie, C., Gatenby, C., & Gore, J. C. (1998). Functional disruption in the organization of the brain for reading in dyslexia. *Proceedings of the National Academy of Sciences of the United States of America, 95,* 2636–2641.

Siegel, L. S. (1989). IQ is irrelevant to the definition of learning disabilities. *Journal of Learning Disabilities, 22,* 469–478.

Siegel, L. S. (1998). The discrepancy formula: Its use and abuse. In B. K. Shapiro, P. J. Accardo, & A. J. Capute (Eds.), *Specific reading disability: A view of the spectrum* (pp. 123–135). Timonium, MD: York Press.

Skottun, B. C. (2000). The magnocellular deficit theory of dyslexia: The evidence from contrast sensitivity. *Vision Research, 40,* 111–127.

Slaghuis, W., & Ryan, J. (1999). Spatio-temporal contrast sensitivity, coherent motion, and visible persistence in developmental dyslexia. *Vision Research, 39,* 651–668.

Stein, J., & Walsh, V. (1997). To see but not to read: The magnocellular theory of dyslexia. *Trends in Neurosciences, 20,* 147–152.

Stein, J. F. (1994). A visual deficit in dyslexics? In A. Facwett & R. Nicolson (Eds.), *Dyslexia in children: Multidisciplinary perspectives*. Hemel Hampstead: Harvester Wheatsheaf.

Stein, J. F., Richardson, A. J., & Fowler, M. S. (2000). Monocular occlusion can improve binocular control and reading in dyslexics. *Brain: A Journal of Neurology, 123,* 164–170.

Stein, J. F., Riddel, P., & Fowler, M. S. (1986). The Dunlop test and reading in primary school children. *British Journal of Opthalmology, 70,* 317.

Stein, J. F., Riddel, P., & Fowler, M. S. (1987). Fine binocular control in dyslexic children. *Eye, 1,* 433–438.

Stein, J. F., Riddel, P., & Fowler, M. S. (1988). Disordered vergence eye movement control in dyslexic children. *British Journal of Opthalmology, 72,* 162–166.

Stein, J., Talcott, J., & Walsh, V. (2000). Controversy about the visual magnocellular deficit in developmental dyslexics. *Trends in Cognitive Sciences, 4,* 209–211.

Studdert-Kennedy, M., & Mody, M. (1995). Auditory temporal perception deficits in the reading-impaired: A critical review of the evidence. *Psychonomic Bulletin & Review, 2,* 508–514.

Suzuki, K., Yamadori, A., Endo, K., Fujii, T., Ezura, M., & Takahashi, A. (1998). Dissociation of letter and picture naming resulting from callosal disconnection. *Neurology, 51,* 1390–1394.

Tallal, P., Miller, S. L., Bedi, G., Byma, G., Wang, X., Nagarajan, S. S., Schreiner, C., Jenkins, W. M., & Merzenich, M. M. (1996). Language comprehension in language-learning impaired children improved with acoustically modified speech. *Science, 271,* 81–84.

Treisman, A., & Gelade, G. (1980). A feature integration theory of attention. *Cognitive Psychology, 12,* 97–136.

Vidyasagar, T. R. (1999). A neuronal model of the attentional spotlight: Parietal guiding the temporal. *Brain Research Reviews, 30,* 66–76.

Vidyasagar, T. R., & Pammer, K. (1999). Impaired visual search in dyslexia relates to the role of the magnocellular pathway in attention. *NeuroReport, 10,* 1283–1287.

Wagner, R. K., Torgesen, J. K., & Rashotte, C. A. (1994). Development of reading-related phonological processing abilities: New evidence of bi-directional causality from a latent variable longitudinal study. *Developmental Psychology, 30,* 73–87.

Willcutt, E. G ., Pennington, B. F., & DeFries, J. C. (2000). Twin study of the etiology of comorbidity between reading disability and attention-deficit/hyperactivity disorder. *American Journal of Medical Genetics, 96,* 293–301.

Williams, M., Molinet, K., & LeCluyse, K. (1989). Visual masking as a measure of temporal processing. *Clinical Vision Sciences, 4,* 137–144.

Witton, C., Talcott, J., Hansen, P., Richardson, A., Griffiths, T., Rees, A., Stein, J., & Green, G. (1998). Sensitivity to dynamic auditory and visual stimuli predicts nonword reading ability in both dyslexic and normal readers. *Current Biology, 8,* 791–797.

Wolff, P. H., Cohen, C., & Drake, C. (1984). Impaired motor timing control in specific reading retardation. *Neuropsychologia, 22,* 587–600.

Wolff, P. H., Michel, G. F., Ovrut, M., & Drake, C. (1990). Rate and timing precision of motor coordination in developmental dyslexia. *Developmental Psychology, 26,* 349–359.

Wright, B. A., Bowen, R. W., & Zecker, S. G. (2000). Nonlinguistic perceptual deficits associated with reading and language disorders. *Current Opinions in Neurobiology, 10,* 482–486.
Ygge, J., Lennerstrand, G., Rydberg, A., Wijecoon, S., & Pettersson, B. M. (1993). Oculomotor functions in a Swedish population of dyslexic and normally reading children. *Acta Ophthalmologica, 71,* 10–21.
Zaidel, E. (1978). Auditory language comprehension in the right hemisphere following cerebral commissurotomy and hemispherectomy: A comparison with child language and aphasia. In A. Caramazza & E. B. Zurif (Eds.), *Language acquisition and language breakdown: Parallels and divergencies* (pp. 229–275). Baltimore, MD: The Johns Hopkins University Press.

V

Two Languages, One Brain

12

The Phonetic Systems of Bilinguals

Molly Mack
University of Illinois at Urbana-Champaign

In their examination of the phonetic systems of bilinguals, researchers have generally used one of three approaches. The first involves the comparison of bilinguals or nonnative speakers to monolinguals and/or native speakers to determine whether their language systems are the same or different and is here termed the *monolingual-comparison approach*. The second attempts to determine the extent to which bilinguals' two languages are interdependent (merged) or independent and is here designated as the *shared-separate approach*. The third deals with the effect of age on the development of a second- or dual-language system among bilinguals and is here called the *age-effect approach*. Most of this chapter is devoted to a consideration of studies representative of these three approaches, which, taken together, provide descriptive and (some) explanatory adequacy. Then attention will be given to three major theories regarding the formation of phonetic systems, which could, if they were supported by further empirical evidence and somewhat refined, provide predictive adequacy. These are Kuhl's native language magnet theory, Best's perceptual assimilation model, and Flege's speech learning model.

Although an emphasis on the phonetic system limits the extent to which generalizations can be made about other linguistic components, studies of the phonetic systems of bilinguals have provided important descriptive and theoretical insights into bilingualism and second-language acquisition. But before considering the phonetic systems of bilinguals it is necessary to define four terms used widely and often differently in bilingual studies—native speaker, monolingual, bilingual, and early bilingual.

DEFINITION OF TERMS

Native speakers are here defined as individuals who have a first language (an L1) nearly always acquired from infancy. Native speakers need not be monolinguals, as is the case among many individuals worldwide who acquire two (or more) languages in infancy (Kachru, 1986, 1992). Some of the confusion surrounding the term *native speaker* arises from equating a native language with the language in which a bilingual is most fluent. Such a proficiency-based definition of the native speaker is not intended here.

Monolinguals are those who have command of only one language, even if they have had some exposure to another. There are also monolingual speakers of a given language who are not native speakers of that language. This occurs, for example, among individuals who have emigrated in infancy from their country of origin and have settled in another country where they no longer use their L1. This interpretation of monolingual native speakers is thus based on a combination of order-of-acquisition and fluency criteria. That is, monolingual native speakers are those who have been exposed exclusively or primarily to one language from infancy and who can subsequently communicate effectively in only one language. Conversely, nonnative speakers are those who have acquired a language or languages after infancy. If they are nonnative speakers of a language due to having acquired a second language (L2) but having lost their L1, then they are simply nonnative but monolingual speakers of that L2 and their proficiency may be essentially identical to that of monolingual native speakers of that language.

Although bilingualism is generally treated dichotomously as one of two possible states (bilingualism vs. monolingualism), there are actually degrees of bilingualism (Baetens Beardsmore, 1986), and bilinguals may function more or less as monolinguals and/or native speakers depending upon language component, task type, context, and speaker variables (Grosjean, 1998). Thus the following is a broad and liberal definition of the term bilingualism as used in the present chapter: If individuals possess two languages and can function reasonably effectively in producing and perceiving both, they are considered bilingual. Hence it is not asserted that individuals must function in a monolingual-like, native-like or, in the terminology of Bloomfield (1933), "perfect" manner in their two languages to be considered bilingual. Conversely, individuals who are able only to read, for example, in an L2 would not be bilinguals. Some researchers use the term *bilingual* more restrictively than is done here, characterizing all or most nonnative users of a language as second-language learners regardless of their level of proficiency. However, whenever appropriate, the term *bilingual* is used throughout the present chapter in reference to individuals who meet these described criteria.

Finally, *early* (versus late) *bilinguals* are here considered individuals who have acquired, in a formal or naturalistic setting, at least two languages prior to about the age of 8 in accord with the convention generally used in bilingual studies. Early bilinguals may use one of their languages dominantly, but they can understand and be understood in both of their languages reasonably well.

APPROACHES TO THE STUDY OF THE PHONETIC SYSTEMS OF BILINGUALS

Many researchers in bilingual speech production and perception have compared bilinguals to monolinguals by examining a variety of components in the phonological system including suprasegmental properties such as stress and intonation. Although these analyses are of practical and theoretical import, the present discussion deals primarily with the segmental properties of speech with a focus on temporal and spectral features.

The Monolingual-Comparison Approach

The monolingual-comparison approach (MCA), which here includes the study of monolinguals and/or native speakers, has arisen primarily out of a desire to analyze bilingual language systems with reference to monolinguals who are often viewed as normative language users. This approach, related to the contrastive analysis hypothesis (CAH) proposed by Lado (1957), is based on the comparative analysis of specific structural properties of two languages to predict which features of the L2 (or target language) should be problematic for a learner or even a fluent bilingual user of that language. An integral component of the CAH is the notion of language transfer—that is, the assertion that the L1 influences the L2 and that, even among native speakers of two languages, there will invariably be unidirectional or bidirectional transfer between the two languages. Although both the CAH and the role of language transfer have been criticized, most often because they cannot account for the variety of phenomena observed in bilingual language systems, a methodology integral to these approaches is still used—the comparative analysis of monolinguals and bilinguals—and it remains central to much of the descriptive and theory-based work on the phonetic systems of bilinguals. Indeed, Mack (1997) argued that the MCA can provide valid and important information about both monolinguals and bilinguals, especially if the notion that monolingualism is somehow superior or preferred to bilingualism is abandoned. (See Grosjean, 1997, for a bilingual-based approach.)

In its simplest form, the MCA is linear and unidimensional (Fig. 12.1). Performance among bilinguals with respect to a given property is examined and compared with performance by monolingual speakers of one or both of the bilinguals' languages. Any one of a number of possible results may obtain. For example, it may be found that a given group of bilinguals performs in a manner approximating but not identical to that of monolinguals (Fig. 12.1a). Or the

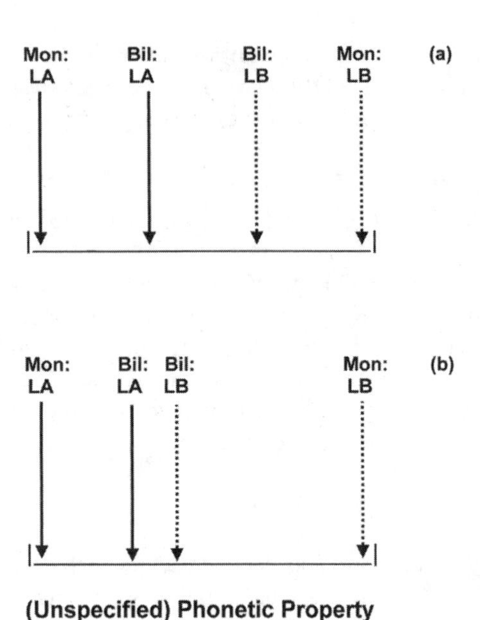

FIG. 12.1. A schematic representation of the monolingual-comparison approach (MCA) in which the two phonetic systems (or properties of those systems) of bilinguals are examined in relation to their proximity to the phonetic systems (or properties of the systems) of monolingual native speakers of those two languages, LA and LB. In (a), neither one of the bilinguals' systems, Bil: LA or Bil: LB, is identical to that of either one of the monolinguals', Mon: LA or Mon: LB. Yet the bilinguals' systems are clearly distinct from one another. In (b), a similar relationship is presented but here the bilinguals 'systems are more closely aligned with one another and with the system of the monolingual speakers of one of the languages. Such might occur if the bilinguals' LA is more dominant than their LB. These are just two examples of the multiplicity of possible monolingual/bilingual-system relationships. (Here LA and LB are used, rather than L1 and L2, to convey neutrality with respect to which language is the native language. Indeed, both languages could be native languages.)

performance of the bilinguals in both of their languages may be more closely aligned with that of the monolingual speakers of only one of their languages (Fig. 12.1b).

Voice-Onset Time and Other Features. One of the most thoroughly investigated aspects of bilinguals' phonetic systems is voice-onset time (VOT)—the time measured in milliseconds between the release of vocal-tract occlusion and the onset of phonation (Fig. 12.2). In English, it is a primary although not sole cue for differentiating homorganic voiced and voiceless consonants (e.g., /b,d,g/ vs. /p,t,k/) and the voicing contrast is acquired quite early in the L1 (Deuchar & Clark, 1996; Mack & Lieberman, 1985; Macken & Barton, 1979; see also Kingston & Diehl, 1994, for a discussion of automatic and con-

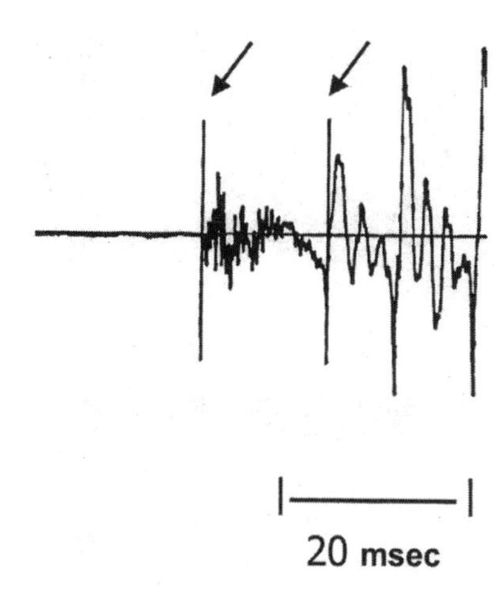

FIG. 12.2. An example of voice-onset time (VOT) in a short-lag stop consonant, preceded by silence and followed by a vowel, displayed using a waveform-editing program. The aperiodic portion of the signal demarcated between the two cursors is the VOT of the consonant and the periodic portion immediately following is the onset of a post-consonantal vowel. As is apparent, the VOT of the stop consonant is readily observable.

trolled processing as related to VOT, and Simos, Molfese, & Brenden, 1997, for a consideration of the neurological substrates of VOT).

VOT has been of particular interest to researchers in bilingualism because the VOT continuum is divided into a small number of modal categories, with languages systematically differing in their use of these categories (Bond & Fokes, 1991; Cho & Ladefoged, 1999; Lisker & Abramson, 1964; Flege & Eefting, 1988). For example, although languages such as French and English have two phonemic VOT categories, their phonetic implementation of these categories differs, as can be seen in Fig. 12.3. (A phoneme is a minimal meaningful unit of sound or, more appropriately, the abstract representation of a cluster of phonetically related sounds, which—although they may vary acoustically/phonetically—are treated as a single unit. Thus in English both the phone [kʰ] when aspirated, as in stressed word-initial position, or the phone [k] when unaspirated, as in unstressed word-final position, are both realizations of a single phoneme /k/.) Languages may differ in terms of their phonemic inventories as well as in the ways in which their phonemes are instantiated in different phonetic environments.

An early study of VOT using the MCA is that of Flege (1980), who compared native speakers of English and speakers of Saudi Arabic who had lived in the United States either less than 1 year or more than 2 years. (Unless stated otherwise, English will refer to American English here and throughout.) Flege examined four acoustic correlates of stop-consonant voicing; only his findings regarding the VOTs of word-initial voiceless stop consonants are considered

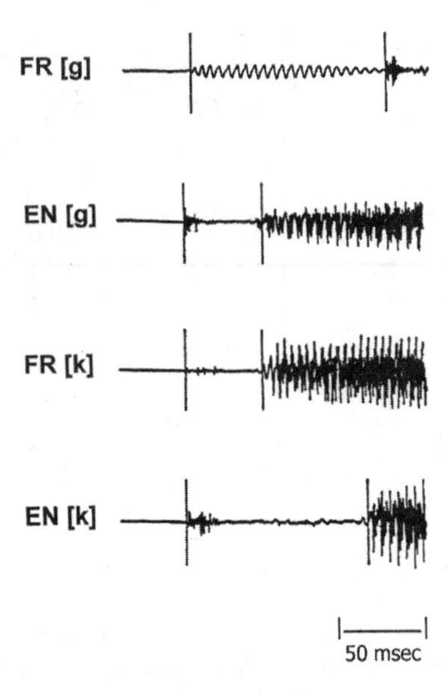

FIG. 12.3. Examples of the phonetic instantiations of the phonemes /g/ and /k/ in French and English as produced by monolingual native French and English speakers. The French voiced stop consonant [g] (top) has a prevoiced VOT of –98 msec, indicating that voicing has begun prior to the release of vocal-tract occlusion at the onset of the stop consonant in contrast to the English voiced [g], which has a short-lag VOT of 40 msec. This value of 40 msec is nearly identical to that of the VOT for the French [k] presented below it. By contrast, the VOT of the English [kʰ] (bottom) is clearly much longer. These examples demonstrate how two "identical" phonemes may be realized, in production, quite differently across languages.

here. In Saudi Arabic, the VOTs for the stop consonants /t/ and /k/ are shorter than in English and, unlike English, there is no phonemic /p/. Flege found that the English VOTs for the two groups of Arabic speakers were not significantly different and their VOTs were shorter than the values obtained from the native speakers of English. Thus both bilingual groups appeared to be using L1-like values in producing their L2. This suggests that fairly extensive exposure to an L2 is required before phonetic values appropriate to it can be produced if, indeed, they even can be among late bilinguals such as those in this study.

This assertion receives support from an early study of another cue to voicing in English—voicing-conditioned vowel duration (Mack, 1982). It has long been recognized that, in English, vowels preceding voiceless consonants, at least in words in stressed prepausal position, are considerably shorter than vowels preceding voiceless consonants, as in the vowels in the minimal pairs *heat–heed* or *tap–tab* (Chen, 1970; Peterson & Lehiste, 1960). The difference is so marked in English that Mack has maintained that it is a strong, secondary, and rule-governed cue to voicing. This is not true of French and many other languages in which the voicing-conditioned durational effect is much weaker and appears to be a consequence of articulatory maneuvers or auditory factors. (See Kluender, Diehl, & Wright, 1988, for a thorough treatment of this topic, and Laeufer, 1992, for consideration of linguistic variables mitigating this effect.)

Thus, Mack measured vowel durations produced in minimal pairs by late adult French–English bilinguals and compared these durations to those produced by English and French monolinguals. Results revealed that, on average, vowels preceding voiceless consonants were 53% the duration of those preceding voiced consonants in English words produced by the English monolinguals but 74% in French words produced by the French monolinguals. The bilinguals' values were nearly identical, in English *and* French, to those of the French monolinguals. Hence the bilinguals seemed to be using their French phonetic system to produce English vowel durations because they were unaware of the English vowel-lengthening rule. Yet when the average differences between the vowel durations in the voiced and voiceless contexts (i.e., the durational ranges) were analyzed, the bilinguals—although still producing ranges in French nearly identical to those of the French monolinguals—produced ranges in English approximating those of the English monolinguals. This indicates that they did, in fact, detect the English temporal distinction but could only partially implement it.

Interestingly, an early French–English bilingual child studied by Mack (1990), who, unlike these bilinguals, did have two distinct voicing-conditioned vowel-duration categories in English and French, exhibited a pattern of durational ranges nearly identical to those of the late bilinguals in Mack (1982). This reveals that, even with respect to a specific temporal property, some features associated with that property may be more susceptible to modification than others and that there are individual differences in the ability to produce elements associated with even a single phonetic feature or rule.

In a study of another aspect of voicing, Flege, Munro, and Skelton (1992) compared the production the /t–d/ contrast in word-final position among late Mandarin–English bilinguals and English monolinguals by examining acoustic correlates associated with the /t–d/ distinction and relating these to predictions made by "equivalence classification" (Flege, 1987b; Flege & Hillenbrand, 1984). Equivalence classification is, Flege stated, "a basic cognitive mechanism which permits humans to perceive constant categories in the face of the inherent sensory variability found in the many physical exemplars which may instantiate a category" (Flege, 1987b, p. 49). Thus it affects the ability of L2 learners to acquire L2 sounds. For example, speakers of English learning French should have more difficulty producing the French vowel /i/ due to its acoustic/phonetic similarity to the English vowel /i/ than in producing the French vowel /y/, which is acoustically and phonetically unlike any English vowel and is thus a "new" vowel for English learners of French. Hence L2 sounds that are similar in the L1 and L2 are assimilated to the L1 system (which itself may then undergo modification due to the influence of the L2), but L2 sounds that are dissimilar in the L1 and L2 are not assimilated and become members of new categories formed in the L2.

Mandarin, unlike English, does not permit obstruents (nonvowel or nonvowel-like sounds) in word-final position, nor does Mandarin exhibit the marked voicing-conditioned vowel duration differences characteristic of English. Thus, it would be predicted that Mandarin–English bilinguals can acquire the English word-final voicing and vowel-duration contrasts because both involve phonetic distinctions nonoccurrent in Mandarin.

Yet Flege et al. found that, contrary to expectation, even the most experienced and presumably fluent Mandarin–English bilinguals did not reliably produce the word-final voicing contrast. Moreover, although the bilinguals exhibited voicing-conditioned vowel duration, the magnitude of the effect was generally smaller than for the English monolinguals. Among the interpretations of these results proposed by Flege et al. is that input directed to native-English-speaking children and adult L2 acquirers of English is different, or that one of their basic premises—that L2 production has a perceptual origin—is simply erroneous. The latter possibility has been disconfirmed in subsequent studies of bilinguals with prolonged exposure to English (Flege, Takagi, & Mann, 1995; Guion, Flege, & Loftin, 2000). The results do, however, have implications for another fundamental issue in bilingual phonetics, and that is the extent to which production and perception are related.

The Relationship Between Production and Perception. It is widely believed that the perception of an L2 phonemic or phonetic unit must be antecedent to its production. In a study of Italian–English bilinguals, Flege, MacKay, and Meador (1999) stated that "phonetic segments in an L2 can be produced in a nativelike fashion only if they are perceived in a nativelike fashion" (p. 2982), and indeed, they did observe a strong correlation between production and perception. However, such correlations have not always been found.

For example, using the MCA in a 1973 study of speech production and perception among early French–English bilinguals, French monolinguals, and English monolinguals, Caramazza, Yeni-Komshian, Zurif, and Carbone found evidence that the productive abilities of bilinguals exceeded their perceptive abilities. Such is also the case in an oft-cited study by Sheldon and Strange (1982) who examined the production and perception of English /r/ and /l/ in adult Japanese–English bilinguals. (Japanese does not have the English /r–l/ contrast.) Sheldon and Strange found that at least some of their subjects could accurately produce the /r–l/ contrast without being able to identify it reliably—a finding also observed among Korean–English bilinguals studied by Mack (1985). In the latter two studies, it is possible that at least some of the subjects received explicit articulatory training in English and hence could use proprioceptive feedback to accurately produce English sounds that they could not differentially perceive, although this would not account for the findings of Caramazza et al. whose subjects apparently acquired their two languages naturalistically, without formal explicit training, in childhood.

A similar production/perception dissociation was obtained in a study of Korean–English bilinguals and English monolinguals by Baker and Trofimovich (in press). Using three sets of English vowel contrasts difficult for Korean–English bilinguals to produce and perceive, they observed that, overall, the bilinguals' accuracy in vowel production and perception was equivalent. But among approximately half of the bilinguals whose production accuracy was rated as intermediate, vowel production exceeded vowel perception. (See also Flege, Bohn, & Jang, 1997, for additional evidence of a production/perception dissociation, and Trofimovich & Baker, 2000, for a discussion of subject-specific effects on production and perception.) Thus there are exceptions to the claim that L2 perception is always more accurate and/or that it invariably precedes L2 production.

Although production and perception have usually been compared using phonemes from one sound class, few studies have used the MCA to examine performance on markedly different sound classes. One such study is that of Mack (1989), who examined consonant and vowel production among early adult French–English bilinguals and English monolinguals. Subjects were tested in their production and perception of the stop consonants /d/ and /t/ and in their production and perception of the vowels /i/ and /I/ (as in the words *beat* and *bit*). Although French and English have the phonemes /d/ and /t/, they are produced differently in the two languages. Likewise, although /i/ occurs in the phonemic inventories of both languages, it too is produced somewhat differently in French and English. Moreover, unlike English, French has no phonemic /I/. Mack assessed subjects' consonant production in measurements of VOT and their vowel production in terms of vowel length, formant frequencies, and other acoustic properties. Perception was assessed using discrimination and identification tasks with continua of computer-synthesized stimuli generated using a cascade/parallel synthesis program (Klatt, 1980).

Results revealed that the bilinguals' VOTs for /d/ and /t/ were nearly identical to those of the monolinguals, as were their average durations for /i/ and /I/. In addition, formant-frequency analyses revealed that the bilinguals' formant-frequency space (the F2–F1 and F3–F2 space), evaluated in hertz and Bark scale (perceptually based) values, were nearly identical to those of the monolinguals, as was their F2 at vowel midpoints. Similarly, the bilinguals' discrimination and identification of /d–t/ and their discrimination of /i–I/ were indistinguishable from those of the English monolinguals. Only in their identification of the /i–I/ continuum did they differ significantly from the monolinguals: Here their crossover boundaries (that point at which 50% of their responses were identified as /i/ and 50% as /I/) were closer to the /i/ end of the continuum, revealing that they accepted fewer of the /i/ and /i/-like vowels as

/i/. This is most likely evidence of the influence of the bilinguals' French vowel system on their English vowel system, for the vowels at or closest to the /i/ endpoint of the continuum (i.e., the most prototypical exemplars of /i/) were acoustically more similar to the French /i/ than were the vowels farther away from the /i/ endpoint.

An alternative explanation is that bilinguals must receive extensive exposure to and/or maintain extensive use of a language in order to form strong "prototypes" for all phonemes. But even among fluent early bilinguals, it is generally not possible to receive the same amount of input and have the same amount of language use in both of their languages as monolinguals do in their (sole) language. Thus, these bilinguals may have had a stronger /i/ than /I/ prototype, because only /i/ occurs in both French and English. Consequently, if Kuhl's assertion (see later discussion of her native language magnet theory) about the "shrinking" of perceptual space in the region of prototypes is correct, one might conclude that the bilinguals' vowels were drawn toward the /i/ end of the continuum to a greater extent than were the monolinguals' vowels because the monolinguals presumably had equally strong /i/ and /I/ prototypes. This did not occur in the bilinguals' identification of the consonants /d/ and /t/, possibly because their /t/ and /d/ prototypes were as strong as the monolinguals', because both French and English have the phonemes /t/ and /d/. Yet both the vowel /i/ and the consonants /d/ and /t/ are phonetically instantiated differently in French and English so, if a prototype model is appropriate here, it would be one requiring a fairly abstract level of representation—something that does not appear to be supported by the discrimination test results of Kuhl and her colleagues.

What is apparent is that these bilinguals' production and perception of English VOT and their production of a number of vowel parameters were indistinguishable from those of English monolinguals. But their identification of a vowel continuum was significantly different. This may indicate that vowels are inherently more susceptible to modification or cross-language influence than are consonants, particularly because there are well-documented differences in how consonants and vowels are perceived (e.g., Pisoni, 1973; Schouten & van Hessen, 1992). Moreover, the finding of a difference in the two groups' vowel identification but not discrimination suggests that the two tasks had different perceptual bases, with identification more likely to require phonological processing than discrimination (Ingram & Park, 1998). Thus, bilingual speech production may be more monolingual-like than bilingual speech perception, depending on which sound classes and task types are used.

Speech Intelligibility. The studies cited thus far have been limited to analyses of segmental properties of the phonetic system in experiments whose methodologies have sometimes been criticized for their lack of "ecological validity" or naturalness. Thus it is of interest to examine results of tests of perception in which speech stimuli have been presented in relatively lengthy and grammatical segments, because it has long been known that the range of possible response alternatives influences perceptual performance (e.g., Miller, Heise, & Lichten, 1951).

To this end, Mack and colleagues at the MIT Lincoln Laboratory and at the University of Illinois conducted a series of experiments utilizing natural (high-quality) and acoustically degraded single words, meaningful sentences, and semantically anomalous sentences presented in English to monolingual (or native) and bilingual speakers of English for whom English was not the L1. A number of researchers have found that acoustically degraded input and perceptually demanding tasks result in a marked decrement in performance among nonnative listeners (Bradlow & Pisoni, 1999; Conrad, 1989; Nábelek & Donahue, 1984; Ozawa & Logan, 1989), so it was of interest to determine how native and fluent nonnative users of English would respond to the variety of stimuli and tests presented. All tests used a subjective performance-based approach to evaluate the intelligibility of the stimuli presented, rather than objective mathematically based methods (e.g., Hansen & Nandkumar, 1995).

Specifically, Mack and Gold (1985) initially undertook sentence-level experiments due to concern that the Diagnostic Rhyme Test (DRT), a then widely used standardized test of speech intelligibility, could be producing ceiling effects. (In the DRT, subjects are presented with minimal pairs differing only in their word-initial consonant, as in *taught* versus *caught*, and they are required to indicate in a forced-choice task which one of the word-initial consonants they have heard.) Hence Mack and Gold developed a test using phonemically balanced semantically anomalous sentences in order to provide lengthy and grammatical segments relatively lacking in contextual (meaning-based) cues, such as *A rapid sailor paid a ripe card*. All sentences were produced by the present author, a native and effectively monolingual speaker of English. Fifty-seven sentences were first presented in natural and computer-processed (vocoded) conditions to native speakers of English who were required to write each sentence as it was presented. It was immediately apparent that this test yielded relatively more errors in perception that did the DRT and was thus a more sensitive measure of perceptual accuracy.

Therefore, Mack and Tierney (1987; see also Mack, 1987, 1988) subsequently administered the anomalous-sentences test to English monolinguals and fluent German–English bilinguals whose L1 was German. Extensive analysis of the results was made, but the findings of relevance to the present discussion are these: The bilinguals made over 11 times as many errors as did the monolinguals in the natural condition but only 1.25 as many errors in the vocoded as in the natural condition; for both groups, the largest number of errors were phonemic; and the bilinguals exhibited evidence of phonological transfer from their L1 as exemplified by the frequency of erroneous word-final obstruent devoicing (e.g., *seed* → *seat*), which occurs in German, and the substitution of *s* for the fricative *th*, which does not occur in German. The bilinguals also had frequent misparsings (e.g., *Modern Leslie* → *Maude and Leslie*), whereas virtually none of the monolinguals did, possibly reflecting the influence of German prosodic cues on English word-boundary identification.

Because even in the natural-speech condition these sentences proved so difficult for the bilinguals, another set of 57 phonemically balanced sentences was developed—a meaningful-sentences test (Mack, Tierney, & Boyle, 1990)—and it was administered along with the DRT and the anomalous-sentences test to a new group of English monolinguals and fluent German–English bilinguals. The bilinguals performed quite well on the vocoded DRT but made many errors even on the meaningful sentences in the natural-speech condition, whereas the monolinguals' performance on these sentences was nearly error free. The bilinguals, unlike the monolinguals, also exhibited evidence of perceptual fatigue, making more errors in the vocoded condition on the final 15 than on the first 15 sentences in both the meaningful and semantically anomalous tests.

A final experiment using the meaningful and anomalous sentences was conducted to evaluate L1-specific effects on processing. Here, the sentences were administered to English monolinguals and French–English bilinguals. (Native speakers of British English were also tested; for details, see Mack, 1992.) Results revealed that the French–English bilinguals made far more errors in both the natural and vocoded conditions than did the previously tested German–English bilinguals, although both groups were as experienced in English and had rated themselves as equally fluent in English. The difference may be attributable to language-specific properties such as phonemic inventory, phoneme-to-grapheme correspondence, and/or segmentation processes. For example, Cutler, Mehler, Norris, and Segui (1986) indicated that French, unlike English and German, is a syllable-timed rather than a stress-timed language. Indeed, Cutler, Mehler, Norris, and Segui (1992) found evidence that even highly fluent French–English bilinguals (whose L1 is French) use French segmentation procedures when processing English, leading Cutler et al. to conclude that, with respect to some aspects of speech processing, bilinguals "may be functionally monolingual" (p. 409).

Another finding in the experiments by Mack and colleagues was that the bilinguals, unlike the monolinguals, appeared to use a bottom-up processing strategy. For example, the bilinguals more accurately perceived low-level non-meaningful components of the sentential stimuli, such as the words *a* and *the*, which the monolinguals often confused. Further, the decrements in performance observed in these experiments were not additive, suggesting that a logarithmic treatment (Boothroyd & Nittrouer, 1988) of the combination of test type, stimulus quality, L1/L2 relatedness, and L2 fluency may be needed to provide a complete account of the difference between bilingual and monolingual performance in tests of speech processing such as these.

General Comments Regarding the Monolingual-Comparison Approach. Empirical evidence using the MCA has demonstrated that many bilinguals function unlike monolinguals in speech production and perception, that—in some cases—their L2 production may be more accurate than their L2 perception, and that tests involving relatively complex processing, even of very high-quality speech, are particularly difficult. Results also indicate that it is inappropriate to treat the phonetic component as a unitary system in comparative analyses of bilinguals and monolinguals because results may vary depending on sound class, modality (production or perception), quality of the stimuli presented, and task demands.

The Shared-Separate Approach

The shared-separate approach (SSA) differs from the MCA less in its methodology than in its objectives. Specifically the SSA does not attempt to determine to what extent bilinguals' phonetic systems are like those of monolinguals, but to what extent bilinguals' two phonetic systems are similar to one another. That is, to what extent are they interdependent (merged or shared) or independent (separate)?

The shared-separate issue first received substantial formal linguistic treatment by Weinreich (1953), who considered ways in which bilinguals' languages may be associated. Specifically, Weinreich presented three possible types of association between bilinguals' language systems—one in which elements from the two languages are represented independently, one in which they are represented interdependently, and one in which elements from one language are mediated by those from the other. These were later termed *coordinate*, *compound*, and *subordinate* types of bilingualism, respectively. Weinreich's typology had major empirical ramifications in the 1960s and 1970s. Indeed, compound bilingualism is closely related to the much-investigated concept of interlanguage in applied linguistics (Corder, 1981; Ioup & Weinberger, 1987). Although Weinreich's typology is now viewed as overly simplistic, an interpretation akin to it, albeit one formulated in a more elaborated and neurolinguistically informed manner, can still be found in hypotheses regarding bilingual language organization proposed by Paradis (1985, 1987, 1997).

Voice-Onset Time and Other Features. A seminal study using the SSA was conducted by Caramazza et al. (1973, cited earlier), who examined the production and perception of voice-onset time among early adult French–English bilinguals (all native speakers of Canadian–French who had acquired English by age 7) and Canadian–French and Canadian–English monolinguals. Results revealed that the monolinguals' VOTs for the voiceless stop consonants (averaged here across /p,t,k/ and rounded to the nearest millisecond) were 24 msec in

French and 74 msec in English, whereas the bilinguals' VOTs were intermediate with values of 28 msec in French and 51 msec in English.

In perception, the subjects were presented with synthesized VOT continua of consonant–vowel (CV) syllables and were required to label the syllable-initial consonant. Because the stimuli were identical for the French and English task, the experimenters attempted to induce a psychological set specific to each of the languages so that the listeners would believe they were hearing French stimuli in one presentation and English in another. The 50% crossover boundary was found to correspond to shorter VOTs for the French than for the English monolinguals. The bilinguals responded differently in the French and English sets but did not respond exactly like the monolinguals in either language, with their crossover boundaries for French and English being nearly identical and falling between those of the French and English monolinguals. Their response functions were also somewhat less monotonic than were those of the English monolinguals, as were those of the French monolinguals, suggesting that, for the bilinguals and French monolinguals, VOT was a less salient cue to voicing than it was for the English monolinguals.

Thus, these bilinguals functioned somewhat differently in their two languages, but more like the monolingual speakers of French than of English. The authors concluded that the acquisition of an L2 sound system might be "a gradual and continuous progression toward a target which may never be attained" (p. 427).

Yet even if the linguistic target is ultimately unattainable, movement toward it appears to occur relatively rapidly, perhaps within a year, at least among children and adolescents, as Williams (1979) found in a study of English VOT produced and perceived by native speakers of Spanish acquiring English between the ages of 8 and 16. In addition, as the English VOTs for the native Spanish speakers in Williams's study began to approximate those of age-matched English monolinguals, their Spanish VOTs restructured, shifting in the direction of the English monolinguals' VOTs and thus revealing bidirectional cross-language influence.

A somewhat different and more complex pattern of findings was obtained in a study by Mack (1990) in which two temporal features—VOT and voicing-conditioned vowel duration—were analyzed in the French and English of a 10-year-old French–English bilingual child whose speech production was compared to that of an age-matched monolingual native speaker of French and of English. The bilingual had been spoken to in French by his native-French-speaking mother from birth, yet had been raised in the United States and had attended only English-language schools and appeared to be English dominant.

The two monolingual children produced average VOTs for the voiced consonants /b,d,g/ of 14 and 20 msec in French and English, respectively—values only slightly shorter than those of the bilingual, whose French and English VOTs were 28 and 24 msec, respectively. More important, the bilingual's

French and English voiced-consonant values were partially shared. Specifically, his voiced consonants had similar VOTs but there were differences in the occurrence of prevoicing associated with them. That is, he prevoiced 17% of his French voiced consonants, quite unlike the French monolingual who prevoiced 97%, and he prevoiced 3% of his English voiced consonants, quite similar to the English monolingual who prevoiced 10%.

Still another finding emerged in this child's VOTs for the voiceless consonants /p,t,k/. Here the monolingual children's values for French and English were 34 and 76 msec, respectively, while the bilingual's values in French and English were 66 and 108 msec, respectively. This indicates that the bilingual's French voiceless VOT value was much closer to that of the English monolingual than to that of the French monolingual. Yet his English VOT was also considerably longer than that of the English monolingual, suggesting that he may have been exaggerating his cross-language voicing contrast: Had he used a VOT close to that of the English monolingual, his voiceless categories in French and English would have coalesced.

Somewhat surprisingly, yet another pattern of temporal values emerged in the bilingual's voicing-conditioned vowel-duration ratios—the ratio of the duration of his vowels preceding voiceless consonants to the duration of his vowels preceding voiced consonants. As will be recalled from Mack (1982, cited earlier), this ratio is far smaller in English than in French. This bilingual's values in French and English were differentiated—but in a direction opposite to that predicted if his French had been influenced by his English. That is, the French and English monolinguals' values were 80% and 59%, respectively (and these values were quite close to those obtained for adult monolingual native speakers of these languages by Mack, 1982). Yet the duration of this bilingual's French vowels in the voiceless context was 65% that of his vowels in the voiced context whereas the duration of his English vowels in the voiceless context was 75% of the duration of his vowels in the voiced context.

Thus in some respects, this bilingual's phonetic systems appeared shared, whereas in other respects they were separate. Moreover some temporal values—in both of his languages—exhibited a shift in the direction of his dominant language, English, whereas others did not, possibly due to differences in the linguistic importance or perceptual salience of the two temporal features examined.

Because these results may have been idiosyncratic, Mack, Bott, and Boronat (in preparation) examined VOT and voicing-conditioned vowel duration in three groups of age-matched children—seven French–English bilinguals, seven French monolinguals, and seven English monolinguals. All of the French-speaking children attended the same school in France, and the bilinguals had native-English-speaking mothers and native-French-speaking fathers. (The father of one of the bilinguals did not reside in the home.) There were two females and five males as well as two sets of siblings in each of the three groups, and the age range of the children in each group was identical (7 to 10 years). All but one of the bilinguals had been exposed to French and English since birth. (One had been exposed to French from age 3.) Language-background information revealed that most of the bilinguals were somewhat dominant in French, and all were highly fluent in French and moderately to highly fluent in English. The monolinguals (and their parents) were all native speakers of one of the two languages involved.

Results involving the analysis of VOT revealed general patterns in production as well as individual differences in the extent to which bilinguals' phonetic systems are shared or separate. Specifically, the bilinguals' average VOTs for each of the three voiceless consonants /p,t,k/ appeared to be intermediate to those of the French and English monolinguals as well as different in French and English (Fig. 12.4). That is, the bilinguals' average VOT for the three voiceless consonants combined was 34 msec in French and 47 msec in English, whereas it was 26 and 78 msec for the French and English monolinguals, respectively. (Interestingly, all four of these values are nearly identical to those obtained in the Caramazza et al. [1973] study of early adult French–English bilinguals.)

However, although these data appear to indicate that the bilinguals' voiceless consonant VOTs for French and English were intermediate to those of the

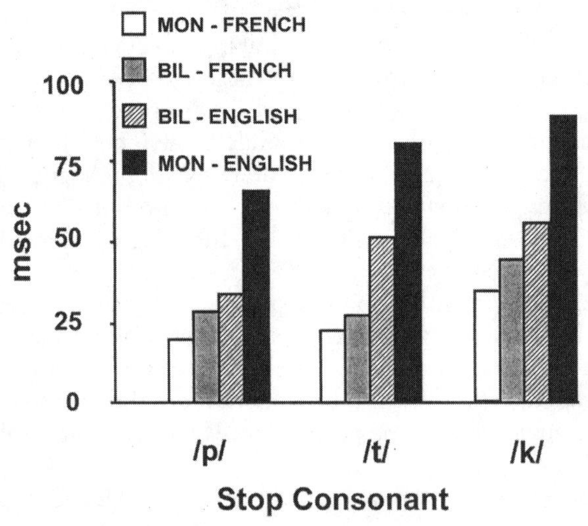

FIG. 12.4. Average VOTs for three voiceless stop consonants, /p,t,k/, produced by seven monolingual native French-speaking children, seven monolingual native English-speaking children, and seven children bilingual in French and English exposed to both languages from birth or very early childhood. Note that although it appears that the bilinguals' values are intermediate to those of the monolinguals and distinct from one another (thus approximating the pattern represented in Figure 1a), these averages do not reveal that there were actually two distinct patterns of voicing among the bilingual children, some of whom had apparently merged their VOT systems for these consonants in French and English.

monolinguals but were still differentiated, examination of the performance of individual bilinguals revealed two distinct subgroups. That is, one subgroup of bilinguals ($n = 3$) had clearly differentiated French and English VOT categories for the voiceless consonants whereas the other ($n = 4$) had nearly identical values for their French and English voiceless VOTs. This may have been due to differences in the two subgroups' dual-language experience: The subgroup with the undifferentiated VOT systems was comprised of two sets of siblings. The children in each of these two sets of siblings had probably had highly similar dual-language experience, and indeed the VOTs of the children in each of the two sets of siblings were quite similar to one another.

The results of a second-language pronunciation study using Quichua–Spanish bilinguals (Guion, et al., 2000) may provide further insight into the existence of the two subgroups of bilinguals found by Mack et al. That is, these researchers proposed a single-system hypothesis (Flege, 1995) in which bilinguals use a common phonological space for the production of their two languages and in which bilinguals' L2 capabilities are inversely correlated with the extent of their L1 use. Although the French–English bilingual children in the Mack et al. study had essentially two native languages rather than an L1 and an L2, they appeared to use French dominantly. To this extent, they were similar to the Quichua–Spanish bilinguals in the Guion et al. study because the latter were early bilinguals who used their L1 (Quichua) regularly and were fluent in their L2.

However, the bilinguals who exhibited two distinct VOT categories in French and English had markedly different amounts of English usage. That is, according to reports by their mothers, English was used in the home 90% of the time by one of these bilinguals whereas English was used in the home only 40% of the time by the other two—a percentage (interestingly) quite similar to that of all four children in the two sibling sets with merged VOT systems, who were reported as using English 50% of the time in the home. Thus, amount of use of the nondominant language cannot entirely account, in the Mack et al. study, for the performance of the bilingual subgroup that had two clearly distinguished VOT categories.

The existence of two bilingual subgroups may have been due to individual differences of yet-to-be-specified origin. This topic has received relatively little attention in studies of bilingual phonetic systems but could prove illuminating, especially if these differences can be related to neuropsychological or neurobiological variables (O' Boyle, 2000). For example, it is possible that *all* of the early French–English bilingual children could detect acoustic/phonetic differences in the VOTs of their two languages but that they differed in their ability to implement those differences motorically. Another possibility is that mechanisms or processes underlying speech production and perception are more closely aligned in some individuals than others.

Thus additional analyses and reanalyses of the data have been undertaken (Mack, in progress), including the examination of VOT in a subset of the words produced (French and English cognate and noncognate words), voicing-conditioned vowel duration, analogous analyses of the French and English speech of the bilinguals' mothers, and more extensive analysis of individual differences. This will permit a more precise characterization of the children's phonetic systems and the nature of their dual-language output and input. For example, the apparent influence of their French on their English may actually have been a reflection of their accurate production of nonnative-like English. For example, preliminary analysis has revealed that the English VOTs of the bilinguals' mothers was shifted away from previously reported English monolingual native-speaker values. This may have been because, at the time of testing, all of the native-English-speaking mothers had lived in France from 9 to 14 years and had thus been exposed to and used French rather extensively.

General Comments Regarding the Shared-Separate Approach. Taken together, the studies discussed above using the shared-separate approach reveal that it is difficult to state, without qualification, that bilinguals' phonetic systems are either shared or separate. Observed effects depend, at the least, on the phonetic property being examined and on learner-specific variables whose origin and impact are still to be ascertained.

The Age-Effect Approach

A third major approach to the study of bilinguals' phonetic systems is the age-effect approach (AEA). That age is a potential determinant in the formation of the L2 sound system was considered as early as 1953 in remarks made by the neurologist Wilder Penfield. He stated that his children, who had been exposed to three languages prior to age 5, exhibited "no confusion, no extra effort, no foreign accents" in any of their language unlike their parents, who in their attempts to acquire second and third languages later in life, did so only with considerable "toil, trouble, and headache"—and with accents (pp. 207–208). In recent decades, Penfield's observations have found shape in numerous studies using the AEA to test one or both of two hypotheses—that early bilinguals outperform late bilinguals in their acquisition of the L2 phonetic system and that there is a critical or sensitive period for the acquisition of an L2. Thus the AEA entails comparative analyses of bilinguals who differ in terms of their age at the onset of exposure to or acquisition of a second language in order to test the "earlier-is-better" proposition and the critical-period hypothesis.

"Earlier is Better." There is abundant anecdotal evidence that, in terms of the acquisition of an L2 phonetic system, early exposure to an L2 is associated with the development of a system that more fully approximates that of monolingual native speakers of that language—that is, that "earlier is better."

For example, Flege and colleagues have spent years examining age-related effects on the development of an L2 phonetic system and concluded that there is a relationship between age at the onset of the acquisition of an L2 and subsequent L2 proficiency. Flege and others, however, have asserted that this relationship need not be an inevitable consequence of developmental changes in the brain but may be related to other variables such as type of exposure to and amount of use of the L2 as well as the way in which the L1 and L2 phonetic systems are structured internally.

For example, Flege (1991) examined the production of Spanish and English VOTs in the phoneme /t/ in Spanish–English bilinguals who had acquired Spanish early (in childhood) and late (in adulthood). One of his findings was that the early bilinguals produced English-monolingual-like values in their English VOTs, whereas the late bilinguals produced compromise values with VOTs in English that fell between those of Spanish and English monolinguals. This is particularly interesting in view of the fact that the late bilinguals had been in the United States from 7 to 25 years and had thus had considerable exposure to their L2. Flege speculated that, unlike late learners, "early L2 learners have an enriched phonetic system that includes all phonetic categories possessed by native speakers of the L1 and L2" (p. 409).

Thornburgh and Ryalls (1998) also conducted a VOT analysis of early and late Spanish–English bilinguals. In this study, the late bilinguals had begun their acquisition of English at the age of 12 or later. They too found a significant difference in the performance of early and late bilinguals and proposed that age of acquisition was a likely determinant in the formation of the bilinguals' consonant production system, although they indicated that other variables that they did not evaluate, such as type and amount of L2 use and motivation to learn the L2, could have contributed to their results.

Another study using the AEA is that of Pallier, Bosch, and Sebastián-Gallés (1997) who examined the role of age of acquisition in two groups of early Spanish–Catalan bilinguals, one of whom had been exposed to Catalan from birth and the other of which had not been exposed to Catalan until attending kindergarten or grade school (but no later than age 6). In their study of the perception of a vowel contrast that occurs in Catalan but not Spanish, they used tests of identification and discrimination as well as category-goodness assessment and found differences between the two groups of early bilinguals, with only those exposed to Catalan from birth able to make the Catalan vowel contrast. They not only concluded that their "data provide strong evidence that the [L2] sound system ... is very biased by the statistics of the first language" (p. B16), but they proposed a "brain-based" explanation for their findings related to a developmental loss in neural plasticity.

The AEA was also used in a vowel study (cited earlier) by Flege, MacKay, and Meador (1999), who compared the production and perception of English vowels among Canadian English monolinguals with that of Italian–English bilinguals who had been born in Italy and had immigrated to Canada at different ages. The bilinguals were divided into three groups based on age of arrival (AOA) in Canada. One of the predictions made by these researchers was that the accuracy of the bilinguals' English vowel production would be inversely correlated with their AOA. Results did reveal that, overall, the bilinguals' vowel production was less accurate than the monolinguals'. However, not one of the vowels produced by the group who had arrived earliest was produced significantly less accurately than the vowels produced by the monolinguals.

To evaluate perception, these researchers used categorial discrimination with a modified oddity format and natural vowels produced by five speakers of English and five speakers of Italian. Such a task thus provides naturalistic stimuli and requires that speaker-specific effects be ignored. Subjects were presented with three stimuli in each trial. In half of the trials, all three stimuli were the same vowel; in the other half, one vowel differed from the other two. Subjects were required to identify the serial position of the dissimilar vowel or indicate "none" if they heard all vowels as the same. Again, the bilinguals with the earliest age of arrival performed as accurately in perceiving English vowels as did the English monolinguals while those with a later AOA did not. Flege et al. thus proposed that early exposure to an L2 may result in the formation of long-term memory representations for vowel contrasts that do not occur in the L1.

The Critical-Period Hypothesis. The name Eric Lenneberg has become inextricably linked with consideration of the critical-period hypothesis (CPH) as it relates to language acquisition: Lenneberg (1967) was the first researcher to articulate a relatively robust neurological explanation for what he believed was an invariable concomitant of the aging process—that is, a time-locked decrease in the ability to fully acquire or, in the case of some brain-damaged individuals, to reacquire language. He attributed this decrease to a progressive loss in hemispheric equipotentiality (the ability of either cerebral hemisphere to subserve language) resulting in the lateralization of language to the left hemisphere, and he further indicated that this lateralization was largely completed by puberty. Regrettably, these two components of his formulation of the CPH have taken firm hold, resulting in the frequent rebuttal of his central premise that there is a critical period (CP) for language acquisition. That is, the notion that there is a CP for language acquisition has often been rejected due to a lack of evidence that cerebral laterality is crucially involved and/or due to evidence that age-based effects on language behavior may end before or extend beyond puberty. Yet one can still posit the existence of a biologically based CP, as Lenneberg did, while rejecting his focus on the importance of laterality and puberty as causal variables.

Attention to this topic is particularly important because the CPH has attracted more interest and controversy among linguists and over a longer period of time than has any other hypothesis about the language systems of bilinguals.

(See, e.g., Birdsong, 1999, for a sample of the divergence of positions on this topic and Paradis, chap. 13, this volume, for a consideration of the relationship between "implicit linguistic competence" and a sensitive period for language acquisition).

Early support for the claim that there is a CP for language acquisition can be found in an oft-cited study by Oyama (1976), who presented speech samples produced by 60 Italian-dominant Italian–English bilinguals to American judges who rated the samples for accentedness. Subjects were grouped according to age of arrival and number of years in the United States, and AOA was found to be a much stronger determinant of accent than number of years in the United States. That is, those who had arrived in the United States earliest (from ages 6 to 10) were judged as having a weaker Italian accent than those who had arrived at a later age. Oyama suggested that this age effect is not due to a generalized loss of neural plasticity for intellectual learning in general but to language in particular, which she, along with Lenneberg, compared to other "biologically programmed" activities, such as walking.

Further support for the CPH is found in a vowel-production study conducted by Kim (1995), who compared Korean–English bilinguals categorized according to age of arrival in the United States with English monolinguals. She found that the bilinguals who had arrived prior to age 16 were able to maintain both a temporal and spectral distinction between /i/ and /I/, even though Korean lacks a phonemic /I/, but those who arrived at the age of 16 or later used only a temporal distinction, producing /i/ with a longer average duration than /I/. (In English, /i/ is inherently longer than /I/, although for native speakers of English this durational distinction is not the primary cue to the difference between these two vowels.) Thus, although they were able to perceive a difference between these vowels in English, they interpreted that difference as one of vowel length—that is, a temporal rather than spectral difference—and implemented it thusly.

This may have reflected the way in which the English /i–I/ contrast is presented pedagogically in Korean schools, where /i/ is often (merely) termed a long vowel and /I/ its shorter equivalent. Or it may indicate that, for some late bilinguals, temporally based contrasts are perceptually more salient than are spectral features—or that some temporally based contrasts in English are inherently more salient than are spectral features for any type of listener.

In a study designed to test the CPH in the acquisition of English vowel categories while statistically controlling for the possible confounding variable of length of exposure to English (operationalized as length of residence in the United States, or LOR), Mack (2001) and Mack, Bott, Trofimovich, and Baker (in progress) tested four groups of 15 Korean–English bilinguals and one group of 15 English native-speaking monolinguals (E. mon.). Subjects were tested in their perception of the /i–I/ and /u–U/ vowel contrasts, with the four vowels being those that occur in the English words *leak*, *lick*, *Luke*, and *look*, respectively. The bilinguals differed based upon age of arrival in the United States, with one group consisting of individuals who had been born in or who had arrived in the United States by the age of 4 and the others consisting of groups who had arrived at ages 5–9, 10–14, and 15 or later (hereafter, 0–4, 5–9, 10–14, and 15+). The /i–I/ and /u–U/ vowel contrasts were selected because, although Korean and English have a phonemic /i/ and /u/, Korean does not have a phonemic /I/ or /U/.

The /i–I/ stimuli and testing protocol were identical to those in Mack's 1989 study of early French-English bilinguals and English monolinguals, and the stimuli for the /u–U/ continuum were synthesized exactly as the stimuli for the /i–I/ continuum had been. (For both vowel pairs, 11-member continua were generated using Klatt's 1980 cascade/parallel software program.) Subjects were required to discriminate and identify the vowel contrasts, and an analysis of covariance (ANCOVA) with LOR as the covariate was used in the analysis of the identification-task crossover boundaries as determined by PROBIT analysis in which response functions were fitted to ogives (s-shaped curves).

In terms of the accuracy of discrimination of vowel pairs in the /i–I/ and /u–U/ continua, there emerged a significant group difference, and the 10–14 and 15+ groups appeared to discriminate vowel pairs in the middle of the continuum (i.e., pairs comprising the least prototypical vowels) less accurately than did the other groups. In the identification of /i–I/, the location of the crossover boundary for the 15+ group was significantly different from that of all other groups, and the group whose boundary was closest to that of (and not significantly different from) the E. mon. group was the 0–4 group. The location of the boundary for the E. mon. group was significantly different from that of all other groups, and the location of the boundary for the 5–9 and 10–14 groups was intermediate to that of the E. mon. and 15+ groups. Thus, there were systematic differences in the manner in which the groups segmented the /i–I/ vowel space. Contrary to expectation, there was no significant group difference in the location of the crossover boundary in the groups' identification of /u–U/.

Of particular interest was that, when age of arrival, experiential, usage, and fluency variables were analyzed statistically, age remained most strongly associated with the bilinguals' identification of /i–I/—but not of /u–U/. Finally, when the identification responses of those bilinguals who had acquired English prior to age 9 were compared with those of the French–English bilinguals in the Mack (1989) study (who had acquired both languages prior to age 8), it was found that both groups responded nearly identically to the /i–I/ continuum. This may reflect the influence of the Korean /i/ and French /i/ on the perception of the English /i/: Unlike the English /i/, which is relatively long and diphthongized, the Korean and French /i/ vowels are relatively short and are not strongly diphthongized. This would also indicate that at least some early bilinguals cannot completely deactivate one of their languages when functioning in the other.

In addition, from an original pool of over 100 potential subjects, far more bilinguals in the 15+ AOA range than in the 5–9 or 10–14 AOA range had to be excluded from the above-described data analysis—i.e., they were not included in the groups of 15 subjects analyzed because they could not reliably make the /i–I/ distinction in identification. Yet all monolinguals and all of the bilinguals in the 0–4 AOA range group were able to do so—a strong indicator that with increasing age at the onset of L2 acquisition comes increasing difficulty in forming certain L2 vowel categories.

Thus, these data provide evidence that, for some vowel contrasts, there is not only an age-of-acquisition effect but possibly a critical-period effect. It is therefore maintained that when bilinguals must form an entirely new category, as the Korean–English bilinguals did for the English vowel /I/, only those with extremely early exposure to that vowel will perform as native monolinguals. If cast in terms of a revised model of the CPH (discussed later) one could thus argue that, with respect to some measures of phonetic performance, exposure to an L2 occurring between birth and about 4 years of age may fall within a critical period whereas exposure between about ages 5 to 14 may fall within a sensitive period. Exposure occurring at about age 15 or later may fall within a sensitive period for some individuals, whereas others must rely upon their ability to apply specific processing strategies to an L2 phonetic task, such as treating a nonnative vowel as an acoustically proximitous native vowel.

A final and related comment is needed regarding the finding of a different pattern of responses to the two vowel pairs in the identification tasks. This may have been due to the shape of the Korean vowel space and its influence upon the bilinguals' perception of the English vowels. That is, Korean has a high-back unrounded vowel /ɯ/ that is acoustically similar to the English /U/ (Fig. 12.5).

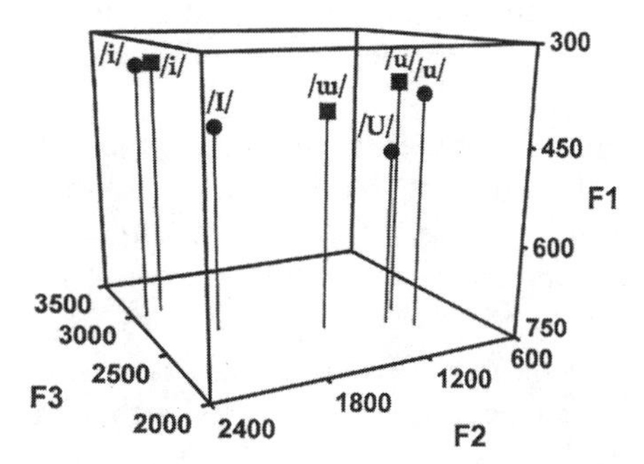

FIG. 12.5. A 3-D plot, using absolute formant-frequency values for F1, F2, and F3, of the English and Korean high front and back vowels. As is apparent, the English and Korean /i/ are quite similar in terms of their formant frequencies, as are the English and Korean /u/. The English /I/ and /U/ are nonoccurrent in Korean, but the Korean high back unrounded vowel /ɯ/ is acoustically proximitous to the English /U/. (Values for English are those obtained from English males by Hillenbrand, Getty, Clark, & Wheeler [1995]; values for Korean are those obtained from Korean males by Yang [1996].)

Thus the late bilinguals in the present study may have appeared to respond as the monolinguals did not because they had a distinct /U/ category but because they perceptually associated the English /U/ with the Korean /ɯ/, while the early bilinguals may have accurately formed distinct categories for English /u/ and /U/. A number of researchers (e.g., Best, 1995; Best, McRoberts, & Sithole, 1998; Flege, 1995) found that differences in the way in which nonnative sound contrasts are perceived are related to the extent to which they can be assimilated to native-language categories.

Here it is proposed that, for bilinguals whose L1 lacks the English phoneme /I/, that phoneme will either be perceived differently by early (0–4) and late (15+) bilinguals, resulting in a different segmentation of the /i–I/ vowel space, or late bilinguals will be completely unable to form a new vowel category and will simply assimilate that phoneme to the L1 vowel perceived as being most similar to it—in this case the Korean /i/. And for those late bilinguals whose L1 lacks the English phoneme /U/ but who are aware of the /u–U/ contrast in English, that phoneme will be assimilated to or treated as the L1 vowel perceived as being most similar to it (in this case /ɯ/), whereas it will be categorized in a monolingual-like manner (as /U/) by early bilinguals. Hence the early and late bilinguals may only have *appeared* to respond similarly to the English /u–U/ contrast—that is, their responses to it in the identification task were nearly identical, but for different reasons.

This proposal is supported by the results of a cross-linguistic vowel perception study conducted by Trofimovich and Baker (2000) in which native-speaking Koreans, grouped according to age of arrival in the United States and amount of experience with English, mapped English vowels onto their Korean counterparts. Results revealed that most of the bilinguals mapped the English vowel /U/ onto the Korean vowel /u/, and when they did not, they mapped it onto the Korean vowel /ɯ/. Moreover, only those bilinguals who had arrived earliest in the United States (at an average age of 9) could discriminate the English /u/ and /U/.

What is thus apparent is that there appear to be age-based effects on the formation of bilinguals' L2 phonetic systems and, with respect to the production and/or perception of some types of sounds, there may be an early and critical period of time in L2 acquisition when monolingual/native-like performance is possible.

Concerns About the Critical-Period Hypothesis. Although the cited studies suggest some support for the hypothesis that there exists a maturationally based period of time during which an L2 sound system can be acquired in a monolingual/native-like manner, there remains a lack of consensus as to when this period ends, possibly due to cross-study differences in subject selection, test stimuli, task type, and data analysis. Nonetheless, no discussion of the CPH would be complete without acknowledging that researchers are often in marked disagreement about the very existence of a critical period in the acquisition of an L2 phonetic system (e.g., Bialystok & Hakuta, 1999; Flege, 1987a; Hakuta, 1986). For example, Flege, Yeni-Komshian, and Liu (1999), although acknowledging the importance of age at the onset of exposure to an L2, attribute an observed age-related declination in L2 pronunciation accuracy to "differences in how, or if, L2 learners perceptually relate L2 sounds to the sounds making up the L1 phonetic inventory ... [possibly leading] to age-related differences in whether new [L2] phonetic categories are or are not established" (p. 99).

Other reasons for the lack of agreement regarding a proposed neurologically based critical period for the acquisition of an L2 system are reflected in the following often-posed questions: If there is a CP for the acquisition of an L1, as data have suggested in examples of L1 deprivation among hearing and deaf individuals (e.g., in the cases of Genie [Curtiss, 1977], Chelsea [Curtiss, 1988], and E. M. [Grimshaw, Adelstein, Bryden, & MacKinnon, 1998), and among learners of ASL [Mayberry & Eichen, 1991; Newport, 1988]), is there perforce a CP for the acquisition of an L2? If there is a CP for the acquisition of an L2 phonetic system, is there a CP for other linguistic components, and does it end at the same time for all components (and modalities and features)? If there is evidence of a CP for the acquisition of an L2 phonetic system, is it actually because age of L2 acquisition is confounded with other variables that affect L2 proficiency? And finally, what constitutes a CP and can it be operationalized in a way that permits researchers to detect neurologically based maturational limitations on the acquisition of an L2 system, and to do so without equating correlation with causality?

Addressing all of these questions is beyond the scope of this chapter, but several appear to have preliminary and promising answers. For example, data from a variety of tests involving the morphosyntactic system suggest that there is a critical period for the acquisition of this component of the L2 system and that it ends earlier than puberty—that is, between age 5 and about 8 or 9 (Bott, 1993; Johnson & Newport, 1989; Kim, 1997; Shim, 1995). It also appears that different modalities, components, and features are subject to different temporal constraints in acquisition (i.e., that there may be multiple critical or sensitive periods), although this conclusion may be due, in part, to cross-study differences in methodology and data analysis. Data are also emerging that point to a causal relationship between brain-based changes and language behavior (Neville et al., 1998), lending credibility to neurological proposals regarding age limitations in language acquisition. But what is most evident is that, due to the heterogeneity of its interpretations and the generality of its applications in language-acquisition studies, the critical-period concept needs clarification and the terms *critical* and *sensitive period* require modification. (See Bornstein, 1987, chap. 1, for an excellent account of the defining characteristics of such a period, and Moltz, 1973, for his distinction between a critical and optimal period, akin to the reformulated version proposed later in this chapter.)

Proposed Revised Definition of the Critical/Sensitive Period. Many researchers have abandoned the term *critical period* in favor of the term *sensitive period* when referring to language acquisition, asserting that, when an age-based declination in linguistic ability occurs, the declination is gradual rather than sudden or abrupt, as would be suggested by the notion of a critical period. Yet one can simply change the size of the intervals on the *x* axis of a graph purporting to demonstrate the presence of a critical period (e.g., change the measurement of time from years to months or weeks) and render gradual what was previously sudden. That is, mere numerical manipulation can make what appears to be a critical period into a sensitive period, and vice versa. (Customarily, in graphic representations of critical or sensitive periods, time is represented on the *x* axis and values associated with a particular trait, physical feature, mental property, ability, or behavior are represented on the *y* axis.)

It is thus proposed that the term *critical* be applied only to that time during which complete acquisition or normal development of a behavior, property, and so on occurs and that the term *sensitive* be applied to that time during which partial acquisition or development of a behavior, property, and so on remains possible—reflected graphically as a linear departure from, then arrival at, asymptote as demonstrated in Fig. 12.6. (Note that some critical periods

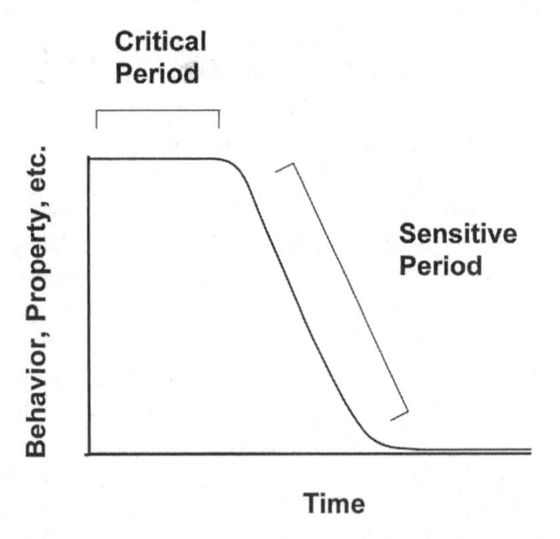

FIG. 12.6 A proposed revised model of the critical period. Here the critical period is only that period of time during which the behavior, property, etc. being examined is at maximal asymptote (top left of the ogive). The sensitive period is that period of time during which that being examined is still suspectible to complete or normal development, yet such susceptibility is subject to linear declination over time. The end of the sensitive period is manifested when that being examined reaches minimal asymptote (bottom right of the ogive). It is unlikely that in the evaluation of language-based behaviors, especially with relatively small samples, such an idealized model will be observed although it might be approximated.

should be represented with an inverted U-shaped function rather than as an ogive.) In other words, during a critical period, the "window of opportunity" is fully open; during a sensitive period, that window is in the process of closing; at the end of the sensitive period, the window has shut.

It then becomes necessary to ask, in terms of bilinguals' phonetic systems for example, "Complete or normal with respect to what or whom?" The answer depends on the judgment of the investigator and the variable(s) selected for examination. Admittedly, there is a lack of objectivity if age-based processes associated with language acquisition are compared to clear evidence of critical periods in embryology, from which the concept was originally derived. For example, one investigator might maintain that the complete or normal acquisition of VOT in one of a bilingual's two languages is equivalent to VOT as used by monolingual native speakers of that language, whereas another might assert that the complete or normal acquisition of VOT is equivalent to VOT as used by individuals who have acquired two native languages in childhood, as commonly occurs in multilingual societies. And another investigator might object to all comparative analyses of native and nonnative speakers, maintaining that no group of language users should be viewed as normative, thus rendering most investigations into a possible CP for L2 acquisition entirely moot.

Nonetheless, it is maintained that the proposed revised definition of critical and sensitive periods could be of considerable value in providing a reasoned approach for researchers who wish to test the possible presence of time-locked maturational constraints on the acquisition of phonetic features or properties, or on the acquisition of other linguistic elements, structures, or rules in bilinguals.

General Comments Regarding the Age-Effect Approach. Research into the correlational and causal relationships between age at the onset of second-language acquisition and subsequent performance in that language continues to be of import and continues to generate controversy. Yet many researchers have now concluded that earlier acquisition of a second language results in a more monolingual/native-like L2 phonetic system than does later acquisition, although these researchers do not all agree why. For example, some have proposed that, with age, language learners experience changes in certain affective variables such as motivation to learn an L2 or desire to acculturate to the community in which the learner's L2 is indigenous, and it is these changes that result in age-related effects in performance. Others have attributed the apparent finding of age-based effects to methodological factors, such as the confounding of age at the onset of L2 acquisition and duration of exposure to an L2.

In contrast, some researchers have taken the "earlier-is-better" assertion a step further by proposing not only that is there a maturational and neurological basis for the apparent advantage conferred by early language acquisition, but also that there is a critical period (or, in the terminology used by many, a sensitive period) for the acquisition of an L2 sound system and possibly for other language components as well.

Clearly what is needed are additional studies in which myriad age-related variables believed to influence the formation of an L2 sound system are controlled. In this way, the proposed primacy of age of acquisition as a determinant in the development of bilinguals' phonetic systems and the possibility that some linguistic components and/or modalities are particularly susceptible to a critical *and* sensitive period may be further evaluated.

RELEVANT MODELS

Although there is a great deal of information about the acquisition of an L1 sound system (see, e.g., Jusczyk, chap. 3, this volume), few formal models have been proposed to account for the development and maintenance of bilinguals' phonetic systems. As indicated in the examples of experiments considered earlier, much of the work done to date has provided descriptions of how dual-language sound systems are organized with reference to those of monolingual and/or native speakers or with reference to one another. Additionally, research has been conducted to determine the extent to which age at the onset of a second language relates to the subsequent formation of an L2 sound system. However, three major models, each of which is relevant to the formation and maintenance of L2 sound systems, have been proposed and may provide much-needed theoretically and empirically based explanations of how bilinguals' phonetic systems develop. These are Kuhl's native language magnet theory, Best's perceptual assimilation model, and Flege's speech learning model.

The Native Language Magnet Theory

Kuhl's native language magnet (NLM) theory is a prototype model. (See Dopkins & Gleason, 1997, for an overview of prototype and exemplar models.) Kuhl et al. (1992, p. 606) characterized speech prototypes as sounds "that are identified by adult speakers of a given language as ideal representatives of a given phonetic category." Moreover, they proposed that prototypes function as "perceptual magnets" (manifested in infants by the age of 6 months) that warp the perceptual space such that prototypes will be perceived as more similar to sounds that are their perceptual variants than will nonprototypes in relation to their variants. Thus it should be more difficult to discriminate a prototypical /i/ from vowels that are proximitous to it acoustically than to discriminate a nonprotypical /i/ from vowels that are proximitous to it. Further, Kuhl stated that perceptual magnets "are a natural result of infants' build-up of representations that code the input of native-language speakers" (1993, p. 130).

Once language-specific magnets develop, infants should be unable to discriminate sounds that they previously could, because "the developing magnet pulls sounds that were once discriminable towards a single magnet, making them no longer discriminable" (Kuhl, 1993, p. 131). This would thus account for the finding that prelinguistic infants are able to discriminate speech sounds that are nonphonemic in their L1 environment, but only until about the age of 10 to 12 months (Werker, Gilbert, Humphrey, & Tees, 1981; Werker & Lalonde, 1988; Werker & Tees, 1983, 1984). It could also provide an explanation for why adult L2 learners find some L2 sounds more difficult to acquire and discriminate than others: If the L2 sound is perceptually similar to an established (prototypical) L1 sound, it will be "pulled" into that L1 sound category. Finally, although the NLM theory appears to be perceptually based, Kuhl and Iverson (1995) stated that speech representations are auditory in the initial stages of language acquisition but that they then guide motoric implementation as speech representations become polymodal.

Some have countered that the proposed perceptual-magnet effect merely reflects the fact that it is easier to discriminate pairs of sounds across than within phonemic categories (e.g., Lotto, Kluender, & Holt, 1998), and others have asserted that there are methodological problems with the intepretation of data purporting to demonstrate the presence of perceptual magnets. Yet the NLM theory continues to generate research and garner support (Diesch, Iverson, Kettermann, & Siebert, 1999; Iverson & Kuhl, 2000). The NLM theory could also provide an explanation for one of the findings reported in Mack (2001) and Mack, Bott, Trofimovich, and Baker (in progress) involving Korean-English bilinguals. As will be recalled, the 10–14 and 15+ bilingual groups discriminated the nonprototypical vowels less accurately than did any other groups. It could be proposed that these late bilinguals had relatively weak English /I/ and /U/ prototypes and therefore weak perceptual-magnet effects, manifested as relatively poorer discrimination on nonprototypical vowels, which should be more accurately discriminated if there are well-established prototypes. Further analyses of the discrimination data, including responses from those bilinguals who were excluded from the original analysis due to their apparent lack of two categories in vowel identification, are being undertaken to determine if this preliminary finding is supported.

However, a perceptual-magnet effect cannot it seems account for the fact that some early bilinguals have two distinct VOT systems whereas others with apparently similar dual-language experience, and hence presumably similar amounts of exposure to prototypical and nonprototypical vowels, do not, as observed in the VOT production of the early French–English bilingual children discussed earlier (Mack, in progress; Mack et al., in progress). Therefore it might be necessary to posit the existence of learner-specific prototypes. If so, it would be important to specify exactly which learner-specific variables determine how or when a prototype is formed—a seemingly daunting task. (However, see Aaltonen et al., 1997, who found differences in one brain-wave component in good versus poor speech-sound categorizers.)

The Perceptual Assimilation Model

Best's perceptual assimilation model (PAM) is, unlike the NLM theory, a fundamentally gestural model. It is also primarily directed at determining how adult L2 learners incorporate L2 sounds into their phonetic system and is based on the widely accepted premise that language-specific experience influences the perception of phonemic contrasts (Best, 1994; Best & Strange, 1992). The extent to which it does so depends largely on differences in the articulatory/phonetic properties of the languages involved (Hallé, Best, & Levitt, 1999).

Specifically, Best advocated a "direct realist view" of L1 acquisition that asserts that perceptual primitives are articulatory gestures. In acquiring their L1, children initially perceive only nonlinguistic information in the speech signal but then "discover correspondences between higher-order invariants of relations among gestures, or gestural constellations, and linguistically functioning elements, ... specific to the language environment" (Best, 1995, p. 178). Moreover, because there is a finite number of gestural possibilities due to the inherent structure of the human supralaryngeal vocal tract, the phonological spaces of different languages overlap, and nonnative speech segments are perceived in relation to segments proximal (or nonproximal) in the phonological space as they are produced. In fact, if the native/nonnative gestural distance is sufficiently large, the nonnative sounds may not only be unassimilated to native categories but may actually be perceived as nonspeech.

Finally, although Best maintained that perceptual learning can occur into adulthood, she acknowledged that children and adults should differ in their ability to perceive nonnative speech sounds due to differences in their "history of experience" with their L1 (1995, p. 198). In this respect, she seems to place greater emphasis on external influences, such as amount of L1 or L2 experience, in the formation of nonnative phonetic systems than on internal influences, such as maturational changes in the brain. Additionally, it is not entirely clear what predictions the PAM would make about the formation of two phonetic systems when simultaneous acquisition of two languages or very early acquisition of an L2 occurs, because it has been applied primarily to cases in which exposure to an L2 system occurs when an L1 system has already been well established. For example, although Guion, Flege, Akahane-Yamada, and Pruitt (2000) found support for the PAM in their study of experienced L2 learners, their subjects were not early bilinguals.

The Speech Learning Model

The speech learning model (SLM), developed by Flege and colleagues, is similar to Best's perceptual assimilation model in terms of the role it ascribes to phonological similarity in the formation of second-language sound systems, yet it includes additional proposals regarding bilinguals' phonetic systems.

Specifically, Flege's SLM (1995) includes a fairly extensive set of postulates and hypotheses whose main features are summarized as follows: The same processes utilized in L1 acquisition can be applied in L2 acquisition regardless of the age of the language learner; phonetic categories established in childhood for the L1 evolve over the life span; bilinguals attempt to maintain a (maximal) contrast between L1 and L2 categories; the greater the perceptual dissimilarity between L1 and L2 sounds, the more likely it is that a new category will be formed for L2 sounds, but if a new category cannot be formed due to equivalence classification, a single category will be used to link L1 and L2 sounds which will eventually resemble one another in production; and the likelihood that there will be differences in L1 and L2 sounds—and between L2 sounds that are noncontrastive in the L1—decreases as age of learning increases.

Flege and colleagues have provided extensive amounts of empirical data supporting these claims and in so doing, quite effectively demonstrated a relationship between age of L2 acquisition and L2 production and perception. However, although Flege agreed in general that "earlier is better," he did not agree with a neurologically based explanation for age-related acquisitional effects based upon maturational changes in the brain. He instead placed relatively more emphasis on the role of experiential, usage, fluency, and language-based variables. Flege also did not believe that there is sufficient evidence of a critical or sensitive period in the acquisition of an L2 phonetic system, citing, for example, empirical data demonstrating a linear relationship between age of L2 acquisition and L2 pronunciation accuracy rather than an abrupt age-associated discontinuity in performance (Flege, Yeni-Komshian, & Liu, 1999). Nonetheless, Flege's SLM is arguably the most ambitious and comprehensive model of the acquisition of L2 phonetic systems and of the maintenance of two phonetic systems in various types of bilinguals.

SUMMARY

In this chapter, three dominant methodological approaches to the study of bilinguals' phonetic systems have been presented—the monolingual-comparison approach, the shared-separate approach, and the age-effect approach. Representative examples of empirical research utilizing these approaches have been discussed and three major theories that could account for at least some of the behavioral phenomena observed have been considered.

Although the data are not yet conclusive, there is mounting evidence that, if tests are sufficiently sensitive, very few bilinguals—regardless of age at the onset of exposure to a second language—will be found to function at the phonetic level exactly as native monolinguals. This is due at least in part to the inevitable influence, however slight, of one system upon the other. Although the two phonetic systems may be effectively shared or separate depending upon experiential, usage, acquisitional, affective, age of acquisition, or other variables, they cannot remain "hermetically sealed" from one another in all respects. Further, it is claimed that age will emerge as a strong predictor of the ultimate structure of bilinguals' phonetic systems due to a maturationally based and possibly nonlinear change in neural plasticity, to the brain's inability to recruit already dedicated neural networks in core areas for speech production and perception, and/or to other yet-to-be-specified developmental changes in the brain.

Such changes may be manifested as a critical or sensitive period for some phonetic features in the spoken and/or auditory modality and could be related to what Greenough and colleagues (e.g., Greenough, Black, & Wallace, 1987) termed an "experience-expectant" process in development. Such a process is characterized by an abundance of synapses (sites of connectivity between neurons) in the brain of an organism, "a subset of which will be selectively preserved by experience-generated neural activity" within a given window of time (Greenough et al., 1987, p. 544). In contrast, an "experience-dependent" process results in the formation of new synapses as a result of certain types of experience and appears not to be temporally bound. It is thus possible that some aspects of bilinguals' speech production or perception are subject to an experience-expectant time-locked process whereas others are not. As Greenough et al. stated, because language acquisition is a relatively long and complex process, "a theory invoking a single, protracted 'sensitive period' may eventually be expanded to reflect the multiple involvement of many brain regions, each with its own time course and experiential sensitivities" (p. 553).

Finally, any one of the three major models discussed—Kuhl's native language magnet theory, Best's perceptual assimilation model, and Flege's speech learning model—can quite capably account for some (even many) aspects of bilingual phonetic performance, yet none of them can yet account for all.

For example, both the native language magnet theory and the perceptual assimilation model focus largely on the formation and structure of the perceptual space, and their premises are based primarily on a combination of results from infant speech perception and the cross-linguistic processing of L2 speech sounds by adults with limited (or no) L2 experience. Thus the extent to which their predictions apply to speech production in fluent or early bilinguals or in bilinguals with two native languages is not readily apparent.

On the other hand, in his speech learning model, Flege addressed both speech production and perception and considered the phonetic systems of early and late bilinguals. He also attempted to operationalize similarity and dissimilarity between phonetic elements in the L1 and L2. Nonetheless, further work is needed in order to develop a standardized L1/L2 distance metric—possibly combining language-user characteristics, articulatory variables, and perceptual features in a model with weighted factors. In this way, specific predictions about the formation and structure of bilinguals' phonetic systems could not only be tested, but findings across studies and researchers could be validly compared. Flege also remained relatively uncommitted regarding the specification of possible neurological mechanisms underlying the processes with which the SLM deals.

Still, all three of the cited models have stimulated a considerable amount of important research and each merits further testing. It would, for example, be of interest to determine how these models would account for the formation of the phonetic systems of multilinguals—individuals with three or more languages—and how they might be modified if additional evidence emerges revealing the presence of neurologically based maturational (and possibly nonlinear) changes in L2 speech perception or production.

CONCLUSION

A number of neuroscientists have used evidence from brain damage, intracranial electro-cortical stimulation, the Wada test (which selectively deactivates one cerebral hemisphere), and brain imaging to determine to what extent bilinguals' languages are monolingual-like, shared or separate, or dependent on age at the onset of L2 acquisition (e.g., Berthier, Starkstein, Lylyk, & Leiguarda, 1990; Chee et al., 1999; Chee, Tan, & Thiel, 1999; Dehaene et al. 1997; Fabbro, Peru, & Skrap, 1997; Gloning & Gloning, 1965; Illes et al., 1999; Klein, Zatorre, Milner, Meyer, & Evans, 1994; Kim, Relkin, Lee, & Hirsch, 1997; Ojemann & Whitaker, 1978; Paradis, 1983; Perani et al., 1996, 1998; Rapport, Tan, & Whitaker, 1983). Yet most of this work has focused on—or has at least accessed—the morphosyntactic or lexicosemantic systems of bilinguals, not solely the phonetic systems. This is due in part to methodological difficulties associated with undertaking dynamic neurofunctional examination of sound systems. For example, imaging techniques that measure changes in regional cerebral blood flow or oxygenation associated with brain activity, such as functional magnetic resonance imaging (fMRI) or positron emission tomography (PET), render it difficult to assess speech production due to the sensitivity of these techniques to movements associated with speaking (Rosen, Ojemann, Ollinger, & Petersen, 2000).

A major attempt to relate bilingual phonetic processing to neurophysiology can be found in dichotic-listening experiments conducted with bilinguals (e.g., Hynd, Teeter, & Stewart, 1980; McKeever, Hunt, Wells, & Yazzie, 1989; Wesche & Schneiderman, 1982). In dichotic listening, stimuli are presented simultaneously to the left and right ears purportedly to determine whether the right or left cerebral hemisphere is preferentially processing the stimuli. (Certain types of speech stimuli presented to the right ear are reported more accurately than are stimuli presented to the left ear when such stimuli are presented simultaneously. Because dichotic listening produces contralateral effects, this finding would be interpreted as evidence of left-hemisphere processing.)

It was once assumed that dichotic listening could reveal the extent to which different types of stimuli are processed by the left or right cerebral hemisphere, although there are now acknowledged methodological and interpretive problems associated with this technique. Moreover, in most dichotic listening experiments conducted with bilinguals, phonetic stimuli have been used not to obtain information about the structure of bilinguals' phonetic systems per se, but to make generalizations about the extent to which an *entire* language system is lateralized to one hemisphere or the other. This renders questionable the use of dichotic listening as an appropriate neurologically based approach to the analysis of bilinguals' phonetic systems.

Thus, if we are to better understand the neurological correlates of the phonetic systems of bilinguals and if we are to provide neurologically based tests of the models considered here, it will be necessary to use and refine clinical and experimental techniques in tests of speech production and perception in order to identify the neural substrates of bilinguals' phonetic systems. Examples of the types of techniques that could be applied to bilinguals include the examination of auditory-evoked potentials in the perception of VOT (Sharma & Dorman, 1999), PET scanning during phonetic discrimination and monitoring (Zatorre, Meyer, Gjedde, & Evans, 1996), and imaging using fMRI in tasks of articulatory and phonetic sequencing (Riecker et al., 2000).

It would also prove fruitful to further examine the relationship between mind and brain (e.g., Fischbach, 1992; Mack, 2002), the role of individual differences in language acquisition and behavior (e.g., Damasio & Damasio, 1992; Shore, 1995), the relationship between brain growth and developmental change (Segalowitz & Rose-Krasnor, 1992), and the strength of the correlation between age-based effects on the formation of an L2 sound-system and brain-based phenomena such as time-locked changes or discontinuities in the development of neuronal structures associated with speech production and perception at the cortical and sub-cortical levels (Jacobs, 1988; Lamendella, 1977; Locke, 1997; Neville, 1985; Pulvermüller & Schumann, 1994). Findings from animal studies in which neurological changes have been correlated with experience and learning might also provide productive models for language-based behaviors (e.g., Greenough et al., 1987; Kandel & Hawkins, 1992).

Finally, there is a need for further study of bilinguals' performance on psycholinguistic and neurolinguistic tests in which the same subjects respond to tasks accessing different linguistic components (e.g., Mack, 1986; Weber-Fox & Neville, 1996). In addition, basic assumptions in theoretical linguistics, such as the existence of a language-acquisition device and constraints on learnability, should be evaluated in terms of their applicability to data obtained in studies of second-language acquisition data and bilingualism.

In conclusion, extending the application of a variety of techniques to the study of language and memory in general and to the examination of bilinguals' phonetic systems in particular would substantially enhance what is known about how dual-language systems are acquired, organized, and maintained. It is hoped that findings from the linguistic, psychological, and neurological sciences will continue to converge and, in so doing, yield important new information about how the sound systems of two languages coexist in one bilingual brain.

ACKNOWLEDGMENTS

Funding for some of the projects described was provided by the Department of the Air Force through the Massachusetts Institute of Technology Lincoln Laboratory and by Research Board grants from the University of Illinois at Urbana-Champaign. Gratitude is extended to Wendy Baker, Sandra Merz Bott, Gabseon Lee, Kyong Hyon Pyo, and Pavel Trofimovich for their assistance in the preparation of this chapter.

REFERENCES

Aaltonen, O., Eerola, O., Hellström, Å., Uusipaikka, E., & Heikki Lang, A. (1997). Perceptual magnet effect in the light of behavioral and psychophysiological data. *Journal of the Acoustical Society of America, 101,* 1090–1105.

Baetens Beardsmore, H. (1986). *Bilingualism: Basic principles* (2nd ed.). Clevedon: Multilingual Matters.

Baker, W., & Trofimovich, P. (in press). Does perception precede production? Evidence from Korean-English bilinguals. In R. Brend, A. Lommel, & A. Melby (Eds.), *LACUS Forum XXVII.* Fullerton, CA: Linguistic Association of Canada and the United States.

Berthier, M. L., Starkstein, S. E., Lylyk, P., & Leiguarda, R. (1990). Differential recovery of languages in a bilingual patient: A case study using selective amytal test. *Brain and Language, 38,* 449–453.

Best, C. T. (1994). The emergence of native-language phonological influences in infants: A perceptual assimilation model. In J. Goodman & H. C. Nusbaum (Eds.), *The development of speech perception: The transition from speech sounds to spoken words* (pp. 167–224). Cambridge, MA: MIT Press.

Best, C. T. (1995). A direct realist view of cross-language speech perception. In W. Strange (Ed.), *Speech perception and linguistic experience: Issues in cross-language research* (pp. 171–204). Timonium, MD: York Press.

Best, C. T., McRoberts, G. W., & Sithole, N. N. (1988). The phonological basis of perceptual loss for non-native contrasts: Maintenance of discrimination among Zulu clicks by English-speaking adults and infants. *Journal of Experimental Psychology: Human Perception and Performance, 14,* 345–360.

Best, C. T., & Strange, W. (1992). Effects of phonological and phonetic factors on cross-language perception of approximants. *Journal of Phonetics, 20,* 305–330.

Bialystok, E., & Hakuta, K. (1999). Confounded age: Linguistic and cognitive factors in age differences for second language acquisition. In D. Birdsong (Ed.), *Second language acquisition and the critical period hypothesis* (pp. 161–182). Mahwah, NJ: Lawrence Erlbaum Associates.

Birdsong, D. (Ed.). (1999). *Second language acquisition and the critical period hypothesis.* Mahwah, NJ: Lawrence Erlbaum Associates.

Bloomfield, L. (1933). *Language.* Chicago: Chicago University Press.

Bond, Z. S., & Fokes, J. (1991). Perception of English voicing by native and nonnative adults. *Studies in Second Language Acquisition, 13,* 471–492.

Boothroyd, A., & Nittrouer, S. (1988). Mathematical treatment of context effects in phoneme and word recognition. *Journal of the Acoustical Society of America, 84,* 101–114.

Bornstein, M. H. (1987). Sensitive periods in development: Definition, existence, utility, and meaning. In M. H. Bornstein (Ed.), *Sensitive periods in development* (pp. 3–17). Hillsdale, NJ: Lawrence Erlbaum Associates.

Bott, S. M. (1993). *Speech intelligibility and bilingualism: The effects of age of acquisition.* Unpublished doctoral dissertation, University of Illinois, Urbana-Champaign.

Bradlow, A. R., & Pisoni, D. B. (1999). Recognition of spoken words by native and non-native listeners: Talker-, listener-, and item-related factors. *Journal of the Acoustical Society of America, 106,* 2074–2085.

Caramazza, A., Yeni-Komshian, G. H., Zurif, E. B., & Carbone, E. (1973). The acquisition of a new phonological contrast: The case of stop consonants in French-English bilinguals. *Journal of the Acoustical Society of America, 54,* 421–428.

Chee, M. W. L., Caplan, D., Soon, C. S., Sriram, N., Tan, E. W. L., Thiel, T., & Weekes, B. (1999). Processing of visually presented sentences in Mandarin and English studied with fMRI. *Neuron, 23,* 127–137.

Chee, M. W. L., Tan, E. W. L., & Thiel, T. (1999). Mandarin and English single word processing studied with functional magnetic resonance imaging. *The Journal of Neuroscience, 19,* 3050–3056.

Chen, M. (1970). Vowel length variation as a function of the voicing of the consonant environment. *Phonetica, 22,* 125–159.

Cho, T., & Ladefoged, P. (1999). Variation and universals in VOT: Evidence from 18 languages. *Journal of Phonetics, 27,* 207–229.

Conrad, L. (1989). The effects of time-compressed speech on native and EFL listening comprehension. *Studies in Second Language Acquisition, 11,* 1–16.

Corder, S. P. (1981). *Error analysis and interlanguage.* Oxford: Oxford University Press.

Curtiss, S. (1977). *Genie: A psycholinguistic study of a modern-day "wild child."* New York: Academic Press.

Curtiss, S. (1988). Abnormal language acquisition and grammar: Evidence for the modularity of language. In L. M. Hyman & C. N. Li (Eds.), *Language, speech, and mind: Studies in honour of Victoria A. Fromkin* (pp. 81–102). London: Routledge.

Cutler, A., Mehler, J., Norris, D., & Segui, J. (1986). The syllable's differing role in the segmentation of French and English. *Journal of Memory and Language, 25,* 385–400.

Cutler, A., Mehler, J., Norris, D., & Segui, J. (1992). The monolingual nature of speech segmentation by bilinguals. *Cognitive Psychology, 24,* 381–410.

Damasio, A. R., & Damasio, H. (1992, September). Brain and language. *Scientific American,* pp. 89–95.

Dehaene, S., Dupoux, E., Mehler, J., Cohen, L., Paulesu, E., Perani, D., van de Moortele, P.-F., Lehéricy, S., & Le Bihan, D. (1997). Anatomical variability in the cortical representation of first and second language. *NeuroReport, 8,* 3809–3815.

Deuchar, M., & Clark, A. (1996). Early bilingual acquisition of the voicing contrast in English and Spanish. *Journal of Phonetics, 24,* 351–365.

Diesch, E., Iverson, P., Kettermann, A., & Siebert, C. (1999). Measuring the perceptual magnet effect in the perception of /i/ by German listeners. *Psychological Research, 62,* 1–19.

Dopkins, S., & Gleason, T. (1997). Comparing exemplar and prototype models of categorization. *Canadian Journal of Experimental Psychology, 5,* 212–230.

Fabbro, F., Peru, A., & Skrap, M. (1997). Language disorders in bilingual patients after thalamic lesions. *Journal of Neurolinguistics, 10,* 347–367.

Fischbach, G. D. (1992, September). Mind and brain. *Scientific American,* pp. 48–57.

Flege, J. E. (1980). Phonetic approximation in second language acquisition. *Language Learning, 30,* 117–134.

Flege, J. E. (1987a). A critical period for learning to pronounce foreign languages? *Applied Linguistics, 8,* 162–177.

Flege, J. E. (1987b). The production of "new" and "similar" phones in a foreign language: Evidence for the effect of equivalence classification. *Journal of Phonetics, 15,* 47–65.

Flege, J. E. (1991). Age of learning affects the authenticity of voice-onset time (VOT) in stop consonants produced in a second language. *Journal of the Acoustical Society of America, 89,* 95–411.

Flege, J. E. (1995). Second language speech learning: Theory, findings, and problems. In W. Strange (Ed.), *Speech perception and linguistic experience: Issues in cross-language research* (pp. 233–277). Timonium, MD: York Press.

Flege, J. E., Bohn, O.-S., & Jang, S. (1997). Effects of experience on non-native speakers' production and perception of English vowels. *Journal of Phonetics, 25,* 437–470.

Flege, J. E., & Eefting, W. (1988). Imitation of a VOT continuum by native speakers of English and Spanish: Evidence for phonetic category formation. *Journal of the Acoustical Society of America, 83,* 729–740.

Flege, J. E., & Hillenbrand, J. (1984). Limits on phonetic accuracy in foreign language speech production. *Journal of the Acoustical Society of America, 76,* 708–721.

Flege, J. E., MacKay, I. R. A., & Meador, D. (1999). Native Italian speakers' perception and production of English vowels. *Journal of the Acoustical Society of America, 106,* 2973–2988.

Flege, J. E., Munro, M. J., & Skelton, L. (1992). Production of the word-final English /t/–/d/ contrast by native speakers of English, Mandarin, and Spanish. *Journal of the Acoustical Society of America, 92,* 128–143.

Flege, J. E., Takagi, N., & Mann, V. (1995). Japanese adults can learn to produce English /r/ and /l/ accurately. *Language and Speech, 38,* 25–55.

Flege, J. E., Yeni-Komshian, G. H., & Liu, S. (1999). Age constraints on second-language acquisition. *Journal of Memory and Language, 41,* 78–104.

Gloning, I., & Gloning, K. (1965). Aphasien bei Polyglotten. *Wiener Zeitschrift für Nervenheilkunde und deren Grenzgebiete, 22,* 362–297.

Greenough, W. T., Black, J. E., & Wallace, C. S. (1987). Experience and brain development. *Child Development, 58,* 539–559.

Grimshaw, G. M., Adelstein, A., Bryden, M. P., & MacKinnon, G. E. (1998). First-language acquisition in adolescence: Evidence for a critical period for verbal language development. *Brain and Language, 63,* 237–255.

Grosjean, F. (1997). Processing mixed language: Issues, findings, and models. In A. M. B. de Groot & J. F. Kroll (Eds.), *Tutorials in bilingualism: Psycholinguistic perspectives* (pp. 225–254). Mahwah, NJ: Lawrence Erlbaum Associates.

Grosjean, F. (1998). Studying bilinguals: Methodological and conceptual issues. *Bilingualism: Language and Cognition, 1,* 131–149.

Guion, S. G., Flege, J. E., Akahane-Yamada, R., & Pruitt, J. C. (2000). An investigation of current models of second language speech perception: The case of Japanese adults' perception of English consonants. *Journal of the Acoustical Society of America, 107,* 2711–2724.

Guion, S. G., Flege, J. E., & Loftin, J. D. (2000). The effect of L1 use on pronunciation in Quichua-Spanish bilinguals. *Journal of Phonetics, 28,* 27–42.

Hakuta, K. (1986). *Mirror of language: The debate on bilingualism.* New York: Basic Books, Inc.

Hallé, P. A., Best, C. T., & Levitt, A. (1999). Phonetic vs. phonological influences on French listeners' perception of American English approximants. *Journal of Phonetics, 27,* 281–306.

Hansen, J. H. L., & Nandkumar, S. (1995). Objective speech quality assessment and the RPE-LTP coding algorithm in different noise and language conditions. *Journal of the Acoustical Society of America, 97,* 609–627.

Hillenbrand, J., Getty, L. A., Clark, M. J., & Wheeler, K. (1995). Acoustic characteristics of American English vowels. *Journal of the Acoustical Society of America, 97,* 3099–3111.

Hynd, G. W., Teeter, A., & Stewart, J. (1980). Acculturation and the lateralization of speech in the bilingual native American. *International Journal of Neuroscience, 11,* 1–7.

Illes, J., Francis, W. S., Desmond, J. E., Gabrieli, J. D. E., Glover, G. H., Poldrack, R., Lee, C. J., & Wagner, A. D. (1999). Convergent cortical representation on semantic processing in bilinguals. *Brain and Language, 70,* 347–363.

Ingram, J. C. L., & Park, S.-G. (1998). Language, context, and speaker effects in the identification and discrimination of English /r/ and /l/ by Japanese and Korean listeners. *Journal of the Acoustical Society of America, 103,* 1161–1174.

Ioup, G., & Weinberger, S. H. (Eds.). (1987). *Interlanguage phonology: The acquisition of a second language sound system.* New York: Newbury House.

Iverson, P., & Kuhl, P. K. (2000). Perceptual magnet and phoneme boundary effects in speech perception: Do they arise from a common mechanism? *Perception & Psychophysics, 62,* 874–886.

Jacobs, B. (1988). Neurobiological differentiation of primary and secondary language acquisition. *Studies in Second Language Acquisition, 10,* 303–337.

Johnson, J., & Newport, E. (1989). Critical period effects in second language learning: The influence of maturational state on the acquisition of English as a second language. *Cognitive Psychology, 21,* 60–99.

Kachru, B. B. (1986). *The alchemy of English: The spread, functions, and models of non-native Englishes.* Oxford: Pergamon.

Kachru, B. B. (1992). Models for non-native Englishes. *The other tongue: English across cultures* (2nd ed., pp. 48–74). Urbana, IL: University of Illinois Press.

Kandel, E. R., & Hawkins, R. D. (1992, September). The biological basis of learning and individuality. *Scientific American,* pp. 79–86.
Kim, E. J., (1997). Maturation constraints on second-language acquisition: A reaction-time (RT) study of lexical-decision and grammaticality-judgment test. *Journal of the Applied Linguistics Association of Korea, 13,* 1–34.
Kim, K. H. S., Relkin, N. R., Lee, K. M., & Hirsch, J. (1997). Distinct cortical areas associated with native and second languages. *Nature,* 388, 171–174.
Kim, R. (1995). The effect of age-of-L2 onset on ultimate L2 production: The English /i–I/ distinction made by Korean speakers. *English Education, 50,* 257–279.
Kingston, J., & Diehl, R. L. (1994). Phonetic knowledge. *Language, 70,* 419–454.
Klatt, D. H. (1980). Software for a cascade/parallel formant synthesizer. *Journal of the Acoustical Society of America, 67,* 971–995.
Klein, D., Zatorre, R. J., Milner, B., Meyer, E., & Evans, A. C. (1994). Left putaminal activation when speaking a second language: Evidence from PET. *NeuroReport, 5,* 2295–2297.
Kluender, K. R., Diehl, R. L., & Wright, B. A. (1988). Vowel-length differences before voiced and voiceless consonants: An auditory explanation. *Journal of Phonetics, 16,* 153–169.
Kuhl, P. K. (1993). Early linguistic experience and phonetic perception: Implications for theories of developmental speech perception. *Journal of Phonetics, 21,* 125–139.
Kuhl, P. K., & Iverson, P. (1995). Linguistic experience and the "perceptual magnet effect." In W. Strange (Ed.), *Speech perception and linguistic experience: Issues in cross-language research* (pp. 121–154). Timonium, MD: York Press.
Kuhl, P. K., Williams, K., Lacerda, F., Stevens, K., & Lindblom, B. (1992). Linguistic experience alters phonetic perception in infants by 6 months of age. *Science, 255,* 606–608.
Lado, R. (1957). *Linguistics across cultures.* Ann Arbor, MI: University of Michigan Press.
Laeufer, C. (1992). Patterns of voicing-conditioned vowel duration in French and English. *Journal of Phonetics, 20,* 411–440.
Lamendella, J. (1977). General principles of neurofunctional organization and their manifestation in primary and non-primary language acquisition. *Language Learning, 27,* 155–196.
Lenneberg, E. H. (1967). *Biological foundations of language.* New York: Wiley.
Lisker, L., & Abramson, A. S. (1964). A cross-language study of voicing in initial stops: Acoustical measurements. *Word, 20,* 384–422.
Locke, J. L. (1997). A theory of neurolinguistic development. *Brain and Language, 59,* 265–326.
Lotto, A. J., Kluender, K. R., & Holt, L. L. (1998). Depolarizing the perceptual magnet effect. *Journal of the Acoustical Society of America, 103,* 3648–3655.
Mack, M. (1982). Voicing-dependent vowel duration in English and French: Monolingual and bilingual production. *Journal of the Acoustical Society of America, 71,* 173–178.
Mack, M. (1985, December). *Vowel production and perception in three linguistically dissimilar groups.* Paper presented at the meeting of the Linguistic Society of America, Seattle, WA.
Mack, M. (1986). A study of semantic and syntactic processing in monolinguals and fluent early bilinguals. *Journal of Psycholinguistic Research, 15,* 463–488.
Mack, M. (1987). The perception of natural and computer-generated speech by English monolinguals and German-English bilinguals. In W. Bahner, J. Schildt, & D. Viehweger (Eds.), *Proceedings of the Fourteenth International Congress of Linguistics* (pp. 470–473). Berlin: Akademie-Verlag.
Mack, M. (1988). Sentence processing by non-native speakers of English: Evidence from the perception of natural and computer-generated anomalous L2 sentences. *Journal of Neurolinguistics, 3,* 293–316.
Mack, M. (1989). Consonant and vowel perception and production: Early English-French bilinguals and English monolinguals. *Perception & Psychophysics, 46,* 187–200.
Mack, M. (1990). Phonetic transfer in a French-English bilingual child. In P. H. Nelde (Ed.)., *Language attitudes and language conflict* (pp. 117–124). Bonn: Dümmler.
Mack, M. (1992). How well is computer-processed speech understood?: A cross-linguistic and cross-dialectal analysis. *World Englishes, 11,* 285–301.
Mack, M. (1997). The monolingual native speaker: Not a norm, but still a necessity. *Studies in the Linguistic Sciences, 27,* 113–146.
Mack, M. (2001, October). *A test of the critical-period hypothesis in Korean-English bilinguals.* Paper presented at the Pacific Second Language Research Forum, University of Hawai'i at Manoa, Honolulu.

Mack, M. (in progress). Voice-onset time and voicing-conditioned vowel duration in early French-English bilingual children and their mothers. Manuscript in preparation.
Mack, M. (2002). The influence of neuroscience upon linguistics from a historical perspective. In. F. Fabbro (Ed.)., *Advances in the neurolinguistics of bilingualism* (pp. 143–191). Udine: Forum.
Mack, M., & Gold, B. (1985). *The intelligibility of non-vocoded and vocoded semantically anomalous sentences* (Tech. Rep. No. 703). Lexington, MA: Massachusetts Institute of Technology Lincoln Laboratory.
Mack, M., Bott, S., & Boronat, C. B. (in progress). An analysis of temporal distinctions in the speech of French-English bilingual children. Manuscript in preparation.
Mack, M., Bott, S., Trofimovich, P., & Baker, W. (in progress). Age-related effects on the acquisition of the English vowel system among Korean-English bilinguals. Manuscript in preparation.
Mack, M., & Lieberman, P. (1985). Acoustic analysis of words produced by a child from 46 to 149 weeks. *Journal of Child Language, 12,* 527–550.
Mack, M., & Tierney, J. (1987). *The intelligibility of natural and vocoded semantically anomalous sentences: A comparative analysis of English monolinguals and German-English bilinguals* (Tech. Rep. No. 792). Lexington, MA: Massachusetts Institute of Technology Lincoln Laboratory.
Mack, M., Tierney, J., & Boyle, M. E. T. (1990). *The intelligibility of natural and LPC-vocoded words and sentences presented to native and non-native speakers of English* (Tech. Rep. No. 869). Lexington, MA: Massachusetts Institute of Technology Lincoln Laboratory.
Macken, M. A., & Barton, D. (1979). The acquisition of the voicing contrast in English: A study of voice onset time in word-initial stop consonants. *Journal of Child Language, 7,* 41–74.
Mayberry, R. I., & Eichen, E. B. (1991). The long-lasting advantage of learning sign language in childhood: Another look at the critical period for language acquisition. *Journal of Memory and Language, 30,* 486–512.
McKeever, W. F., Hunt, L. J., Wells, S., & Yazzie, C. (1989). Language laterality in Navajo reservation children: Dichotic test results depend on the language context of the testing. *Brain and Language, 36,* 148–158.
Miller, G. A., Heise, G. A., & Lichten, W. (1951). The intelligibility of speech as a function of the context of the test materials. *Journal of Experimental Psychology, 41,* 329–335.
Moltz, H. (1973). Some implications of the critical period hypothesis. *Annals of the New York Academy of Sciences, 223,* 144–146.
Nábelek, A. K., & Donahue, A. M. (1984). Perception of consonants in reverberation by native and non-native listeners. *Journal of the Acoustical Society of America, 75,* 632–634.
Neville, H. J. (1985). Effects of early sensory and language experience on the development of the human brain. In J. Mehler & R. Fox (Eds.), *Neonate cognition: Beyond the blooming buzzing confusion* (pp. 349–363). Hillsdale, NJ: Lawrence Erlbaum Associates.
Neville, H. J., Bavelier, D., Cornia, D., Rauschecker, J., Kari, A., Lalwani, A., Braun, A., Clark, V., Jezzard, P., & Turner, R. (1998). Cerebral organization for language in deaf and hearing subjects: Biological constraints and effects of experience. *Proceedings of the National Academy of Sciences, USA, 95,* 922–929.
Newport, E. L. (1988). Constraints on learning and their role in language acquisition: Studies of the acquisition of American sign language. *Language Science, 10,* 147–172.
O' Boyle, M. W. (2000). A new millennium in cognitive neuropsychology research: The era of individual differences? *Brain and Cognition, 42,* 135–138.
Ojemann, G. A., & Whitaker, H. A. (1978). The bilingual brain. *Archives of Neurology, 35,* 409–412.
Oyama, S. (1976). A sensitive period for the acquisition of a nonnative phonological system. *Journal of Psycholinguistic Research, 5,* 261–283.
Ozawa, K., & Logan, J. S. (1989). Perceptual evaluation of two speech coding methods by native and non-native speakers of English. *Computer Speech and Language, 3,* 53–59.
Pallier, C., Bosch, L., & Sebastián-Gallés, N. (1997). A limit on behavioral plasticity in speech perception. *Cognition, 64,* B9–B17.
Paradis, M. (Ed.). (1983). *Readings on aphasia in bilinguals and polyglots.* Montreal: Didier.
Paradis, M. (1985). On the representation of two languages in one brain. *Language Sciences, 7,* 1–39.
Paradis, M. (1987). *The assessment of bilingual aphasia.* Hillsdale, NJ: Lawrence Erlbaum Associates.
Paradis, M. (1997). The cognitive neuropsychology of bilingualism. In A. M. B. de Groot & J. F. Kroll (Eds.), *Tutorials in bilingualism: Psycholinguistic perspectives* (pp. 331–354). Mahwah, NJ: Lawrence Erlbaum Associates.

Penfield, W. (1953). A consideration of the neurophysiological mechanisms of speech and some educational consequences. *Proceedings of the American Academy of Arts and Sciences, 82,* 201–214.
Perani, D., Dehaene, F. G., Cohen, L., Cappa, S. F., Dupoux, E., Fazio, F., & Mehler, J. (1996). Brain processing of native and foreign languages. *Cognitive Neuroscience and Neuropsychology, 7,* 2439–2444.
Perani, D., Paulesu, E., Sebastián Gallés, N., Dupoux, E., Dehaene, S., Bettinardi, V., Cappa, S. F., Fazio, F., & Mehler, J. (1998). The bilingual brain: Proficiency and age of acquisition of the second language. *Brain, 121,* 1841–1852.
Peterson, G. E., & Lehiste, I. (1960). Duration of syllable nuclei in English. *Journal of the Acoustical Society of America, 32,* 693–703.
Pisoni, D. B. (1973). Auditory and phonetic memory codes in the discrimination of consonants and vowels. *Perception & Psychophysics, 13,* 253–260.
Pulvermüller, F., & Schumann, J. H. (1994). Neurobiological mechanisms of language acquisition. *Language Learning, 4,* 681–734.
Rapport, R. L., Tan, C. T., & Whitaker, H. A. (1983). Language function and dysfunction among Chinese and English speaking polyglots: Cortical simulation, Wada testing, and clinical studies. *Brain and Language, 18,* 342–366.
Riecker, A., Ackermann, H., Wildgruber, D., Meyer, J., Dogil, G., Haider, H., & Grodd, W. (2000). Articulatory/phonetic sequencing at the level of the anterior perisylvian cortex: A functional magnetic resonance imaging (fMRI) study. *Brain and Language, 75,* 259–276.
Rosen, H. J., Ojemann, J. G., Ollinger, J. M., & Petersen, S. E. (2000). Comparison of brain activation during word retrieval done silently and aloud using fMRI. *Brain and Cognition, 42,* 201–217.
Schouten, M. E. H., & van Hessen, A. J. (1992). Modeling phoneme perception. I: Categorical perception. *Journal of the Acoustical Society of America, 92,* 1841–1855.
Segalowitz, S. J., & Rose-Krasnor, L. (1992). The construct of brain maturation in theories of child development. *Brain and Cognition, 20,* 1–7.
Sharma, A., & Dorman, M. F. (1999). Cortical auditory evoked potential correlates of categorical perception of voice-onset time. *Journal of the Acoustical Society of America, 106,* 1078–1083.
Sheldon, A., & Strange, W. (1982). The acquisition of /r/ and /l/ by Japanese learners of English: Evidence that speech production can precede speech perception. *Applied Psycholinguistics, 3,* 243–261.
Shim, R. J. (1995). *The sensitive period for second-language acquisition: An experimental study of age effects on universal grammar and language transfer.* Seoul: Thaehaksa.
Shore, C. M. (1995). *Individual differences in language development.* Thousand Oaks, CA: Sage.
Simos, P. G., Molfese, D. L., & Brenden, R. A. (1997). Behavioral and electrophysiological indices of voicing cue discrimination: Laterality patterns and development. *Brain and Language, 57,* 122–150.
Thornburgh, D. F., & Ryalls, J. H. (1998). Voice onset time in Spanish-English bilinguals: Early versus late learners of English. *Journal of Communication Disorders, 31,* 215–229.
Trofimovich, P., & Baker, W. (2000, March). *Korean-English bilinguals' perception and production of American-English vowels: Effects of age, experience, and native language phonology.* Paper presented at the annual meeting of the American Association for Applied Linguistics, Vancouver, BC.
Weber-Fox, C., & Neville, H. (1996). Functional neural systems are differentially affected by delays in second language immersion: ERP and behavioral evidence in bilinguals. In D. Birdsong (Ed.), *Second language acquisition and the critical period hypothesis* (pp. 23–38). Mahwah, NJ: Lawrence Erlbaum Associates.
Weinreich, U. (1953). *Languages in contact: Findings and problems.* The Hague: Mouton.
Werker, J. F., Gilbert, J. H. V., Humphrey, K., & Tees, R. C. (1981). Developmental aspects of cross-language speech perception. *Child Development, 52,* 349–355.
Werker, J. F., & Lalonde, C. E. (1988). Cross-language speech perception: Initial capabilities and developmental change. *Developmental Psychology, 24,* 672–683.
Werker, J. F., & Tees, R. C. (1983). Developmental changes across childhood in the perception of non-native speech sounds. *Canadian Journal of Psychology, 37,* 278–286.
Werker, J. F., & Tees, R. C. (1984). Cross-language speech perception: Evidence for perceptual reorganization during the first year of life. *Infant Behaviour and Development, 7,* 49–63.
Wesche, M., & Schneiderman, E. I. (1982). Language lateralization in adult bilinguals. *Studies in Second Language Acquisition, 4,* 153–169.

Williams, L. (1979). The modification of speech perception and production in second-language learning. *Perception & Psychophysics, 26,* 95–104.
Yang, B. (1996). A comparative study of American English and Korean vowels produced by male and female speakers. *Journal of Phonetics, 24,* 245–261.
Zatorre, R. J., Meyer, E., Gjedde, A., & Evans, A. C. (1996). PET studies of phonetic processing of speech: Review, replication, and reanalysis. *Cerebral Cortex, 6,* 21–30.

13

Differential Use of Cerebral Mechanisms in Bilinguals

Michel Paradis
Department of Linguistics, McGill University

For the past hundred years, in aphasiology and the neuropsychology of language in general, the term "language" has referred to the language system or what linguists today call the grammar—namely, phonology, morphology, syntax, and semantics. This has come to be known as *implicit linguistic competence*, and it has been traditionally associated with activity in the perisylvian cortex of the left hemisphere. Throughout this chapter, *competence* refers to each individual's actual neurofunctional competence, not that of an idealized speaker-hearer. The *grammar* thus refers to the description of the inferred competence of a given individual, at a given time.

But over the past 15 years or so, researchers investigating behavioral deficits exhibited by right-hemisphere damaged patients (Brookshire & Nicholas, 1984; Brownell, 1988; Brownell, Gardner, Prather, & Martino, 1995; Brownell, Potter, Bihrle, & Gardner, 1986; Dipper, Bryan, & Tyson, 1997; Dwyer & Rinn, 1981; Foldi, 1987; Gardner, Brownell, Wapner, & Michelow, 1983; Hier & Kaplan, 1980; Joanette & Brownell, 1990; Joanette, Goulet, & Hannequin, 1990; Kaplan, Brownell, Jacobs, & Gardner, 1990; McDonald & Wales, 1986; Ross, 1981, 1984; Weylman, Brownell, Roman, & Gardner, 1989) have made us aware of the fact that there is much more to verbal communicative behavior than grammar, and that pragmatic competence (i.e., the ability to infer the intended meaning of an utterance from the situational and discursive context and general knowledge) is at least of equal importance in the normal use of language.

The study of students' second-language performance and investigations of amnesia have drawn attention to a third cerebral system—that which subserves *explicit metalinguistic knowledge* (Bialystok, 1981; Paradis, 1994), distributed bilaterally over multiple specific cortical areas as is all declarative knowledge (Cohen & Eichenbaum, 1993). As discussed here, most of the grammar is subserved by procedural memory whereas at least some aspects of words are declarative (Paradis, 1994; Ullman, 2001; Ullman et al., 1997).

The extreme variability in success among second-language learners (Byalistok, 1994) has drawn attention to the important dimension of motivation (Gardner & Lambert, 1972), identified as a major predictor of performance, and to its cerebral counterpart, the subcortical cerebral structures involved in motivation and emotion (Lamendella, 1977), namely, the amygdaloid complex and the emotive dopaminergic structures within the limbic system (Schumann, 1990, 1997).

In this chapter, the contribution of these four systems (implicit competence, metalinguistic knowledge, pragmatic competence, and motivation) in subserving the representation and processing of language are examined, as they pertain to various bilingual populations. It is relevant to indicate here that I prefer to speak of implicit *competence* as that which has been acquired without *knowledge*—that is, incidentally—and of explicit knowledge as that which has been consciously learned. Thus, the term "acquisition" is used when competence or skills are concerned, and "learning" when conscious knowledge is concerned.

Before proceeding, it is important to define the term "bilingual." Bilinguals, people who speak two languages, differ among themselves along several dimensions including (at the least) degree of proficiency, accuracy, context of acquisition and/or learning, age of appropriation, degree of motivation, context of use, and structural distance between the languages, with each of these dimensions having several variables (see Paradis, 1987, Fig. 1.1, p. 6). Because the claims in this chapter are that there are no qualitative differences between any types of bilinguals, but that all make use of the same mechanisms to different extents, the data and conclusions proposed here are relevant to all bilinguals, irrespective of the definition one wishes to adopt. The general argument runs as follows: To the extent that X is the case, Y shall ensue. To the extent that individuals are more or less motivated, that they appropriate the language incidentally or consciously, and that they compensate for gaps in their linguistic competence by relying on pragmatics, they will involve the left-hemisphere perisylvian language areas, the amygdala and dopaminergic system, the basal ganglia, striatum and cerebellum, and the hippocampal system and cortical areas relevant to the storage of metalinguistic knowledge. To the extent that degree of metalinguistic knowledge differs among unilinguals, there will be differences in the degree of involvement of the relevant cerebral mechanisms in unilinguals too. (The term "unilingual" is here preferred to the oft-used "monolingual" because it is well-formed with a Latinate prefix on a Latinate word.)

Even though second-language and foreign-language appropriation differ in terms of a number of parameters, again the differences are immaterial for our purposes, because they are taken care of by the "To-the-extent-that" formula, and implications for differential cerebral processing follow from it.

In addition, the term "early bilingual" refers to individuals having acquired both languages concurrently, from infancy. The term "late bilingual" or "fluent second-language speaker" refers to an individual who has appropriated (acquired or learned) a second or foreign language later. To the extent that early bilinguals are balanced (i.e., have been exposed in equal proportion to their two languages, in similar settings, with equal sociolinguistic value attached to each), they will show the activation of the same mechanisms as unilinguals, and to the same extent. They may show differences in the *contents* of their representations (e.g., lexical semantic field or voice-onset time for certain consonants may differ from those of unilingual speakers of the respective languages, but not in the manner in which they are represented—i.e., a concrete noun is represented as a concrete noun and a phoneme is processed as a phoneme, whether or not its quality is identical to that of the unilingual counterpart). To the extent that the exposure to each language during the normal period of language development differs, not only the contents of the representations may differ, but the amount of representations may differ as well (e.g., in one of their languages, their vocabulary may be less extensive, or they may lack a register). They may, however, be expected to process their two languages in the same manner as respective unilinguals.

The phrase "various bilingual populations" underscores the notion that bilinguals do not constitute a homogeneous group. Although there are nontrivial differences among unilinguals—in fact, differences much greater than have been usually assumed because theoretical linguistics has focused on the idealized speaker-hearer, a nevertheless useful theoretical construct—there is not even such an entity as the idealized bilingual, unless we refer to persons who are bilingual from infancy, or at least, say, by age 5, to be on the safe side (Weber-Fox & Neville, 1996). As with any biological maturational trait, there are individual differences: Some individuals mature earlier than others. However, group studies generally show a difference in language acquisition after age 7, as compared to prior to age 7 (i.e., among early bilinguals, as shown in Weber-Fox & Neville, 1996). The degree of maturation between the ages of 5 and 7 will likely vary, such that some 6-year-olds will function more like average 5-year-olds, and others more like average 7-year-olds.

Nonetheless, early bilinguals, as they are often called, share with the proverbial idealized speaker-hearer the property of being sufficiently homogeneous that differences are negligible and generalizations with respect to the cerebral mechanisms involved are of the same degree of validity as the generalizations made about unilingual speakers. (The *contents* of the representations may differ, in that they may deviate with respect to the unilingual norm, but there is no reason to believe that the principles governing their acquisition, storage, and processing are any different.)

Late bilinguals, on the other hand, individuals having acquired or learned a second language after the age of 7 years, exhibit much greater variability in the cerebral representation and processing of their later appropriated language than early bilinguals (Dehaene et al., 1997; Weber-Fox & Neville, 1996; Perani et al., 1996), so that no generalizations—even about idealized individuals—are possible, other than in relative terms: Specifically, to the extent that speakers rely on strategy X (e.g., conscious learning) they will utilize cerebral mechanism A (declarative memory); to the extent that they rely on strategy Y (e.g., incidental acquisition) they will utilize cerebral mechanism B (procedural memory); and so on for the four cerebral systems identified so far as being involved in subserving the normal use of language in unilinguals and bilinguals.

I now examine each of these four cerebral systems in turn, and the components of verbal communication that they subserve.

IMPLICIT LINGUISTIC COMPETENCE

The distinction between *knowing that* and *knowing how*, or between declarative and procedural memory, is based in part upon studies of anterograde amnesia. For example, Patient H. M., who has become one of the most famous subjects in the neuropsychological literature, in part for having been studied so extensively for a period of more than 40 years (MacKay, Stewart, & Burke, 1998; Scoville & Milner, 1957), developed severe symptoms of anterograde amnesia after the surgical removal of parts of his hippocampus and surrounding tissue bilaterally. He was, and still is, incapable of forming new memories. He cannot remember any event even a few minutes after it has occurred. As soon as he is distracted by some other information, the memory is gone. H. M. still thinks that the President of the United States is Dwight Eisenhower, he does not know his own age because it changes every year, and he cannot remember what he had for breakfast. (In fact, he can't remember *whether* he had breakfast.) Researchers serendipitously discovered that, in spite of all this, H. M. was able to acquire new motor skills and that he improved with practice at the same rate as normal individuals—although of course he did not remember having ever practiced any particular task on which he was trained. It was later discovered that he was able to acquire not only motor skills, but cognitive skills as well. However, he was never able to learn new words. For example, despite the many attempts to teach him the meaning of the word *cupidity*, he still does not know it, as indicated by Cohen (1991). (Cupidity is not one of the most frequently used words in English, which explains why H. M. did not know this word. Most of my English-speaking students do not know it either. However, once I present it to them, along with its meaning, all but 2 or 3 out of about 50 can remember it 1 week later, and if I tell them once more, all of them know it the following week, and they still know its meaning at the end of the term.)

Information about H. M. has led to the realization that implicit linguistic competence is subserved by procedural memory—namely, the memory that subserves automatized skills, involving the striatum (Saint-Cyr, Taylor, & Lang, 1988), some of the basal ganglia (Aglioti, 1997; Crosson, Zawacki, Brinson, Lu, & Sadek, 1997), and the cerebellum (Fabbro, 2000; Gordon, 1996; Leiner, Leiner, & Dow, 1991; Molinari et al., 1997; Thach, 1996). On the other hand, the aspects of the lexicon of which the speaker is conscious, namely, the sound and referential meanings of words, of which speakers are aware, are subserved by declarative memory, which underlies the appropriation and use of explicit knowledge (Paradis, 1994).

Implicit linguistic competence refers to the covert procedures that linguists infer allow speakers to understand and produce all well-formed sentences in their language, including those they have never heard before. All aspects of the language system (phonology, morphology, syntax, and corresponding aspects of the lexicon, such as the number of arguments a verb must take, or whether a noun is a count or a mass noun) are components of implicit linguistic competence. It is acquired incidentally (i.e., by focusing attention on some aspect of the stimulus other than what is actually internalized). For example, individuals may focus on the acoustic properties of a word while acquiring the proprioceptive programs that allow them to articulate the word, or focus on the meaning of an utterance while internalizing its underlying syntactic form—which is not there to be observed. It is stored implicitly, in that it remains forever opaque to introspection, as is made clear by the numerous unsuccessful attempts at characterizing the underlying structure of sentences since the emergence of Chomky's early work on the representation of syntactic structures. This difficulty has continued to present itself in a variety of approaches to linguistic analysis, including structural, transformational, government-binding, and minimalist approaches to generative grammar, and to stratificational, tagmemic, relational, cognitive, and functional grammars, not to mention pedagogical grammars that are encountered in the course of learning a second language. Implicit linguistic competence is used automatically, that is, without our conscious control. In other words, the entire process of language internalization is beyond awareness. It improves with practice, without our knowing what underlying procedure is implemented, just like the acquired skill of riding a bicycle or hitting a tennis ball: It simply gets better, without our knowing the underlying mechanism that allows us to perform as we do.

To give a concrete example: When at the age of seventeen I was learning how to pronounce English, I was unable to produce the sound "aw" as in law. I would produce approximations of the vowel in this word, but never the appropriate vowel. A very patient roommate kept on providing the model that I was trying to imitate, without much success, until one day, all of a sudden, it came out right. Amazed that such a sound came out of my oral cavity, I repeated it, over and over, with other words, like "claw" and "paw"—and from then on, I was able to produce words with this same vowel sound. To this day I am not aware of the various muscles involved, whether the tip of my tongue touches my palate, or what happens to my larynx, but I do produce these words without giving them a second thought. I was aware of the acoustic properties of the sound, but not of the proprioceptive feedback that eventually built a kinesthetic program that allowed me to produce the sound automatically, that is, without conscious control. Thus we are aware of *what* we produce, not of *how* we produce it. This is of course the way that children acquire the phonology of their first language as well.

Another piece of anecdotal evidence will drive the point home: In a recent semester, as I was walking down the hall toward my office, I passed the open door of a seminar room where a Brazilian teaching assistant was explaining to a group of English-speaking phonetics students how they were producing the sounds of their language. The students, who had spoken English as their native language for the past 20 years, were amazed to notice, by placing their fingers on their throat, which consonants were voiced and which were not, and awed at the idea that their tongue was in this or that particular configuration. They knew perfectly well how to make the appropriate sounds, but they did not have the faintest idea of the means by which they were doing it. On the other hand, the teaching assistant, who knew how they were doing it and was explaining it to them in detail, spoke English with his characteristic Brazilian accent. He had explicit knowledge but no implicit competence; the students had implicit competence, but no explicit knowledge.

METALINGUISTIC KNOWLEDGE

Metalinguistic knowledge is acquired consciously, and it is stored explicitly. That is, its contents can be recalled to conscious awareness and can possibly be verbalized. It comprises all the knowledge speakers are aware of, such as the rules of pedagogical grammars that they have learned in school. They are also aware of the outcome of procedural linguistic competence: The surface structure of utterances is observable, although not the computational procedures that generate them. The underlying structure can only be inferred from the systematic verbal behavior of speakers; it cannot be observed. After all, this is why competence is called implicit in the first place, and why professional linguists to this day do not yet agree on the nature of the correct representation of the grammar (rules, trees, parallel distributed processing with weighted connections based on statistical probabilities and frequency of use, etc.), let alone its form. It is therefore unlikely that children who acquire the ability to automatically understand and produce a particular sentence do so by proceeding through the steps described in any available grammar, including the generative model of the 1995 Quebec referendum question, "Do you agree that Quebec should become sovereign after having made a formal offer to Canada for a new economic and political partnership within the scope of the bill respecting the future of Quebec and of the agreement signed on June twelfth nineteen ninety-five?" (Fig. 13.1; the phonetic transcription is provided below it).

Declarative memory, on which metalinguistic knowledge relies, requires an intact hippocampal system, and probably intact amygdala and medial temporal lobes, for the consolidation of new information whose representations are then distributed over multiple (albeit specific) cortical areas. Procedural memory, on the other hand, tends to be represented in the circumscribed cortical areas that are required in its acquisition. Hence, implicit linguistic competence is represented in the classical perisylvian areas of the left hemisphere generally referred

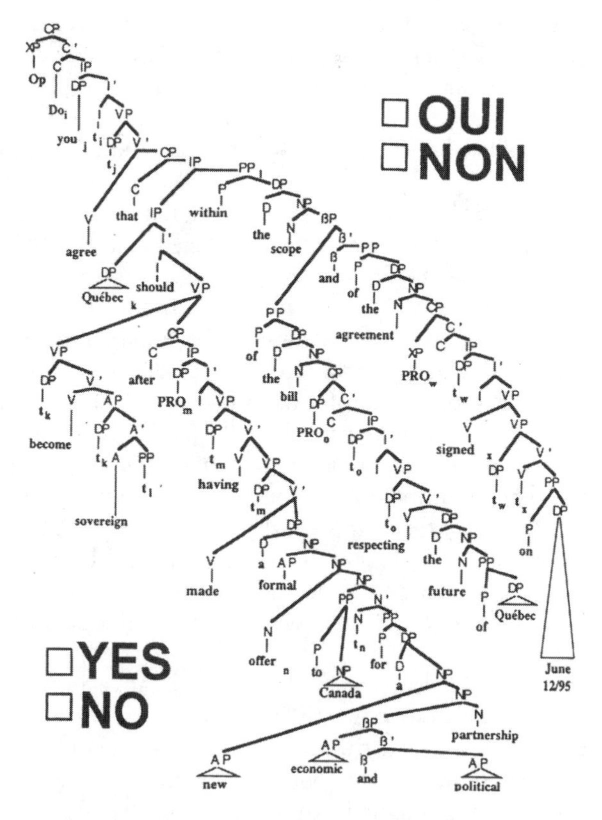

dú ju əgrí ðæt kwəbɛ́k ʃud bikʌ́m sávrən ɑftr̩ hávɪŋ méjd ə fórməl
ɑ́fr̩ tu kǽnədə for ə njú ɛkənámɪk æn pəlɪ́rɪkəl pártnərʃɪp wɪðɪ́n
ðə skóp əv ðə bɪ́l rəspɛ́ktɪŋ də fjútʃr̩ əv kwəbɛ́k ænd əv ði
əgrímənt sájnd an dʒún twɛ́lfθ nájntin naynti fajv

FIG. 13.1 A principles and Parameters phrase structure of the 1995 Quebec referendum question, as it appeared on the Society of Linguistics Undergraduates at McGill (SLUM) T-shirts, courtesy of Lisa Travis (Syntactician). Phonetic transcription by Heather Goad (Phonologist).

to as Broca's and Wernicke's areas. Focal lesions in these areas cause specific linguistic deficits known as aphasia. It is interesting to note that lesions in the basal ganglia and the cerebellum (which structures are associated with procedural memory) also result in deficits of implicit linguistic competence (i.e., deficits in phonology, morphology, syntax, and implicit aspects of the lexicon).

Implicit and explicit memory have been doubly dissociated in patients with Alzheimer's disease (Gabrieli, Reminger, Grosse & Wilson, 1992), alcoholic Korsakoff's syndrome (Canavan, Hömberg, & Stelmach, 1992; Parker, 1992), anterograde amnesia (Corkin, 1992; Keane, Clarke, & Corkin, 1992), and Parkinson's disease (Saint-Cyr et al., 1987). Patients with Alzheimer's Disease, Korsakoff's syndrome, or amnesia show evidence of impaired explicit memory but intact implicit memory; patients with Parkinson's disease demonstrate a selective impairment of procedural memory; patients with aphasia have impaired implicit memory for language (or of the automatic use thereof) without loss of explicit knowledge. Lesion sites associated with these symptoms are distinct.

Thus, metalinguistic knowledge is of a different nature than implicit linguistic competence. That is, it is declarative, not procedural, and therefore is concerned with knowing *that*, not knowing *how*; it consists of conscious knowledge, as opposed to a skill; it bears on different objects (conscious information, such as pedagogical grammar rules); and it is subserved by different neural structures. Hence, explicit metalinguistic knowledge cannot be expected to ever become, turn into, or be converted or transformed into implicit competence. Implicit linguistic competence is acquired incidentally (and independently) through practice, and then coexists alongside the metalinguistic knowledge, which remains as it was. The acquisition of the ability to automatically produce French phrases of the type "*la chaise que j'ai prise*" or "*le fauteuil que j'ai pris*" is not the result of applying ever faster and faster the conscious rule, "Make the past participle agree with the preceding direct object if it is a verb conjugated with the auxiliary *avoir* or a reflexive verb, and with the subject if it is a verb conjugated with the auxiliary *être*."

Metalinguistic knowledge remains in the declarative memory of second language learners and can still be verbalized after the corresponding implicit competence has been acquired through practice. Implicit competence exists most often in the absence of corresponding metalinguistic knowledge. This is not to claim that metalinguistic knowledge is useless. It indirectly facilitates the acquisition of implicit competence by pointing out those structures that need to be practiced, and it serves as a monitor that consciously censures the output of implicit competence (before or after it has been actually uttered), thus allowing the gradual internalization of the correct form through the repetition of the correct model. Every self-correction leads to the eventual automatization of the production of the proper form in the appropriate context.

Whereas some aspects of the lexicon are explicit (e.g., we know the sound and meaning of words), *access* to the lexicon is implicit (we do not know how we search our mental lexicon for a word, either alphabetically, by rhythm, or by semantic field—or all three concurrently). Some tasks may combine implicit and explicit elements. But Parkin (1989) argued that the double dissociation observed between the implicit and explicit components of a task reflects the activity of two independent systems. In other words, the two systems never merge nor metamorphose one into the other, although they may be used simultaneously on different aspects of a task, or in rapid succession

PRAGMATIC COMPETENCE

Patients with right-hemisphere lesions do not typically exhibit deficits of linguistic competence. They do, however, often show clear deficits of pragmatic competence, or dyshyponoia. Dyshyponoia, from the Greek ὑπονοῶ—to grasp what is "understood" in an utterance, albeit unsaid, in the sense of the French "*sous-entendu*"—is the impairment of the use of linguistic pragmatics as in the inability to draw appropriate inferences from the context or from general knowledge, leading to problems with the interpretation of indirect speech acts, metaphors, and in general of the unsaid component of utterances.

That is, such patients have difficulty in inferring the correct interpretation of an utterance from the situational or the discursive context. They understand what is said, but not what is meant if any extralinguistic context is necessary to interpret the utterance beyond its literal meaning. Yet adults speaking to adults rarely say what they mean, not because they are devious, but because this is the way language works. Most of the time, we do not say *all* that we mean. It would in fact be very strange if we stated the obvious. We do this only when speaking to infants (e.g., "Now we put your little hand through this sleeve, and the other hand through this one; now we button up the first little button here"). We often say something different from what we mean literally (as when we use idioms, figurative speech, metaphors, indirect speech acts) or even the opposite of what we mean (as in the case of sarcasm or irony), but that does not prevent non-brain-damaged speakers from understanding the intended meaning. Hence individuals with dyshyponoia suffer a considerable handicap, arguably with greater social consequences than individuals with aphasia—particularly because their deficit is less conspicuous: They have no obvious problems with phonology, morphology, syntax, or the lexicon (save perhaps a sometimes mild aprosody), and their behavior becomes socially questionable. Imagine simply answering, "Yes" and not passing the salt when someone at dinner asks, "Is there any salt on the table?" or not telling the time when someone looks at your watch and asks, "Do you have the time?" Even 5-year-olds understand the indirect command in the form of the question, "Do you know what time it is?" when it is obviously past bedtime and the tone of voice and facial expression leave no room for doubt as to the parent's intention.

In fact, children learn to use indirect speech acts and are able to interpret figurative speech literally for comic effect quite early. The 5-year-old son of one of our graduate students once stated, as he was standing next to the desk of one of our professors, "My daddy has candy in his drawer." And as the professor continued writing without picking up the hint, the child added, "Do you?" He was obviously well mannered and had been taught not to make such requests. So, he wasn't: He merely stated some facts and inquired about facts. Yet both he and the professor knew exactly what he was up to. In a related example, when my younger son, Fred, was 3, we had guests in the house and the children were put to bed. But every 5 minutes, Fred would come back asking for a drink of water, or wanting to go to the bathroom, and so on (the range of excuses was very broad). So after the *n*th time, I gave him what he wanted, told him this was the last time I wanted to see him out of bed, using the French idiomatic expression, "*Je ne veux plus te voir le bout du nez*" (literally, "I don't want to see the tip of your nose again"). Five minutes later he appeared in the living room with a big grin on his face, hiding the tip of his nose in his little fist. He knew exactly what he was doing and got the effect he was seeking. Everybody laughed and he got away with it.

Thus, interestingly, we have two independent systems that necessarily collaborate in the interpretation of every utterance—linguistic competence (what linguists describe as sentence grammar) subserved by areas of the left hemisphere, and pragmatic competence (the ability to make inferences from various types of contexts to arrive at the appropriate meaning of utterances) subserved by areas of the right hemisphere. Both systems are necessary and neither alone is sufficient for the normal use of language (Paradis, 1998).

MOTIVATION

Different kinds of general motivation behind the learning of a second language have been identified, from instrumental (e.g., the perception of the need to learn a language to improve one's professional status) to integrative (e.g., the desire to become part of another linguistic community). Anecdotal evidence abounds in support of the strong facilitating effect of learning the language of a significant other (especially during courtship). This situation is facilitative probably for a number of reasons, including the motivation to be accepted as a valid partner, which not only stimulates the dopaminergic system, but also encourages the learner to multiply practice sessions, thus facilitating incidental acquisition. Schumann (1990) further postulated that the attitude toward the L2 and the L2 speaking community has an influence on the acquisition of the L2: Efficiency of L2 appropriation is a function of the emotional appraisal of the linguistic input and the learning situation. Second-language teachers will often assert that degree of motivation is one of the best predictors of success in L2 learning. Such observations find their neurofunctional explanation in Schumann's proposal that one of the functions of the amygdala is to appraise the subjective emotional significance of incoming sensory stimuli. Hence, in a positively evaluated environment, the learner would be much more receptive to intake, given that the amygdala would project opiates in greater quantity to the specific sensory processing cortical systems involved and thereby facilitate retention of the material in long-term-memory.

In addition to these general motivations to learn a language, there is another more specific motivation that is present in infants (but not necessarily in second-language learners). It is the need or strong desire to be understood by their interlocutors and to understand every utterance that their interlocutors address to them. Thus, during the acquisition of the native language (or native languages), the first phase of the microgenesis of an utterance is the desire to communicate a message, a phase that is absent in most language teaching contexts. The microgenesis of a sentence is the generation of an actual utterance as it develops from the intention to communicate a message to its acoustic realization, through its logical, syntactic, morphological, and phonological processing in real time. Children learning their native language are strongly motivated to understand every utterance they hear addressed to them, and to produce every utterance they address to others. This specific motivation is absent in the classroom when sentences are produced on demand, without any real need or desire, among the students, to communicate the particular message that the sentence conveys. For example, in a classroom, students may ask for an aspirin, not because they have a headache, but because it is their turn to ask the question at the top of page 24 in their textbook. Even in simulated situations, as when a student asks, "Where is the pharmacy?," the motivational force to utter that specific utterance is not a need or desire to obtain the requested information, but the willingness to play a game of make-believe, which does not quite have the same effect on the brain as the perception of a real need.

In communicative approaches to second-language learning, when the learner is placed in a game-like situation in which success at communicating the relevant information is the key to winning—and individuals are generally motivated to win—it might possibly be assumed that the initial phase of the microgenesis of utterances somewhat approximates that in the infant, thus providing the beneficial surge of dopamine.

The emotional input from the relevant parts of the limbic system into the processing of utterances may be assumed to lower an activation threshold in the same way that frequency of use does. This is compatible with the observation that emotional impact seems to have the same effect as rehearsal in strengthening a memory trace. This would be a direct way of affecting L2 acquisition. An additional indirect effect is that motivation also likely encourages practice, which in turn positively affects L2 acquisition.

EARLY VERSUS LATE BILINGUALISM

A number of recent studies have reported neuropsychological evidence for a distinction between early and late bilinguals in the way they process language, stemming from event-related potentials (ERPs), positron emission tomography (PET), and functional magnetic resonance imaging (fMRI). Early bilinguals have been shown to process each of their languages in the same manner as their respective native speakers. Late bilinguals, on the other hand, have been shown to treat function words in a way that differs from the way unilinguals and early bilinguals treat them (Weber-Fox & Neville, 1996), and to involve to a lesser extent those areas that subserve implicit linguistic competence while at the same time involving to a greater extent those areas that are associated with declarative memory (Perani et al., 1996) and those associated with explicit control (Dehaene et al., 1997). A picture therefore emerges whereby late bilinguals seem to compensate for their gaps in implicit linguistic competence by a greater reliance on controlled declarative memory-based metalinguistic knowledge and right-hemisphere-based pragmatic competence.

More specifically, Weber-Fox and Neville (1996) report a pattern of ERP activation for function words (e.g., prepositions such as "at," "to," and "of") and conjunctions (e.g., "but," "and," "if") that, in unilinguals and early bilinguals but not in late bilinguals, differs from the pattern of ERP activation for lexical items (also known as "content words," or words carrying a significant information load), making the processing of function words in late bilinguals resemble that of the processing of lexical items, involving greater right-hemisphere participation. Because the meaning of words is consciously known by the speaker, the meaning component of the word, subserved by declarative memory, is expected to be more bilaterally represented, having connections to the various sensory modalities involved (the sound, shape, texture, smell, taste, color of the word's referent), whereas the syntactic properties of the word, its more structural components, being implicit, are expected to be represented in the classical perisylvian language areas of the left hemisphere, with the rest of implicit linguistic competence. Pulvermüller (1999) postulated that function words possess a less extensive semantic component than lexical items and hence are more strongly lateralized (i.e., have more connections to the left hemisphere). This follows from Damasio's (1989) proposal that the meaning of lexical items, being conceptually connected to numerous sensory modalities, would have representations in cortical associative areas associated bilaterally with different modalities. Moreover, meaning is one of the declarative word features and hence it is more widely distributed over various cortical areas. We may thus assume that late bilinguals have a tendency to treat function words declaratively, attributing to them an overt meaning, rather than implicitly like other syntactic aspects of language processing, as early bilinguals do.

Patterns of brain activation as measured by brain imaging studies suggest that a second language learned after an individual is about 7 years of age activates the various brain regions associated with language processing to different extents (some more, some less) than the native language. For example, Perani et al. (1996) reported that, for their subjects' native language (Italian), activation of the classical perisylvian language areas, including the angular gyrus (Brodmann's area 39), the superior and middle temporal gyri (areas 22 and 21), the inferior frontal gyrus (area 45), and the temporal pole (area 38) in the left hemisphere, as well as the right superior and middle temporal gyri, the right temporal pole, the posterior portion of the cingular gyrus (area 31), and a focus in the right cerebellum was observed. For their foreign language, English, learned in school (and of which the subjects had a good understanding), the set of language areas was considerably reduced. Only the left and right superior and middle temporal areas remained active, but there was also a bilateral activation of the parahippocampal gyri, suggesting an increased participation of declarative-memory-related structures. The authors conclude that the organization of the classical language areas has been shaped by exposure to the native language during childhood. These areas are not responsive to a second language acquired after an individual is beyond the age of 7. Moreover, there is great interindividual variability—but for the foreign language only. Areas associated with implicit linguistic competence (i.e., the classical left-hemisphere perisylvian language areas) are not necessarily activated when subjects are engaged in the processing of a foreign language that they have learned through limited exposure later in life.

Using fMRI, Dehaene et al. (1997) also reported a remarkable consistency in the activated areas of the left hemisphere during the processing of their subjects' native language (in this case, French). All subjects showed activity in the superior and temporal gyri, extending to the temporal pole, with similar activity in the right temporal lobe in six of the eight subjects, although it was weaker and highly variable from subject to subject. There was also a consistent focus of activation superior to Broca's area in the left hemisphere of six subjects and in the right hemisphere of three subjects. English, the foreign language, evinced much greater intersubject variability, including activation of the left temporal lobe with considerable dispersion in six subjects, activation of the right temporal lobe and the anterior portion of the left cingular gyrus in all subjects and, in six subjects, the activation of frontal areas above Broca's area and its homologous site in the right hemisphere. It is interesting to note that the anterior cingulate region, active only in the processing of the foreign language, is considered to be implicated in attentive, controlled, or central executive processing tasks (Devinksy, Morell, & Vogt, 1995), suggesting that some subjects used metalinguistic knowledge in a consciously guided manner. The authors concluded that a dedicated network of left-hemisphere cerebral areas underlies native-speech comprehension but fails to be consistently recruited for foreign-language comprehension in late, moderately proficient learners. They further implied that different methods of teaching a foreign language may favor different strategies for language processing, and hence distinct cerebral circuits (presumably, as suggested by Paradis [1992, 1993a], depending on the degree of inherent motivation and the extent of occasions for incidental acquisition and explicit learning). They concluded that behavioral and brain-imaging evidence suggests that maturational changes affect the ability to acquire a second language.

The data from the Perani et al. (1996) PET study and the Dehaene et al. (1997) fMRI study suggest that the left hemisphere of late (nonbalanced) bilinguals is activated in proportion to their reliance on implicit linguistic competence, and the activation of other areas reflects their increased reliance on metalinguistic knowledge and/or pragmatic competence. To the extent that implicit linguistic competence in the second language is native-like, bilinguals activate the same areas to the same extent as in their native language; to the extent that their implicit linguistic competence is weaker in the second language, they use compensatory mechanisms that are less procedural (and hence less homogeneous among individuals, because different individuals may adopt diverse compensatory strategies in various proportions). Patterns of brain activation may thus reveal the degree to which a person's second language is processed in a native-like fashion. In a more recent publication investigating very fluent, late bilinguals, Perani et al. (1998) found many more similarities between the activation patterns of the (very fluent) second language and the first language of their subjects than they had found previously in less fluent second language speakers. Nevertheless, for L2, the authors report activation foci *bilaterally* in hippocampal structures, indicating greater reliance on declarative memory when using L2 than L1.

IMPLICATIONS

One clear implication of some of the brain-imaging studies is that there is a sensitive period from about age 2 to 5 after which implicit linguistic competence is attained only with great difficulty and possibly never completely. These studies provide information on the issue of the critical period by showing that areas subserving procedural memory for language are less activated for languages acquired after the age of 7 years than for those acquired earlier (Dehaene et al., 1997; Kim, Relkin, Lee, & Hirsh, 1997; Perani et al., 1996), and that language components are processed differently (Neville, Mills, & Lawson, 1992; Weber-Fox & Neville, 1996) in early and late bilinguals. Late bilinguals are able to compensate to a certain extent for this difficulty in obtaining full competence by using both pragmatics and metalinguistic knowledge, the way individuals with genetic dysphasia have been shown to compensate for their language deficit in the use of their native language (Paradis & Gopnik, 1997). Of interest is the finding that children with familial specific language impairment have been shown to memorize rules that they consciously apply when forming the past tense of regular verbs (e.g., "walk/walked") and the plural of regular nouns (e.g., "cat/cats") the way nonimpaired children learn irregular verbs (e.g., "buy/bought") and irregular plurals (e.g., "woman/women"), instead of generating the regular forms automatically, the way nonimpaired children eventually do. (For details, see the special issue on genetic dysphasia in the *Journal of Neurolinguistics*, vol. 11, 1997, and the special issue on cross-linguistic evidence for genetic dysphasia in *Folia Phoniatrica et Logopaedica*, vol. 51, 1999.)

Indeed, some of the more paradoxical recovery patterns of bilingual aphasic patients who better recovered the language they spoke the least fluently before insult may well be the result of their greater metalinguistic knowledge in the formally learned but less fluent foreign language than in their informally acquired (fluent) native language. If aphasia is the impairment of implicit linguistic competence, that is, of the procedural memory underlying the automatic use of the grammar, then metalinguistic knowledge, subserved by declarative memory, should still be available to the patients, along with their pragmatic competence. In fact, both are capitalized on and used as compensatory strategies in much current language therapy practice (see Paradis, 1993b).

A Word of Caution

With any type of neuroimaging, the procedure is likely to measure only a part or an aspect of the complex process being measured. The question then is, which one? The answer is only as good as the theoretical framework used to interpret the data, that is, to infer which component of what function is activated where—and why?

For example, in the late 1970s and early 1980s, David Ingvar (personal communication, 1981) was puzzled by the right-hemisphere activation he was observing for language tasks in which regional cerebral blood flow was measured, using the low level of gamma radiation emitted by inhaled xenon-133 (Lassen, Ingvar, & Skinhøj, 1978). It was assumed at the time that perhaps the result was due to the hemodynamics of the neurovascular system, with similar contralateral flow maintaining symmetry. Another explanation, of course, is that right-hemisphere-based pragmatic competence is just as necessary as what was then considered "language" in the processing of verbal material.

Moreover, some of the activation may not be detected (because of limitations of a particular procedure), and individual differences may reflect different processing strategies, not necessarily topologically diverse representations.

When someone recently asked me what the French word "ver" meant in English, two possibilities came to mind—either "green" (*vert*) or "toward" (*vers*)—so I asked my interlocutor for a context, and the translation turned out to be the word "worm" (*ver*). The fact that, as pronounced, this word could also have meant "glass" (*verre*) had not even occurred to me. (All four of these words are homophonous in French.) In other words, what gets activated depends on context, and this fact can never be overlooked. The activation detected using neuroimaging techniques may depend not only on the task but also on the context in which stimuli are presented.

Specifically, the same stimulus may be processed one way or another depending on whether it is perceived as speech or not. Wang (1973) reported that, in an electroencephalograph (EEG) study, when French speakers in a group were asked to "listen to the following words" (all stimuli were comsonant–vowel [CV] words—the vast majority of CV syllables are real words in French—e.g., *peu, pas, pis, pot, pus, pou, pois, pain, pan, pont*), the subjects' left hemispheres showed increased activation. When asked to "listen to the following sounds" with the same stimuli presented to them, the subjects showed equal activation in both cerebral hemispheres. The mental set is a factor that cannot be ignored: Activated cortical sites are not necessarily an indication that they are involved in subserving the particular function that is being investigated, nor is the absence of activation an indication that the site is not involved in the function being investigated, but may simply be the result of the subject using a different strategy. (In a word-reading task, for instance, it is difficult to know whether a stimulus word is read via grapheme-to-phoneme correspondence without access to the semantic representation or through direct pattern recognition of the entire word, with or without semantic lookup.)

This does not mean that we should disregard neuroimaging data—only that we should be fully aware of their limitations, and of the different limitations for each procedure, and then be aware that the validity of our interpretation of the results is directly related to the theoretical framework used to infer what is happening. Moreover, our rationale should be compatible with the data we obtain from many other sources, including clinical data. Discrepancies should receive a reasonable explanation, again, unavoidably based on a hypothesis that itself has, it is hoped, been constructed on the basis of many observations from different sources. Our interpretations will depend on what we know about the tasks and about the brain—in other words, on our current working hypotheses—which will be as valid as they are richly informed, coming from many converging pieces of evidence from various sources (positron emission tomography, functional magnetic resonance imaging, magnetoencephalography, clinical observations, and anatomical data, among others).

CONCLUSION

Normal verbal communication involves left-hemisphere-based implicit linguistic competence—that is, the internalized computational procedures that underlie the comprehension and production of the possible sentences in a language; right-hemisphere-based inference mechanisms or pragmatic competence; bilaterally distributed metalinguistic knowledge; and the activity of the (subcortical) amygdaloid complex and midbrain dopaminergic motivational systems. All four systems are involved in the acquisition and processing of (first as well as second) language and conspire to make late language appropriation different from early acquisition with respect to the degree of reliance on each system.

In summary, these four generalizations can be made:

1. The specific motivation to communicate a message is absent at the onset of the microgenesis of utterances during appropriation, and general instrumental or integrative motivation varies between individuals, hence the differential impact of the amygdaloid and dopaminergic systems on language intake.
2. Incidental learning diminishes significantly as declarative memory—and hence metalinguistic knowledge—increases (Parkin & Steele, 1988; Parkin, 1989), thus seriously limiting the capacity to acquire implicit linguistic skills. As a result of the decline of implicit linguistic competence, the other two systems are used to compensate for gaps in the procedural memory for grammar.
3. The use of these compensatory mechanisms results in a greater reliance on declarative-memory-based metalinguistic knowledge.
4. There is also greater reliance on the right hemisphere to infer from various contexts what the syntax does not provide automatically.

Thus, to the extent that bilingual individuals differ in degree of mastery of the second language and to the extent that they differ in the degree of reliance on one rather than the other available compensatory mechanism, they will differ from each other, as illustrated by the observed interindividual variability in PET and fMRI studies; also to the extent that they have not developed complete linguistic competence, they will all differ from early bilinguals and unilinguals. Moreover, to the extent that early bilinguals have acquired both languages in the same circumstances as unilinguals have acquired theirs, bilingual cerebral representation and the processing of language will involve the same mechanisms as unilingual language representation and processing, and to a similar degree.

REFERENCES

Aglioti, S. (1997). The role of the thalamus and basal ganglia in human cognition. *Journal of Neurolinguistics, 10*, 255–265.

Bialystok, E. (1981). Some evidence for the integrity and interaction of two language sources. In R. W. Andersen (Ed.), *New dimensions in second language acquisition research* (pp. 62–74). Rowley, MA: Newbury House.

Bialystok, E. (1994). Representation and ways of knowing: Three issues in second language acquisition. In N. Ellis (Ed.), *Implicit and explicit learning of languages* (pp. 549–569). London: Academic Press.

Brookshire, R. H., & Nicholas, L. E. (1984). Comprehension of directly and indirectly stated main ideas and details in discourse by brain-damaged and non-brain-damaged listeners. *Brain and Language, 21*, 21–36.

Brownell, H. H. (1988). Appreciation of metaphoric and connotative word meaning by brain-damaged patients. In C. Chiarello (Ed.), *Right hemisphere contributions to lexical semantics* (pp. 19–32). New York: Springer-Verlag.

Brownell, H. H., Gardner, H., Prather, P., & Martino, G. (1995). Language, communication, and the right hemisphere. In H. S. Kirshner (Ed.), *Handbook of neurological speech and language disorders* (pp. 325–349). New York: Marcel Dekker.

Brownell, H. H., Potter, H. H., Bihrle, A. M., & Gardner, H. (1986). Inference deficits in right brain-damaged patients. *Brain and Language, 27*, 310–321.

Canavan, A. G. M., Hömberg, V., & Stelmach, G. E. (1992, October). *Separating declarative memory and procedural learning in alcoholic amnesics*. Paper presented at the 22nd Annual Meeting of the Society for Neuroscience, Anaheim, CA.

Cohen, N. (1991, November). *Memory, amnesia and the hippocampal system*. Paper given at the Cognitive and Neuroscience Colloquium, McGill University.

Cohen, N., & Eichenbaum, H. (1993). Memory, amnesia, and the hippocampal system. Cambridge, MA: MIT Press.

Corkin, S. (1992, April). *Implicit memory*. Paper given at the Seminar in Cognitive Neuroscience, Montreal Neurological Institute and Hospital.

Crosson, B., Zawacki, T., Brinson, G., Lu, L., & Sadek, J. (1997). Models of subcortical functions in language: Current status. *Journal of Neurolinguistics, 10*, 277–300.

Damasio, A. (1989). Concepts in the brain. *Mind and Language*, 4, 24–28.

Dehaene, S., Dupoux, E., Mehler, J., Cohen, L., Paulescu, E., Perani, D., van Moortele, P. F., Lehéricy, S., & Le Bihan, D. (1997). Anatomical variability in the cortical representation of first and second language. *NeuroReport, 8*, 3809–3815.

Devinsky, O., Morell, M. J., & Vogt, B. A. (1995). Contributions of anterior cingulated cortex to behavior. *Brian*, 118–306.

Dipper, L. T., Bryan, K. L., & Tyson, J. (1997). Bridging inference and relevance theory: An account of right hemisphere inference. *Clinical Linguistics and Phonetics, 11*, 213–228.

Dwyer, J., & Rinn, W. (1981). The role of the right hemisphere in contextual inference. *Neuropsychologia, 19*, 479–482.

Fabbro, F. (Ed.). (2000). Language and the cerebellum. [Special issue] *Journal of Neurolinguistics, 13*(3–4), 81–225.

Foldi, N. S. (1987). Appreciation of pragmatic interpretations of indirect commands: Comparison of right and left hemisphere brain-damaged patients. *Brain and Language*, 31, 88–108.

Gabrieli, J. D. E., Reminger, S. L., Grosse, D. A., & Wilson, R. S. (1992, October). *Implicit memory for representational and novel visual materials in patients with Alzheimer's disease*. Paper presented at the 22nd Annual Meeting of the Society for Neuroscience, Anaheim, CA.

Gardner, H., Brownell, H., Wapner, W., & Michelow, D. (1983). Missing the point: The role of the right hemisphere in the processing of complex linguistic materials. In E. Perecman (Ed.), *Cognitive processing in the right hemisphere* (pp. 169–191). Orlando, FL: Academic Press.

Gardner, R., & Lambert W. (1972). *Attitudes and motivation in second-language learning*. Rowley, MA: Newbury House.

Gordon, N. (1996). Speech, language, and the cerebellum. *European Journal of Disorders of Communication, 31*, 359–367.

Hier, D. B., & Kaplan, J. (1980). Verbal comprehension deficits after right hemisphere damage. *Applied Psycholinguistics, 1*, 279–294.

Joanette, Y., & Brownell, H. (Eds.). (1990). *Discourse ability and brain damage: Theoretical and empirical perspectives*. New York: Springer Verlag.

Joanette, Y., Goulet, P., & Hannequin, D. (1990). *Right Hemisphere and Verbal communication*. New York: Springer Verlag.

Kaplan, J. A., Brownell, H. H., Jacobs, J. R., & Gardner, H. (1990). The effects of right hemisphere damage on the pragmatic interpretation of conversational remarks. *Brain and Language*, 38, 315–333.

Keane, M. M., Clarke, H., & Corkin, S. (1992, October). *Impaired perceptual priming and intact conceptual priming in a patient with bilateral posterior cerebral lesions*. Paper presented at the 22nd Annual Meeting of the Society for Neuroscience, Anaheim, CA.

Kim, K. H., Relkin, N. R., Lee, K. M., & Hirsch, J. (1997). Distinct cortical areas associated with native and second languages. *Nature, 388*, 171–174.
Lamendella, J. (1977). General principles of neurofunctional organization and their manifrestation in primary and nonprimary language acquisition. *Language Learning, 27*, 155–196.
Lassen, N., Ingvar, D., & Skinhøj, E. (1978). Brain function and blood flow. *Scientific American, 239*(4), 62–71.
Leiner, H., Leiner, A., & Dow, R. (1991). The human cerebro-cerebellar system: Its computing, cognitive, and language skills. *Behavioural Brain Research, 44*, 113–128.
MacKay, D., Stewart, R., & Burke, D. (1998). H.M. revisited: Relations between language comprehension, memory, and the hippocampal system. *Journal of Cognitive Neuroscience, 10*, 377–394.
McDonald, S., & Wales, R. (1986). An investigation of the ability to process inferences in language following right hemisphere brain damage. *Brain and Language, 29*, 68–80.
Molinari, M., Leggio, M., Solida, A., Ciorra, R., Misciagnia, S., Silveri, M., & Petrosini, L. (1997). Cerebellum and procedural learning: Evidence from focal cerebellar lesions. *Brain, 120*, 1753–1762.
Neville, H., Mills, D., & Lawson, D. (1992). Fractionating language: Different neural systems with different sensitive periods. *Cerebral Cortex, 2*, 244–258.
Paradis, M. (1987). Neurolinguistic perspectives on bilingualsim. In M. Paradis & G. Libben (Eds.), *The assesment of bilingual aphasia* (pp. 1–17). Hillsdale, NJ: Lawrence Erlbaum Associates.
Paradis, M. (1992). Neurolinguistics and language learning. In D. Girard (Ed.), *Language teaching in today's world* (pp. 20–31). Paris: Hachette.
Paradis, M. (1993a). Implication de mécanismes mnésiques cérébraux différents selon les méthodes d'apprentissage. In J. Chapelle & M. T. Claes (Eds.), *Memory and memorization in acquiring and learning languages* (pp. 205–223). Brussels: CLL.
Paradis, M. (Ed.). (1993b). *Foundations of aphasia rehabilitation*. Oxford: Pergamon Press.
Paradis, M. (1994). Neurolinguistic aspects of implicit and explicit memory: implications for bilingualism and SLA. In N. Ellis (Ed.), *Implicit and explicit learning of languages* (pp. 393–419). London: Academic Press.
Paradis, M. (1998). The other side of language: Pragmatic competence. *Journal of Neurolinguistics, 11*, 1–10.
Paradis, M., & Gopnik, M. (1997). Compensatory strategies in genetic dysphasia: Declarative memory. *Journal of Neurolinguistics, 10*, 173–186.
Parker, W. (1992, October). *Verbal implicit recall of subject performed tasks but not verbal tasks in alcoholic Korsakoff's amnesics*. Paper presented at the Society for Neuroscience 22nd Annual Meeting, Anaheim, CA. Also: *Society for Neuroscience Abstracts, 18*, 1213.
Parkin, A. J. (1989). The development and nature of implicit memory. In S. Lewandowsky, J. C. Dunn, & K. Kirsner (Eds.), *Implicit memory: Theoretical issues* (pp. 231–240). Hillsdale, NJ: Lawrence Erlbaum Associates.
Parkin, A.J., & Streete, S. (1988). Implicit and explicit memory in young children and adults. *British Journal of Psychology, 79*, 361–369.
Perani, D., Dehaene, S., Grassi, F., Cohen, L., Cappa, S., Paulesu, E., Dupoux, E., Fazio, F., & Mehler, J. (1996). Brain processing of native and foreign languages. *NeuroReport, 7*, 2439–2444.
Perani, D., Paulesu, E., Sebastian Galles, N., Dupoux, E., Dehaene, S., Bettinardi, V., Cappa, S., Fazio, F., & Mehler, J. (1998). The bilingual brain. Proficiency and age of acquisition of the second language. *Brain, 121*, 1841–1852.
Pulvermüller, F. (1999). Words in the brain's language. *Brain and Behavioral Science, 22*(2), 253–336.
Ross, E. D. (1981). The aprosodias: Functional-anatomical organization of the affective components of language in the right hemisphere. *Archives of Neurology, 38*, 561–569.
Ross, E. D. (1984). Right hemisphere's role in language, affective behavior and emotion. *Trends in Neurosciences, 7*, 342–346.
Saint-Cyr, J., Taylor, A., & Lang, A. (1988). Procedural learning and neostriatal dysfunction in man. *Brain, 111*, 941–959.
Schumann, J. H. (1990). The role of the amygdala as a mediator of affect and cognition in second language acquisition. *GURT*, 169–176.
Schumann, J. H. (1997). *The neurobiology of affect in language*. Language Learning Monograph Series. East Lansing, MI: Blackwell.
Scoville, W., & Milner, B. (1957). Loss of recent memory after bilateral hippocampal lesions. *Journal of Neurology, Nuerosurgery, and Psychiatry, 20*, 11–21.

Thach, W. (1996). On the specific role of the cerebellum in motor learning and cognition: Clues from PET activation and lesion studies in man. *Behavioral and Brain Sciences*, *19*, 411–431.
Ullman, M.T. (2001). The neural basis of lexicon and grammar in first and second language: The declarative/procedural model. *Bilingualism: Language and Cognition*, 4, 105–122.
Ullman, M., Corkin, S., Coppola, M., Hickock, G., Growdon, J., Koroshetz, W., & Pinker, S. (1997). A neural dissociation within language: Evidence that the mental dictionary is part of declarative memory, and that grammatical rules are processed by the procedural system. *Journal of Cognitive Neuroscience*, 9, 266–276.
Wang, W. (1973, August). *Phonological theory*. Course given at the LSA Institute, University of Michigan, East Lansing.
Weber-Fox, C., & Neville, H. (1996). Maturational constraints on functional specializations for language processing: ERP and behavioral evidence in bilingual speakers. *Journal of Cognitive Neuroscience*, 8, 231–256.
Weylman, S. T., Brownell, H. H., Roman, M., & Gardner, H. (1989). Appreciation of indirect requests by left and right brain-damaged patients: The effects of verbal context and conventionality of wording. *Brain and Language*, 36, 580–591.

Author Index

Note: Page numbers in *italic* indicate bibliography references. Those followed by "n" refer to footnotes.

A

Aaltonen, O., 338, *343*
Abernethy, M., 238, *244*
Aboitiz, F., 286, 294, *302*
Abrahamson, A., 106, *109*
Abramson, A. S., 313, *346*
Ackermann, H., 342, *348*
Adelstein, A., 333, *345*
Adjukiewicz, K., 121, *140*
Aglioti, S., 355, *367*
Akahane-Yamada, R., 338, *345*
Alavi, A., *21*
Aldridge, J. W., 12, *20*
Alexander, A. W., 291, *303*
Alexander, G. E., 10, *20*
Alho, K., 291, *303*
Allen, J., 70, *80*
Allport, D. A., 268, 268n, 269, *277*
Alpert, N., 194, *208*, 259, 263, *281*
Altmann, G., 179, *203*
Amiel-Tison, C., 63–64, *82*
Anaki, D., 239, *244*
Anderson, B., 225, *226*
Anderson, J. A., 143, *164*, *165*
Anderson, R. C., 158, *164*
Andreason, P., 286, *304*
Angluin, D., 131, *140*
Aosaki, T., 12, 13, *21*
Aquino, T., 286, 298, *304*
Arbib, M. A., 269, *279*
Arezzo, J., 219, *227*
Aronson, S., 17, *21*
Aslin, R. N., 70, *79*, *81*, *82*, *83*
Atran, S., 30–31, *56*
Awh, E., 15, 17, 18, *20*, 263, 281

B

Baayen, H., 37n, *56*
Babkoff, H., 233, 240, *245*
Baddeley, A. D., 17, 18, *20*
Baetens Beardsmore, H., 310, *343*
Bahrick, L. E., *79*
Baker, C., 256, *278*
Baker, W., 317, 329, 332, 337, *343*, *347*, *348*
Bakker, D. J., 297, *301*
Bandettini, P. A., 218, *226*
Banich, M. T., 297, 300, *301*
Bard, E. G., 186, *203*, *208*
Barker, W. W., 298, *302*
Baron-Cohen, S., 92, 103, *110*
Barrett, S. E., 182, *203*, *208*
Bartke, S., 102, *109*
Barton, D., 312, *347*
Bashore, T. R., 197, *207*
Bates, E., 10, 20, *20*, 106, *109*, 275, *277*, *278*
Bauby, J. D., 91, *109*

Bauman, A., 73, *81*
Bavelier, D., 284, *301*, 333, *347*
Baynes, K., 237, *246*
Beaton, A. A., 298, *301*
Bechtel, W., 106, *109*
Bedi, G., 290, *305*
Beeman, M., 232, 237, 239, 241, *244*
Belin, P., 219, 225, 226, *226*, *227*
Belliveau, J. W., 178, *204*
Bellugi, U., 39, *59*, 62, *80*, 93, *109*
Bennardo, G., 25, 36n, 45, 45n, 48, 48n, 49, 50, 50n, 51, 54, *56*, *58*
Bentin, S., 174, 178, *206*
Berger, M., 20, *21*
Berlin, B., 29, 29n, 30, 31, *56*
Berndt, R. S., 258, 258n, 262, 275, *277*, *278*, *280*
Berridge, K. C., 12, *20*
Bersick, M., 189, *207*
Berthier, M. L., 341, *343*
Bertoncini, J., 63–64, *82*
Besson, M., 184, *206*
Best, C. T., 65, *79*, 298, *303*, 332, 338, *343*, *345*
Best, M., 294, *302*
Bettinardi, V., 269, *280*, *348*, 364, *369*
Bever, T. G., 154, *166*, 185, *204*, *205*
Bialystok, E., 333, *343*, 352, *367*
Bickerton, D., 6, 19, *20*
Bihrle, A., 92, *109*, 351, *368*
Binder, J., 212, 213, 218, *226*
Bird, H., 257, 261, 275, *278*
Birdsong, D., 103, *109*, 329, *343*
Biscaldi, M., 296, *302*
Bishop, D., 289, *302*
Bishop, D. V. M., 101, *109*
Bishop, S., 289, *302*
Black, J. E., 340, 342, *345*
Blackburn, P., 136, *140*
Blanz, B., 288, *302*
Bloch, D. E., *281*
Bloomfield, L., 310, *343*
Blumstein, S. E., 15, *20*, 212, 218, 219, 221, *226*, 234, *245*, 264, 268, *279*
Boas, F., 25, 26, 32, *56*
Boatman, D. F., 255, *278*
Bock, J. K., 195, 200, *203*, 257, 262, 275, *278*
Boder, E., 290, *302*
Bogen, J. E., 231, 232, *246*
Bohn, O. S., 66, *82*, 317, *344*
Bolinger, D. L., 70, *79*
Bond, Z. S., 313, *343*
Bookman, M. O., 288, *304*
Boothroyd, A., 320, *343*
Bornstein, M. H., 333, *343*
Boronat, C. B., 323, *347*
Bosch, L., 64, *80*, 327, *347*
Bostantzopoulou, S., 10, *21*
Bott, S. M., 323, 329, 333, 337, *344*, *347*
Bowden, E., 241, *244*
Bowen, R. W., 291, *306*
Bowerman, M., 24, 41, 42, *56*, 107, *109*
Boyle, M. E. T., 320, *347*
Boyton, G., 294, *302*
Bradley, L., 295, *302*
Bradlow, A. R., 319, *344*
Bradshaw, J. L., 10, 13, *20*, 232, *245*
Braine, M. D. S., 62, *80*
Brandt, M. E., 183, *208*
Braun, A., 284, *301*, 333, *347*
Breedin, S. D., 264, 265, 275, 276, *278*, *281*
Breen, N., 105, *109*
Breitmeyer, B. G., 294, *302*
Brenden, R. A., 235, *246*, 313, *348*
Brent, M. R., 70, *80*
Bressi, S., 269, *280*
Brinson, G., 355, *368*
Broca, P., 252, *278*
Brooker, B. H., 196, *203*
Brookhuis, K. A., 197, *207*
Brookshire, R. H., 351, *368*
Broschart, J., 45, 51, *56*
Brown, A. S., 196, *203*
Brown, C. M., 172, 185, 188, 189, 190–191, 196, 197, 199, *203*, *205*, *209*, 237, *246*
Brown, P., 37n, *56*
Brown, R., 62, *80*
Brown, W. S., 299, *303*, *304*
Brownell, H. H., 351, *368*, *370*
Bruck, M., 288, *302*
Bruckert, R., 274, *279*
Bryan, K. L., 351, *368*
Bryden, M. P., 234, *246*, 333, *345*
Buckner, R. L., 178, *204*
Bucy, P. C., 269, *279*
Burgess, C., 236, 237, 238, 239, 241, *245*
Burgund, E. D., 244, *245*
Burke, D., 354, *369*
Burling, R., 32, *57*
Burton, M. W., 218, 219, *226*
Buxbuam, L., 268, 269, *278*
Bybee, J. L., 153, *164*

Byma, G., 290, *305*

C

Cairns, P., 70, *80*
Calvin, W., 6
Canavan, A. G. M., 358, *368*
Caplan, D., 179, 194, *203, 208,* 255, 256, 259, 259n, 260, 263, 272, *278, 281,* 341, *344*
Cappa, S. F., 269, *280,* 341, *348,* 362, 363, 364, *369*
Caramazza, A., 186, 196, *205, 208,* 256, 258, 267, 270, 274, 275, *278, 279, 280,* 316, 321, 324, *344*
Carbone, E., 316, 321, 324, *344*
Cardebat, D., 217, 219, *226*
Carew, T. G., 269, *278*
Carey, S., 91, *110*
CARG (Cognitive Anthropology Research Group), 50, *57*
Carlyon, R., 289, *302*
Carmo, I., 301, *302*
Carpenter, P. A., 184, 185, 186, 194, *204, 205, 208,* 259, 259n, 260, 263, *279, 280*
Carpenter, R., 120, *140*
Carroll, J. M., 272, *281*
Carson-Radvansky, L., 37, *57*
Carston, R., 88, 104, *109*
Carter, B., 288, *303*
Carter, D. M., *80*
Cartwright, T. A., 70, *80*
Carvell, S., 10, *21,* 155, *165*
Casanova, M., 298, *304*
Castet, E., 293, 295, *302*
Castles, A., 301, *302*
Castro-Caldas, A., 301, *302*
Caviness, V. S., 222, *227*
Cazden, C., 62, *80*
Ceci, S. J., 236, *247*
Chapman, R. M., 188, *204*
Charles-Luce, J., 69, 70, *81, 82*
Charniak, E., 133, *140*
Chase, C., 292, *302*
Chater, N., 70, *80*
Chee, M. W. L., 341, *344*
Chen, M., 314, *344*
Cheney, D. L., 8, *20*
Chiarello, C., 232, 233, 236, 237, 239, 241, 242n, *244, 245, 246*
Chiat, S., 265, *280*
Childers, J. B., 70, *80*
Cho, T., 313, *344*
Chollet, F., 213, 217, 218, 219, *226, 227*
Chomsky, N., 25, 29, 53, *57,* 62, *80,* 87, 98, 100, 102, 103, *109,* 119, 122, 123, 124–125, 126, 128, 136, 139, *140,* 145, 146, 158, *164*
Christiansen, M. H., 70, *80*
Church, K. W., 70, *80*
Churchland, P. S., 144, *167,* 229, *245*
Churchward, C. M., 51, *57*
Ciorra, R., 355, *369*
Clahsen, H., 102, 103, 106, *109,* 183, *207*
Clark, A., 312, *344*
Clark, H. H., 39, *57, 203*
Clark, M. J., 331n, *345*
Clark, V. P., 284, *301,* 333, *347*
Clarke, H., 358, *368*
Cleeremans, A., 144, *164*
Clifton, C., 158, *165*
Cohen, C., 299, *305*
Cohen, L., 341, *344, 348,* 354, 362, 363, 364, *368, 369*
Cohen, N., 352, 354, *368*
Cohen, R., 39, *57*
Cohen, R. M., 286, *304*
Coles, M. G. H., 174, 177, 197, *203, 207, 208*
Coley, J. D., 47, *57*
Collins, A. M., 180, *203*
Collins, D., 222, *226*
Colombo, L., 180, *204*
Coltheart, M., 88, 105, *109,* 154, 155, *164, 166,* 264, 267, 270, *278, 281*
Conesco-Gonzales, E., 260, *279*
Coney, J., 238, *244*
Conners, F., 289, *304*
Conrad, L., 319, *344*
Constable, R. T., 286, *305*
Cooper, R. P., *82*
Cooper, W., 15, *20,* 234, *245*
Coppola, M., 154, 156, 157, *167,* 352, *370*
Corballis, P. M., 299, *302*
Corder, S. P., 321, *344*
Corina, D., 284, *301*
Corkin, S., 154, 156, 157, *167,* 352, 358, *368, 370*
Cornelissen, P., 295, *302*
Cornell, T. L., 260, *280*
Cornia, D., 333, *347*
Coslett, H. B., 264, 265, *278, 281*

Cossu, G., 287, *302*
Cottrell, G. W., 154, *164*, *165*
Coulson, S., 177, 180, 189, *204*, *206*, *209*
Cowie, F., 131, 132, 134, *140*
Cox, R., 212, 213, *226*
Crain, S., 145, *165*
Crick, F. H. C., 146, *165*
Crosson, B., 355, *368*
Crowhurst, M. J., 70, *80*
Crozier, S., 219, 225, *226*
Crystal, D., 31n, *57*
Cummings, J. L., 10, 17, 18, *20*
Cunnington, R., 10, 13, *20*
Curtiss, S., 333, *344*
Cutler, A., 65, 69, 70, *79*, *80*, *81*, 179, 180, 186, *207*, *208*, 320, 344

D

Dale, A. M., 174, 178, *204*, *205*
Damasio, A. R., 342, *344*, 362, *368*
Damasio, H., 19, *22*, 342, *344*
D'Amico, S., *278*
Daneman, M., *204*
Daniele, A., 265, *279*
Danziger, E., 37n, 56
Darwin, C., 5, *20*
Datta, H., 289, 301, *304*
Datto, H., *302*
Daugherty, K., 154, *165*
Davidson, R. J., 298, 299, *302*, *303*
Davies, L., 102, *109*
Davis, B. L., 150, *166*
Davis, K. R., 256, *280*
Deacon, T. W., 19, *20*
Deecke, L., 196, *205*
Deeks, J., 289, *302*
Deese, J., 180, *204*
DeFries, J. C., 289, 297, *304*, *305*
Dehaene, F. G., 341, *348*
Dehaene, S., 103, *109*, 341, *344*, *348*, 354, 362, 363, 364, *368*, *369*
Dejerine, J. J., 254, *278*
Dell, G. S., 144, *165*, 195, 196, *204*, 270, 271–272, 273, *278*, *280*, *281*
Delong, M. R., 10, *20*
Demb, J. B., 294, *302*
Demonet, J.-F., 255, *279*
Démonet, J. F., 217, 219, *226*
Demopoulos, W., 131, *140*
DeRenzi, E., *278*
deSa, V. R., 236, *246*
de Saussure, F., 26, *57*
Desmond, J. E., 341, *345*
Deuchar, M., 312, *344*
Deutsch, G., 233n, 234, *246*
DeVaughn, N., 298, *304*
Devescovi, A., 273, *278*
Devinsky, O., 363, *368*
Diamond, S., 237, *244*
Dicla-Soares, E., 301, *302*
Diehl, R. L., 312, 315, *346*
Diesch, E., 337, *344*
Dipper, L. T., 351, *368*
Dogli, G., 342, *348*
Donahue, A. M., 319, *347*
Donald, M. W., 196, *203*
Donchin, E., 196, 197, *206*, *207*
Donohue, B. C., 284, 286, *303*, *304*
Dopkins, S., 336, *344*
Dorman, M. F., 342, *348*
Dougherty, J. D., 30, 31, 32, 46, *57*
Dow, R., 355, *369*
Doyle, M. C., 183, *204*
Drake, C., 291, 299, *305*
Drislane, F., 294, *303*
Druss, B., 75, *81*
Duara, R., 298, *302*
Duhamel, 269, *281*
Duncan, G. W., 256, *280*
Dupoux, E., 65, *82*, 341, *344*, *348*, 354, 362, 363, 364, *368*, *369*
Dwyer, J., 351, *368*

E

Eberhard, K. M., 160, *165*
Echols, C. H., 70, 76, 80
Eddy, W. F., 194, *205*, 259, 263, *279*
Eden, G. F., 294, 297, *302*
Edwards, T. J., *81*
Eefting, W., 313, *344*
Eerola, O., 338, *343*
Eglin, M., 236, *245*
Eichen, E. B., 333, *347*
Eichenbaum, H., 352, *368*
Eimas, P. D., 62, 63, *80*, *82*
Eimer, M., 199, *204*
Eliopulos, D., 298, *303*
Ellen, P., 48, *57*
Ellis, A. W., 235, *247*
Elman, J., 10, 20, *20*, 106, 107, *109*, 144, 154, 164, *165*, 180, *207*
Emple, E., 300, *303*

Endo, K., 299, *305*
Engen, B., 17, *21*
Ericsson, K. A., *204*
Ervin, S., *80*
Estkowski, L. D., 218, *226*
Evans, A., 214, 215, 218, 219, 221, 222, 225, *226*, *226*, *227*, 341, 342, *346*, *349*
Evans, E. F., 219, *227*
Eviatar, Z., 235, *245*
Ezura, M., 299, *305*

F

Fabbro, F., 341, *344*, 355, *368*
Facoetti, A., 296, *302*
Farah, M. J., 267, 268, *278*
Farmer, M. E., 290, *302*
Fatigue, L., 269, *279*
Faust, M., 233, 240, 241, *244*, *245*
Fawcett, A., 290, *302*
Fazio, F., 269, *280*, *348*, 354, 362, 363, 364, *369*
Federmeier, K. D., 174, 177, *206*
Feldman, L. S., 8, 10, 14, 15, 17, 18, *21*
Fellbaum, C., 180, *207*
Fernald, A., 74, *80*, *83*
Ferreira, F., 158, *165*
Fifer, W. P., *82*
Fillmore, C. W., 128, 136, *140*
Finkelstein, S., 256, *280*
Fischbach, G. D., 342, *344*
Fischl, B. R., 178, *204*
Fisher, C. L., 75, *80*
Fisher, F. W., 288, *303*
Fitch, R., 219, *225*, *227*
Fize, D., 199, *209*
Flaherty, A. W., 12, 13, *21*
Flege, J. E., 313–314, 315, 316, 317, 325, 327, 332, 333, 338, 339, *344*, *345*
Fletcher, J. M., 286, *305*
Florey, M. J., 51, *57*
Flowers, K. A., 15, 16, *20*
Fodor, J., 11, *21*, 29, 39, *57*, 87, 88, *109*, 128, *140*, 145, 154, *165*, 185, *204*, *205*, 272, 273, *278*
Fodor, J. D., 188, *204*
Fokes, J., 313, *343*
Foldi, N. S., 351, *368*
Foley, A. W., 34, *57*
Fontaine, A., 219, *225*, *226*
Ford, J. M., 199, *208*
Forsberg, H., 289, *304*
Fowler, M. S., 293, 295, *302*, *305*
Fox, P., 214, 218, *227*, 297, *304*
Frackowiak, R., 213, 217, 218, 219, *226*, *227*, 300, *304*
Francis, W. N., 149, *166*, 184, *204*
Francis, W. S., 341, *345*
Frank, R., 19, *22*
Franklin, S., 257, 261, 275, *278*
Fraser, C., *80*
Frazier, L., 158, *165*, 272, *279*
Frege, G., 46, *57*
Freud, S., 255, *279*
Friederici, A. D., 68–69, *79*, *80*, *81*, 188, 189, *204*
Friedman, J., 8, 10, 14, 15, 18, *21*
Friedman, R. B., 237, *244*
Friston, K., 213, 218, *227*
Frith, C. D., 300, *304*
Frith, U., 102, *109*, 300, *304*
Fromkin, V. A., 257, 260, *279*, *280*
Frost, J., 212, 213, *226*
Fujii, T., 299, *305*
Fulker, D., 289, *304*
Fullbright, R. K., 286, *305*
Funkenstein, H. H., 256, *280*
Funnell, E., 264, 276, *279*
Funnell, M. G., 299, *302*
Furbee, L. N., 28, *57*
Futter, C., 260, *278*

G

Gabrieli, J. D. E., 300, *303*, 341, *345*, 358, *368*
Gagnon, D. A., 271–272, 273, *280*
Gainotti, G., 265, *279*, *281*
Galaburda, A. M., 221, *227*, 286, 294, *302*, *303*, *304*
Gallagher, A., 300, *304*
Gallistel, C. R., 48, *57*
Gandour, J., 218, *227*
Ganz, L., 294, *302*
Gardner, B. T., 7, *21*
Gardner, H., 351, *368*, *370*
Gardner, R., 352, *368*
Gardner, R. A., 7, *21*
Garnsey, S. M., 188, *204*
Garrett, M. E., 185, 188, 195, *204*, *205*, 257, 270, *279*
Gatenby, C., 286, *305*
Gayan, J., 289, 301, *302*, *304*
Gazdar, G., 119, 120, 121, *140*

Gazzaniga, M., 224, *227*, 231, 232, *245*, *246*, 299, *302*
Gelade, G., 296, *305*
Gelman, S. A., 29, 47, 55, *57*
Gemba, H., 199, *205*, *208*
Georgiewa, P., 288, *302*
Gerken, L. A., 75, 76, *80*, *83*
Gernsbacher, M. A., 184, *205*, 239, 241, *244*, *245*
Gerstman, L. J., 70, *79*
Geschwind, N., 272, *279*, 286, 294, *302*
Getty, L. A., 331n, *345*
Gezeck, S., 296, *302*
Gilbert, J. H. V., 337, *348*
Giraud, K., 299, *303*
Giustolisi, L., 265, *279*
Gjedde, A., 214, 218, 219, *227*, 342, *349*
Gladstone, M., 298, *303*
Glauche, W., 288, *302*
Gleason, T., 336, *344*
Gleitman, H., 76, *80*
Gleitman, L., 76, *80*, *81*
Gloning, I., 341, *345*
Gloning, K., 341, *345*
Glover, G. H., 341, *345*
Gold, B., 319, *347*
Gold, E. M., 129–130, *140*
Goldinger, S. D., 179, *206*
Goldman-Rakic, P. S., 194, *205*
Goldstein, M. D., 218, *226*
Gollner, S., 102, *109*
Gollump, S., 10, *21*, 155, *165*
Goodall, J., 8, *21*
Goodenough, W., 31, 32, *57*
Goodglass, H., 15, *20*, 255, 256, 259, 264, 268, 274, *279*, *280*
Gopnik, M., 101, 102, *109*, 364, *369*
Gordon, B., 186, *205*, 255, *278*
Gordon, N., 355, *368*
Gore, J. C., 286, *305*
Gorno-Tempini, M., 269, *280*
Gottfried, G. M., 47, *57*
Gottleib, J., 15, *20*
Gough, P. B., 288, *303*
Goulding, P. J., 264, *281*
Goulet, P., 232, *246*, 351, *368*
Grafman, J., 237, *244*
Grafton, S. T., 269, *279*
Graham, K. S., 155, *165*
Graham, N., 264, *279*
Grant, J., 92, 103, *110*
Grassi, F., 354, 362, 363, 364, *369*
Graybiel, A. M., 12, 13, *21*
Green, G., 291, *305*
Green, P. A., 288, *304*
Greenough, W. T., 340, 342, *345*
Grieser, D., *81*
Griffiths, T., 291, *305*
Grimshaw, G. M., 333, *345*
Grodd, W., 342, *348*
Grodzinsky, Y., 257, 260, *279*
Groothusen, J., 188, 189, *205*
Grosjean, F., 310, 311, *345*
Grosse, D. A., 358, *368*
Gross-Glenn, K., 298, *302*
Grossman, M., 10, *21*, 155, *165*
Grouios, G., 10, *21*
Growdon, J. H., 154, 156, 157, *167*, 352, *370*
Guion, S. G., 316, 325, 338, *345*
Gunter, T. C., 189, *205*

H

Haarmaan, H. J., 260, *279*
Habib, M., 255, *279*, 298, 299, *303*, *304*
Hadar, U., 213, 218, *227*
Haendiges, A., 258, 275, *278*
Hagoort, P., 172, 185, 188, 189, 190–191, 196, 197, 199, *203*, *205*, *209*, 237, *246*
Hahne, A., 188, *204*
Haider, H., 342, *348*
Haith, M. M., 288, *304*
Hakuta, K., 333, *343*, *345*
Halgren, E., 178, *204*
Hall, J., 298, *303*
Halle, M., 145, *164*
Hallé, P. A., 338, *345*
Hallgren, B., 288, *303*
Halstead, N., 63–64, *82*
Hamburger, S. D., 286, 298, *304*
Hammeke, T., 212, 213, 218, *226*
Hannequin, D., 232, *246*, 351, *368*
Hansen, J. H. L., 319, *345*
Hansen, P., 291, *305*
Happé, F., 102, *109*
Hardin, C. L., 30, *57*
Hare, M., 154, *165*
Hargreaves, D. J., 184, *205*
Hari, R., 291, *303*
Harm, M., 163, *165*
Harris, C., *277*
Hassbrooke, R., 239, *246*

Haughton, V. M., 218, *226*
Haussler, D., 133, *140*
Haviland, 40n
Havinga, J., 196, 199, *206*
Hawkins, R. D., 342, *346*
Haxby, J. V., *21*, 269, *280*
Head, H., 255, *279*
Hedehus, M., 300, *303*
Heeger, D. J., 294, *302*
Heikki Lang, A., 338, *343*
Heilman, K. M., 291, *303*
Heise, G. A., 319, *347*
Helenius, P., 291, *303*
Heller, W., 297, *301*
Hellige, J. B., 232, 244, *246*, 297, *303*
Hellström, Å, 338, *343*
Henaff Gonon, M., 274, *279*
Henderson, V. W., 284, *303*
Herman, M., 12, *20*
Hermelin, B., 103, *109*, *110*
Hernandez, A., *278*
Hickock, G., 260, *279*, 352, *370*
Hicock, G., 154, 156, 157, *167*
Hier, D. B., 351, *368*
Hildebrandt, N., 259n, *278*
Hill, D., 51, *57*
Hill, J. H., 28, *57*
Hillenbrand, J., 315, 331n, *345*
Hillenbrand, J. M., *81*
Hillis, A. E., 275, *279*
Hillyard, S. A., 177, 183, 188, *205*, *206*
Hinshelwood, J., 286, *303*
Hinton, G. E., 143, 145, 156, *165*, *167*
Hirsch, J., 341, *346*, 364, *369*
Hirschfeld, L. A., 29, 55, *57*
Hirsh-Pasek, K., 70, 75, *81*, *82*
Hockett, C. F., *81*
Hodges, J. R., 154, 155, *165*, *166*, 259, 264, 276, *279*
Hoeffner, J., 154, *165*, *167*
Hoeien, T., *303*
Hoffman, J. E., 296, *303*
Hoffner, E., 213, 218, *227*
Hohne, E. A., 67, 73, 74, *81*
Hoijer, H., 28, *57*
Holcomb, P. J., 172, 177, 183, 188, *205*, *207*
Holt, L. L., 337, *346*
Hömberg, V., 358, *368*
Hopf, J.-M., 288, *302*
Horowitz, B., 286, *304*
Horwitz, B., 284, *303*
Houde, J. F., 148, *165*
Houston, D. M., 70–71, *81*
Howard, D., 218, *227*
Hubel, D. H., 30, *57*, 292, *303*
Huijbers, P., 195, *205*
Hukari, T. E., 120, *140*
Humphrey, K., 337, *348*
Humphreys, G. W., *280*, 286, 288, *304*
Humphreys, P., *303*
Hunt, L. J., 341, *347*
Hurtig, H. I., 10, *21*, 155, *165*
Hutchins, G., 218, *227*
Hutsler, J., 224, *227*
Hyde, J. S., 218, *226*
Hyde, M. R., 264, 268, *279*
Hynd, G. W., 298, *303*, 341, *345*
Hyslop, C., 51, *57*

I

Iacaboni, M., 235, *246*
Iansek, R., 10, 13, *20*
Illes, J., 341, *345*
Ingram, D., 153, *165*
Ingram, J. C. L., 318, *345*
Ingvar, D., 365, *369*
Inhelder, B., 91, *109*, *110*
Ioup, G., 321, *345*
Irwin, D., 37, *57*
Iverson, P., 337, *344*, *345*, *346*
Ivry, R., 234, 235, 244, *246*

J

Jackendoff, R., 25, 29, 38, 40, 43–45, 47, 53, 55, *57*, *58*
Jacobs, B., 342, *345*
Jacobs, J. R., 351, *368*
Jaeger, J. J., 154, *165*
Jain, S., 131, *140*
Jallad, B., 298, *302*
Jang, S., 317, *344*
Jenkins, J. J., 272, *281*
Jenkins, W. M., 290, *305*
Jenner, A. R., 292, *302*
Jescheniak, J. D., 186, *205*
Jesmanowicz, A., 218, *226*
Jezzard, P., 284, *301*, 333, *347*
Jiminez, E. B., 8, 10, 14, 15, 18, *21*
Joanette, Y., 232, *246*, 351, *368*
Joanisse, M., 101, 102, *109*, 146, 153–158, 163, *165*

Job, R., 267, *281*
Jodo, E., 199, *205*
Johannes, S., 189, 191, *207*
Johnson, D. E., 136, *140*
Johnson, E. K., 64, *82*
Johnson, J., 333, *345*
Johnson, M., 10, 20, *20*, *58*, 106, *109*
Johnson-Laird, P. N., 47, 48, *58*
Jones, R. S., 143, *164*
Jonides, J., 15, 17, 18, *20*, 263, *281*
Joos, M., 225, *227*
Jordan, M. I., 148, *165*, *166*
Joshi, A., 120, *140*
Jusczyk, A. M., 68, 74, 75, *81*, *82*
Jusczyk, P. W., 62, 63–64, 65, 67, 68, 69, 70–71, 72, 73, 75, 77, *79*, *80*, *81*, *82*, *83*, 104, *109*, 147, *165*, 336
Just, M. A., 184, 185, 186, 194, *208*, 259, 259n, 260, 263, *279*, *280*
Just, M. M., *205*

K

Kachru, B. B., 310, *345*
Kacinik, N., 242n, *245*
Kaiser, W.-A., 288, *302*
Kako, E. T., 8, 10, 14, 15, 18, *21*
Kallio, J., 291, *303*
Kandel, E. R., 174, *206*, 342, *346*
Kanki, B. G., 18, *21*
Kaplan, J. A., 351, *368*
Kari, A., 333, *347*
Karmiloff-Smith, A., 10, 20, *20*, 92, 103, 104, 106, *109*, *110*
Karni, A., 284, *301*
Katsarou, Z., 10, *21*
Katz, J. J., 62, *81*, 128, *140*
Katz, L., 286, 287, *302*, *305*
Katz, R., 264, *279*
Katz, S., 15, 17, 18, *20*
Kaufmann, W., 286, *303*
Kavé, G., 89, 102, *110*
Kawamoto, A. H., 159, *166*
Kay, P., 29, 29n, 30, *56*, *58*, 136, *140*
Kayama, Y., 199, *205*
Keane, M. M., 358, *368*
Keenan, E. L., 122, *140*
Keil, E. C., 268, *279*
Keller, C. M., 25, 32, 45n, 46, 54, *57*, *58*
Keller, F., 129, *140*
Keller, J. D., 46, 47, 54, *58*
Keller, T. A., 194, *205*, 259, 263, *279*
Kelley, B. F., 51, *57*
Kello, C. T., 146, 147–153, 155, 163, *167*
Kemler Nelson, D. G., 70, 75, *81*, *82*
Kemmerer, D. L., 154, *165*
Kempen, G., 195, *205*
Kemper, T. L., 286, *302*
Kennedy, L., 75, *81*
Kertesz, A., 251, 255, *279*
Kettermann, A., 337, *344*
Khalak, H. G., 154, *165*
Kim, E. J., 333, *346*
Kim, K. H. S., 341, *346*, 364, *369*
Kim, R., 329, *346*
Kimura, M., 12, 13, *21*
King, A. C., 286, *304*
King, J. W., 174, 177, 178, 184, 186, 187, 189, 192, 193, *204*, *205*, *206*, *207*
Kingston, J., 312, *346*
Kintsch, W., 160, *167*, 192, *204*, *205*, 239, *246*
Klatt, D. H., 70, *81*, 317, *346*
Klein, D., 341, *346*
Klein, E., 119, 120, 121, *140*
Klein, R. E., *81*
Klein, R. M., 290, *302*
Klima, E., 92, 103, *110*
Klingberg, T., 300, *303*
Kluender, K. R., 315, 337, *346*
Kluender, R., 183, *205*, *209*
Kluver, H., 269, *279*
Knab, R., 288, *302*
Knight, R. T., 237, *246*
Koch, C., 144, *167*
Koeppe, R. A., 15, 17, 18, *20*, 263, *281*
Koivisto, M., 237–238, *246*
Kolk, H. H. J., 258, 260, 262, *279*
Kopell, B. S., 199, *208*
Kornhuber, H. H., 196, *205*
Koroshetz, W. J., 154, 156, 157, *167*, 352, *370*
Kosslyn, S. M., 39, *58*, 233–234, *246*
Kravetz, S., 233, 239, 240, *244*, *245*
Kritchevsky, M., 39, *59*, 275, *277*
Krueger, L. E., 235, *246*
Kucera, H., 149, *166*, 184, *204*
Kuhl, P. K., 63, 66, *81*, 336, 337, *345*, *346*
Kuhn, T. S., 28, *58*
Kujala, T., 291, *303*
Kushch, A., 298, *302*
Kutas, M., 172, 174, 177, 178, 183, 184, 185, 186, 187, 188, 189, 190–191, 192,

193, 194, 196, 199, 200, 201, 202, *203, 204, 205, 206, 207, 208, 209,* 284, 291

L

Lacadie, C., 286, *305*
Lacerda, F., *81,* 336, *346*
Lachter, J., 154, *166*
Ladefoged, P., 313, *344*
Lado, R., 311, *346*
Laeufer, C., *346*
Lakoff, G., 136, *140*
Lalonde, C. E., 337, *348*
Lalwani, A., 284, *301,* 333, *347*
Lambert, W., 352, *368*
Lambertz, G., 63–64, *82*
Lamendella, J., 342, *346,* 352, *369*
Landau, B., 44, 47, *58,* 76, *80*
Lang, A., 355, *369*
Langacker, R. W., 124, *140*
Langdon, R., 105, *109*
Larsen, J. P., *303*
Lashley, K. S., 9, *21*
Lasky, R. E., *81*
Lasnik, H., 114, 117, 122, 123, *140*
Lassen, N., 365, *369*
Lawson, D. S., 186, *207,* 364, *369*
Leavitt, L. A., *83*
Lebby, P. C., 234, *246*
Le Bihan, D., 341, *344,* 354, 362, 363, 364, *368*
LeCluyse, K., 294, *305*
Lee, C. J., 341, *345*
Lee, K. M., 341, *346,* 364, *369*
Lefly, D. L., 288, *304*
Leggio, M., 355, *369*
Lehéricy, S., 341, *344,* 354, 362, 363, 364, *368*
Lehiste, I., 70, *82,* 314, *348*
Lehman, F. K., 25, 32, 45, 45n, 46, 47, 49, *58*
Leiberman, P., *82*
Leiguarda, R., 341, *343*
Leinbach, J., 154, *166*
Leiner, A., 355, *369*
Leiner, H., 355, *369*
Lenneberg, E., 28, 29, *58,* 328, *346*
Lennerstrand, G., 295, *306*
Leote, F., 301, *302*
Leslie, A., 102, *109, 110*
Lesser, R. P., 255, *278*
Lettich, E., 20, *21*
Levelt, W. J. M., 35, 37, 38, 48, *58,* 181, 186, 195, 196, 199, 200, *203, 205, 206, 208,* 255, 257, 258, 271, *278, 279, 281*
Levin, B., 298, *302*
Levine, R. D., 120, *140*
Levinson, S. C., 23–24, 33, 35–40, 36n, 37, 37n, 38, 48, 48n, 50, 53, *58*
Levitt, A., 338, *345*
Levy, J., 70, *80*
Levy, Y., 89, 102, *110*
Lewine, J. D., 178, *204*
Ley, R. G., 234, *246*
Liben, L. S., 39, *59*
Liberman, A. M., *82,* 147, *166,* 219, *227,* 291, *303, 305*
Liberman, I. Y., 287, 288, *302*
Lichten, W., 319, *347*
Lichtheim, L., *21,* 254, *279*
Lieberman, P., 4, 6, 7, 8, 10, 11, 14, 15, 17, 18, *21,* 312, *347*
Lindblom, B., *81,* 336, *346*
Lindsay, M. B., 237, *244*
Linebarger, M., 259, 259n, 260, 261, *279, 280, 281*
Lisker, L., 313, *346*
Liu, A. K., 178, *204*
Liu, S., 242n, *245,* 333, 339, *345*
Lively, S. E., 179, *206*
Livingstone, M., 292, 294, *303*
Locke, J. L., 148, 149, *166,* 342, *346*
Lockwood, A. H., 154, *165*
Loewenstein, D. A., 298, *302*
Loftin, J. D., 316, 325, *345*
Loftus, E. F., 180, *203*
Logan, J. S., 319, *347*
Logothetis, J., 10, *21*
Lotto, A. J., 337, *346*
Lounsbury, F. G., 31, *59*
Lovegrove, B., 292, 293, 295, *303*
Lu, L., 355, *368*
Lucchelli, F., *278*
Luce, P. A., 69, 72, *81, 82*
Lucy, J., 23–24, 27, 30, 34, *59*
Lundberg, I., 287, *303*
Lylyk, P., 341, *343*

M

MacDonald, J. D., 215, 221, 222, 225, *227*
MacDonald, M. C., 159, 162, *166,* 262, 273, *280*
Mack, M., 311, 312, 314, 315, 316, 317, 319, 320, 322, 323, 325, 329, 330, 337, 342, *346, 347*

MacKay, D., 354, *369*
MacKay, I. R. A., 316, 327, *345*
Macken, M. A., 312, *347*
MacKinnon, G. E., 333, *345*
MacLaury, R. E., 30, *59*
Maclay, H., 180, *206*
MacNeilage, P. F., 150, *166*
MacWhinney, B., 154, *166*
Maffi, L., 30, *57*
Maisog, J. M., 286, *302, 304*
Mandel, D. R., 75, *80, 82*
Mann, V., 316, *345*
Mannheim, B., 28, *57*
Mannheim, G. B., 298, *304*
Marangolo, P., *278*
Marcel, A. J., 154, *166*
Marchione, K. E., 286, *305*
Marchman, V. A., 154, *166, 167*, 275, *277*
Marcus, G., 106, *110*
Marcus, M. P., 158, *166*
Marie, P., 255, *280*
Marin, J. W., 196, *207*
Marin, O. S. M., 255, 264, *280, 281*
Markee, T., 299, *303, 304*
Marks, S., 93, *109*
Marlot, C., 199, *209*
Marsden, C. D., 10, 14, *21*
Marshall, J., 265, *280*
Marshall, J. C., 154, *166*
Marslen-Wilson, W., 154, 160, *166*, 180, *206*
Marsolek, C. J., 233–234, 244, *245, 246*
Martin, A., *21*, 269, *280*
Martin, F., 293, *303*
Martin, J. H., 174, *206*
Martin, N., 262, 270, 271–272, 273, *280*
Martino, G., 351, *368*
Marzola, V., 296, *302*
Mascetti, G., 296, *302*
Mason, C., 174, *206*
Masson, G. S., 293, 295, *302*
Masson, M. E. J., 236, *246*
Masure, M. C., 219, 225, *226*
Matarrese, M., 269, *280*
Matsuzaki, R., 199, *208*
Matthews, R. J., 135, *140*
Matthies, M. L., 148, *166*
Mattingly, I. G., 219, *227*
Mattys, S., 72, *82*
Matzke, M., 189, 191, *207*
Mauner, G., 260, *280*
Maunsell, J. H. B., 273, *280*
Mayberry, R. I., 333, *347*
Mayr, 5, 14
Mazzucchi, A., 259, *280*
McAnally, K., 291, *303*
McCarthy, G., 174, 178, *206*
McCarthy, R., 267, 269, *280, 281*
McClelland, J. L., 143, 144, 145, 146, 153, 154, 158–162, 163, *164, 165, 166, 167*, 180, *207*, 235, *246*, 267, 268, 272, 273, 276, *278, 280*
McDaniel, C., 30, *58*
McDonald, S., 351, *369*
McIsaac, H., 183, *209*
McKeever, W. F., 341, *347*
McKoon, G., 159, *166*
McLaughlin, J., 189, *207*
McLeod, P., 146, *166*
McNeill, D., 62, 74, *82*
McQueen, J. M., 179, 180, *207*
McRae, K., 236, *246*
McRoberts, G. W., 65, 74, *79, 80*, 332, *343*
Meador, D., 316, 327, *345*
Mecklinger, A., 189, *204*
Medin, D. L., 47, *59*
Mehler, J., 63–64, 65, *80, 82*, 146, *167*, 320, 341, *344, 348*, 354, 362, 363, 364, *368, 369*
Meier, R. P., *82*
Meltzoff, A. N., 149, *166*
Mencl, W. E., 286, *305*
Menn, L., 148, *166*, 259, *280*
Mentenopoulos, G., 10, *21*
Merzenich, M. M., 290, *305*
Mesulam, M. M., 10, *21*
Meyer, A. S., 181, 195, 196, 199, 200, *206, 208*, 258, 271, *279, 281*
Meyer, D. E., 197, *207*
Meyer, E., 214, 218, 219, 226, *227*, 341, 342, *346, 349*
Meyer, J., 342, *348*
Meyer-Viol, W., 136, *140*
Miceli, G., 256, 259, *280*
Michel, F., 274, *279*
Michel, G. F., 291, *305*
Michelow, D., 351, *368*
Miller, G. A., 48, *59*, 180, *207*, 319, *347*
Miller, J., 197, *207*
Miller, J. L., 63, *80, 82*
Miller, S., 219, 225, *227*
Miller, S. L., 290, *305*
Mills, D. L., 186, *207*, 364, *369*
Milner, B., 341, *346*, 354, *369*
Minifie, F. D., *81*

Minoshima, S., 263, *281*
Mintun, M., 214, 218, *227*
Miozzo, M., 274, *278*, *280*
Miranda, P. C., 301, *302*
Mirenowicz, J., *21*
Misciagnia, S., 355, *369*
Mishkin, M., 219, *227*
Mitchiner, M., 183, *209*
Mitchum, C., 258, 275, *278*
Miyake, A., 259n, 260, *280*
Mody, M., 290, *305*
Moffitt, A. R., *82*
Mohr, J. P., 256, *280*
Molfese, D. L., 235, *246*, 291, *304*, 313, *348*
Molfese, V. J., 235, *246*
Molinari, M., 355, *369*
Molinet, K., 294, *305*
Moltz, H., 333, *347*
Montague, R., 121, *140*
Moon, C., *82*
Moore, C. J., 288, *304*
Moore, L. H., 299, *303*, *304*
Moore, M. K., 149, *166*
Moore, T. E., 39, *59*
Morell, M. J., 363, *368*
Morgan, G., 96, *110*
Morgan, J. L., 70, 72, *82*
Morrison, D., *21*
Morse, P. A., *82*, *83*
Morton, J., 102, *109*, 300, *304*
Moseley, M. E., 300, *303*
Mulder, G. M., 189, 197, *205*, *207*
Mulder, L. J. M., 197, *207*
Mullennix, J., 63, *81*
Müller, H. M., 192, 193, *207*
Munro, M. J., 315, *345*
Münte, T. F., 177, 183, 189, 191, 194, 199, 200, 201, 202, *206*, *207*, *208*
Murphy, B. W., 154, *165*
Murphy, G. L., 47, *59*
Myers, J., 70, *82*
Myllyviita, K., 291, *303*

N

Näätänen, R., 199, *207*, 291, *303*
Nábelek, A. K., 319, *347*
Nace, K. L., 286, *304*
Nagarajan, S. S., 290, *305*
Nambu, A., 199, *208*
Nandkumar, S., 319, *345*
Natsopoulos, D., 10, *21*
Nazzi, T., 64, 75, *82*
Neary, D., 264, *281*
Nebes, R. D., 232, 236, *246*
Neelin, P., 222, *226*
Neely, J. H., 236, *246*
Nespor, M., *82*
Nespoulous, J. L., 217, 219, *226*
Nettleton, N. C., 232, *245*
Neville, H. J., 186, *207*, *347*, 284, *301*, 333, 342, *348*, 353, 354, 362, 364, *369*, *370*
Newcombe, N., 39, *59*
Newport, E. L., 76, *80*, *82*, *83*, *333*, *347*, *345*
Newsome, M., 70–71, *81*
Newsome, W. T., 273, *280*
Nicholas, C. D., *246*
Nicholas, L. E., 351, *368*
Nittrouer, S., 320, *343*
Nobre, A. C., 174, 178, *206*
Nocentini, U., *280*
Norris, D. G., 65, 70, *80*, 180, *207*, 320, *344*
Novey, E. S., 298, *303*
Nuding, S., 233, 236, *245*
Nunez, P. L., 174, *207*

O

Obeso, J. A., 10, 14, *21*
O'Boyle, M. W., 325, *347*
O'Connor, N., 103, *110*
Oden, G., 158, *166*
Oedegaard, H., 298, *303*
Ojemann, F., 20, *21*
Ojemann, G. A., 20, *21*, 212, *227*, 341, *347*
Ojemann, J. G., 341, *348*
Ollinger, J. M., 341, *348*
Olofsson, A., 287, *303*
Olson, R. K., 288, 289, 301, *302*, *304*
O'Reilly, R. C., 146, *166*
Orton, S. T., 297, *304*
Ortony, A., 158, *164*
O'Seaghdha, P. G., 196, *204*, *207*, 271, *278*
Osgood, C. E., 180, *206*
Osherson, D., 131, *140*
Osman, A., 197, *207*
Osterhout, L., 172, 177, 188, 189, *207*
Ouhalla, J., 96, 99, *110*
Ovrut, M., 291, *305*
Owen, A. M., 194, *207*
Oxbury, S., 264, 276, *279*
Oyama, S., 329, *347*
Ozanne-Rivierre, F., 51, *59*

Ozawa, K., 319, *347*

P

Padmanabhan, S., 284, *301*
Paganoni, P., 296, *302*
Paivio, A., 264, *280*
Pallier, C., 327, *347*
Palmer, S., 51, *59*
Pammer, K., 296, *305*
Paradis, M., 321, 329, 341, *347*, 352, 355, 360, 364, 365, *369*
Parisi, D., 10, 20, *20*, 106, *109*
Park, S.-G., 318, *345*
Parker, W., 358, *369*
Parkin, A. J., 359, 367, *369*
Parks, M., 180, *209*
Paronas, N., 298, *304*
Parsons, C., 235, *246*
Pascal, S., 298, *302*
Pate, D. S., 259n, 260, *281*
Patterson, A. H., 39, *59*
Patterson, K., 154, 155, 163, *165*, *166*, *167*, 186, *207*, 218, *227*, 259, 264, 276, *279*
Paulesu, E., 300, *304*, 341, *344*, *348*, 354, 362, 363, 364, *368*, *369*
Paus, T., 219, 221, *227*
PDP Research Group, 143, 146, *166*, *167*
Pearlmutter, N. J., 159, 162, *166*, 262, 273, *280*
Pechmann, T., 196, 199, *206*
Pederson, E., 37n, *59*
Pegg, J. E., 67–68, *82*
Penfield, W., 212, *227*, 251n, *280*, 326, *348*
Penhune, V. B., 214–215, 221, 222, 225, 226, *227*
Pennington, B. F., 288, 289, 297, *304*, *305*
Perani, D., 269, *280*, 341, *344*, *348*, 354, 362, 363, 364, *368*, *369*
Perez, E., 237, *244*
Perkell, J. S., 148, *166*
Perlmutter, D. M., 123, *140*
Perry, D., 219, 221, *227*
Peru, A., 341, *344*
Pessin, M. S., 256, *280*
Peters, A., *82*
Peters, P. S., *140*
Peters, T., 222, *226*
Petersen, S. E., 214, 218, *227*, *297*, *304*, 341, *348*
Peterson, G. E., 314, *348*
Petersson, B. M., 295, *306*
Petrides, M., 194, *207*
Petrosini, L., 355, *369*
Pfefferbaum, A., 199, *208*
Pfeifer, E., 188, *204*
Philips, J. G., 10, 13, *20*
Piaget, J., *110*
Pick, H. L., 39, *59*
Pickens, J. N., *79*
Picton, T. W., 177, *205*
Pikus, A., 286, *304*
Pinker, S., *22*, 55, *59*, 145, 146, 153, 154, 156, 157, *165*, *166*, *167*, 352, *370*
Pinto, J. P., 74, *80*, *83*
Pisoni, D. B., 63, *79*, *81*, 179, *206*, 318, 319, *344*, *348*
Piwoz, J., 75, *81*
Pizzamiglio, L., *278*
Plante, E., 180, *209*
Plaut, D. C., 146, 147–153, 154, 155, 163, 164, *167*
Plunkett, K., 10, 20, *20*, 74, *83*, 106, *109*, 146, 154, *164*, *165*, *166*, *167*, 272, 288
Poldrack, R. A., 300, *303*, 341, *345*
Polka, L., 65, 66, *82*
Pollock, A., 233, 236, 237, *245*
Poncet, M., 269, *281*
Pons, T., 219, *227*
Posner, M., 214, 218, *227*
Postal, P. M., 123, 136, *140*, *141*
Potter, H. H., 351, *368*
Powers, R. E., 225, *226*
Praamstra, P., 181, *208*
Prather, P., 351, *368*
Preilowski, B., 299, *304*
Price, C., 217, 218, 219, *226*, *227*, 288, *304*
Prince, A., 154, *167*
Pring, T., 265, *280*
Prinster, A., 284, *301*
Pritchard, W. S., 183, *208*
Protopapas, A., 18, *21*
Pruitt, J. C., 338, *345*
Pugh, K. R., 286, *305*
Pullum, G. K., 119, 120, 121, 131, *140*, *141*, 188
Pulvermüller, F., 186, *208*, 342, *348*, 362, *369*
Pylyshyn, Z. W., 145, 154, *165*

Q

Quan, N., 242n, *245*
Quine, W. V. O., 91, *110*
Quinlan, P., 146, *167*

R

Rabin, M., 298, *302*
Rack, J., 288, *304*
Rademacher, J., 222, *227*
Raichle, M., 214, 218, *227*, 297, *304*
Ramsay, S., 217, 218, 219, *226*, *227*
Rao, S., 212, 213, 218, *226*
Rapoport, J. L., 286, *304*
Rapp, B. C., 196, *208*
Rapport, R. L., 341, *348*
Rascol, A., 217, 219, *226*
Rashotte, C. A., 287, *305*
Ratcliff, R., 159, *166*
Rauch, S., 194, *208*, 259, 263, *281*
Rauschecker, J. P., 219, *227*, 284, *301*, 333, *347*
Rayman, J., 297, *304*
Raymond, J. E., 294, *304*
Rayner, K., 295, *304*
Razzano, C., *278*
Redanz, N., 69, *79*, *81*
Reed, E., 18, *21*
Rees, A., 291, *305*
Reich, P. A., 196, *204*, 270, *278*
Reis, A., 301, *302*
Reivich, *21*
Relkin, N. R., 341, *346*, 364, *369*
Remez, R. E., 76, *80*
Reminger, S. L., 358, *368*
Requin, J., 197, *207*
Ribeiro, C., 301, *302*
Richards, L., 236, 237, 239, *245*, *246*
Richardson, A. J., 291, 293, *305*
Richman, J. M., 286, *304*
Riddel, P., 295, *305*
Riecker, A., 342, *348*
Riehle, A., 197, *207*
Rinn, W., 351, *368*
Ritter, W., 199, *208*
Ritz, S. A., 143, *164*
Rizzolatti, G., 269, *279*
Roberts, J., 28, 29, *58*
Roberts, L., 212, *227*, 251n, *280*
Robertson, C., 15, 16, *20*
Robertson, L. C., 234, 235, 244, *246*
Robichon, F., 298, *304*
Robson, J., 265, *280*
Rodriguez-Fornells, A., 201–202, *208*
Roelofs, A., 37n, *59*, 195, 196, 199, 200, *206*, *208*, 258, *279*
Roeper, T., 62, *82*
Rogers, J., 136, *141*
Rohde, D. L. T., 164, *167*
Rolls, E. T., 146, *166*
Roman, M., 351, *370*
Rose-Krasnor, L., 342, *348*
Rosen, G. D., 286, 294, *302*, *303*, *304*
Rosen, H. J., 341, *348*
Ross, E. D., 351, *369*
Royer, J. S., 131, *140*
Rubin, S., 180, *209*
Rugg, M. D., 174, 177, 182, 183, *203*, *204*, *208*
Rumbaugh, D., 7, *22*
Rumelhart, D. E., 143, 144, 145, 146, 148, 153, 156, *165*, *166*, *167*, 235, *246*
Rumsey, J. M., 284, 286, 298, *302*, *303*, *304*
Rutter, M., 283, *304*
Ryalls, J. H., 327, *348*
Ryan, J., 293, 294, *305*
Rydberg, A., 295, *306*
Rzanny, R., 288, *302*

S

Sabo, H., 92, *109*
Sacchett, C., *280*
Sadek, J., 355, *368*
Saffran, E. M., 180, *208*, 216, 255, 258n, 259, 259n, 260, 261, 262, 264, 265, 267, 268, 270, 271–272, 273, 275, 276, *278*, *280*, *281*, 284, 289
Saffran, J. R., 70, *82*, *83*
Sag, I. A., 119, 121, 136, *140*
Saint-Cyr, J., 355, *369*
Samson, S., 216, 226, *227*
Samson, Y., 219, 225, *226*
Sandson, J., 275, *278*
Santelmann, L., 77, *83*
Sapir, E., 26, 29, *59*
Saron, C. D., 299, *302*
Sartori, G., 267, *281*
Sasaki, K., 199, *205*, *208*
Satz, T., 300, *303*
Savage-Rumbaugh, E. S., 7, *22*
Say, T., 183, *207*
Schacter, D. L., *246*
Schafer, G., 74, *83*
Schiltz, K., 183, 194, 200, 201, *207*, *208*
Schmitt, B. M., 199, 200, 201, 202, *208*, 284, 291
Schneiderman, E. I., 341, *348*
Scholz, B. C., 131, *141*, 188

Schouten, M. E. H., 318, *348*
Schreiner, C., 290, *305*
Schriefers, H., 196, 199, *206, 208,* 271, *281*
Schroeder, C., 219, *227*
Schuell, H., 272, *281*
Schultz, W., *21*
Schumacher, E. H., 15, 17, 18, *20,* 263, *281*
Schumann, J. H., 342, *348,* 352, 360, *369*
Schütze, C., 126, 128, *141*
Schwartz, J., 290, *304*
Schwartz, M. F., 155, *167,* 258n, 259, 259n, 260, 261, 264, 265, 269, 271–272, 273, 275, *278, 280, 281*
Scoville, W., 354, *369*
Sebastiàn-Gallés, N., 64, *80,* 327, *347, 348,* 364, *369*
Segalowitz, S. J., 342, *348*
Segui, J., 65, *80, 82,* 320, *344*
Seidenberg, M. S., 70, *80,* 101, 102, *109,* 145, 146, 153–158, 159, 162, 163, *165, 166, 167,* 236, *246,* 262, 273, *280*
Sejnowski, T. J., 144, *167,* 229, *245*
Seldon, H., 224, *227*
Selkirk, E. O., *83*
Semendeferi, K., 19, *22*
Senehi, J., 233, 236, *245*
Senft, G., 37n, *56*
Sereno, M. I., 178, *204*
Servan-Schreiber, D., 144, *164*
Seuren, Pieter A. M., 119, *141*
Seyfarth, R. M., 8, *20*
Shady, M. E., 76–77, *83*
Shafer, V., 76, *83*
Shallice, T., 145, *165,* 256, 267, 269, 273, *281*
Shankweiler, D. P., 286, 287, 288, *302, 303, 305*
Shappell, S. A., 183, *208*
Sharma, A., 131, *140,* 342, *348*
Shaul, D. L., 28, *57*
Shaywitz, B. A., 286, *305*
Shaywitz, S. E., 286, *305*
Shears, C., 242n, *245*
Sheldon, A., 316, *348*
Sheldon, J., 298, *302*
Shelton, J. R., 267, 270, *278*
Sherman, G., 286, 294, *302, 304*
Shewell, C., 186, *207*
Shillcock, R., 70, *80,* 179, 186, *203, 208*
Shim, R. J., 333, *348*
Sholl, A., 180, *208,* 264, 265, 267, 270, *280*
Shore, C. M., 342, *348*
Shucard, D., 76, *83*
Shucard, J., 76, *83*
Siebert, C., 337, *344*
Siegel, L. S., 283, *305*
Sieratzki, J. S., 103, *110*
Silveri, M. C., 256, 265, *279, 280, 281,* 355, *369*
Silverstein, J. W., 143, *164*
Simos, P. G., 235, *246,* 313, *348*
Simpson, G. B., 238, 239, 241, *245*
Simson, R., 199, *208*
Siqueland, E. R., 62, *80*
Sirigu, A., 269, *281*
Sithole, N. M., 65, *79,* 332, *343*
Skelton, L., 315, *345*
Skinhøj, E., 365, *369*
Skottun, B. C., 292, 293, *305*
Skrap, M., 341, *344*
Skudlarsi, P., *305*
Slaghuis, W., 293, 294, *305*
Slobin, D., 91, *110,* 153, *164*
Slobin, I. D., 24, 41, *59*
Sloboda, J., 90, *110*
Small, S. L., 218, 219, *226*
Smid, H. G. O. M., 197, *207*
Smith, E. E., 263, *281*
Smith, N. V., 89, 93, 94, 96, 97, 98, 99, 100, 103, 104, 106, 107, *110*
Smith, R. E., 15, 17, 18, *20*
Smith, S. D., 288, *304*
Snowden, J. S., 264, *281*
Snowling, M., 288, 300, *304*
Snyder, A. Z., 297, *304*
Soja, N., 91, *110*
Solida, A., 355, *369*
Soon, C. S., 341, *344*
Sorensen, R. E., 294, *304*
Soulier, M., 233, *245*
Southern, B. D., 225, *226*
Spelke, E., 91, *110*
Spencer, D. D., 174, 178, *206*
Sperber, D., 104–105, *110*
Sperry, R. W., 231, 232, *245, 246*
Spivey-Knowlton, M. J., 160, *165*
Springer, S. P., 233n, 234, *246*
Squire, L. R., 233–234, *246*
Srinivas, K., 265, *281*
Sriram, N., 341, *344*
St. John, M., 146, 158–162, 163, *166, 167,* 272, 273, 276, *280*
Stabler, E., 122, *140*

Starkstein, S. E., 341, *343*
Statlender, H., 15, *20*
Steedman, M., 121, *141*
Stein, J. F., 291, 292, 293, 294, 295, 296, 297, *302, 303, 305*
Steinmetz, H., 221, *227*
Steinschneider, M., 219, *227*
Stelmach, G. E., 358, *368*
Stern, M. B., 10, *21*, 155, *165*
Stevens, K. N., *81*, 336, *346*
Stewart, J., 341, *345*
Stewart, R., 354, *369*
Stiles-Davis, J., 39, *59*
Stoel-Gammon, C., 148, *166*
Stollwerck, L., 101, *111*
Stone, L. V., 286, *304*
Stowe, L. A., 189, *205*
Strange, W., 316, 338, *343, 348*
Streete, S., 367, *369*
Streeter, L. A., *83*
Strick, P. L., 10, *20*
Stromswold, K., 194, *208*, 259, 263, *281*
Studdert-Kennedy, M. G., *82*, 148, *167*, 290, *305*
Stuhr, V., 296, *302*
Subramaniam, B., 296, *303*
Suomi, K., *83*
Suzuki, K., 299, *305*
Svenkerud, V. Y., 68, *81*
Svirsky, M. A., 148, *166*
Swaab, T., 237, *246*
Swingley, D., 74, *80, 83*
Swinney, D. A., 186, *208*
Swoboda, P., *83*
Syrdal-Lasky, A., *81*

T

Tajchman, G., 8, 10, 14, 15, 18, *21*
Takagi, N., 316, *345*
Takahashi, A., 299, *305*
Talairach, J., *227*
Talcott, J., 291, 292, 293, 295, *305*
Tallal, P., 101, *110*, 219, 225, *227*, 290, *304, 305*
Talmy, L., 41, 50n, *59*
Tan, C. T., 341, *348*
Tan, E. W. L., *344*
Tanaka, K., 174, *208*
Tanenhaus, M. K., 159, 160, *165, 167*, 188, *204*
Taraban, R., 146, 158, 159, *166*, 272, 273, 276, *280*
Taylor, A., 355, *369*
Tchekhoff, C., 51, *59*
Tees, R. C., 65, *83*, 337, *348*
Teeter, A., 341, *345*
Tervaniemi, M., 291, *303*
Thach, W., 355, *370*
Theberge, D. C., 299, *303, 304*
Thibadeau, R., 186, *208*
Thiel, T., 341, *344*
Thinus-Blanc, C., 48, *57*
Thivard, L., 219, *225, 226*
Thornburgh, D. F., 327, *348*
Thorpe, S., 199, *209*
Thulborn, K. R., 194, *205*, 259, 263, *279*
Tian, B., 219, *227*
Tierney, J., 319, 320, *347*
Tincoff, R., *83*
Tokura, H., 75, *80*
Tola, G., 287, *302*
Torgesen, J. K., 287, *305*
Tournoux, P., *227*
Trauner, D., 20, *20*
Treffert, D. A., 93, *110*
Trehub, S. E., *83*
Treisman, A., 296, *305*
Trofimovich, P., 317, 329, 332, 337, *343, 347, 348*
Trueswell, J., 159, *167*
Tseng, C.-Y., 15, *21*
Tsimpli, I.-M., 89, 93, 94, 96, 97, 98, 99, 100, 103, *110*
Tsujimoto, T., 199, *208*
Turatto, M., 296, *302*
Turner, R., 284, *301*, 333, *347*
Tyler, L. K., 154, 160, *166*, 259, *281*
Tyson, J., 351, *368*

U

Ullman, M. T., 154, 156, 157, *167*, 352, *370*
Ungerleider, L. G., *21*, 269, *280*
Uusipaikka, E., 338, *343*
Uutela, K., 291, *303*

V

Valiant, L., *141*
Vallar, G., 256, *281*
Van Berkum, J. J. A., 185, 191, *203, 209*

van de Moortele, P.-F., 341, *344*, 354, 362, 363, 364, *368*
van der Lely, H. K. J., 101, 102, *110*, *111*
van Dijk, T. A., 160, *167*
van Gelder, T., 145, *167*
van Hessen, A. J., 318, *348*
Van Hoesen, G. W., 19, *22*
Vanier, M., 256, *278*
VanMeter, J. W., *302*
Van Orden, G. C., 288, *304*
Van Petten, C. K., 172, 174, 180, 183, 184, 185, 186, *206*, *209*
Van Turennout, M., 196, 197, 199, *209*
Van Valin, R. D. Jr., 154, *165*
Vaughan, H., 219, *227*
Vaughan, H. G., 199, *208*
Vernon, G., 10, *21*
Vicari, S., 20, *20*
Vidyasagar, T. R., 296, *305*
Vigorito, J., 62, *80*
Vihman, M. M., 147, 148, *167*
Vijay-Shanker, K., 121, *141*
Villa, 256
Voeller, K., 291, *303*
Vogel, I., *82*
Vogt, B. A., 363, *368*
Vorberg, D., 196, 199, 206

W

Wada, J., *281*
Wagner, A. D., 341, *345*
Wagner, K. R., 151n, *167*
Wagner, R. K., 287, *305*
Wales, R., 351, *369*
Walker, E., 236, *247*
Wall, S., 287, *303*
Wallace, A. F. C., 32, *59*
Wallace, C. S., 340, 342, *345*
Walsh, M. A., 288, *303*
Walsh, V., 292, 293, 295, *305*
Wang, W., 366, *370*
Wang, X., 290, *305*
Wanner, E., 76, *80*, *81*
Wapner, W., 351, *368*
Warrington, E. K., 267, 269, *280*, *281*
Wasow, 119, 121, 136
Weber-Fox, C., 342, *348*, 353, 354, 362, 364, *370*
Webster, R., 297, *303*
Weekes, B., 341, *344*
Weinberg, A., 74, *80*
Weinberger, S. H., 321, *345*
Weinreich, U., 321, *348*
Weir, D. J., 121, *141*
Weisberg, R., *280*
Weller, B. J., 199, *208*
Wells, S., 341, *347*
Wells, T., 183, *204*
Welsh, A., 180, *206*
Werker, J. F., 65, 66, 67–68, *82*, *83*, 337, *348*
Wernicke, C., 252, *281*
Wesche, M., 341, *348*
Wessels, J. M. I., 68–69, *80*, *81*
Wexler, K., 104, *111*
Weylman, S. T., 351, *370*
Whalen, D. H., 291, *303*
Wheeldon, L., 37n, *56*
Wheeler, K., 331n, *345*
Whitaker, H. A., 341, *347*, *348*
Whitfield, I. C., 219, *227*
Whorf, B. L., 26, 27, 27n, 35–36, *59*
Wiggs, C. L., *21*, 269, *280*
Wijecoon, S., 295, *306*
Wijers, A. A., 197, *207*
Wildgruber, D., 342, *348*
Willcutt, E. G., 297, *305*
Williams, E., 62, *82*
Williams, K. A., *81*, 336, *346*
Williams, L., 322, *349*
Williams, M., 294, *305*
Williams, R. J., 145, 156, *167*
Wilson, D., 105, *110*
Wilson, R. S., 358, *368*
Wingfield, A., 255, 274, *279*
Wise, B., 289, *304*
Wise, D., 286, *304*
Wise, R., 213, 217, 218, 219, *226*, *227*, 288, *304*
Witton, C., 291, *305*
Witz, K., 32, *58*
Wohlert, A. B., 196, *209*
Wolff, P. H., 291, 299, *305*
Woll, B., 96, 103, *110*
Wong, D., 218, *227*
Wong, E. C., 218, *226*
Wood, F. B., 297, *302*
Woods, R. P., *302*
Woodward, A., 70, 75, *81*, *82*
Worsley, K., 219, 221, *227*
Wright, B. A., 291, *306*, 315, *346*
Wright Cassidy, K., 75, *81*

Wulfeck, B., 275, *277*
Wynn, K., 103, *111*

Y

Yamadori, A., 299, *305*
Yang, B., 331n, *349*
Yazzie, C., 341, *347*
Yeni-Komshian, G., 255, *280*, 316, 321, 324, 333, 339, *344*, *345*
Yetkin, F. Z., 218, *226*
Ygge, J., 295, *306*
Young, A. W., 235, *247*
Youngs, J. W., 18, *21*
Yule, W., 283, *304*

Z

Zaake, W., 200, 201, 207, *208*
Zaidel, D., 232, 236, *246*
Zaidel, E., 232, 235, *245*, *246*, *247*, 297, *304*, *306*
Zametkin, A. J., 286, *304*
Zatorre, R., 214, 215, 216, 218, 219, 221, 222, 225, 226, *227*, 284, 341, *346*, *349*
Zawacki, T., 355, *368*
Zecker, S. G., 291, *306*
Zeffiro, T. A., *302*
Zilbovicius, M., 219, 225, *226*
Zimmer, L., 12, *20*
Zurif, E. B., 186, *208*, 258, 260, *278*, *279*, 316, 321, 324, *344*
Zvi, J. C., 299, *304*
Zwitserlood, P., 180, *209*

Subject Index

Note: Page numbers in italic refer to figures; those in boldface refer to tables.
Page numbers followed by 'n' refer to footnotes.

A

Abstract word superiority, 264–265
Age-effect approach (AEA), 326–336, 331, 339–340
Agrammatism, 256–263, 260, 277
Agreement Deficit, 102
Alexia, 284, 286–287
Allophonic cues, in word segmentation, 73
Alzheimer's disease, 154–158, 358
Amnesia, 354, 358
Angular gyrus, 284, 284, 286
Anomalous-sentences test, 319–320
Anti-Whorfian argument, 46
Aphasia
    Broca's, 14–15, 252, 256–263
    conceptual knowledge in, 263–270, 266
    defined, 358
    as evidence in Broca's-Wernicke's area theory, 10
    lexical organization in, 270–272
    syntactic processing in, 256–263
    transcortical sensory, 254
    Wernicke's, 253
Arabic speakers, 313–314
Argument from poverty of the stimulus, 131
Attentional functioning, in dyslexia, 295–297
Attractor network, 144
Auditory cortex, 221–226, 223, 224
Auditory processing, in dyslexia, 290–291
Australian Aboriginals. *See* Guugu Yimithirr
Autism, 94

B

Babbling, in phonological development model, 150
Back-propagation, 145–146
Basal ganglia, 4, 10, 11–18, 261n, 358
Bilingualism
    age-effect approach to, 326–336, 331, 339–340
    defined, 310, 352
    early versus late, 310–311, 353, 362–364
    future research in, 342
    implicit linguistic competence in, 351, 354–356, 365
    metalinguistic knowledge in, 352, 356–359, 365
    monolingual-comparison approach to, 311–321, 312
    motivation in, 352, 360–361
    phonetic system models of, 336–341
    pragmatic competence in, 351, 359–360, 365
    shared-separate approach to, 321–326
    Weinreich's typology, 321
Binding theory, 124–125
Binocular vergance control, 295
Broca's aphasia, 14–15, 252, 256–263
Broca's area, 10, 211–212, 212, 216–219, 217, 252–256, 253, 358

C

Case theory, 101

Categorial grammar, 121–122
Central nervous system, 229–230, 230
Central syntactic deficit hypothesis, 258–259
Central system, in modularity theories, 87–89, 89, 90
Chomsky
 binding theory, 124
 model of modularity, 88–89, 90, 101, 101n
 universal grammar, 4–6
Chomskyan revolution, 32
Classifier languages, 23n
Cognitive Anthropology Research Group, 37n
Cognitive architecture
 Dougherty, Keller, Lehman's, 46–47
 Fodor and Chomsky's, 87–89, 89, 90
 Jackendoff's, 43–45, 45
Color, 29–30
Conceptual knowledge, 263–270, 266, 268
Conceptual structures, 44–45, 53
Connectionism (historical use), 254–255
Connectionist models
 described, 143–146
 future work in, 163–164
 inflectional morphology model, 153–158, 155, 163
 versus modularity, 105–107, 272–273
 phonological development model, 147–153, 148, 150, 152, 163
 sentence comprehension model, 158–162, 159, 161, 162, 163
Conservation tasks, 91–92, 92
Constellation, 46–47
Construction grammar, 136
Contrastive analysis hypothesis (CAH), 311
Corpus collosum, 298–301
Cosmological theory, 47
Covert categories, 26–27, 27n
Critical-period hypothesis, 328–335, 334, 340
Culture, defined, 53

D

Declarative memory, 354–355, 357–359
Derivation, 115–118
Derived linguistic features, versus primitive, 3–4, 7–9
Diagnostic Rhyme Test (DRT), 319
Dichotic listening, 234–235, 341–342
Diffusion tensor magnetic resonance imaging, 300
Direct route, 288
Dissociation
 as evidence of modularity, 89–93
 in inflectional morphology, 153–158, 157
 in savant syndrome, 93–100, 102–103
 in specific language impairment, 101–102
Distributed knowledge system, 268, 269
Distributed representations, in connectionist model, 144–145
Dual-route model, 288–289
Dual-route theories, 153–154
Dutch speakers, 37
Dyslexia
 versus alexia, 284, 286–287
 defined, 283
 inflectional morphology in, 154–158
 interhemispheric interaction in, 297–301
 phonological awareness in, 285, 287–297
Dysphonetic dyslexics. *See* Dyslexia

E

Early bilinguals, 310–311, 353, 362–364
Encoding
 semantic versus phonological, 197–199, 197, 198
 semantic versus syntactic, 200–202, 201
English speakers
 age-related effects in, 329–332, 331
 enumeration in, 34–35
 linguistic relativity paradigm and, 24
 spatial relationships in, 41–42
 voice-onset time in, 312–316, 312, 321–326, 324
 word segmentation development in, 74–78
Epun, 97–100
Equivalence classification, 315
Ethnobotany, 30–31
Event related potentials (ERPS)
 in comprehension, 179–187, 182, 184, 185. 187
 introduction to, 172–179, 175
 in production, 195–202, 201
 syntactic violations and, 188–195, 189, 190, 192, 193, 195
Evolution of language
 basal ganglia and, 4, 10, 11–18

biological versus psychological, 4–9
functional language system and, 9–11
innateness and, 20
Experience-dependent process, 340
Experience-expectant process, 340

F

False belief, 94
Feedforward architecture, 144
Fodor model, 87–88, 89
Folk biology, 30–31
Forward model, 148
Frame of reference, 36–40, 36n, 48–53, 49, 52
French speakers
production and perception in, 316–318
speech intelligibility in, 320
voice-onset time in, 313, 314, 321–326, 324
Frequency sensitive negativity (FSN), 186–187, 187
Functional autonomy, 89–90, 213
Functional language system (FLS), 6, 9–11
Functional magnetic resonance imaging (fMRI), 172, 213. *See also* Functional neuroimaging
Functional neuroimaging
cerebral areas identified with, 211–212
shortcomings of, 172, 365–366
speech perception studies with, 213–221

G

Generalized phrase structure grammar (GPSG), 121
Generative-enumerative grammars
with constraints, 123–129
described, 118–119
expressions as trees in, 119–123
Genetics, in dyslexia, 288–289
German speakers, 24, 200, 319–320
Gold theorems, 129–135
Go/no go paradigm, 197, 197–202, 198, 201
Gradient ungrammaticality, 125–129
Guugu Yimithirr, 23–24, 36–40, 54

H

Habitual thought, 27, 35, 40
Head-driven phrase structure grammar (HPSG), 121
Hebrew speakers, 24
Hemispheric asymmetries
evidence of, 231–233
generalizations about, 242–244
semantic priming and, 236–239, 238
sentence priming and, 239–241, 240
in word recognition, 233–235
Heschl's gyrus, 214–215, 215, 222–226, 223, 224

I

Imitation, in phonological development model, 151
Immediate update, 160
Implicit linguistic competence, 351, 354–356, 365
Implicit Rule Formation Deficit, 102
Impossible language, 97–100
Infantile hypercalcemia, 92–93
Inflectional morphology, 153–158, 155, 163
Informational encapsulation, 88
Innateness, 20
Input systems, 87–88
Intensional approach to cognition, 55
Intentional naming, in phonological development model, 151
Interhemispheric interaction, in dyslexia, 297–301
Irregular words, 288
Italian speakers, 316, 327–328

J

Japanese speakers, 316–317

K

Kinship, 31–33
Korean speakers
age-related effects in, 329–332, 331
linguistic relativity paradigm and, 24
production and perception in, 317
spatial relationships in, 24
Korsakoff's syndrome, 358

L

Language, defined, 53
Language acquisition
early research in, 61–62
unlearnability paradox, 129–135
Language acquisition device (LAD), 62
Language-brain relationships

conceptual knowledge in, 263–270, 268
history of, 252–256, 253, 254
lexical organization in, 270–272
opposing views of, 272–276
syntactic processing in, 256–263, 260
Language comprehension
ERPS in, 179–187, 182, 184, 185. 187
in phonological development, 147–153
Language production, ERPS in, 195–202
Last Resort, 102
Late bilinguals, defined, 310–311, 353, 362–364
Lateral geniculate nucleus, 293–294
Lateralized readiness potential (LRP), 196–199
Learning
from an informant, 132
in connectionist models, 145–146
from text, 129–135
Left hemisphere. *See also* Implicit linguistic competence
in dyslexia, 297–301
functional regions in, 211–212, 212
hemispheric-systems view of, 229–233, 242–244
semantic priming and, 236–239
sentence priming and, 239–241, 240
word recognition and, 233–235
Lexical categories
ERPS and, 186–187
in phrase structure grammars, 114
Lexical domains, and LR paradigm, 29–33
Lexical organization, 270–272
Lexical processing negativity (LPN), 186–187, 187
Lichtheim model, 253–255
Linguistic relativity paradigm
challenges to, 29–33
contemporary research in, 33–43
continued interest in, 53
development of, 25–29
strong versus weak form of, 24, 33
Living things impairment, 265–270, 266
Localist representation, 144

M

Magnetic resonance imaging. *See* Functional magnetic resonance imaging
Magnetoencephalogram (MEG), 172
Magnocellular system, 292–295
Mandarin speakers, 315–316
Mapping deficit hypothesis, 260–261, 263
Matter versus shape, 34–35
Mayan speakers, 23, 34–35
Meaningful-sentences test, 320
Mental lexicon, 179–180
Metalinguistic knowledge, 352, 356–359, 365
Metarepresentational module, 105
Metrical segmentation strategy (MSS), 70–72
Model-theoretic grammars, 135–139
Modularity
alternatives to, 104–107
versus connectionist models, 105–107, 272–273
versus functional language system, 11
models of, 87–89, 89, 90
versus parallel distributed processing, 171–172
quasi- and sub-modules, 100–103
Monolingual-comparison approach (MCA), 311–321, 312
Monolinguals, defined, 310
Motivation, 352, 360–361
Motor cortex, 212, 253
Motor production, 291
Müller-Lyer optical illusion, 88, 88
Myelination, in dyslexics, 300–301

N

N200, 199–202, 201
N400, 183–186, 184, 185
Native language magnet theory (NLM), 336–338, 340
Native speakers, defined, 310
Natural selection, 5
Negative evidence, in language acquisition, 132–134
Neural circuits, 9–11

O

Overt categories, 26–27, 27n

P

P600, 188–191, 189, 190
Parallel distributed processing, 172

Parkinson's disease, 13–15, 154–158, 358
Parvocellular system, 292, 294–295
Perceptual assimilation model (PAM), 338, 340
Perceptual deficit hypothesis, 267
Perceptual magnet effect, 65–66
Perislyvian cortex, 256, 357–358, 363
Phonemes, 67–68, 313
Phonetic rehearsal, 17–18
Phonological awareness, 285, 287–297
Phonological development, 147–153, 148, 150, 152, 163
Phonological processing
  ERPS and, 181–183, 182
  versus semantic, 197–200, 197, 198
Phonological route, 287
Phonology, defined, 147
Phrasal categories, 114
Phrase structure grammar, 114–118
Phrenology, 252
Pitch processing, 214–216, 226
Positron emission tomography (PET), 172, 213. *See also* Functional neuroimaging
Pragmatic competence, 351, 359–360, 365
Predaptation, 5
Primary genealogical space (PGS), 32
Primitive linguistic features, versus derived, 3–4, 7–9
Procedural memory, 354–355, 357–359

Q

Quasi-modules, 100–103
Quasi-regular domain, 153
Quebec referendum question, 356–357, 357
Quichua-Spanish speakers, 325

R

Readiness potential (RP), 196
Reading disorders. *See* Dyslexia
Recurrent architecture, 144, 148, 159
Representational Deficit with Dependent Relationships, 102
Representational modularity, 43–45
Representational redescription hypothesis, 104
Representational systems, 38
Rewrite rules, 31, 31n
Rhyming, 181–183, 319
Rhythmic organization, in speech perception, 64. *See also* Metrical segmentation strategy (MSS)
Right hemisphere. *See also* Pragmatic competence
  in dyslexia, 297
  hemispheric-systems view of, 229–233, 242–244
  in pitch processing, 216
  semantic priming and, 236–239
  sentence priming and, 239–241, 240
  word recognition and, 233–235

S

Saccades, 294–295
Sapir-Whorf hypothesis, 28
Savant syndrome, 93–100, 93, 94
Second-language acquisition, in savants, 95–100
Semantic dementia, 264, 269, 276
Semantic memory, 263–270, 268
Semantic priming, 236–239, 238
Semantic processing, 197–202, 197, 198, 201
Sensitive period, versus critical period, 334–335, 334, 340
Sentence comprehension, 158–162, 159, 161, 162, 163
Sentence Gestalt model, 159–161
Sentence priming, 239–241, 240
Sentence processing, 191–195, 193, 195
Seriation tasks, 91–92, 92
Shape, 34–35
Shared-separate approach (SSA), 321–326
Simple phrase structure grammar, 114–118
Single-route model, 288–289
Sound pattern discrimination, 62–63, 67–68
Spanish speakers
  age-related effects in, 327
  linguistic relativity paradigm and, 24
  spatial relationships in, 41–42
  voice-onset time in, 322
Spatial relationships
  Bennardo proposal, 47–53, 49, 52
  Levinson research, 35–40
Slobin and Bowerman research, 41–42
Spatial representation module, 44, 47–53
Specific language impairment (SLI), 101–102
Speech intelligibility, 318–320
Speech learning model (SLM), 338–341

Speech perception
- in bilinguals, 316–318
- cerebral areas involved in, 211–212, 212
- discriminative capacities in, 62–65
- functional imaging studies in, 213–221
- non-native contrasts in, 65–69
- structural imaging studies in, 221–226
- syntactic organization in, 74–78
- word segmentation in, 69–74

Speech production
- in bilinguals, 316–318
- cerebral areas involved in, 211–212, 212
- in phonological development, 147–153
- syntax and, 17–18

Speech prototypes, 336
Split-brain patients, 231–233
Stress cues, in word segmentation, 70–73
Structure dependence, 98–100
Sub-modules, 100–103
Summation priming, 237
Superfinite languages, 130
Sylvian fissure, 253, 256
Syntactic organization, 74–78
Syntactic positive shift, 188–191, 189, 190
Syntactic processing
- disruptions in, 256–263, 260
- versus semantic processing, 200–202, 201
- speech production and, 17–18

Syntactic violations, 188–195, 189, 190, 192, 193, 195

T

Temporal processing, in dyslexia, 290–291
Thai speakers, 218
Thinking for speaking, 41
Tongan, 45, 47–54
Transcortical sensory aphasia, 254
Transformational-generative grammar (TG), 122–123, 124
Transformations, 122
Translability/Incommensurability of FOR, 38–40
Tree adjoining grammar (TAG), 120
Tzetal, 37n, 39

U

Universal grammar, 4–6
Unlearnability paradox, 129–135

V

Visual half-field, 231, 231
Visual processing, in dyslexia, 292–295
Voice-onset time
- in monolingual-comparison approach, 312–316, 313, 314
- in Parkinson's patients and aphasiacs, 14–15
- in shared-separate approach, 321–326

Voicing-conditioned vowel duration, 314–316, 322–324
Voluntary versus bound behavior, 7–9

W

Wernicke's aphasia, 253
Wernicke's area, 10, 211–212, 212, 252–256, 253, 358
Whorfian effect, 36–40, 42
Williams syndrome, 92–93, 103, 103n
Word recognition, 233–235
Word segmentation, 69–74
Word-superiority effect, 235
Working memory, 17–18, 191–195, 193, 195

Y

Yucatec Maya, 23, 34–35